The Translator and Editor

CHARLES MARTIN is Professor Emeritus at Queensborough Community College of the City University of New York. His verse translation of the *Metamorphoses* of Ovid was winner of the Harold Morton Landon Award from the Academy of American Poets for 2004. His most recent book of poems, *Starting from Sleep: New and Selected Poems*, was a finalist for the Lenore Marshall Award of the Academy of American Poets. He is the recipient of a Bess Hokin Prize for Poetry, a Pushcart Prize, and fellowships from the Ingram Merrill Foundation and the National Endowment for the Arts. In 2005, he received an Award for Literature from the American Academy of Arts and Letters.

W. W. NORTON & COMPANY, INC.
Also Publishes

ENGLISH RENAISSANCE DRAMA
edited by David Bevington et al.

THE NORTON ANTHOLOGY OF AFRICAN AMERICAN LITERATURE
edited by Henry Louis Gates Jr. and Nellie Y. McKay et al.

THE NORTON ANTHOLOGY OF AMERICAN LITERATURE
edited by Nina Baym et al.

THE NORTON ANTHOLOGY OF CHILDREN'S LITERATURE
edited by Jack Zipes et al.

THE NORTON ANTHOLOGY OF CONTEMPORARY FICTION
edited by R. V. Cassill and Joyce Carol Oates

THE NORTON ANTHOLOGY OF DRAMA
edited by J. Ellen Gainor, Stanton B. Garner Jr., and Martin Puchner

THE NORTON ANTHOLOGY OF ENGLISH LITERATURE
edited by M. H. Abrams and Stephen Greenblatt et al.

THE NORTON ANTHOLOGY OF LITERATURE BY WOMEN
edited by Sandra M. Gilbert and Susan Gubar

THE NORTON ANTHOLOGY OF MODERN AND CONTEMPORARY POETRY
edited by Jahan Ramazani, Richard Ellmann, and Robert O'Clair

THE NORTON ANTHOLOGY OF POETRY
edited by Margaret Ferguson, Mary Jo Salter, and Jon Stallworthy

THE NORTON ANTHOLOGY OF SHORT FICTION
edited by R. V. Cassill and Richard Bausch

THE NORTON ANTHOLOGY OF THEORY AND CRITICISM
edited by Vincent B. Leitch et al.

THE NORTON ANTHOLOGY OF WORLD LITERATURE
edited by Sarah Lawall et al.

THE NORTON FACSIMILE OF THE FIRST FOLIO OF SHAKESPEARE
prepared by Charlton Hinman

THE NORTON INTRODUCTION TO LITERATURE
edited by Alison Booth and Kelly J. Mays

THE NORTON READER
edited by Linda H. Peterson and John C. Brereton

THE NORTON SAMPLER
edited by Thomas Cooley

THE NORTON SHAKESPEARE, BASED ON THE OXFORD EDITION
edited by Stephen Greenblatt et al.

For a complete list of Norton Critical Editions, visit
www.wwnorton.com/college/English/nce_home.htm

A NORTON CRITICAL EDITION

Ovid

METAMORPHOSES

A NEW TRANSLATION
CONTEXTS
CRITICISM

Translated and Edited by

CHARLES MARTIN

QUEENSBOROUGH COMMUNITY COLLEGE
CITY UNIVERSITY OF NEW YORK

W. W. NORTON & COMPANY
New York • London

W. W. Norton & Company has been independent since its founding in 1923, when William Warder Norton and Mary D. Herter Norton first published lectures delivered at the People's Institute, the adult education division of New York City's Cooper Union. The firm soon expanded its program beyond the Institute, publishing books by celebrated academics from America and abroad. By mid-century, the two major pillars of Norton's publishing program—trade books and college texts—were firmly established. In the 1950s, the Norton family transferred control of the company to its employees, and today—with a staff of four hundred and a comparable number of trade, college, and professional titles published each year—W. W. Norton & Company stands as the largest and oldest publishing house owned wholly by its employees.

The text of this book is composed in Fairfield Medium
with the display set in Bernhard Modern.
Book design by Antonina Krass.
Composition by TexTech International Pvt. Ltd.
Manufacturing by the Courier Companies—Westford division
Production manager: Eric Pier-Hocking.

Library of Congress Cataloging-in-Publication Data

Ovid, 43 B.C.–17 or 18 A.D.
  [Metamorphoses. English]
  Metamorphoses : a new translation, contexts, criticism / translated and edited
by Charles Martin. — 1st ed.
       p. cm. — (A Norton critical edition)
  Includes bibliographical references.
  ISBN 978-0-393-92534-0 (pbk.)
  1.   Fables, Latin—Translations into English. 2.   Metamorphoses—
Mythology—Poetry. 3.   Mythology, Classical—Poetry.   I. Martin, Charles,
1942- II. Title.
  PA6522.M2M44 2010
  873'.01 —dc22

                                                          2009024625

W. W. Norton & Company, Inc., 500 Fifth Avenue
New York, N.Y. 10110-0017
www.wwnorton.com

W. W. Norton & Company Ltd., Castle House
75/76 Wells Street, London W1T 3QT

2 3 4 5 6 7 8 9 0

To Johanna

Contents

Criticism

Preface

Ovid's *Metamorphoses* presents itself as a unity, an epic-length poem in which we find considerable diversity: 250 variations on the theme of transformation that the poet speaks of in its opening lines. How is it to be read in our time? Critics who value unity will search, as Brooks Otis did, for "the plan of Ovid's epic," finding in it not only what Ovid said was there, "one continuous song (*carmen perpetuum*) going down from the world's beginnings to his own times,"[1] but also a good deal more that Ovid was silent about. The poet's own comments on such matters go only a little beyond admitting a temporal structure; in the *Tristia*, he speaks of having written a poem "of changed forms in three times five books (*ter quinque volumina formae mutatae*),"[2] and one might extrapolate from this remark a notion that each of these sets of five has its own kind of internal consistency, thematic or otherwise. Otis goes much further than this simple division and finds in the poem not only a temporal but an architectural structure as well, a significant and expressive arrangement of tales in a cunning strategy of balances and antitheses, an elaborate and well-mirrored auctorial funhouse that exhibits the formal unity he seeks.

Critics who read the poem for its variety will have little or no sympathy for Otis's activity or his conclusions, and will see *Metamorphoses,* as the distinguished poet and translator Daryl Hine does, as "a loosely affiliated farrago of generally discreditable stories about the Greco-Roman gods . . . a skewed and partial compendium of classical mythology. . . . "[3] Hine's vigorously stated position is not original with him: in the late nineteenth century, J. W. Mackail described Ovid's technique as yielding us "a vast mass of multifarious stories, whose only connection is the casual fact of their involving or alluding to some transformation of human beings into stones, trees, plants, beasts, birds and the like. . . . "[4]

1. Brooks Otis, *Ovid as an Epic Poet* (Cambridge: Cambridge UP, 1966), 45.
2. Arthur Leslie Wheeler, trans. *Ovid Tristia Ex Ponto* (Cambridge: Harvard UP, 1924), Tristia III, xiv, 19, p. 154.
3. Daryl Hine in *Poetry: The Translation Issue*, Vol. CXCII, Number 1, April 2008, 32.
4. J. W. Mackail, *Latin Literature* (London: J. Murray, 1895), 140.

Though I myself feel more comfortable among the *"ter quinque"* crew, in truth, most of us begin reading Ovid's *Metamorphoses* not as literature but as a collection of detachable tales dealing with those absorbing myths of the Greek and Roman past. Whether we first read it in the original or in translation, in prose or in verse, we will likely be oblivious of (or at least indifferent to) any evidence of its unity and coherence. My own first reading of Ovid was actually a reading of Thomas Bulfinch's bowdlerized adaptation of Ovid's stories, hammered out in Bulfinch's undistinguished prose. I had no idea that I was missing something, and even later, when I read Horace Gregory's translation, I cannot say that I was aware of a great poem embodying the fascinating stories. Ovid's work has often been seen as detachable, and the interest it arouses is often an extraliterary interest: T. S. Eliot's comment in *The Waste Land* on Ovid's account of Tiresias's sex change is typical and unexceptional: "The whole passage from Ovid is of great anthropological interest."

But if we read enough of the poem in the original or in a translation at least as good as Horace Gregory's, we will become aware of an Ovidian voice, of the way in which the narrator of the poem is shaping the stories that he tells to create certain effects. We will also become aware of the protean shiftiness of that voice, discovering in it various levels, shallows and depths, commitments and evasions that seem to reveal the complexity of the person behind the poem. Ovid could say as Walt Whitman did, "Who touches this book touches a man." And yet, if we ask what *kind* of man, the book may yield contradictory answers. (It may be helpful to recall that Whitman also said, "Do I contradict myself? Very well then I contradict myself. [I am large, I contain multitudes]") Is Ovid, as Italo Calvino argues, the poet who does not take sides, the poet who is always searching for the unknown god, so as not to offend any of them? Is he the dutiful supporter of the Augustan regime, or the subtle antagonist, the antimilitarist described by Diane Middlebrook, with his own agenda for showing in poetry the triumph of Venus over Mars? Could he possibly be all of these things at once?

The issue of Ovid's sympathies is not easily settled. One of our most basic human needs is to believe that there is justice in our relationships, yet so many of the stories that Ovid tells have characters unequal in their powers and conclusions that are blatantly unjust: Callisto, raped by Jove, is transformed into a bear. The innocent Itys is butchered and cooked by his own mother, Philomela, and served by her as a dish to his father, Tereus, as Philomela's revenge for violating her sister Procne. Dryope, after having been raped and discarded by Apollo, innocently picks some lotus flowers to delight her infant son and is turned forever into a tree by a nymph hidden in the flowers; some in our time argued that she should have known better, but none that I know of has argued that her punishment was proportionate to her offense.

Where do the poet's sympathies lie? With a writer like Chekhov, one can see through whatever ironies may present themselves to grasp the author's feeling for his suffering characters. Ovid is simply not like that, and when he is—as in the narrator's overwhelming outpouring of grief for the death of Orpheus in Book X—the reader may suspect that Ovid is putting us on. There is a moment in his description of the aftermath of the helpless Callisto's rape by Jove when the poet seems to be the world through her eyes, but there is no such moment for helpless Itys, and Ovid appears to be viewing the banquet scene through lenses provided by the boy's deranged mother and aunt. Some have argued that Ovid is trying to show us such horrors not only from a human perspective, but even as the gods see them; that is to say, without undue emotion, and this coolness in the presence of suffering is actually meant to say to us, "See? This is how the gods and bosses behave. We can't say it too openly, but I know it and you do too."

Perhaps that is why other artists have felt intuitively that Ovid was on their side, especially those who, like Ovid, suffered political repression at the hands of an autocratic regime: the Russian poet Osip Mandelstam took Ovid's title *Tristia* for one of his own books, apparently finding in Ovid's situation vis-à-vis Augustus, an analog for his own with Joseph Stalin, who also took a very personal interest in *his* poets. It may be that Augustus truly thought that Ovid was of his own court, an Augustan at heart, and so the poet's betrayal was wholly unforgivable. (If Stalin had read Ovid, perhaps he would have thought him a Stalinist.) But wouldn't Augustus have seen through the excessive flattery in the hymn of praise to his rule that ends the *Metamorphoses*? Perhaps not. It appears that if we think well of ourselves, nothing is easier to believe than that Ovid is on our side.

The voice of the Ovidian narrator is rich in ironies, ambiguities, and contradictions, scripting its various scenarios of commitment and evasion: if his poem is indeed more than "a loosely affiliated farrago" of stories, its structure would likely exhibit patterns of commitment and evasion similar to those we find in that voice. The clearest example of these is surely Ovid's elastic notion of the possibilities latent in the word *book*. The first book of Ovid's *Metamorphoses* gives us a beginning and the last book gives us a conclusion, but the first book ends with a continuation to the next, and the last book begins with a continuation from the one before; the thirteen books in between are both continuous and inconclusive. The relationships that they exhibit between "stories" and "books" display shifting patterns of commitment and evasion, as themes emerge from their context and then dissolve back into it, only to reappear, subtly changed—or to disappear completely. The model for this continual transformation within and between books seems less like the elaborate and static structure described by Otis than the dynamic motions of an actor or dancer performing one role and then transforming himself (while still onstage) to perform another. One is tempted to paraphrase T. S. Eliot and say that the structure of this poem (rather than its meaning) is a bone thrown by a burglar to distract the mind's watchdog while the poem goes about its own deeper business.

What that business may be is difficult to define, but easy enough to illustrate. Book XIII of Ovid's *Metamorphoses* begins with an outgrowth of the account of Achilles's death that closes Book XII. This is a lengthy debate between Ulysses and Ajax—brains versus brawn—over the armor of the fallen hero. Brains triumph, as Ulysses walks off with the coveted booty and Ajax kills himself. The hypermasculine self-aggrandizement of their argument segues into a consideration of Hecuba and the women of Troy, who after the fall of the city have been reduced to yet another form of plunder, erotic rather than martial. We move from an imitation of speeches and arguments heard in a Roman law court to scenes from Greek tragedy: Ovid's treatment of Hecuba follows Euripedes's eponymous play. Hecuba is being tormented by the shade of Achilles, who demands the death of her last surviving daughter, Polyxena, as a funeral sacrifice. Polyxena goes to her fate with a courage that none of the men portrayed in this book can match or even come near in showing, and a new theme, the bravery of women, is introduced and will be developed in two of the next stories of the book. First we see the goddess Aurora mourning the loss of her mortal son Memnon, much as we have seen Hecuba grieving for her lost children. In the tale of the daughters of Anius that follows, we continue with life after the Triojan War: the character of Aeneas is introduced and we have, told as an ecphrasis, the story of the heroic, self-sacrificing daughters of Anius. Time moves back to the period before the Trojan War for the next tale, that of the daughters of Orion, who are betrayed by male cowardice. The story of Ajax's loss to Ulysses is revisited when the one-eyed monster Polyphemos vies with the adorable if ineffective (typically male!) Acis for the love of the beautiful Galatea. Here Ovid imitates two genres, the epic and the pastoral: Homer had represented Polyphemos as a violent monster, and the poet Theocritus represented him as a comical lover in his *Idylls*. Polyphemos succeeds in eliminating his rival but loses the prize he has sought. Now the theme of unrequited love rises again to the surface (literally) to be developed in the last tale of the book, "Scylla and Glaucus," in which another nymph is pursued by a different kind of monster, a tale that will continue on past the physical ending of Book XIII and into the beginning of Book XIV.

Whether one can call it a structure or not, there is something created by the continuity of Homeric references, the variety of literary genres illustrated, and the thematic twists and turns, like Proteus moving from one figure to another, as the Book progresses. And whether the "structure" of Ovid's *Metamorphoses* is as real as Brooks Otis believed or as illusory as the extended vistas of Roman wall painting in Ovid's time, those metamorphic patterns of commitment and evasion in the telling of the stories seem to me to reflect something that is real in the poem, something one can actually feel in reading it.

Consideration of structure yields, or perhaps drives us back to, a consideration of voice, and that may lead us to see the poem, as Diane Middlebrook argues, as an epic whose only hero is its all-knowing narrator. That narrator will never replace the stories for us, but the "Ovid" whom we hear when we read his poem is at least as protean as his poem is. He seems to point the way from the definable epic of his time to its distant future, when, in the hands of Wordsworth and Whitman, Eliot and Pound, Louis Zukofsky and David Jones, it would be as indefinable as he perhaps imagined it could be, a poem of varied experiences filtered through a single, expansive sensibility, describing its own process, celebrating itself, serving as a means of transmission for stories that its author wants to tell, while perhaps repeating the words of the poet Nennius, "I have made a great heap of all I have found."

Acknowledgments

I wish to thank the editors of the following publications, in which portions of this work have previously appeared:

Arion: "The Wrath of Juno," "Deucalion and Pyrrha," "Medea,"
  "The Plague at Aegina," and "Cephalus and Procris"
Barrow Street: "The House of Rumor"
Cumberland Poetry Review: "Tereus, Procne, and Philomela"
Eclectic Literary Forum: "The Sun and Leucothoë"
The Formalist: "The Mortal Child of an Immortal's Lust"
Parnassus: "Polyphemus, Galatea, and Acis"
Pivot: "The Daughters of Pierus"
The Tennessee Quarterly: "Echo and Narcissus"
TriQuarterly: "Of Praise and Punishment: Arachne"

I am grateful for the frequent PSC-CUNY Research Awards that have given me time to work on this project.

I have benefited greatly from the very close attention that two advisory editors gave to earlier versions of this translation. Bernard Knox's enthusiastic encouragement for this undertaking has been a source of inspiration from the beginning, and his comments on that earlier text were invaluable to me. I am similarly indebted to John Hollander, whose superb ear helped me find my way into Ovid's verse; his conversations on Ovid and on translation are warmly recalled.

William S. Anderson's two-volume commentary on Ovid's *Metamorphoses* has been my constant companion in this venture, a treasure for any reader of the poem.

Over the years, friends have offered advice, suggestions, solutions, partial solutions, and venues wherein I have had the chance to talk (formally or informally) about my work and read from it: my thanks to John Gery, Dana Gioia and Michael Peich, Rachel Hadas, Emily Martin, David Mason, Wyatt Prunty, Mark Rudman, Nigel Thompson, Rosanna Warren, and the late Katharine Washburn.

In preparing this Norton Critical Edition, I was given similar opportunities to talk about Ovid and about translating him by my colleague at Syracuse University, Dympna Callaghan; by Isaac Cates at Long Island University; by Paula Deitz of *The Hudson Review*, Wyatt Prunty at the Sewanee Writers' Conference, and Deborah Warren at the Nicholas Roerich Museum. I must thank Christopher Brunelle, of St. Olaf College, not only for inviting me to speak to his students, but also for the thoroughness with which he read my text. His corrections have been incorporated in this edition.

John Mardirosian first welcomed me to Norton; my manuscript and I both learned much from Ann R. Tappert's thoughtful copyediting of the trade edition, and it is a pleasure to acknowledge the continuing helpfulness of Rivka Genesen, Ben Reynolds, and Brian Baker. I am most grateful to Carol Bemis, whose enthusiasm, dedication, and patience have done much to make these remarks both possible and necessary.

A Note on This Translation

Ovid ends the *Metamorphoses* with the word *vivam*, which I have unremarkably translated as "I will live." A poet survives only if his poem does, and if his poem survives, it does so either in its own language or in translation; there are no other possibilities. In our time, the *Metamorphoses* has many more readers in English and in other living languages than it has in the Latin in which Ovid composed it: this does not mean that it is less alive in Latin than in translation, only that it is less frequently alive in Latin. The loss of Latin as a living language makes translation essential if most of us are to enjoy Ovid's work at all, but it also means that an entire world of connotation and association has been lost with it.

In his time, Ovid's *Metamorphoses* was centered in a web of cultural and political relations to which it was bound by allusions of various kinds. For Ovid's first readers, his brief introduction—the first four lines of his poem—not only set out his own intentions for it, but referred to two of his own earlier works in a very different genre and illustrated in verse his turn from the elegiac couplets he had previously written to the hexameter lines proper to the Latin epic. Not only personal history but cultural: the reader of his time would have also noticed allusions not just to Ovid's earlier work but also to the *Iliad* and the *Odyssey*, the *Argonautica* of Apollonius, and to the issue of whether the poet should write a traditional, chronologically arranged epic or the more refined variety preached and practiced by the Alexandrian Callimachus and his later Roman followers.

What Ovid's Pythagoras would call "the gnawing tooth of time" has left us the poem intact but has fragmented the web surrounding it: Ovid's personal history and the larger cultural issues of his day have little resonance in our age; if a translator could bring across those allusions into modern English, a contemporary reader would still have little or no idea what was at issue; in that sense, they are lost to translation. Throughout the *Metamorphoses*, for example, Ovid is engaged in a complex and competitive relationship with the poet Virgil and with the *other* epic of the Augustan era, Virgil's *Aeneid*. Many contemporary readers will have their first hint of this in Book XIII, when Aeneas himself makes his appearance; unlike Virgil's Aeneas, however, Ovid's hero bumbles along like a celebrity tourist on a guided tour, opening his mouth only to get in trouble for saying the wrong thing and otherwise avoiding memorable speech and action. Very odd indeed for an epic hero, and in the past, his behavior in the poem has often been seen as ineptitude on Ovid's part rather than as a clever element of a deliberately parodic strategy.

Other, more subtle allusions to Virgil's poem may be misunderstood or lost entirely. In Book III of the *Metamorphoses*, the goddess Juno bitterly complains about her husband Jove's affair with Semele and is about to launch into a great tirade when she stops to remind herself of her own importance and to threaten vengeance on her enemy:

> "*profeci quid enim totiens per iurgia?" dixit,*
> "*ipsa petenda mihi est; ipsam, si maxima Iuno*
> *rite vocor, perdam, si me gemmantia dextra*
> *sceptra tenere decet, si sum regina Iovisque*
> *et soror et coniunx—*"

> "But when have I won anything by shouting?"
> she asked. "No: I must attack and ruin her,
> if I am rightly styled as almighty Juno,
> if it is right for me to bear the scepter,
> if I am certainly the queen of Jove,
> his sister, his wife—"

Part of the fun in this passage is that Ovid has taken a speech of Juno from Book I of the *Aeneid*, in which she laments her inability to prevent Aeneas from reaching Italy, an issue of cosmic importance, and applied it to the rather more comical situation of the latest infidelity of her perpetually straying husband, Jove, the omnipotent ruler of heaven; Ovid's last phrase in this passage, "*regina Iovisque et soror et coniunx*," "the queen of Jove, his sister and wife," is taken directly from Virgil; to it Ovid adds one more phrase, deflating Juno's epic dignity just as surely as Groucho Marx did Margaret Dumont's: "*certe soror*," "well, certainly his sister."

This is not to say that Ovid is completely without respect for Virgil; his borrowing and echoing of Virgilian phrases throughout the *Metamorphoses* indicate that he clearly realized the older poet's genius; but to Virgil's gravitas he opposed that "thoughtful lightness" that Italo Calvino finds in his work; to Virgil's single story of how one man, Aeneas, refused to be sidetracked from coming to Italy and establishing a dynasty that led to the rule of Augustus, Ovid opposes so many stories told by so many voices that it is hard to be sure we have counted them accurately.

Ovid's relationship with Virgil, important as it may have been for him in staking out his poetic turf, is impossible to convey in translation, since the existence of Virgil himself largely depends on translations. Unless there were a translation of the *Aeneid* so distinctive in its diction or rhythm that the translator of the *Metamorphoses* could count on his readers recognizing an allusion to it— but even to suggest this is to recognize its unlikeliness.

And what of Ovid's relationship to Augustus himself, the "first citizen" of the Roman state and the official sponsor of Virgil and his literary vision? In Book I, Ovid describes a boisterous convocation of the Olympian gods in which an obstreperous Jove lords it over the other gods and decides to wipe out the human race altogether, for . . . its cruelty! Ovid explicitly compares Jove to Augustus in this scene, and then goes on to show Jove, in the remainder of Book I and subsequent books, as a successful rapist and clumsy seducer of essentially defenseless women. In Book XV, Ovid again compares Augustus to Jove and praises him so extravagantly, in a tone so different from anything else in the *Metamorphoses*, that it is hard to believe Ovid is being serious. "Praise undeserv'd is scandal in disguise," said Alexander Pope, and this seems almost a formula for what Ovid is doing here. Between these episodes are others in which Ovid appears to raise serious questions about the character of Augustus and the legitimacy of his reign. If the Olympian gods often seem in Ovid's treatment of them to be the spoiled members of a dysfunctional family, then Ovid's comparison of Augustus to Jove becomes an act of political subversion, and the *Metamorphoses* may be read as a social and political commentary, an allegorical reflection of its times, and not—it never was intended to be—a timeless and canonical collection of myths.

The translator may suggest such things, but they must be left for the critic to develop: they belong to what has already been lost, that world of context in which Ovid's poem once moved. What the translator can hope for is to bring over as best he may those elements of Ovid's style that *can* be translated. Chief among these would be that "thoughtful lightness" that Italo Calvino has spoken of in his *Six Memos for the Next Millennium*.[1] One can see it in the irony that so often undercuts the noble and the heroic, either by an inappropriate admission (as in Juno's monologue cited above) or by a simile that brings us from tragedy to comedy with no stops in between, as when Pyramus (in Book IV) nobly decides to take his own life in emulation of his beloved Thisbe:

> "'Drink *my* blood now,' he says, drawing his sword,
> and thrusting it at once in his own guts:
> a fatal blow; dying, he draws the blade

---

1. Italo Calvino, *Six Memos for the Next Millennium* (Cambridge: Harvard UP, 1988).

out of his burning wound, and his lifeblood
follows it, jetting high into the air,
as he lies on his back upon the ground.
    "It was as when a water pipe is ruptured
where the lead has rotted, and it springs a leak . . .

The reader is torn from the world of undying love and thrown into one
in which we are trying to find a twenty-four-hour plumbing service.

So then, there is the speed of the narration, the casualness of tone,
the rapid changes in point of view, the alternation between apparent
sympathy for his characters and apparent indifference to their fates;
there is the wordplay, the elaborate rhetorical and prosodic figures,
the whimsical erudition, and the coining of new words: more than
enough to keep a translator busy. If the translator cannot reproduce
one of Ovid's jokes, he may perhaps substitute one of his own in a different place to give a sense of Ovid's playfulness.

Other effects are impossible to reproduce. Latin allows the poet
the liberty to create lines, such as the so-called Golden Line, which
Virgil and Ovid both employed, in which a pair of adjectives and
their respective nouns at either end enclose a verb in the middle.
English will rarely stand still for this sort of thing, but occasionally
something like it may occur to the translator, as in the passage in
Book I where Io's poor father laments her having been discovered in
her current condition as a heifer:

"Lost, you were less a grief than you are, found!"

Though this is not a reflection of the metrical arrangement of the
original lines, I used it anyway, since the artificiality of the arrangement tells us something about the way in which we are to understand Io's (temporary) metamorphosis.

When I began my own process of translation, I set out in medias res,
with the opening of Book III, to see what doing Ovid would be like:

Iamque deus posita fallacies imagine tauri
se confessus erat dictaeque rura tenebat,
cum pater ignarus Cadmo perquirere raptam
imperat et poenam, si non invenerit, addit
exilium, facto pius et sceleratus eodem.

My first question was, what kind of meter will work for this? My earliest version used a line whose length and irregularly placed stresses
would seem, I hoped, analogous to Ovid's dactylic hexameter:

And now, no longer misrepresenting himself as a bull,
Jove in his own form arrived at Crete, while the captive

girl's baffled father orders her brother Cadmus
to search for her, and—perverse but paternal—threatens
to banish the son if he doesn't come up with the daughter.

This lumbered along genially enough, with some lines sagging toward the middle, but I kept thinking of it as a blunt club, battering Ovid into submission. With those few lines, I realized that Ovid does not stop or slow down to take prisoners: he moves swiftly, from one detail to another, one story to another. A second version tried for a shorter line and greater speed:

And now, no longer impersonating a bull,
Jove was on Crete, exposed as himself, while the captive
girl's baffled father (in an action both
paternal and perverse) orders her brother Cadmus
to go out and find her or face banishment.

In subsequent versions, my line moved closer and closer to blank verse—the iambic pentameter line—until I realized that blank verse was what I was looking for:

And now, his taurine imitation ended,
the god exposed himself for what he was
to cowed Europa on the isle of Crete.

In an action both paternal and perverse,
the captured maiden's baffled father bids
her brother Cadmus to locate the girl
or face an endless term of banishment.

In blank verse I found both an analogue to Ovid's dactylic hexameter and a willing and patient warhorse, infinitely adaptable and responsible to the demands placed upon it. Since contemporary poetry has for the most part yielded storytelling to prose, I have organized my verse into paragraphs, as both an acceptance of that fact and a challenge to it.

And so, blank verse it has been, for the most part. There are a few passages where I have departed from its rule; in Book IV, for instance, I have the demonic Tisiphone speak in rhymed couplets because I did not know how else to convey the sheer strangeness of that scene; couplets occasionally managed to slip in elsewhere, either alone or in small groups, where I had not expected them: a number of them found their way into Book X at a place where I was perhaps thinking of Pope's "Eloisa to Abelard." The hymn to Bacchus at the beginning of Book IV is rendered in a meter associated with hymns in English; and the awkward, boxy quatrains of the Athenians' song of praise to Theseus in Book VII are meant to resemble an old-fashioned kind of amateur verse.

In Book V, Ovid tells how the goddess Minerva visits the immortal Muses, the nine daughters of Memory, and learns that they had recently been challenged in song by the nine human daughters of Pierus, who were defeated in the ensuing contest and changed into birds. I do not know what Ovid really thought of the daughters of Pierus, but he does give them a much more interesting song than he gives the Muses. It occurred to me that the contest might be represented as one between the voices of Poesy and those of the Downtown Scene. Thus, the Pierides became the P-Airides, and their song is presented in the diction and meter of contemporary rap. Because Ovid was imitating song here and not speech, I now needed a meter different from the blank verse I had been using and one that would reflect the formality of the Muses' opposing song. Since it seemed fitting that the Muse Calliope would speak in poetry, I settled on a loose five-beat line, relatively irregular as to placement of stresses, but to my ear a lot like Latin dactylic hexameter.

At this point I noticed that in addition to the fifth book, Ovid also turns from the imitation of conversation to the imitation of poetry in the tenth and fifteenth books of his poem. In Book V, it is the song of the Muse Calliope; in Book X, it is the songs of her son, Orpheus; and in Book XV, it is the long, inspired (so *he* says) monologue of the philosopher Pythagoras, whose teachings—written out in Greek hexameter lines—were known in a collection called *The Golden Sayings*. All three figures are related: Calliope and Orpheus are mother and son, and Pythagoras is bound to both of them by his habit of writing in verse and by the emphasis that Pythagorean thought placed on the mystical importance of music. Whether Ovid is using these figures to signal that his epic of fifteen books can be structurally divided into three equal parts, I cannot say: Ovid is very skillful at playing with our structural expectations. However, because of the relationship between these speakers, and because they are all speaking poetry, as it were, I have used the same meter for all three of them.

Though I have generally resisted the urge to add anything to an already abundant original, there are three areas in which I have supplied some information that Ovid left out.

By allowing his stories to jump from one book to the next, and by abrupt, often fortuitous-seeming transitions between stories, Ovid deliberately gives most of the fifteen books of the *Metamorphoses* the appearance of mutability; though they are permeable, they also have a certain underlying coherence, and so I have supplied titles that indicate what I take to be the major theme of each book. I have also supplied running titles for each of the stories, at about the place— and opinions will differ on this—where one story changes to another.

Finally, there are some places, usually near the end of a story, where Ovid withholds information necessary to complete the reader's understanding of what he has just read; often Ovid will leave out entirely the names of some of his more significant characters: Aesculapius, for instance, or Europa, or Callisto, all unnamed in the tales told of them. These omissions may simply be Ovid's way of assuring his readers that he knows they are already familiar with the story, a mild form of flattery, and a means of inviting their participation in the poem: if they aren't familiar with it, how long will it take them to discover the identity of the protagonist?

Unnamed characters are far less numerous than those who are named. For the more important of these, as well as for settings and allegorical figures named by Ovid, the reader may find it helpful to consult Persons, Places, and Personifications in the *Metamorphoses*, on page 531.

Since Ovid's contemporary readers are not as familiar with the figures of myth and legend as his first readers were, I have taken the liberty of slipping the names into the tales, either in the running titles or occasionally in a bracketed line or two in the text itself. I apologize in advance to those who find this obtrusive; the alternative, sending the reader to footnotes at a crucial moment in the story, seemed to me even more so.

Translators hope to be stalking horses for those readers who will discover the work in their own language for the first time and make something new out of it. Shakespeare found in Golding's version of Ovid a source for the cruelties of *Titus Andronicus* and the refined magic of *The Tempest*. After a long period in which Ovid seemed to have little to say to Western readers, his text is once again coming to be seen as a source.

It is perhaps too early to say what it will be a source of, but in his *Six Memos for the Next Millennium*, Italo Calvino describes what he calls "the manifold text, which replaces the oneness of the thinking 'I' with a multiplicity of subjects, voices and views of the world." Calvino goes on to describe the possibilities it opens: "Think what it would be like to have a work conceived from outside the self, a work that would let us escape the limited perspective of the individual ego, not only to enter into selves like our own but to give speech to that which has no language, to the bird perching on the edge of the gutter, to the tree in spring and the tree in fall, to cement, to plastic." One ancient source of the manifold text in Western literature is of course Ovid's *Metamorphoses*, as Calvino clearly recognizes when he asks, "Was this not perhaps what Ovid was aiming at when he wrote about the continuity of forms?"[2]

2. Calvino, 117, 124.

A Brief Life of Ovid

Publius Ovidius Naso was born on March 20 in 43 B.C. to a well-to-do landowning family of the equestrian class in Sulmo (now Sulmona), a town set among the Abruzzi mountains, about forty miles east of Rome. The times were perilous: Julius Caesar had been murdered only a year earlier, and in the year of Ovid's birth the Roman republic, still tottering from the shock of his death, finally collapsed. A catastrophic civil war ensued, lasting until Caesar's adopted heir, his great-nephew Octavian, was able to consolidate power and establish his own autocratic, dynastic rule in Rome in 27 B.C. Ovid's family evidently took no part in the troubles of that period, nor did they suffer from the confiscations of property and wealth common at the time.

Ovid tells us that his father sent him and his brother, exactly one year older than he was, to Rome for their education, where both were encouraged to pursue careers in law. Ovid however betrayed a precocious interest in and gift for the writing of verse, which his father attempted to discourage. "Homer," he warned his son, "left nothing when he died." Ovid dutifully attended lectures given by two of the most important teachers of rhetoric of his time, Arellius Fuscus and Porcius Latro, and attempted to renounce poetry altogether. Still, despite real or feigned enthusiasm for the studies that would have led him to a career in public life, he found it impossible to suppress his poetic talent.

When Ovid was twenty, his brother died, and after fulfilling a few minor judicial offices, Ovid decided against pursuing that line of work. Instead he gave himself over to a life of poetry and self-indulgence, supported no doubt by the Roman equivalent of a trust fund. His gift for making verses had triumphed over his father's good sense. It might also have occurred to Ovid that, with all political power in the hands of one man, a career in public life would have been either pointless or dangerous. At any rate, he says that even though the senate house awaited him—he would have been the first senator in his family, a great distinction—he turned away from competition for public office, on the grounds that such service would have been too great a burden both for his body and his mind. Ambition for civic honor could not match the lure of the Muses.

The Roman literary world in which he would quickly find a place was dominated by the work and influence of earlier generations of poets, soon to become canonical. Lucretius and Catullus, the great poets of the late republic, were dead before Ovid was born, and their successors, Virgil and Horace, were both more than twenty years older than Ovid. The younger poet says that he delighted in hearing Horace read his poems, but only saw Virgil. Those two poets had lived and suffered through the social and political chaos between the death of Julius Caesar and his kinsman's accession to power. They had many good reasons to support Octavian, who had overseen the transition from a dying republic to a newborn empire and had brought peace to a war-weary nation. For these services Octavian was rewarded by the Roman Senate in 27 B.C. with the title Augustus, meaning the illustrious or exalted one. Through the patronage of Augustus's friend Maecenas, he had provided both of the older poets with generous livings. It must have seemed to Ovid, who came to his maturity after that period, and who was beyond needing patronage, that he was alive in a time of constraint against political and social liberties.

Ovid quickly found himself a member of a different, for the most part younger, coterie of poets. With one of them, Aemilius Macer, Ovid spent several years making a Grand Tour, traveling and stopping for various periods of time in Athens and Sicily and seeing the sights and sites of the famous cities of Asia Minor, including the (supposed) ruins of Troy. Other members of the coterie included two poets nearer to him in age: Tibullus (who died before they could become close friends) and Propertius (a comrade, as he says) in age and sensibility. Following their examples, Ovid wrote erotic poems in elegiac couplets. These were immediately popular: Ovid tells us that he was giving readings shortly after he began shaving. In his early twenties, he began to publish: first came the five books (later reduced to three) of his *Amores*, a series of poems written in elegiac couplets, whose subjects were love and poetry, both treated with a great deal of playfulness. This work preceded (or perhaps followed: we don't have a dependable chronology for Ovid's early writings) the *Heroides*, a series of fifteen verse epistles in the voices of the abandoned women of myth and legend. Ovid's female characters are abandoned in both senses of the word: Dido writes a letter to Aeneas after he has left her, but Phaedra writes one to her stepson Hippolytus, professing her ardent (and of course scandalous) love for him. Somewhere around this time, Ovid also wrote a tragedy in Latin, his *Medea*, which has not survived.

Much of the poetry written by Virgil and Horace may be seen as, if not outright propaganda for Augustus, then at least supportive of his regime and programs, which included an attempted reformation of

Roman morals. Barring the *Medea*, about which we know nothing, Ovid's earliest works could never have been seen as supportive of Augustan morality: a collection of erotic verses, happily unconcerned with the thoughts of censorious elders, and a collection of poems in the voices of women who had crossed the line between propriety and publicity were no doubt greatly entertaining to the sophisticated young people of Rome, but probably not to the Autocrat of the Palatine Hill. When he was not writing poetry, Ovid seems to have pursued the life of pleasure that must have given him ample materials not only for the *Amores* but also for the books that immediately followed it. He also managed to find time for two brief, youthful marriages: the first wife, he says, was unworthy of him, and the second, though blameless, was fated not to be his for long. His second wife gave him a daughter who married twice and provided him with grandchildren. A third wife, of whom he wrote with affection and respect, brought into his life a stepdaughter named Perilla.

After the spicy *Amores*, worse was to come: three tongue-in-cheek didactic poems added to his reputation for salaciousness. The first of these was his *Medicamini Faciei*, or *The Art of Cosmetics*, a poem which has survived only in part; it was followed by the *Ars Amatoria*, or *Art of Love*, which poses as a how-to book, teaching men the fine art of seducing women. Its sequel, the *Remedia Amoris*, or *Remedies for Love*, was the poet's attempt to give women the benefit of his own experience and to help them evade the toils of the seducer. Together, these three poems constitute one of Western literature's first experiences of the mock-heroic: serious-sounding poems on subjects more often treated in jokes than in Latin elegiac couplets.

In Ovid's time, Roman women were still forced into marriages against their will, and coming from a privileged background only made this a likelier prospect. The Emperor's daughter Julia offers a case in point: after three dynastic marriages (to the emperor's nephew, Marcellus; then to the emperor's lieutenant, Agrippa; and finally to the emperor's successor, Tiberius), her frequent attempts to find personal satisfaction through a string of increasingly notorious love affairs led to her exile. Though a more tragic case than others, there is no reason to believe her singular in her situation. Many women of her class and background would have sought the same satisfactions the same way, and no doubt Ovid's racy trilogy gave them and their lovers in Rome's fast set the pleasure of seeing the preoccupations of their lives reflected in poetry of the first order.

Around the year 1 A.D., Ovid, then in his early forties, set about writing his epic poem on transformations in fifteen books of dactylic hexameter, his *Metamorphoses*. At the same time, he began the *Fasti*, a poem that has come down to us as six books of elegiac couplets on the first six months of the Roman calendar. The *Fasti* purports to explain the origins of various religious rituals, and in the course of doing so tells a great many stories interspersed with erudite bits such as astrological calculations.

Ovid's *Metamorphoses* is his major work, and in itself and in its influence is one of the most important poems of the Western tradition. When Ovid was nearly finished writing it in 8 A.D., and when advance copies of the poem had begun circulating in Rome, his career was suddenly and permanently turned in a different direction by Augustus, who ordered him exiled to the settlement of Tomis on the Black Sea, at the easternmost end of Roman influence. The conditions of his banishment (in a form called *relegatio*) were relatively light: he did not forfeit any property and was allowed to communicate with his wife (who remained in Rome) and friends. From this exile, he was never to return.

Ovid is our only source for the cause of his banishment, and he really tells us only that it was precipitated by "*carmen et error*"; a poem and a mistake of some kind were responsible. Ovid tells us that the poem was his *Ars Amatoria*, and it may have been, though that work had appeared eight years earlier—was Augustus a slow reader, or did he just have a very long fuse? Many have doubted that the *Ars Amatoria* was indeed the culprit. Given the subversive nature of just about everything else that Ovid had written up to this point, one might expect to find transgressive elements in the *Metamorphoses*, elements that might have been seen as far more destabilizing to the Augustan regime. It is difficult to ignore that a poem built on constant metamorphosis points to a radical instability in the social world, a concept totally opposed to the secure dynasty that Augustus had hoped to leave behind him. It is at least suggestive that Ovid was banished just as copies of that poem began to circulate in Rome.

About the error he had committed, Ovid is far less explicit: it was something that he had overheard and whose significance he had overlooked until it was too late for him to bring it to the attention of the proper authorities. To be more explicit, he tells us, would only pain the emperor more. It is perhaps not unreasonable to connect his banishment with the exile of another scandalous Julia in the First Family: this time Augustus's granddaughter, whom he sent into perpetual exile the same year he banished Ovid.

It took Ovid almost a year to reach Tomis, the settlement at the end of the world, where he would spend the rest of his life, and during that time he began writing the five books of elegiac poems known as the *Tristia*, or *Sorrows*. The second book consists of a single poem appealing to Augustus to restore him; the rest of the poems are letters to friends, asking for their help in getting back and complaining about life in Tomis. This was followed by another series of letters home, the *Epistulae ex Pontus*, or *Letters from Pontus*. At

Rome, Augustus died and was succeeded by his stepson Tiberius. In Tomis, the most sophisticated poet of his age languished in isolation, often cold, frequently ill, terrified of barbarians attacking the town with their poisoned arrows. He learned enough of the local language, Getic, to write a poem in it, but the poem has not survived. He died in 17 A.D.

The Text of
METAMORPHOSES

BOOK I

The Shaping of Changes

Proem[1]

My mind leads me to speak now of forms changed
into new bodies; O gods above, inspire
this undertaking (which you've changed as well)
and guide my poem in its epic sweep
from the world's beginning to the present day.   5

The Creation[2]

Before the seas and lands had been created,
before the sky that covers everything,
Nature displayed a single aspect only
throughout the cosmos; Chaos was its name,
a shapeless, unwrought mass of inert bulk   10
and nothing more, with the discordant seeds
of disconnected elements all heaped
together in anarchic disarray.
   The sun as yet did not light up the earth,
nor did the crescent moon renew her horns,   15
nor was the earth suspended in midair,
balanced by her own weight, nor did the ocean
extend her arms to the margins of the land.
   Although the land and sea and air were present,
land was unstable, the sea unfit for swimming,   20
and air lacked light; shapes shifted constantly,
and all things were at odds with one another,
for in a single mass cold strove with warm,
wet was opposed to dry and soft to hard,
and weightlessness to matter having weight.   25
   Some god (or kinder nature) settled this
dispute by separating earth from heaven,
and then by separating sea from earth
and fluid aether from the denser air;[3]
and after these were separated out   30

1. Ovid divided his *Metamorphoses* into fifteen books, and spoke of it as three times five volumes, suggesting that each five books constituted a kind of unity. The titles of books and the subtitles within books are the translator's. In the opening lines of his poem, Ovid addresses its major theme of metamorphosis, and its chronological range from the creation to his own time.
2. Ovid's universe is not created from nothing; it begins with an already existing Chaos, consisting of formless matter. Something happens, by intervention of a nameless god or by Nature, and Chaos begins to assume form. Creation is a process of increasing definition, the shaping of changes.
3. Romans believed that the atmosphere was divided into two parts: the air we breathe, which was heavy and dense, and the lighter aether, which rose to float above it and fill the upper regions of the heavens.

and liberated from the primal heap,
he bound the disentangled elements
each in its place and all in harmony.
   The fiery and weightless aether leapt
to heaven's vault and claimed its citadel;   35
the next in lightness to be placed was air;
the denser earth drew down gross elements
and was compressed by its own gravity;
encircling water lastly found its place,
encompassing the solid earth entire.   40
   Now when that god (whichever one it was)
had given Chaos form, dividing it
in parts which he arranged, he molded earth
into the shape of an enormous globe,
so that it should be uniform throughout.   45
   And afterward he sent the waters streaming
in all directions, ordered waves to swell
under the sweeping winds, and sent the flood
to form new shores on the surrounded earth;
he added springs, great standing swamps and lakes,   50
as well as sloping rivers fixed between
their narrow banks, whose plunging waters (all
in varied places, each in its own channel)
are partly taken back into the earth
and in part flow until they reach the sea,   55
when they—received into the larger field
of a freer flood—beat against shores, not banks.
He ordered open plains to spread themselves,
valleys to sink, the stony peaks to rise,
and forests to put on their coats of green.   60
   And as the vault of heaven is divided
by two zones[4] on the right and two on the left,
with a central zone, much hotter, in between,
so, by the care of this creator god,
the mass that was enclosed now by the sky   65
was zoned in the same way, with the same lines
inscribed upon the surface of the earth.
Heat makes the middle zone unlivable,
and the two outer zones are deep in snow;
between these two extremes, he placed two others   70
of temperate climate, blending cold and warmth.
   Air was suspended over all of this,
proportionately heavier than aether,
as earth is heavier than water is.

---

4. Just as there are five different climate zones on earth—a central tropical region, with a
   temperate zone on either side, and a frigid zone at each extreme—so there are five analogous zones in the heavens.

He ordered mists and clouds into position,   75
and thunder, to make test of our resolve,
and winds creating thunderbolts and lightning.
   Nor did that world-creating god permit
the winds to roam ungoverned through the air;
for even now, with each of them in charge   80
of his own kingdom, and their blasts controlled,
they scarcely can be kept from shattering
the world, such is the discord between brothers.
   Eurus went eastward, to the lands of Dawn,
the kingdoms of Arabia and Persia,   85
and to the mountain peaks that lie below
the morning's rays; and Zephyr took his place
on the western shores warmed by the setting sun.
The frozen north and Scythia were seized
by bristling Boreas; the lands opposite,   90
continually drenched by fog and rain,
are where the south wind, known as Auster, dwells.
Above these winds, he set the weightless aether,
a liquid free of every earthly toxin.
   No sooner had he separated all   95
within defining limits, when the stars,
which formerly had been concealed in darkness,
began to blaze up all throughout the heavens;
and so that every region of the world
should have its own distinctive forms of life,   100
the constellations and the shapes of gods
occupied the lower part of heaven;
the seas gave shelter to the shining fishes,
earth received beasts, and flighty air, the birds.
   An animal more like the gods than these,   105
more intellectually capable
and able to control the other beasts,
had not as yet appeared: now man was born,
either because the framer of all things,
the fabricator of this better world,   110
created man out of his own divine
substance—or else because Prometheus[5]
took up a clod (so lately broken off
from lofty aether that it still contained
some elements in common with its kin),   115
and mixing it with water, molded it
into the shape of gods, who govern all.
   And even though all other animals
lean forward and look down toward the ground,

5. One legend had Prometheus create the first man and woman on earth from clay and animate them with the fire he had stolen from heaven.

he gave to man a face that is uplifted,   120
and ordered him to stand erect and look
directly up into the vaulted heavens
and turn his countenance to meet the stars;
the earth, that was so lately rude and formless,
was changed by taking on the shapes of men.   125

The Four Ages[6]

Golden, that first age, which, though ignorant
of laws, yet of its own will, uncoerced,
fostered responsibility and virtue;
men had no fear of any punishment,
nor did they read of threatened penalties   130
engraved on bronze;[7] no throng of suppliants
trembled before the visage of a judge
or sought protection from the laws themselves.
     As yet no pine tree on its mountaintop
had been chopped down and fitted out to ship   135
for foreign lands; men kept to their own shores;
steep moats did not yet girdle besieged towns;
there were no straight bronze trumpets, no curved horns,
no swords or helmets; without warfare, all
the nations lived, securely indolent.   140
     No rake had been familiar with the earth,
no plowshare had yet wronged her; untaxed, she gave
of herself freely, providing all essentials.
Content with food acquired without effort,
men gathered fruit from the arbutus tree,   145
wild strawberries on mountainsides, small cherries,
and acorns fallen from Jove's spreading oak.
     Spring was the only season that there was,
and the warm breath of gentle Zephyr stroked
flowers that sprang up from the ground, unsown.   150
Later—though still untilled—the earth bore grain,
and fields, unfallowed, whitened with their wheat;
now streams of milk, now streams of nectar flowed,
and from the green oak, golden honey dripped.
     When Saturn was dispatched to Tartarus,[8]   155
Jove ruled the world; the silver race appeared,

---

6. In his poem *Works and Days*, the Greek poet Hesiod (fl. ca. 700 B.C.) described five generations of progressively degenerating humanity (see p. 453 ff.). In Ovid's scheme, there are
   four ages: golden, silver, bronze, and iron, at which point Jove is persuaded by the corrupt
   state of mankind to destroy it and start over again.
7. In the ancient world, laws were commonly inscribed on stone or bronze tablets.
8. The Italian god Saturn was identified with the Greek Cronos, who devoured all his children but Zeus (identified with Jove) who in turn overthrew Cronos and confined him to
   the underworld. Saturn presided over the Golden Age, Jove over the Silver and subsequent ages. Tartarus was a region of the underworld where the wicked were punished.

less dear than gold, but costlier than bronze.
Jupiter made the ancient springtime shorter
by adding onto it three seasons more:
now winter, summer, an erratic fall,   160
and a brief spring filled out the fourfold year.
      Then the scorched air first burned and glowed with heat,
and icicles dangled in the freezing wind;
then houses first appeared, in the form of caves,
or crude shelters hidden in dense thickets,   165
or huts of branches bound with strips of bark.
At that time, grain was first sown in long furrows,
and bullocks groaned, whose shoulders bore the yoke.
      The third age followed with the race of bronze,
crueler by nature and much more disposed   170
to savage warfare, but not yet corrupt.
      Last was the age of iron: suddenly,
all forms of evil burst upon this time
of baser mettle; modesty, fidelity,
and truth departed; in their absence, came   175
fraud, guile, deceit, the use of violence,
and shameful lusting after acquisitions.
      Now ships spread sail, though sailors until now
knew nothing of them; pines that formerly
had stood upon the summits of their mountains,   180
turned into keels, now prance among the waves;
and land—which formerly was held in common,
as sunlight is and as the breezes are—
is given boundaries by the surveyor.
      Now men demand that the rich earth provide   185
more than the crops and sustenance it owes,
and piercing to the bowels of the earth,
the wealth long hidden in Stygian gloom[9]
is excavated and induces evil;
for iron, which is harmful, and the more   190
pernicious gold (now first produced) create
grim warfare, which has need of both; now arms
are grasped in bloodstained hands; men live off plunder,
and guest has no protection from his host,
nor father-in-law from his daughter's husband,   195
and kindness between brothers is infrequent;
husband and wife both wish each other dead,
and wicked stepmothers concoct the bilious
poisons that turn their youthful victims pale;
a son goes to a soothsayer to learn   200
the date when he will change from heir to owner,

---

9. The darkness associated with the river Styx, which ran through the underworld.

and piety lies vanquished here below.
   Virgin Astraea,[1] the last immortal left
on the bloodstained earth, withdraws from it in horror.

War with the Giants

So that the skies above might be no more   205
secure than earth, the race of Giants[2] plotted
(we hear) to rule in heaven by themselves:
they brought together mountains in a heap
and piled them up to reach the lofty stars;
then the omnipotent father launched a bolt   210
that shattered Mount Olympus at the base,
so Pelion came crashing down from Ossa.[3]
   When their enormous corpses all lay crushed
beneath the great weight of each other's bodies,
their Mother Earth (or so the story goes)   215
drenched with their steaming gore, gave life to it;
and lest no memory at all remain
of her offspring, she gave them human shape;
her stock was marked by hatred of the gods,
by cruelty and eagerness for slaughter: 220
you would have recognized their bloody nature.

Lycaon's Feast

Now when great Jove, the son of Saturn, saw
all this from his high citadel, he groaned,
recalling an event then still too recent
to be widely known: Lycaon's filthy banquet!   225
And stirred by anger worthy of himself,
he called a council of the gods[4] to session:
none of those summoned was the least bit late.
   When the nighttime sky is clear, there can be seen
a highway visible in heaven, named   230
the Milky Way, distinguished for its whiteness.
Gods take this path to the royal apartments

---

1. The goddess representing the virtue of Justice. After Astraea's withdrawal, she was placed among the constellations of the zodiac as Virgo.
2. The race of Giants was related to the gods and strove with them for domination. Jove and the Olympian gods (with help from Hercules) prevailed over them.
3. The Giants piled Ossa on Olympus and Pelion on Ossa; Jove shattered the mountain at the bottom to bring the whole structure crashing down.
4. A traditional epic scene, but Ovid presents the council session as a meeting of the Roman senate, with an outraged and indignant Jove presiding and the other gods as impotent and sycophantic senators. As will become clear, Augustus is Ovid's target.

of Jove the Thunderer; on either side
are palaces with folding doors flung wide,
and filled with guests of their distinguished owners;   235
plebeian gods[5] reside in other sections,
but here in this exclusive neighborhood,
the most renowned of heaven's occupants
have *their* own household deities enshrined;
and if I were permitted to speak freely,   240
I would not hesitate to call this enclave
the Palatine[6] of heaven's ruling class.
    So when, within their marble council chamber,
all of the gods assembled took their seats,
and Jove, above the others, leaned upon   245
his staff of ivory and shook three times
and four his awe-inspiring thick head
of hair, which makes the very cosmos tremble,
these words escaped from his indignant lips:
    "I've never been more anxious for my realm,   250
not even when the serpent-footed Giants
were each preparing to take heaven captive
in the fierce embrace of his one hundred arms!
—That enemy was savage, to be sure,
but all the trouble came from just one source,   255
yet now, wherever Nereus is heard
resounding as he flows around the world,
the human race must perish; this I swear
by the rivers flowing underneath the earth
through Stygian groves; we have tried everything   260
to find a cure, but now the surgeon's blade
must cut away what is untreatable,
lest the infection spread to healthy parts.
    "I have my demigods to think about,
rustic divinities, the nymphs, the fauns,   265
the Satyrs, and the spirits of the forest
that dwell on mountainsides; although, as yet,
we haven't honored them with residence
in heaven, we must guarantee their safety
upon the earth which we have given them.   270
    "But can we? O my gods, can you believe
they will be safe, when I, who lord it over

---

5. Ovid's celestial society mirrors that of Rome, with its division between the nobility and
    those of lower rank. Just as Roman families had shrines for their household gods, so do
    Ovid's Olympians.
6. The Palatine hill, one of Rome's best addresses in Ovid's time, was where Augustus had
    his home.

lesser immortals *and* the thunderbolt,
have had snares set against me by a mortal
noted for beastliness? I mean—Lycaon!"   275
    All hell broke loose in heaven—what an uproar,
with everyone excitedly demanding
a punishment to fit such infamy!
It was as when that band of traitors raged
to annihilate the name of Rome by shedding   280
the blood of Caesar's heir;[7] stunned by the frightful
prospect of utter ruin, the human race
throughout the world, as one, began to shudder;
nor was the piety of your own subjects,
Augustus, any less agreeable   285
to you than that of Jove's had been to him.
By voice and gesture, he suppressed the riot.
All held their peace.
                        When the clamor had subsided,
curbed by the weight of his authority,
great Jove once more broke silence with these words: 290
"He has been dealt with—have no fears of that!
But I will now inform you of his crimes
and of their punishment.
                        "The age's infamy
had reached our ears; hoping to disprove it,
I glided down from the summit of Olympus,   295
concealing my godhood in a human form,
and walked upon the earth. Long would it take
to enumerate the evils that I found
in such abundance, everywhere I went:
the truth was even worse than I had heard.   300
    "I crossed Maenala, where the wild beasts roam,
Cyllene, and the pine groves of Lycaeus;
then on to the inhospitable abode
and seat of the tyrant of Arcadia,[8]
approaching it as evening turned night.   305
    "By signs I let them know a god had come,
and common folk began to offer prayers;
at first Lycaon mocked their piety,
and then he said, 'I will make trial of him,
and prove beyond a shadow of a doubt   310
whether this fellow is a god or man.'
    "He planned to take me, overcome with sleep,
and murder me as I lay unawares;

7. Ovid probably refers to an unsuccessful attempt on the life of Augustus, rather than (as
   some believe) to the assassination of Julius Caesar in 44 B.C.
8. Lycaon.

that was his way of getting at the truth.
Nor was he satisfied with this: he took   315
a hostage sent by the Molossians,
and after severing his windpipe, cut
his body into pieces and then put
the throbbing parts up to be boiled or broiled.
   "As soon as he had set this on the table,   320
I loosed my vengeful bolts until that house
collapsed on its deserving household gods!
   "Frightened, he runs off to the silent fields
and howls aloud, attempting speech in vain;
foam gathers at the corners of his mouth;   325
he turns his lust for slaughter on the flocks,
and mangles them, rejoicing still in blood.
   "His garments now become a shaggy pelt;
his arms turn into legs, and he, to wolf
while still retaining traces of the man: 330
grayness the same, the same cruel visage,
the same cold eyes and bestial appearance.
   "One house has fallen: many more deserve to;
over the broad earth, bestiality
prevails and stirs the Furies up to vengeance."   335

The Great Flood

Some of the gods give voice to their approval
of Jove's words and aggravate his grumbling,
while others play their roles with mute assent.
   Nevertheless, all of them were saddened
by the proposed destruction of the human race   340
and wondered what the future form of earth
could possibly be like, without men on it:
why, who would bring the incense to their altars?
   Was it his purpose to surrender earth
for wild beasts to plunder? As they debated,   345
the king of gods bade them not to worry,
for he would tend to everything himself,
and promised to provide them with a race
which, quite unlike the one he would destroy,
would be miraculous in its origin.   350
   Now he was just about to sprinkle earth
with thunderbolts,[9] yet held back out of fear
that such a conflagration could ignite
the sacred heavens and set the skies ablaze;

---

9. Jove's most impressive weapon, created by the race of Cyclopes in a forge under volcanic
   Mount Etna.

and he recalled a time the Fates predicted,   355
when land and seas and heaven's palaces,
the universe so artfully devised,
should come to total ruin in a fire.
　　He puts away those bolts the Cyclopes forged;
another punishment now pleases him: 360
to sink the mortal race beneath the waves
and send down sheets of rain from up above.
　　At once he seals the north wind in the cave
of Aeolus, along with all those winds
that scatter clouds; the south wind is set loose   365
and flies off swiftly on his dripping wings,
his awful face concealed in pitchy blackness;
his beard is utterly suffused with rain
that runs in channels down his streaming locks;
upon his forehead gather clouds of gloom,   370
and his flowing robes are—literally—flowing.
　　And when his broad hands squeeze low cloud formations,
a crash is heard, and they give up their rain.
Iris, the messenger of Juno, clad
in many-colored robes, draws water up   375
to heaven, where she nourishes the clouds.
　　Ripening grain that was the farmer's hope,
to his despair, now lies completely ruined;
the long year's labor has been all for naught.
　　Jove's own sky cannot yield sufficient water   380
to ease his wrath: Neptune, his sky-blue[1] brother,
aids him with waves of fresh auxiliaries.
The tyrant calls his rivers to assemble
beneath his roof and tells them only this:
　　"No point in lengthy battlefield harangues.   385
Pour yourselves into this with all your strength,
that's what is needed! Open all your doors,
release the floodgates of your dams and dikes,
let all your rivers run without restraint!"
　　Those are his orders: back the rivers go   390
and loose the reins about their fountainheads;
unbridled streams go racing to the sea.
　　Now with his trident, Neptune strikes the earth,
who shudders at the blow and opens wide
new waterways. Delivered from their courses,   395
the rivers rush across the open fields,
and bear away not only figs and flocks,
but folks who tend them, with their dwelling places;
they also sink the shrines of household gods!

---

1. Azure was the color of immortality for Romans.

If any roof has managed to resist,   400
untoppled, this unnatural disaster,
the waves embrace above it nonetheless;
its highest turrets lie beneath the flood.
There are no longer boundaries between
earth and the sea, for everything is sea,   405
and the sea is everywhere without a shore.
    One takes to the hills, another to his skiff,
rowing where once he plowed the earth in rows,
while yet another sails above his grainfields,
or glimpses, far below, his sunken villa;   410
and here in the topmost branches of an elm
is someone casting out a fishing line;
an anchor grazes in a meadow's grasses,
or a curved keel sweeps above a vineyard,
and the seal's misshapen figure lies at rest   415
where the slender goats were lately fond of browsing.
    The Nereids marvel at the sight of groves,
cities, and dwelling places all submerged,
while dolphins take possession of the woods
and shake the lofty branches of the oak   420
as they brush by. The wolf swims among sheep,
the tawny lion and the tiger both
are carried helplessly upon the waves;
the boar's great power, like a lightning bolt,
does not avail, nor do the stag's swift limbs.   425
After his long search for a landing place,
the bird with weary wings collapses seaward.
    Now unrestrained, the sea conceals the hills,
and strange new waves beat at the mountaintops;
the greater part are drowned beneath the waves,   430
while those spared drowning perish of starvation.

Deucalion and Pyrrha

The land of Phocis separates Boeotia
from the Oetaean fields—a fertile land,
when it *was* land—but now part of the sea,
a broad field, rather quickly inundated.   435
    There Mount Parnassus raises its twin peaks,
piercing the clouds and seeking out the stars;
in this place (which alone was unsubmerged)
Deucalion, and she who shared his bed,
borne on a little raft, had come to land.   440
Immediately they set out to worship
the local nymphs, the mountain deities,
and Themis, who, in those days, was in charge

of giving answers through the oracles;[2]
there lived no better nor more upright man,   445
no wife more reverential than his own.
    When Jupiter realized the world was now
thoroughly inundated, and observed
only a single man and woman left
out of the many thousands there had been,   450
and that they both were blameless and devout,
he tore the clouds apart and drove them off
with the blustery north wind; then he revealed
the heavens and the earth to one another.
    The sea's great rage subsides now, as its lord   455
deactivates his triple-pointed spear
and soothes the waters; then he summons Triton,
a sea god, blue as is the sea itself,
who rises from the vasty deeps, displaying
a colony of shellfish on his shoulders,   460
and bids him blow on his resounding conch shell
to signal the retreat of floods and streams.
    He lifts the hollow shell of his great horn,
which twists, expanding in diameter
as it revolves around its spiral base;   465
and when he blows upon it in midocean,
its voice reverberates from shore to shore
along the daily route that Phoebus travels.[3]
    So after he had pressed it to his lips,
wet from that streaming beard of his, and blew   470
retreat as he had been commanded to,
the waters everywhere, on land and sea,
all heard that sound, and were at once restrained.
    Now seas have shores, and streams their swollen beds,
and hills appear again as floods subside;   475
land rises and earth waxes as waves wane;
after so long a period of time,
the treetops are uncovered in the woods,
showing the muck still clinging to their leaves.
    The world was certainly restored, but when   480
Deucalion perceived the emptiness
and silent desolation of its lands,
tears rose within him as he turned to Pyrrha:
"O sister,[4] wife, and only woman left,

---

2. Themis was a goddess who like Astraea was associated with Justice. Oracles were places
   where the questions that men asked the gods about private and public affairs were
   answered, though often ambiguously.
3. The journey of the sun.
4. Ovid exaggerates their familial relationship: the two are actually cousins.

you, whom the bonds of race and family   485
and our marriage bed have joined to me,
we are now joined by our common perils—
for we two are the crowd that fills the lands
seen by the rising and the setting sun—
we two are all: the sea now has the others.   490
And our claim upon our lives is still
doubtful, for those storm clouds frighten me!
    "And how would you be feeling, my poor wretch,
if fate had snatched you from the flood without me?
How would you bear this terror all alone?   495
Who would console you in your unshared grief?
For trust me, if the sea had taken you,
I would have followed then, my wife; the sea
would not have taken one of us, but two.
    "Oh, would that I were able to repair   500
these losses by the skills my father had
of breathing spirit into molded clay,
for then I could restore the human race!
    "But now humanity depends on us;
so heaven wills, and wills that we alone   505
remain the only models of mankind."
He finished speaking. For a while they wept
and then decided to entreat the heavens
and seek aid through the sacred oracles.
    So side by side, the couple went at once   510
to the Cephisus, which, though not yet clear,
was now confined to its accustomed bed.
They sprinkled drops of water in libation
upon their heads and garments, then went off
to worship at the sacred shrine of Themis,   515
its gables all discolored with foul moss,
and altars with no sacrificial fires.
    As soon as they approached the temple steps
both fell upon the ground in reverence,
kissing the cold stone with trembling lips: 520
"If heaven may be softened by the prayers
of the just, and godly anger be deflected,
then tell us, Themis, by what methods may
this ruined race of ours be restored,
and aid, most merciful, this world immersed!"   525
    Moved by their words, the goddess offered them
an oracle: "Go from my temple now,
with your heads covered and your robes unbound;
behind you, toss the bones of your great mother!"
    Bewildered, were they, for the longest time: 530
Pyrrha broke the silence first, refusing

to carry out the orders of the goddess;
begging her pardon, though, with quivering lip,
but mother's shade would surely be offended
by such a casual treatment of her bones.   535
    And meanwhile they repeat the oracle's
obscurities, those words whose sense is hidden,
turning them over in their puzzled minds,
until at last the son of Prometheus
spoke soothing words to Epimetheus' daughter: 540
    "The righteous oracles can't counsel evil,
so if I am not very much mistaken,
our 'great mother' is the earth itself;
I reckon that the 'bones' the goddess meant
are merely stones in the body of the earth: 545
it's stones we're meant to throw behind our backs!"
    Though Pyrrha was excited by her husband's
interpretation of the oracle,
it seemed a rather doubtful hope at best,
for neither of them had much confidence   550
in heaven's admonitions—still, what harm
could come from trying it?
                            As they descend,
they veil their heads and loosen up their robes,
and cast the stones behind them as the goddess
bade them to do—and as they did, these stones   555
(you needn't take this part of it on faith,
for it's supported by an old tradition)—
these stones at once begin to lose their hardness
and their rigidity; slowly they soften;
once softened, they begin to take on shapes.   560
    Then presently, when they'd increased in size
and grown more merciful in character,
they bore a certain incomplete resemblance
to the human form, much like those images
created by a sculptor when he begins   565
roughly modeling his marble figures.
    That part in them which was both moist and earthy
was used for the creation of their flesh,
while what was solid and incapable
of bending turned to bone; what had been veins   570
continued on, still having the same name.
    By heaven's will, in very little time,
stones that the man threw took the forms of men,
while those thrown from the woman's hand repaired
the loss of women: the hardness of our race   575
and great capacity for heavy labor
give evidence of our origins.

The Second Creation

The earth spontaneously generated
the varied forms of other animals
after the standing water had been warmed   580
by the sun's rays; for then the sodden marshes
swelled up with heat, and fecund seeds of life
grew in that soil as in a mother's womb,
and from its richness took distinctive forms;
so when the Nile that flows with seven mouths,   585
retreating from the fields it irrigates,
has settled back into its ancient bed
and the still-damp slime was heated by the sun,
then farmers, as they tilled the soil, discovered
numerous kinds of animated life;   590
some, just begun, were not yet quite alive,
while others showed some sort of imperfection,
and often in the same form one could see
that this part lived, while that part was raw earth.
It is when heat and moisture join as one   595
that life is generated; all living forms
originate from these opposing sources;
for even though they are at odds by nature,
the two of them create all living things,
and their discordant harmony is suited   600
to foster varied offspring in abundance.
So when the earth, still completely covered
with fresh muck from that just receded flood,
was heated by the sun's rays, she produced
countless species; some were the old ones, restored,   605
and others were monsters, novel in their shapes.

Apollo and the Python

Unwillingly, the earth bore *you*, as well,
enormous Python,[5] serpent quite unknown
to all prior ages—you, who would become
a terror to the newly fashioned folk,   610
so very like a mountainside you were;
the archer god (with lethal bow unused
before, except for hunting does and she-goats)
destroyed this beast by ventilating him
with almost every arrow in his quiver,   615
and the snake's venom poured through his black wounds.

5. A monstrous serpent sprung from the fertile postdiluvian earth.

And, lest the centuries should wear away
the glory of his deed, he instituted
the sacred games whose contests all would throng to,
and named them Pythian,[6] to celebrate   620
his victory against the vanquished serpent;
at these events, the youths who won in trial
of hand or foot or fleet-wheeled chariot
were given, as their prize, an oaken garland,
for laurel wasn't in existence yet;   625
in those days, Phoebus bound his flowing locks
in garlands made from any tree whatever.

Apollo and Daphne

Daphne, the daughter of the river god
Peneus, was the first love of Apollo;
this happened not by chance, but by the cruel   630
outrage of Cupid; Phoebus, in the triumph
of his great victory against the Python,
observed him bending back his bow and said,
    "What are *you* doing with such manly arms,
lascivious boy? That bow befits *our* brawn,   635
wherewith we deal out wounds to savage beasts
and other mortal foes, unerringly:
just now with our innumerable arrows
we managed to lay low the mighty Python,
whose pestilential belly covered acres!   640
Content yourself with kindling love affairs
with your wee torch—and don't claim *our* glory!"
    The son of Venus answered him with this:
"Your arrow, Phoebus, may strike everything;
mine will strike you: as animals to gods,   645
your glory is so much the less than mine!"
    He spoke, and soaring upward through the air
on wings that thundered, in no time at all
had landed on Parnassus' shaded height;
and from his quiver drew two arrows out   650
which operated at cross purposes,
for one engendered flight, the other, love;
the latter has a polished tip of gold,
the former has a tip of dull, blunt lead;
with this one, Cupid struck Peneus' daughter,   655
while the other pierced Apollo to his marrow.

---

6. A Greek national festival second in importance to the Olympics, the Pythian Games were
   celebrated every four years from 586 B.C. to about 394 A.D. at a venue near Delphi, in
   honor of Apollo's victory over the Python.

One is in love now, and the other one
won't hear of it, for Daphne calls it joy
to roam within the forest's deep seclusion,
where she, in emulation of the chaste   660
goddess Phoebe, devotes herself to hunting;
one ribbon only bound her straying tresses.
    Many men sought her, but she spurned her suitors,
loath to have anything to do with men,
and rambled through the wild and trackless groves   665
untroubled by a thought for love or marriage.
    Often her father said, "You owe it to me,
child, to provide me with a son-in-law
and grandchildren!"
                "Let me remain a virgin,
father most dear," she said, "as once before   670
Diana's father, Jove, gave her that gift."
    Although Peneus yielded to you, Daphne,
your beauty kept your wish from coming true,
your comeliness conflicting with your vow:
at first sight, Phoebus loves her and desires   675
to sleep with her; desire turns to hope,
and his own prophecy deceives the god.
    Now just as in a field the harvest stubble
is all burned off, or as hedges are set ablaze
when, if by chance, some careless traveler   680
should brush one with his torch or toss away
the still-smoldering brand at break of day—
just so the smitten god went up in flames
until his heart was utterly afire,
and hope sustained his unrequited passion.   685
    He gazes on her hair without adornment:
"What if it were done up a bit?" he asks,
and gazes on her eyes, as bright as stars,
and on that darling little mouth of hers,
though sight is not enough to satisfy;   690
he praises everything that he can see—
her fingers, hands, and arms, bare to her shoulders—
and what is hidden prizes even more.
    She flees more swiftly than the lightest breeze,
nor will she halt when he calls out to her: 695
"Daughter of Peneus, I pray, hold still,
hold still! I'm not a foe in grim pursuit!
Thus lamb flees wolf, thus dove from eagle flies
on trembling wings, thus deer from lioness,
thus any creature flees its enemy,   700
but I am stalking you because of love!

"Wretch that I am: I'm fearful that you'll fall,
brambles will tear your flesh because of me!
The ground you're racing over's very rocky,
slow down, I beg you, restrain yourself in flight,   705
and I will follow at a lesser speed.

"Just ask yourself who finds you so attractive!
I'm not a caveman, not some shepherd boy,
no shaggy guardian of flocks and herds—
you've no idea, rash girl, you've no idea   710
whom you are fleeing, that is why you flee!

"Delphi, Claros, Tenedos are all mine,
I'm worshiped in the city of Patara!7
Jove is my father, I alone reveal
what was, what is, and what will come to be!   715
The plucked strings answer my demand with song!

"Although my aim is sure, another's arrow
proved even more so, and my careless heart
was badly wounded—the art of medicine
is my invention, by the way, the source   720
of my worldwide fame as a practitioner
of healing through the natural strength of herbs.

"Alas, there is no herbal remedy
for the love that I must suffer, and the arts
that heal all others cannot heal their lord—"   725

He had much more to say to her, but Daphne
pursued her fearful course and left him speechless,
though no less lovely fleeing him; indeed,
disheveled by the wind that bared her limbs
and pressed the blown robes to her straining body   730
even as it whipped up her hair behind her,
the maiden was more beautiful in flight!

But the young god had no further interest
in wasting his fine words on her; admonished
by his own passion, he accelerates,   735
and runs as swiftly as a Gallic hound
chasing a rabbit through an open field;
the one seeks shelter and the other, prey—
he clings to her, is just about to spring,
with his long muzzle straining at her heels,   740
while she, not knowing whether she's been caught,
in one swift burst, eludes those snapping jaws,
no longer the anticipated feast;
so he in hope and she in terror race.

7. All are Greek cities connected with the worship of Apollo.

But her pursuer, driven by his passion,   745
outspeeds the girl, giving her no pause,
one step behind her, breathing down her neck;
her strength is gone; she blanches at the thought
of the effort of her swift flight overcome,
but at the sight of Peneus, she cries,   750
"Help me, dear father! If your waters hold
divinity, transform me and destroy
that beauty by which I have too well pleased!"
　　Her prayer was scarcely finished when she feels
a torpor take possession of her limbs—   755
her supple trunk is girdled with a thin
layer of fine bark over her smooth skin;
her hair turns into foliage, her arms
grow into branches, sluggish roots adhere
to feet that were so recently so swift,   760
her head becomes the summit of a tree;
all that remains of her is a warm glow.
　　Loving her still, the god puts his right hand
against the trunk, and even now can feel
her heart as it beats under the new bark;   765
he hugs her limbs as if they were still human,
and then he puts his lips against the wood,
which, even now, is adverse to his kiss.
　　"Although you cannot be my bride," he says,
"you will assuredly be my own tree,   770
O Laurel, and will always find yourself
girding my locks, my lyre, and my quiver too—
you will adorn great Roman generals
when every voice cries out in joyful triumph
along the route up to the Capitol;[8]   775
you will protect the portals of Augustus,
guarding, on either side, his crown of oak;[9]
and as I am—perpetually youthful,
my flowing locks unknown to the barber's shears—
so you will be an evergreen forever   780
bearing your brilliant foliage with glory!"
　　Phoebus concluded. Laurel shook her branches
and seemed to nod her summit in assent.

---

8. Triumphs were victory parades awarded to successful Roman generals; they proceeded
　　from the forum below to the temple of Jupiter Optimus Maximus on the highest point of
　　the *capitolium*, the southern summit of Rome's Capitoline Hill.
9. When the Roman senate gave Julius Caesar's nephew Octavian the title of Augustus in
　　27 B.C., it awarded him a crown of oak to symbolize his preservation of the lives of the
　　Roman people by his victory in the civil war. The crown, surrounded by protective laurels,
　　was mounted over the door of his house on the Palatine hill.

Jove and Io (1)

There is a grove in Thessaly, enclosed
on every side by high and wooded hills: 785
they call it Tempe. The river Peneus,
which rises deep within the Pindus range,
pours its turbulent waters through this gorge
and over a cataract that deafens all
its neighbors far and near, creating clouds   790
that drive a fine, cool mist along, until
it drips down through the summits of the trees.
    Here is the house, the seat, the inner chambers
of the great river; here Peneus holds court[1]
in his rocky cavern and lays down the law   795
to water nymphs and tributary streams.
    First to assemble were the native rivers,
uncertain whether to congratulate
or to commiserate with Daphne's father:
the Sperchios, whose banks are lined with poplars,   800
the ancient Apidanus and the mild
Aeas and Amprysus; others came later—
rivers who, by whatever course they take,
eventually bring their flowing streams,
weary of their meandering, to sea.   805
    Inachus was the only river absent,
concealed in the recesses of his cave:
he added to his volume with the tears
he grimly wept for his lost daughter Io,
not knowing whether she still lived or not;   810
but since he couldn't find her anywhere,
assumed that she was nowhere to be found—
and in his heart, he feared a fate far worse.
    For Jupiter had seen the girl returning
from her father's banks and had accosted her: 815
"O maiden worthy of almighty Jove
and destined to delight some lucky fellow
(I know not whom) upon your wedding night,
come find some shade," he said, "in these deep woods—"
(showing her where the woods were *very* shady)   820
"while the sun blazes high above the earth!
    "But if you're worried about entering
the haunts of savage beasts all by yourself,
why, under the protection of a god
you will be safe within the deepest woods—   825
and no plebeian god, for I am he

---

1. Throughout the *Metamorphoses*, rivers are not only places but persons—river gods of
often very distinctive personalities.

who bears the celestial scepter in his hand,
I am he who hurls the roaming thunderbolt—
don't run from me!"
               But run she did, through Lerna
and Lyrcea, until the god concealed   830
the land entirely beneath a dense
dark mist and seized her and dishonored her.
    Juno, however, happened to look down
on Argos, where she noticed something odd:
swift-flying clouds had turned day into night   835
long before nighttime. She realized
that neither falling mist nor rising fog
could be the cause of this phenomenon,
and looked about at once to find her husband,
as one too well aware of the connivings   840
of a mate so often taken in the act.
    When he could not be found above, she said,
"Either I'm mad—or I am being had."
She glided down to earth from heaven's summit
immediately and dispersed the clouds.   845
    Having intuited his wife's approach,
Jove had already metamorphosed Io
into a gleaming heifer—a beauty still,
even as a cow. Despite herself,
Juno gave this illusion her approval,   850
and feigning ignorance, asked him whose herd
this heifer had come out of, and where from;
Jove, lying to forestall all inquiries
as to her origin and pedigree,
replied that she was born out of the earth.   855
Then Juno asked him for her as a gift.
    What could he do? Here is his beloved:
to hand her over is unnatural,
but not to do so would arouse suspicion;
shame urged him onward while love held him back.   860
Love surely would have triumphed over shame,
except that to deny so slight a gift
to one who was his wife and sister both
would make it seem that this was no mere cow!
    Her rival given up to her at last,   865
Juno feared Jove had more such tricks in mind,
and couldn't feel entirely secure
until she'd placed this heifer in the care
of Argus, the watchman with a hundred eyes:
in strict rotation, his eyes slept in pairs,   870
while those that were not sleeping stayed on guard.
No matter where he stood, he looked at Io,
even when he had turned his back on her.

He let her graze in daylight; when the sun
set far beneath the earth, he penned her in   875
and placed a collar on her indignant neck.
She fed on leaves from trees and bitter grasses,
and had no bed to sleep on, the poor thing,
but lay upon the ground, not always grassy,
and drank the muddy waters from the streams.   880
  Having no arms, she could not stretch them out
in supplication to her warden, Argus;
and when she tried to utter a complaint
she only mooed—a sound which terrified her,
fearful as she now was of her own voice.   885
  Io at last came to the riverbank
where she had often played; when she beheld
her own slack jaws and newly sprouted horns
in the clear water, she fled, terrified!
  Neither her naiad sisters nor her father   890
knew who this heifer was who followed them
and let herself be petted and admired.
Inachus fed her grasses from his hand;
she licked it and pressed kisses on his palm,
unable to restrain her flowing tears.   895
  If words would just have come, she would have spoken,
telling them who she was, how this had happened,
and begging their assistance in her case;
but with her hoof, she drew lines in the dust,
and letters of the words she could not speak   900
told the sad story of her transformation.
  "Oh, wretched me," cried Io's father, clinging
to the lowing calf's horns and snowy neck.
"Oh, wretched me!" he groaned. "Are you the child
for whom I searched the earth in every part?   905
Lost, you were less a grief than you are, found!
  "You make no answer, unable to respond
to our speech in language of your own,
but from your breast come resonant deep sighs
and—all that you can manage now—you *moo!*   910
  "But I—all unaware of this—was busy
arranging marriage for you, in the hopes
of having a son-in-law and grandchildren.
Now I must pick your husband from my herd,
and now must find your offspring there as well!   915
  "Nor can I end this suffering by death;
it is a hurtful thing to be a god,
for the gates of death are firmly closed against me,
and our sorrows must go on forever."
  And while the father mourned his daughter's loss,   920
Argus of the hundred eyes removed her

to pastures farther off and placed himself
high on a mountain peak, a vantage point
from which he could keep watch in all directions.
      The ruler of the heavens cannot bear   925
the sufferings of Io any longer,
and calls his son, born of the Pleiades,[2]
and orders him to do away with Argus.
      Without delay, he takes his winged sandals,
his magic, sleep-inducing wand, and cap;   930
and so equipped, the son of father Jove
glides down from heaven's summit to the earth,
where he removes and leaves behind his cap
and winged sandals, but retains the wand;
and sets out as a shepherd, wandering   935
far from the beaten path, driving before him
a flock of goats he rounds up as he goes,
while playing tunes upon his pipe of reeds.
      The guardian of Juno is quite taken
by this new sound: "Whoever you might be,   940
why not come sit with me upon this rock,"
said Argus, "for that flock of yours will find
the grass is nowhere greener, and you see
that there is shade here suitable for shepherds."
      The grandson of great Atlas takes his seat   945
and whiles away the hours, chattering
of this and that—and playing on his pipes,
he tries to overcome the watchfulness
of Argus, struggling to stay awake;
even though Slumber closes down some eyes,   950
others stay vigilant. Argus inquired
how the reed pipes, so recently invented,
had come to be, and Mercury responded:

Pan and Syrinx

"On the idyllic mountains of Arcadia,
among the hamadryads of Nonacris,   955
one was renowned, and Syrinx[3] was her name.
Often she fled—successfully—from Satyrs,
and deities of every kind as well,
those of the shady wood and fruited plain.
      "In her pursuits and in virginity   960
Diana was her model, and she wore
her robe hitched up and girt above the knees
just as her goddess did; and if her bow

---

2. Mercury, Jove's messenger, was the son of Maia, one of the stars in the Pleiades constellation.
3. Hamadryads were nymphs who lived in trees. *Syrinx* is the Greek name for reed.

had been made out of gold, instead of horn,
anyone seeing her might well have thought   965
she *was* the goddess—as, indeed, some did.
    "Wearing his crown of sharp pine needles, Pan
saw her returning once from Mount Lycaeus,
and began to say. . . . "
                      There remained to tell
of how the maiden, having spurned his pleas,   970
fled through the trackless wilds until she came
to where the gently flowing Ladon stopped
her in her flight; how she begged the water nymphs
to change her shape, and how the god, assuming
that he had captured Syrinx, grasped instead   975
a handful of marsh reeds! And while he sighed,
the reeds in his hands, stirred by his own breath,
gave forth a similar, low-pitched complaint!
    The god, much taken by the sweet new voice
of an unprecedented instrument,   980
said this to her: "At least we may converse
with one another—I can have that much."
    That pipe of reeds, unequal in their lengths,
and joined together one-on-one with wax,
took the girl's name, and bears it to this day.   985
    Now Mercury was ready to continue
until he saw that Argus had succumbed,
for all his eyes had been closed down by sleep.
He silences himself and waves his wand
above those languid orbs to fix the spell.   990
    Without delay he grasps the nodding head
and where it joins the neck, he severs it
with his curved blade and flings it bleeding down
the steep rock face, staining it with gore.
O Argus, you are fallen, and the light   995
in all your lamps is utterly put out:
one hundred eyes, one darkness all the same!

Jove and Io (2)

But Saturn's daughter[4] rescued them and set
those eyes upon the feathers of her bird,
filling his tail with constellated gems.   1000
    Her rage demanded satisfaction, *now*:
the goddess set a horrifying Fury
before the eyes and the imagination
of her Grecian rival; and in her heart

---

4. Juno.

she fixed a prod that goaded Io on,   1005
driving her in terror through the world
until at last, O Nile, you let her rest
from endless labor; having reached your banks,
she went down awkwardly upon her knees,
and with her neck bent backward, raised her face   1010
as only she could do it, to the stars;
and with her groans and tears and mournful mooing,
entreated Jove, it seemed, to put an end
to her great suffering.
                Jove threw his arms
around the neck of Juno in embrace,   1015
imploring her to end this punishment:
"In future," he said, "put your fears aside:
never again will you have cause to worry—
about *this* one." And swore upon the Styx.[5]

   The goddess was now pacified, and Io   1020
at once began regaining her lost looks,
till she became what she had been before;
her body lost all of its bristling hair,
her horns shrank down, her eyes grew narrower,
her jaws contracted, arms and hands returned,   1025
and hooves divided themselves into nails;
nothing remained of her bovine nature,
unless it was the whiteness of her body.
She had some trouble getting her legs back,
and for a time feared speaking, lest she moo,   1030
and so quite timidly regained her speech.

   She is a celebrated goddess now,
and worshiped by the linen-clad Egyptians.
Her son, Epaphus, is believed to be
sprung from the potent seed of mighty Jove,   1035
and temples may be found in every city
wherein the boy is honored with his parent.

Phaëthon

He had a friend, like him in age and spirit,
named Phaëthon, the sun god's child. One day
this boy was boasting, and in vanity   1040
would not take second place to Epaphus,
so proud he was that Phoebus was his father.
   The grandson of Inachus could not bear it:
"You *are* a fool—to trust your mother's lies!
You're swollen with false notions of your father!"   1045

---

5. The river Styx, which flowed nine times around the underworld, was held in great venera-
tion by the gods. The oaths they swore by it were irrevocable.

Phaëthon blushed, and in embarrassment,
repressed the awful anger that he felt;
he went back to his mother, Clymene,
and told her what the other boy had said.
"And so that you may feel this pain the more,   1050
dear mother," he said, "I who am so bold,
so very spirited, could not reply!
It shames me that I listened to such insults
unable to respond or to refute them!
    "If I am truly of immortal seed,   1055
give me sure proof of my exalted birth,
and a status equal to my origin!"
    He spoke and threw his arms around her neck,
imploring her upon his very life,
and on that of his stepfather, Merops,   1060
and by the wedding torches of his sisters,
to give him proof of who his father was.
    Clymene, moved by Phaëthon's petition
(or by the insult to her own good name),
lifted her arms and stretched them out to heaven   1065
and gazing right into the sun, replied,
"By this great radiance, my child, I swear,
by this bright orb which sees and hears us now,
that from this being which you now behold,
and which rules the world, you have your origin,   1070
child of the Sun! And if I speak a lie,
never may I look on his face again;
may this light be the last light that I see!
    "It will not be a great task to discover
the place where your father keeps his household gods.   1075
The house from whence he rises is on land
contiguous to ours: if you dare,
set out and ask your question of the Sun."
    Already full of heaven in his mind,
his mother's words inspire him with joy,   1080
and after crossing Ethiopia,
his native land, and passing through the realm
of India that lies beneath the sun,
he comes at last to where his father rises.

BOOK II

Of Mortal Children and
Immortal Lusts

Phaëthon[1]

There stood the regal palace of the Sun,
soaring upon its many lofty columns,
with roof of gold and fire-flashing bronze,
and ceilings intricate with ivory,
and double-folding doors that shone with silver.   5
    Its art surpassed the stuff that it was made of,
for Vulcan had engraved upon those doors
the seas that gird the middle of the earth,
the circling lands and the overhanging sky.
    The waves displayed their gods of cerulean hue: 10
harmonious Triton, inconstant Proteus,
huge Aegaeon, who lifts enormous whales,
and Doris with her daughters, the sea nymphs;
some are depicted swimming, others sit
upon a rock to dry their sea-green hair,   15
and others are shown riding upon fishes,
their features neither utterly alike
nor wholly different, but rather mixed,
as those of sisters ought to be.
                  On land
were scenes of men in cities, beasts in forests,   20
rivers and nymphs and rural deities;
and over this he set the zodiac,
six figures each upon the left and right.
    Soon as the son of Clymene had climbed
the steep path leading to the dwelling place   25
of his reputed parent, he went in
and turned at once to meet his father's gaze—
though at some distance, for he could not bear
such brightness any closer.
                 Phoebus[2] sat
in robes of purple high upon a throne   30
that glittered brilliantly with emeralds;
and in attendance on his left and right
stood Day and Month and Year and Century,
and all the Hours, evenly divided;

---

1. Ovid delights in having his tales break the boundaries normally imposed by the idea of division implied in the term "book"; as here, he allows them to flow over into the next, equally permeable container.
2. Ovid here calls the sun god Phoebus, though he usually reserves that title for Apollo. According to William S. Anderson, "The distinction between Helios and Phoebus Apollo, which prevailed in Homer and earlier Greek literature, has vanished by this time." (Anderson, ed., Ovid's Metamorphoses Books 1–5 [Norman: U of Oklahoma P, 1997], 233.)

fresh Spring was there, adorned with floral crown,   35
and Summer, naked, bearing ripened grain,
and Autumn, stained from treading out her grapes,
and Winter with his gray and frosty locks.
    And sitting in the middle of these figures,
the all-seeing Sun looked upon that youth,   40
who quaked with terror at such novel sights.
"What brings you here?" he asked. "What do you seek
in this high tower, Phaëthon—you, an heir
no parent would deny?"
                        The youth responded:
"O Phoebus, our universal light,   45
and father—if you let me use that name!
—If Clymene is not concealing guilt
under false pretenses, then give me proof
by which I might have credibility
as your true son, and free my mind of doubt!"   50
So the boy spoke.
                 The father put aside
his shining crown and told him to draw nearer
and took him in his arms: "It would not be
appropriate for me to disavow
our relationship," he said, "for Clymene   55
has spoken truly of your parentage.
    "But so that you may have no doubts at all,
whatever gift you ask me will be given you;
and this I promise by the marshy Styx,
which all of the immortals swear upon—   60
a sight which I, of course, have never seen."[3]
    He'd scarcely finished speaking when the boy
asked for his father's chariot—and permission
to guide his winged horses for a day.
The father's oath now filled him with regret;   65
three times and four he struck his lustrous brow:
"Your deed reveals the rashness of my speech!
Would that I were permitted to rescind
the promise I have given! I confess
that this alone I would deny you, son!   70
    "At least I am permitted to dissuade you:
what you desire is most dangerous!
You seek a gift that is too great for you,
beyond your strength, beyond your boyish years;
your fate is mortal: what you ask for isn't.   75
    "Out of your ignorance, you seek much more
than even gods are able to control,

---

3. Because the Sun's daily journey across the sky stops short of the underworld.

for though each god may do just as he pleases,
none but myself may set his heel upon
the fire-bearing axle. No—not even he   80
who governs vast Olympus and who flings
the thunderbolt may drive this chariot:
and what force is more powerful than Jove?

"The journey starts off steeply, and my team,
emerging from their stables in the morning,   85
must struggle to ascend—and barely do:
the midpoint of the heavens is so high
that when I look down on the earth and seas,
fear often makes me tremble, and the heart
within my breast is seized with palpitations!   90

"The last part of the journey is a steep
descent that needs a skilled hand on the reins;
then, even Tethys,[4] waiting to receive me
beneath the waves, must fear that I will crash!

"Besides, there is the whirling vault of heaven   95
that draws the stars along and sets them spinning;
I press against this force which overcomes
all others, and I overcome it by
opposing the revolving universe.[5]

"Suppose the chariot were in *your* hands: 100
what would *you* do? Would you have the power
to go against the whirling of the poles,
lest their rotation sweep you off completely?

"Perhaps you think that there are sacred groves
and cities of the gods along the way,   105
temples displaying all the gifts of wealth?
Not so: your path is full of lurking perils
as well as images of savage beasts.

"And if you hold this course unswervingly,
you'll find the horns of Taurus in your way,   110
the Archer and the gaping jaws of Leo,
and Scorpio, whose long and curving arms
sweep one way, while the curving arms of Cancer
sweep broadly in the opposite direction.[6]

"Nor will you find it easy to control   115
my fire-breathing steeds, who challenge me
to hold them back when they get heated up,
and their wild necks rebel against the reins.

---

4. A sea goddess and mother of Clymene, hence Phaëthon's grandmother; as the wife of
   Ocean, she attends the Sun as he rises up from the water in the morning and returns to it
   in the evening.
5. The sky is depicted as rotating counter to the motion of the Sun.
6. Ovid has the Sun exaggerate, probably to frighten Phaëthon; the Sun would not encounter
   so many of the signs of the zodiac in his journey, just the one that was prominent at the
   time.

"I would not be the giver of a gift
that would prove fatal to you, son—beware,   120
and change your asking while it may be changed!
You seek assurance that you are my son?
I give you such assurance by my fears,
and by my dread, I show myself your father.
Look, look, upon my countenance—I wish   125
that you could look into my heart as well,
and there discover my paternal cares!

"Whatever wealth this ample world affords
is yours to have: just cast your eyes about
the plenitude of sky and earth and ocean   130
and ask for any of the goods you see:
I will deny you nothing that you wish.

"Only one thing I beg you not to ask for,
a punishment, if truly understood,
and not a gift, although you think it so—   135
a punishment indeed, my Phaëthon.

"Why do you throw your arms around my neck,
you foolish child? Why do you beseech me?
It will be given to you! Have no doubt!
I've sworn it by the waters of the Styx,   140
whatever you wish for—only wish more wisely!"
But his rebellious son refused to listen
and adamantly kept to his design,
so great his passion for the chariot.

And so, after delaying for as long   145
as possible, the father led his son
to Vulcan's gift, the noble chariot.
Golden its axle, golden too, its shaft,
and golden the outer surface of its wheels,
adorned with radiating silver spokes;   150
its yoke, inlaid with golden chrysolites,[7]
returned the light of Phoebus in reflection.

And while the overreaching Phaëthon
gazed upon it in admiration, look—
Aurora, wakeful in the gleaming east,   155
has once more opened wide her purple gates,
and now her rosy courtyard is displayed;
the stars all scatter, and bright Lucifer[8]
brings up the rear, the last to leave his post.

When the father noticed that the morning star   160
was setting, and the world was growing red,

7. Precious gemstones.
8. The planet Venus in its appearance as the morning star.

and the Moon's pale horns were vanishing, he ordered
the passing Hours to prepare his steeds.
Swiftly they brought his fire-breathing horses
from the lofty stalls where they had been well fed   165
on heavenly ambrosia, and harnessed them:
they shook their jangling reins impatiently.
    Then Phoebus smeared his son's face with an ointment
to keep him safe from the consuming flames,
and placed the radiant crown upon his head.   170
Foreseeing grief, his breast heaved as he spoke:
"You have so far ignored your father's warnings,
but listen now, and—if you can—heed these:
spare the whip, boy, and rein your horses in,
for on their own, they will go fast enough—   175
your task is to restrain them in their flight.
    "Do not attempt to go directly through
the five zones of heaven, but rather take
the curving route that leads through only three,
and thus avoids extremes of north and south.   180
    "That is the right way—you will clearly see
the ruts worn in the pathway by my wheels.
To heat the earth and sky both evenly,
don't hug the earth, don't rise to the upper air
or you will either set the sky ablaze   185
or the earth below: the middle way is safest.
    "Avoid the coiled-up Serpent on your right
and the low-lying Altar[9] on your left—
keep in between! I leave the rest to Fortune,
and trust that she will be a better guide   190
than you yourself have been.
                    "But while I speak,
the humid night has reached the western shore—
we may delay no longer. We are called:
Dawn is conspicuously present now,
and shadows all are fled. Take up the reins,   195
or, if that heart of yours can be persuaded,
take my advice—and *not* my chariot!
    "Change your mind now, while change is still permitted,
while both your feet are firmly on the ground—
before you mount and set out on this course   200
which, in your ignorance, you foolishly desire—
look on in safety while I light the world!"
But the boy is in the chariot already

9. Having cautioned Phaëthon to avoid extremes, the Sun illustrates with two constellations: the Serpent is at the highest point in the heavens, and the Altar is just above the
horizon.

and stands there proudly as he takes the reins
and offers thanks to his unwilling father.   205
    Meanwhile, the flying horses of the Sun,
Pyrois, Eous, Aethon, and Phlegon,[1]
filled all the air with fiery whinnying,
and kicked the bars that held them back.
                                    When Tethys
(not knowing what her grandson's fate would be)   210
released them, and all heaven opened up,
they took off with their hooves shredding the mists
of morning in their way as they flew past
the east winds in the quadrants where they rise.
    But the burden that the horses of the Sun   215
were used to bearing was much heavier,
and their yoke lacked its customary weight;
just as a ship that is unballasted
rolls all about, unsteadied by its lightness,
and goes off course, so too the chariot,   220
without the weight it usually carries,
leaps in the air, bucking, tossed all about
as though it had no passenger at all;
and once they're all aware of this, the horses
bolt from the rutted track in four directions.   225
    Now terrified, it is impossible
for him to use the reins that he was given,
or find his way; nor, if he were to find it,
could he control his steeds. For the first time, then,
the Great and Little Bears knew the sun's heat   230
and tried—in vain, for it was not permitted—
to plunge into the sea. And the Serpent, who
lies nearest to the frigid northern Pole,
and who has been, in sluggish hibernation,
a threat to no one, suddenly became   235
a raging terror, stirred up by the heat.
Folks say that even you, Boötes, fled,
slow as you are, and hampered by your oxcart.[2]
    But when, from heaven's summit, he looked down
at the lands that lay so distantly beneath him,   240
unlucky Phaëthon at once turned pale,
and suddenly his knees began to shake
with terror, and his eyes were darkened by

---

1. Other poets had supplied the Sun with a four-horse chariot. The names of the steeds,
   Greek and suggestively cosmic, are Ovid's invention.
2. The Sun, off course now, begins to have disastrous effects above. The Great and Little
   Bears, two constellations so far north that they had never felt the Sun's heat, try to cool
   themselves. The Serpent comes out of hibernation, and Boötes the plowman is pictured
   as trying madly to flee the catastrophe, hindered by his oxcart.

excessive light; and now the god's true son
regrets he ever touched his father's horses,   245
is sorry to have found his origins,
and sorry that his prayer was ever answered;
he wishes to be called the son of Merops,[3]
this boy now like a ship caught in a gale
and driven by the furious north wind,   250
whose helmsman lets the useless tiller go
and puts his trust in heaven and in prayer.
    Much of the sky already lies behind him,
much more remains ahead: what can he do?
He turns this matter over in his mind,   255
now looking to the west (which he is fated
never to reach), now looking eastward: no
solution to his problem may be found,
and stunned by ignorance, cannot decide
if he should hold the reins or let them go—   260
he doesn't even know his horses' names!
    And scattered everywhere throughout the sky,
he sees the terrifying images
of enormous beasts, which aggravate his fears.
There is a place where two gigantic arms   265
bend into bows, and arms and tail extended,
Scorpio wholly occupies two zones:
when the boy sees this venom-sweating monster
bend its tail back to strike at him, his mind
goes blank with icy fear. He drops the reins,   270
which slackly lie upon the horses' backs;
and now his steeds, completely unrestrained,
go galloping off course through the unknown
regions of the upper air, wherever
impulse proposes, purposeless, and knock   275
against the fixed stars set within the sky,
dragging their chariot through trackless space.
    Now they seek heaven's summit, now they drop
and carry themselves closer to the earth;
Luna now marvels at her brother's horses   280
below her own, at scorched clouds trailing smoke!
Earth at its highest point bursts into flame,
deep fissures open up, and its juices dry;
the ripe grain whitens, trees and leaves all burn,
and the dry crop provides itself as fuel.   285
    What I lament is nothing to what comes:
great cities perish and their walls collapse,

---

3. Phaëthon's human stepfather.

entire nations are reduced to ash;
the woods burn with their mountains: Athos burns,
Cilician Taurus and Timolus burn,   290
and Oeta, too; Mount Ida, which had once
been full of fountains, now runs dry and burns;
Muse-haunted Helicon and Haemus (not
yet associated with Oeagrus);[4]
Etna (already blazing) blazes twice;   295
twin-peaked Parnassus, Eryx, Cynthus, Othrys,
and Rhodope (about to lose its snows),
Mymas and Dindyma, Mycale and Cithaeron
(famed for Apollo's rites) are now ablaze;
Scythia's frigid climate does not spare it;   300
Caucasus burns, and Ossa burns with Pindus,
and greater than the pair of them, Olympus;
whole ranges burn: the Alps, the Apennines.
    Then Phaëthon in truth beholds the world
in every part aflame, and cannot bear   305
the overwhelming heat; each breath he draws
seems like an exhalation from an oven;
his chariot is white-hot underfoot.
    Unable to endure the sparks and ashes
whirling about him, shrouded in black smoke,   310
he has no way of knowing where he is,
or where he is going through the darkness, borne
wherever the flying horses wish to take him.
    And it was then, according to some folks,
that the inhabitants of Ethiopia   315
turned black, when blood was drawn up to their skins;
and then that Libya became a desert,
and nymphs lamented their lost springs and pools:
Boeotia mourned Dirce; Argus, Amymone;
and Corinth mourned the spring at Pirene.[5]   320
    Broad-channeled rivers were no better off:
unquietly the distant Don flows, steaming;
Old Man Peneus, Mysian Caïcus,
swift-running Ismenus, Arcadian Erymanthus,
and Xanthus (destined to blaze up again);   325
the yellow Lycormas and the Maeander,
that playfully meanders in its course,
the Thracian Melas and Spartan Eurotas;
in Babylon, the wide Euphrates burns,
and the Orontes burns in Syria,   330

---

4. Orpheus, the son of Oeagrus, was slain here.
5. Ovid's catalogue of mountains is followed by a catalogue of springs: burning rivers will
   follow as all the world catches fire.

as do the rapid Thermodon, the Ganges,
the river Phasis and the blue Danube;
Alpheus blazes through Olympia,
and the banks of Sperchios in Thessaly;
the Tagus is so hot that its gold melts![6]   335
In Lydia the celebrated swans
that sing upon the Cayster have been scorched;
the Nile in terror seeks a place of refuge
and hides its head—where it is hidden still:
its seven mouths lie empty, choked with dust,   340
its seven channels all without a stream.
Likewise the Hebrus and the Strymon shrivel,
as in the west, the Rhone, the Rhine, the Po,
and—fated for later greatness—our Tiber.[7]
    The soil cracks everywhere, and now the light   345
seeps to the underworld and terrifies
its ruler and his wife;[8] the sea contracts,
and what had been until quite recently
a sheet of water is a field of sand,
and peaks that once were covered by the waves   350
are new additions to the Cyclades!
    Fish seek the bottom, and no dolphins dare
to trust their curving bodies to the air,
the dying sea calves bob upon their backs,
and it is said that even Nereus,   355
with Doris and the Nereids, attempted
to hide themselves in underwater caves
from the blazing heat.
                Three times great Neptune strove
to lift his head and torso from the waves
and three times failed, unable to endure   360
the fiery air.
          Kind Mother Earth, surrounded
by the sea and by the waters of the deep
and by her streams, contracting everywhere
as they took shelter in her shady womb,
though heat-oppressed, still lifted up her head   365
and placed a hand upon her fevered brow;
and after a tremor that shook everything
had subsided somewhat, she spoke out to Jove
in a dry, cracked voice:
                 "If it should please you
that I merit this, greatest of all gods,   370

---

6. A Portuguese river famous for its golden sands.
7. Rome has not yet emerged onto the historical scene and will not appear in Ovid's poem
   until Book XIV.
8. Dis and Proserpina, respectively.

why keep your lightnings back? If I must die
of fire, why not let me die of yours:
knowing that *you* are author of my doom
will make it more endurable to me.
I'm scarcely able to pronounce these words—"   375
(through choking smoke)
                    "—Just look at my singed hair,
the glowing ashes in my eyes and face!
    "Do I deserve this? Is this the reward
for my unflagging fruitfulness? For bearing,
year after year, the wounds of plow and mattock?   380
And for providing flocks with pasturage,
the human race with ripened grain to eat,
the gods with incense smoking on their altars?
    "But even assuming I deserve destruction,
why is your brother[9] equally deserving?   385
Why are those waters, which were his by lot,
so much diminished, so far now from the sky?
    "If neither Earth nor Sea deserve your favor,
have pity on the heavens! Look around you!
Both poles are smoking now! If flames destroy them,   390
the palaces of heaven will collapse!
    "Atlas is scarcely able to support
the white-hot heavens on his bare shoulder![1]
Now if the sea, the lands, the heavens perish,
all will be plunged in chaos once again!   395
    "Save from the flames whatever is still left,
take measures to preserve the universe!"
    So spoke the Earth, and with no more to say,
unable any longer to endure
the heat, retreated deep within herself   400
and took up chambers nearer the underworld.
    Before he would commit himself, however,
the father almighty made the other gods
(especially the god who gave his son
the chariot) swear that the gravest fate   405
hung over all, unless he should take action.
    And then he sought the pinnacle of heaven,
whence he was wont to parcel out the rain clouds
widely over the earth, and whence he moved
the thunder and sent forth his lightning bolts;   410
but now he had no rain clouds to distribute,
nor any rain to send down from the heavens;

9. Neptune.
1. The Titan Atlas, having been turned into the North African Mount Atlas, was so large that
   the ancients believed the heavens rested upon it. Atlas is frequently represented supporting the world on his shoulders.

and so he thundered and released a bolt
of lightning from beside his ear that drove
the hapless driver from his spinning wheels   415
and from his life: fires put cruel fires out.
    In consternation then, his horses reared
and slipped their yoke and fled from their restraints;
the chariot breaks up now: here the reins
come falling from the sky, and here the pole   420
now breaks off from its axle, and the spokes
of the shattered wheels fall to another spot,
and wreckage litters a wide area.
    But Phaëthon, his bright red hair ablaze,
is whirled headlong, and tracing out an arc,   425
seems like a comet with a tail of fire,
or like a star about to fall that doesn't.
In Italy, far distant from his homeland,
the river Eridanus [now the Po]
receives his corpse and bathes his seething face.   430

    Italian naiads lay his broken body,
still smoking from that three-forked thunderbolt,
within a tomb prepared for it and carve
this epitaph in verse upon the stone:

    Young Phaëthon lies here, poor lad, who dreamt   435
    Of mastering his father's sky-borne carriage;
    Although he sadly died in the attempt,
    Great was his daring, which none may disparage.

    His miserable father, sick with grief,
drew his cloak up around his head in mourning;   440
for one whole day then, if the tale is true,
the sun was quite put out. The conflagration
(for the world was still ablaze) provided light;
that was a time some good came out of evil.
    After Clymene said what might be said   445
of such an awful situation, she
wandered the world, her mind quite gone with grief,
beating her breast, and seeking first to gather
his lifeless limbs, then to collect his bones,
which she at last found in a foreign tomb;   450
collapsing, she threw herself upon the stone
that bore his name, and bathing it in tears,
she pressed her naked breast on the inscription.

The Heliades

Nor did her daughters, the Heliades,
hold back their empty gift of lamentation;   455

their cruel hands raised bruises on their breasts,
while night and day they cried to Phaëthon
(who would not hear their wretched wails of grief)
and cast themselves upon his sepulcher.

    Four months went by; according to their custom   460
(which their persistence had established), they
continued grieving; one day, Phaëthusa,
the eldest of the sisters, while attempting
to fling herself upon the tomb, complained
of a rigidity down in her feet;   465
and when a second sister, luminous
Lampetia, attempted to approach her,
she suddenly felt rooted to the earth.

    Now the third sister, tearing at her hair,
grasps foliage; now this one grieves to find   470
her ankles sealed in wood, that one to feel
her slender arms becoming lengthy branches;
and as they marvel at these happenings,
their private parts are wrapped in sheaths of bark,
which, from their loins, move upward to surround   475
their bellies, breasts and shoulders, arms and hands—
fixed to the ground, they call out to their mother.

    What can she do? Where impulse carries her,
she dashes off, now this way and now that,
encouraging their kisses, while she can.   480
To no avail! Now frantic, she attempts
to strip their bodies of this new veneer
and breaks the little twigs off with her hands,
releasing drops of blood, as from a wound.

    "Pray spare me, mother!" comes from each of them,   485
the selfsame cry repeated: "Spare me, pray!
It is my body wounded in this tree!
Farewell now, mother!" The conclusive bark
immediately weaves itself upon
those last words of the daughters of the Sun.   490

    Their tears continue flowing, and, sun-hardened,
fall from the trees; borne onward by the Po,
they will one day adorn the brides of Rome.
[And so, in myth, mourning becomes *electrum*;
the sisters' tears are, now and forever, amber.]   495

Cycnus

Cycnus,[2] the son of Sthenelus, observed
this marvelous event, O Phaëthon!

---

2. If your name was Cycnus, the Latin word for swan, you evidently had a very good chance
of being changed into your namesake, as happens to all three Cycnuses mentioned by
Ovid.

Although related to you through his mother,
he was more closely joined to you by passion,
and so your death was devastating to him.   500
    Abandoning his kingdom (for he ruled
the people and cities of Liguria)
he wept and wailed along the Po's green banks
and in those woods so recently augmented
by the Heliades.
                    His voice becomes   505
attenuated, and white feathers grow
over the hair upon his face and body;
a lengthy neck extends far from his chest,
a membrane starts between his reddish toes,
wings hide his sides, and a blunt bill, his mouth.   510
    So Cycnus was turned into something new:
a bird that had no faith in Jove or heaven,
recalling all too well the thunderbolt
unjustly hurled. His habitat is now
the surface of a standing pond or lake;   515
detesting fire, he calls water home,
preferring flumes to flames—their opposite.

The Sun's Complaint

Phoebus, meanwhile, mourning his lost son,
ignores appearances, as is his wont
whenever he goes into an eclipse: 520
hating the light of day and his own being,
he gives himself entirely to grief,
and in his anger threatens to resign:
    "Enough!" he cries. "Why, ever since creation
my lot has been incessant restlessness,   525
work unrewarded, going on forever!
Let someone else—whoever wishes to,
be driver of the chariot of light!
    "If no one else of all the gods will do it,
if none admits that he is able to,   530
why not just let the Governor[3] take charge:
at least while he is struggling with the reins
he'll have to put aside the thunderbolt
fated to rob fathers of their children!
    "Then he will know—once he has gauged the mettle   535
of those fire-footed horses—that my son,
who was unable to control the team,
did not deserve to die!"
                    The other gods

3. Jove.

all stand around the Sun beseeching him,
as humble suppliants, to keep the darkness   540
from covering the world; Jove goes so far
as to defend himself for hurling fire,
but adds (as royals will) threats to entreaties.
    Then Phoebus gathers up his team and yokes them,
still trembling and wild-eyed with their fear,   545
and in his grief torments them with his whip
(torments them truly!) and reproaches them,
holding them liable for his son's death.

Jove, Callisto, and Arcas

Now Jupiter omnipotent sets out
on an inspection tour of heaven's walls   550
after the fire, in order to make certain
that nothing is in danger of collapsing.
And once he sees that all is up to strength,
he turns toward earth, where the affairs of men,
their varied labors, come into his ken.   555
    Arcadia, his birthplace, above all
is dearest to him; he at once restores
her springs and streams (which had not dared to flow),
gives grass back to the earth, gives leaves to trees,
and bids the blackened woods grow green again.   560
    And as he comes and goes about his business,
he gets stuck on an Arcadian nymph,
Callisto [although Ovid doesn't name her],
and passion burns into his deepest marrow.
    She did not spend her days before the loom   565
nor in the artful styling of her hair;
a modest brooch was her one ornament,
and a white headband bound her otherwise
neglected tresses; so artlessly adorned,
with sometimes her swift javelin in hand,   570
sometimes a bow, she was Diana's soldier,
and no nymph pleased the goddess more than she did,
there on Mount Maenalus: but influence
cannot be counted on to last for long.
    Just as the Sun had passed his highest point,   575
she set foot in that grove which had not known
the felling of a tree since time began;
putting aside her arrows and unstringing
her resistant bow, she fell upon the grass
and used her painted quiver for a pillow.   580
    When Jupiter beheld the girl, exhausted
and off her guard, he said, "That wife of mine

will never learn about this escapade!
But if she happens to discover it,
a little scolding is small price to pay!"   585
    At once he was Diana in appearance,
and greeted her: "Dear maiden of my band,
where, on what mountain, did you hunt today?"
The virgin sprang up from her grassy couch:
"Hail, goddess far superior to Jove—   590
a judgment I would stand by in his presence!"
    He laughed to be preferred above himself,
and joined their lips together with a kiss
much less than modest, more than maidenly;
as she began recounting the day's hunt,   595
he interrupted her with an embrace
that clearly showed his criminal intent.
    She did as much as any woman could
(if only you had been a witness, Juno,
your judgment would have been much less severe);   600
she fought against him but was just a girl;
and can a mere girl fight off a grown man?
Can anyone fight off great Jupiter?
    Victorious, Jove now withdraws to heaven
leaving the Arcadian behind him   605
to trace her way back from that knowing grove,
now hateful to her—and almost forgetting
her quiver full of arrows and her bow.
    But look—the goddess with her company
approaches on the slopes of Maenalus,   610
well pleased with that day's feral body count,
and calls out when she sees her. Terrified
that it is Jove disguised again, she flees;
but when she sees the nymphs around the goddess,
she is relieved and joins their company.   615
    How difficult it is not to reveal
a guilty conscience in one's countenance!
She does not lift her gaze up from the ground,
nor walk beside the goddess as she used to,
nor take the lead; and she is silent now—   620
that and her blushing show her loss of honor.
    The countless indications of her guilt
went by Diana, much too innocent
to recognize loss of virginity—
they say her nymphs were well aware of it.   625
    Nine months elapsed. Now wearied of the heat,
the goddess broke off her pursuits and came
to a gelid grove in which a babbling brook
poured over polished sands. She approved the place

and stirred the shallow water with her foot;   630
it, too, won her approval: "No one is near
to spy on us," she said. "Come—let us undress
and take a dip in this pellucid stream."
     And while the rest of them undressed at once,
one blushed and sought excuses for delay,   635
until the others snatched away her shift,
baring her body—and her crime as well.
     The dumbstruck girl attempted to conceal
her swollen belly. "Get away from here!"
Diana said. "Do not defile this spring!"   640
And with that drove her from their company.
     The consort of almighty Jupiter
had long since learned about this situation,
but put off vengeance till the time was ripe;
no reason to postpone it any longer,   645
for now a boy named Arcas had been born
to Lady Juno's husband's concubine,
a further source of grief. And now she turned
her baleful eyes and mind in their direction:
     "Oh, very nice indeed," she said. "Homewrecker!   650
Nothing would do but that you must conceive,
and publish the disservice that you've done me,
bearing your witness to my lord's disgrace!
Ah! But you will not get away with it;
I'll take away the beauty that delights   655
you and my husband both, you thoughtless thing!"
     And with those words, she seized her by the hair
and threw her down, face-forward on the ground.
The girl stretched out her arms in supplication;
her arms began to bristle with black hairs,   660
her hands now served as feet, tipped with sharp claws,
and the mouth that Jove had praised so recently
was now a pair of widely gaping jaws!
     To keep her from successfully appealing
to Jupiter, her speech was snatched away: 665
only a growl from deep within her chest,
a rumble, hoarse and menacing, remained.
     Within the bear, there was a human mind,
however; constant groans expressed her grief
as she reared up and raised her hands to heaven,   670
her gestures showing what she could not say:
the pain of Jovian ingratitude.
     How often she would be too terrified
to lie down by herself in the deep woods,
and wandered to the fields near her old home!   675
How often had a baying pack of hounds

driven her upward through the steep ravines;
how many times the huntress was the hunted.
Often she hid herself at the sight of beasts,
forgetting that she was a beast herself.   680
And the bear was frightened by the sight of bears
up in the mountains—and afraid of wolves,
although her father had been changed to one.[4]
   And now here is Lycaon's grandson, Arcas;
at age fifteen, the special circumstances   685
of his conception are unknown to him;
while he pursues his quarry through ravines
and on the mountain pastures they prefer,
while he wraps up the woods of Arcady
in woven nets, he comes upon his mother.   690
   And when she sees him, she stands motionless
and seems to recognize him as her son;
fearing he knows not what, he flees from her
unmoving eyes that fix on him forever;
and as she tries to close the gap between them,   695
he turns to thrust his spear into her breast!
   Jove stayed his hand and then expunged together
their abominations and identities,
bearing them upward through the empty air
and imposing them on heaven in the form   700
of two adjacent constellations.[5]
                              When
her husband's mistress gleamed among the stars,
rage-swollen Juno descended to the level
of white-haired Tethys and venerable Oceanus,
gods whom the others often reverence.   705
   And when they asked what brought her there, she said:
"You wish to know why I, the queen of heaven,
have come here from my airy habitation?
Another has usurped my lofty place!
Call me a liar if you do not see,   710
when darkness has obscured the nighttime sky,
there, in the place of highest honor, where
the smallest circle revolves around the pole,
two constellations put out to insult me!
   "And truly, why should any hesitate   715
to take on Juno or to fear her wrath,
who only helps the ones that she would harm?
How vast my power and how great my deeds!
I would not let her keep her human form,

---

4. Callisto's father is Lycaon, changed into a wolf by Jove in Book I.
5. The Great Bear and Boötes, also known as the Bear-Watcher.

and the result is—she is a goddess now!   720
Thus do I punish those who do me wrong!
Thus do I wield my great authority!
    "Let him restore her former face and figure,
eliminating all the beastliness,
as once before he did—in Io's case: 725
since Juno is deposed, why shouldn't he
remarry—and become Lycaon's son-in-law?
    "But if the disdain he shows your foster child[6]
arouses you to anger, then deny
this constellation your cerulean depths,   730
drive off these interlopers who have been
turned into stars—the wages paid to sin!
—and keep this slut from dipping in your waters."
    Tethys and Oceanus gave assent,
and Juno in her handy chariot   735
was carried upward through the melting air
by peacocks fitted out with Argus' eyes
quite recently—in fact, at the same time
that your white plumage suddenly turned black,
loquacious raven.

The Raven and the Crow

                For once upon a time   740
those wings of his were silvery snow-white,
immaculate as are the wings of doves,
or as those geese whose vocal vigilance
would one day keep the Capitol from harm,[7]
and no less white than the water-loving swan.   745
It was that tongue of his that did him in;
through his loquacity, he came to ruin
and turned from white into its opposite.
    There was no one in all of Thessaly
more beautiful than Coronis of Larissa,   750
and surely a delight to you, Apollo,
while she was either true—or undetected.
Apollo's raven caught her in the act
and that inexorable tattletale
went flying off to see his lord and master   755
in order to disclose her guilty secret.
    Eager for news, that chatterbox, the crow,
caught up to him and flapped along beside,

---

6. Tethys was Juno's wet nurse.
7. In the fourth century B.C., when invading Gauls attempted to sneak up the Capitoline
   Hill in the middle of the night, a honking flock of geese gave the alarm. Ovid's simile
   points out that there was a time when squawking birds were appreciated.

but when he learned the journey's purpose, said,
"This course will get you nowhere, friend, believe me!   760
Do not dismiss my warning: pay attention
to what I once was and to what I am now,
then ask why I deserved this transformation.
You will discover that my loyalty
was what destroyed me!
                    "Once upon a time,   765
a boy named Erichthonius was born
without a mother.[8] Minerva hid the child
in a woven basket of the Attic kind,
and ordered the three virgin daughters of
the monster Cecrops to watch over him,   770
and not to take a peek inside the basket.
    "Concealed within an elm tree's greenery,
I spied on them to see what they would do;
two of the sisters, Pandrosos and Herse,
were careful, honest watchers—but the third,   775
Aglauros, called the other sisters cowards,
and opened up the basket to peek in:
she saw the infant stretched beside a serpent.
    "I carried my report back to the goddess,
expecting a reward, but for my troubles   780
I was deposed as Minerva's favorite,
and—even worse—demoted to a rank
below that of the noxious bird of nighttime![9]
    "All birds should be reminded by my loss
not to seek trouble by loquacity,   785
and not to bring bad tidings to the boss.
    "Perhaps you'll say she did not seek me out
as her companion, of her own accord,
when I had no such notion in my mind.
Why don't you go and ask the goddess? She   790
may still be angry, but she won't deny it.
    "For I was not always as you see me now;
the land of Phocis was my place of birth,
my father was the famous Coroneus,
as everyone knows; and, as a princess, I   795
was wooed by many wealthy noblemen.
    "My beauty was my ruin, for, one day,
while I was promenading on the beach
as usual, Neptune, god of the sea,
saw me and right away grew passionate;   800

---

8. Erichthonius sprang from the semen of Vulcan, which he spilled inadvertently while attempting to rape the goddess Minerva.
9. The owl, regarded by the ancients as a bringer of bad omens.

when prayers and blandishments proved wasted time,
he chased me, threatening to force the issue.
    "I called upon the gods and men for aid,
but no one was around to hear my cries;
a virgin's plight aroused the virgin goddess   805
and she delivered me: I stretched my arms out
and they began to darken with pinfeathers;
I tried to tear the clothing from my shoulders
but it was feathered, rooted in my skin;
I strove to beat my bare breast with my hands,   810
but found that I had neither hands nor breasts.
I tried to run but now I glided over
the unrestraining surface of the sand,
and soon I soared aloft, high in the air,
and then was given to Minerva as   815
her chaste companion.
                        "What good does that do me,
if someone who was turned into a bird
to punish her for her appalling crimes—
I mean Nyctimene—now takes my place?[1]
    "Or have you somehow managed not to hear   820
the story that is famous everywhere,
throughout all Lesbos—how Nyctimene
outraged the honor of her father's bed?
    "Although a bird now, she still feels her guilt
and flees the sight of men and light of day,   825
concealing shame in darkness, driven out
of the clear sky by all the other birds."
    "We spurn your foolish omens," said the raven.
"May all your efforts to arrest my flight
redound upon you!" Onward raven flew   830
and told his master he had seen Coronis
lie with a young Thessalian.
                        When Apollo heard
the accusation brought against his lover,
the laurel resting on his brow slipped down;
in not as much time as it takes to tell,   835
his face, his lyre, his high color fell!
Swelling with rage, he seized his customary
weapon and bent it toward him from the tips;
then his inexorable arrow flew
into that breast so often pressed to his.   840
    Coronis groaned, and when the arrowhead
was drawn out, her white limbs were drenched in gore:

---

1. Nyctimene, after committing incest with her father, was changed into an owl. Like
Myrrha in Book X, she was aided by her nurse.

"O Phoebus, I deserved your punishment,"
she said. "But not before I'd given birth—
for now another perishes with me."   845
And with her blood, the life poured out of her;
soon, with its spirit gone, her body lay
frigid in death.
                    Now he is sorry for
his cruel punishment, belatedly,
and hates himself for what he listened to,   850
and for his furious response to it:
he hates the bird who forced him into this,
the cause both of his crime and of his grief;
he hates the hand and bow, and with the hand,
he hates his thoughtless arrows for good measure;   855
he strokes the fallen girl, too late, and tries
to overcome her fate: too late again,
for his attempt to bring her back to life
through the arts of medicine are all for naught.

    Now when he saw that these had no effect,   860
and that her funeral pyre was prepared
for the flames that would soon shrivel up her limbs,
the groans (for the immortal gods, you see,
are not permitted tears upon their cheeks)
from deep within him came, not unlike those   865
a young cow utters when she sees the hammer
come crashing down into the rounded skull
of her own suckling calf. The deity
pours fragrance on her unresponsive breast,
embraces her one last time and performs,   870
improperly, rites proper to the dead.
    But Phoebus could not bear for his own seed
to perish in those flames—and so he ripped
the unborn child out of its mother's womb
and brought it to the centaur Chiron's cave;   875
and raven, who had hoped to be rewarded
for his truth-telling was prohibited
from taking his old place among white birds.

The Prophecies of Ocyrhoë

Meanwhile, the centaur was rejoicing in
his foster child's immortal lineage,   880
delighted by the thought of raising him,
an onerous, yet honorable task,
when look—here comes the centaur's human daughter,
distinguished by her shoulder-length red hair,
and named Ocyrhoë, for the swift stream   885

upon whose banks the naiad Chariclo
gave birth to her: besides her father's arts,
she learned how to foretell fate's mysteries.

    And so, when the prophetic fit came on her,
and a god's fire burned within her breast,   890
she looked upon that infant and she said,
"Grow up, Boychild, bringer of good health
to the whole world![2] The sick will often be
indebted to you, and you will be permitted
to bring back spirits who were snatched away,   895
once and once only: for when you attempt
to bring the dead to life a second time
in spite of heaven, you will be halted by
a lightning bolt from your grandfather Jove.

    "No longer godlike in your power then,   900
but a lifeless corpse until changed yet again—
into a real god now, and so your fate
will be renewed for yet a second time.

    "You, father dear, who are immortal too,
destined from birth to live on earth forever,   905
will beg the gods to be allowed to die,
when the foul Hydra's blood has poisoned you;
heaven will finally permit your death,
and the three goddesses will snap the thread."[3]

    Still other fortunes waited to be told,   910
but with a deep sigh and flowing tears, she said,
"The fate that changes me prohibits speech,
and makes my own voice inaccessible.
Those arts by which I have earned heaven's wrath
are scarcely worth the price I pay for them!   915
—I'd rather not know what the future holds!
It seems my human form is being taken:
the thought of grass for dinner pleases me,
and open fields, where I can freely ride
as I become my relative—a mare!   920
Whole horse? But why? My father is but a centaur!"

    Her whining, waning, becomes whinnying,
as mind and speech both grow confused together,
and for a moment seemed a sound between
the noise a horse makes and a human word,   925
more like someone who imitates a horse,
before the sound turned clearly into neighing,
as she went on all fours through the tall grass.

2. The centaur's foster child is the god Aesculapius, the healer. For an account of how this
   Greek god was imported into the Roman pantheon, see Book XV, *Aesculapius*, p. 428.
3. The Fates, three sisters, known to the Romans as the Parcae: one sister, Clotho, spins the
   thread of life; a second, Lachesis, measures it; and the third sister, Atropos, snips it.

Her fingers fused together and a single
band of light horn surrounded them, a hoof.   930
Her neck and mouth were both increased in size
and her long robe was turned into a tail
while the hair that used to stray across her neck
became a mane that fell on her right side;
made over now in voice and form completely,   935
this transformation gave her a new name.

Mercury and the Tattletale

Heroic Chiron, son of Philyra, wept,
and sought your help, O Phoebus, but in vain,
for you could not revoke the orders of
almighty Jove—and even if you could,   940
you had gone off to Elis and Messenia.[4]
     That was the time when you were clothed in homespun
and carried, in your left hand or the other,
a shepherd's crook, and played the pipes of Pan:
love was the care you eased with country music,   945
and your unguarded herd went wandering
into the fields of Pylos.
                         Mercury,
that crafty rustler, sees your cattle there
and drives them off and hides them in the woods.
     And no one knows about this theft except   950
for one old man well known to everyone
within that area. They called him Battus,
the hired hand of wealthy Neleus,
who watched his herd of mares, all thoroughbreds,
in nearby glades and grassy pasturelands.   955
     Young Mercury gladhands the aged rustic
and taking him aside, inveigles him:
"If anyone should ask about a herd,
deny that you saw cattle passing through.
So that your kindness may not lack reward,   960
select one of these heifers for yourself."
     He gave one to the old man, who replied:
"Your secret's safe with me! Why, that stone there—"
(and as he spoke, he pointed to a rock)
"—will tell about your theft before I will!"   965
     The son of Jove appeared to go away
but soon returned with a new identity:

---

4. Apollo's grief was not without term; suitably attired, he had already taken off to console
   himself with a young herdsman.

"Say there, Hayseed," he said, "if you've just seen
a herd of cattle being moved through here,
don't keep silent—help me—they've been stolen!   970
Your prize will be a heifer—and a bull."
    The doubled bribe appealed to the old man:
"Foot of yon mountain there is where you'll find 'em,"
the rustic said, and that was where they were.
    Mercury laughed at him: "Will you betray me,   975
you rogue? Betray me even to myself?"
And he turned that hardened criminal to stone,
a peak still known there as "the Tattletale";
unmerited, the ancient libel clings.

Mercury and Aglauros (1)

On wings that steadied him, young Mercury   980
flew off until from high above he looked
on the land which is Minerva's special love,
the fields of Athens and its learnèd grove.
    He happened to have shown up on the day
on which Minerva's festival was kept,   985
when maidens carried sacred gifts in baskets,
poised on their heads, up to the Parthenon.[5]
    The winged god gave them the once-over
as they returned, and, altering his flight plan,
made after them in a wide, sweeping arc,   990
as when that swiftest of all birds, the kite,
has glimpsed the entrails of the sacrifice—
but while the priests are crowded round, it fears
to fly too near, yet fears to fly away,
so hovers high above its longed-for prey;   995
just so the nimble Mercury in flight
made circles over the Acropolis.[6]
    Just as the morning star outshines all others,
and as the moon is to the morning star,
so Herse was to her companions there,   1000
her beauty singular in their procession.
    The son of Jupiter was stupified
and in suspension burned with passion's flame:
as when a Balearic sling lets fly
and its leaden load goes whizzing on its way,[7]   1005

---

5. The temple in Athens, sacred to the cult of Athena, who was associated by the Romans
with the goddess Minerva.
6. The citadel of Athens.
7. Used in hunting and combat, the Balearic sling released an egg-sized "bullet" of clay or lead.

heated by its own speed until it finds
a warmth unknown before within the clouds.
    He left the sky and came down to the earth
without disguise, so great his confidence
in his own beauty, which, though not misplaced,   1010
was aided by the care he took of it,
smoothing his hair, which had been mussed in flight,
arranging his cloak so that it hung just so,
letting its pricey golden border show,
and making sure that the wand in his right hand   1015
(with which he brings sleep on or drives it off)
was freshly shined, and seeing that the wings
were gleaming brightly on his shapely feet.
    Expensive ivory and tortoiseshell
adorned the women's quarters,[8] which held three   1020
bedchambers; yours, Pandrosos, on the right,
Aglauros' on the left, Herse's in between.
She on the left first noticed the approach
of Mercury, and dared to ask his name
and reason for his visit.
                        The grandson   1025
of Atlas and Pleione answered her:
"Let me get to the point directly: I
am the airborne messenger of my father Jove,
and you should wish to be loyal to your sister
and famous as the aunt of our offspring,   1030
for Herse is the reason I am here;
I pray you favor me in my request."
    Aglauros looked at him in the same way
that she had only recently looked on
the mysteries of golden-haired Minerva;   1035
and for his services, demanded gold
in quantity; and Mercury, meanwhile,
was ordered to vacate the premises.

The House of Envy

Now bellicose Minerva turned the fierce
fire of her gaze upon Aglauros,   1040
sighing so deeply that her breast was shaken
beneath the aegis that defended it;
for she realized that this was the same one
who had gone against her orders and profaned
her mysteries by peeking at Apollo's   1045

---

8. Separate women's quarters were a Greek, rather than a Roman, arrangement.

motherless child; and now this one would be
a god's delight and pleasing to her sister,
and rich with what her avarice demanded!
     She headed straight to Envy's squalid quarters,
black with corruption, hidden deep within   1050
a sunless valley where no breezes blow,
a sad and sluggish place, richly frigid,
where cheerful fires die upon the hearth
and fog that never lifts embraces all.
     Arriving here, the warlike maiden stood   1055
before the house (for heaven's law denied
her entrance) and with her spear tip rapped
upon the doors, which instantly flew open,
revealing Envy at her feast of snakes,
a fitting meal for her corrupted nature: 1060
from such a sight, the goddess turned away.
     The object of her visit sluggishly
arises from the ground where she'd been sitting,
leaving behind her interrupted dinner
of half-eaten reptiles. Stiffly she advances,   1065
and when she sees the beauty of the goddess
and of her armor, she cannot help but groan,
and makes a face, and sighs a wretched sigh.
     Then she grows pale, and her body shrivels up.
Her glance is sidewise and her teeth are black;   1070
her nipples drip with poisonous green bile,
and venom from her dinner coats her tongue;
she only smiles at sight of another's grief,
nor does she know, disturbed by wakeful cares,
the benefits of slumber; when she beholds   1075
another's joy, she falls into decay,
and rips down only to be ripped apart,
herself the punishment for being her.
     Although the goddess hated Envy, she
addressed her nonetheless with these few words: 1080
"Infect one of the daughters of the Cecrops.
That is the task. Aglauros is the one."
With not another word, the goddess fled,
placing the tip of her spear against the ground
and using it to vault back up to heaven.   1085
     Muttering sourly beneath her breath,
she eyes the fleeing goddess with distrust,
already saddened by Minerva's joy.
She takes her staff, bristling with thorns,
and sets off in a mantle of black clouds,   1090
flicking the heads off flowers as she passes,

blighting the grasses and destroying trees,
her breath polluting houses, cities, states.
    At last she sees the city of the goddess;
its wealth, its work, its joyous flourishing   1095
and peaceful temper all affect her so,
she's scarcely able to prevent herself
from weeping—for there's nothing here to weep for.
    Once in the chambers of Aglauros, Envy
obeys her orders, touching the girl's breast   1100
with her rust-stained hand and filling it with thorns;
now Envy breathes her poison in the girl,
and spreads her venom right into her bones,
and so that she would have a cause for grief,
draws her a picture of her sister's fortune,   1105
her blessed marriage to the handsome god,
enlarging on it in imagination.
    Aglauros, maddened, feasts on her own heart
in secret wretchedness as anxious day
succeeds each anxious night; groaning, she slowly   1110
wastes away, dissolving, just as ice does
in the uncertain light of early spring.

Mercury and Aglauros (2)

Her envy of her sister's happiness
consumed her, and she burned as does a fire
that smolders in a pile of thorny scrub.   1115
Often she wished to die in order not
to see such happiness and often wished
to bring the news of it to her stern parents;
and finally she sat down on the threshold
to keep the god from entering.
                    His prayers   1120
and his most honeyed words proved unavailing:
"Stop it," she said. "I will not move from here
until you have been thwarted in your purpose!"
    "You have," said Mercury the swift, "a deal!"
And with his wand, he opened up the door;   1125
but she, attempting to get to her feet,
discovered that the parts one bends when sitting
could not be moved, so heavy they had grown;
she tried to stand up, but her knees had stiffened,
and a chill crept down to her extremities   1130
and pallor drained her body of its color;
as cancer, that incurable disease,
spreads its roots widely while it makes its way,

infecting healthy tissue from unhealthy,
so lethal winter gradually came   1135
into her breast and closed the passages
of life and slowly suffocated her;
she no more tried to speak, and if she had,
would not have found a passage for her voice.
    Her neck was turned to rock. Her features hardened   1140
until she sat, a bloodless effigy;
nor was that stone white, but stained as by her soul.

Jove and Europa

When Mercury had punished her for these
impieties of thought and word, he left
Athena's city, and on beating wings   1145
returned to heaven where his father Jove
took him aside and (without telling him
that his new passion was the reason) said:
    "Dear son, who does my bidding faithfully,
do not delay, but with your usual   1150
swiftness fly down to earth and find the land
that looks up to your mother on the left,
called Sidon[9] by the natives; there you will see
a herd of royal cattle some way off
upon a mountain; drive them down to shore."   1155
    He spoke and it was done as he had ordered:
the cattle were immediately driven
down to a certain place along the shore
where the daughter of a great king used to play,
accompanied by maidens all of Tyre.   1160
    Majestic power and erotic love
do not get on together very well,
nor do they linger long in the same place:
the father and the ruler of all gods,
who holds the lightning bolt in his right hand   1165
and shakes the world when he but nods his head,
now relinquishes authority and power,
assuming the appearance of a bull
to mingle with the other cattle, lowing
as gorgeously he strolls in the new grass.   1170
    He is as white as the untrampled snow
before the south wind turns it into slush.
The muscles stand out bulging on his neck,
and the dewlap dangles on his ample chest;
his horns are crooked, but appear handmade,   1175

9. Sidon was the capital city of Phoenicia.

and flawless as a pair of matching gems.
His brow is quite unthreatening, his eye
excites no terror, and his countenance
is calm.
      The daughter of King Agenor[1]
admires him, astonished by the presence   1180
of peacefulness and beauty in the beast;
yet even though he seems a gentle creature,
at first she fears to get too close to him,
but soon approaching, reaches out her hand
and pushes flowers into his white mouth.   1185
    The lover, quite beside himself, rejoices,
and as a preview of delights to come,
kisses her fingers, getting so excited
that he can scarcely keep from doing it!
    Now he disports himself upon the grass,   1190
and lays his whiteness on the yellow sands;
and as she slowly overcomes her fear
he offers up his breast for her caresses
and lets her decorate his horns with flowers;
the princess dares to sit upon his back   1195
not knowing who it is that she has mounted,
and he begins to set out from dry land,
a few steps on false feet into the shallows,
then further out and further to the middle
of the great sea he carries off his booty;   1200
she trembles as she sees the shore receding
and holds the creature's horn in her right hand
and with the other clings to his broad back,
her garments streaming in the wind behind her.

---

1. Europa.

BOOK III

The Wrath of Juno

Jove and Europa[1]

And now, his taurine imitation ended,
the god exposed himself for what he was
to cowed Europa on the isle of Crete.
      In an action both paternal and perverse,
the captured maiden's baffled father bids   5
her brother Cadmus to locate the girl
or face an endless term of banishment.
Ilis search was fruitless, for who can discover
Jove's secret snatches? The son of Agenor,
shunning alike his parent's realm and wrath,   10
supplicates the oracle of Phoebus
and asks him for a land to colonize.[2]

Cadmus Founds Thebes

"You will meet a heifer in a trackless place,"
says Phoebus, "one who has not borne the yoke,
nor broken up the earth with a curved plow.   15
Follow her lead; wherever she reposes,
there build your city. Name the land Boeotia."[3]
      Cadmus had just come down from the Castalian
grotto, when he discovered an unguarded
heifer who ambled on ahead of him,   20
her neck unscarred by any signs of service.
He fell in after, following her tracks,
and as he walked, gave silent thanks to Phoebus,
who instigated this.
                        The heifer crossed
the shallows of the river called Cephisus,   25
then passed beyond the meadows of Panope,
and then abruptly halted; lifting up
her lovely rack of horns to heaven, she
bellowed repeatedly: then, with a glance
over her shoulder at the men behind her,   30
knelt and resigned her flank to the soft grasses.

1. One might expect the story to be continued here, but after creating in words a motif, the abduction of Europa, that countless artists would translate into iconic images, Ovid moves on to develop one of its consequences: the founding of Thebes by Cadmus, who sets out from the Phoenician city of Tyre, where his father Agenor is king. Juno's anger at Jove for his dalliance will have consequences for many of Cadmus's descendants.
2. Cadmus consults the oracle of Apollo at Delphi, visiting one of its famous springs, the Castalian grotto.
3. A region of ancient Greece, north of the Gulf of Corinth, whose name comes from the Greek word for cow.

Gratefully, Cadmus kissed the foreign soil
and reverenced the unknown fields and mountains.
    A sacrifice to Jove is now in order:
Cadmus sends his attendants off to find   35
the necessary spring of running water.
Nearby there was a stand of virgin timber,
and deep within, a cave whose mouth was screened
by undergrowth and stones all mixed together;
fresh water poured across the arch it made.   40
    Deep in this cave, there lurked a golden-crested
serpent that Mars had chosen as his own:
his eyes flashed fire and his coiling bulk
was swollen up with venom, while his tongue
(divided at its tip into three parts)   45
flickered past teeth arranged in triple rows.
    When the doomed Tyrians had reached this grove
and started to draw water from the spring,
their careless clattering and splashing woke
the serpent, who, from deep within the cave   50
thrust his head out, hissing at them fiercely:
the pitchers tumble from their frightened hands
as in their veins the warm blood ices over,
and their agitated limbs convulse with tremors.
    Twisting his scaly coils in rolling knots,   55
with a great leap he flexes like a bow,
and then, by more than half his height, he thrusts
himself up through the unresisting air;
so huge he was that if you could have seen
the whole of him, he would have seemed the Snake   60
that keeps the Greater from the Lesser Bear.
    At once he falls upon the Tyrians,
whether they now prepare to fight or flee
or simply stand there, paralyzed by fear;
those who escape his fangs live but to die   65
crushed in his coils or poisoned by his breath.
    At midpoint now, the sun draws shadows in,
and Cadmus, wondering what keeps his mates,
sets out to find them: his shield, a lion pelt;
his arms, a javelin and thrusting spear;   70
no weapon, though, was greater than his courage.
    Soon at the grove, he sees their broken bodies,
and towering above them sways their huge
enemy, triumphant, his bloody tongue
licking at their sad wounds. The hero cries,   75
"Most faithful souls! I will avenge your deaths
or else I'll join you," and with his right hand
lifts up a huge rock, straining, and then hurls it.

   Such a great blow would easily have toppled
steep walls and lofty towers; but the serpent,   80
protected by the armor of his scales
and by his adamantine hide beneath,
repels the stroke unscathed, though not the spear
that slips through writhing coils to pin his spine,
its tip of iron buried in his innards.   85
   Frenzied, he twists his head round to examine
his wounded back, then bites down on the shaft,
and with great effort barely manages
to tear it loose, although the tip stays in,
adding new fuel to the well-banked ire   90
of customary rage: the veins throb in his throat,
his gaping horrid jaws are flecked with foam;
buffed by his scales, the bare earth resonates,
and his infernal breath infects the air.
   He coils his roundness up into enormous   95
spirals, then winds out upright, tall as a tree;
and now comes pouring like a stream in flood,
his huge breast sweeping forests on before it.
   Cadmus falls back: his shield of lion skin
receives the blows, while he wards off the jaws   100
with sharp spear jabs; enraged, the serpent bites
into the palate-piercing iron tip;
now blood begins to trickle from his throat,
and spatters the fresh grass with its new color.
   The wound is light though, since he keeps retreating,   105
moving his injured neck back from the spear,
yielding more ground, while he prevents the hero
from working on that wound. Relentlessly
Cadmus engages him, maneuvering
until he gets him right before an oak,   110
then thrusts and pins the monster to the tree,
which now bends in the middle from his weight,
and groans in bass, lashed by the serpent's tail.
   And while he stared at his enormous trophy,
the winner heard an unexpected voice,   115
distinctly clear, but unlocatable:
"Why do you gape at the slain serpent, Cadmus,
when you yourself are fated to become
a spectacle, a serpent well worth seeing?"[4]
   And for a long time, faint and colorless,   120
he stood there, trembling with icy fear,
his hair erect. But look: his patroness
glides down from heaven and stands by his side:

---

4. A prophecy that will be fulfilled in Book IV, *Cadmus and Harmonia*, p. 109.

Pallas Athena, who now bids him sow
the agitated earth with the viper's teeth,   125
seed of a race to come. Obeying her,
he opens furrows with a plow, then sprinkles
that mortal seed of teeth into the ground.
    And then, incredibly, the dull clods stir:
at first only the little tips of spears   130
are visible, emerging from the furrows,
but these, almost at once are followed by
the brightly painted waving crests of helmets,
then shoulders, breasts, and arms heavy with weapons,
and finally a dense-packed mass of shields: 135
no different from what you will have seen
on feast days, in the theater, when the curtain
lifts from the pit,[5] and the images of men
painted upon it seem to rise: heads first,
and then the rest of them, little by little,   140
drawn up in one unbroken wave until
the tiny figures stand erect onstage,
complete in all respects, from head to feet.
    Cadmus, alarmed by this new enemy,
prepared to arm himself: "Don't take up arms,"   145
cried one of those created in the earth.
"It's our civil war—stay out of it!"
    And closing in on one of his earthborn
brothers, he hacked him with his rigid sword,
and then was felled by someone else's spear;   150
and just a moment later, that one too
yielded the breath he'd only just received.
    Now all of them were equally enraged!
These brothers of a moment slew each other,
until young men, whose lives had just begun,   155
lay beating the breast of their ensanguined[6] mother.
    And now just five remained: one was Echion,[7]
who, warned by Pallas, threw his weapons down,
seeking and giving securities for peace
among his brothers; these were the companions   160
Sidonian[8] Cadmus had when he built the city
granted him by the oracle of Phoebus.

5. In Roman theaters curtains were raised, rather than lowered, at the end of an act or the
   end of a play; figures painted on the curtain would appear to be gradually rising, just as
   the tiny warriors do.
6. Bloodstained.
7. Echion goes on to marry Cadmus's daughter Agave, becoming the father of King
   Pentheus.
8. From Sidon, the Phoenician capital.

Actaeon and Diana

Thebes has been founded now, and even though
an exile still, you might seem fortunate
in having Mars and Venus as your in-laws,[9]   165
Cadmus; nor is this all, for in addition
are offspring worthy of your noble wife,
your sons and daughters, the pledges of your love,
and grandsons too, already grown to manhood.
But "fortunate"? A judgment best reserved   170
for a man's last day: call no one blest, until
he dies and the last rites are said for him.
      Not all your riches could console you, Cadmus,
grieving for the grandson that you lost
when those unlikely horns sprang from his brow,   175
and his own dogs were sated with his blood.
You'll find—if you look closely—that the fault
here was with Fortune, not with the young man,
for can it really be a crime to err?
      When the sun stood equidistant from its goals   180
at shadowless midday, upon a mountain
polluted with the blood of divers beasts,
Actaeon languidly addressed his mates,
who had been hunting in the trackless wood:
"Fortune has been sufficient to the day: 185
our nets and spears are steeped in beastly gore.
Let us renew our labors when Aurora
next brings the day back in her saffron car,
for now at midpoint, Phoebus sweats the fields;
stop what you're doing and take in the nets."   190
They did as he commanded them to do,
and abruptly brought their labors to an end.
      There is a grove of pine and cypresses
known as Gargaphie, a hidden place
most sacred to the celibate Diana;   195
and deep in its recesses is a grotto
artlessly fabricated by the genius
of Nature, which, in imitating Art,
had shaped a natural organic arch
out of the living pumice and light tufa.   200
      Before this little grotto, on the right,
a fountain burbles; its pellucid stream
widens to form a pool edged round with turf;

---

9. Ovid leaps forward: Cadmus has married Harmonia, daughter of Mars and Venus, and
    has founded the city of Thebes. He is the father of four daughters, by whom he has the
    three grandsons who will play important roles in Book III: Actaeon, Bacchus, and
    Pentheus.

here the great goddess of the woods would come
to bathe her virgin limbs in its cool waters,   205
when hunting wearied her.
                    She is here today;
arriving, she hands the Armoress of Nymphs[1]
her spear, her quiver, and her unstrung bow;
and while one nymph folds her discarded robe
over an arm, two more remove her sandals,   210
and that accomplished Theban nymph, Crocale,
gathers the stray hairs on Diana's neck
into a knot (we cannot help but notice
that her own hair is left in careless freedom!);
five other nymphs, whose names are Nephele,   215
Hyale, Rhanis, Psecas, and Phiale,
fetch and pour water from enormous urns.
    And while Diana bathes as usual,
see where Actaeon on a holiday,
wandering clueless through the unfamiliar   220
forest, now finds his way into her grove,
for so Fate had arranged.
                 At sight of him
within the misty precincts of their grotto,
the naked nymphs began to beat their breasts
and filled the grove with shrill and startled cries;   225
in their concern, they poured around Diana,
attempting to conceal her with a screen
of their own bodies, but to no avail,
for the goddess towered over all of them.
    The color taken from the setting sun   230
by western clouds, so similar to that
which rosy-tinted Dawn so often shows,
was the same color on Diana's face
when she was seen undressed. And even though
her virgin comrades squeezed themselves around her,   235
she managed to turn sideways and look back
as if she wished she had her arrows handy—
but making do with what she had, scooped up
water and flung it in Actaeon's face,
sprinkling his hair with the avenging droplets,   240
and adding words that prophesied his doom:
"Now you may tell of how you saw me naked,
tell it if you can, you may!"
                 No further warning:
the brow which she has sprinkled jets the horns
of a lively stag; she elongates his neck,   245

---

1. A purely honorific title, which Ovid grants Arethusa in Book V, line 797 (p. 137).

narrows his eartips down to tiny points,
converts his hands to hooves, his arms to legs,
and clothes his body in a spotted pelt.
Lastly, the goddess endows him with trembling fear:
that heroic son of Autonoe[2] flees,　　　　　　　　　　250
surprised to find himself so swift a runner.
　　But when he stopped and looked into a pool
at the reflection of his horns and muzzle—
"Poor me!" he tried to say, but no words came,
only a groaning sound, by which he learned　　　　　　255
that groaning was now speech; tears streamed down cheeks
that were no longer his: only his mind
was left unaltered by Diana's wrath.
What should he do? Return home to the palace,
or find a hiding place deep in the woods?　　　　　　　260
Shame kept him from one course, and fear, the other.
　　And while he stands bewildered, he observes
his pack of hunting dogs[3] approaching him
with Tracker and keen Blackfoot in the lead
(Tracker's a Cretan, Blackfoot's out of Sparta)　　　265
baying the good news to the dogs behind,
the whole pack rushing at him like a storm:
Gazelle and Greedy and Ridge Rover, all
Arcadians, with Killdeer and Tornado,
and sturdy Hunter, fearsome Birdie, Gwen,　　　　　　270
and savage Sylvia (who'd lately been
gored by a boar) and Snap (a wolf, her dam)
and faithful Shepherdess along with Snare
and two of the pups from her last litter;
ravenous Raptor the Siconian,　　　　　　　　　　　275
then Runner, Grinder, Spot, Tigress, Terror,
snow-colored Whitey, Soot as black as ashes,
powerful Sparta, devastating Whirlwind,
Speedy, and Wolf, the Cyprian, her brother,
and Trap (with that distinctive little white patch　　280
right in the middle of his black brow);
and after them came Blackie, Shag, and two
dogs of mixed Cretan-Spartan ancestry,
Fury and Fang, a little one named Yipper,
and many more too numerous to mention,　　　　　　285
all out to taste his blood, all unrelenting;
through steep, and sheer, and inaccessible,
through difficult and through impossible
places, they track him, and he flees the hunt

2. Actaeon's mother Autonoe is one of the daughters of Cadmus and Harmonia.
3. Ovid's epic catalogue of dogs is a brilliant tour de force.

he has so often led, longing to cry out   290
to the pack behind him, "It's me! Actaeon!
Recognize your master!" But the words
betray him and the air resounds with baying.

    Now Brownie and Buster leap onto his back
while Mountain Climber dangles from one shoulder;   295
they'd started late but figured out a shortcut
across the hilltop; now he's held at bay
until the pack can gather and begin
to savage him: torn by their teeth, he makes
a sound no man would make and no stag either,   300
a cry that echoes through those well-known heights;
and kneeling like a suppliant at prayer,
he turns toward them, pleading with his eyes,
as a man would with his hands.

                           But his companions
loudly encourage the ferocious pack,   305
all unaware: they look around for him,
call out to him as though he weren't there;
"*Actaeon!*" "Pity he's not here with us!"

    And hearing his own name, he turns his head:
he might wish to be elsewhere, but he's present,   310
and might wish merely to be watching this,
rather than feeling the frenzy of his dogs
who press around him, thrusting pointed snouts
into the savaged body of their master,
convinced that he's a stag.

                        And it is said   315
he did not die until his countless wounds
had satisfied Diana's awful wrath.

Juno, Jove, and Semele

Folks were divided: there were those who found
the goddess's actions cruel and unjust,
while others considered them appropriate   320
to the defense of her austere virginity.

    As usual, both parties had their reasons.
Jove's wife alone refrained from passing judgment,
rejoicing as she did when some misfortune
fell upon one of Agenor's descendants,   325
for her undying hatred of her husband's
Tyrian mistress had been redirected
more generally against Europa's kin.

    But look: her husband's at it once again:
Semele's womb is swollen with the seed   330
of almighty Jove, and Juno is dismayed;

this so reminds her of earlier episodes
that a great tirade rises to her lips:
    "But when have I won anything by shouting?"
she asked. "No: I must attack and ruin her,   335
if I am rightly styled as almighty Juno,
if it is right for me to bear the scepter,
if I am certainly the queen of Jove,
his sister, his wife—well, certainly his sister.[4]
    "Why bother, though? She's just a one-night stand,   340
a momentary insult to my conjugal rights.
But this one carries shame that can't be hidden
in her tumescent womb—and that *is* new;
her fondest wish is to become the mother
of a child by Jove—an honor I'm denied.   345
    "She's proud of her good looks: I'll have that pride
betray her; say that I'm not Saturn's daughter
if that one doesn't end up in the Styx,
and plunged there by almighty Jove himself!
    She left her throne and journeyed to the house   350
of Semele, wrapped in a golden cloud,
until she'd made herself into a crone
with whitened hair and wrinkle-furrowed skin
who walked bent over double, tottering
on trembling limbs, and spoke up in a voice   355
that quavered with old age; as such she seemed
Beroë, Semele's Epidaurian nurse.
    A long, inveigling chat of this and that,
until Jove's name came up. Nurse sighed and said,
"I *hope* he's Jupiter—although I doubt it: 360
the divinity plea? An all-too-common ploy
among seducers. Suppose he is, though:
make him provide assurance of his love;
if he's the real thing, ask him to put on
all of the trappings of his high office   365
and embrace you, showing such almighty splendor
as when he is received by Lady Juno."
    Thus the goddess schooled the clueless daughter
of Cadmus, who went quickly off to Jove
and asked him for a gift, nature unspecified.   370
    "Ask it," he said. "I will deny you nothing!
So that you may believe me all the more,
I'll swear it by the sacred, roiling Styx,
the god that terrifies the rest of us."
    Tickled to death by her appalling fate   375
and demanding from her too-indulgent lover

---

4. Ovid's parody of Juno's monologue in Book I of the *Aeneid*, lines 36ff.

a gift soon to undo her, Semele said,
"Just as you are when Lady Juno receives you
in her embraces and you initiate
the pact of Venus,[5] hidden from all others—   380
come likewise unto me." Even as she spoke
the god would have prevented her from speaking,
but all too swiftly had her words been uttered,
which, like his oath, could not be taken back.

He groans, distraught, and then ascends to heaven,   385
and with a glance, the mists are summoned round;
dark clouds are laced with lightning and high winds,
and thunder too, and inescapable fire;
as best he can, he moderates his force,
leaving upon its shelf the thunderbolt   390
with which he hurled the hundred-handed Typhoeus[6]
into the fire: that would have been too much.

Instead, he picks a bolt the Cyclops forged,[7]
one with reduced anger and a lower flame
(they call such weapons his Light Artillery);   395
and so appareled, came to Semele;
but she, whose mortal body could not bear
such heavenly excitement, burst into flames
and was incinerated by Jove's gift.

Her child was torn out of her womb unfinished,   400
and—this part is scarcely credible—was sewn
into his father's thigh, where he was brought to term.
His mother's sister, Ino, secretly
cared for the babe and then surrendered him
to nymphs on Nysa,[8] who hid him in their cave   405
and nourished him with milk.
                              And so, on earth,
the cradle of the twice-born baby Bacchus
was kept from harm by Fate's decree.

The Judgment of Tiresias

                              Meanwhile,
they say that in heaven Jove had put aside
his weighty cares, and, drink in hand, was busy   410
killing time in repartee with Juno:
"Women get far more pleasure out of sex
than men do," he said. And when she denied this,
they both agreed to seek the arbitration
of the transsexual sage, Tiresias,   415

5. Sexual intercourse.
6. One of the Titans.
7. On the race of Cyclopes as celestial blacksmiths, see note 9, p. 13.
8. The god Mercury took charge of Bacchus after his birth and gave him to be raised by the
   nymphs of Nysa in India.

who, in a leafy forest, had once profaned
the coupling of two enormous serpents,
by giving them a blow with his walking stick.
　　A wonder, for at once he was transformed
into a woman[9] and remained as such   420
for seven years. But when the eighth year came,
he saw the same two serpents once again
and said, "Since striking you has the effect
of turning one into one's opposite,
I'll strike you once again."
　　　　　　　　　　And having done so,   425
became the image of his former self.
　　The sage agreed to settle their dispute,
a trifling one, or so he must have thought,
when he agreed with Jove. But Saturn's daughter
reacted badly when he gave his judgment,   430
and many thought her anger was excessive,
when, for an issue of no great importance,
she damned Tiresias to eternal blindness.
　　But one god can't undo another's doing,
and so Jove gave Tiresias the gift   435
of foresight to replace the vision lost,
tempering punishment with the high esteem
he was soon held in, throughout all Boeotia,
for the unerring answers that he gave
to those who came to him and sought his counsel.   440
　　First to consult him was Liriope,
the sky-blue nymph who had been ravished by
the river god Cephisus when he snared her
between his winding banks; she bore a child,
who even as an infant was adorable,   445
and whom she called Narcissus.
　　　　　　　　　　When she asked
whether her son would live to ripe old age,
Tiresias responded with these words:
"If he knows himself—not." For a long time
that prophecy appeared completely groundless,   450
until the boy's unusual obsession,
which took his life, proved the foretelling true.

Narcissus and Echo[1]

Narcissus at sixteen seemed to be both
boy and man, and many boys and women
desired him; but in his yielding beauty   455

---

9. In another version of the myth, Tiresias is changed into a woman after he catches sight of the naked Athena.
1. Ovid was the first writer to put these two figures together in the same story.

was such inflexibility and pride
that no young man or woman ever moved him.
    Once, as he drove the trembling deer to his nets,
resounding Echo sighted him, a nymph
unable to keep still when someone spoke,   460
or speak at all before another did.
    Until this time, Echo had a body;
though voluble, she wasn't just a voice,
as she is now—although she used her voice
no oftener than she does now, repeating   465
just the last words of any speech she heard.
    Juno had done this to her, for whenever
Saturn's daughter was poised to apprehend
Jove in his dalliance with a mountain nymph,
Echo, who knew full well what she was doing,   470
detained the goddess with a long recital
of idle chatter while the nymphs escaped.
    But Juno figured out what she was up to:
"Once too often has your tongue beguiled me;
from now on you'll have little use for it!"   475
And that is why Echo skips now to the end
of any speech she hears and then repeats it.
    One day Narcissus happened to be roaming
the countryside when Echo happened by,
and at the very sight of him grew hot;   480
she secretly pursued him through the woods,
her heat increasing as she overtook him,
as torches smeared with highly flammable
sulfur ignite themselves, brought near a flame.
    Often she wanted to come on to him,   485
accost him with endearments, tender prayers—
but her nature won't permit such forwardness:
advances are denied her, though she may
repeat, in her own voice, a sound she hears.
    That day he was cut off from his companions,   490
and called out, "Anyone here?"
                               "*Here!*" answered Echo.
Narcissus searches all around, astounded:
cries out more loudly,
                 "Come!" His cry returns;
he turns around, but there's no one approaching:
"Why do you run away from me?" he asks,   495
and the very same words are given back to him.
    He halts, astounded by that other voice:
"Here let us come together," he cries out,
and Echo gave her heart with her reply,
"*Come! Together!*" And leapt out of the woods,   500

eager to give her words a little help
by swiftly embracing the desired neck;
he flees, and fleeing, cries, "Hands off! No hugs!
I'll die before you'll have your way with me!"
"You'll have your way with me," Echo replied.   505
    Spurned, shamefaced, she slipped into the woods
and hid herself, living alone in caves
from that time on. And yet her love endured,
increased even, by feeding on her sorrow:
unsleeping grief wasted her sad body,   510
reducing her to dried out skin and bones,
then voice and bones only; her skeleton
turned, they say, into stone. Now, only voice
is left of her, on wooded mountainsides,
unseen by any, although heard by all;   515
for only the sound that lived in her lives on.

Narcissus

He'd trifled with her and so many others,
water nymphs, nymphs of the wooded mountains,
as well as a host of male admirers.
One of those spurned raised his hands to heaven: 520
"May he himself love as I have loved him,"
he said, "without obtaining his beloved,"
and Nemesis[2] assented to his prayer.
    There was a clear pool of reflecting water
unfrequented by shepherds with their flocks   525
or grazing mountain goats; no bird or beast,
not even a fallen twig stirred its surface;
its presence nourished greenery around it,
and the surrounding trees would keep it cool.
    Worn out and overheated from the chase,   530
here comes the boy, attracted to this pool
as to its setting, and reclines beside it.
And as he strives to satisfy one thirst,
another is born; drinking, he's overcome
by the beauty of the image that he sees;   535
he falls in love with an immaterial hope,
a shadow that he wrongly takes for substance.
    Transfixed, suspended like a figure carved
from marble, he looks down at his own face;
stretched out on the ground, stares into his own eyes   540
and sees a pair of stars worthy of Bacchus,
a head of hair that might adorn Apollo;

2. The goddess of vengeance.

those beardless cheeks, that neck of ivory,
the decorative beauty of his face,
and the blushing snow of his complexion;   545
he admires all that he's admired for,
for it is he that he himself desires,
all unaware; he praises and is praised,
seeks and is the one that he is seeking;
kindles the flame and is consumed by it.   550

　　How many times, in vain, he leans to kiss
the pool's deceptive surface or to plunge
his arms into the water, keen to clasp
the neck he glimpses but cannot embrace;
and ignorant of what it is he looks at,   555
he burns for what he sees there all the same,
aroused by the illusion that deceives him.

　　Why even try to stay this passing fancy?
Child, what you seek is nowhere to be found,
your beloved is lost when you avert your eyes: 560
that image of an image, without substance,
arrives with you and with you it remains,
and it will leave when you leave—if you can!

　　For neither his hunger nor his need for rest
can draw him off; prone on the shaded grass,   565
his insatiate stare fixed on that false shape,
he perishes by his own eyes.

　　　　　　　　　　　　Lifting himself,
he spreads his arms out toward the nearby woods:
"O woods," he cries, "tell me if any other
has ever suffered any more than I have,   570
for surely you would know, you who have been
a likely lurking place for so many lovers—
was there ever one, in all the ages past
that you recall, who was consumed like me?
I like what I look at, but what I look at and like   575
I can't locate—"
　　　　　　　　　(So great is the confusion
in which this lover wanders, lost!)
　　　　　　　　　　　　　　　"My pain
is even greater, for no ocean lies
between us, nor some highway without end,
nor mountain range to cross, nor gates to scale: 580
only this shallow pool! He *would* be held,
for every time I lean down to the surface
and offer him my willing mouth to kiss,
he, on his back, lifts up his lips toward mine—
you'd think he could be touched!
　　　　　　　　　　　　　　"So very small   585

a thing it is that keeps us from our loving!
Come out and show yourself! Why do you mock me,
singular boy? Where do you take yourself?
Surely I'm young and sufficiently attractive
to stay your flight! Why, even nymphs have loved me!   590
  "I've no idea what hopes you mean to raise
with that come-hither look of yours, but when
I've reached down toward you, you've reached up again,
and when I laughed, why, you laughed too, and often
I have seen tears on *your* cheeks when I wept;   595
you second all my motions, and the movement
of your bow-shaped lips suggests that you respond
with words to mine—although I never hear them!
  "But *now* I get it! *I* am that other one!
I've finally seen through my own image!   600
I burn with love for—*me*! The spark I kindle
is the torch I carry: whatever can I do?
Am I the favor-seeker, or the favor sought?
  "Why seek at all, when all that I desire
is mine already? Riches in such abundance   605
that I've been left completely without means!
  "Oh, would that I were able to secede
from my own body, depart from what I love!
(Now *that's* an odd request from any lover.)
My grief is draining me, my end is near;   610
soon I will be extinguished in my prime.
This death is no grave matter, for it brings
an end to sorrow. Of course, I would have been
delighted if my beloved could have lived on,
but now in death we two will merge as one."   615
  Maddened by grief, he spoke and then turned back
to his image in the water, which his tears
had troubled; when he saw it darkly wavering,
he cried out, "Stay! Where are you going? O cruel,
to desert your lover! Touch may be forbidden,   620
but looking isn't: then let me look at you
and feed my wretched frenzy on your image."
  And while he mourned, he lifted up his tunic
and with hard palms, he beat on his bare breast
until his skin took on a rosy color,   625
as parti-colored apples blanch and blush,
or clustered grapes, that sometimes will assume
a tinge of purple in their unripened state;
the water clears; he sees what he has done
and can bear no more; just as the golden wax   630
melts when it's warmed, or as the morning's frost
retreats before the early sun's scant heat,

so he dissolves, wasted by his passion,
slowly consumed by fires deep within.
　　Now is no more the blushing white complexion,   635
the manly strength and all that pleased the eye,
the figure that was once quite dear to Echo.
　　And seeing this, she mourned, although still mindful
of her angry pain; as often as the wretched
boy cried, "Alas!" she answered with "*Alas!*"   640
And when he struck his torso with his fists,
Echo responded with the same tattoo.
　　His last words were directed to the pool:
"Alas, dear boy, whom I have vainly cherished!"
Those words returned to him again, and when   645
he cried "Farewell!" "*Farewell!*" cried Echo back.
　　His weary head sank to the grass; death closed
those eyes transfixed once by their master's beauty,
but on the ferry ride across the Styx,
his gaze into its current did not waver.   650
　　The water nymphs, his sisters, cut their locks
in mourning for him, and the wood nymphs, too,
and Echo echoed all their lamentations;
but after they'd arranged his funeral,
gotten the logs, the bier, the brandished torches,   655
the boy's remains were nowhere to be found;
instead, a flower,[3] whose white petals fit
closely around a saffron-colored center.

Bacchus and Pentheus[4]

Once news of this affair had circulated
throughout the Grecian cities, the seer's fame   660
increased deservedly; of all men, only
King Pentheus (who mocked the gods) despised him,
deriding his prophetic speech, and cruelly
throwing in his face the sudden blindness
which he had been afflicted with by Juno.   665
　　But the old man shook his white head in warning:
"Better, far better, had it been for you
if you too were blind: you would then be spared
the sight of Bacchus' rites," replied the seer.
　　"The day of his arrival is not distant,   670
this new god who is sprung from Semele,
and if you fail to show him fitting honors,
the god will tear your mangled corpse to pieces
and scatter them, your blood will stain the trees—

3. That flower is, of course, the narcissus.
4. The two are cousins.

will stain your mother and her sisters too!   675
—It will be so! You will ignore the god,
and you will say that in my blindness, I
saw far too much!"
                      The son of Echion
drove the seer off before he finished speaking,
but what he said would happen came to pass.   680

    Liber has come! The fields reverberate
with the ululations of the revelers;
people come pouring from the city's gates,
ignoring all distinctions of rank and gender:
men with matrons, matrons with young marrieds,   685
nobles and nobodies all hastening
together to these novel rites of Bacchus.

    "Children of Mars! Offspring of the Serpent!"[5]
cried Pentheus. "What madness clouds your judgment?
Will clashing cymbals, blaring hornpipes, tawdry   690
illusions conquer those who have endured
a line of flashing spears, who've drawn their swords,
advancing as one man when the charge was sounded?
Will these be overcome by women's voices,
by wine-soaked madness, drums and debauchery?   695

    "And you, elders—should I not find it strange
that you who crossed the sea to found New Tyre,
and made a home here for your exiled gods,
will yield it up without a fight?
                              "And you,
my comrades, warlike men of my own age—   700
have you decided to exchange your arms
and helmets for the thyrsus[6] and green garlands?

    "I pray you keep in mind the stock you spring from,
take as your own the spirit of the Serpent,
one who slew many; he died in the defense   705
of his own lair, but you for glory's sake;
he slew heroes; you must drive off sissies
to keep your nation's honor bright.
                              "If fate
denies long life to Thebes, I'd rather see
her walls fall to men and the engines of war,   710
in tumult of iron and fire! Our wretchedness
would be no crime then, we could mourn our lot
openly, unshamed by our tears.

    "But Thebes has been captured by a sissyboy,
untutored in the arts of war, unaided   715

5. A reference to the serpent overcome by Cadmus earlier in Book III.
6. A staff, wrapped in ivy vine leaves and crowned with a pinecone, carried by Bacchus and
   by those who celebrated the god's rites.

by spears or cavalry: the city taken
by slicked and scented hair, by tender garlands,
by robes embroidered with rich gold and purple!
    "Out of my way! I'll force him to admit
the truth about his lofty parentage   720
and concocted rites! Didn't Acrisius[7]
show what he was made of when he banned
this empty deity and closed the gates
of Argos to him and his crowd? Will Pentheus
and all of Thebes take fright at his approach?   725
Go quickly, slaves, bring me their leader back
in chains: do as I bid without delay!"
    His grandfather and Athamas[8] rebuke him,
and all the counselors that press around,
vainly attempting to contain his anger;   730
their warnings, ineffectual, enrage him,
and his wrath increases as they urge restraint.
    So I have sometime seen a stream in torrent
make no more than a murmur as it flowed on,
unobstructed; but where it met resistance   735
from logs and rocks, it boiled and foamed, turning
its waters white with an opposing rage.
    But look: his slaves are back, all smeared with blood,
and when he asks for Bacchus, they reply
that even though no Bacchus could be found,   740
they nonetheless have captured his companion,
a Bacchic priest, hauled up before the king
with his arms tightly bound behind his back.
    Almost unable to restrain himself,
Pentheus casts a dreadful eye on him: 745
"You who are about to die, and by your death
serve as a warning to all others, speak:
tell us your name, your ancestry, your nation,
and why you devote yourself to these new rites."
    He spoke up fearlessly: "My name's Acoetes,   750
my land's Maeonia; my people, humble;
my father didn't leave me a young bull
to help the cultivation of the fields
he didn't leave me any of besides;
no herds of sheep, nor any other beasts.   755
    "He was, in fact, a pauper, baiting hooks
and casting out to where the fish were leaping;
that skill was all his wealth and property,
and when he passed it on to me, he said,

---

7. Grandfather of the hero Perseus, Acrisius also resisted the cult of Bacchus.
8. Cadmus is the grandfather of Pentheus, and Athamas is his uncle.

'Accept the only riches that I have,   760
my sole successor, heir of my enterprise.'
    "And so it was that my inheritance
consisted totally of liquid assets:
dying, he left me nothing but the water.
    "Then, so as not to have to spend my life   765
forever stuck on one rock and the same,
I added to my repertoire the arts
of navigation: I learned how to steer
and set a course for ships by the positions
of the Goat, the Pleiades, the Hyades, the Bear;   770
I studied the directions of the winds
and learned which ports make the safest harbors.
    "Happened one day that as we made for Delos,
we were becalmed and lay to, off the coast
of Chios, until with our practiced oars,   775
we brought the ship to shore, leapt to wet sand,
and beached her there. And there we spent the night.
    "At dawn, I rose and sent the men for water
from a nearby spring I showed them where to find,
while I went up a hill to read the winds,   780
and when I finished, summoned them aboard.
'All present and accounted for,' answered Opheltes,
the first of my crew members to return
with booty (as he thought) found in a field:
a little boy formed like a little girl.   785
    "The child seemed to totter, stumbling along
as though dulled by sleep. I noted carefully
the refinement of his bearing, the *look* of him—
nothing I saw there made me think him mortal.
Sensed it at once, and told my crew,
                                            "'What god   790
impersonates that child I do not know,
but there's a god in him, I'm sure of that!
Whoever you are, oh, show us grace and favor,
aid our undertakings, and forgive
these men for their offense.'
                              "'Don't pray for us,'   795
said Dictys, who would scramble like a monkey
into the rigging and right back down again.
Libys concurred with him, as did the lookout,
blond Melanthus; Alcimedon joined in
and Epopeus, who timed the rowers' strokes,   800
and all the others went along with them,
blinded alike by greediness for plunder.
    "'I won't allow this ship to be defiled
by profaning acts,' I said. 'My own authority

must have the greater weight and precedence.'   805
I held them back from boarding, but Lycabas,
the most abandoned, most headstrong of that crew,
exiled from Tuscany for manslaughter,
flew at my throat, enraged, in mortal combat;
choked me until I very nearly fainted,   810
and would have sent me flying into the water
had I not grabbed a rope and clung to it.
     "The filthy rabble all approved. At last,
Bacchus (for it was he), as though awakened
by our racket, asked, half-drunkenly,   815
'What's going on here, sailors? Why this fuss?
How did I get here? What will you do with me?'
     "'Don't you fret none,' said Proreus. 'Just say
which port you want and we'll deliver you
straight to whatever land your heart is set on.'   820
     "'Naxos!' cried Liber:[9] 'Change your heading to starboard!
That is my home, and there you will be welcomed!'
     "Those liars swore by the sea, by all the gods,
it would be so, and ordered me to sail.
Naxos lay to starboard; starboard was my heading,   825
but men kept coming up to me and muttering,
'What are you doing, madman?' 'What's gotten into you,
Acoetes?' 'Tack to port and hold steady!'
Some made their meaning clear with a nod or wink,
while others whispered openly. I balked: 830
'Have someone else take over then,' I said,
letting them know I'd have no part in this.
     "They all began to murmur and rebuke me,
and from their midst Aethelion emerged:
'Sure,' he said, 'Sure—as if our safety   835
depends on one man—you!' He took the helm
and set sail to port, away from Naxos.
     "The god began to toy with them, pretending
he'd only just now seen through their deceit,
and gazing out at the sea from the curved prow   840
in feigned tears, he cried, 'This is not the shore
you promised, sailors, nor the land I sought:
What have I done to you? What glory is gained,
if a boy is tricked by men? Or one by many?'
     "I had long been weeping. My indecent crew   845
laughed at my tears and rowed at double speed.

9. The Aegean isle of Naxos plays an important role in the cult of Bacchus because the adult
   Bacchus discovered Ariadne there after her abandonment by Theseus. "Liber" is one of
   the cult names of the god.

Now, by the presence of the god himself
(a god more truly present than all others)
I swear that what I tell you next is truth,
though past belief: the ship stood still in the sea—   850
as though it had been lifted up in dry dock!
    "The men, although astounded, persevere,
redoubling their strokes and letting sail out,
hoping to break loose one way or another.
But now the oars are tangled up in ivy,[1]   855
and twining strands of it coil round their bodies,
ascend the mast and decorate the sails
with ivy berries in enormous clusters.
    "And now the god reveals himself at last,
his brow festooned with leaves and grapes in bunches,   860
shaking a spear with vine leaves wrapped around it!
About him tigers and the bodiless
forms of lynxes and fierce leopards lie!
    "Insanity or terror drives my crew,
and they leap overboard: Medon's whole body   865
begins to darken and his spine is molded
in a dramatic curve:
                    "'What sort of specimen
is it you're turning into?' asks Lycabas,
but even as he speaks his jaws gape wide,
his nose protrudes, his skin gets rough and scaly.   870
And while he leans against unmoving oars,
Libys becomes aware his hands are shrinking
until they aren't even hands—but fins.
    "Another only learns he's lost his arms
when he attempts to wrap them round a rope: 875
limbless, he does a back-flip into the sea,
to demonstrate the tail that he now sports,
curved like the crescent horns of a new moon!
    "Now they leap up and splash back, frolicking
in the water all around us, everywhere!   880
They carry on like dancers, leaping wildly,
sucking in water and spraying it into the air!
    "Out of the twenty men that vessel carried,
I alone was left: trembling, cold with terror,
scarcely myself, until the god encouraged me: 885
'Dismiss your fears,' he said. 'Set sail for Naxos!'
And since the time of my arrival there,
I've been devoted to the god and to his rites."

1. The appearance of the god is signaled by dead wood sprouting green leaves, ivy, or
grapevines.

"We've listened patiently, too patiently,
to this long-winded drivel, meant to dissipate   890
our anger by delaying punishment,"
said Pentheus. "Off with him quickly, boys,
go break his bones and rack him with dread torments
and plunge him lifeless into Stygian gloom!"
    At once Acoetes was dragged out and chained   895
in a thick-walled cell. While they prepared
the instruments of torture and hot irons,
the doors flew open, folks said, on their own,
and just like that, the chains fell from his shoulders!
    But Pentheus kept up his opposition.   900
No longer sending others, he himself
went to Cithaeron, the appointed site
for the performance of the mysteries,
and heard the songs and loud cries of Bacchantes;[2]
and as a warhorse, eager for some action,   905
snorts and whinnies when the brazen trumpet sounds
the charge, and his old love of battle surges,
so Pentheus was roused by their wild cries,
his wrath rekindled by the savage clamor.
    Halfway up the mountain was a clearing   910
surrounded by woods, but wholly visible.
And here, as he observed the mysteries
with his profaning eyes, the very first
to sight him and pursue him in a frenzy,
the first to wound him, with the wand she hurled,   915
was his own mother: "Sisters," she cried, "come here:
a great boar has blundered into our field,
a boar that I must slay!"
                              In a seething mass
they rush out after him from every side,
driving him on; and he, now terrified,   920
the autocratic no longer, speaking mildly,
admits to them the error of his ways.
Wounded, he cries out, "Help, Aunt Autonoe,
yield to the spirit of your son, Actaeon!"
    But who is this Actaeon he has mentioned?   925
How would *she* know? She tears off his right arm,
while Ino in rapture savages the left.
He has no arms to stretch out to his mother,
unlucky man, but cries out, "Mother, look!"
and shows her his torso with its missing limbs.   930
    Tossing her hair in frenzy and exulting
at the grim sight, Agave tears her son's

---

2. Female worshippers of Bacchus.

head from his trunk and fiercely gripping it
in a bloody fist maniacally cries,
"Comrades! The deed, the victory are ours!"   935
    Swift as the wind that tears the last few leaves
clinging to trees touched by autumnal frost,
those impious hands tore him all asunder;
by that example warned, Thebans observe
the new rite, bringing incense to its altars.   940

BOOK IV

Spinning Yarns and Weaving Tales

The Daughters of Minyas[1]

But not Alcithoë: Minyas' daughter considers
the rites of Bacchus unacceptable,
and goes so far as to deny that Jove
fathered the new god, an impiety
her sisters also hold.
    A priest commands   5
the people celebrate a festival:
all servant girls to be excused from work;
they and their mistresses to dress in hides,
unbind their hair, wreathe their heads in garlands,
and lift the leafy thyrsus in procession;   10
failure to comply with these instructions,
he prophecies, will move the slighted god
to cruel anger.
    Old wives and young comply:
the piles of weaving, baskets full of wool,
all the unfinished business of the day   15
is thrust aside; incense is burned, and Bacchus
summoned by his many names and titles:
"Great Thunderer![2] Sweet Bringer of Release!"
"Child whose father was his second mother!"
"Child torn from woman, and reborn of Jove!"   20
"Unshorn Son of Semele Translated!"
"Lenaeus, Planter of the Genial Grape!"
"Nocturnal Orgiast!"
       "Father of Cries!"
"Eleleus!"
   "Iacchus!
     "Euhan!"
    "And by whatever other names unmentioned   25
here in our litany belong to you,
Liber, among the multitudes of Greece:

1. Another abrupt beginning: the scene has moved from Thebes to Orchomenus, a city about forty miles away. The three daughters of its king, Minyas, challenge the powers of Bacchus and pay dearly for their presumption.
2. Names of the god derived from his characteristics and from aspects of his worship. "Great Thunderer" attests to the noisy nature of his rites; "Sweet Bringer of Release" reminds us that Bacchus is god of wine. The next three references are to Jove's taking over the duties of pregnancy after Semele's destruction. "Lenaeus" is a name derived from an Athenian festival in the god's honor. "Nocturnal Orgiast" and "Father of Cries" point to the frenzied nature of the rites. "Eleleus" and "Euhan" were ritual cries of the worshippers, and "Iacchus" was another name for the god, as was "Liber." After the summons comes a hymn of praise to the god.

91

"O Youth undimmed, Eternal Boy,
   Fairest in the heavens;
Without your horns,[3] your countenance   30
   Is lovely as a maiden's;

"Now all the Orient admits
   The godhead that is yours,
Even as far as India,
   Where the dark Ganges pours;   35

"Worshipful god, King Pentheus
   Died of your great wrath,
And Lycurgus,[4] who swung his axe;
   Blasphemers were they both.

"You threw the changed Tyrrhenian   40
   Sailors in the ocean,
But you reward your devotees
   Who offer their devotion;

"Lynxes in harness draw your car,
   Bacchantes and Satyrs follow;   45
The boxwood flutes begin to wail,
   Their music fills the hollow;

"Your revelers collapse in laughter,
   As swaying on his mule,
Or staggering drunkenly after,   50
   Silenus[5] plays the fool!

"Intoxicating clamor trails
   You upon your rambles:
The ululations of your horde,
   Their tambourines and cymbals!"   55

   "Be reconciled, be gentle," cry the Theban
women as they perform the rites demanded;
only the daughters of Minyas keep within,
spoiling the new god's feast with their untimely
spinning and weaving, the diurnal tasks   60
they and their servants are kept busy with.

---

3. Bacchus was often depicted with horns, a suggestion of the bestial violence associated
   with his worship.
4. A Thracian king who drove Bacchus out of his kingdom and was severely punished for
   this impiety.
5. The nurse, teacher, and attendant of Bacchus, Silenus is represented as a jolly old man
   riding on an ass in a state of perpetual intoxication.

One sister, lightly drawing thread, observes,
"Though other women cease their work and hasten
to *his* concocted rites, a superior
divinity has kept us in our places: 65
Pallas Athena! No reason why we shouldn't
lighten the useful labor of these hands
by taking our turns at telling stories:
such give and take will pass the time more quickly,
and be a kindness to those listening."   70
　　Her joyful sisters bid her to begin,
but which of the many stories that she knows
should she relate? Long she pondered, doubtful:
your story, Babylonian Dercetis?[6]
A woman who, as Syria supposes,   75
was changed into a scaly thing that swims
now in a little pool? Or how her daughter,
transformed into a dove of purest white,
spent her last years perched on lofty towers?
Or how, by potent herbs and incantations,   80
a nymph changed little boys to fish, until
she underwent the very same conversion?
Or how the mulberry, which once bore white,
bears dark fruit now, since it's been stained with blood?
That one will please them with its novelty!   85
And as she weaves, begins to spin her yarn:

Pyramus and Thisbe

"Pyramus, who was handsomest of men,
and Thisbe, of a loveliness unrivaled
in all the East, lived next to one another
in Babylon, the city that Semiramis   90
surrounded with a wall made out of brick.
　　"Proximity saw to it that this couple
would get acquainted; soon, they fell in love,
and wedding torches would have flared for them
had both their parents not forbidden it,   95
although they weren't able to prevent
two captive hearts from burning equally.
　　"These lovers had no go-between, yet managed
a silent conversation with the signs
and gestures they alone could understand: 100
their fire burned more hotly, being hidden.

---

6. The nameless first sister proposes and rejects three stories from the Near East. Dercetis is
another name of the Syrian goddess Atargatis; her daughter was Semiramis, the notori-
ously promiscuous queen of Babylon, in whose city the story of Pyramus and Thisbe takes
place. The third tale mentioned is known only from what Ovid says about it here.

"In the common wall that ran between their houses,
there was a narrow cleft made by the builders
during construction and unnoticed since.
Love misses nothing! You two first descried it,   105
and made that little crack the medium
that passed your barely audible endearments.

"Often, when they had taken up positions,
Pyramus on one side, Thisbe on the other,
and each had listened to each other's panting,   110
'O grudging wall,' they cried, 'why must you block us?
Is it too much to ask you to let lovers
embrace without impediment of stone?
Or if it is, won't you *please* let us kiss?
It's not that we're ungrateful—we admit   115
all that we both owe you, for allowing
our words to pass into attentive ears!'

"So they (in pointless separation) spoke.
When night came on, each said goodbye and pressed
a kiss—which went no further—on the stone.   120

"When next Aurora had put out the stars
and the Sun had burned the hoarfrost from the meadow,
they found themselves at their familiar spot,
and after much whispered lamentation,
agreed that just as soon as it was night,   125
they'd slip their guardians and leave their houses,
and once outdoors, flee from the city too.

"And so as not to end up wandering
those open spaces by themselves, they chose
the tomb of Ninus[7] as their meeting place: 130
nearby, there was a fountain and a tall
mulberry tree, abounding with white berries;
in its dense shadows they would find concealment.
They were delighted by this plan of theirs;
daylight seemed loath to leave, but at long last,   135
the sun extinguished itself in the sea,
and from its waters came—at last—the night.

"Discretely veiled, Thisbe unlocks her door,
lets herself out and slips into the darkness;
emboldened by love, she finds the tomb and sits   ·140
beneath the tree. But look! A lioness,
whose jaws are dripping from a recent kill,
approaches the fountain to assuage her thirst.

"From far off, Thisbe sees her in the moonlight,
and with trembling steps, runs into a dark cave.   145
But in her flight, she drops her cloak and leaves it

---

7. Some local color: Ninus was king of Babylon, husband of Semiramis. Presumably his
tomb would have been prominent enough for the lovers to find in the dark.

behind her on the ground. Now, when the savage
lioness has had her fill of water
and heads back to the woods, by chance she finds
that cloak (without the girl) and pauses there   150
to mangle it in her ferocious jaws.
    "Arriving later, Pyramus discovers
tracks in the dust, as plain as day: he blanches,
and when he finds her bloodstained garment, cries,
'On this one night, two lovers come to grief!   155
For she, far more than I, deserved long life!
Mine is the guilt, poor miserable dear,
since it was I most surely who destroyed you,
bidding you come by night to this drear place,
and me not here before you!
                            "'Come now, you lions   160
inhabiting the caves beneath this rock,
tear me to pieces and consume me quite!
But only cowards merely *beg* for death.'
    "He carries Thisbe's cloak to the tree of their pact,
and presses tears and kisses on the fabric.   165
'Drink *my* blood now,' he says, drawing his sword,
and thrusting it at once in his own guts:
a fatal blow; dying, he draws the blade
out of his burning wound, and his lifeblood
follows it, jetting high into the air,   170
as he lies on his back upon the ground.
    "It was as when a water pipe is ruptured
where the lead has rotted, and it springs a leak:
a column of water goes hissing through the hole
and parts the air with its pulsating thrusts;   175
splashed with his gore, the tree's pale fruit grow dark;
blood soaks its roots and surges up to dye
the hanging berries purple with its color.
    "But look! Where frightened still, but frightened more
that by her absence she might fail her lover,   180
Thisbe comes seeking him with eyes and soul,
all eagerness to tell him of the perils
she has escaped. But can this be the place?
That tree has a familiar shape, although
the color of its fruit leaves her uncertain.   185
    "And as she hesitates she notices
a knot of writhing limbs on the bloodstained earth;
in horror, she leaps back, as white as boxwood;
a tremor runs right through her, and she shivers
as the sea does when a breeze stirs on its surface.   190
    "In the next moment, Thisbe recognizes
her lover's body and begins to beat
her unoffending arms with small, hard fists,

tearing her hair out; she embraces him,
and the tears she sheds there mingle with his blood.   195
Kissing his cold lips, she cries, 'Pyramus,
what grave mischance has taken you from me?
Answer me, Pyramus, your darling Thisbe
is calling: hear me, raise your fallen head!'

   "And he, responding to his darling's name,   200
opens his eyes, so heavy with his death,
to close them on the image of her face.

   "And now she recognizes her own cloak
and sees his sword and its sheath of ebony:
'O poor unfortunate! You've lost your life   205
by your own hand and by your love for me!
In my hand too, there's strength to do the same,
and love that will give power to my stroke!

   "'I'll follow you until the very end;
it will be said of me I was the cause   210
as well as the companion of your ruin.
Death once had strength to keep us separate;
it cannot keep me now from joining you!

   "'And may our wretched parents, mine and yours,
be moved by this petition to allow us,   215
joined in the same last hour by unwavering love,
to lie together in a single tomb.

   "'And you, O mulberry, whose limbs now shade
one wretched corpse and soon will shelter two,
display the markings of our deaths forever   220
in the crimson of your fruit, the likeliest
memorial for two who perished here.'

   "She holds the sword tip underneath her breast
and then falls forward on the still-warm blade.
Her parents and the gods yield to her prayers;   225
for now the mulberry's ripe fruit is dark
and their blent ashes share a single urn."

Mars and Venus

And so it ended. A brief pause ensued,
and then Leuconoë began to weave
another story for her silent sisters: 230

   "Even the Sun, who with his own light governs
all other stars, has felt love's agitation:
I will relate the passions of the Sun.

   "Since this god sees whatever happens first,
the Sun is reckoned to have first uncovered   235
the extramarital affair of Mars
and Venus. Scandalized, the Sun informed

the husband of the goddess, shedding light
on the very couch where two had sinned together!
    "Vulcan at once dropped what he was doing: 240
immediately he devised a brilliant
trap for the guilty pair, a net of bronze links
so finely woven that it fooled the eye.
No thread of mortal weaving was as slender
as this one was: finer than the spider's,   245
and more responsive to the slightest touch.
    "He spread it craftily across the bed,
and when his wife and her gallant had come
together on the couch, by her husband's art
and by the chains he'd cleverly devised,   250
the two of them were caught in the very act,
clinging together in mutual embrace.
    "Vulcan at once threw wide the folding doors
of ivory, and sent the other gods
inside to see the lovers where they lay   255
trapped in each other's arms most shamefully!
    "And one of the immortals who was present
was heard by all the others there to wish—
not at all sadly—that he too might be
embarrassed so. The others howled with laughter,   260
and for a long time that was the one story
any of them told in all of heaven.

The Sun and Leucothoë

"But Venus knew who her betrayer was,
and soon devised appropriate revenge:
the spoiler of her naughty little secret   265
would find himself no less destroyed by love.
—O son of Hyperion,[8] what use to you
your beauty, your brightness, your radiant beams?
You who scorch earth with fire of your own
are burned now by an unaccustomed flame!   270
You who should gaze on all, impartially,
have eyes but for the virgin Leucothoë!
    "And now you rise too early in the morning
and drop into the sea too late at night;
your lingering glance prolongs brief winter days,   275
and now and then you even fail completely,
as the unshakable obsession in your mind
passes through your eyes, and its obscureness
is terrifying to all mortal hearts!

8. The Sun is the offspring of Hyperion, one of the Titans.

"It's not as though the moon had interposed   280
its own pallor between the earth and you:
love is the force that leaves you colorless!
You've chosen this one, and no longer care
for Clymene, for Rhodos, or for Circe's
most attractive mother; you neglect   285
poor Clytie, who, although you scorn her,
is very eager to make love to you,
and even now is languishing, heartbroken.

"For Leucothoë has chased them from your mind,
the daughter of Eurynome, the fairest   290
in the land of spices;[9] just as *her* mother's beauty
surpassed that of all other women, she,
when she grew up, surpassed her mother's beauty.
Her father Orchamus was king of Persia,
the seventh in descent from ancient Belus,   295
the kingdom's founder.
                                   "Under western skies
are meadows where the horses of the Sun
are pastured, feeding on divine ambrosia
instead of ordinary grass; and here,
exhausted by their efforts of the day,   300
this nourishment sustains them and renews
their vigor for the labors of the morrow.

"And while his horses browse on their immortal
pasturage, and Night goes to work, the Sun
takes on the form of Leucothoë's mother,   305
Eurynome, and slips into her bedroom;
lamplight reveals his darling with her servants,
winding fine strands of wool upon her spindle.
Then kissing her as her fond mother would,
he says, 'A secret matter, servants: leave!   310
Respect a mother's right to privacy!'

"Once witnesses are gone, the god emerges:
'I am that one who measures the long year,
who sees all things, and by whom all may see;
I am the world's eye and believe me, you   315
are something really special, quite a sight!'

"She trembles uncontrollably with fear;
distaff and spindle slip from her slack grip.
Her fear arouses him: at once he resumes
his former shape and his accustomed splendor.   320

"This unexpected apparition frightens
the virgin, but its radiance overwhelms her,
and she gives in to him without complaint.

9. The East in general, Persia in particular.

"Now Clytie, whose own love for the Sun
was boundless, raged with envy of her rival: 325
she spread around the story of her fall,
and brought her ruined state to the attention
of the girl's father.

                  "Like a savage beast
he mercilessly scorns his daughter's pleas,
her hands uplifted to the Sun in prayer,   330
and her own explanation of events:
'He plundered me! I did not pleasure him!'

    "He buries her alive, and then heaps up
an enormous mound of sand upon her grave.
The Sun's rays melt it down, so that you might   335
lift your head proudly in the world once more;
but worn out by the weight of earth you bear,
you cannot raise yourself, poor nymph, and lie
with all the life crushed out of you.

                     "They said
that not since the fiery death of Phaëthon   340
had the governor of swiftly flying horses
seen anything as sad as he attempted
to revive those icy limbs with his warm rays
and call the living warmth back to her body.

    "And although Fate prevents him from succeeding,   345
he sprinkles her body and the site around it
with fragrant nectar; and after he had mourned her,
he cries out loudly in his lamentation,
'In spite of Fate, you *will* reach up to heaven!'

    "Her body, steeped in those divine aromas,   350
dissolved at once in earth-delighting odors.
A slip (not of a girl now, but of fragrant incense)
broke through the apex of that hillock, while
its roots drove down and deeply gripped the soil.

    "Though Clytie might well have made the case   355
that love brought her to grief, and grief to tattle,
because the Lord of Light no longer wanted
to sleep with her as he had used to do,
her passion turned into consuming madness.

    "Unable to endure the other nymphs,   360
naked she sat on the uncovered earth
by day and night, beneath the open sky,
her hair a straggly mess, and for nine days
subsisting on no more than dew and teardrops,
in motion only when she turned her face   365
to keep it always fixed upon her god.

    "Her limbs (they say) attached themselves to earth,
her pallor turned in part to bloodless plant,

and where her face had been, a trace of color
yielded a little violet-like flower.[1]   370
Rooted in earth, she turns now toward the Sun,
and, although changed, preserves her changeless love."

The Fountain of Salmacis

She ended, and the marvels she related
held every ear: some sisters would deny
that anything like that could ever happen,   375
while some declare that any real gods may
do anything at all that they've a mind to,
though Bacchus surely isn't one of these.
    Now when the sisters have composed themselves
once more, Alcithoë is called upon,   380
and as she swiftly and expertly draws
the shuttle through the warp, she thinks aloud:
    "I will not mention here the too-familiar
loves of the Idaean shepherd Daphnis,[2]
turned into stone for a nymph's rage at a rival: 385
how thwarted lovers burn! Nor will I speak
of how a law of nature was repealed
when Sithon changed at will from man to woman;
nor of you, Celmis, now adamant, but once
the most faithful guardian of baby Jove;   390
nor how the Curetes emerged from a downpour;
nor will I speak of Crocus and his Smilax,
turned into tiny flowers—these I pass by,
choosing to keep your attentions with a tale
commended by the charm of novelty: 395
    "I will explain the way in which the fountain
of Salmacis, whose enervating waters
effeminate the limbs of any man
who bathes in it, came by its reputation,
for though the fountain's ill effects are famous,   400
their cause has never been revealed before.
    "Venus of Cythera and Mercury
together made a boy raised by the naiads

---

1. It might seem likelier that Clytie would turn into a sunflower, but the violet color suggests
   a heliotrope, which turns its face toward the sun.
2. Ovid learned the rhetorical trope of paraleipsis ("I will not mention here . . . Nor will I
   speak of . . .") when he studied oratory as a young man. A jealous nymph turned Daphnis
   into stone as punishment for his infidelity; Sithon's tale is otherwise unknown—it may
   have been an inferior version of the one finally selected; Celmis protected baby Jove on
   Crete from the rage of his father, Saturn, and then was changed into stone by Jove for
   questioning his divinity. The Curetes were Cretan defenders of Jove. Crocus (a boy) and
   Smilax (a nymph) were changed into flowers of the same names.

in caves upon Mount Ida. His face and name
made evident their offspring's origins.[3]   405
    "At fifteen he took off for parts unknown,
leaving maternal Ida and the mountains
of his fatherland, and wandered, pleased to see
strange lands and rivers likewise new to him,
his keenness making molehills out of mountains.   410
    "He traveled to the cities of Lycia
and to the Carians, who dwell nearby.
And there he saw a pool of crystal-clear
water, not choked with reeds and spiky rushes,
but fluidly transparent, with a border   415
of well-kept lawn, landscaped with evergreens.
    "A nymph dwelled here, who was not keen on hunting,
not up for archery, unfit for footraces;
the only nymph not in Diana's posse.
Often, the story goes, her sisters said,   420
'Choose one, Salmacis, javelin or bow,
and interrupt your leisure for the chase!'
    "But she would not choose javelin or bow,
or interrupt her leisure for the chase;
for she would rather bathe her shapely limbs   425
and then spend hours working on her hair,
using the waters as a mirror to
reflect the look that made her look most lovely.
    "And after that, in a transparent gown,
she chose between the softness of the leaves   430
or the lawn's softness to lie down upon.
Often she gathered flowers. As it happened,
one day while so engaged, she saw the boy,
and realized that she just *had* to have him.
    "But eager as she was, she still hung back: 435
composed herself and then arranged her hair
and struck a fetching pose; and having done
her utmost to be seen as beautiful,
she only then came up to him and spoke:
    "'O boy, most worthy to be taken for   440
a god, if you're a god, why you'd be Cupid,
but if you're not a god, if you're just mortal,
why, blessed are the parents who produced you,
happy your brother and fortunate indeed
your sister, if you have one, and the nurse   445
who gave her breasts to you, but far more blest
than any one of these is your betrothed,

---

3. The boy is the son of Mercury (Greek Hermes) and Venus (Greek Aphrodite); their Greek
   names, when joined, allude to the outcome of the story.

if you're already promised to another,
if that's the case I'll bed you secretly—
but if there is no other I would be   450
the one to share a wedding couch with you.'
  "The nymph fell silent, and the boy's cheeks reddened,
for though he'd no experience of love,
he blushed attractively.
                    "The color seemed
like that of apples in a sunny orchard,   455
or painted ivory, or like the moon
eclipsed, when red is glimpsed around her rim,
and brazen vessels are beaten in the vain
effort of the pious to restore her.
  "The nymph kept pestering him for a kiss,   460
a friendly kiss, the kind a sister gets—
while readying herself to fling her arms
around his ivory neck in an embrace.
'Stop that,' he said, 'or I'll leave you here alone!'
This terrifies Salmacis, who replies,   465
'Stranger, this place is yours; I freely yield it.'
  "She walked away, pretending to depart,
but only went into a nearby thicket
and hid herself, crouching on bended knee;
he seemed to think that he was all alone   470
and unobserved, and so went wandering
along the grassy margins of the pool,
testing the playful waters with his toes
and then his feet, and then—no more delay,
the tepid water summoned him, and he   475
removed the garments from his slender body.
  "Salmacis is delighted by the sight
and burns with passion for his nakedness;
her eyes light up as though he were the Sun
and they were mirrors filled with his reflection.   480
Delay seems unendurable and joy
will suffer no postponement; scarcely able
to still her passion, she must have him now!
  "And after splashing water on his body
with his cupped palms, he dives into the pond,   485
and breaks the surface with an easy crawl,
glowing within that liquid as though lilies
or an ivory figurine has been sealed up
in clearest glass.
                    "'I've won, the boy is mine!'
the nymph cries out, and tearing off her clothing,   490
she dives into the middle of the pool,
and though he fights her, holds him in her clutches,

seizing the kisses he is loath to yield;
her hands surprise him, coming from below,
caressing that reluctant breast of his—   495
although he strives to tear himself away,
the nymph—now here, now there—surrounds her prey,
just as the serpent wraps herself around
the eagle when he grasps her in his talons
and takes her up: dangling from his claws,   500
she twines herself between his head and feet
and with her tail, immobilizes him;
or just as ivy winds around a tree,
and as the octopus beneath the sea
securely binds the prey that it has captured   505
with tentacles sent out in all directions;
yet still the boy denies the nymph her bliss.
     "She presses her whole body against his
as though stuck on him, crying, 'Willful boy,
you can resist me, but you can't escape!   510
O gods, so order it that from this day
he will not part from me—nor I from him!'
     "Her wish was granted: their two bodies blent,
both face and figure, to a single form;
so when a twig is grafted to a tree,   515
they join together in maturity.
     "Now these two figures in their close embrace
were two no longer, but were something else,
no longer to be called a man and woman,
and although neither, nonetheless seemed both.   520
     "And when he understood about the water,
how he had dived into it as a man,
but left it otherwise, with softened limbs,
Hermaphroditus raised both hands to heaven
and cried out in a voice no longer virile: 525
     "'O father and mother, after whom I'm named,
grant me, as consolation, this one boon:
may any man who sets foot in this pool
depart from it without virility,
instantly softened by the water's touch.'   530
     "Hermes and Aphrodite heard the prayer
of their one child, in whom both sexes were,
and gave the fountain that defiling power."

The Daughters of Minyas Transformed

Alcithoë concluded, while the daughters
of Minyas continued with their work,   535
spurning the god, dishonoring his feast;

when suddenly a dissonant outburst
from unseen tambours, flutes, and cymbals broke
upon them with a loud, disturbing clamor—
the air now smelled of saffron and of myrrh,   540
and, unbelievably, their weaving *greened*.
    Some of their hanging tapestries burst forth
with ivy, while the others turned to grape vines,
and what had lately been unliving threads
are vine sprouts now, while soft vine tendrils trail   545
from the distaff, and brightly clustered grapes
now seek to match the woven purple dye!
    The day was ended and that time had come
which you could say was neither light nor dark,
uncertain night, when yet some day remains.   550
It seemed as though the house suddenly shuddered,
and unaccountably the oil lamps flared
and blazing torches lit up every room,
and howling all around them everywhere
were the false images of savage beasts.   555
    Meanwhile, the sisters have been seeking refuge
in various places from the glaring flames,
and as they try to slip into the shadows,
a slender membrane glides over their limbs
and meager wings enclose their withered arms;   560
darkness conceals from them the true extent
of the great changes now come over them;
not downy feathers, but translucent wings
sustain their flight, and when they try to speak,
their much diminished bodies now emit   565
only the very tiniest of voices,
telling their woes in little, high-pitched squeaks.
    Shunning the woods, they congregate in houses,
nocturnal fliers fearful of the day,
creatures named for the time they first appear: 570
vespertilians. [Or, as we say, bats.]

Juno in Hades; Ino and Athamas

After this incident, the divinity
of Bacchus was much remarked on throughout Thebes,
and the god's aunt, Ino, boasted of his powers
everywhere, for only she had been   575
spared the great grief that her three sisters knew,
save for her tears of sympathy with them.
    Juno could not but notice Ino's pride
in her son and in her husband, Athamas,
and—yes!—in her immortal foster child!   580

Quite unendurable, she told herself:
"My rival's son is able to transform
men into fishes and plunge them in the sea,
to make a mother dismember her own child,
and slip weird new wings over on the three   585
daughters of Minyas: what can Juno do,
but weep for slights and insults unavenged?
    "Should that content me? That be my one power?
My enemy instructs me (as is fitting)
in my course of action: the death of Pentheus   590
reveals beyond the shadow of a doubt
what madness may achieve: why shouldn't Ino
be goaded into frenzy like her sisters?"
    There is a road on both sides darkened by
funereal yew trees as it descends   595
through speechless silence to the nether world,
where sluggish Styx exhales its rotten breath;
shades of the recent dead tread down that path
when their last rites have been attended to;
and in that cold and featureless wasteland,   600
souls newly come are at a loss to find
the Stygian city and palace of black Dis.
    There are a thousand ways into this city,
and open gates on all sides; as the ocean
receives the rivers from around the world,   605
so this place gathers in all mortal souls,
and never fills, however many come.
    Here bloodless, boneless, bodiless shades stray:
some make their way to the forum; others seek
the palace of the ruler of the dead,   610
or take up once again the crafts they lived by.
    Motivated by her ferocious hatred,
Saturnian Juno found the fortitude
to come here after leaving heaven's realm.
Pressed by her sacred body on arrival,   615
the threshold groaned, and Cerberus raised up
his three heads baying all in unison.
    Juno summons those sisters born of Night,[4]
implacable grave powers, where they sit
before the adamantine prison's gates,   620
combing the snakes from their hair; as soon as they
saw who it was approaching through the gloom,
the sisters rose at once and greeted her.

---

4. The Furies, three sisters—Tisiphone, Megara, and Alecto—who were the inexorable
ministers of the vengeance of the gods on earth and in the afterlife.

This is the place where infamy is punished;[5]
here Tityos endures evisceration,   625
pegged down over nine acres; here you, Tantalus,
lower your lips to the receding flood
and raise them to the ever-rising fruit;
here, Sisyphus, you push or you pursue
the rock that always rolls back to its place;   630
here Ixion, bound on his turning wheel
both flees himself and follows after; here
the Belides, who slew their cousin-husbands,
must carry water in their leaky vessels.

    Juno looked daggers at these felons all,   635
at Ixion especially, then turned
her glance to Sisyphus again, and said,
"Why is it that of all the brothers, he
should be eternally tormented, when
Athamas and his wife, who scorned my godhead,   640
live grandly in a palace up above?"

    Juno sets out before them all the reasons
why hatred had compelled her to this journey,
and tells them what she wishes, which was this:
the ruination of the house of Cadmus,   645
and that the vengeful Furies should employ
Athamas as an instrument of evil;
she bids them, begs, beseeches their support
in a flood of words.

            When Juno stopped at last,
Tisiphone shook out her matted locks,   650
and brushed the snakes away so she could speak:
"It's no big thing," she said, "no reason for
a song and dance about it. Say no more:
consider it done exactly as you bid;
and now from this unlovable abode,   655
return at once to heaven's sweeter airs."
Thither celestial Juno repairs,
and on arrival, Iris, Thaumas' daughter,
besprinkles her with purifying water.

    At once the ominous Tisiphone   660
selected a torch that had been steeped in blood,
put on a robe reddened with dripping gore,
and a belt of live snakes. And so appareled,

---

5. Ovid supplies a brief catalogue of legendary figures whose behavior has earned them a
place in Tartarus, the penitential part of the underworld. Tityos, a giant, attempted to
rape the goddess Latona; Tantalus attempted to deceive the gods by serving them a feast
consisting of his murdered son, Pelops; Sisyphus was guilty of slyness, nature unspecified; Ixion attempted to rape Juno; the Belides, more commonly known as the Danaides,
were fifty daughters of Danaus, forty-nine of whom murdered their husbands (though not
without provocation) on their wedding night.

set out from home accompanied by Grief,
with Fear and Terror and convulsive Madness.   665
    They say the doorposts shuddered when she stood
on the threshold of the house of Aeolus;
the polished oaken doors lost all their luster,
and the Sun went in. Ino and Athamas
were blocked, when, terrified, they tried to flee   670
the ill-omened Fury there before them,
who spreads her arms, alive with tangled snakes,
and shakes her locks out: stunned, more serpents fall,
some to her shoulders, others to her breast,
hissing and vomiting their deadly slaver.   675
    And then she seizes two from her coiffure
and hurls them at her victims, but the snakes
glide easily across their torsos, breathing
their poison out, though not to harm their bodies:
it is their minds that take the fatal blows.   680
    Besides the serpents, she had brought along
assorted other poisons and distempers:
slaver from Cerberus, venom from the Hydra,
Hallucination, Blindness, Mindlessness,
with Sin and Tears and Rage and Blood-Lust too,   685
all ground together into a fine powder,
mixed with fresh blood and then brought to a boil
in a great kettle made of bronze, and stirred
with a fresh green wand cut from a hemlock tree.
    And while they stood there trembling, she poured   690
her potion on their breasts; at once it sank
into the very center of their feelings.
Then snatching up her torch, she whirled it round
so swiftly that its flames burst into flame!
    And having done what she set out to do,   695
victorious Tisiphone returned
to the insubstantial kingdom of black Dis
and slipped out of the serpents she was wearing.
    Athamas, raging in his palace, cries,
"Ah, comrades! Spread your nets here in these woods,   700
for I have just now seen a lioness
with her twin cubs!"
                    Dementedly he stalked
his wife as though she were a savage beast;
laughing at this, his infant son, Learchus,
was reaching toward him with his little arms,   705
when the madman snatched him from his mother's breast
and whirled him in the air just like a sling,
two or three times, before he smashed the child's
head on a rock.
                Then, maddened by her grief

or by the poison she'd been sprinkled with,   710
Ino flees, shrieking, with her hair disheveled,
and you, Melicertes, clutched in her bare arms.
"*Euhoe, Bacchus!*" she cried, and at the sound
of Bacchus' name, Juno laughed and said,
"May he always bless you so, your foster son!"   715
    There is a cliff that juts into the ocean;
the waves had worn away its lower face,
leaving a shelf to keep away the rain;
its high peak thrust far out above the tide.
    She reached this point, for Madness gave her strength,   720
and unrestrained by any normal fears,
leapt with her burden out into the sea,
whose pounding waves churned the dark waters white.
    But Venus, out of pity for her grandchild's
unmerited distress, addressed her uncle   725
caressingly: "O Neptune, god of waters,
and second in command in all of heaven,
I realize that I am asking much,
but these are mine: I beg you pity them,
who, as you know, are plunged in the immense   730
reaches of the vast Ionian Sea,
and let them join you now as water gods.
    "For after all, the sea owes me a favor,[6]
if it is true indeed that I arose
from sea foam in the depths, on that occasion   735
commemorated by my name in Greek."
    Neptune nodded, assenting to her prayer,
and raised them up no longer mortal,
but in their majesties most worshipful;
new names and shapes were also given them: 740
Palaemon was the name of the new god;
his goddess mother was named Leucothoë.
    Ino's attendants caught up to her in time
to see her leaping from the summit's edge;
her death assured, they mourned the house of Cadmus,   745
beating their breasts, tearing their hair and garments,
and reproving the goddess for the cruel
injustice shown the wife of Athamas.
    Juno would not hear it: "My cruelty?
Yourselves will be its greatest monuments!"   750
No sooner had she spoken when it happened,
as Ino's most devoted servant cried,
"I will attend upon her in the waves,"
and poised in the very moment of her leap,

---

6. Venus alludes to the story, frequently represented by artists, of her origin from sea foam,
the substance from which her Greek name Aphrodite derives.

she froze, as though connected to the rock;   755
another, who'd been beating her own breasts,
felt her arms stiffen as she lifted them;
a third, who, as it happened, stretched her hands
over the waters, turned into a figure
of stone, her hands outstretched to that same ocean;   760
and yet another of the women froze
just as she started tearing out her hair.
    Each one inhabited her final gesture,
and those of the attendants who escaped
this cruel fate, were turned into seabirds,   765
who skim the surface of those troubled waters.

Cadmus and Harmonia

Now Cadmus had no notion that his daughter
and little grandson had become sea gods;
but overwhelmed by evil upon evil,
by all of the misfortunes he'd endured   770
and by the many portents that he'd seen,
went out of Thebes, the city he had founded,
as though not his, but *its* fortune oppressed him;
and driven to wandering for many years,
he and his wife came to the Illyrian coast,   775
where all the ills they had so long endured
weighed down on them, and they stopped to consider
the fates of their offspring and their own distress.
    "Was it a sacred serpent that I speared,"
asked Cadmus, "when, newly come from Sidon,   780
I sprinkled the viper's teeth upon the ground,
and seeded a new crop of human beings?
If that is what the gods have been avenging
by their unwavering wrath for all these years,
why then, I pray that I might be extended   785
into a serpent with a gut-like shape—"
    And as he said it he became a serpent[7]
with a gut-like shape. At once he felt the scales
begin to grow out on his thickened skin,
and his dark body lighten up with patches   790
of iridescent blue; he fell upon his breast,
and his two legs were blended into one,
which, gradually lengthening, became
an elegant and sharply pointed tail.
    His arms remained unchanged; he held them out,   795
and as the tears coursed down his cheeks (which were
still—for the moment—human), he exclaimed,

---

7. Minerva's prophecy in Book III is at last fulfilled.

"Come closer to me, O most wretched wife,
and while there is still something left of me,
before I am entirely transformed   800
to serpent, touch me, take these hands in yours!"

He would have said much more, but suddenly
the tip of his tongue divided into two,
and words no longer would obey his wishes,
so that whenever he tried to complain   805
or grieve, he hissed, and could not manage more,
for he had been left with no other voice.

Now striking her bare breast, his wife cries out,
"Cadmus! Stay as you are! Put off these strange
shapes now possessing you, unfortunate man!   810
Cadmus, what's happening? Where are your feet?
Your face? Complexion? Even as I speak,
where is the rest of you! Heavenly beings,
will you not also turn me to a snake?"

The creature's tongue flicked lightly over her lips,   815
and he slipped in between her cherished breasts
as though he were familiar with the place,
embraced her, and slid right around her neck.

Those of his companions who were present
were horrified, but she just calmly stroked   820
the smooth, sleek neck of the crested dragon,
and at once there were two serpents intertwined,
who presently went crawling off and found
a hiding place within a nearby grove.

But these days, they no longer flee from men,   825
nor do they harm them; mindful of their former
identities, they're very gentle dragons.

Perseus and Atlas

Nevertheless, their mighty nephew Bacchus
was comfort to them both in their changed shapes,
worshiped as he was throughout defeated   830
India,[8] and in crowded Grecian temples;
only Acrisius, his relative,
will not admit him to his city, Argos;
Acrisius makes war against the god,
whom he denies was the true son of Jove,   835
and says the very same thing about Perseus,
conceived by Danaë in a rain of gold.[9]

8. A reference to the way in which the god's cult spread through the East.
9. Confined in a brazen tower by her father, Danaë was impregnated by a smitten Jove in the
   form of a shower of gold; Perseus was the offspring of that union.

So mighty is the force of truth revealed
that not long after this, Acrisius
repented of his outrage to the god   840
and of the way he slighted his own grandson.
    One is installed in heaven now, the other,
returning with his memorable trophy
after the snake-coiffed monster had been slain,
goes gliding through thin air on humming wings,   845
and while he overflies harsh Libya,
the blood drops trickle from the Gorgon's head;
reaching the ground, these come to life as snakes
of various kinds; and that is why today
serpents infest that whole unpleasant land.   850
    Driven this way and that by sparring winds
through heaven's great immensity, as though
of no more substance than the dewy mist,
he looked down from a great height onto earth
as he flew over it; thrice to the frigid north,   855
thrice to the far south; to the west often,
and just as often to the east he flew.
    The setting sun made further flight too risky;
he landed on the borders of the west
in the realm of Atlas, where he sought his ease   860
until the morning star should summon Dawn,
and Dawn bring forth the carriage of the Day.
    Atlas, the son of Iapetas, was huge,
greater in bulk than all men put together.
He ruled earth's western border and the sea   865
which welcomed the panting horses of the Sun
and his worn-out chariot at end of day.
    A thousand herds of cattle and as many
flocks of fat sheep were grazing on his meadows;
there were no neighbors nearby to confine him.   870
A tree he had, whose leaves of shining gold
concealed gold fruit and branches underneath.
    "Mine host," said Perseus, "if the renown
of noble birth is what impresses you,
why, I'm the son of Jove! If mighty deeds   875
are what you marvel at, marvel at mine!
I seek both hospitality and rest."
    But Atlas called to mind the prophecy
given him by Themis of Parnassus:
"A time will come when your bright golden tree   880
will be despoiled, Atlas; and the spoils will go
to one who styles himself the son of Jove."
    In order to forestall this, Atlas built
a mighty wall to fence his orchard in,

and set an enormous dragon to patrol   885
his boundaries and keep all strangers out.
"Go far from here," said Atlas. "All these lies
about your deeds of glory won't avail you,
and as for Jupiter—he's nowhere near!"

 Now Atlas tries to drive the stranger off   890
with force as well as threats, but Perseus
stands up to him, yet tries to calm him down
with pacifying speech. At length, perceiving
himself—who wouldn't be?—the weaker, says,
"Well, since the little favor that I ask   895
seems too important to you to be granted,
take this instead!" The hero turned his back
to Atlas and raised up in his left hand
the unkempt horror of Medusa's head.[1]

 Atlas became a mountain just as large   900
as the man had been. His hair and beard became
a forest, and his arms and shoulders turned
into adjacent ridges; his head was now
the mountain's summit and his bones were rock.
Each part grew to extraordinary size   905
(as you immortals had ordained), until
the weight of heaven rested on his shoulders.

Perseus and Andromeda

Aeolus had just finished locking up
the winds in prison underneath Mount Etna,
and the morning star that summons men to work   910
had risen brightly in the eastern sky.
Perseus strapped his wings onto his feet
and armed himself again with his hooked sword,
and with his swift-winged sandals split the air.

 The world fell back away from him in flight   915
till he saw Ethiopia beneath him
and near it, the kingdom ruled by Cepheus,
where Ammon had condemned Andromeda
(the one unjust, the other innocent)
to pay the price for her own mother's speech.[2]   920

 At sight of her, bound high upon a cliff,
he would have thought that she'd been carved from stone
were it not for the breeze that stirred her hair

---

1. Medusa (whose story will be told later) was once a beautiful woman; her hair was turned
 into writhing serpents, and anyone who looks upon her visage is turned into stone.
2. Her mother, Cassiope, boasted of her own beauty and so irritated the Nereids that they
 persuaded Neptune to punish the kingdom with a flood. The oracle of Ammon revealed
 that only the sacrifice of Andromeda would relieve the kingdom.

and for the warm tears flowing from her eyes;
the woman's beauty quite astounded him,   925
and left him witless, to the point that he
almost forgot to keep his wings in motion.
   "Oh!" he said. "These chains don't do you justice;
the only chains that you should wear are those
that ardent lovers put on in their passion.   930
But what's your name and land of origin,
and why *are* you chained up?"
                                    At first the maiden
would not address the man, for modesty,
and would have used her hands to hide her face
were they not tightly bound; her eyes, however,   935
as they welled up with tears, said everything.
   At his insistence, she (lest she appear
to be concealing some fault of her own)
told him her name, and land of origin,
and how it happened that her mother's trust   940
in her own beauty brought her to this pass;
and in the middle of her tale, the sea
erupted with the roar of a great beast
who rose up as he breasted the wide water.
   The virgin screams, her parents mourn with her,   945
all miserable—though she has greatest cause.
They have no help to offer her, except
for weeping, wailing, thumping on their breasts,
and clinging to the chains around her body,
as is appropriate to the occasion.   950
   The stranger said, "There will be time enough
for weeping, by and by—but brief indeed
the time in which bold actions may succeed!
If I, as Perseus, the son of Jove
and she to whom he came in a rain of gold,   955
had sought your daughter—Perseus, the hero
who slew the snake-haired Gorgon and was bold
to take to the air, borne on soaring wings—
I would no doubt have been preferred to all
suitors as son-in-law material.   960
But, with the gods' permission, I will try
to add to these endowments by my service;
the deal is that she's mine if I can save her."
They take his offer (who would hesitate?)
and promise him a kingdom as his dowry.   965
   But look! Just as the beak of a swift ship
ploughs through the waves when all its oarsmen strain,
that beast divides the water with his breast,
no farther from the rocks than one could send

a shot launched from a Balearic sling;   970
when suddenly the young man leapt from earth
into the clouds; his shadow on the sea
provoked the beast to strike at it in fury.
    And just as when Jove's bird, the eagle, sees
a snake sunning itself idly in a field,   975
he strikes from behind, avoiding the fierce maw,
and sinks his talons in the scaly back;
so Perseus, through the resistless air
swoops and dives at the monster from behind,
and plunges his sword right up to the hilt   980
into the shoulder of the raging beast.
    Tormented by that wound, it rises up
into the air, it crashes to the water
and turns in terror and confusion, like
a boar surrounded by the baying pack.   985
    The hero flees its jaws on speedy wings,
and where the beast is vulnerable, strikes
with his hooked blade: now slashes at the back,
inlaid with barnacles, now jabs the sides,
and now strikes where the beast is slenderest,   990
at that place where its tail spreads like a fish's.
    The serpent vomits up a purple froth
of blood and salty water in a spray
that dampens our hero's drooping pinions,
which he no longer can rely upon;   995
he spies a rock whose summit breaks the water
when the sea is calm, but otherwise is hidden;
bracing himself against its surface, he
clutches the jagged rock with his left hand,
and with his right, he time and time again   1000
plunges his sword into the serpent's guts.
    Applause reverberates along the shore
and from the mansions of the gods above;
Cepheus and Cassiope, the parents,
rejoice in their new son-in-law, and hail him   1005
as prop and savior of their family;
the unbound virgin steps forth from her chains,
well worth the trouble that her troubles caused him.
    Water is drawn: before the hero washes
his serpent-slaying hands, he carefully   1010
constructs a little nest there on the beach,
of some soft leaves with seaweed strewn upon them,
and there he rests Medusa's snake-fringed head,
lest she be damaged by the beach's gravel.
    Thirsty fresh twigs, still living, still absorbent,   1015
soak up the monster's force, and at its touch

rigidify through every branch and leaf.
Astounded sea nymphs try experiments
on other twigs and get the same results;
delighted, they toss them back into the sea   1020
as seeds to propagate this new species!
Coral today shows the same properties;
its branches harden when exposed to air,
and what was—in the water—a spry twig
becomes a rock when lifted out of it.   1025
      The hero builds three altars out of turf:
one on the left for Mercury, and one
for the warlike virgin goddess on the right,
and in between, an altar for great Jove;
a cow is slain for Minerva, and a calf   1030
for the swift god with wings upon his feet,
but a bull to thee, highest of all gods.
At once the hero takes Andromeda
without a dowry, given that she herself
is a reward sufficient to his labors.   1035
      Now Love and Marriage shake the wedding torches,
and burning aromatics scent the air;
houses are garlanded, and everywhere
are lyres, flutes, and singers singing songs
that make their argument for happiness.   1040
      The folding doors are opened to reveal
a golden hall where a great banquet is about to start,
attended by the princes of the realm.

Perseus and Medusa

When they had finished dinner and were all
gladdened by the liberal gifts of Bacchus,   1045
Perseus asked his hosts about the region,
the manner and mores of the folk that lived there.
After responding, his informant said,
"Now tell us, gallant Perseus, how strength
and cleverness let you lay hands upon   1050
that head whose hair is woven through with snakes."
      So Perseus told them of that place beneath
frigid Mount Atlas, guarded by its bulk,
within whose entryway two sisters live,
daughters of Phorcys,[3] who shared a single eye: 1055
while one was passing it off to the other,
her pass was intercepted by our hero,
who palmed it cleverly and slipped away.

---

3. Medusa's two sisters.

And then by trekking through remote and distant
byways, through fearful forests and rough rocks,   1060
he came at last to where the Gorgon[4] lived.
And everywhere, in fields, along the roads,
he witnessed the sad forms of men and beasts
no more themselves, but changed now into stone,
misfortunates, who'd glimpsed Medusa once.   1065
   He too had once looked upon her image,
but it had been reflected in the shield
of bronze our hero bore in his left hand;
and while sleep held Medusa and her snakes,
he struck her head off; from their mother's blood   1070
sprang swift Pegasus and his brother[5] both.
   And then he told more stories, just as true,
of lands and seas he'd seen from high above,
and of the stars his wings had whisked him past;
and ended there, before it was expected.   1075
But one of that company of nobles asked
why none of her sisters but Medusa wore
those serpents interwoven in her hair.
   The guest responded: "Since what you would know
happens to be a story worth relating,   1080
listen to me and I will tell you why.
   "She was at one time very beautiful,
the hope of many suitors all contending,
and her outstanding feature was her hair
(this I have learned from one who saw her then).   1085
But it is said that Neptune ravished her,
and in the temple of Minerva, where
Jove's daughter turned away from the outrage
and chastely hid her eyes behind her aegis.[6]
   "So that this action should not go unpunished,   1090
she turned the Gorgon's hair into foul snakes;
and she, to overwhelm her foes with terror,
bears on her breast the serpents she created."

---

4. Medusa. She and her two sisters comprised the Gorgons.
5. Pegasus was the flying horse, a darling of the Muses; his brother was Chrysaor, a mortal
   otherwise unnoticed in the *Metamorphoses*.
6. Others said that Medusa yielded without a struggle, turning Minerva and her wrath
   against her. An attribute of Minerva, the aegis was usually represented as a breastplate or
   shield with the head of Medusa depicted in its center, surrounded by a fringe of serpents.

BOOK V

Contests of Arms and Song

Perseus and the Suitors[1]

While Danaë's heroic son regaled
the Ethiopians surrounding him
with his adventures, raucous tumult filled
the hall of the palace: this was not the clamor
which signifies a wedding feast in progress,   5
but that which tells of warfare breaking out,
as, unexpectedly, the marriage banquet
became a riot, which you might compare
to when the sea's calm waters, angered by
the rabid winds, make agitated waves.   10
    Phineus was the first to take up arms,
the instigator of this thoughtless action,
who shook his bronze-tipped ash-wood spear, and said,
"Look over here at me, come to avenge
my stolen bride: your wings will not avail you,   15
nor Jupiter, transformed into fool's gold,[2]
defend you from the havoc I will wreak!"
    As Phineus prepared to cast his spear,
his brother Cepheus cried out to him,
"What are you doing? What insanity   20
is urging you to perpetrate this outrage?
Do his great services deserve such thanks?
Will you repay the saving of a life
with such a dowry? For to tell the truth,
it was not Perseus who took her from you,   25
but the grim deity of the Nereids,
and Ammon of the horns, and the sea monster
who came to sate his hunger on my child;
you lost her at the moment she was taken
to be destroyed—unless your cruelty   30
would have her dead to cover up your shame,
and ease *your* grief at the expense of mine!
    "That you, her uncle and her fiancé,
could see her bound and not attempt a rescue,
that should have ended any claim *you* had.   35

---

1. Ovid continues the story of Perseus directly from Book IV. Ovid is credited with developing the theme of rivalry between Perseus and Phineus (Andromeda's unsuccessful suitor) into an epic battle, whose comically extravagant violence points in the direction of satire. For Ovid, "epic" is the epic mockery of heroes who talk big but do little, and often ineptly. This battle may be seen as a parody of the battle between Odysseus and Penelope's suitors in the *Odyssey*, and of the struggle between Aeneas and Turnus for the hand of Lavinia in the *Aeneid*.
2. Phineus dismisses the legend of the hero's divine conception in a shower of gold.

119

But now, because another saved the girl,
will you cry foul and try to take his prize?
If his reward now seems excessive to you,
you should have tried to win it on the rocks,
when she was chained to them. Now let that man,   40
who has delivered me from an old age
that would have lacked the comfort of a daughter,
keep what his actions—and my pledge—have won him,
and realize that he has been preferred
not to you, merely, but to certain death."   45
　　He made no answer, but looked back and forth
to Perseus and to the other man,
unable to decide which one should get it,
but after a few moments' hesitation,
he hurled his mighty spear at Perseus.   50
　　It stuck out from the couch beside the hero,
who, when he noticed it at last, leapt up
ferociously, and sent it whizzing back;
it would have torn the breast of Phineus
were he not hiding out behind the altar,   55
where, shamefully, that criminal found refuge.
　　Nevertheless, his throw could not be said
to be entirely without effect:
the spear caught Rhoetus full in the face,
and after it was plucked out of his skull,   60
he lay there writhing in his agony,
and spattered the table settings with his gore.
　　The crowd went totally ballistic, then;
spears filled the air, and there were those who said
that Cepheus should die with Perseus,   65
but the old man had already slipped away,
swearing by Faith and Justice and the gods
of hospitality that this was done
against his will. Warlike Athena appeared
and covered up her brother[3] with her shield   70
and gave him courage.
　　　　　　　　From India had come
a youth named Athis, whom the nymph Limnaee
(herself a daughter of the river Ganges)
gave birth to, underneath its glassy surface,
or so they say. The exceptional good looks   75
of this still adolescent innocent
were well enhanced by his distinguished wardrobe,
especially his gold-fringed purple mantle;

3. The goddess Athena was born from Zeus's head; this would make her something like
　　Perseus's half-sister.

a golden necklace ornamented his neck,
and a headband held his perfumed locks in place;   80
he was a master of the javelin,
quite capable of hitting a bull's-eye
from far away, and even more accomplished
with the bow, which, at that moment, he was bending,
when Perseus snatched up a smoking brand   85
from the sacrificial fires of the altar
and struck him with it, shattering his face.

    Now when Assyrian Lycabas saw
that much-admired beauty wallowing
in his own blood, expiring beneath   90
that bitter wound, he wept for his true love
and closest mate, then took up his friend's bow
and said, "I will provide you with a contest;
you will not long rejoice in this boy's fate,
which brings you far more odium than glory."   95

    He had not finished saying all of this
when the penetrating dart leapt from its string
to miss the mark and dangle helplessly
from the robe of Perseus, who turned on him
and thrust into his breast that scimitar   100
first tested in the slaughter of Medusa.
His vision blurry with advancing night,
he sought a glimpse of Athis as he died,
and fell upon him, bearing to his grave
the solace that they were now joined in death.   105

    But look, where Phorbas, son of Metion,
and Amphimedon, a Libyan, appear,
both eager to commit themselves to battle,
both skidding helplessly, then crashing down
into the blood that made the floor all slippery;   110
and as they struggled to regain their footing,
one caught it in the ribs, and one, the throat.

    But Perseus did not employ his sword
when he found Eurytus, the son of Actor,
whose weapon was the double-headed axe;   115
he hoisted in both hands a huge and weighty
wine-mixing bowl, artistically engraved,
and sent it crashing down onto the man,
who fell upon his back, expiring
in the bright red blood that he had vomited,   120
and his head thumped in spasms on the floor.

    Then Perseus struck down Polydegmon
(who was descended from Queen Semiramis),
Caucasian Abaris, Lycetus of Thessaly,
unbarbered Helices, Phlegyas, and Clitus,   125
and trod upon that heap of dying men.

Phineus did not dare engage in close
combat, but hurled a javelin instead,
which accidentally struck Idas, who
had vainly sought to maintain neutrality.   130
Idas, dying, glared at the man and said,
"Since I have been forced to take sides in this,
accept the enemy you've made of me,
and pay the price for that wound now, with *this* one—"
He had withdrawn that weapon from his body   135
and was about to hurl it back at him,
when he collapsed, completely drained of blood.
    Then Hodites, the second in command
to Cepheus, was slain by Clymenus,
and Hypseus struck down Prothoenor,   140
and was himself transfixed by Lyncides.
    There was an old man named Emathion,
a friend of justice and of piety;
since he was kept from combat by his age,
he warred with words, and boldly now stepped up   145
to execrate their irreligious arms;
as he clung tremulously to the altar,
a blow from Chromis' sword cut off his head
which dropped at once onto the altar stone,
and his half-conscious tongue continued to   150
upbraid them till his failing breath no longer
stirred sacrificial flames.
                            The next to fall
were Broteas and Ammon, who were twins;
unbeaten in the ring, they would have won,
if boxing gloves were any match for swords: 155
in close combat, Phineus slew them both.
    Ampycus, priest of Ceres, with his brows
adorned in sacramental fillets, fell;
you also fell, Lampetides, not meant
to shine in situations such as these;   160
yours were the deeds of peace, reciting poems
which you accompanied upon the lute;
you had been summoned here to solemnize
the wedding feast with song.
                            Pedasus, grinning,
saw how he kept himself and his instrument   165
out of harm's way, and shouted to him, "Sing
the remainder of your song to the shades below,"
lodging his shaft above the bard's left eye;
and as he fell, his dying fingers struck
the lyre's strings, and on that plaintive note   170
the poet and his song came to an end.

Infuriated by that sight, Lycormas
did not allow him to go unavenged,
but seized a beam from the right side of the door
and brought it crashing down upon the spine   175
of grinning Pedasus, and broke his neck,
and he collapsed like a sacrificial bull.
　　　Pelates, a North African, attempted
to tear out a pillar on the left-hand side,
and as he struggled, his right hand was pinned   180
against the wooden beam with a spear cast
by Corythus, come from Marmarica.
And as he hung there, Abas cut him open
and bled him dry; he did not fall to the ground,
but dangled helplessly until he died.   185
　　　And Melaneus too was overcome,
one of the followers of Perseus;
and Dorylas as well, the wealthiest
in Libya, where no one else possessed
estates or heaps of spice as vast as his;   190
a spear cast from the side tore through his groin,
a fatal place.
　　　　　　　When Halcyoneus
of Bactria, who'd given him that wound,
observed his victim gasping up his soul
and rolling his eyes in agony, he said,   195
"Of all the many properties you own,
you may keep only what you lie upon,"
and left his lifeless corpse.
　　　　　　　　　But Perseus,
avenging him, snatched from the still-warm wound
the bloody spear and flung it back at him;   200
it broke his nose and drove right through his neck,
projecting from the front and from behind.
　　　While Fortune favored him, the hero slew
Clytis and Clanis, who, though both were born
of the same mother, died of different wounds,   205
for Clytis had been shafted through both thighs
while Clanis ate the spear that did him in.
　　　Then Celadon of Mendes also fell,
and Astreus (his mother Syrian,
his father dubious) and Aethion,   210
once shrewd enough at seeing what would come,
now victimized by a deceptive omen;
and Thoactes, the royal armorer,
and Agyrtes, the ill-famed patricide.
　　　Although worn-out by all that he had done,   215
there was still more to do: it was one man

against a mob united to destroy him;
from all sides he was set on by opponents,
a moving front, the servants of a cause
assailing his merit and the promise made him.   220
    On *his* side, he could count on the support
of his father-in-law and his new bride
and the bride's mother—all filling up the hall
with pointless lamentation, now drowned out
by the groans of the dying warriors,   225
as fierce Bellona shames the household gods
with fresh-spilled blood and stirs the conflict up.
    Phineus and his thousand followers
surround one man: past him the missiles whiz
on either side, beyond his eyes and ears,   230
thicker than hailstones in a winter storm.
He leans his shoulders flat against a column,
and with his back safe, faces his opponents
massed on both sides and ready to attack:
Chaonian Molpeus leads the left   235
and Nabataean Ethemon, the right.
    Just as a tigress, goaded by her hunger,
who has heard the lowing of two separate herds
in different valleys, cannot quite decide
which to take on, but burns to take on both,   240
so our Perseus is hesitant
as to which side he ought to strike at first:
Molpeus takes a spear shaft in the shin
and is permitted to remove himself,
but Ethemon cuts Perseus no slack,   245
and charges, with his sword held shoulder high,
aiming to wound our hero in the neck,
a powerful, though ill-considered thrust:
he strikes the column and his shattered blade
rebounds and lodges in its master's throat.   250
    That wound was not sufficient to dispatch
the helpless man, who raised up trembling hands
in unsuccessful prayer as Perseus
now ran him through with Mercury's curved sword.
    Then seeing that the mob would overwhelm him,   255
Perseus said, "You've forced me into this;
I will seek aid from my own enemies!
If there are any friends here, hide your eyes,"
and speaking, lifted up the Gorgon's head.
    "Find someone else to worry with your wonders,"   260
said Thescalus, who raised his deadly spear
to cast it, but was frozen in that gesture,
as motionless as any marble statue.

And then came Ampyx, rich in self-esteem,
who, with his sword tip, sought the hero's heart,   265
and as he sought it, his right hand grew stiff
and powerless to move the sword it held.
　　But Nileus, who falsely claimed descent
from the Nile, whose seven mouths were all engraved
in gold or silver on his shield, cried out,   270
"Look, Perseus, upon my origin:
it will much comfort you when you are dead
and wandering among the silent shades,
that you were slain by such a one as I—"
but the last part of what he said was stifled;   275
it would have seemed to you as though his mouth
opened to speak, but words could not pass through.
　　Then Eryx scornfully rebuked them, saying
"Defective courage, not effect of Gorgon,
brings on this inertia—attack with me,   280
and cast him and his magic weapons down!"
He started in; the earth clung to his feet,
and he remained there, having turned to flint,
the immobilized shape of an armed man.
　　Now all of these deserved their punishment,   285
but one of them, a soldier on the side
of Perseus named Aconteus, didn't:
while he was fighting for our hero, he beheld
the Gorgon's face and hardened into rock;
supposing that the man was still alive,   290
Astyages struck him with his long sword
which leapt back, clanging shrilly from the blow.
While Astyages stood there all astounded,
the very same force turned him into marble
and left him an astonishment of stone.   295
　　It really would take far too long to name
the ordinary soldiers; when it ended,
two hundred men returned to their own side,
two hundred others were left petrified
from looking at Medusa's horrid visage.   300
　　Now Phineus has finally repented
of his unjust war, but what is he to do?
He sees these likenesses in diverse poses,
and realizes that they are his men,
and calling each by name, asks for his help,   305
and reaches out to touch the nearest man
in disbelief—all are made of marble!
　　He turns his face away but holds his hands out
in supplication, confessing his defeat:
"O Perseus," he cries, "you win! Just take away   310

that fright of yours, that petrifying head
of this Medusa, whatever she may be—
get rid of it, get rid of it, I beg you!
I *never* hated you! I *never* wanted
to rule in your place! What got me into this,　　315
what moved me to take up arms against you,
was my promised bride—I had the prior claim,
but on the merits, you deserved to win.
I'm not at all ashamed at having lost;
grant me my life and nothing in addition—　　320
yours be the spoils, greathearted Perseus!"

　　And as he spoke, he did not even dare
to look upon that other, who replied,
"Fear not, fainthearted Phineus: the gift
that lies within my power to bestow　　325
(and what a tribute to your cowardice it is!)
I now confer: no sword will injure you.
You will remain a monument forever,
displayed in the house of my father-in-law;
my wife will find great solace," said the hero,　　330
"in gazing at her fiancé's still form,"
and carried the Medusa's head around
to the agitated gaze of Phineus.

　　Then, even as he strove to turn away,
his neck grew rigid, and, upon his cheeks,　　335
the tears that he was shedding turned to stone,
and fixed forever in the marble were
the frightened face and suppliant expression,
the pleading hands and abject attitude.

　　And now, accompanied by his new bride,　　340
triumphant Perseus returns to Argos,
the high-walled city of his birth; and there,
in order to avenge his undeserving
grandfather, Acrisius,[4] he wages war
on his granduncle, Proetus, who drove　　345
Acrisius away by force of arms
and seized his citadel. But neither arms
nor the citadel that he had wrongly seized
allowed Proetus to prevail against
the fierce gaze of the serpent-bearing monster.　　350

---

4. In the usual version of the myth, Acrisius is the villain: believing a prophecy that the son of his daughter Danaë will kill him, he shuts her in a tower to which Jove comes as a shower of gold. She and her son Perseus are thrown into the sea in a wooden box and rescued by Polydectes, for whom see the following note. Perseus later finds Acrisius and accidentally slays him, as Apollo slays Hyacinthus, with a discus. Ovid, however, casts Acrisius as the victim of his villainous brother Proetus, avenged by Perseus.

But you, O Polydectes,[5] governor
of tiny Seriphos, unmollified
by the young man's excellence, so often shown
in the trials and tribulations he went through—
you were inflexible in hating him   355
and unrelenting in your unjust anger;
you went so far as to deny him praise,
and claimed Medusa's death to be a lie.
      "We'll give you evidence right now," said Perseus.
"Protect your eyes!" He raised Medusa's face   360
up to the king's and turned him into stone.

Minerva Visits the Muses

Up until now, Minerva had companioned
her gold-begotten brother in his travels;
but then, surrounded by a hollow cloud,
she slipped out of Seriphos; on her right,   365
the isles of Cythnus and Gyarus fell away,
as, by the most direct route she could take
across the sea, she headed right for Thebes
and Helicon, where the virgin Muses[6] dwell.
      She landed on their mountain and addressed   370
those erudite and skillful sisters nine:
"We have heard much of this new spring of yours,[7]
which Pegasus, Medusa's flying horse,
created when his hoof broke through the earth.
That is what brings me here: I wish to see   375
this miracle—I have already seen
the horse himself, born from his mother's blood."
      Urania replied: "Whatever cause
brings you to visit our home, O goddess,
you are a welcome presence in our hearts;   380
the tale that you have heard is true indeed,
for it was Pegasus produced this spring."
She led Minerva to the sacred waters.
      The goddess long stood rapt in admiration
of the spring made by a blow from the horse's hoof,   385
and gazed about her at the ancient woods,

---

5. In the alternative version, Polydectes rescues Perseus and Danaë after Acrisius tries to
   drown them, and later inspires Perseus to go after Medusa in order to have the chance to
   seduce Danaë.
6. Helicon was the mountain home of the Muses, the nine daughters of Zeus and
   Mnemosyne, the goddess of Memory. Each was charged with being the patron of a different kind of art. Urania here appears to be their Mother Superior; Calliope, chosen by
   them to respond to the song of the Pierides, was the muse of epic poetry, a genre that
   Ovid has just treated somewhat less than reverentially in the previous tale.
7. The Hippocrene, whose waters were said to inspire poets.

the grottoes, and the varied kinds of grasses
displaying their innumerable flowers,
and called the daughters of Mnemosyne
doubly blest—both by their eagerness to learn   390
and by their home.
                    One of them answered her:
"O goddess, more than welcome in our choir—
had not your worthiness selected you
for greater tasks—you speak the truth in praising
the arts we practice and the home we share.   395

    "We *would* be happy were we safe in it,
but these days wickedness is unrestrained,
and maiden sensibilities like ours
are easily affrighted: before our eyes
we still can see him—fierce king Pyreneus;   400
that scare we have not yet recovered from.

    "For with his Thracian forces, he had seized
rich Daulis and the fields of Phocea,
whose folk he tyrannized; we were en route
to our temple high on Mount Parnassus,   405
when he noticed us as we were passing through,
and recognizing us, put on a face
that showed false reverence for our godhead.
'Daughters of Memory,' he said, 'stop here!
Take refuge without hesitation, please,   410
from gloomy skies and rain (for it was raining)
beneath my roof—for often deities
have taken shelter in much humbler homes.'

    "Persuaded by his words and by the weather,
we yielded and set foot in his front room.   415
The rain soon ceased: the north wind having won
its struggle with the south wind, the dull clouds
were promptly purged and exiled from the sky.
We wished to leave; he shut us up within,
thinking to have his way with us by force,   420
and so we put our wings on to escape.

    "He perched on the summit of his citadel,
as though intending to come after us:
'Whither thou goest, I shall go the same,'
he said, and threw himself from the high tower   425
and landed on his head, which shattered it,
and dyed the earth with his indecent blood."

The Daughters of Pierus

As the Muse spoke, Minerva could hear wings
beating on air, and cries of greeting came

from high in the trees. She peered into the foliage,   430
attempting to discover where those sounds,
the speech of human beings to be sure,
were emanating from: why, from some birds!
Bewailing their sad fate, a flock of nine
magpies (which mimic anyone they wish to)   435
had settled in the branches overhead.

    Minerva having shown astonishment,
the Muse gave her a little goddess-chat:
"This lot has only recently been added
to the throngs of birds. Why? They lost a contest!   440
Their father was Pierus, lord of Pella,
their mother was Evippe of Paeonia;
nine times she called upon Lucina's[8] aid
and nine times she delivered. Swollen up
with foolish pride because they were so many,   445
that crowd of simpleminded sisters went
through all Haemonia and through Achaea too,
arriving here to challenge us in song:

    "'We'll show you girls just what real class is
Give up tryin' to deceive the masses   450
Your rhymes are fake: accept our wager
Learn which of us is minor and which is major
There's nine of us here and there's nine of you
And you'll be nowhere long before we're through
Nothin's gonna save you 'cuz your songs are lame   455
And the way you sing 'em is really a shame
So stop with, "Well I *never*!" and "This *can't* be real!"
We're the newest New Thing and here is our deal
If we beat you, obsolete you, then you just get gone
From these classy haunts on Mount Helicon   460
We give you Macedonia—*if* we lose
An' that's an offer you just can't refuse
So take the wings off, sisters, get down and jam
And let the nymphs be the judges of our poetry slam!'

    "Shameful it was to strive against such creatures;   465
more shameful not to. Nymphs were picked as judges,
sworn into service on their river banks,
and took their seats on benches made of tufa.

    "And then—not even drawing lots!—the one
who claimed to be their champion commenced;   470
she sang of war between the gods and Giants,[9]

---

8. Goddess of childbirth.
9. Angered by the defeat of the Titans, to whom they were related, Typhoeus and the other
    giants conspired to destroy Jove and the Olympians, who, terrified, fled to Egypt, where
    they disguised themselves as animals.

giving the latter credit more than due
and deprecating all that the great gods did;
how Typhoeus, from earth's lowest depths,
struck fear in every celestial heart,   475
so that they all turned tail and fled, until,
exhausted, they found refuge down in Egypt,
where the Nile flows from seven distinct mouths;
she sang of how earthborn Typhoeus
pursued them even here and forced the gods   480
to hide themselves by taking fictive shapes:
        "'In Libya the Giants told the gods to scram
The boss god they worship there has horns like a ram[1]
'Cuz Jupiter laid low as the leader of a flock
And Delius his homey really got a shock   485
When the Giants left him with no place to go:
"Fuggedabout Apollo—make me a crow!"
And if you believe that Phoebus was a wuss
His sister Phoebe turned into a puss
Bacchus takes refuge in the skin of a goat   490
And Juno as a cow with a snow-white coat
Venus the queen of the downtown scene, yuh know what her wish is?
"Gimme a body just like a fish's"
Mercury takes on an ibis's shape
And that's how the mighty (**cheep cheep**) gods escape'   495
        "And then her song, accompanied on the lute,
came to an end, and it was our turn—
but possibly you haven't got the time
to listen to our song?"
                        "Oh, don't think that,"
Minerva said. "I want it word for word: 500
sing it for me just as you sang it then."
        The Muse replied: "We turned the contest over
to one of us, Calliope, who rose,
and after binding up her hair in ivy
and lightly strumming a few plaintive chords,   505
she vigorously launched into her song:

Calliope's Hymn to Ceres:[2] Proem

"'Ceres was first to break up the soil with a curved plowshare,
the first to give us the earth's fruits and to nourish us gently,
and the first to give laws: every gift comes from Ceres.

---

1. In Libya, Jove was worshipped as Ammon, in the form of a ram.
2. Based on the Homeric Hymn to Demeter, the song of Calliope is the first of three "poetic" interludes occurring at the end of each five books of the *Metamorphoses* and discussed in "A Note on This Translation," p. xvii. Critics who see Ovid as culturally transgressive read it as satire; Ovid's irony may be difficult for the modern reader to see here, but it should not go unsuspected.

The goddess must now be my subject. Would that I *could* sing   510
a hymn that is worthy of her, for she surely deserves it.

The Rape of Proserpina

" 'Vigorous Sicily sprawled across the gigantic body
of one who had dared aspire to rule in the heavens;
the island's weight held Typhoeus firmly beneath it.[3]
Often exerting himself, he strives yet again to rise up,   515
but there in the north, his right hand is held down by Pelorus,
his left hand by you, Pachynus; off in the west, Lilybaeum[4]
weighs on his legs, while Mount Etna presses his head, as
under it, raging Typhoeus coughs ashes and vomits up fire.
Often he struggles, attempting to shake off the earth's weight   520
and roll its cities and mountains away from his body.

" 'This causes tremors and panics the Lord of the Silent,[5]
who fears that the earth's crust will crack and break open,
and daylight, let in, will frighten the trembling phantoms;
dreading disaster, the tyrant left his tenebrous kingdom;   525
borne in his chariot drawn by its team of black horses,
he crisscrossed Sicily, checking the island's foundation.

" 'After his explorations had left him persuaded
that none of its parts were in imminent danger of falling,
his fears were forgotten, and Venus, there on Mount Eryx,   530
observed him relaxing, and said, as she drew Cupid near her,
"My son, my sword, my strong right arm and source of my power,
take up that weapon by which all your victims are vanquished
and send your swift arrows into the breast of the deity
to whom the last part of the threefold realm[6] was allotted.   535

" ' "You govern the gods and their ruler; you rule the defeated
gods of the ocean and govern the one who rules them, too;
why give up on the dead, when we can extend our empire
into their realm? A third part of the world is involved here!
And yet the celestial gods spurn our forbearance,   540
and the prestige of Love is diminished, even as mine is.
Do you not see how Athena and huntress Diana
have both taken leave of me? The virgin daughter of Ceres
desires to do likewise—and will, if we let her!
But if you take pride in our alliance, advance it   545
by joining her to her uncle!"[7]

" 'Venus ceased speaking and Cupid
loosened his quiver, and, just as his mother had ordered,

---

3. During the battle of the Giants, Jove got his nerve back and hurled thunderbolts against
   Typhoeus, driving him off to Sicily, where he was crushed under Mount Etna.
4. Pelorus, Pachynus, and Lilybaeum are the three capes of Sicily.
5. Dis, the god of the underworld.
6. Jove rules the heavens and earth, Neptune the seas, and Dis the underworld.
7. Proserpina was the daughter of Ceres and Jove, and so the niece of Jove's brother Dis.

selected, from thousands of missiles, the one that was sharpest
and surest and paid his bow the closest attention,
and using one knee to bend its horn back almost double,   550
he pierces the heart of Dis with his barb-tipped arrow.
    "'Near Henna's walls stands a deep pool of water, called Pergus:
not even the river Cayster, flowing serenely,
hears more songs from its swans; this pool is completely
        surrounded
by a ring of tall trees, whose foliage, just like an awning,   555
keeps out the sun and preserves the water's refreshing coolness;
the moist ground is covered with flowers of Tyrian purple;
here it is springtime forever. And here Proserpina
was playfully picking its white lilies and violets,
and, while competing to gather up more than her playmates,   560
filling her basket and stuffing the rest in her bosom,
Dis saw her, was smitten, seized her and carried her off;
his love was that hasty. The terrified goddess cried out
for her mother, her playmates—but for her mother most often,
since she had torn the uppermost seam of her garment,   565
and the gathered flowers rained down from her negligent tunic;
because of her tender years and her childish simplicity,
even this loss could move her to maidenly sorrow.
    "'Her abductor rushed off in his chariot, urging his horses,
calling each one by its name and flicking the somber,   570
rust-colored reins over their backs as they galloped
through the deep lakes and the sulphurous pools of Palike
that boil up through the ruptured earth, and where the Bacchiadae,
a race sprung from Corinth, that city between the two seas,
had raised their own walls between two unequal harbors.   575
    "'There is a bay that is landlocked almost completely
between the two pools of Cyane and Pisaean Arethusa,
the residence of the most famous nymph in all Sicily,
Cyane, who gave her very own name to the fountain.
She showed herself now, emerged from her pool at waist level,   580
and recognizing the goddess, told Dis, "Go no further!
You cannot become the son-in-law of great Ceres
against her will: you should have asked and not taken!
If it is right for me to compare lesser with greater,
I accepted Anapis when he desired to have me,   585
yielding to pleas and not—as in *this* case—to terror."
She spoke, and stretching her arms out in either direction,
kept him from passing. That son of Saturn could scarcely
hold back his anger; he urged on his frightening horses,
and then, with his strong right arm, he hurled his scepter   590
directly into the very base of the fountain;
the stricken earth opened a path to the underworld
and took in the chariot rushing down into its crater.

"'Cyane, lamenting not just the goddess abducted,
but also the disrespect shown for *her* rights as a fountain,   595
tacitly nursed in her heart an inconsolable sorrow;
and she who had once been its presiding spirit,
reduced to tears, dissolved right into its substance.
You would have seen her members beginning to soften,
her bones and her fingertips starting to lose their old firmness;   600
her slenderest parts were the first to be turned into fluid:
her feet, her legs, her sea-dark tresses, her fingers
(for the parts with least flesh turn into liquid most quickly);
and after these, her shoulders and back and her bosom
and flanks completely vanished in trickling liquid;   605
and lastly the living blood in her veins is replaced by
springwater, and nothing remains that you could have seized on.
  "'Meanwhile, the terrified mother was pointlessly seeking
her daughter all over the earth and deep in the ocean.
Neither Aurora, appearing with dew-dampened tresses,   610
nor Hesperus knew her to quit; igniting two torches
of pine from the fires of Etna, the care-ridden goddess
used them to illumine the wintery shadows of nighttime;
and when the dear day had once more dimmed out the bright stars,
she searched again for her daughter from sunrise to sunset.   615

Stellio

  "'Worn out by her labors and suffering thirst, with no fountain
to wet her lips at, she happened upon a thatched hovel
and knocked at its humble door, from which there came forth
a crone who looked at the goddess, and, when asked for water,
gave her a sweet drink, sprinkled with toasted barley.   620
And, as she drank it, a boy with a sharp face and bold manner
stood right before her and mocked her and said she was greedy.
Angered by what he was saying, the goddess drenched him
with all she had not yet drunk of the barley mixture.
The boy's face thirstily drank up the spots as his arms were   625
turned into legs, and a tail was joined to his changed limbs;
so that he should now be harmless, the boy was diminished,
and he was transformed into a very small lizard.
Astonished, the old woman wept and reached out to touch him,
but the marvelous creature fled her, seeking a hideout.   630
He now has a name appropriate to his complexion,
Stellio, from the cons*tella*tions spotting his body.
  "'To speak of the lands and seas the goddess mistakenly searched
would take far too long; the earth exhausted her seeking;
she came back to Sicily; and, as she once more traversed it,   635
arrived at Cyane, who would have told her the story
had she not herself been changed; but, though willing in spirit,

her mouth, tongue, and vocal apparatus were absent;
nevertheless, she gave proof that was clear to the mother:
Persephone's girdle (which happened by chance to have fallen   640
into the fountain) now lay exposed on its surface.

"'Once recognizing it, the goddess knew that her daughter
had been taken, and tore her hair into utter disorder,
and repeatedly struck her breasts with the palms of both hands.
With her daughter's location a mystery still, she reproaches   645
the whole earth as ungrateful, unworthy her gift of grain crops,
and Sicily more than the others, where she has discovered
the proof of her loss; and so it was here that her fierce hand
shattered the earth-turning plows, here that the farmers and cattle
perished alike, and here that she bade the plowed fields   650
default on their trust by blighting the seeds in their keeping.
Sicilian fertility, which had been everywhere famous,
was given the lie when the crops died as they sprouted,
now ruined by too much heat, and now by too heavy a rainfall;
stars and winds harmed them, and the greedy birds devoured   655
the seed as it was sown; the harvest of wheat was defeated
by thorns and darnels and unappeasable grasses.

"'Then Arethusa[8] lifted her head from the Elean waters
and swept her dripping hair back away from her forehead,
saying, "O Mother of Grain—and mother, too, of that virgin   660
sought through the whole world—here end your incessant labors,
lest your great anger should injure the earth you once trusted,
and which, unwillingly pillaged, has done nothing ignoble;
nor do I plead for my nation, since I am a guest here:
my nation is Pisa, I am descended from Elis,   665
and live as a stranger in Sicily—this land that delights me
more than all others on earth; here Arethusa
dwells with her household gods. Spare it, merciful goddess,
and when your cares and countenance both have been lightened,
there will come an opportune time to tell you the reason   670
why I was taken from home and borne off to Ortygia
over a waste of waters. The earth gave me access,
showed me a path, and, swept on through underground caverns,
I raised my head here to an unfamiliar night sky.
But while gliding under the earth on a Stygian river,   675
I saw with my very own eyes your dear Proserpina;
grief and terror were still to be seen in her features,
yet she was nonetheless queen of that shadowy kingdom,
the all-powerful consort of the underworld's ruler."

"'The mother was petrified by the speech of the fountain,   680
and stood for a very long time as though she were senseless,

---

8. The fountain Arethusa will have her own tale to tell; see p. 136.

until her madness had been driven off by her outrage,
and then she set out in her chariot for the ethereal regions;
once there, with her face clouded over and hair all disheveled,
she planted herself before Jove and fiercely addressed him: 685
"Jupiter, I have come here as a suppliant, speaking
for my child—and yours: if you have no regard for her mother,
relent as her father—don't hold her unworthy, I beg you,
simply because *I* am the child's other parent!
The daughter I sought for so long is at last recovered,   690
if to recover means only to lose much more surely,
or if to recover means just to learn her location!
Her theft could be borne—if only he would return her!
Then let him do it, for surely *Jove's* daughter is worthy
of a mate who's no brigand, even if *my* daughter isn't."   695
    "'Jupiter answered her, "She is indeed *our* daughter,
the pledge of our love and our common concern,
but if you will kindly agree to give things their right names,
this is not an injury requiring my retribution,
but an act of love by a son-in-law who won't shame you,   700
goddess, if you give approval; though much were lacking,
how much it is to be Jove's brother! But he lacks nothing,
and only yields to me that which the Fates have allotted.
Still, if you're so keen on parting them, your Proserpina
may come back to heaven—but only on one condition: 705
that she has not touched food, for so the Fates have required."

Ascalaphus

"'He spoke and Ceres was sure she would get back her daughter,
though the Fates were not, for the girl had already placated
her hunger while guilelessly roaming death's formal gardens,
where, from a low-hanging branch, she had plucked without
        thinking   710
a pomegranate, and peeling its pale bark off, devoured
seven of its seeds.[9] No one saw her but Ascalaphus
(whom it is said that Orphne, a not undistinguished
nymph among those of Avernus, pregnant by Acheron,
gave birth to there in the underworld's dark-shadowed forest);   715
he saw, and by his disclosure, kept her from returning.
    "'Raging, the Queen of the Underworld turned that informer
into a bird of ill omen: sprinkling the waters
of Phlegethon[1] into the face of Ascalaphus,
she gave him a beak and plumage and eyes quite enormous.   720
Lost to himself, he is clad now in yellow-brown pinions,

---

9. The pomegranate as a symbol of immortality became associated with Proserpina. In other
    versions of the tale she eats only one seed, which suffices.
1. One of the rivers of the underworld.

his head increases in size and his nails turn to talons,
but the feathers that spring from his motionless arms scarcely
    flutter;
a filthy bird he's become, the grim announcer of mourning,
a slothful portent of evil to mortals—the owl.   725

The Daughters of Acheloüs

"'That one, because of his tattling tongue, seems quite worthy
of punishment,—but you, daughters of Acheloüs,
why do you have the plumage of birds and the faces of virgins?
Is it because while Proserpina gathered her flowers,
you, artful Sirens, were numbered among her companions?   730
No sooner had you scoured the whole earth in vain for her
than you desired the vast seas to feel your devotion,
and prayed to the gods, whom you found willing to help you,
that you might skim over the flood upon oars that were pinions,
then saw your limbs turn suddenly golden with plumage.   735
And so that your tunefulness, which the ear finds so pleasing,
should not be lost, nor your gifts of vocal expression,
your maidenly faces remain, along with your voices.

Proserpina Transformed

"'But poised between his sorrowing sister and brother,
great Jove divided the year into two equal portions,   740
so now in two realms the shared goddess holds sway,
and as many months spent with her mother are spent with her husband.
She changed her mind then, and changed her expression to
    match it,
and now her fair face, which even Dis found depressing,
beams as the sun does, when, after having been hidden   745
before in dark clouds, at last it emerges in triumph.

Arethusa's Tale

"'Her daughter safely restored to her, kindhearted Ceres
wishes to hear *your* story now, Arethusa—
what did you flee from and what changed you into a fountain?
The splashing waters are stilled: the goddess raises   750
her head from their depths and wrings dry her virid tresses,
then tells the old tale of the river Alpheus' passion.
    "'"Once I was one of the nymphs who dwell in Achaea,"
she said, "and none had more zeal than I for traversing
the mountain pastures or setting out snares for small game.   755
But even though I did not seek to find fame as a beauty,
men called me that, my courage and strength notwithstanding;

nor was I pleased that my beauty was lauded so often,
and for my corporeal nature (which most other maidens
are wont to take pleasure in) I blushed like a rustic,   760
thinking it wrong to please men.
                            """Exhausted from hunting,
I was on my way back from the Stymphalian forest,
and the fierce heat of the day was doubled by my exertions.
By chance I came on a stream, gently and silently flowing,
clear to the bottom, where you could count every pebble,   765
water so still you would scarcely believe it was moving.
Silvery willows and poplars, which the stream nourished,
artlessly shaded its banks as they sloped to the water.
    """At once I approach and wiggle my toes in its wetness,
then wade in up to my knees—not satisfied wholly,   770
I strip off my garments and hang them up on a willow,
and, naked, merge with the waters. I strike and stroke them,
gliding below and thrashing about on the surface,
then hear a strange murmur that seems to come from the bottom,
which sends me scampering onto the near bank in terror: 775
'Why the great rush?' Alpheus cries from his waters,
then hoarsely repeating, 'Why the great rush, Arethusa?'
Just as I am, I flee without clothing (my garments
were on the bank opposite); aroused, Alpheus pursues me,
my nakedness making me seem more ripe for the taking.   780
    """Thus did I run, and thus did that fierce one press after,
as doves on trembling pinions flee from the kestrel,
as kestrels pursue the trembling doves and assault them.
To Orchomenus and past, to Psophis, Cyllene,
the folds of Maenalia, Erymanthus, and Elis,   785
I continued to run, nor was he faster than I was;
but since Alpheus was so much stronger, I couldn't
outrun him for long, given his greater endurance.
    """Nonetheless, I still managed to keep on running
across the wide fields, up wooded mountains,   790
on bare rocks, steep cliffs, in wastes wild and trackless;
with the sun at my back, I could see his shadow before me,
stretched out on the ground, unless my panic deceived me;
but surely I *did* hear those frightening footsteps behind me,
and felt his hot breath lifting the hair from my shoulders.   795
    """Worn with exertion, I cried out, 'Help! Or I'm taken!
Aid your armoress, Diana—to whom you have often
entrusted your bow, along with your quiver of arrows!'
The goddess was moved by my plea and at once I was hidden
in a dense cloud of fine mist: the river god, clueless,   800
circled around me, hidden in darkness, searching;
twice he unknowingly passed by the place where the goddess
had hidden me, and twice he called, 'Yo! Arethusa!'

How wretched was I? Why, even as the lamb is,
at hearing the howling of wolves around the sheepfold,   805
or as the rabbit in the briar patch who glimpses
the dog's fierce muzzle and feels too frightened to tremble.
    """Alpheus remained there, for as he noticed no footprints
heading away from the cloud, he continued to watch it.
An icy sweat thoroughly drenched the limbs that he looked for,   810
and the dark drops poured from every part of my body;
wherever my foot had been, there was a puddle,
and my hair shed moisture. More swiftly than I can tell it,
I turned into liquid—even so, he recognized me,
his darling there in the water, and promptly discarded   815
the human form he had assumed for the occasion,
reverting to river, so that our fluids might mingle.
Diana shattered the earth's crust; I sank down,
and was swept on through sightless caverns, off to Ortygia,
so pleasing to me because it's the goddess's birthplace;   820
and here I first rose up into the air as a fountain.""

Triptolemus and Lyncus

"'Here Arethusa concluded. The fruitful goddess summoned
her team of dragons and yoked them onto her chariot;
and guiding their heads with the reins, she was transported
up through the middle air that lies between earth and heaven   825
until she arrived in Athens, and, giving her carriage
to Triptolemus,[2] ordered him to go off and scatter
grain on the earth—some on land that had never been broken,
and some on land that had been a long time fallow.
    "'The young man was carried high up over Europe and Asia   830
until at last he came to the kingdom of Scythia.
Lyncus[3] was king here; he brought him into his palace,
and asked him his name, his homeland, the cause of his journey,
and how he had come there.
                    """My well-known homeland," he answered,
"is Athens; I am Triptolemus; neither by ship upon water   835
nor foot upon land have I come here; the air itself parted
to make me a path on which I coursed through the heavens.
I bear you the gifts of Ceres, which, sown in your broad fields,
will yield a bountiful harvest of nourishing produce."
    "'This the barbarian heard with great envy, and wishing   840
that he himself might be perceived as the donor,

---

2. The favorite of Ceres, whom she sent around the world in a serpent-drawn chariot to foster the growth of agriculture.
3. The story of Lyncus occurs only in Ovid, but it is remarkably similar to Lycaon's tale in
Book I.

took him in as a guest, and while the young man was sleeping,
approached with a sword, and as he attempted to stab him,
Ceres changed *Lyncus* to *lynx*, and ordered Triptolemus
to drive her sacred team through the air back to Athens.'   845

The P-Airides

"When our eldest sister had concluded
her superb performance, with one voice
the nymphs awarded victory to . . . the Muses!
    "And when the others, in defeat, reviled us,
I answered them: 'Since you display such nerve   850
in challenging the Muses, you deserve
chastisement—even more so since you've added
insult to outrage: our wise forbearance
is not without its limits, as you'll learn
when we get to the penalties, and vent   855
our righteous anger on your worthless selves.'
    "Then the Pierides mock our threats,
and as they try to answer us by shouting
vulgarities and giving us the finger,
their fingers take on feathers and their arms   860
turn into pinions! Each one sees a beak
replace a sister's face, as a new bird
is added to the species of the forest;
and as they try to beat upon their breasts,
bewailing their new situation, they   865
all hang suspended, flapping in the air,
the forest's scandal—the P-Airides!
    "And even though they are all feathered now,
their speech remains as fluent as it was,
and they are famous for their noisiness   870
as well as for their love of argument."

BOOK VI

Of Praise and Punishment

Arachne

After she'd listened to their tale, Minerva[1]
gave her approval to the Muses' song
and to the anger that it justified.
"To praise is insufficient," she reflected;
"we will be praised—and we will not permit   5
those who belittle our divinity
to go unpunished!"
              Her attention turned
to the undoing of Maeonian Arachne,
who (it was said) accepted praise that set her
above the goddess in the art of weaving,   10
a girl renowned not for her place of birth
nor for her family, but for her art:
her father, Idmon, came from Colophon,
and (like the mother that Arachne lost)
was of plebeian origin, a tradesman   15
who steeped the thirsty wool in purple dye.
    Nevertheless, her art had made her famous
throughout the many cities of Lydia,
although her home was every bit as humble
as Hypaepa, the hamlet where she lived.   20
    To see her wonderwork, the nymphs would leave
their vineyards on the slope of Mount Timolus
or their haunts along the winding Pactolus.
They came not *just* to see the finished product,
but to watch her working, for such comeliness   25
and grace were present when she plied her art,
whether she shaped the crude wool in a ball,
or with her fingers softened it and drew
the fleecy mass into a single thread
spun out between the distaff and the spindle,   30
or worked a pattern into what she wove
with her embroidery.
              You would have known
that only Pallas[2] could have been her teacher.

---

1. The theme of much of Book VI is clearly stated in Minerva's first words. Rivalry between the gods and mortals was present in the contest between the Muses and the Pierides in Book V, but it faded into the background with the elaboration of the hymn to Ceres and Arethusa's tale. With *Arachne, Niobe, Latona,* and *Marsyas,* Ovid develops the theme once again in the context of increasing self-assertion on the part of mortals. With the tale of *Tereus, Procne, and Philomela,* we see humans behaving with a psychopathic cruelty perhaps unimagined by the gods.
2. Another name for Athena or Minerva. The word means "wisdom" in Greek.

Nevertheless, as though offended by
the very thought, the girl denied it, saying,   35
"Let her compete with me, and if she wins
I'll pay whatever penalty she sets!"
    Pallas disguises herself as a crone:
puts on a wig of counterfeit gray hair
and, with a staff to prop her tottering limbs,   40
begins to speak: "Old age is not to be
wholly despised, for with it wisdom comes.
Heed my advice: seek all the fame you wish
as best of mortal weavers, but admit
the goddess as your superior in skill;   45
beg her to pardon you for your presumption
in an appropriately humble manner—
forgiveness will be given, if you ask it."
    Arachne drops the work she had begun,
and scarcely able to restrain her hand,   50
expresses outrage through her glaring eyes,
cutting the goddess short with these sharp words:
"You've lived too long, you senile nincompoop,
that's what your trouble is! Try telling that
to your own daughter or your daughter-in-law,   55
if you have any children; as for me,
I'll take my own advice, thanks very much!
    "And so you shouldn't think you've made your case,
my own opinion hasn't changed at all:
why does the goddess shun a match with me?   60
Why won't she come to challenge me herself?"
    The goddess answered her with, "She has come,"
and casting off the image of old age,
revealed herself as Pallas; the Phrygian
matrons and the nymphs bowed down before her.   65
    All were quite terrified except Arachne,
although she reddened when a sudden flush
stained her unwilling cheeks, then disappeared,
as when the sky turns crimson just at dawn,
but then grows pale again as the sun rises.   70
    Yet she persists in what she has begun;
in her desire for the foolish palm
of victory, she rushes to her fate;
Jove's daughter does not turn Arachne down,
or warn her further, or postpone the match.   75
    At once the two of them select their sites
and set the uprights of their frames in place,
then draw the slender threads of the warp between
the horizontal crossbeams of the yoke;
the warp is separated with a reed,   80

and dexterous fingers, busy at the shuttle,
draw woof through warp,[3] then tap it into place
with the comb's notched teeth.
                              Then they go to it,
hitching their robes up underneath their breasts,
their well-instructed fingers swiftly flying,   85
and zeal for the contest making light of labor.
   Into their fabrics they weave purple threads
of Tyrian dye, and place beside them shades
that lighten imperceptibly from these;
as when a storm ends and the sun comes out,   90
a rainbow's arc illuminates the sky;
although a thousand colors shine in it,
the eye cannot say where one color ends
and another starts, so gradual the verging;
there in the middle, the colors look the same,   95
while, at the edges, they seem different.
Into the fabrics they weave threads of gold,
as on each loom appears an oft-told tale:
   Minerva shows the Areopagus,
site of that contest held once to determine   100
a city's name.[4] Twelve deities are seated
in august assurance, weighty on their thrones,
Jove in the middle; ranged on either side,
the gods all look like their own images;
how regal Jove seems!
                         Next, she depicts   105
how Neptune with his trident strikes the rugged
rock from which a spring of water gushes,
the pledge by which he hopes to claim the city.
   Then she displays herself, armed with a shield
and a sharp spear; a helmet guards her head,   110
her breast is well protected by the aegis;
she represents that moment when the earth,
struck by her spear tip, instantly produces
a full-grown olive tree,[5] laden with ripe fruit.
The gods all marvel, and she takes the prize.   115
   And then, to give Arachne an idea
of the reward this upstart can expect
for her audacious bid for praise and glory,

---

3. The two contestants construct their looms on the spot. "Warp" refers to the threads that
   are stretched lengthwise on the loom, and "woof" refers to those that cross the loom from
   side to side.
4. Neptune (Greek Poseidon) and Minerva (Greek Athena) held a contest to determine
   whose name would be given to the city built around its citadel, the Acropolis. An illustra-
   tion of the goddess's victory is followed by the representation of a series of episodes in
   which presumptuous mortals are punished for their impudence—an obvious warning to
   Arachne.
5. Athena's favorite tree and her city's symbol.

the goddess then expertly represents,
in each of the four corners of her work,   120
a different contest, each in miniature,
and each with its distinctive color scheme.
   In the first scene, two Thracians, Rhodope
and Haemus, who were mortals once, are turned
into a pair of mountains, for assuming   125
the names of Jove and Juno as their own;
and in the second corner she depicted
the terrifying fate of the Pygmy queen:
when Juno had defeated her, she ordered
her to transform herself into a crane   130
and then make war upon her former subjects;
in the third corner is Antigone,
who once dared struggle with Jove's mighty consort
and whom Queen Juno turned into a stork;
not Ilion, nor Laomedon, her father,   135
could save the girl: she put white feathers on,
and now applauds herself with clacking beak;
the final corner shows a grieving man:
Cinyras, clinging to the temple steps
that used to be the limbs of his own daughters,   140
and weeping what appear to be real tears.[6]
   Around her work, the goddess wove a border
of peaceful olive leaves; that finished it,
and with her tree, her labors, too, were done.
   Arachne shows Europa tricked by Jove   145
in semblance of a bull upon the sea,
and done so naturally you would have thought
the bull and the waves he breasted were both real;
the girl seems to look back at her lost land,
cries out to her companions and withdraws   150
her feet in terror from the surging flood.[7]
   Asterie is shown in an eagle's grip,
and Leda, lying under a swan's wing;
Arachne shows how, in a Satyr's guise,
Jupiter filled Antiope with twins;   155
how, as Amphitryon, he hoodwinked you,
Alcmena; and how Danaë was deceived
by a golden shower; Aegina by a flame;
how Mnemosyne was cozened by a shepherd

---

6. Four instances of human overreaching: Rhodope and Haemus impersonated the gods and
were punished for their boasting; the nameless Pygmy queen causes a state of unending
war between her former subjects and the cranes; the Trojan princess Antigone apparently
boasted that her beauty was superior to Juno's; Cinyras is otherwise unknown, but his
daughters may have made the same claim as did Antigone.
7. Ovid revisits the climax of Book III with the abduction of Europa.

and Proserpina, child of Demeter,   160
was ruined by a many-colored serpent.[8]
    And she depicted you as well, Neptune,
transformed into the fiercest-looking bull,
with the Aeolian maiden, Canace;
as Enipeus, you were shown begetting   165
Otos and Ephialtes, the Aloidae,
and as a ram, deceiving Theophane;
immortal Demeter, the golden-haired
and infinitely mild mother of grain,
knew you as a horse; while to Medusa,   170
mother of Pegasus, you seemed a bird,
and seemed just like a dolphin to Melantho;
she rendered all of them just as they were,
and each with an appropriate background.[9]
    And there's Apollo, tricked out as a rustic,   175
now dressed in feathers, now a lion skin,
or as a shepherd to take Isse in;
and Bacchus, out to trick Erigone
with grapes that aren't really grapes at all;
there's Saturn, breeding Chiron on a mare,   180
and all around the edge, a deftly woven
border of flowers plaited into ivy.[1]
    Not even Envy could have faulted this;
Pallas did not, yet, bitterly resenting
her rival's success, the goddess warrior   185
ripped it, with its convincing evidence
of celestial misconduct, all asunder;
and with her shuttle of Cytorian boxwood,[2]
struck at Arachne's face repeatedly!
    She could not bear this, the ill-omened girl,   190
and bravely fixed a noose around her throat;
while she was hanging, Pallas, stirred to mercy,
lifted her up and said:
                    "Though you will hang,
you must indeed live on, you wicked child:

---

8. Arachne lists Jove's many seductions through deception. Asterie and Leda were both
   taken by Jove in two different bird forms; disguised as a satyr, Jove raped Antiope; impersonating her husband Amphitryon, Jove slept with the unknowing Alcmena; in the form
   of gold, he impregnated Danaë; as a flame, he did the same for Aegina; as a shepherd, he
   fathered the nine Muses on Mnemosyne; and as a serpent, he slept with his own daughter, Proserpina. Arachne then enumerates Neptune's similar seductions.
9. Ovid seems to have chosen the seductions of Neptune to create a kind of celestial bes-
   tiary. Jove mounting Medusa as a bird perhaps accounts for the wings on Pegasus.
1. Three more gods, with one seduction each. Though Erigone's story is unknown, all three
   stories emphasize deception and rape.
2. Mount Cytorus was the ancient source for boxwood. The shuttle was a sharp, heavy
   implement used in weaving to draw the threads of the woof back in between the threads
   of the warp.

so that your future will be no less fearful   195
than your present is, may the same punishment
remain in place for you and yours forever!"

    Then, as the goddess turned to go, she sprinkled
Arachne with the juice of Hecate's herb,[3]
and at the touch of that grim preparation,   200
she lost her hair, then lost her nose and ears;
her head got smaller and her body, too;
her slender fingers were now legs that dangled
close to her sides; now she was very small,
but what remained of her turned into belly,   205
from which she now continually spins
a thread, and as a spider, carries on
the art of weaving as she used to do.

Niobe

Now all of Lydia is in an uproar
and farther to the east, the story spreads   210
from town to town through Phrygia,
until the great world speaks of nothing other
than Arachne's fate.

                    Before her wedding day,
when she was living in Maeonia,
Niobe knew this girl;[4] nevertheless,   215
the punishment her countrywoman suffered
did not convince Niobe to defer
to the immortals, and to treat with them
as with superiors.

                    Her pride had many
sources, as it happened, but in fact,   220
neither her husband's great artistic skills,
nor their distinguished lists of ancestors,
nor the power of their realm—no, none of these
gave her such pleasure (even though, of course,
all of the items mentioned gave her pleasure)   225
as did her progeny. All would have hailed
Niobe as most fortunate of mothers
had she not gotten there ahead of them.

    Then Manto, daughter of Tiresias,
and like her father skilled at divination,   230
went all throughout the city, prophesying,
"Women of Thebes! Go to Latona's temple,

---

3. A potion administered by the tripartite goddess—Luna in heaven, Diana on earth, Proserpina in the underworld—who presided over magic and enchantments.
4. One of Ovid's more casual bridges between stories, though there is a strong thematic connection between Arachne's tale and Niobe's.

and offer her and the twin gods she bore[5]
the gifts of incense and your dutiful worship,
binding your brows with laurel as the goddess,   235
speaking through me, commands."
                            The Theban women
obediently bind their brows with laurel,
and offer prayers and incense at her altar.
    But look, where in the midst of her attendants,
Niobe comes, a sight well worth the seeing,   240
in gold-embroidered robes from Phrygia,
and lovely, insofar as her great anger
would let her be.
                Tossing her fine head
so that her hair spills over both shoulders,
she halts and draws herself up to full height,   245
and fixes the women with a haughty look:
    "What madness is this," she said, "to prefer
gods that you've only heard of to the ones
you've actually seen? Why cultivate
Latona's altars and deny me mine?[6]   250
    "My lineage is highly worshipful:
only one man has ever been permitted
to lie among the gods at their high table,
my father, Tantalus. And Dione,
my mother, is a sister of the famous   255
Pleiades; my grandfather on her side
is mighty Atlas, who bears heaven's weight
upon his shoulders; on my father's side,
why, my grandfather is Jupiter himself,
who raped my husband's mother and became   260
the father-in-law that I am proud to claim.[7]
    "Feared by the Phrygians, I am a queen
in the line that traces its descent from Cadmus,
and with my husband Amphion, I rule
the folk within these walls, which rose as though   265
by magic when he played upon the lyre.[8]
    "I gaze around my palace, and I see
the spectacle of riches everywhere;
my beauty is quite worthy of a goddess,
and in addition, I have seven daughters   270

5. Latona is the mother of the heavenly twins Apollo and Diana, whom Ovid refers to as
   Phoebus and Phoebe to emphasize their twinship.
6. In her claim to *be* a goddess, Niobe goes beyond Arachne's claim of artistic superiority.
7. The fate of Atlas foreshadows Niobe's. Jupiter raped Antiope (an episode depicted by
   Arachne in her weaving) and produced Niobe's husband Amphion. Niobe does not let the
   impropriety of the act prevent her from emphasizing the connection with a distinguished
   in-law.
8. Amphion, a skilled poet and musician, was given his lyre by the god Mercury.

and seven sons, all soon to multiply
my holdings by their spouses when they marry—
and you still ask what cause have I for pride?
    "Then *dare* prefer Latona's cult to mine,
that daughter of the Titan Coeus,   275
whoever *he's* supposed to be! Latona,
denied the barest spot for giving birth!
There was no place in heaven nor on earth
nor on the sea that would receive your goddess,
an exile driven over the wide world   280
until the Isle of Delos pitied her:
'You wander homeless on the earth,' he said,
'as I upon the waters do the same.'[9]
He gave her a place, unstable though it was,
where she became the parent of—just two!   285
One seventh of the yield of our womb!
    "Blessèd am I (who ever would deny it?),
and (who can doubt it?) blessèd will I be
forever, safely kept by my abundance.
Fortune would find me far too great to harm: 290
though she took many, I'd have many more.
    "Such wealth drives fear away! But just suppose
some part of that vast nation of my offspring
was taken from me: not even so reduced
would I be left with two—Latona's horde,   295
wherewith she staves off utter childlessness!
    "So stop these ceremonies now, and go—
and take that laurel from your hair!" They did,
abandoning their uncompleted rites,
yet offering Latona what they could,   300
their reverence expressed in silent prayers.
    Seething with indignation at this treatment,
Latona, on the summit of Mount Cynthus,
addressed her children, the immortal twins:
"Just look at this, now! I, a goddess who   305
gives way to no one else, except for Juno,
and proud of having borne the pair of you,
now find my divinity called into doubt!
    "My altars will forever be neglected,
unless you two come to my aid at once!   310
There's more, besides: this child of Tantalus
adds insult to these injuries, preferring
her own offspring to you! And calling me—
Oh, may that word come back to her—*bereft!*
She shows her father's gift for blasphemy!"   315

9. One of the Cycladic islands, Delos was thought to have wandered over the seas until the
   birth of Apollo and Diana.

She would have added prayers to her complaint,
but Phoebus broke in: "Enough! This lengthy screed
serves only to delay her punishment."
Phoebe concurred, and in a trice the two
had touched down on the citadel of Thebes.   320
    Below the walls there lay a level field,
pounded incessantly by horses' hooves
and by the thronging wheels of chariots:
here some of the seven sons of Amphion
were putting their spirited chargers through their paces,   325
gaily caparisoned with saddlecloths
dyed in Tyrian purple, and with golden reins.
    Here as he wheeled his steed round in a circle,
forcing the bit against its jaws, Ismenus,
the earliest burden of his mother's womb,   330
cried out, "Ah, me!" as the arrow pierced his breast
and the reins slid between his lifeless fingers
and he dismounted slowly from the right,
toppling over the shoulder of his steed.
    The next was Sipylus, who, having heard   335
the clattering of arrows in a quiver,
at once gave full rein to his horse, fleeing
as when a helmsman sees a distant cloud,
the harbinger of an approaching storm,
and crowds on sail to take advantage of   340
the slightest breeze; though he gave full rein,
the inevitable arrow overtook him;
while its steel tip projected from his throat,
its feathered shaft stood trembling in his nape;
as he was leaning forward, so he pitched   345
over his horse's mane and fell beneath
its galloping legs, defiling Mother Earth
with his warm blood.
               Ill-fated Phaedimus
and Tantalus (the grandson of the hero)
had finished with their horses and moved on   350
to boyish pleasures in the wrestling ring;
their well-oiled bodies glistening, they gripped
each other, breast to breast, in a tight clinch;
a bowstring is drawn back and then released:
a single arrow pierces both of them.   355
They groan together and together fall,
together writhing in death's agony;
they roll their eyes and breathe their last together.
    Alphenor saw this and flew toward the pair,
beating his grief-stricken breast, and as he   360
lifted their limbs, already cold, in his embrace,
he, in that act of piety, was felled

when Delian Apollo drove a shaft
right through his diaphragm: when they withdrew it,
a part of his torn lung stuck on the barb;   365
his lifeblood followed, gushing in the air.

    Longhaired Damascithon came to a more
complicated end, struck by an arrow
between the ligaments behind his knee;
and as he struggled with that fatal shaft,   370
a second arrow punched right through his throat,
up to the feathers. His hot blood expelled it,
drilling the air through in a slender column.

    Ilioneus was the last to die;
raising his arms to heaven in a prayer   375
that would prove ineffectual, he cried
in desperation,"Spare me, all you gods!"
(not knowing that not *all* gods needed asking!).
Although the god who bent the bow was moved,
his arrow (not to be recalled) sped on: 380
nevertheless, a slight wound did for him,
for the arrow didn't pierce his heart—too deeply.

    Rumor of evil spreads across the city,
touching with sorrow every group it meets,
until her own attendants, now in tears,   385
assure the mother of her certain ruin;
she can't believe that this could happen to her,
and that it had happened was outrageous;
that the gods could dare so, were within their rights;
that father Amphion had killed himself,   390
putting one end to sorrow and to life.

    How sadly different is this Niobe
from that Niobe who so recently
dispersed the people at Latona's shrine,
who sailed so proudly down the city's streets   395
with head held high, the envy of her friends—
who now is pitied even by her foes!

    She flings herself onto the lifeless corpses
in her derangement, kisses them farewell,
then lifts her bruised arms to the sky and says,   400
"Now feast your cruel heart upon our grief,
feast yourself, Latona, till you're sated!
Glut your bloodthirsty heart! These seven deaths
have ruined me: exult then, in the triumph
of the victor over her defeated foe!   405

    "But who is victor? In my wretchedness
I still have far more children left to me
than you in all your bliss! Thus, even after
so many deaths, I am the victor still!"

No sooner had she spoken when the taut   410
bowstring twanged with its release, a sound
that terrified them all except Niobe:
ruin had made her reckless.

                        The seven sisters stood,
in black for mourning, with their hair unbound,
before the corpses laid out in a row;   415
the first sister, attempting to remove
an arrow threaded through a brother's guts,
collapsed and died, her lifeless cheek on his;
the second sister, trying to console
her grieving mother, suddenly bent over   420
in agony, struck by an unseen wound.
    This one dies fleeing; that one falls upon
a sister's corpse; this one hides, and that one
stands up where you can see her shivering;
now six, diversely wounded, have been slain;   425
the last of them still lives; her mother stretches
her body and her garment over her,
and cries, "Leave me my youngest one at least,
spare me but one, the youngest of my many!"
    And as she prayed, the one for whom she prayed   430
fell dead, the last of them; and now bereft,
she sits, surrounded by the lifeless bodies
of her sons, her daughters, and her husband,
she sits there stilly, rigid in her grief:
not a hair upon her head stirs in the breeze,   435
her face is colorless, and her eyes fixed,
and in this image of her nothing lives;
her tongue is stone, frozen to her palate,
her veins no longer move; she cannot turn
her head nor raise her hand nor move a foot;   440
her viscera are stone; and yet Niobe wept.
    A whirlwind carried her back to her homeland;
there, set upon the summit of a mountain,
Niobe weeps, and even to this day,
she bathes the marble with her flowing tears.   445
    And now, for certain, men and women fear
the revelation of Latona's wrath,
and tend her altars with a greater ardor,
showing their awe before the power of
the goddess-mother of the sacred twins.   450

Latona

And as so often happens in such cases,
recent events remind folks of old stories,

until one says, "Something like this took place
in fruitful Lycia, once, long ago,
when peasants spurned the goddess to their grief;   455
only the humble birth of those involved
has kept this tale from being better known,
yet it's amazing—with my own eyes I saw
the pond, the place touched by that miracle.
It happened like this.

                  "My father, being then   460
too far advanced in years to brave the rigors
of cattle driving, ordered me to move
some fancy stock of his out of that region,
and gave me a local fellow for a guide.

    "And as we made our way through the grasslands,   465
I saw, right in the middle of a lake,
surrounded by reeds that trembled in the breeze,
an ancient altar coated with a crust
of black ash from sacrificial fires.

    "He stopped right there and whispered fearfully,   470
'Show me your favor!' And I did likewise.
'So now,' I ask him, 'would that be an altar
to Faunus?[1] The naiads? Some local god perhaps?'

    "The fellow answers, 'Young sir, that there altar
hasn't to do with any mountain god: 475
she calls it hers whom once the queen of heaven
put earth off-limits to, until (but just)
the floating island Delos took her in.

    "'She braced herself against a pair of trees,
the olive and the palm, Latona did,   480
and brought forth twins upon that very spot,
in spite of all their stepmother[2] could do.

    "'She fled, they say: the goddess-mother left
with the baby deities upon her breast,
until she reached the borders of Lycia,   485
where the Chimaeras live. A blazing sun
scorched the fields bare; assailed by heat and thirst,
her breasts drained dry by her greedy nurslings,
it happened that she saw, down in a dell,
a lake of modest size; there, at its edges,   490
peasants were gathering bushy osiers
and other useful grasses from the marsh.

    "'The Titan's daughter came to them, and knelt
at the lake's margin for a cooling drink;

---

1. A rural deity with the legs, feet, and ears of a goat, known by the Greeks as a Satyr.
2. Ovid is speaking, somewhat ironically, of Juno as the stepmother of Phoebus and Phoebe, since Latona was impregnated by Jove. Latona was driven from place to place by Juno's continuing wrath.

the rustic mob forbade her. She appealed: 495
"And why do you prohibit me from drinking?
Surely the water is for everyone.
Nature has given no one ownership
of sunlight, air, and water! I have come
to exercise what is a public right; 500
nevertheless, it's as a suppliant
that I am here to beg this gift from you.
    """I have not come to bathe my weary limbs,
but to relieve my thirst: for I'm so dry
that I can hardly speak, my throat is parched, 505
and I have almost no voice left at all!
A draft of water will be nectar to me,
and I will say I've been restored to life,
yes, it is life you give me with this water!
    """And let my little children move you too, 510
my pretty babes, who even now beseech you,
stretching their tiny arms out from my breast!"
(And as it happened, they stretched out their arms!)
    "'And who would not have been won over by
such winning words? But they, despite her pleas, 515
continued to restrain her, threatening
to do her harm unless she goes away,
and adding insults to such injuries.
    "'Nor did that end it, for they roiled the pond
with hands and feet, and from its bottom stirred 520
the oozy muck by jumping up and down,
out of no other motive than pure meanness.
    "'Anger put thirst off, for the Titan's daughter
now would no longer beg unworthily,
nor could she bear not speaking as a goddess. 525
Turning her palms up to the stars, she cried,
"Dwell in this pond of yours forevermore!"
    "'And as the goddess ordered, so it was.
It pleases them, the underwater life,
sometime to hide, submerged in muck completely, 530
sometime to poke a head out or to swim
across the surface of the pond, or sit,
as they quite often do, along its banks,
only to leap on back into its cool water;
but now, as in the past, they exercise 535
their foul tongues in shameless quarreling,
and even underwater, utter curses.
    "'They've raucous voices now and swollen throats,
and constant quarreling has given them
distended jaws; their heads now seem to sit 540
on shoulders without benefit of necks;

green are their backs and white their bellies (now
their largest parts); no longer laboring,
they all cavort in ponds and mucky bogs,
after their transformation into—frogs.'"   545

Marsyas

No sooner had that nameless fellow finished
his tale of how the Lycians came to ruin,
than someone called to mind the old story
of how Latona's son trounced the Satyr[3]
in a match played upon Minerva's pipes,   550
then punished him:
                "Why do you deconstruct me?"
cried the Satyr. "Oh! I am mortified!
What a great price I'm paying for this flute!"
    And as he cries, the skin is stripped from his body
until he's all entirely one wound: 555
blood runs out everywhere, and his uncovered
sinews lie utterly exposed to view;
his pulsing veins were flickering, and you
could number all his writhing viscera
and the gleaming organs underneath his sternum.   560
    Then came the country folk to weep for him,
gods of the forest, nymphs and fauns, his fellow
Satyrs, and his favorite boy, Olympus,
along with shepherds who, in mountain pastures,
tended their woolly flocks and horny herds.   565
    All wept for him, drenching the fertile earth;
she then absorbed their transitory tears
into her veins and turned them into droplets
of vapor. Sent back out into the air,
they gathered together in a single stream   570
descending swiftly between narrow banks
until it reached the ocean; that stream is known
as the clearest river in all Phrygia,
and takes its name from his: the Marsyas.

Pelops

Immediately after this, the crowd   575
turned to the present day, mourning the death
of Amphion, destroyed with all his offspring.

---

3. Accounts vary on the details, but agree that Marsyas the Satyr challenged Apollo to a
   musical contest, he on the pipes, Apollo on the lyre. In the judgment of the Muses Apollo
   won, and Marsyas was flayed alive.

All blame the mother; nonetheless, folks say
one man, her brother Pelops, mourned for her,
and when he ripped his garment from his breast,   580
revealed the ivory patch on his left shoulder.
    At birth, both shoulders were the same in color
and both were made of flesh; when Tantalus,
his father, chopped him up in little pieces,
they say the gods put him back together,   585
and all the other parts of him were found
except for one between his arm and neck.
    An ivory chip replaced the missing piece,
and Pelops was made once again complete.[4]

Tereus, Procne, and Philomela[5]

Neighboring nobles assembled, and nearby cities   590
encouraged their kings to pay condolence calls:
Argos, Sparta, Pelopeidean Mycenae,
and Calydon (which had not yet acquired
the emnity of fierce Diana);[6] fertile
Orchomenus and Corinth (famed for bronze);   595
fearsome Messene and Patrae and low-lying Cleonae;
and Nelean Pylos and Troezen (not yet ruled
by Pittheus); and all the other cities
to the north and south of Corinth
sent delegates to pay their last respects.   600
    Who would believe that only you, Athens,
did nothing? Warfare kept you from your duty,
for a barbaric horde from overseas
had marched its terror right up to your walls.
    Tereus of Thrace had raised that siege   605
with his auxiliaries, had driven off the foe,
and now was famous for his victory.
And since he was a man of wealth and power,
and a descendant of the god of war,
King Pandion had bonded with Tereus   610
by joining him in marriage to his daughter,
Procne.
            But neither Juno, who presides
at weddings, nor the wedding god himself,

---

4. A foreshadowing of the conclusion of the next tale: Tantalus murdered his young son
   Pelops, and then cooked and served him in a feast he set before the gods to see if they
   were really omniscient. Only Demeter, momentarily distracted, ate a portion, which
   proved to be Pelops's left shoulder; this she later replaced, when he was resurrected, with
   the ivory patch.
5. So far, the gods have been responsible for the pain inflicted on mortals; in this tale we discover that mortals can do it for themselves.
6. A foreshadowing reference to the tale of *Meleager and Althaea* in Book VIII (p. 211).

Hymenaeus, nor the required Graces
attended theirs. Instead, the Furies shook   615
the torches they had snatched from funerals,
and turned down the coverlet upon their bed;
and all night long, an evil owl perched
and brooded on the roof of their bedchamber.

    Under these omens, Tereus and Procne   620
are wed; and under them, their child is born;
and naturally all of Thrace is one
in its felicitations to the parents,
who offer up their own thanks to the gods.

    That day is now proclaimed a festival   625
on which the king of Athens gave his daughter
to the distinguished ruler, and the day
as well on which Itys, their son, was born.
What does us good is to a great extent
concealed from us.

           Five autumns passed,   630
then Procne coaxed her husband with these words:
"If I am at all pleasing in your sight,
then either let me visit with my sister
or let her visit me; you must assure
my father we won't keep her for too long!   635
The sight of her would be the finest gift
that you could give me!"

            So he orders ships
brought down to waterside, then sail and oar
swiftly convey Tereus overseas
to Athens and the harbor at Piraeus.   640
Admitted to the presence of the king
upon arrival, it so happens that
the two men clasp each other's hands and start
their conversation on that lucky omen.

    He had just mentioned his young wife's request   645
to see her sister, and assured the king
that she, if sent, would be sent promptly back,
when look! where Philomela now appears
richly adorned, but richer still in beauty,
one to be spoken of in the same terms   650
as often we hear used of nymphs and dryads
glimpsed in the woods—if only they were dressed
as well as she and were quite as refined.

    When he first saw her, Tereus caught fire
as instantly as ripe grain or dry leaves,   655
or as hay stored in a barn goes up in blazes.
Her beauty surely justified such passion,
but he was driven by an innate lust,

a bent that Thracians have for lechery:
he burned with his and with his nation's heat.[7]   660
    What tack to take here? Bribe her attendants?
Make his way to her through her faithful nurse?
Seduce the girl with rare and precious gifts,
even at the cost of his whole kingdom?
Or seize her and defend his theft with warfare?   665
Nothing at all he would not dare to do
in his unbridled passion, so fierce the flames
that would not be contained within his breast.
    And now delay was unendurable:
he eagerly repeated Procne's speech,   670
and raised his own desires under hers.
Love lent him eloquence, and when he seemed
to go beyond the mandate he'd been given,
he said that this was merely Procne's wish,
and added tears, as though they too were part   675
of his commission. By the gods above,
what utter blindness dwells in human hearts!
Here Tereus achieves a reputation
for piety while plotting wickedness,
and criminal behavior wins him praise!   680
    What made it even easier for him
was Philomela's acquiesence: she
wishes the very same thing for herself,
and puts her arms around her father's neck,
and in a captivating manner begs   685
that she might go and visit with her sister,
for all the good—none!—that will come of this.
    Pricked on by lust, by sights that feed his madness,
Tereus looks at her and sees himself
with her already, doing it to her!   690
He watches as she flings her arms around
her father's neck and chastely kisses him,
and as he watches them in their embrace,
he yearns to take the father's part, although
his motives would be no less impious.   695
    The father is won over by the prayers
of both his daughters. The nearer one rejoices,
and thanks him, for she thinks, unhappy child,
that what must turn out ill will turn out well
for both the daughters. Little labor now   700
remained for Phoebus, whose straining horses fly
on pounding hooves across the western sky.

---

7. An inadequate explanation of the horrors to come, but Ovid may be saying that Tereus
   simply does not reflect on his motives.

A regal banquet is provided next,
and Bacchus too, in golden chalices.
Then sated bodies seek untroubled sleep.   705
But even though the Thracian has retired,
he burns for her, recalling now her face,
her gestures, and the way her body moved,
imagining what he has not yet seen,
and feeding the fires burning in his heart,   710
sleep driven off by his anxiety.
     Light came, and with tears welling in his eyes,
King Pandion embraces Tereus,
committing his daughter to the Thracian's care:
"Compelled, dear son-in-law, by your desires,   715
as well as by the urgings of my daughters,
I give her to you; by faith and by the ties
between us, by the gods above, I beg
that you protect her with a father's love,
and send back home, as soon as possible   720
(for any delay will be unbearable),
the sweet alleviation of my years.
     "You also, Philomela, must return
as soon as possible, if you would be
dutiful in your relationship with me: 725
one daughter's absence is enough to bear."
     With these commands, he kisses her goodbye,
the ripe tears falling even as he speaks,
and makes the two of them join hands together
in pledge of faith, and begs them to remember   730
him to his absent daughter and her son,
and with abundant sobs bids them farewell,
a grim foreboding troubling his mind.
     Once Philomela had been brought aboard
the painted ship, they rowed out of the harbor   735
into the channel and lost sight of land.
"My victory!" he cried. "At last the prize
that I have wished for is aboard this boat!"
     And scarcely able to defer his lust,
the barbarian exults, and keeps his eyes   740
fixed firmly on his now defenseless prize,
exactly as when Jove's great bird of prey,
the eagle, drops into his lofty nest
the hare gripped in his talons, and the prey
and captor both know there is no escape.   745
     Their journey done, the ship is brought to shore:
Tereus drags the daughter of the king
to an upland hut, deep in those ancient woods,
where pallid, trembling, utterly in terror,

she tearfully asks where her sister is;   750
he locks her in and openly admits
his shameful passion and his wicked plan,
then overwhelms the virgin all alone.
In vain she cries repeatedly for help
from father, sister, from the gods above.   755
    And after he was done with her, she shuddered
like a young lamb, broken by an old gray wolf
and flung aside, who cannot yet believe
that she is safe; or like a wounded dove,
her plumage brightly stained with her own blood,   760
who trembles with her dread that the sharp claws
which have embraced and raked her will return.
    When she recovered from her shock, she tore
her unbound hair and scratched and beat her arms
like one bereft. With hands turned out, she cried,   765
"Oh, what a dreadful thing you've done to me,
barbarian! You bloody-minded rogue!
Neither the charge my father laid on you,
nor his loving tears, nor my sister's care,
nor my virginity, nor your wedding vows—   770
none of these things meant anything to you!
    "And now the very order of our lives,
our relationships, are all confused!
I have been made the rival of my sister,
and you a bigamist! Procne my enemy!   775
O treacherous man! Why don't you kill me now,
and leave no heinous crime still uncommitted!
Would you had done so before bedding me
so shamefully, for then I would have gone,
an innocent shade, down to the world below.   780
    "Nevertheless, if the gods are watching this,
if heavenly power means anything at all,
if, with my honor, all has not been lost,
somehow or other I will punish you;
I'll cast aside my modesty and speak   785
of what you've done; if I escape this place,
I'll go among the people with my tale;
imprisoned here, my voice will fill the trees
and wring great sobs of grief from senseless rocks!
Heaven will hear me, and what gods there are,   790
if there are any gods in all of heaven!"
    Such words provoke the savage tyrant's wrath
and fear in equal measure; spurred by both,
he draws the sword he carried from its sheath
and, seizing her by her hair, forces her arms   795
behind her back and binds her.

Philomela,
for whom the sword had given hope of death,
eagerly offers him her throat, but he,
with a pair of pincers, takes her tongue instead,
which calls (as though protesting this offense)   800
her father's name out in a garbled voice,
before the tyrant's sword has severed it.

    Its stump throbs in her mouth, while the tongue itself
falls to the black earth trembling and murmuring,
and twitching as it flings itself about,   805
just as a serpent's severed tail will do;
and with what little life is left it, seeks
its mistress's feet. And even after this—
one scarcely can believe it, but they say
that even after this, the man continued   810
to violate her mutilated body.

    And after these outrages, he returned
to Procne, who at sight of him inquired
about her sister. Tereus replied
with practiced sobs and a convincing tale   815
of how she died—a story that his tears
made altogether credible. His wife
rips from her back the golden-bordered robe
and puts on black for mourning, and constructs
a needless sepulcher; and with the hands   820
that his lies have deceived, she offers gifts
in expiation of her sister's death,
and prematurely mourns her sister's fate.

    And now the Sun has journeyed through one year;
what can poor Philomela do? A guard   825
is set upon her to prevent escape,
a wall of solid stone surrounds her hut;
her speechless lips cannot address the wrongs
that have been done her.
                  And yet from suffering
comes native wit, and often cleverness   830
is born of misery. Upon her loom,
she hangs a Thracian web and starts to weave
threads of deep purple on a white background,
depicting the crime.
             And when her work is done,
she rolls it up and hands it to the slave   835
attending her; and by mute gestures asks
the slave to bring this package to her mistress;
and so she does, not knowing what it holds.

    The wife of the cruel tyrant opens it

and in it reads her sister's wretched fate,   840
and (it is quite amazing that she can)
keeps silent, for her grief restrains her speech;
her questing tongue cannot produce the words
sufficient to her outrage: no tears now,
for good and evil are all heaped together,   845
and her imagination wholly bent
on one and only one course: punishment.
    Every third year the Thracian women join
in a great throng to celebrate the rites
of Bacchus: now that time has come again.   850
Night is aware of what is happening;
by night Mount Rhodope is resonant
with the disturbing sound of clashing cymbals;
by night the queen emerges from her palace,
outfits and arms herself as for the frenzy: 855
she wraps her head in vines and drapes a deerskin
over her left shoulder—in her left hand
a staff the Bacchantes carry, called the thyrsus.
    Now through the woods she hastens with a crowd
of her attendants; roused to madness by   860
her grief, O Bacchus, she pretends your frenzy:
comes to that hut far from the beaten path
and crying out, "*Ulula!*" and "*Euhoy!*"[8]
breaks the door down, snatches up her sister
and outfits her as one of the Bacchantes,   865
conceals her ravaged face with ivy leaves,
and brings the stunned girl back into her palace.
    As soon as Philomela understood
she was inside *his* unspeakable abode,
the poor girl shuddered and turned pale with dread;   870
but Procne brought her to a hiding place,
where she removed her ritual adornments,
showing the face a monstrous crime had shamed,
and held her closely in a warm embrace;
but Philomela could not bear to meet   875
her sister's pleading eyes, for in her own,
the wrong done her had wronged her sister too.
    She kept her glance fixed firmly on the ground,
yearning to swear by all the gods in heaven
that her disgrace was brought about by force,   880
if only hands could speak.
                  But Procne blazed,
unable to control her anger, and,

---

8. Ritual cries of the Bacchantes.

sweeping aside her sister's tears, she said,
"No weeping now—it is the time for swords,
or for whatever else surpasses swords: 885
my sister, there is no abomination
that I am unprepared to undertake,
whether I torch the palace roof and fling
Tereus, the mastermind of all our woes,
into the blazing ruins of this house,   890
or pluck his tongue out or remove his eyes,
or sever the member which has brought you shame,
or by a thousand wounds minutely given,
expel the guilty spirit from his body!
I am prepared for some important work,   895
but what it will be, I am still uncertain."
      While Procne was still speaking to her sister,
Itys came to his mother, who at once
realized what she could do, and said,
taking him in with her unfeeling eyes,   900
"How very like his father the boy is!"
And that was all she said. Outwardly silent
yet inwardly ablaze, she planned the crime.
      And yet, when he came up and greeted her,
throwing his little arms around her neck,   905
and kissed her with all the innocence of youth,
she was quite moved by this; her anger broke,
and her unwilling eyes were suddenly
full of hot tears that she could not control;
but as she felt her sense of purpose falter   910
out of an excess of maternal love,
she turned to look upon her sister's face,
and then turned back and forth between them, wildly:
      "And why does this one babble pleasantries,
while that one's silent? What has got her tongue?   915
How can it be that this one calls me mother,
while that one cannot call me sister? Look!
Your husband is the answer to this riddle,
unworthy daughter of royal Pandion!
The only crime against a man like this   920
is to behave with natural affection!"
      Now resolute, she carries Itys off,
just as a tiger on the Ganges' banks
will drag a nursing fawn through the dense woods,
until they reach an unfrequented room   925
deep within the palace.
                        He pleads with his hands,
aware of what is just about to happen,
and cries out, "Mother!" reaching for her neck,

as Procne drives the blade into his side
and does not turn away. That single blow   930
sufficed to kill the boy, but Philomela
severed his windpipe also with the sword.

    He was still alive as they dismembered him.
Gobbets of flesh in the cauldron wildly
danced as she made a fine broth of the boy,   935
while other parts were hissing on the grill.

    Now Tereus, all unaware, receives
an invitation to attend a feast
which his wife falsely claims to be a rite
of the Athenians: husbands only may   940
partake of it; all slaves are sent away
and all attendants: Tereus dines alone.

    And he, on his ancestral banquet throne
begins to feed and shortly stuffs his gut
with flesh and blood that he himself begot,   945
and in the blindness of his heart, commands,
"Bring Itys here!"
                  Procne is unable
to hide her savage joy; and eager now
to be the bearer of misfortune cries,
"The one that you are seeking is within!"   950

    He looks about and asks, where can he be?
He calls and asks once more; until, disheveled,
her long hair matted with the stain of slaughter,
Philomela leaps up and flings the bloody
head of young Itys in his father's face,   955
and never more than then did she desire
the faculty of speech, so that she might
most fittingly express the joy she felt!

    With a great cry he overturns the table
and calls upon the Furies to assist him;   960
and now, if only he were able to,
he'd open up his own breast and remove
the half-digested remnants of that feast;
he weeps and calls himself his own son's tomb;
and with his naked blade pursues the two   965
daughters of Pandion; you would have thought
that the Athenians were poised on wings:
and so they were! One flies off to the woods,
the other finds her refuge under roofs.

    And even now, the signs of what they did   970
are visible in marks upon their breasts
and in the bloody stains upon their plumage.

    Fast to fly after them, he's given wings
by grief and by desire for revenge—

he turns into a stiffly crested bird   975
with a huge beak in place of his long sword:
the hoopoe, which seems armed as though for war.[9]

Boreas and Orithyia

Pandion's life was shortened by this grief,
which sent his shade to Tartarus before
old age could claim him. The royal scepter   980
and management of Athens and its affairs
passed on to Erectheus, who was famed
equally for justice and for skill in war.
    Four sons he sired and four daughters too,
and of the latter, two were famous beauties: 985
Aeolus' grandson, Cephalus, was made
a happy man, with Procris as his wife;
but Boreas, a northerner like Tereus,[1]
of Thrace, was blamed for what his kinsman did,
and for a great long while, the god was kept   990
from Orithyia, the prize he sought,
while he proceeded by pleas and prayers
to court her, rather than by using force.
    And when his fancy speeches got him nowhere,
reverted to his usual harsh anger: 995
"Why did I ever give my weapons up?"
he asked. "For without Cruelty and Might,
my Rage and Menace, I deserved to lose!
    "Most unbecoming of me to rely
on prayers to move them! Force is my strong suit: 1000
by force I drive the heavy-laden clouds,
by force I agitate the ocean's waves
and uproot the knotty oak; I heap the earth
with snow, I pelt the ground with icy hail;
likewise, when I get going in the sky   1005
with my brother winds, why, I contend so fiercely
that middle heaven rings with our concourse
and fires burst forth from the hollow clouds;
likewise, when I descend to the vaulted caves
below the surface of the earth, and brace   1010
my back against the lower vaults and heave,
why, even shades in the underworld are shaken!
    "Now that's the sort of tack I should have taken

9. Procne turns into a nightingale and Philomela becomes a house swallow.
1. Boreas is presented to us first as a person, then as a personification of the north wind.
   Ovid concludes this book with another tale of rape, but one where brutality is concealed
   by narrative discretion and the comic bluster of its protagonist. The tale ends happily,
   with the birth of two winged heroes, Zetes and Calaïs, unnamed by Ovid.

to get myself a wife; I should have *made*
Erectheus my kinsman—not just prayed!"   1015
    And with these words (or words no less impressive)
Boreas smartly clapped his wings together,
which shook the earth and terrified the ocean;
he trailed his dusty mantle over mountains
and swept the plains below; concealed in darkness,   1020
he gathered up the trembling Orithyia
in his tawny wings; and as he flew, their action
more fiercely fanned the fires of his love,
nor did her captor check his flight
until he reached the city of the Cicones;   1025
here the Athenian became the bride
of the frigid tyrant, and in time became
a mother too, when she delivered twins
who had her features but their father's wings,
though not at birth: both boys were wingless then,   1030
and beardless underneath their golden locks;
but when their beards came in, the wings did too,
sprouting on either side as bird's wings do,
and cheeks grew tawny with new facial hair.[2]
    And so, when childhood passed and they were men,   1035
they sailed (together with the Minyans)[3]
over an unknown ocean in the first ship ever,
to seek the brightly shining Golden Fleece.[4]

2. A feathery transformation ends this tale, as in the one before it.
3. Many of the Argonauts were descended from Minyas, king of Orchomenos, whose daughters turned into bats in Book IV.
4. The prize sought by Jason and the band of Greek heroes aboard the *Argo*: the fleece of the ram that carried Phrixus, son of Athamas and Ino, to safety in the realm of Colchis when his parents sought to kill him. Received there by King Aeetes, Phrixus sacrificed the ram and presented its fleece to the king, with whom it remained until Jason captured it.

BOOK VII

Of the Ties That Bind

Medea and Jason[1]

Now they were plowing through the ocean's waves,
the Argonauts, in their Thessalian craft,
and Phineus they had already seen,
dragging his weary way through scant old age
in never-ending night; and the young sons   5
of the north wind had driven off the Harpies
that snatched the food out of the poor man's mouth;[2]
and after undergoing many trials
at the command of their famous leader, Jason,
they reached at last the swift and turbulent   10
brown waters of the river Phasis.
                 There,
while they present themselves and their demands
for the fleece that had been given to the king,
and he describes the great and terrible
labors they must accomplish to attain it,   15
the daughter of the king is overcome
by a passion which she struggles to resist
for a long time.
             But when her raging madness
will not submit to reason, she cries out,
"All your resistance is in vain, Medea;   20
what god opposes you, I do not know—
I wonder if this isn't love, so called,
or something rather like it—for why else
would these ordeals imposed upon the strangers
by my own father seem too harsh to me?   25
Because they *are!*
             "Why do I fear that one
whom I have only just now seen will die?
What is the power that can cause such fear?
There is a fire in your untried heart,
poor wretched girl! Dislodge it if you can!   30
I'd act more sanely, if I only could,
but this new power overwhelms my will;
reason advises this, and passion, that;

---

1. The book begins with the arrival of the Argonauts at the court of King Aeetes, and the kindling of Medea's passion for the hero Jason; her monologue reveals an interiority explored
at length with subtlety and understanding.
2. After blinding his own children, Phineus, a Thracian king, received the same punishment
from Jove, who ordered the Harpies (a trio of winged monsters, with women's faces and
vultures' bodies) to further torment him. He was saved by Zetes and Calaïs, the sons of
Boreas.

I see the better way, and I approve it,
while I pursue the worse.

                "O royal virgin, 35
why is it that you blaze now for this stranger?
Why dream of marriage in another world?
You love *this* land: surely it can furnish
a husband worthy of you?

                    "This man's fate—
whether he lives or dies—is up to heaven. 40
May he live, then! It's quite appropriate
for me to offer such a prayer as that,
even without my loving him at all.

    "But look at the heroic deeds of Jason!
What heartless wretch could be indifferent 45
to youth and breeding joined with manliness?
Absent these qualities, who would not be
moved by the beauty of his countenance?
My heart was moved by it, most certainly.

    "And now, unless I come to Jason's aid, 50
he will be scorched by fire-breathing bulls
and clash with enemies sprung from the soil
that he himself has seeded, or be given
as sacrifice to sate the greedy dragon!

    "If I permit this, I'll confess myself 55
a tiger's daughter with a heart of stone!
But why can I not look upon his dying
and not defile my eyes? Why can't I urge
his enemies against him, cheer on the bull,
the earthborn warriors, the sleepless dragon? 60
Because the gods wish him a better fate!
And yet not prayers are needed here, but deeds!

    "Will I betray the kingdom of my father,
only to have the stranger whom I save
set sail without me for another's bed, 65
leaving Medea to her punishment?
If he could do that, leave me for another,
let the ingrate die!

                "But no: that isn't in him,
not in his face, not in his noble spirit,
not in a man as beautiful as he, 70
that I should fear duplicity from him,
or his neglecting what I am deserved.

    "Besides, he'll give his word to me beforehand,
and I will call the gods as witnesses
of our compact. Why fear, when all is safe? 75
Prepare for action now, without delay;
you will have Jason's gratitude forever,

he'll join himself to you with solemn vows,
and you'll be praised as his deliverer
by throngs of women throughout all of Greece!   80
    "So shall I then sail off, abandoning
my sister, brother, father, gods, and homeland?
My father is cruel and my homeland crude;
my brother is no more than a mere child,
and my sister sides with *me* in this affair.   85
Within my breast the greatest of all gods
has found his residence! I do not leave
greatness, but elope with him to seek it!
    "I will be called 'Savior of Grecian Youth,'
and come to know a better land, and cities   90
famous, even here, for art and culture;
and that young man, whom I would not exchange
for all the wealth of this world, at my side;
and with him as my husband, in felicity,
I'll be considered heaven's favorite,   95
and with my forehead I will touch the stars.
    "But what of . . . oh, what *are* their names, those clashing
mountains in midocean people speak of?
And what of ship-devouring Charybdis,
that sucks the sea in and then spits it out?   100
What of rapacious Scylla, surrounded by
her savage dogs, baying off Sicily?[3]
    "Nothing to me: holding the one I love,
lying contentedly in Jason's lap,
I'll make the long sea voyage in his arms,   105
and nothing fear unless I fear for him.
    "Marriage you call it then, Medea, do you?
Aren't you merely covering your guilt
with a deceptive name? Just look ahead:
how great a sin it is you're thinking of!   110
Turn from this crime and flee while you are able."
She spoke: before her stood stern Rectitude,
earnest Devotion, blushing Modesty;
and Love, defeated, now prepared to fly.
    Then she went off to Hecate's ancient altar,   115
hidden deep in the forest's deepest shades.
Here she was resolute, and her impulsive
ardor would appear to be extinguished—
but broke out once again at sight of Jason:
her cheeks reddened, and a suffusing glow   120

---

3. Medea turns her mind to the terrors of the journey: the Symplegades were two large rocks
  in the Euxine Sea that occasionally crashed together, smashing anything between them;
  Charybdis was a whirlpool that sucked in and spewed out seawater; Scylla, a sea monster,
  is described in Books XIII (p. 203) and XIV (p. 379).

spread across her countenance completely,
as when a spark that has been hidden under
a crust of ash is nourished by a breeze
and comes to life again as it's stirred up,
regaining all the vigor it once had;   125
just so her smoldering love, which you'd have thought
was almost out, came blazing up anew,
to see the young man standing in her presence,
and—as it happened—looking even better
than usual. You would have understood   130
and pardoned her for her infatuation.

    And when he took her hand and spoke to her
in a modest tone, and pleaded for her help,
and gave his word that he would marry her,
she wept profusely as she answered him: 135
"I clearly see what I'm about to do:
not ignorance beguiles me now, but love.
Through my good offices, you will be saved;
fulfill the promise you have made me then!"

    He swore by Hecate and by whatever other   140
deities might dwell within that grove,
and by the father of his own prospective
father-in-law, the all-beholding Sun,[4]
and by the peril of his coming trials;
so she believed him and at once passed on   145
the magic herbs; from her, he learned their uses,
then joyfully withdrew to his own tent.

    The flickering stars were scattered by the Dawn:
the folk assembled on the field of Mars,
then placed themselves on the surrounding heights;   150
and in their midst, the king himself was seated,
conspicuously clad in purple robes
and holding a scepter carved from ivory.

    But look! Two fire-breathing, bronze-shod bulls,
exhaling, scorch the grasses underfoot!   155
And just as fiery furnaces resound,
or limestone hisses in an earthen kiln
and then ignites when sprinkled with fresh water,
so those two rumbled with their pent-up blaze,
and bellowed from scorched throats; nevertheless,   160
the son of Aeson[5] dares to stand against them.
At his approach, they turn their dreadful faces
to glare at him and drop their mighty horns,
tipped with iron; now their cloven hooves

---

4. King Aeetes is the offspring of the Sun.
5. Jason.

pound the powdery earth, and now they fill   165
the smoky air with bellowing that blazes!
   The Agonauts are paralyzed with fear;
Jason ignores those flaming exhalations
and presses on (what potent medications
Medea has given him!), ever closer,   170
until his right hand daringly caresses
their dangling dewlaps.
               Now he yokes
his team, and makes them draw the plow across
that field unused to prior cultivation:
the Colchians marvel, and the Argonauts   175
raise a great cry that lifts up every spirit.
   Then, from a bronze helmet, Jason removes
the serpent's teeth and sows them in the field.
Earth softens seed that had been steeped beforehand
in virulent poison; and now, as growth begins,   180
those scattered teeth commence to take new forms,
as when an infant in its mother's womb
takes on a human shape, and not until
its separate parts have been composed together
does it emerge into the common air;   185
so when their human forms had been accomplished
in the quickened womb of pregnant Mother Earth,
they rose up from that newly fertile field,
and—an even greater miracle—the arms
they bore to warfare had been born with them!   190
   But when the Greeks observed the men preparing
to fling their sharpened spears at Jason's head,
their faces and their spirits fell together;
and even she who'd made him safe was frightened
at seeing one man set on by so many,   195
and turning pale, she sat there cold and bloodless.
And fearful that her magic herbs should prove
ineffectual, she murmured incantations
and summoned secret powers to his aid.
   He lifts a heavy rock and sends it flying   200
into their midst, which redirects their rage
against each other: those earthborn brothers
die of mutual wounds in bitter civil war.
   The Greeks congratulate the winner then,
eager to hold him warmly in embrace;   205
you also wanted to embrace the winner,
barbarian maiden, but restrained yourself
out of your fear of what the folk would say.
You did what was permitted you to do:
gave joyful thanks in silence for the charms   210
and for the gods who had accomplished this.

All that remained was to deploy your herbs
against the vigilant custodian
whose elevated crest and thrice-forked tongue
and curving fangs proclaim him as the dragon   215
who guards the tree that holds the Golden Fleece.
    But after Jason doused the wakeful snake
with juice of the plant that brings oblivion,
and thrice recited words to summon sleep,
the spell that pacifies the raging seas   220
and stills the roaring brook, a slumber sealed
those eyes that had not known its sway before.
    And now that haughty hero, Aeson's son,
obtained the golden trophy and—the one
who'd made it possible—his trophy bride,   225
and carried both off to Iolchos harbor.[6]

Medea and Aeson

Delighted that their sons have all returned,
Thessalian parents gratefully bring gifts
and burn great heaps of incense on the pyre,
as a dedicated bull with gilded horns   230
falls to the blade.
                    But Aeson absents himself
from the solemnities of this thanksgiving,
worn-out by the great weight of all his years
and near to death.
                    His son, the hero, says,
"Dearest, to whom I must confess I owe   235
my very life, although you've given all,
and even though all that you've given me
has far exceeded all my expectations,
if by your spells you could accomplish this
(and nothing is impossible for them!),   240
I'd have you take some years from my own life
and add the subtracted portion to my father's!"
He wept without restraint.
                    Medea was moved
by the great devotion shown in his request;
the image of the father she'd abandoned   245
came to her mind, so unlike her husband's.
    Without revealing how she felt, she said,
"Dearest, what blasphemy falls from your lips!
Do you believe me able to take years
from you and give them to another man?   250

6. Iolchos was Jason's birthplace in Thessaly.

Why, Hecate will never grant me this—
you ask for what has never been permitted.
  "But Jason, I will nonetheless attempt
to offer you an even greater gift:
with my own feats of magic, I will try   255
to lengthen your father's life by many years,
and not by revoking any years of yours,
if Hecate will only aid me now,
and nod assent to this great enterprise."[7]
  Three nights must pass before the moon's horns close   260
into a circle; now when it is complete,
and in its fullness gazes down on earth,
she sets out walking barefoot from her house,
with garments loosened and with unbound hair
cascading down her back, and makes her way   265
without companion, straying through the deep
silence of midnight, when men and birds and beasts
are all released into profound repose,
with not a peep or murmur from the hedgerow,
and in the trees the leaves are stilly silent,   270
and even the dewy air is motionless;
she lifts her arms up to the brilliant stars,
and spins around: once, twice, thrice;
and thrice she pours branch water on her hair,
and thrice she cries out wailing in the night,   275
and then kneels down upon the earth to pray:
  "O Night," she cries, "most faithful guardian
of secrecies, and you, O golden Stars,
who with the moon relieve the blazing sun;
and you as well, three-headed Hecate,   280
who are aware of our undertakings,
and who assist the mage's spells and arts;
and you too, Earth, provider of potent herbs,
you, Breezes, Winds, Mountains, Rivers, Lakes,
you gods of every grove, and every god   285
of night, be present now! For with your aid,
when I have willed it, I have caused the streams
to flow back in between their startled banks
up to their sources; I've calmed the raging flood
and I've enraged the calm seas with my spells;   290
I drive the clouds off, and I bring them back;
I chase the winds away, and I recall them;
I break the jaws of serpents with my spells,
and I uproot the living rocks and oaks;

7. Medea now reveals herself as an accomplished magician.

I make whole forests move; by my command   295
the mountains tremble, and the deep earth groans,
and spirits of the dead come from their tombs.
    "You also, Moon, I draw you from the sky,
though clattering bronze attempt to aid your labors;[8]
the chariot of my grandfather Sun   300
grows pale at the power of my incantations,
and Dawn grows pale from thinking of my poisons.
    "For me you dulled the sharp flames of the bulls,
bending their fretful necks to bear the plow;
you brought the serpent-born to slay themselves   305
in cruel warfare, and you lulled the rude
protector of the Golden Fleece to sleep,
and with its guardian beguiled, you sent
his treasure sailing off to Grecian cities.
    "Now I must have a potion to renew   310
old age, restoring it to youthful bloom.
And you will give me one, for not in vain
do the stars above me flicker their assent,
and not in vain does my chariot appear,
drawn by its matched pair of flying dragons."   315
    And there it was: her chariot, sent down
from the aethereal regions. Once aboard,
she stroked her dragons' necks and flicked their reins
lightly, and they ascended; below her lay
Thessalian Tempe; she set her dragons for   320
those regions that were sources of her herbs:
and she descried below plants found on Ossa
and lofty Pelion, on Othrys, on Pindus,
and (larger than that last one) on Olympus;
the herbs that pleased her she took, root and all,   325
or snipped off leaves with her bronze pruning hook.
    Many appealing herbs were found along
the banks of the Apidanus, and many more
along the Amphrysus, nor were *you* exempt,
Enipeus, from her provisioning,   330
and Peneus and Sperchios and Boebe;
and from Euboean Anthedon she seized
a life-prolonging herb not yet made famous
by the effects that it produced on Glaucus.[9]
    After nine days and nights had seen Medea   335
in her dragon-driven chariot, traversing
the skies above those regions, she returned

---

8. Making a great deal of noise with pots and pans was the approved Roman way of getting an eclipse to end.
9. Glaucus describes the effect himself in Book XIII (p. 203).

to her own home; her reptiles had been touched
only by the *odors* of those herbs,
and yet they shed the skins of their old age!   340
    Nearing her house she halted on its threshold:
and there, beneath the blue sky's canopy,
without allowing Jason to embrace her,
she built two altars out of turf; on the right
was Hecate's—and Youth she gave the other.   345
    She decorated them with sacred boughs
fetched out of the forest; near the altars,
she dug a pair of trenches in the earth,
and there performed her rites. She slit the throat
of a black sheep and let his blood drain out   350
into the trenches; over it she poured
a goblet full of honey, liquified,
and then a goblet full of tepid milk,
while praying to the gods who dwell below,
begging the king of shadows and his bride,   355
stolen from earth, that they should be less eager
to cheat an old man of the breath of life.
    And then, when by her prayers and incantations
the underworld was calmed, she had them bring
Aeson's exhausted body to the altars;   360
and once her spells had put him in a sleep
resembling death, she stretched the old man out
on a bed of strewn grasses, then sent her mate
and his attendants off, commanding them
to keep far hence, lest their profaning eyes   365
should violate the mysteries.
                            They left
as she had ordered them, and then, her hair
unbound like one of the Bacchantes, Medea
walked all around the blazing altars, steeping
her torches in the trenches black with blood,   370
until, igniting them upon the altar stones,
she purified the old man three times each,
with water and with fire and with sulphur.
    Meanwhile the potent brew in her bronze cauldron
is on the boil, leaping with thick white foam;   375
in it are roots dug up in Thessaly
cooking with seeds and flowers and black juice;
she adds some pebbles from the Orient,
some sand grains washed by Ocean's ebbing tide,
some hoarfrost gathered in the full moon's light,   380
the nasty wings and flesh of a screech owl,
the innards of a werewolf, which can change
his feral mask into a human face,

the scaly skin of a Libyan water snake,
an old stag's liver, and the head and eggs   385
of an ancient crow that had lived longer than
nine human generations.

                    When, with these,
and with a thousand other such ingredients
(whose names we needn't bother mentioning),
the miracle to come had been arranged,   390
the foreign woman took a long-dead branch
from a fruitful olive tree and stirred her pot,
mixing it thoroughly from top to bottom.

   But look! Almost at once, that stick turned green,
and just a short time later put out leaves,   395
and suddenly was loaded down with fruit!
Wherever her bronze cauldron overflowed
and the hot potion splashed upon the ground,
flowers and tender grass turned the earth green.

   Medea, seeing this, unsheathed her sword   400
and slit the old man's throat to drain his blood,
which she at once replaced with her elixir;
as soon as Aeson had consumed the stuff
(poured either in his mouth or in his wound),
his beard and hair immediately changed   405
from white to black, his gauntness and his pallor
and aura of decay took their departure,
as all his wrinkles filled out with new flesh
and withered limbs regained their muscle tone:
Aeson was now astonished to recall   410
himself as he had been four decades past!

   (Bacchus observed this wonder from on high,
and realizing how his aged nurses
could be rejuvenated by her gift
at once obtained it from the sorceress.)[1]   415

Medea and Pelias[2]

Now, so that guile might not go out of fashion,
Medea feigned a breakup with her husband
and ran off as a suppliant to Pelias;
since he himself was burdened with the weight
of old age too, his daughters welcomed her;   420
pretending friendship, the cunning Colchian

---

1. Ovid's fleeting reference implies the existence of a tale about Bacchus no longer in circulation.
2. Other versions describe a history of trouble between the half-brothers Aeson and Pelias: Pelias sends Jason off on the quest for the Golden Fleece and, in one version, kills Aeson while his son is away; when Jason returns, Medea persuades him to let her avenge him.

took the girls in and shortly won them over.
   And while she entertained them all with stories
of her remarkable accomplishments,
she told at length of how she had restored   425
Aeson to his prime. Her story raised the hope
among her listeners that by such arts
their father too could be rejuvenated:
they begged her aid, imploring her to name
her own reward, however great it was.   430
   A moment's silence while she seemed in doubt,
as by her fictive indecisiveness
she kept the pleading girls in high suspense—
but when she'd given them her word, she added,
"We'll have a demonstration, so that you   435
may be more confident about this gift
I offer you: your oldest sheep, the aged
bellwether of your flock, will soon become,
through my concoctions, a young lamb again."
   Worn-out by his innumerable years,   440
the woolly one, with great horns curving round
his bulging temples, was brought forth at once;
slitting his throat with her Thessalian blade
(which his exhausted blood could barely stain)
the sorcer woman quickly plunged his carcass   445
into the cauldron, where the heat reduced it,
and where his horns (and years) were burned away.
   A feeble "*Baa, baa*" comes from deep within:
to their astonishment, a little lamb
skips out and eagerly essays a bleat,   450
then scampers off—to find a milky teat!
   The daughters of Pelias were dumbstruck then,
for she had done exactly as she promised!
Even more eagerly, they urged her on.
Three times now Phoebus had unyoked his team   455
after their plunge into the western stream;
on the fourth night, the stars were glittering
when the deceitful daughter of Aeetes
brought up to boil a cauldron of clear water,
and added to it herbs of no real power.   460
A death-like sleep (produced by magic spells)
had quite unstrung the king and his defenders.
   As ordered by the Colchian, his daughters,
slipping across the threshold of his room,
surround his bed: "Slackers! Why hesitate?   465
Unsheathe your swords and spill his ancient gore,
and I'll refill his veins with youthful blood.
Your aged father's life is in your hands;

if you have any love for him at all,
if you're not merely stirred by empty hopes,   470
then give your father what you owe him, now:
drive his old age off with your sharp weapons,
let his blood out by plunging in your swords!"

　　Urged on by her and by their piety,
each child commits the worst crime that a child   475
can possibly commit against a parent,
and only to avoid a much worse crime!
Unable nonetheless to watch themselves,
they turn away and blindly strike at him.

　　Bleeding profusely, leaning on one elbow,   480
he struggles to get up, though slashed to ribbons,
and as he raises arms in supplication
amid a thicket of swords, cries out to them,
"What are you doing, daughters? Why arm yourselves
to slay your father?" Their hands—and spirits—fall;   485
he would have gone on speaking, but Medea
slit his throat and plunged his mangled body
into the cauldron full of boiling water.

The Flight of Medea[3]

And she, had she not taken to the air,
escaping in her dragon-driven carriage,   490
would not have gone unpunished for that deed.

　　Aloft, she fled above Mount Pelion,
where Chiron makes his home, and over Othrys,
famed site of the adventures of Cerambus,
who managed to escape Deucalion's flood   495
on wings provided him by mountain nymphs
when the heavy earth was being overwhelmed
by the engulfing waters of the sea.

　　On her left she passed Aeolian Pitane
with its gigantic serpent made of stone,   500
and Ida's grove, where once the son of Bacchus
rustled a calf; in order to protect him,
his father changed the boy into a stag;
she passed the site where Helen's lover lies
beneath a meager monument of sand,   505
and passed those fields which Maera terrified
with her strange barking; flew above the city
of Eurypylus, where the Coan women
were changed to cows when Hercules set off
on his great expedition against Troy;   510

---

3. Ovid's own invention, a travelogue of minor metamorphoses, none meriting further development or annotation, by means of which Medea gets to Athens and Theseus gets into the story.

and over Rhodes, that island dear to Phoebus,
and Ialysos, home of the Telechines,
whose eyes so blighted everything they saw
that Jupiter condemned them to be plunged
under the waters governed by his brother;   515
she passed the ancient city of Carthaea
on the Isle of Cea, where Alcidamas once
would find himself astonished by the strange
metamorphosis of daughter into dove.

   And after that she saw the Hyrian lake   520
and Tempe, home of Cycnus, celebrated
for his sudden transformation into swan:
for at this boy's imperious command,
Phylius tamed wild birds and a fierce lion
and brought them to him as love-offerings;   525
ordered to overcome a bull as well,
he did so, but when he saw his passion
so utterly ignored and unrewarded,
refused to give the latest of these presents
to the one who sought it; enraged, the boy   530
cried out, "You'll wish you had!" and straightway leapt
from a high rock: all thought he had been slain,
but changed into a swan, he hung in midair,
supported by strong pinions, white as snow;
his mother, Hyrie, quite unaware   535
of his deliverance, dissolved in tears,
and turned into the lake that bears her name.

   Nearby is Pleuron, where, on fluttering wings,
Combe, the daughter of Ophius, escaped
the death her sons had planned. Medea saw   540
the fields of Latona's Calaurea,
fields well aware of how a king and queen
were also changed to birds. Now on her right,
Cyllene passes by, where Menephron,
just like a beast, would bed down with his mother;   545
and in the distance she beholds Cephisus,
weeping for the end his grandson came to,
changed to a tumid sea calf by Apollo;
and near him was Eumelus, who had tears
because his son had changed into a bird.   550
   To Corinth then she came[4] on dragon wing,
Corinth, the city of the sacred spring;

---

4. Ovid briskly summarizes the tragic events following Medea's arrival; when Jason aban-
   dons her for the daughter of Creon, the Corinthian king, she poisons both father and
   daughter and then murders the children she had by Jason, from whose wrath she flees in
   her dragon-borne chariot. These events would have been familiar to Ovid's audience from
   their treatment in Euripedes's *Medea* and perhaps from the lost tragedy that Ovid wrote
   on this subject.

for here, according to an old tradition,
mankind sprang from wet funguses by fission.[5]
  But after the new bride that Jason took   555
was poisoned by the old wife he forsook,
and fisherfolk off Corinth glimpsed through haze
the ruined palace of the king ablaze,
the blade that dripped with her own children's gore
enraged their father, whom she fled before,   560
her fatal vengeance leaving all undone!
  Now, once again, the dragons of the Sun
bore her aloft, off to the citadel
of Athens, where the citizens all tell
the tale of Phene, their most righteous queen,   565
who, with her mate, Periphas, was last seen
flying side by side in tight formation;
and they recount another transformation,
that of Polypemon's Alcyone,
leaning on her new wings—a halcyon!   570
  Aegeus[6] welcomed the new refugee,
and by that act of hospitality
condemned himself; the king, not satisfied
to have her as his guest, made her his bride.

Medea, Aegeus, and Theseus

Then Theseus appeared, a son unknown   575
to his own father;[7] the valorous young man
has pacified the land between two seas.
Medea, wishing to destroy him, mixed
a cup with poison brought from Scythia
a long time past; they say this poison came   580
from the jaws of Cerberus.
         There is a cave
as black as blindness, with a gloomy mouth,
and a path that leads down to the underworld.
Upward along that path, great Hercules
dragged Cerberus on adamantine chains,   585
while the great beast struggled hard against him,
and turned his eyes away from the harsh daylight.

---

5. A tradition known only from what Ovid says about it here.
6. Having fled Corinth, Medea arrives at Athens, where Ovid cannot resist two more metamorphoses. Periphas, a king so just that he was given honors belonging to Zeus, provoked
the latter's envy; Zeus turned the king into an eagle and his wife Phene into a vulture.
Alcyone, granddaughter of Polypemon, was turned into a halcyon. (See Ovid's tales *Ceyx
and Alcyone* in Book XI.)
7. Theseus was born out of wedlock to Aethra, the daughter of Pittheus, king of Troezene.
Theseus was raised in Troezene, unacknowledged by his father Aegeus until Theseus's
arrival in Athens.

Now goaded to a frenzy by his rage,
he filled the air with barking from three throats,
and spattered the green fields with his white foam.   590
They say those foam flecks grew, and taking root
were nourished by the richness of that soil,
and found in it the power to do ill;
the rustics call them, since they grow on rocks,
the aconites, or "flowers lacking soil."   595
    This poison, through Medea's treachery,
father Aegeus offered his own son
as to an enemy, and Theseus,
all unaware of any ill intent,
had taken it and raised the cup to drink,   600
when his father recognized the family crest
on the ivory hilt of the hero's sword,
and swept the poisoned goblet from his lips.
Medea fled the death that would have followed
in a cloud cover summoned by her spells.   605
    The father, though delighted by his son's
deliverance, was nonetheless astounded
by just how closely they had come to ruin
and so had fires kindled on the altars
and offered gifts up to the gods; now hefty   610
axe blows descended on the brawny necks
of bulls whose horns were gaily draped with ribbons.
    No day more festive ever dawned on Athens,
say the Athenians, than this one was,
as elders and those of undistinguished rank   615
commingled happily, with wine inspiring
the song of praise they made up for the hero:[8]

"Now *Marathon* lies at your feet,
The slayer of the *Bull of Crete*;
To you the men of *Cromyon* bow   620
For sticking the *Enormous Sow*;

"You sent the hero, *Periphetes,*
With giant club, right to his knees
In *Epidauria,* and you slew
Fierce, club-wielding *Procrustes,* too!   625

8. The hero is praised by an enumeration of his glorious exploits: he slew a great bull that
was terrifying the farmers of Marathon, and (like Hercules) killed a wild pig rampaging at
Cromyon. Procrustes famously tied his prisoners to a bed that they were either length-
ened or shortened to fit. Cercyon challenged travelers to fight with him and was slain by
Theseus, as was Sinis; Sciron was another criminal dispatched by the hero and metamorphosed by the poet. The episodes are not in chronological order.

"In *Eleusis*, the dear town
Of *Ceres*, you killed *Cercyon*;
Sinis you killed, and with due cause,
Who violated our laws:

"He'd bend two pine trees of great height   630
Until their tips were touching, quite;
The victim in between them tied,
Released, was scattered far and wide;

"The coastal road is now secure
Since vicious *Sciron* is no more: 635
Even his bones were long denied
A resting place by the restless tide

"Until they hardened, as folks claim,
Into those cliffs which bear his name;
Count your good deeds and then your days,   640
Deeds are more numerous to praise;

"To honor the heroic labors
Of our prince, his subject-neighbors
In gratitude now offer up
Libations poured from every cup."   645

    Prayers and applause inspired by the hero
filled the palace; and nowhere in that city
was there a place where sorrow could be found.

King Minos Threatens War[9]

And yet, no joy is ever unalloyed,
and worry worms its way into delight;   650
so Aegeus, rejoicing in his son's
return, was not completely without care,
for Minos was preparing to make war;
though powerful in fleet and infantry,
his greatest strength was his paternal wrath   655
over the death of his son, Androgeos,
whom he intended, justly, to avenge.[1]
    Before declaring war, he sought out allies,
ranging the Aegean in that swift fleet

---

9. The Athenians are now threatened by the great maritime power of Cretan Minos. This
   episode may be Ovid's invention, meant to shift the scene now to the island of Aegina.
1. Androgeos was slain when King Aegeus either sent him to battle the Bull of Marathon or
   had him killed in an ambush. As punishment, Minos demanded seven Athenian youths
   and seven maidens to be sent to him every nine years as a sacrifice to the Minotaur.

by which his awesome power was maintained.   660
He brought Anaphe over to his cause
by promises, and Astypalaea
by threats of war; low-lying Mykonos
came over next, then chalk-famed Cimolus
and Syros, known for its abundant thyme;   665
then level Seriphos, the marble cliffs
of Paros, and then Siphnos, once betrayed
by wicked Arne, who, acquiring
the gold her avarice implored, became
a thieving jackdaw with black feet and wings,   670
who even now takes pleasure in bright gold.
    However, Oliaros and Didyme,
as well as Tenos, Andros and Gyaros,
and Peparethos, rich in glistening olives,
declined to aid the fleet.   Then Minos sailed   675
west to Oenopia, the realm of Aeacus,
for that was the name given to this island
in the old days, until the present king
renamed it for his mother, Aegina.
    A crowd surged forward, eager to become   680
acquainted with a man of such great fame.
Telamon greeted him, then Peleus,
and Phocus, youngest of the king's three sons,
and then the king himself appeared, Aeacus,
slow with the burden of his many years,   685
and asked King Minos what had brought him there.
    At this reminder of his paternal grief,
the ruler of a hundred cities sighed
and answered him: "I must have your assistance
in a war which I am undertaking now   690
for my dead son's sake; serve under my command
in a just cause: I act for his repose."
    The aged king replied, "You ask in vain
for something which my city cannot offer:
no region is more closely linked to Athens,   695
and there are treaties binding us to them."
    Grimly King Minos turned away and said,
"Those treaties will be kept at a great cost."
He thought it much more useful just to threaten,
instead of waging, war—and thus avoided   700
using up his warriors beforehand.

Cephalus Arrives at Aegina

The Cretan fleet could still be sighted from
the city's walls when there appeared a ship

flying from Athens under crowded sail,
which put in to the friendly harbor, bearing   705
Cephalus and the greetings of his country.
      Although it had been long since they'd last seen him,
the three young princes of Aeacus' line
immediately recognized Cephalus,[2]
embracing him and leading him within   710
their father's house; the hero, well worth seeing,
still with some traces of his former beauty,
entered the palace carrying a branch
of the olive tree, native to his country.
      He stood between a pair of younger men,   715
Clytus and Butes, who were sons of Pallas.
And after an exchange of formal greetings,
the emissary laid out his commission,
appealed for aid, referring to the treaty
and the ancestral league between the cities,   720
adding that Minos sought dominion over
not only Athens, but the mainland, too.
      His eloquence did justice to his cause;
Aeacus, his left hand resting on his scepter, spoke:
"Do not come *seeking* aid, Athenian: 725
assume it! Count as yours whatever men
this isle may boast of and whatever else
the present state of my affairs can offer;
my forces are at strength, and quite sufficient
to defend Aegina and to mount offenses;   730
thanks to the gods, the times are fortunate,
and offer us no reason for inaction!"
      "May it be so, indeed," Cephalus said,
"and may your city grow in citizens;
on my way in, joy took me when I saw   735
so many young men coming out to meet me,
so similar in beauty and in age.
And yet I miss many of the men I saw
when I came to this city, years ago."
      Aeacus groaned and sadly answered him: 740
"Though better fortune followed, what came first
was cause for sorrow: would that I were able
to call to mind the one without the other!
      "But I will tell you all, as it occurred,
nor beat about the bushes any further: 745
those whom you ask for are now bones and ashes,
and with them perished much of my own kingdom.

---

2. Ovid invents what appears to have been a previous visit by Cephalus in order to have him
   comment on the change in the populace he notices in lines 733–39.

The Plague at Aegina

"A fearful plague came down among the people,
brought on when cruel Juno's anger turned
against the land that bore her rival's name.   750
While we were ignorant of what had caused it,
and while it still appeared to us to be
a natural disaster, it was fought
with all the arts of medicine, and still
it vanquished all of our stratagems!   755
    "At first the sky pressed down against the earth
in a dense darkness; clouds helped to contain
the enervating heat, and while the moon
filled out its horns four times, and four times waned,
the south wind warmed us with its fatal breath.   760
    "Our pools and springs became infected next,
when multitudes of serpents slithered through
the empty fields and left our streams and rivers
stained with their venom.
                        "At first the animals
alone succumbed: the plague confined itself   765
to dogs, birds, sheep, cattle, and wild beasts:
the luckless plowman is quite stunned to see
his healthy bulls collapsing at their work,
falling in midfurrow; woolly flocks
give a few feeble bleats, then, without help,   770
shed their thick coats, grow wasted and soon die;
the stall-bound horse, once famous for his speed,
but now unworthy of his victories,
ignores his former honors, whinnying
as death prepares to scratch him from the race.   775
    "The boar does not remember now to rage,
nor the deer to trust in swiftness, nor the bear
to cull the great herds with his fierce attacks;
a languor seizes all; in woods, in fields,
along the roads, the fetid corpses lie   780
until the air is blighted with the stench.
    "I'll tell you something quite astonishing:
the greedy dogs and vultures—even wolves!—
left them untouched; those bodies fell apart,
sickening us with their appalling odor   785
and spreading foul contagion everywhere.
    "The plague, grown stronger, now advances on
the wretched country folk, then rules within
the walls of the great city. Its first symptom
is a fierce burning in the viscera,   790
the hidden fire indicated by

a flushed complexion, pain in drawing breath;
the patient's roughened tongue swells up with fever,
and lips that have been parched by the hot winds
gape widely, snatching at the torpid air—   795
no bed nor covering is bearable;
they fling themselves facedown upon the ground
to cool their bodies off; but no: the heat
of their poor bodies warms the earth instead!

    "Ungovernable plague! The doctors die,   800
their arts a harm to their practitioners,
and those who are the closest to the sick,
who serve most faithfully, are first to fall!

    "Now as the hope of health abandons them,
they realize that their disease will end   805
only in death and give in to their desires,
having no care at all for what might cure them,
since nothing can. They sprawl about all over,
without a thought for decency—they lie
in springs, in streams, and in capacious wells;   810
bloated by water, many cannot rise
and so they die—where others come to drink!

    "They find their beds too painful to endure
and leap from them; but if they cannot stand,
they roll their bodies right along the ground,   815
fleeing the homes that now seem charnel houses;
the cause unknown, the place itself is blamed;
you would have seen some wandering the roadways,
half-dead, perhaps, but capable of standing,
and others lying on the ground in tears,   820
at the point of death: they roll their eyes and die.
Others lift arms up to oppressive heaven;
here, there—wherever death overtakes them—
they breathe their last and silently expire.

    "Can you imagine what my feelings were?   825
Like those of anyone in such a case:
I hated life and longed to share the fate
of my own kind, for everywhere I looked
the dead were strewn in heaps, without distinction,
like rotten apples shaken from the bough   830
or acorns that the wind strips from an oak.

    "Do you see that temple there, the lofty one
with the long approach? It is Jupiter's.
And who among us did not offer up
the unavailing incense on its altars?   835
How often, for his wife, the husband came,
and for his dying son, the father, who
gave up the ghost while he was still at prayer

upon the unmoved altar—in his hand
a portion of the incense, unconsumed!   840
How often, in that temple, while the priest
at prayer was pouring wine between the horns
of sacrificial bulls, the beasts collapsed
even before the anticipated blow!
    While I myself was sacrificing there   845
for my own good and for my sons and nation,
the beast began to bellow horribly,
and instantly collapsed without a stroke:
it barely stained the knife with its thin blood;
the entrails, too, were sickly, and had lost   850
those signs by which the truth and heaven's will
are made apparent, for this grim disease
had penetrated to the viscera!
I saw cadavers flung by temple doors,
and even thrown—as though to shame the gods   855
for their indifference—before the altars!
    "Some freed themselves from the fear they had of death
by taking their own lives—summoning Fate
even as Fate prepared to summon them.
No longer were the bodies of the dead   860
carried in processions from the city
for burial with the customary rites:
no gates were wide enough for such a throng.
    "Either they lay unburied on the ground
or, without services, were stacked and burned;   865
and now there are no honors for the dead;
dying, men struggle over scraps of wood,
and are cremated with a stranger's flame.
    "With none to mourn them, unlamented souls
of parents and their children, the young, the old,   870
wander about, their journey uncompleted:
no wood is left to burn their bodies now,
no bit of land where they may be interred.
    "And stunned by such a whirlwind of disasters,
I cried, 'O Jupiter, if what folks say   875
is not untrue, that you have lain in love
with Aegina, the daughter of Asopus,
and that you're not ashamed to be our father,[3]
either restore to me those who are mine,
or else give me a sepulcher as well!'   880
    "Jove answered favorably with a flash
of lightning followed by a thunderbolt.
'I take this omen, and I pray that these

---

3. Aeacus was said to be the child of Jove and Aegina.

signs of your purpose augur well for us,'
I said, 'for I accept them as your promise.'   885
   "It happened that there was an oak nearby,
one with unusually widespread branches;
this tree, whose seed had come from Dodona,
was therefore sacred to almighty Jove;[4]
here we observed a swarm, in single file,   890
each bearing a great load in tiny jaws:
a busy company of grain-gathering ants,
making its way across the wrinkled bark!
   "Astonished by that multitude, I cried,
'O best of fathers, give me just as many   895
new subjects and fill up my lifeless city!'
That lofty oak tree trembled, and its limbs
groaned as they moved in the unmoving air;
I shook with terror and my hair stood up;
and even though I kissed the earth and oak,   900
could not admit—not even to myself—
the hopes I had. And yet, I hoped, indeed,
and in my heart I cherished my desires.
   "Night fell, and sleep claimed our bodies, worn
by ceaseless cares. Before my eyes I seemed   905
to see the oak that I had seen before,
with just as many branches and the same
number of creatures swarming over them,
and the limbs swaying as they had before:
the grain-bearing ants were shaken to the ground,   910
where they at once seemed to grow much larger,
lifting themselves from where they'd fallen off,
to stand with upright torsos; they put aside
their former leanness, monotonous black hue,
and many of their feet, while they assumed   915
a human form and human attributes.
   "Sleep fled: waking, I had no confidence
in what my vision had disclosed to me;
no help, I thought, from heaven.
                            "But within,
a great hubbub arose; it seemed to me   920
I heard what I'd been long unused to hearing:
the sound of human voices!
                            "While I still thought
myself asleep and dreaming, Telamon
came bursting in on me and cried out, 'Father,
come forth, and you will see a miracle   925
greater than you had hoped for or believed in!'

4. Dodona in Thessaly was the site of a temple to Jove surrounded by prophetic oaks.

"I went on out, and there they were: the very
men that I had just seen in my dream—
now wide awake, I recognized the fellows!
Approaching, they saluted me as king.   930
I offered thanks to Jove and portioned out
my city and my fields, now tenantless,
to these new citizens. I called this folk
the Myrmidons [from the Greek word for ant],
a name that doesn't hide their origins.   935
    "You've seen their bodies; well, their character
and dispositions have remained the same:
they are a thrifty race, industrious,
acquisitive, and keep their acquisitions.
    "All similar in age and bravery,   940
these are the ones who'll follow you to war
when the east wind, which so propitiously
brought you here, shall veer round to the south."
    Such conversation filled the lengthy day;
the evening was set aside for feasting,   945
and the night for sleep. Now when the Sun
had brought his radiance to light, the east wind still
prevented the Athenians' return.
    The sons of Pallas came to Cephalus
(who was their elder), and together they   950
went to Aeacus, whom they found still sleeping.
The king's son Phocus met them on the threshold,
for Telamon and Peleus were busy
mustering the Myrmidons for warfare.
    So Phocus conducted the Athenians   955
into a handsome chamber deep within
the palace, where they all sat down together.
And here he saw the gold-tipped javelin
that Cephalus was carrying, its shaft
made from a kind of wood unknown to him.   960
    After a brief exchange, the young man said,
"Woodlore and hunting are my specialties,
but for a while now I've been wondering
what kind of wood your javelin is made from:
if it were ash, it would be tawnier;   965
if it were dogwood, there would be more burls.
—I can't say what it is, and yet I'm certain
these eyes of mine have never seen a spear
more beautiful in its design than this one!"
    One of the two Athenian brothers said,   970
"You will discover more to marvel at
than just its beauty," he said, "for it strikes
the target that it seeks, unruled by chance,

and then—quite on its own—comes flying back,
with bloodstained tip, into its owner's hand."   975
    And then, of course, young Phocus had to know
everything about it: How could this be?
Where was it from? Who gave him such a gift?
Cephalus tells him all he wants to know,
or all, at least, that decency allows: 980
shame keeps him from revealing the concession
by which he gained it.[5]
                    Silence.

                            Then, touched by grief
for his lost wife, he wept, and said to them,
"It is this weapon which incites my tears,
son of the goddess—who would think it so?   985
But so it does and for a long time will,
however long the life my fate decrees,
for this has ruined me and my poor wife:
would that I never had this gift at all!

Cephalus, Procris, and Aurora

"Her name was Procris: it's likelier you've heard   990
about her ravished sister, Orithyia,
but were you to compare the two of them
in looks and manner, Procris was more worthy
of being ravished! Her father Erectheus
joined me to her as Love joined her to me.   995
I was called 'fortunate,' and so I was;
and had the gods not otherwise ordained,
I would perhaps still know felicity.
    "But in the second month of our marriage,
while I was setting nets out to take deer,   1000
high on the peak of flowering Hymettus,
pale Aurora, fresh from driving off
nocturnal gloom, first saw, then ravished me,
against my will! Now may it please the goddess,
I am permitted to report the truth: 1005
and by her rosy mouth (a sight worth seeing),
and by her power over night and day,
and by that nectar she was nurtured on,
I still loved Procris! *She* was in my heart,

---

5. Ovid is apparently suppressing another aspect of the story, even more embarrassing to
   Cephalus: others say that his wife in disguise seduced him into agreeing to commit a
   homosexual act in order to show him that he too was corruptible. Something like that is
   implied here: see also lines 1072–74.

her name was always trembling on my lips.   1010
I spoke of nothing but the ties that bound us,
of fresh delights and recent pleasures proven,
of the first doings on our deserted bed.
 "Such talk upset Aurora: 'Stop your whining,
you thankless dolt! You may have your Procris,   1015
but if I've any gift at all of foresight,
you'll wish you hadn't!' Angrily she sent me
back to my wife, and, while I was returning,
I turned her warnings over in my mind,
and—as I thought on them—began to fear   1020
that my young wife had not observed my rights.
 "Her youth and beauty led me to believe her
an adulteress; her character forbade me
to believe it. Nonetheless, the one
from whom I was just now returning set   1025
quite a good example of misconduct—
besides, we lovers are a fearful lot.
 "I settled upon making myself wretched
by trying to disturb her constant nature
through bribery. Aurora churned my fear,   1030
and helped me out by altering my looks.
(It seemed to me that I could feel the change.)
 "Unrecognized, I slipped into Athena's
beloved city, and entered my own home:
there were no signs of anything amiss;   1035
all were concerned about their vanished master,
and only by a thousand stratagems
did I contrive an audience with Procris.
 "Dumbstruck at sight of her, I nearly dropped
my scheme for testing her fidelity;   1040
I barely kept from blurting out the truth
and giving her the kisses she deserved.
 "Though she was sad, none could be lovelier
than she was in her sorrow, longing for
the husband taken from her. Imagine, Phocus,   1045
how beautiful this woman must have been
when even grief served as her ornament!
Why tell how often her modesty withstood
my challenges, how often she would meet
my offers with, 'I keep myself for one,   1050
wherever he may be; him I love, only.'
 "What man in his right mind would not have been
contented by such proof of loyalty?
I was not satisfied. Out to draw blood
(my own!) I battled on, and offered her   1055

a fortune just to spend one night with me,
then added even more to what I'd offered,
and finally got her to hesitate—
at which, unlucky winner, I cried out,
'O wretch! Here was a false adulterer;   1060
I was your own true husband! Faithless one,
by my own witness, you are apprehended!'

    "But she made no response to me at all,
and silenced by her overwhelming shame,
fled her deceitful husband and his house;   1065
detesting the entire race of men
because of the wrong that I had done to her,
she roamed the mountains, giving herself over
to the preoccupations of Diana.

    "Abandoned, I was desolate: a fire   1070
scorched me right to the marrow of my bones.
I begged her pardon and confessed my sins,
admitting that I too might have succumbed,
tempted by such gifts—if they'd been offered.

    "And when I had confessed such things to her,   1075
after avenging her injured honor, she
returned to me; years passed in sweet agreement.

    "And, as if she herself were not gift enough,
she gave me another one: a hunting dog,
a present from her very own Diana,   1080
and said, 'He will be fastest of them all.'
At the same time she gave me this javelin,
which, as you see, I'm holding in my hands.
You're curious about the other gift?
Then listen to this marvelous account;   1085
you'll find excitement in its novel plot:

The Plague at Thebes[6]

"The son of Laius, Oedipus, had solved
the riddle of the Sphinx,[7] which none before him
had ever done; straightway, the dark prophet
leapt headfirst from the summit of a cliff,   1090
heedless of her own ambiguities.

---

6. A different kind of plague than the one at Aegina: in the ancient world, famines were
   often described as plagues and personified as ravenous beasts.
7. A monster sent by Juno to Thebes to punish the line of Cadmus. She proposed riddles to
   passersby and devoured those unable to answer them. Oedipus eventually solved her
   riddle, "What animal walks on four legs in the morning, two at midday, and three in the
   evening?", answering that man crawled on four legs as an infant, walked upright in maturity, and relied on a cane in old age. The Sphinx, a sore loser, killed herself immediately
   thereafter.

"At once, another plague was loosed on Thebes,
and this fierce beast left many of the farm folk
frightened for themselves and for their flocks.
We local lads came out and drew a cordon   1095
around the fields; lightly the swift beast
leapt over the highest point of our nets!
    "The dogs were loosed, but she escaped them all,
and mocked the hunting party with her speed,
by flying no more slowly than a bird!   1100
The others begged me to release my "Storm"
(which was the name my present had been given);
he'd long been struggling against the leash
and straining at his collar; on release,
he disappeared, was nowhere to be found.   1105
    "Instead, we saw his tracks left in the dust,
but he himself had vanished from our sight,
No spear, no ball of lead shot from a sling,
no reedy arrow from a Cretan bow
was ever swifter in its flight than he.   1110
    "There was a nearby hill whose summit gave
a view of the surrounding fields below.
I climbed it and observed this novel race,
wherein the beast seemed almost to be caught
yet slipped—it seemed—out of his very mouth!   1115
Nor did the sly one run in a straight line,
but to deceive the jaws that followed her,
she circled round to keep her foe from springing.
    "I thought it time to use my javelin,
and as I balanced it in my right hand   1120
and fit my fingers to the throwing loop,
I took my eyes from them for just a moment,
and when I looked again at where they were,
I saw (oh, marvelous!) the two of them,
now marble figures standing in midfield!   1125
You would have thought that she appeared to flee,
and he to capture her. Most certainly
some god had wished that neither know defeat—
if any god had been attending them."

Cephalus, Aura, and Procris

At this point he fell silent. Phocus asked,   1130
"What charge do you bring against the javelin?"
The other man then set out his indictment:
    "From our joys, dear Phocus, sprang our sorrows.
I will speak first of our happiness,
for it is pleasing to recall those first   1135

years of our marriage, when, as husband and wife,
we were both equally blest in our loves,
and closely bound to one another by
mutual care and loving comradeship.
    "No one could come between us: if great Jove   1140
had offered marriage, she would have declined;
and I was interested in no other,
not even Venus, if she herself appeared,
for in our hearts the flames burned equally.
    "In early morning, when the sun's first rays   1145
touched on the hilltops, youthful eagerness
to go off hunting drew me to the woods;
no horse, no servants, and no keen-nosed hounds
would come along with me on these excursions,
nor did I bring my knotted nets: for safety,   1150
all that I needed was my javelin.
    "When I was sated with the slaughter of game,
I would go seek some cool refreshing shade
and gentle breeze that emanated from
the chilly hollows. I named that cool breeze 'Aura,'   1155
and sought her gentle breath in midday heat,
waiting for her to refresh me from my labors.
    "I had a song that I would sing to her
that went, as I recall, like this: 'Sweet Aura, come,
please me and ease me now with your embrace,   1160
most welcome one—and as you do so well,
relieve me of the fever which consumes me!'
    Perhaps I added (as Fate led me to)
additional endearments to the breeze:
'You give me such great pleasure,' I would say,   1165
'you are my dear refreshment and delight,
you make me love these woods and lonely places;
what joy to catch your breath upon my lips!'
    "Now someone overheard these words of mine
and misinterpreted their ambiguities;   1170
and hearing me so often summon 'Aura,'
assumed that I was speaking to a nymph
of the same name, whom he thought my lover!
    "At once this rash informer went to Procris
and whispered in her ear the false story   1175
of my alleged infidelity!
How credulous love is! My wife collapsed
from grief (I later learned) in a dead swoon.
    "Recovering at last, she called herself
the wretched victim of a cruel fate,   1180
complained of my betrayal, and, aroused

by an insubstantial charge, by *nothing*, really,
grew frightened of this phantom with a name,
and wept—my luckless darling—just as though
her rival had been real.
               "Often, however,   1185
she doubted and she hoped, in her wretchedness,
that she might be mistaken, and rejected
what she had heard as unreliable;
she would not hold her husband to be sinful,
unless she witnessed his misdeeds herself.   1190
    "On the next day, when Aurora's early light
had driven night off, I made for the woods,
and after a successful hunt, reclined
on the soft grass and called out, 'Aura, come,
alleviate the stresses of my labors!'   1195
    "And suddenly, while I was calling her,
I thought I heard a groaning sound, and yet
I cried out once more, 'Come, my dearest, come!'
Hearing a rustling in the fallen leaves,
I took it for some beast and hurled my javelin: 1200
Procris emerged, clutching her wounded breast,
and cried out, 'Woe is me!'
               "As soon as I
had recognized my faithful darling's voice,
I rushed to where I heard it coming from,
beside myself with fear of what I'd find: 1205
and found her dying, with her garments soaked
and soiled in her own blood, and, oh, how awful!
    "Attempting to withdraw from her torn breast
the very present she had given me,
I raised her body, dearer than my own,   1210
and tore the bloody garment from her wound
and wrapped and bandaged it as best I could,
in an attempt to stanch the flow of blood;
I prayed she would not die and leave me
guilty of her murder.
             "Though she was failing   1215
and very close to death, she forced herself
to speak these few words: 'By our faithful vows,
and by the gods above—and by those gods
soon mine below—by what is owed my love,
unchanging even as I die—the love   1220
that is the very cause of my own death—
do not let Aura take my place in bed!'
    "She spoke, and I immediately knew
how she had been mistaken about the name,

and I explained the truth of it to her,   1225
but to what end was any explanation?
    "She fell back in my arms, and her last strength
fled with her blood. As long as she could fix
her eyes on anything, she looked at me,
and on my lips I caught her luckless spirit;   1230
but she died easily and seemed content."
    With copiously flowing tears, the hero
brought this to mind again. But look—Aeacus
enters, accompanied by his two sons
and by his newly recruited citizens,   1235
impressive in their weaponry and armor,
all gratefully received by Cephalus.

BOOK VIII

Impious Acts and Exemplary Lives

Nisus and Scylla[1]

And now when Lucifer had driven off
the night, revealing the next brand-new day,
the east wind fell and wet, dark clouds arose;
the south wind mildly offered safe return
to Cephalus and his assembled troops,   5
bringing them home much sooner than expected.
    Meanwhile, along Megara's coast, King Minos
was pillaging, and trying out his forces
against its capital, now held by Nisus,
who had, among the venerable locks   10
of gray upon his head, a tuft of purple,[2]
which guaranteed the safety of his realm.
    The war was entering its sixth month, still
undecided, as wingèd Victory
flew back and forth uncertainly between   15
the two combatants. A royal tower rose
upon those singing walls,[3] where, it is said,
Apollo had set his golden lyre down:
its music lingered still within the stones.
    In peacetime, Scylla, daughter of King Nisus,   20
would often come and toss a pebble here
to make the rocks sing; now, in time of war,
she came as often to observe the duels,
and as the war dragged on, not only learned
the names of the chief contenders on both sides,   25
but recognized them by the arms they bore,
their horses, styles of dress, and Cretan quivers;
she knew Europa's son the best of all,
the countenance of Minos being more
familiar to her than it should have been.   30
    What if his face is hidden in a helmet?
Why, helmets frame his beauty! And that shield

---

1. The first in a series of tales in which passions of one kind or another cause protagonists to behave in ways that offend against piety, considered here as the duty one owes to a member of one's family—so Scylla betrays Nisus because of her passion for Minos, Icarus disobeys his father, and Daedalus murders his nephew, while for Althaea the only possibilities are to betray either her brothers or her son.
2. Ovid provides no reason for Nisus's tonsorial distinction. In other versions of the story the lock is gold, which may provide a clue: grapes may be purple or gold, and the Greek word *bótrys* means both a lock of hair and a cluster of grapes. Meleager is likewise protected by a fetish, a piece of wood whose preservation guarantees his safety and whose loss, his destruction.
3. While Apollo was helping to build the walls of Megara, he put his harp down on a stone, infusing it with his own music; struck by a pebble, the stone resounds like a plucked string.

he carries, hammered out of gleaming bronze—
how well the gleaming shield becomes the man!
And does he cast his javelin with vigor?   35
Then she commends his skillful manliness.
And does he draw the bowstring to his ear?
Why, no—that must be Phoebus with the bow!
     But when he raised his visor to reveal
his countenance, and purple-cloaked, he clenched   40
his horse's back and sat that milk-white steed,
using the reins upon its foaming jaws,
why then, the virgin daughter of King Nisus
lost herself almost, almost lost her mind:
happy the spear that his hand grasped, she thought,   45
and happy the reins that lay within his grip.
     She would go off to him, were it permitted,
a virgin treading through the enemy lines,
or from her tower fly into his camp,
or turn the city over to the foe—   50
or do whatever else Minos might wish.
     As she sat gazing at his tents, she said,
"What should I feel about this dreadful war?
Should I rejoice or grieve? I cannot say:
I grieve for my beloved enemy,   55
but without war, I never would have known him!
Were I his hostage, he could end it now,
I'd be with him and be his pledge of peace!
     "If she who bore you were as beautiful
as you are, O my loveliest of kings,   60
no wonder, then, that Jove was mad for her!
Thrice happy would I be if I had wings
to fly into his camp, and there confess
my passion for him and demand to know
what dowry the great king would have me for!   65
     "As long as it were not my city's life!
Far better that my dreams of marriage die
than that they should be realized by treason!
—Though many, on the other hand, have found it
most useful to be vanquished by a foe   70
who, when appeased, grants them his clemency.
     "And certainly, he wages a just war
of retribution for his murdered son;
his motive will prevail, as will the arms
advancing it. I think that we are lost.   75
     "Then, if it is the end for our city,
why should his martial skills, and not my love,
unbolt the gates? Much better would it be

for him to conquer us without delay,
without exterminating our folk   80
or being hurt himself. That being so,
Minos, I'll have no cause to fear, unless
someone should unintentionally wound you,
for who could be so cruel as to dare
deliberately cast a spear at you?   85
    "These undertakings please me. I resolve
to surrender to him, and give my country
as my dowry—and by acting, end the war.
    "But mere desire will not be enough!
A sentry guards my father in his sleep: 90
my father holds the keys that keep the city;
he is the source of all my fear and sorrow,
and he alone delays my love's fulfillment:
would that the gods could make me fatherless!
    "But each of us is his own divinity,   95
and Fortune spurns the coward's useless prayers.
Another woman in my situation
would long ago have happily destroyed
whatever stood between her and her love!
    "Why should another be more brave than I?   100
I would endure the fire and the sword,
but in this situation, there's no need
for sword or fire: all that I have need of
is but a single lock of my father's hair!
That would be far more valuable than gold!   105
One lock of purple hair will make me blest,
and give me everything that I've desired."
    Now Night, the greatest nurse of mortal cares,
broke in on these reflections; in the darkness,
her boldness grew. In time of first repose,   110
when Slumber finds its way into the heart
exhausted by its daily round, the daughter
slips silently into her father's chambers
and robs him of his fated lock of hair.
    Oh, what an awful crime! And with this prize   115
she flees the city, passing through its foes,
and confident of her reception comes
and makes her presentation to the king,
who quails at the sight of her:
                                    "Love has led me
into this betrayal; I am Scylla,   120
the daughter of King Nisus; I surrender
myself, my nation, and my gods as well,
and seek no other recompense but you;

receive this pledge that guarantees my love,
this purple lock—which is no lock at all,   125
but my father's head!"
                              She stretched out her foul hand
with the proffered gift as Minos shrank away,
shocked by the sight of this unholy act:
"Shame of the age," he said, "may the gods forbid you
their kingdom, and may land and sea deny you!   130
Be sure that I will never let so vile
a monster into Crete, which is my realm
and the sacred cradle of the infant Jove!"[4]
    That upright leader spoke, and, just as soon
as terms had been imposed upon the vanquished,   135
ordered his captains to release their moorings,
and the bronze-keeled fleet was rowed away from shore.
    Once Scylla saw the ships already launched
and realized that their commander had
no notion of rewarding her wrongdoing,   140
and that her prayers were pointless, she became
enraged with him, and with her arms outstretched
and hair disheveled, cried out in a frenzy:
"Where do you run to now, abandoning
the only reason for your victory?   145
Where do you flee, you savage man, who took
my nation and my father's place? To whom
our victory was both my crime and glory!
Are you unmoved by all I've done for you?
Unmoved by my great passion and my trust?   150
    "Where can I go, abandoned? To my homeland?
It has been conquered. Suppose it hadn't been:
my treachery has closed it off to me.
Should I return now to my father's presence?
But I've already given him to you!   155
    "My countrymen detest me, and my neighbors
fear my example: I have made myself
an exile everywhere, throughout the world,
that only Crete might offer me its shelter;
if you refuse me Crete as well, you ingrate,   160
and leave me here, then legend has it wrong:
Europa did not give birth to you, King Minos,
it was that tigress from Armenia,
inhospitable Syrtis! Raging Charybdis!
    "Your father was not Jove, your mother, not misled   165
by the counterfeit appearance of a bull!

---

4. The infant Jove, some say, was hidden on Crete to keep him from the murderous designs
   of his father, Saturn.

The story of your origin is false!
In truth, it *was* a bull that sired you!
    "O father, punish me! Walls I have betrayed
so recently, take pleasure in my pain!   170
For I confess that I deserve to perish,
but by the hand of someone I have harmed;
you who have profited from our crime—
why should *you* be the one to punish it?
You should regard this crime against my father   175
and country as a service to your cause!
    "That wife of yours is worthy, to be sure,
who tricked the fierce bull into lechery
and bore its unnatural offspring in her womb![5]
    "Can you hear my voice? Or do the selfsame winds   180
that fill your sails out, you ungrateful man,
break up my words and scatter them?
                                        "Now, now,
I see it is no wonder Pasiphaë
preferred the bull to you: you are much more
a savage beast than it could ever be!   185
    "Alas for me! He orders double-speed!
The waves resound as his oars beat on them;
my land and I both disappear from view!
    "It will avail you nothing to forget
what I have merited! Against your will,   190
I'll overtake you, cling to your curved plow,
and be dragged through the long furrows of the sea!"
    She'd scarcely finished speaking when she leapt
into the water and struck out for the ship,
her passion giving her the strength required.   195
A hateful guest now clung to the Cretan keel.
    Her father, hovering on yellow wings
(for he had just been changed into an osprey),
caught sight of her and dove to the attack,
prepared to savage her with his curved beak.   200
    She lost her grip in terror; as she fell,
the light air bore her up—or so it seemed,
so that she lightly skimmed above the surface.
    Feathers appear upon her hands; transformed
into a bird, she is now known as *Ciris*,   205
and has this name from the clipped lock of hair
[because the Greek verb *kerein* means "to cut"].

5. Pasiphaë, the wife of Minos, became infatuated by a bull; she had the artisan Daedalus
   build her a hollow cow form, in which she was able to satisfy her desire. The offspring of
   their union was the Minotaur, a half-man, half-bull, who lived in the labyrinth that
   Daedalus built for him.

Minos and Ariadne

As soon as he had disembarked on Crete,
Minos discharged his debt to Jove by slaying
a hundred bulls, then hung the spoils of war   210
as decorations on his palace walls.
    The scandal of his family had grown
past all concealment; now the mother's foul
adultery was proven by the strange
form of the Minotaur, half man, half bull.   215
Minos determined to remove the cause
of this opprobrium from his abode,
enclosing it within a labyrinth
devised and built by Daedalus, the most
distinguished of all living architects,   220
who framed confusion and seduced the eye
into a maze of wandering passages.
    Not otherwise than when Maeander plays
his liquid games in the Phrygian fields[6]
and flowing back and forth uncertainly,   225
observes its own waves bearing down on it,
and sends its doubtful waters on their ways
back to their source or down to the open sea:
so Daedalus provided numberless
confusing corridors and was himself   230
just barely able to find his way out,
so utterly deceitful was that place.
    Minos confined that monstrous form within
the labyrinth, and twice it had been fed
on the blood of sacrificed Athenians;   235
after another nine-year interval,
the third demand for tribute doomed the creature,
when, by the aid of Princess Ariadne,
the path back to the hidden entranceway,
which none before had ever reached again,   240
was rediscovered when the thread was wound;
then Theseus abducted Minos' daughter
and sailed to Dia, where he cruelly
abandoned his companion to her wailing.[7]
    Bacchus brought love and comfort to the girl,   245
and so that she would shine among the stars,

---

6. The river Maeander in Asia Minor was famous for its windings, which, it is said, inspired Daedalus to build the labyrinth; because of it, we speak of a *meandering* river.
7. Theseus went with the Athenian contingent to be sacrificed to the Minotaur; Minos's daughter Ariadne fell in love with the hero and betrayed her half-brother for him, providing Theseus with a thread by which he found his way through the labyrinth. After slaying the Minotaur, Theseus carried Ariadne off to the isle of Dia or Naxos, where he abandoned her.

he sent her diadem up into heaven;
it flew through the thin air, and where it flew
its precious stones were turned to brilliant fires;
now in appearance still a crown, it's found   250
between Ophiucus and Hercules.[8]

Daedalus and Icarus

Meanwhile, detesting Crete and his long exile,
and longing to return to his own nation,
Daedalus found that an escape by sea
was closed to him:
                    "Though he may bar the earth   255
and seas," he said, "without a doubt, the sky
above is open; that is how we'll go:
Minos rules everything except the air."
    He spoke and turned his mind to arts unknown,
and changed the face of nature, for he placed   260
a row of feathers in ascending order,
smallest to largest, so you would have thought
that they had all grown that way on a slope;
thus antic panpipes with unequal reeds
will rise above each other; these were bound   265
together in the middle with flaxen thread
and then joined at the quills with molded wax;
and finally, he bent them just a bit,
so they resembled bird's wings.
                    Icarus,
his boy, was standing close by, unaware   270
of any danger in the things he handled;
he smiled as he snatched at wisps of feathers blown
from his father's workbench by a passing breeze,
or left a thumbprint in the golden wax
and playfully got in his father's way.   275
    The wondrous work continued nonetheless,
and when he'd put the final touches to it,
the artisan himself hung poised between
the wings upon his shoulders in midair,
and offered these instructions to his son: 280
    "Listen to me: keep to the middle course,
dear Icarus, for if you fly too low,
the waves will weight your wings down with their moisture;
and if you fly too high, flames will consume them;
stay in the middle and don't set your course   285

8. Ariadne was discovered on the island by Bacchus, who cherished her and gave her a
   crown of seven stars, which became a constellation (which Ovid wrongly believed was
   located between the two others that he names) after her death.

by gazing at the stars: ignore Boötes,
the Dipper, and Orion's unsheathed sword;
keep to my path and follow where I lead you."
And while he was instructing him in flight,
he fit the untried wings to the boy's shoulders.   290

   And as he works and as he warns the boy,
the old man's cheeks are dampened by his tears;
the father's hands are trembling as he gives
his son a not-to-be-repeated kiss,
and lifts off on his wings into the air;   295
he flies ahead, afraid for his companion,
just like a bird who leads her young in flight
from their high nest, and as he flies along,
exhorts the boy to follow in his path,
instructing him in their transgressive art,   300
as he employs his wings in flight and watches
his fledgling Icarus attempt his own.

   Some fisherman whose line jerks with his catch,
some idle shepherd leaning on his crook,
some plowman at his plow, looks up and sees   305
something astonishing, and thinks them gods,
who have the power to pass through the air.

   Now on their left, they had already passed
the Isle of Samos, Juno's favorite,
Delos and Paros too; and on their right,   310
Lebinthos and Calymne, honey-rich,
when the boy audaciously began to play
and driven by desire for the sky,
deserts his leader and seeks altitude.

   The sun's consuming rays, much nearer now,   315
soften the fragrant wax that bound his wings
until it melts.

                 He agitates his arms,
but without wings, they cannot grip the air,
and with his father's name on them, his lips
are taken under by the deep blue sea   320
that bears his name,[9] even to the present.

   And his unlucky father, now no more
a father, cries out, "Icarus, where are you,
where, in what region, shall I look for you?"

   And then he saw the feathers on the waves   325
and cursed his arts; he built his son a tomb
in the land that takes its name from Icarus.[1]

9. The Icarian Sea.
1. Icaria.

Daedalus and Perdix

As he entombs his child's pathetic corpse,
he is observed, from where a rank ditch drips,
by a chatty partridge, who chirps cheerfully   330
and makes his wing tips flutter in applause:
a novel and unprecedented bird,
and one who'd only lately been transformed,
O Daedalus, because of a misdeed
that, for a long time, will be held against you.   335

    For, as it happened, the inventor's sister,
quite unaware of what the Fates intended,
entrusted her own son to his instruction,
a likely lad of twelve, who had a mind
with the capacity for principles and precepts;   340
and from his observation of the spines
of fishes, which he'd taken as his model,
incised a row of teeth in an iron strip
and thereby managed to invent the saw.
Likewise, he was the first to bind two arms   345
of iron at a joint, so one is fixed
and the other, as it moves, inscribes a circle.

    Daedalus envied him, and headlong hurled
this lad of precepts from a precipice,
the steep acropolis Minerva loves,   350
and lying, said the lad had slipped and fallen.

    But Athena, who takes care of clever people,
snatched him from harm, changed him to a bird,
and covered him with feathers in midair.
His former brilliance, like his former name,   355
he kept, although the former was transformed
into the swiftness of his wings and feet.

    Although a bird, she does not soar aloft,
and does not build her nest high up in trees
or on lofty peaks; she flies close to the ground   360
and lays her eggs in hedges; remembering
that fall of long ago, she fears the heights.
[*Perdix* is the word Greeks had for partridge.]

Meleager and Althaea

And then, exhausted Daedalus found rest
in Sicily, where Cocalus the king   365
waged war on his behalf against the Cretans.[2]

---

2. The Sicilian king gave Daedalus shelter when he fled from the wrath of Minos. When Minos invaded his land, he was betrayed and murdered by his daughters.

Now, thanks to Theseus, the Athenians
no longer had to pay their mournful tribute;
the temple is all wrapped around with flowers,
and the people praise the bellicose Minerva,   370
along with Jove and all the other gods,
whose altars they now sacrifice before,
leaving them gifts and burning pungent incense;
Rumor had gone racing through the towns
of Greece, bearing the name of Theseus,   375
and everywhere Achaean folk implored
the hero to deliver them from dangers.

    Calydon sought his help, although she had
a hero of her own, named Meleager;
a pig it was that prompted her petition,   380
hostile Diana's attendant and avenger.[3]

    For they say that Oeneus of Calydon,
in gratitude for an abundant harvest,
offered the firstfruits of the grain to Ceres
and the first squeezings of his grapes to Bacchus   385
and poured out a libation of her oil,
as golden as her hair is, to Minerva.

    Commencing with the rural deities,
the gods all got the honors they desired;
only Diana's altar was ignored,   390
and left, they say, without a gift of incense.
Even the gods may be provoked to anger!
"We will not let them get away with this,"
Diana said. "Dishonored we may be;
but none will say that we were unavenged!"   395

    And the spurned goddess sent her vengeful boar
straightway onto the fields of Calydon:
a beast as great as the bulls of Epirus,
and mightier than those of Sicily,
with blood and fire shining from his eyes   400
and a neck stiff with bristles just like spear shafts;
and as his chest heaved with his grating breath,
his heavy shoulders dripped with seething spume;
in length his tusks were like an elephant's,
and bolts of lightning issued from his mouth,   405
and when he exhaled, trees turned black and died.

    Now he destroys the grain while it is growing,
and now it is a field of ripened wheat
some farmer has occasion to lament;
the mills and granaries await in vain   410

---

3. The story of the hunt for the Calydonian Boar possessed an attraction for poets and
artists that Ovid seems to have felt largely as a challenge to his gift for irony and ridicule.
His target is the heroic ideal.

their promised harvests. He destroys the grapes
in weighty clusters with their trailing vines
and the leafy olive's berry-laden branches.
He raged against the herds of cattle too,
and neither herdsmen nor their dogs were able   415
to guard them, nor the bulls defend their own.
    Folks fled the countryside and thought themselves
safe only when inside a city's walls,
till Meleager with his chosen band
of youths assembled, desirous of glory:[4]   420
Leda's twin boys, one famous for his boxing,
the other skilled as an equestrian;
Jason, the world's first sailor; Theseus
and Pirithoüs, a single-minded pair;
Meleager's uncles; the sons of Thestius;   425
Lyncaeus and swift Idas, who were sons
of Aphareius; and Caeneus, who
was no more a woman; fierce Leucippus;
Acastus, famous for his javelin,
and Hippothous, with Dryas, and the son   430
of Amyntor, named Phoenix, with the two
sons of Actor; Phylius of Elis;
the brothers Telamon and Peleus
(the father of magnificent Achilles)
were neither of them absent, nor the son   435
of Pheres nor Boeotian Iolaüs;
and likewise present were Eurytion
the diligent, and rapid Echion,
and Lelex the Locrian; Panopeus
and Hyleus and fierce Hippasus too,   440
and Nestor in his prime, and those sent by
Hippocoon from ancient Amyclae;
the father of Penelope's beloved;
Arcadian Ancaeus and the son
of Ampyx, famous for his prophecies;   445
the son of Oecleus, who was as yet
unruined by his wife; and finally,
the pride of Arcadia's Mount Lycaeus,
Tegean Atalanta:[5] at her neck,
a polished buckle kept her garments fastened;   450

---

4. An Ovidian catalogue of distinguished Greek heroes, whose amazing incompetence
makes an epic mockery of this grand beginning. Among the more important are Leda's
twins, Castor and Pollux; Jason, the leader of the Argonauts; Theseus and his companion
Pirithous; Meleager's uncles, who cause trouble later; Caeneus, whose story will be told
in Book XII; Ulysses's father Laertes; and the son of Oecleus, Amphiarus, a seer whose
wife, Eriphyle, betrayed him for a golden necklace.
5. Ovid does not mention Atalanta's name; its appearance in the next line and thereafter are
my own additions. Given that she will prove more competent than any of the heroes save
Meleager, Ovid's description of her gender ambiguity is significant.

her hair was gathered in a single knot,
a style that was simplicity itself.
      The maiden held a bow in her left hand,
and from her shoulder swung an ivory
quiver, whose arrows clattered as she walked.   455
So much for her attire: as for looks,
it wouldn't be inaccurate to say
that she was somewhat girlish for a boy
and really rather boyish for a girl.
      As soon as our hero saw her face,   460
he ached for what the gods would not allow,
and wasted by love's hidden fires, said:
"Oh, fortunate, the fellow that she chooses—
if she should choose one."
                              But the occasion
and his own sense of decency forbade   465
all further speech: a far, far greater task—
this mighty contest—summons him to action.
      The scene: an old-growth forest, never cut,
which, rising from a plain, looks down upon
fields sloping off in mild declivity.   470
The men arrive: while some spread out the nets,
others unleash the dogs, and others still,
pursuing danger, start to track the beast.
      Within that forest was a hollow, soaked
by constant rain: the pliant willow grew   475
upon its swampy floor, accompanied
by sedge and osier, tall rushes and short reeds:
out of this dell, the boar came hurtling
against his foes in furious assault
as lightning issues from colliding clouds,   480
overwhelming the whole grove with his attack,
for the trees came down as he crashed into them.
      The young men raise a cry and hold their spears
with the broad, glinting tips aimed at the beast
who rushes them and strews the hounds about   485
as they attempt to block his frenzied charge,
obliquely sweeping at them with his tusks.
      Echion hurled the first spear, but in vain:
it struck and left a maple slightly wounded;
the next seemed sure to stick in the boar's back,   490
and would have done so—had not Jason thrown
with so much force it overshot its mark:
      Mopsus, the son of Ampyx, cried, "O Phoebus,
if I once worshiped and still worship you,
allow me what I ask for: let my spear   495
attain its goal unerringly!"
                              The god

complied, so far as he was able to;
the blow was struck, but left the boar unwounded:
Diana snatched the spear tip in midflight,
and the now pointless shaft flew on its way.   500
    The beast was stirred to anger by the blow
and burned more fiercely than the lightning does:
his eyes glittered and his exhalations blazed,
and as a stone slung from a catapult
seeks out a wall or tower full of soldiers,   505
just so that bloody-minded pig deployed
his overwhelming force against the men.
    Now Pelagon and Hippalmus, who held
the right flank, were bowled over by his charge;
companions snatched them both out of harm's way,   510
but Enaesimus, son of Hippocoon
could not escape the boar's death-dealing blows;
while timidly preparing to turn tail,
he was hamstrung, and his legs collapsed
beneath him.
        And Nestor of Pylos, too,   515
might well have died before the Trojan War,
had he not had the strength to use his spear
to vault himself into a nearby oak,
from whose convenient branches he looked down
in safety at the enemy below.   520
    Now having sharpened up its blunted tusks
against the oak that Nestor nestled in,
and confident of its refurbished weapons,
the beast was out for blood: raking its snout,
it savages the thigh of Hippasus.   525
    And now the Gemini (not yet promoted
to constellations,[6] being brothers still),
conspicuous both, both mounted upon steeds
whiter than snow, both fiercely brandishing
great javelins that quivered in the air—   530
for sure they would have dealt it a great wound,
had not the beast retreated to a thicket
impervious to horses and to spears.
    Telamon followed, eager and incautious,
and tripping over a projecting root   535
fell flat upon his face.
        While Peleus
was helping him get up, swift Atalanta
drew back her bowstring smartly and released
an arrow which, though high, creased the boar's back
and pricked it slightly, right beneath the ear;   540

6. Castor and Pollux, who became twin constellations after their deaths.

a little blood now trickled down its bristles.
    She took no greater pleasure in her hit
than Meleager did, who was the first
to see the blood and show it to the others:
"How manly of you!" he said. "You deserve   545
the honor and acclaim you will receive!"
    The men all reddened with embarrassment
and yelled encouragement to one another;
becoming braver from the noise they made,
they launched their spears together in a jumble   550
that missed the mark they were intended for.
    But look where Arcas, raging, rushes off
to meet his fate, armed with a two-edged axe:
"Now you will learn how the weapons of a man
surpass those of a woman," Arcas said.   555
"Stand back now, fellows, leave the job to me:
why, even if Diana could protect
the beast with her own weapons, nonetheless,
I would destroy him with my strong right hand!"
    Swollen by such magniloquence, he rose   560
and hoisting high his double-headed axe
above his head, he gripped it with both hands
and stood on tiptoes, poised to bring it down;
but the boar anticipated his next move
and looking for the fastest way to kill him,   565
drove both its tusks into his private parts.
Ancaeus fell, and his intestines spilled
like a great ball of thread unraveling
all bloody, and the earth was stained with his gore.
    The son of Ixion, Pirithoüs,   570
was next of them to face the enemy,
shaking the hunting spear in his right hand.
"Don't get too close to it!" warned Theseus.
"You who are dearer to me than my soul,
my other half! For heroes are permitted   575
to do their acts of valor from afar;
learn from Ancaeus how rash courage fares!"
He spoke and cast his heavy, bronze-tipped spear;
though hurled with force and with good augury,
it ran into an oak tree's leafy branch.   580
    And then the son of Aeson threw his spear
which, by an accident, turned from its mark
to fall among the pack of hunting dogs
and pin one by its privates to the ground.
    But Meleager, son of Oeneus,   585
achieved a very different result:

the first of his two spears fell short to ground,
the second struck the boar right in its back,
and as it raged and spun itself around,
it jetted hissing spume mixed with fresh blood;   590
the giver of the wound goaded his foe,
then drove his splendid spear into its heart.

　　His comrades testify to their great joy
by making a commotion with their mouths,
crowding around to press the victor's hand,   595
and gazing in wonder at the savage beast
which takes up so much room upon the earth
that even now they are afraid to touch it,
although they dip their spears into its blood.

　　Then Meleager set his foot upon   600
that ruinous head and said to Atalanta,
"Take, by my right, these spoils, Arcadian,
and let my glory come in part to you."
He offered her the bristling pelt and head
distinguished for the size of its curved tusks.   605
The giver of the gift was just as pleasing
to her as the gift was.
　　　　　　　　　　An envious murmur
arises from the ranks of the companions:
shaking their fists, the sons of Thestius
[who happen to be Meleager's uncles,   610
the brothers of his mother, Althaea]
raise a great ruckus: "Let it go now, woman,
do not usurp the prizes rightly ours,
and do not think too highly of your beauty:
your lover may not always be so near."   615

　　They seize his gifts, denying him the right
to offer them to anyone he chooses.
That son of Mars[7] cannot endure such treatment,
and grinding his teeth in anger, he cries out,
"You scavengers of someone else's honors!   620
Now you will learn how great a difference
there is between an action and a threat!"
And without warning, thrusts his wicked blade
into the fearful heart of Plexippus.
While Toxeus considers what to do,   625
wanting to avenge his brother's murder,
but scared of sharing in his brother's fate,
he has but little time to think it over:
the blade still warm from slaughtering the one

7. Not meant to imply anything other than warlike.

is soon reheated in the other's blood.   630
   Althaea[8] was already in the temple
thanking the gods for her son's victory
when she saw her brothers' corpses carried in.
Now Meleager's mother beat her breasts
and raised a lamentation audible   635
throughout the city; she at once replaced
the golden robes she wore with mourning weeds.
But when she learned who was the murderer,
her grief left her completely, and she turned
from weeping to a desire for revenge.   640
   When Althaea was in the throes of labor,
the Threefold Sisters[9] dropped a block of wood
into the fire; and as they wove the threads
of life beneath their fingertips, they sang,
"We give an equal span of time to you   645
and to this piece of wood, O newborn babe."
   As soon as their prophetic recitation
was over and the Fates had disappeared,
the mother snatched the branch out of the fire
and sprinkled it with water. Many years   650
it lay within its secret hiding place,
and guarded there, it guarded you, young man.
   She brought the piece of wood out now and ordered
her servants to supply the gummy pine
and kindling bits, then lit the cruel flames.   655
   And then she tried—four times—to thrust the branch
into the fire, and drew back each time;
mother and sister strove with one another
and those two names were tugging at one heart.
Often she turned pale, thinking of the crime   660
she wanted to commit—and just as often
her eyes took on the color of her rage.
   Now she resembled some unfeeling menace,
and now you would have thought her pitiful;
and when her angry heart had stopped her tears,   665
her tears would flow again; as when a ship,
driven in one direction by the wind
and in the other by an opposing tide,
feels those two equal forces struggling,
and yields herself uncertainly to both;   670
that was Althaea, wandering between
wavering passions; now her burning rage
is stifled, now it's started up again.

8. Meleager's mother; this is her first appearance in the tale.
9. The Fates, for whom see note 3 on p. 54.

The sister, nonetheless, began to win,
and so that blood might pacify the shades   675
of her own blood, her brothers, she resolves
to do a pious deed, impiously.
For when that fire had blazed up, she said,
"Let this be the cremation of my womb!"

And as she stood before her brothers' biers,   680
with the deadly piece of wood in her grim hand,
the miserable woman raised a cry:
"Now turn your faces to our dreadful rites,
O Threefold Goddesses, O Gracious Ones!
Avenging one abomination, I   685
commit another: death must expiate death,
crime be added onto crime, burial
to burial, until the weight of woe
accumulated overwhelms at last
this impious household! Shall fortunate   690
Oeneus rejoice in his son's victory?
Shall Thestius mourn? Better you both grieve.

"And you now, brothers, dead so recently,
appreciate the office I perform;
accept the sacrifice prepared for you   695
by your own sister at such dreadful cost,
the wicked tribute of a mother's womb.

"Oh, god! What am I rushing into here?
Brothers, forgive a mother's wavering,
my hands rebel from what they have begun!   700
Yes, I admit that he deserves to die,
but it displeases me to do the deed.

"Shall he then walk away from this, unpunished,
alive, a victor, swollen with his triumph,
inheriting the realm of Calydon   705
while your thin ashes lie in icy darkness?
But I could not endure that. Let him die,
the criminal, and with him take the hopes
his father had for him and for his kingdom.

"But where are my maternal feelings? Where   710
is that devotion any parent has?
The pains I bore until my son was born?

"O would that you had died in infancy,
when that first fire blazed up in my sight!
Mine were the gifts that you have conquered by;   715
of your own merit you deserve to die!
Now pay the penalty for what you've done;
twice I have given you the gift of life,
once at birth, once when I snatched the branch
out of the fire; now return the gift   720

or put me with my brothers in the grave!
    "But I cannot accomplish what I wish for.
What is my problem? Here before my eyes
is the image of my brothers' bloody wounds,
and now the mother in me melts my heart.   725
    "Oh, wretched me! It is a wickedness
that you shall win, my brothers, but you shall!
Provided that you offer me the solace
I give you now, and let me follow you!"
    She turned away and with a trembling hand   730
flung the funereal torch into the fire;
and then it gave—or seemed to give—a groan,
as it burned in flames that bent away from it.
    All unaware of that far-distant fire,
Meleager felt his viscera consumed   735
by hidden flames and bore great suffering
with courage, although he was grieved to die
far from a battlefield;[1] Ancaeus seemed
most fortunate in dying as he did.
    He cries out to his superannuated   740
father, his brothers, his devoted sisters;
and, groaning, to his wife and bedmate; then,
summoning up his last breath, calls upon
his mother, as it happened.
                            Flames rose and fell
as did his pain, and both died down together;   745
his spirit gradually slipped away
and mixed in the air as gradually
as ashes settle over glowing coals.
    High Calydon is now brought low by grief:
princes and proles, old men and young men mourn,   750
the matrons on the banks of the Euenus
tear out their hair in grief and beat their breasts;
his father, lying on the ground, befouls
his white hair and his ancient head with dust,
and angrily rebukes his length of years.   755
For now his mother, cognizant at last
of the wickedness her hand has caused,
has seen fit to exact her punishment,
and thrusts a sword into her viscera!
    Not even if some god had given me   760
a hundred mouths, each fitted with a tongue,
and genius suitable to the occasion,
and all of Helicon for inspiration,

---

1. Ovid's nod to the heroic ideal.

not even then would I be able to
describe the sad fate of his wretched sisters, 765
who, careless of decorum, beat their breasts,
and while his corpse was still displayed among them,
caressed him constantly and gave him kisses,
and even kissed the bier he was laid out on;
they gathered up his ashes in an urn 770
and pressed it to their breasts, and threw themselves
onto his grave mound and embraced the stone
and bathed the name carved on it with their tears.
 At last Diana, being satisfied
with the destruction of Oeneus' house, 775
caused feathers to appear upon their bodies,
excepting Gorge and [Deianira]
the daughter-in-law of highborn Alcmena,
and having fitted out their arms with wings
and given each of them a horny beak, 780
she sent them, thus transformed, into the air
[as *meleagrides*, or guinea hens].

Acheloüs and Theseus

Theseus, meanwhile, having done his part
in the joint effort, headed back to Athens.
Swollen from recent rains, the Acheloüs[2] 785
prevented him from going on his way:
"Abide with me," he said, "beneath my roof,
O celebrated son of Aegeus,
do not entrust yourself to the greedy flood;
why, I have seen it seize and carry off 790
enormous tree trunks, even mighty boulders,
and send them spinning, now this way, now that,
with a huge roar! I have seen great stables,
constructed on the bank here, carried off
with all their herds; neither the oxen's strength 795
nor the horses' speed availed against the flood.
 "When springtime torrents are created by
snow melting in the mountains, strong young men
are swept away and drowned in its seething eddies.
Much safer would it be for you to stay 800
until the waters once more learn their limits,
and the thin stream gets back into its bed."
 The son of Aegeus, assenting, said,
"You offer me your counsel and your home;

---

2. As usual in Ovid, he is both a river and a river-god.

I will take both." And take them both he did.   805
He passed into the river's entrance hall
made of poriferous pumice and rough tufa;
its earthen floor was squishy with wet moss,
its ceiling done in alternating rows
of inlaid seashells, conch, and purple murex.   810
    The Sun had finished two-thirds of his journey
when the hero and his companions of the hunt
arranged themselves in couches round the table.
Here sat the son of Ixion, and there
sat Lelex, the great hero of Troezen,   815
a smattering of gray hair at his temples,
and others too, deemed worthy of this honor
by the river-god, delighted to be hosting
the mightiest of heroes, Theseus.
    At once came barefoot nymphs to set the table,   820
bring out the feast, and clear away the courses,
before they filled the jeweled cups with wine.

The Echinades and Perimele

While gazing at the waters of the gulf,
Theseus, pointing with one finger, asked,
"What is that place? What is that island's name?   825
Though it doesn't seem to be *one* island, just."
    "It isn't," said the river in response;
"what you perceive is not one isle, but five:
perception is misled at such a distance.
And so that you may find Diana's actions,   830
when she was slighted, less astonishing,
those islands that you see were naiads once,
who, when they had slaughtered ten young bullocks,
extended invitations to their feast
to all the local gods, except yours truly,   835
forgotten as they led their choral dancing.
    "Infuriated, I became as full
as ever I get when my water rises,
and as my mind made waves, I overwhelmed,
and tore away the forests from their forests,   840
fields from their fields: I carried off the nymphs,
mindful of me at last, *with* their habitat,
down to the sea; there, where I join the gulf,
together we divided up the land
into those diverse portions you behold   845
off in the water, called the Echinades.
    "But further off, you'll see another island
more dear to me, which mariners have named

Perimele, a maiden whom I prized;
but when I took her maidenhead from her,   850
her father, Hippodamas, was enraged,
and sent her hurtling headlong from a cliff
into the sea below. I caught her as she fell,
and keeping her afloat, I cried to heaven,
'O trident-bearing Neptune, drawn by lot   855
to rule over the nearby world of waves,
answer my prayer and give to one
drowned by her father's cruelty, a place—
or, if she cannot *have*, then let her *be* one.'
     "And even as I spoke, new earth began   860
to gather her in its embrace, and from
her transformed shape the solid land emerged."

Baucis and Philemon[3]

The river then fell silent. All were moved
save Pirithoüs, son of Ixion,
a freethinker, dismissive of the gods,   865
who ridiculed their host's credulity:
"The fables that you tell, Acheloüs,
attribute too much power to the gods,
if they can change the shapes of things like that."
     The others were all shocked by what he said,   870
and disapproved, Lelex especially,
whose judgment had been ripened by his years:
"Omnipotent and limitless is heaven,
and what the gods desire is accomplished;
and so that you may come to doubt it less,   875
know that on a hillside in Phrygia,
there stand an oak and linden, side by side,
surrounded by an undistinguished wall;
once, on a mission for King Pittheus,
I saw the very site of which I speak.   880
     "There is a marsh nearby; no longer fit
for men to dwell in, it is now the haunt
of coots and seagulls only; Jupiter
came to this area, disguised as a mortal,
with Mercury, who'd taken off his wings.   885
     "A thousand homes they came to, seeking rest;
a thousand doors were bolted fast against them;
one home received them, humble, just a hut,
and thatched with reeds and stubble from the swamp,

---

3. The exemplary lives of this book's title.

but most devout; Baucis and Philemon,   890
a couple equally advanced in years,
were wed there in their youth, and there grew old
together, making light of poverty
by cheerfully admitting it and bearing
its deprivations with composure; seek   895
no servants in that house, nor masters neither,
for there were only two there, and the one
commanding was the same one who obeyed.

   "So, when the gods came to their humble home
and stooped to pass through its ramshackle door,   900
the old man bade them rest upon a bench
which Baucis, busy bustling about,
had covered with a roughly woven blanket;
and after sweeping ashes from the hearth,
she had resuscitated yesterday's   905
still-glowing coals, restoring them to life
with a diet of leaf mold and dry bark;
and then she added twigs and bits of kindling
which she fetched down from overhead and chopped
still smaller, before placing them beneath   910
her little cooking pot: she huffed and puffed
until she managed to produce a flame,
then trimmed the cabbage which her mate had picked
from their well-watered garden.   "He, meanwhile,
had fetched a hunk of what had once been bacon   915
down from its hook upon a sooty rafter,
an inexpensive, sinewy old chine
and not at all improved by long-term storage;
she carefully snipped off a frugal piece
and put it in the pot to learn some manners.   920

   "While they beguiled the hours before dinner
with talk that kept delay from being felt,
he filled a beechwood basin with warm water,
then bathed the travelers' exhausted limbs
as they sat on a mattress stuffed with grass,   925
perched on a couch with frame and feet of willow.

   "Over this piece, a coverlet was thrown,
brought out on feast days only, yet a match
in age and value for the willow couch.

   "The gods reclined. And with her skirts hitched up,   930
the trembling old lady set the table,
correcting its imbalance with a potsherd
slipped underneath the shortest of its legs;
and when the table had been stabilized,
she scrubbed its surface clean with fragrant mint.   935

"She set out berries from Minerva's tree,[4]
and autumn-ripened cornel cherry pickles,
with endives, radishes, fresh cheese, and eggs
that had been lightly roasted in the coals.
    "She put out everything on earthenware;   940
a bowl for mixing wine and water in
(ordered, no doubt, from the same catalogue)
appeared upon the table, joined by cups
of beechwood, all patched up with yellow wax.
    "A moment, and the hearth sent out its steaming feast,   945
and once again the wine—a recent vintage—
returned to table, briefly, set aside
to make some room now for the second course
of nuts and varied fruits: figs, dates, and plums,
sweet-smelling apples rolling from their baskets,   950
and purple grapes just taken from the vine;
and right there, in the middle of the table,
an oozing honeycomb. But more than these
were beaming looks, expressions of goodwill,
the very opposite of poverty.   955
    "Meanwhile, they saw that when the mixing bowl
was emptied out, it filled right up again
of its own accord, as though from underneath;
astonished and frightened by this miracle,
old Baucis and fainthearted Philemon   960
pressed their palms upward and recited prayers,
and begged the gods' indulgence for their meal
and the meager preparations they had made.
    "They had a single goose, the guardian
of their small villa, whom they now prepared   965
to sacrifice to their immortal guests;
his swiftness, though, left the old pair exhausted.
    "Time after time, he slipped out of their grasp,
and then, it seemed, sought refuge with the gods,
who would not let the couple do him in: 970
'We are gods,' they said. 'This irreligious
region will now be punished as it should be;
you two will be exempted from the evil,
so leave your house together now and climb
that difficult steep mountain there with us.'   975
    "Leaning on walking sticks, the pair obeyed,
and struggled to find their footing on its slope.
When they were just a bowshot from its summit,
they looked back and saw everything submerged
in the waters of the swamp—save for their house!   980

4. Olives: their tree was sacred to the goddess.

They marveled at this, and they shed some tears
for their neighbors' fate.
                "And that house of theirs,
which had been crowded with just two of them,
was turned into a temple: columns replaced
the wooden beams supporting its front gable,   985
the yellow thatch became a roof of gold,
and doors appeared, inlaid with artful bronze,
and—where bare dirt had been—a marble courtyard!

    "The son of Saturn quietly addressed them:
'Decent old man, wife worthy of her mate,   990
what can we do for you now? Tell us, please.'
Philemon turned and spoke to Baucis briefly,
and then revealed their mutual decision:
'We ask to be allowed to guard your temple
as its priests, and, since we have lived together   995
so many years in harmony, we ask
that the same hour take us both together,
and that I should not live to see her tomb
nor she survive to bury me in mine.'

    "Their prayers were granted. Their remaining years   1000
were spent in taking care of the new temple,
till finally, exhausted by old age,
the two of them were standing by its columns,
speaking of what had happened to them there,
when Baucis saw Philemon come into leaf,   1005
and Philemon saw Baucis put forth leaves.
Then, as their faces both were covered over
by the growing treetop, while it was allowed them,
they spoke and answered one another's speech:
'Farewell, dear spouse!' they both cried out together,   1010
just as their lips were sealed in leafiness.

    "And even now, the peasants in that region
will show you two trees standing side by side,
sprung from a single trunk; sensible seniors,
who had no earthly reason to deceive me,   1015
told me this tale, and my own eyes have seen
the votive garlands hanging from the branches,
and as I hung fresh garlands there, I said,
'Let those who are beloved of the gods
be gods themselves; let those who reverence   1020
the gods be reverenced as gods as well.'"

Erysichthon and His Daughter

He ceased, and his whole audience was moved
by the substance of the tale and by its teller,
especially Theseus, who wished to hear

more of the gods and their astounding deeds.   1025
    Propped on his elbow, Acheloüs responded:
"O bravest of all heroes, there are those
whose forms, once changed, forevermore remain
in their new state; others there are for whom
continual transformation is the rule,   1030
as is *your* case, O Proteus,[5] who live
in the sea that wraps itself around the earth;
at one time men have seen you as a youth,
at others as a lion, a wild boar,
a snake that everyone must fear to touch;   1035
now horns have made you into a wild bull;
often you could appear to be a stone,
often a tree; and every now and then,
taking the shape that flowing water makes,
you were a river; occasionally you   1040
became the opposite of water, flame.
    "The daughter of Erysichthon, who wed
Autolycus,[6] had powers great as those;
her father was a man who spurned the gods
and would not offer fragrant sacrifice;   1045
why, it is even said he violated
the sacred grove of Ceres with his axe,
defiling ancient woods with man-made iron.
    "There stood a giant oak of many years,
a veritable grove all by itself,   1050
girdled with ribbons, garlands, votive tablets—
all witnesses to efficacious prayer.
    "Often beneath its branches, dryads danced,
and linking hands, encircled the great oak,
no less than fifteen ells[7] circumference;   1055
it stood as high above the other trees
as they stood to the grasses underneath them.
    "Its character provided Erysichthon
no reason to restrain from ordering
his slaves—the criminal—to cut it down.   1060
And when he saw them hesitate, he snatched
the axe away from one of them, and said,
'Why, even if this were not *just* the tree
that Ceres loves, but were itself the goddess,
its leafy tip would touch the ground!'
                            "He spoke,   1065
and held the axe suspended for the blow:
the sacred oak gave out a groan and shuddered,

---

5. The wise old man of the sea, famous for his shape-shifting ability.
6. Mercury's son, one of the Argonauts, a great thief, and the real father of Ulysses.
7. About fifty-six inches around.

and its leaves, its acorns, and its branches paled.
   "But when he struck with his defiling hand,
blood issued from its severed bark, as when   1070
a bull is sacrificed before the altar
and the warm blood pours from its severed throat.
   "All were astounded by this miracle,
and one more daring than the others tried
to hold his cruel axe back from a crime,   1075
deterring it from an impiety:
'Take this reward for your religious bent,'
Erysichthon muttered when he saw him,
and turning from the tree toward the man,
truncated him by severing his head.   1080
   "But as he struck the oak repeatedly
a voice was heard from deep within the wood:
'Beneath the surface of this tree I dwell,
a nymph of Ceres; dying, I foresee
your punishment at hand, and pleased, foretell   1085
the consolation that your death will be.'
   "The criminal at last succeeded: shaken
by many blows and hauled on by thick ropes,
it fell and brought down the surrounding woods.
Grief-stricken by their loss and by the grove's,   1090
the dryad sisters went to Ceres, weeping
and wearing black, and begged her with their prayers
to punish Erysichthon for his crimes.
   "The loveliest of goddesses assented,
nodding her head—and by that motion shook   1095
fields freighted with a harvest yet to come.
Ceres contrived a punishment for him
that would have stirred to pity, were it not
for the unpitiable nature of his deeds:
he should be lashed by pestilential Famine.   1100
   "Because the goddess could not go herself
upon this mission (for the Fates forbid
Ceres and Famine ever to connect),
she called upon a mountain nymph of hers
to go instead of her, with this command: 1105
'There is a place in icy Scythia's
northernmost reaches where the barren soil
will not support a tree or field of grain;
sluggish Frigidity inhabits it,
with Pallor, Shivering, and Famine too;   1110
command this last one to conceal herself
in the stomach of this sacrilegious rogue,
and order her to overcome Abundance
and Fruitfulness—the powers that I wield.

And, lest the distance should dishearten you,   1115
accept these dragons with my chariot.'
And she placed the reins that guide them in her hands.
    "Borne through the air in Ceres' vehicle,
she came to Scythia; on a forbidding peak
(called the Caucasus) she unyoked her steeds,   1120
and there she found the Famine that she sought,
picking stray grasses in a field of stones:
    "Her unkempt hair was matted and her eyes
seemed hollowed out; gray was her complexion,
and gray her lips, from want of frequent use;   1125
her throat was rusted from inactivity,
and her skin was stretched so tightly you could see
the viscera beneath; hip bones protruded
from underneath her withered, sunken loins,
her belly, nothing more than an indication   1130
of where a belly might be found; her breasts,
dependents of her spine; her joints were all
exaggerated by emaciation;
her knees and ankles were great shapeless lumps.
    "Now when the mountain nymph caught sight of Famine   1135
from far away (not daring to come near)
she wasted no time giving her her orders;
although she kept her distance from the other
and really hadn't been there very long,
she felt herself beginning to feel famished,   1140
and so she leapt into her chariot
and headed the dragons back to Thessaly.
    "Famine obeyed the orders Ceres gave her
(although their functions are in opposition)
and swift upon the wind passed through the air   1145
until she came to Erysichthon's house
and introduced herself at once into
the bedroom of the sacrilegious one,
sunk in deep slumber, for it was the night;
she wrapped both arms around him in embrace,   1150
and breathed herself, her essence, into him,
exhaling on his throat, his breast, his lips,
till hunger circulated through his veins;
her mission done, she fled the fruitful world,
returning to the homes of emptiness   1155
and her accustomed caverns.
                              "Gentle Sleep
fans Erysichthon with emollient wings;
in dreams he seeks imaginary feasts,
and opens wide to gobble nothingness;
he wears his teeth down, grinding one another,   1160

deludes his throat with insubstantial food,
and for his banquet feasts on empty air.
    "Awakened, the desire to devour
raged within him; reason was overruled
by greed of gorge and appetite of maw.   1165
    "At once he sought whatever edibles
that the earth or air or ocean could supply
and moaned with hunger at the groaning board,
looking for feasts even as he feasted;
what would have been enough for a whole city,   1170
or for a nation, did not suffice for one,
and as he fed it, his desire grew.
    "Just as the sea receives from round the world
its rivers, and is never satisfied,
no matter from what distant source they flow,   1175
and as a raging fire spurns no fuel,
devouring innumerable logs
and wanting more with every one it gets,
growing more voracious from abundance,
just so the greedy lips of Erysichthon,   1180
even as they took in, were seeking out;
the cause of one feast was the one before,
and all his eating only left him empty.
    "When Famine and his belly's bottomless
abyss had eaten up all his estates,   1185
he nonetheless remained insatiable;
the fire in his gullet raged full blast,
devouring his wealth and property
until a daughter (who deserved a better
father) was all that still remained to him: 1190
a man now without means, he sold her too.
    "The noble girl refused to have a master
and went down to the seaside there to pray:
'Oh, take me from my master, you who took
the gift of my virginity,' she said,   1195
for Neptune had already taken it,
and now the god did not ignore her prayer,
although the master in pursuit had seen her;
Neptune gave her a new form and countenance,
and made her look just like a fisherman.   1200
    "And catching up to her, the master said,
'O regulator of the reedy rod,
who hides the dangling hook in balls of bait,
so may the sea lie nice and flat for you,
and may the fish be wholly credulous,   1205
and never sense your presence till they're hooked;
but just now on this shore, there stood a girl—

I know this, for I saw her standing there—
a girl dressed like a slave with unkempt hair:
please tell me where she is, for her tracks lead   1210
right up to you, and do not go beyond.'
     "From what her master said, she realized
that Neptune's gift was working; with these words
she interrupted his interrogation:
'I beg your pardon, sir, whoever you are,   1215
but I have not looked up from here at all,
so taken have I been with my pursuit;
but so that you should doubt me less, I swear
by Neptune's aid upon my enterprise
that for a great long while, there has not been   1220
a soul upon this shore except for me,
and no one here that you might call a girl.'
     "The master trusted her and turned around
and left the beach, deluded utterly;
the girl changed back then to her other form.   1225
     "But once the father realized that she
was able to transform her body's shape,
he sold her off to master after master,
and she, as mare, or bird, or cow, or deer,
would slip away, dishonestly providing   1230
her greedy father with the food he craved.
     "But when at last his illness had consumed
all that she brought him, and he still craved more,
the wretched man began to tear his limbs
asunder, mangling them in his maw,   1235
and fed his body as he shrank away.
     "But why do I linger over others' tales
of metamorphoses? Often, young friends,
I have myself turned into something else,
although my choices have been limited: 1240
at times I seem to be as I am now,
at other times I coil into a snake,
and sometimes as the leader of the herd,
a bull with potent horns—did I say horns?
     "Once I had two—but now, as you can see,   1245
one of the weapons on my brow is gone!"
And after speaking, he let out a groan.

BOOK IX

Desire, Deceit, and Difficult Deliveries

Acheloüs and Hercules[1]

Theseus asked the river why he groaned,
and how he happened to have lost his horn;
and after binding up his hair in reeds,
Acheloüs began to answer him:
    "The task you set before me is a sad one,   5
for who indeed takes pleasure in recalling
the battles he has lost? Nevertheless,
I will recount this story as it happened,
because there is less shame in being beaten
than honor in my being a contender,   10
and solace to have lost to such a hero.
    "You may have heard the name of Deianira,[2]
at one time the most beautiful of maidens,
and a great cause of jealousy among
her many suitors. When all of us had entered   15
the palace of her father, I spoke up:
'Accept me as your son-in-law, Oeneus,'
and Hercules beside me said the same.
The others yielded to the two of us.
    "He spoke first, repeating the old story   20
of how he was the son of Jupiter,
and boasting of the fame of his great labors,
all undertaken by command of Juno.[3]
    "Then it was my turn. I responded, saying,
'It is indecent for a god to yield before   25
a mortal (for at that time Hercules
had not yet been transformed into a god);
in me you have the master of the streams
that through your realm meander; I will be
one of your own, no distant son-in-law,   30
a countryman and part of your own kingdom.
    "'Juno doesn't hate me, that is true,
and I was never forced into her service—
I only hope this won't be held against me!

---

1. The setting of the last part of Book VIII continues, but with a new subject: the career of the hero Hercules.
2. Ovid actually goes out of his way *not* to mention her name at the end of the tale of her brother, Meleager, in Book VIII. Ovid's placement of this tale is hardly fortuitous: note the similarities between Althaea's behavior and Deianira's.
3. The son of Jove and Alcmena, Hercules attracted Juno's wrath even before his birth: see *Alcmena's Tale*, p. 245. The twelve labors imposed on the hero later in his life were an indirect result of Juno's enmity.

"'And as for that paternity *you* boast of,   35
great Hercules, why, you must take your choice:
either it's false that Jupiter's your father,
or else it's true that you're a bastard born;
you seek a father in your mother's sin![4]
Which will you have then, son of Alcmena,   40
a fictive parent or a shameful birth?'

    "Long after I had finished speaking, he
still glowered at me, smoldering with rage,
and displaying little self-control, replied,
'Your tongue is far more dexterous than mine,   45
but just as long as *I* can win with punches,
I'll let *you* have the victory with words.'

    "Then he advanced upon me, savagely,
and after such big talk, I would have been
dishonored to fall back: I shed my green robe   50
and raised my hands, and crouching, took my stance
in opposition, with my arms widespread,
and so prepared myself to wrestle him.

    "He tosses a handful of dust in my direction,[5]
and he himself takes on its tawny color.   55
He lunges then and feints as though to seize
me by the neck or legs or private parts,
attacking everywhere. He seeks in vain:
I am defended by my weightiness,
not otherwise than when a seaside bluff,   60
assaulted by the waves that pound against it,
endures, protected by its mighty bulk.

    "We separate for just a little while,
and then we come together once again,
each holding firm and neither backing down,   65
and stand there, toe to toe, fingers knotted,
breast against breast, and forehead pressed to forehead:
I've seen two mighty bulls rush at each other
in competition for the herd's prize heifer:
the rest of the herd all look on in terror,   70
not knowing which contender will achieve
the victory—and with it, gain a realm.

    "Three times, without success, Hercules strives
to push my breast away from his; the fourth,
he knocks away my arms and breaks my hold,   75
and as I tumble forward, off balance,
—I have to tell this just the way it happened—

---

4. Hercules can't have it both ways: either he is the legitimate son of a mere mortal, Amphytrion, or the bastard son of Jove.
5. Wrestlers threw dust at their opponents' oiled bodies in order to give themselves a better grip.

gives me a slap that turns me all around
and then comes down on me with all his weight.
   "If you can credit this—I do not seek   80
to garner glory by exaggeration—
I felt I had a mountain on my back!
I barely had the strength to work my arms—
the sweat was *pouring* off them—under his,
and barely freed myself from his fierce grip.   85
   "He pressed against me as I gasped for breath
and kept me from recovering my strength,
then got me in a stranglehold—my knees
connected with the earth and I ate dust.
   "Clearly deficient in the manly virtues,   90
I opted to try trickery instead,
and changing to a snake, I glided out
from under his strong grip. But after I
had wound my body up into tight coils
and showed him my forked tongue, and hissed a bit,   95
Hercules laughed and ridiculed my arts:
'While I was in my cradle, I whipped snakes;
supposing you surpass the lot of them,
what portion of the many-headed Hydra[6]
will you—a single serpent—prove to be,   100
Acheloüs? The blows I dealt that beast
just strengthened it: no sooner did I sever
one of its heads than two more took its place!
   "'This creature, branching out with serpents sprung
from death, delighted in destruction—*yes!*   105
I overwhelmed the monster and I *diced* it!
What do you think will happen in *your* case?
—Why, even as a snake you're an imposter,
fighting with borrowed weapons, in a form
that is not yours—and subject to recall!'   110
   "He spoke and wrapped his fingers like thick chains
around my throat and dug in with his thumbs:
gripped by those pinchers, I was passing out,
and fought to get his digits off my throat.
   "So, since I had been vanquished as a snake,   115
the only refuge left was my third form,
that of a raging bull. And thus transformed
in all my parts, I now renewed the struggle.
He got his arms around my neck again,
and dragged his heels beside me as I galloped,   120

---

6. When Hercules was only eight months old, Juno slipped a pair of serpents into his cradle, which he dispatched heroically; the destruction of the Lernaean hydra was the second of the twelve labors that Hercules undertook as an adult.

until he pushed my horns down to the ground
and plowed my poor head deep into the dirt.
    "Nor was this all: grasping my rigid horn
in his right hand and cruelly breaking it,
he tore it from my mutilated forehead.   125
The naiads immortalized this incident,
filling my horn with fruit and fragrant flowers;
known as the cornucopia, it now
enriches the sweet goddess of Abundance."
    He finished speaking and a nymph stepped up,   130
dressed like Diana, with her hair unbound:
one of his attendants, who produced
their second course out of that horn of plenty,
the ripe fruit which are bountiful in autumn.
    The sun appeared, and as the mountaintops   135
were touched by its first rays, the young men left,
even before the river had found peace
and the flood-driven waters had subsided;
Acheloüs concealed his rustic looks
and mutilated brow beneath the waves.   140

Hercules, Deianira, and Nessus

His only grief, though, was to be deprived
of his lovely horn—he was fine, otherwise,
and that one loss was easily repaired
by willow leaves and reeds wrapped round his head;
you, on the other hand, impulsive Nessus,   145
passionate centaur who loved Deianira—-
an arrow through the back cost you your life.
    While Hercules was heading back to Thebes,
the city he called home, with his new bride,
he came to the swift waters of Evenus,   150
higher than normal, swollen with winter rains,
and full of whirlpools—impassable, in short.
Though Hercules was fearless for himself,
concern for Deianira made him anxious.
    Along came Nessus, powerfully built,   155
and knowing where the river could be forded:
"With my assistance, Hercules, your bride
will be set down on the opposing bank,"
he said, "and you can swim across yourself."
    Although she was as frightened by the centaur   160
as by the raging river, Hercules
entrusted her to Nessus, and at once,
still weighed down with his lion skin and quiver

(for he had thrown his club and curving bow
across to the far bank), the hero said,   165
"One river I've already overcome;
I'll conquer this one just as handily."
    And without hesitating, or attempting
to find a calmer place to cross it at,
he spurned the help of more compliant waters;   170
and after he had reached the other bank,
as he was picking up the articles
sent over in advance, he recognized
his wife's voice, and he shouted to the centaur,
who was preparing to violate his trust: 175
    "To what unhappy end will that misplaced
self-confidence of yours betray you, rapist?
—Yes, I mean *you*, double-dealing Nessus!
Listen, don't interfere with what is mine—
if not for the respect you ought to show me,   180
then for the memory of Ixion,
your father, who lies bound upon a wheel
for all eternity—the price *he* paid
for *his* attempting a forbidden rape.[7]
It won't be possible for you to flee,   185
however much you count on equine speed:
my weapon, not my feet, will run you down!"
    It happened as he said: with those last words,
he drilled an arrow through the centaur's back,
whose barbed tip exited beneath his breast.   190
When he removed it, blood that had been mixed
with the Hydra's poison spurted from those wounds.
    The centaur let it soak into his tunic,
"Lest I should die," he said, "without revenge,"
and gave the garment steeped in his warm blood   195
to Deianira as a magic charm
that would induce a lost love to return.
    Many years passed, and the heroic deeds
of Hercules endeared him to the world
and made his father's wife[8] despise him less.   200
    After one famous foreign victory
over Eurytus, king of Oechalia,
he was preparing to give thanks to Jove
by sacrificing to him at Cenaeum,
when Rumor, madly chattering, appears   205

---

7. Ixion had attempted to rape Juno.
8. Juno does not relent until the apotheosis of Hercules, and even then, her change of heart
   does not seem heartfelt: see lines 383–86.

and whispers, Deianira, in your ears;
Rumor, whose wide range and jurisdiction,
increasing with each mix of fact and fiction,
announces that your mate has got a thing
for Iole, the daughter of the king!   210
     The story of this new love was widespread,
and loving him, his wife of course believed it;
surrendering to tears at first, she grieved
and poured her heart out.
                              But soon enough she asked,
"What am I weeping for? These tears of mine   215
can only be a comfort to my rival!
Since she approaches, I should use the time
to plan some unexpected stratagem,
before this woman takes my place in bed.
Loudly complain—or suffer it in silence?   220
Decamp to Calydon—or linger here?
Yield her the house—or stay and be obstructive,
if I can do no more? But what if I—
recall that I'm your sister, Meleager—
if I should happen to devise a crime,   225
and by destruction of my rival, show
how great a deed the grief and injury
of a woman scorned is capable of causing!"
     And after mulling over all these options,
Deianira finally decided   230
to send him the garment soaked in Nessus' gore,
which had the power to restore lost love.
     With honeyed words the wretched woman bids
her husband's servant, Lichas (unaware
of what it is that he is carrying),   235
to bring this gift to mighty Hercules—
and all unwittingly, seals her own doom.

The Passion of Hercules

Suspecting nothing, he receives her gift,
and drapes the poisoned tunic on his shoulders.
He prayed and offered incense to the fire,   240
and poured out wine upon the altar stone;
freed by the flames, the pestilential venom
warmed to its task and spread throughout his body.
While he was able to, he suppressed his groans
with manly strength; when his impassivity   245
at last was overcome by violence,
he overturned the altar, and his screams

reverberated through the woods of Oeta.
  He first tried to remove the fatal tunic,
but when he tore it off, his skin came too,   250
for (sickening to speak of) it would cling
fiercely to his limbs; removed by force,
it bared his muscles and enormous bones.
  His blood (as when a heated iron bar
is plunged into the blacksmith's icy trough)   255
boiled up and hissed with fiery hot venom;
with nothing to restrain them, the greedy flames
fed upon his heart; dark sweat drenched his body,
and his scorched nerves unnervingly sang out,
while deep within his bones the marrow melted;   260
he raised both hands to heaven and cried out,
"Look down from your high seat upon this plague,
O cruel Juno—feast your bestial heart
on my destruction till your greed is sated!
Or if I may be pitied even by   265
an enemy, that is to say, by you—
then take from me my much-despised existence,
my life of labor, sickened by these torments.
My death would be a gift! And what gift more
appropriate from my stepmother's hands?   270
  "Did I subdue Busiris, who defiled
Egyptian temples with the blood of pilgrims,
to come to *this*? Was it for *this* that I tore
Antaeus from his mother's nourishment?
—That I withstood three-headed Geryon   275
the Spanish shepherd, and that dog from hell,
fierce Cerberus, who had three heads as well?
  "And you, my hands—was this the reason why
you wrenched the horns off Neptune's mighty bull?
—Was this the reason why you toiled at Elis?   280
At Stymphalus? In the Parthenian groves?
—Was this the reason why you carried off
Hippolyte's gold belt from Thermidon
and the apples guarded by the sleepless dragon?
—Was it for this that the centaurs fell before me,   285
and the boar that devastated Arcadia?
—That the Hydra who grew stronger from his losses
regenerated heads to no avail?
—That when I saw those horses fat with blood,
and saw their mangers full of chopped-up men,   290
I slew the Thracian king and his steeds too?
  "These biceps flattened the Nemean lion,
this neck upheld the world! Jove's cruel mate

is worn out now with issuing commands;
I have outlasted Juno's savage hate;   295
unwearied still of doing are my hands.[9]
    "But now my strength cannot resist this plague,
nor force of arms. This all-consuming fire
has penetrated deep into my lungs
and feeds itself on each and every limb.   300
But is Eurystheus still vigorous?
And are there those who still believe in gods?"[1]
    The gravely wounded hero finished speaking
and then climbed Oeta to its highest range,
and nothing more resembled than a bull   305
still carrying the hunting spear's barbed tip,
long after his assassin has escaped.
    You would have seen him there upon the mountain,
and heard his groaning and his roars of pain
as once again he struggled to tear off   310
the poisoned tunic, and in agony
plucked trees up by the roots and scattered them,
and raised his arms to heaven in despair.

Lichas

He catches sight of Lichas cowering
in fear, attempting to conceal himself   315
within a hollow rock, and all his rage
is gathered up and focused on one man:
"Are you the giver of the fatal gift,
Lichas? Would you achieve undying fame
by causing my demise?"
                        Lichas trembled   320
in terror, trying to excuse himself,

---

9. Highlights of Hercules's career as a hero: Busiris was an Egyptian king who murdered
   strangers in his kingdom, until Hercules killed him; Antaeus, a giant, was lifted by Hercules from the ground, thus separated from the nourishment of his mother earth; Geryon
   was a Spanish shepherd with a herd of red cattle, rustled by Hercules, who also dragged
   Cerberus, the three-headed watchdog of the underworld, up into daylight; Elis was the
   site of the stables of King Augeias, filled with the dung of three thousand cattle, which
   Hercules cleaned up in a single day; Stymphalus was the site of a lake full of monstrous,
   man-eating birds, which Hercules drove away with arrows; Hercules captured the golden-
   horned, brass-footed deer of the goddess Diana in the Parthenian groves; Hyppolite's
   golden belt was captured from the Amazon queen; the apples guarded by the sleepless
   dragon were the golden apples of the Hesperides; the centaurs who fell before him and
   the boar recall a battle in the cave of the centaur Pholos, while our hero was stalking the
   Erymanthian boar; the hydra was slain by Hercules and his companion Iolaus; the
   "horses fat with blood" belonged to Diomedes, king of Thrace, who fed them on human
   flesh; the Nemean lion was strangled by Hercules; and Hercules's neck upheld the world
   while Atlas went off to fetch him the apples of the Hesperides.
1. Eurystheus was a relative of Hercules. Whichever of the two was born later would be subservient to the other. Thanks to Juno's trickery, Hercules's mother was kept from delivering the hero (see Alcmena's Tale, p. 245) until Eurystheus was born. Later he gained
   mastery over Hercules and imposed on him the twelve labors.

but even as he spoke, while he attempted
to clasp the hero's knees in supplication,
Hercules seized him, spun him round and round,
then catapulted him into the sea.   325
He hardened as he hung there in midair,
as rain (they say) congeals in a frigid wind,
until it changes into snow, whose flakes
turn first to slush and then to frozen hail;
so he, hurled through the void by Hercules,   330
bloodless with fear, all humors vaporized,
turned into rigid flint, tradition says.

　　And even now, in the Eubocan Sea,
a small rock rises just above the waves,
maintaining still its former, human shape;   335
sailors believe that it is sentient,
and will not walk upon it in their shoes.
They call it Lichas.

The Death of Hercules

　　　　　　　　　　But you, famed son of Jove,
having denuded Mount Oeta of its trees,
constructed your enormous funeral pyre   340
and ordered Philoctetes, son of Poeas
(who torched it from the base), to take your bow
and arrows and your quiver in exchange,
armaments destined to return to Troy.[2]

　　And as the eager flames began to spread,   345
you draped the pelt of the Nemean lion
over the top, and pillowing your head
upon your club, you lay there at your ease,
not otherwise than as you would have been
reclining at a banquet, flower-wreathed,   350
with wine to drink from cups always refilled.
Now spreading out in every direction,
the crackling flames came after Hercules,
whose carefree limbs received them with contempt.

Jove and the Apotheosis of Hercules

The gods were frightened for the earth's protector,   355
and when he realized this, Jove was pleased
by their concern and happily addressed them:
"It gives me pleasure to observe your fear,
O deities; I congratulate myself
quite unreservedly, that I am called   360

---

2. According to a prophecy, Troy would not fall to the Greeks without the bow of
　　Philoctetes.

the father and the rector of such a race
of mindful subjects—and that my progeny
is given the protection of your favor,
for even though you organize this tribute
to honor him for his impressive deeds,   365
I nonetheless am much obliged to you.

    "But let your hearts not quake with empty fear;
ignore those flames rising from Mount Oeta—
he who has vanquished all will vanquish them!
Only his mother's part will feel the fires: 370
immortal is the part he has from me;
it cannot die or be subdued by flames.

    "And when he has been discharged from the earth,
I will receive him on the shores of heaven;
and I am utterly convinced that *all* of you   375
will find my action a great source of joy.

    "But if there should be *any*one among you,
anyone *at all*, I say, who might be pained
by Hercules' becoming an immortal,
that one may wish him not to have this gift,   380
but will acknowledge that it is deserved,
and—even though unwillingly—approve it."

    The gods assented—and even Juno seemed
to find his speech not difficult to bear,
until its ending, when she lost composure,   385
embarrassed to be singled out in public.

    Meanwhile, whatever parts of Hercules
were flammable, the fire burned away,
till naught that could be recognized remained,
and none of what his mother's gifts had been;   390
now all that he retained derived from Jove.

    And as a serpent who has shed his skin
sheds old age too, rejoicing in new life,
and glitters with new scales; so Hercules,
when he had cast off his mortality,   395
became more vigorous in his better part,
and he began to seem much more impressive,
more worshipful in his augmented size.

    Almighty Jupiter bore him aloft
and (in his chariot) through hollow clouds   400
up to his place among the radiant stars.

    Atlas could feel an increase in the weight
upon his shoulders; yet not even now
did Eurystheus let go of his anger:
the hatred that he had for Hercules   405
was redirected against his descendants.[3]

---

3. He persecuted the children of Hercules until the hero's son Hyllus killed him.

Alcmena's Tale

But the hero's mother, Alcmena, consumed
by lifelong cares, had now, in Iole,
someone to whom she could relate the tales
of the legendary labors of her son   410
and of her own labors and misfortunes.
For Hyllus, as commanded by his father,
had taken Iole to heart and bed
and magnanimously filled her womb with seed.
    Alcmena began telling her this story: 415
"I pray the gods will favor you at least
by shortening your time of delivery
when you are due, and call on Ilithyia,[4]
the patron-goddess of all frightened mothers,
whom Juno's anger influenced against me.   420
    "For when the time came for me to deliver
the child who took on labors of his own,
and the Sun's weight pressed upon the tenth house,[5]
the burden of my womb was so enormous,
my size so great, that you could tell the cause   425
could be no other than almighty Jove.
I could not bear the pains a moment longer!
    "Grief seizes me as I recall it now,
and horror grips me even as I speak
and a cold shiver runs throughout my limbs.   430
For seven nights and days, I was in torment;
wrung out by suffering, I called upon
Lucina and the Nixi, goddesses
who offer aid to women in their pangs.
    "Lucina came—but having taken bribes   435
from cruel Juno, who desired my death,
she sat outside the house upon an altar,
with her right knee pressed tightly on her left,
and fingers interlaced across them both;
and as she listened to my screams, the goddess   440
recited spells and charms in a low voice
that kept delivery from taking place.
    "I strain, and mad with agony, reproach
ungrateful Jove; I want to die, my words
would stir unfeeling stones! The women of Thebes   445
offer up prayers and try to comfort me.
    "Galanthis, a plebeian servant girl
with bright red hair, appears, quick to take orders,
and pleasing to me for her diligence.

---

4. A goddess also known as Juno Lucina, who presided over the travails of women in labor.
5. Alcmena has finished nine months of her pregnancy and is entering the tenth; the sun in
   its annual journey is pressing on the tenth of the twelve signs of the zodiac.

She realizes Juno is against me   450
and up to mischief. As she comes and goes,
she sees the goddess sitting on the altar,
her knees pressed close, her fingers laced around them:
'Whoever you are,' she said, 'congratulate
our mistress, for Alcmena is delivered   455
of a boychild, and our prayers are answered!'
        "That influential goddess of the womb
leaps up, unclenching both her hands and knees,
and I give birth as soon as the chains drop!
        "They say Galanthis mocked the cheated goddess,   460
who seized the girl, still laughing, by her hair,
and wiped the ground with her; and as she struggled,
the goddess changed her arms into forelegs;
she kept her former quickness, and her body
now has the color that her hair once had,   465
although her form is rather different.
        "Because of the deception of her lips,
she must now bear her offspring through her mouth;[6]
she dwells (as formerly) within our homes."
[Galanthis has been turned into a weasel.]   470

Iole's Tale of Dryope

Alcmena finished speaking, and she groaned,
upset to think of what had happened to
her former servant.
                        While she grieved, Iole
addressed her in these words: "Nevertheless,
dear mother, it's the transformation of   475
a stranger that you find upsetting—what
if I should tell you the astounding tale
of my own sister's fate? And yet my tears
impede me and prohibit me from speaking!
        "Dryope was her mother's only daughter   480
(for I was born to my father's second wife),
by far the fairest in Oechalia.
The god who rules at Delphos and Delos[7]
desired her virginity and forced her,
and then she was accepted by Andraemon,   485
who was considered lucky in his marriage.
        "There is a lake whose banks are crowned with myrtle,
whose shores slope gently down to meet the water;
here Dryope came, ignorant of fate,

6. As weasels were believed to do.
7. Apollo.

and—so your indignation may be greater—   490
to gather myrtle garlands for the nymphs!
She carried the sweet burden of her boy,
an infant, really, not yet one year old,
and nourished him with milk warm from her breast.

    "Close to the water's edge, a lotus bloomed,   495
whose purple blossoms, bright as Tyrian dye,
foretold of berries. Dryope reached in
and picked some flowers to delight her son,
and I was just about to follow suit,
for I was present, too—but just in time,   500
I saw the drops of blood those flowers shed
and saw the branches quivering with dread!

    "For as you know, the local boors still tell
how the nymph Lotis, fleeing from obscene
Priapus, found a refuge as this flower,   505
and kept her name, though changing her appearance.
My sister had known nothing of all this:
when she in fright attempted to turn back
and leave, while begging pardon of the nymphs,
her feet, as though turned roots, clung to the ground.   510

    "She fought to tear herself away from it,
yet nothing but her torso could now move;
a shell of bark wound upward from below,
little by little, till it sheathed her loins.
She tried to tear the hair out of her head,   515
but found her hands were full of leaves instead.
Her child, Amphissus (given that name by
his grandfather, Oechalian Eurytus),
could feel his mother's titty growing rigid
and was no longer able to take suck.   520

    "I was a witness to your cruel fate,
my sister, powerless to bring you aid,
yet did as much as I was able to;
with my embraces, I delayed the change
by clinging to your burgeoning new growth   525
at trunk and branches. O sister, I confess,
I wished to hide myself beneath that bark!

    "But look, to where her husband Andraemon
and her most wretched father now appear,
seeking Dryope. The Dryope they seek,   530
as I point out, is now a lotus tree.
And having thrown themselves upon the ground,
they cling to its roots and kiss the still-warm wood.

    "Now only my beloved sister's face
had not yet been transformed into the wood: 535
your tears were trickling down upon the leaves
made from your body; while it could, your mouth

responded to the promptings of your voice
and filled the air with rending lamentation:
   "'If those in wretchedness may truly swear,   540
why then I swear by all the gods in heaven,
I have done nothing to deserve this evil!
I bear a punishment that has no crime!
I've lived a blameless life—and if I lie,
then let my foliage shrivel up and die   545
and may the axe and flame consume me quite!
   "'But take my baby from his mother's limbs
and give him to a wet nurse who will bring
him here and nurse him underneath this tree,
and let him play here too; when my poor babe   550
has learned to speak, let him come to this place
and greet his mother here and sadly say,
"My mother is hidden underneath this bark."
Let him be frightened of the lake, and mindful
never to pluck the flowers from the trees,   555
and think that in each bush a goddess hides!
   "'Farewell, dear husband—sister—father!
If you can show compassionate respect,
then keep the sharpened pruning hook far hence,
and guard my foliage from browsing flocks.   560
   "'And since I am forbidden to bow down,
raise yourselves up to where my limbs branch out
and let us kiss while I am able to;
lift up my little boy! I can say no more;
the bloodless bark crawls over my soft neck   565
and what I am is hidden in its tip.
But do not offer me the services
given to the dead—for without your hands
the upward crawling bark will close my eyes.'
   "She ceased her speaking—and ceased at once to be,   570
but for a long while her new branches held
her body's warmth, now changed entirely."

Iolaüs and Hebe's Prophecy

While Iole told this amazing story,
and while Alcmena (who was weeping too)
with sympathetic thumbs erased the tears   575
cascading down the storyteller's cheeks,
a new occurrence drove away their sorrow:
right there above them on the threshold stood
a boy with his first beard upon his cheeks,
Iolaüs,[8] restored to prime of life.   580

---

8. At the hero's request, the goddess Hebe, Hercules's divine bride, restored the youth of
   Hercules's companion Iolaüs.

For Hebe, Hercules' immortal bride
and Juno's daughter, worn down by her mate's
entreaties, had just given him this gift.
And nevermore, she was about to swear,
would she confer such gifts on anyone,   585
when Themis broke in with a prophecy:[9]
    "Why, even now, Thebes suffers the commotion
of civil war," she said, "and Capaneus
will be invincible to all but Jove;
the two brothers will inflict mortal wounds   590
on one another; the still-living seer
will disappear into the gaping earth
and find the spirits which he once controlled;
in a crime of piety his son will slay
his mother to avenge his father's death;   595
stunned by the horror of this crime, expelled
from home and driven mad, he will be chased
by the raging Furies and his mother's ghost
until his wife demands from him the fatal
golden necklace, and the sword of Phegeius   600
will find its way into his kinsman's side.
    "And then, at last, Callirhoë, his wife,
the daughter of Acheloüs, will be
given by Jove the gift that will allow
her sons to change from infancy to manhood,   605
so that their father's murder may not go
unpunished; and then Jupiter, won over
by her petitioning shall claim the gifts
of Hebe in advance for them, and change
the prepubescent boys into young men."   610
    When Themis, who was prescient, had told them
what was to come, the other gods began
to grumble openly; a groundswell rose;
Why was this same gift not allowed to others?
    Aurora railed about her ancient spouse   615
Tithonus, and mild-mannered Ceres moaned
for Iasion's white locks; Vulcan demanded
renewed life for his son Erichthonius,
and Venus also, looking to the future,
insisted that Anchises be restored.[1]   620
    Each of the gods there had a favorite,
and argued from a partisan position
against the others, until Jove spoke up:
"O gods! If you have any reverence
for us at all, why leap to such confusions?   625

9. A complicated prophecy whose events refer to the legend of the seven against Thebes.
1. The immortals named are all attached by bonds of love to mortals who must age and die,
   a situation that these gods would like to alter.

Does anyone here imagine himself able
to overcome the limits set by Fate?
Iolaüs was given back the years
he was in need of by the will of Fate;
not by ambition, not by skill in combat   630
will Callirhoë's sons turn into men
from infancy, but by the will of Fate,
which governs even us; I tell you this
that you might put a better face on it—
yes, *you* are ruled by Fate, and *I* am too.   635
      "If I were able to oppose its force,
the years would not have bent Aeacus down,
and Rhadamanthus would be always young,
and Minos too, now held in disregard
by reason of the bitter weight of age,   640
no longer ruling as he used to do."[2]
      The words of Jove calmed everybody down:
none of the gods was able to complain
when he saw Rhadamanthus worn with years,
and Aeacus, and Minos, who, when young,   645
could frighten mighty nations with one word:
Minos. He was decrepit now and feared
Miletus, son of Deione and Phoebus,
a young man proud of his strength and lineage.
Minos believed Miletus would rise up   650
against his realm, but still he did not dare
to banish him from his ancestral lands.
      You fled, Miletus, of your own accord,
traversing the Aegean in your swift ship,
and in the land of Asia you established   655
that city which still bears its founder's name.
Here you had knowledge of the nymph Cyanee
(the daughter of that winding stream, Maeander)
while she was straying on her father's banks;
and from that union came a pair of twins,   660
Byblis and Caunus, famous for their beauty.

Byblis and Caunus

Now Byblis, who was driven by desire
for her own brother, the grandson of Apollo—
this Byblis serves to illustrate a moral:
that girls should not desire what's forbidden;   665
she did not love her brother as a brother,
or as a sister should.
                  Indeed, at first,

2. Three sons of Jove.

she didn't even recognize her passion,
nor did she think it wrong to kiss him often,
or throw her arms around her brother's neck;   670
and she herself was for some time deceived
by the appearance of affectionate devotion.
 Her feelings for him gradually changed,
and not for the better; when she visited
her brother, she was elegantly dressed,   675
and anxious that he find her beautiful,
and envious of those who seemed more lovely.
 She was, as yet, unconscious of her feelings,
and offered up no prayers for satisfaction,
but burned with inner fire, nonetheless.   680
She calls him "Master" now, and now detests
the thought that they are siblings, and prefers
that he should call her "Byblis" and not "Sister."
 Nevertheless, she did not dare admit
such impure hopes into her wakeful thoughts;   685
often, however, when relaxed in sleep,
an image of her passion came to her,
an image of her lying with her brother,
that made her, even sleeping, blush with shame.
 Sleep fled, and for a long time she lay still,   690
revisiting the dream of her desire,
until, at last, she spoke out, doubtfully:
"I am so wretched! Whatever can they mean,
these visions that appear in the wordless night?
I would not have it so! Why do I see   695
such things while I am sleeping? He is indeed
most pleasing, even to a hostile eye,
and I could love him, not unworthily,
if he were not my brother! I am wronged,
and all the harm is—that I am his sister!   700
 "But even if I keep them out of mind,
there is no wrong in *dreaming* of such things
as often as I want to, in my sleep!
There are no witnesses to our dreams,
and they provide a pleasure almost real!   705
 "O Cupid and sweet Venus, what great joys
were given to me! And how real they seemed!
My marrow melted as I lay asleep!
How pleasing to remember! But how brief
those pleasures were—the night, with breakneck speed,   710
snatched them away, when they had just begun!
 "If I could be allowed to change my name
and marry you, dear Caunus, what a fine
daughter-in-law I would make your father!
What a fine son-in-law you would make mine!   715

We would have everything in common then,
except grandparents—yours should be the nobler!
Yes, I would have it so! But all too soon,
you will take someone else to be your wife,
most beautiful of men—and you will be,   720
by virtue of parental lottery,
my brother only. There is the harm of it,
that we will have no more than that in common.

 "What are they telling me, these dreams of mine?
What weight do dreams have? Have they any weight?   725
Oh, may the gods send better dreams than these!

 "The gods took their own sisters, to be sure!
So Saturn had Ops, Oceanus had his Tethys,
the ruler of Olympus had his Juno:[3]
the gods, though, are a law unto themselves!   730
—Why should I try to use them as my models
when their behavior is so unlike ours?

 "Passion suppressed will either leave my heart,
or, if I am unable to suppress it,
I pray that I might die and not surrender;   735
and when I have been laid upon my bier,
may my dear brother kiss me on the lips!
Such a decision should be jointly made:
what pleases me might seem a crime to him!

 "The sons of Aeolus[4] were not afraid   740
to sleep with their sisters! How do I know this,
and why have I come up with this example?
Where is this leading me? Depart, indecent thoughts,
and let me love my brother not at all,
unless my love is sisterly and lawful!   745

 "Nevertheless, if he had been seized first
by love for me, I might indulge his passion.
And so, since I would never turn him down,
I will go after him! *Can you admit this?*
Will you be able to confess it?   750
Compelled by love, I will be able to!
If Shame should press her finger to my lips,
a silent letter will confess my hidden feelings."

 This purpose pleases her and overcomes
her mind's uncertainties. Still in her bed,   755
she lifts herself up and leans on her left elbow:
"Now let him see," she says, "my decadence!
What slope am I beginning to descend?
What fire is conceived within my heart?"

---

3. Brother-sister relationships as well as husband-wife.
4. According to Homer in Book 10 of the *Odyssey*, the sons and daughters of Aeolus, the god
 of winds, married one another.

Her shaking hands set down the practiced words: 760
she grips the iron stylus in her right,
and holds the blank wax tablet in her left.[5]
She starts and stops. Sets down—and then condemns.
Adds and deletes. Doubts; finds fault with; approves.
She throws the tablet down, then picks it up!   765
She cannot say what she is striving for,
and every tack she takes displeases her,
who sometimes seems ashamed, and sometimes bold.
    She first wrote "Sister" down—and then decided
to take the "Sister" out—and then inscribed   770
these words on the corrected wax:
                                    "My dearest—
One who so holds *you*, one who will not have
a dearest, if not you, now sends you this,
who cannot, out of shame, reveal herself,
but if you wish to know what I desire,   775
it is that, nameless, I might plead my case
unrecognized as Byblis, undiscovered
until my wish were certain to be granted.
    "You might have sensed I was in love with you
from my drained complexion and stressed countenance,   780
my eyes so often filling up with tears,
the sighs brought on by no apparent cause,
my constant need to throw my arms about you—
and, if by any chance you noticed them,
the kisses that were more than sisterly.   785
    "And yet, despite the burden of my wound,
despite the fury of that inner fire,
I did my best—the gods will witness this!—
to bring myself again to sanity;
unfortunate, I've struggled for so long   790
to get away from Cupid's fierce encounters,
enduring more—I think you would agree—
than any girl could bear.
                            "Now overwhelmed
by my great passion and compelled to speak,
I seek your help with this fainthearted prayer,   795
for you will be my rescue—or my ruin:
the choice is yours and you must make it now.
    "I pray to you not as an enemy,
but as the one most closely joined to you,
who yet desires to be nearer still,   800
more closely linked by even stricter chains.

---

5. Typical writing instruments of Ovid's time; the wax could be easily erased and used again.
   This is the only tale in the *Metamorphoses* in which we see someone writing.

"Let old men know what is and is not proper,
distinguish 'decent' from 'indecencies,'
and keep the fine distinctions of the law.
Heedless passion accords with our youth.   805
We have not learned yet what may be allowed,
so we believe that everything may be,
and follow the example of the gods!

"In our case, we haven't a strict father
or a concern for what the people say,   810
or fear to serve as an impediment;
and should there be occasion for our fear,
our pleasurable thefts will be concealed
by our relationship—for as your sister,
I am allowed to speak with you in private,   815
and openly embrace and give you kisses.

"The little that is lacking—is it too much?
Have pity, then, on one who speaks her love
but would not speak unless compelled by passion;
and let it not be written on my stone   820
that by refusing me, you caused my death."

When she had finished setting down these words
on tablets which were filled right to their edges
(though pointlessly, as it will soon appear),
she sealed the wicked missive with her signet,   825
dampened—her mouth was dry—by flowing tears.

Shamefaced, she called a servant to her side
and gave him orders in a shaky voice:
"Take these, most faithful one, to our—"
and after a long pause, she got out,
                                    "—brother."   830
She dropped the tablets she was giving him,
but sent them anyway—despite that omen.
And when he thought it was appropriate,
the servant gave the message to her brother,
who read it halfway through, then threw it down,   835
astonished and enraged by what he'd read,
and scarcely able to restrain himself
from tearing out the frightened servant's throat:
"Flee while you can," Maeander's grandson said,
"you agent of my sister's filthy lust—   840
if your death were not linked to our dishonor,
then surely you would die, you vicious rogue!"

He fled in terror, bringing to his mistress
her brother's fierce response. When she heard the news
of his rejection, Byblis lost all color   845
and shivered uncontrollably from chills.

As soon as she became herself again,
her passion for her brother came back too,
and barely audible, she gave it voice:
"Deserved, indeed! Why have I been so foolish   850
as to reveal my very soul to him!
So swiftly to set down upon the page
what should have been concealed! I should have tried
to understand his feelings for me first,
with speech that hinted but did not commit.   855
    "I should have checked which way the wind was blowing
before I set my sails out, to be safe;
I set them out too soon; a wind came up
and now I have been driven on the rocks;
the whole force of the ocean overwhelms me,   860
and I have no way to regain my course.
    "By unambiguous omens I was warned
not to give in to my desires, when,
while ordering my servant to deliver
the letter, it—and all my hopes—both fell.   865
Should I have changed the day—or my whole purpose?
    "Better to change the day! Almighty Jove
admonished me in no uncertain terms,
which I would not have missed, had I been sane.
I should have *spoken* to him, and confessed   870
the feelings that I have for him in person,
and not put them in writing in the wax.
He would have seen his tearful lover's face;
I could have said much more than any letter.
    "With no encouragement, I could have thrown   875
my arms around his neck, and if he spurned me,
I would have made it seem like I was dying,
and clinging to his knees, begged for my life.
    "I should have left nothing unattempted:
though any of my stratagems could fail,   880
the lot of them together might prevail
against the hardness of my brother's heart.
The fault—it may be—of my messenger,
ineptly showing up at the wrong time,
seeking him out when he was not at leisure,   885
I'm sure of it.
                    "All this has injured me.
But after all, he is no tiger's son
with heart of iron or of adamant,
nor was he suckled by a lioness.
He will be overcome! I will pursue him   890
once more, and not give up while I have breath!

"If I could just undo what I have done,
that would have been best: not to have begun;
the second best is now for me to do
all that it takes to see this journey through.   895
        "For if I now should alter my intent
he could not think of me as innocent,
and if I give him up now, I must seem
a light thing, undeserving of esteem,
or else a temptress trying every way   900
she knows to lead the virtuous astray.
He will not think I have within my breast
that god whose urgent flames give me no rest,
but rather that I am provoked by lust.
        "Nothing I do now will regain his trust,   905
since he has read the letters that I traced;
desire revealed may never be erased.
Though I do nothing more, I must appear
guilty to him; with hope, and without fear,
I may still win my bliss and end my pain,   910
and nothing to lose means only much to gain."
        She spoke, and her confusion was so great
that while she wept for what she had attempted,
she wanted to attempt it yet again;
at every approach, rejection came.   915
Her brother fled his homeland, and his sister's
abominations; when her grim pursuit
seemed endless to him, he went off and founded
a city of his own on foreign soil.
        And then, they say, she truly lost her mind,   920
and ripped apart the garments on her breast
and beat her arms and shoulders in her fury;
her madness unconcealed now, she confesses
the hope of her forbidden love, and flees
her homeland and its now-detested hearth,   925
and sets out after her self-exiled brother.
        It is as when your devotees, O Bacchus,
the frenzied women of Ismaria,
all come together at your triennial rites;
not otherwise the women of Bibassus   930
saw Byblis raving all across the fields.
        And afterward, she roamed through Caria,
and among the Leleges and Lycians.
Now she has passed Cragus and Limyre,
and the river Xanthus, and that mountain range   935
the fire-breathing Chimaera inhabits,
who boasts a lion's head and serpent's tail.

The woods grew sparse. Worn out by your pursuit,
you tumble to the ground, and lie there, Byblis,
your unbound hair on the unyielding earth,   940
and your mouth pressed against the fallen leaves.
    Often the Lelegeian nymphs attempted
to lift her up in their sympathetic arms,
and urged upon the unresponsive girl
the remedies they had for lovesickness;   945
Byblis just lies there silently and clutches
the grasses in her fingers, as she waters
the vegetation with her flowing tears.
The naiads, it is said, replaced that font
with one incapable of running dry: 950
what greater gift could naiads have to give?
    As pitch drops drip from gashes in pine bark,
as gummy asphalt oozes from dense soil,
as frozen water, touched by the soft breath
of the west wind, now melts beneath the sun,   955
so Byblis, quite consumed by her own tears,
is changed at once into a flowing spring
which, in these parts, still bears its mistress' name,
and has its source beneath a shrub-oak tree.

Iphis and Isis

Rumor might very well have spread the news   960
of this unprecedented transformation
throughout the hundred towns of Crete, if they
had not just had a wonder of their own
to talk about—the change that came to Iphis.
    For, once upon a time, there lived in Phaestus,   965
not far from the royal capital at Cnossus,
a freeborn plebeian[6] named Ligdus, who
was otherwise unknown and undistinguished,
with no more property than fame or status,
and yet devout, and blameless in his life.   970
    His wife was pregnant. When her time had come,
he gave her his instructions with these words:
"There are two things I pray to heaven for
on your account: an easy birth and a son.
The other fate is much too burdensome,   975
for daughters need what Fortune has denied us:
a dowry.
        "Therefore—and may God prevent

---

6. Ovid's conceit: plebeian was a Roman, rather than Greek, social distinction.

this happening, but if, by chance, it does
and you should be delivered of a girl,
unwillingly I order this, and beg   980
pardon for my impiety—*But let it die!*"[7]
    He spoke, and tears profusely bathed the cheeks
of the instructor and instructed both.
Telethusa continued to implore
her husband, praying him not to confine   985
their hopes so narrowly—to no avail,
for he would not be moved from his decision.
    Now scarcely able to endure the weight
of her womb's burden, as she lay in bed
at midnight, a dream-vision came to her: 990
the goddess Io[8] stood (or seemed to stand)
before her troubled bed, accompanied
with solemn pomp by all her mysteries.
    She wore her crescent horns upon her brow
and a garland made of gleaming sheaves of wheat,   995
and a queenly diadem; behind her stood
the dog-faced god Anubis, and divine
Bubastis (who defends the lives of cats),
and Apis as a bull clothed in a hide
of varied colors, with Harpocrates,   1000
the god whose fingers, pressed against his lips,
command our silence; and one often sought
by his devoted worshipers—Osiris;
and the asp, so rich in sleep-inducing drops.
She seemed to wake, and saw them all quite clearly.   1005
    These were the words the goddess spoke to her:
"O Telethusa, faithful devotee,
put off your heavy cares! Disobey your spouse,
and do not hesitate, when Lucina
has lightened the burden of your labor,   1010
to raise this child, whatever it will be.
I am that goddess who, when asked, delivers,
and you will have no reason to complain
that honors you have paid me were in vain."
After instructing her, the goddess left.   1015

---

7. Greeks and Romans alike exposed their unwanted babies in waste places, either to die or
   to be taken up by those who wanted them. In a letter from a Roman citizen to his wife,
   said to date from 1 B.C. there is a remarkable parallel to Ligdus's instructions to his wife:
   "Know that I am still in Alexandria. [. . .] I ask and beg you to take good care of our baby
   son, and as soon as I receive payment I shall send it you, If you are delivered [before I
   come home], if it is a boy, keep it, if a girl, discard it." (Lewis Naphtali, ed., "Papyrus
   Oxyrhynchus 744," *Life in Egypt Under Roman Rule* [Oxford: Oxford UP, 1985], 54).
8. Io, transformed into the goddess Isis at the end of her tale, appears in her Egyptian
   panoply, accompanied by her attendant gods.

The Cretan woman rose up joyfully,
lifted her hands up to the stars, and prayed
that her dream-vision would be ratified.
     Then going into labor, she brought forth
a daughter—though her husband did not know it.   1020
The mother (with intention to deceive)
told them *to feed the boy*. Deception prospered,
since no one knew the truth except the nurse.
     The father thanked the gods and named the child
for its grandfather, Iphis; since this name   1025
was given men and women both, his mother
was pleased, for she could use it honestly.
So from her pious lie, deception grew.
She dressed it as a boy—its face was such
that whether boy or girl, it was a beauty.   1030
     Meanwhile, the years went by, thirteen of them:
your father, Iphis, has arranged for you
a marriage to the golden-haired Ianthe,
the daughter of a Cretan named Telestes,
the maid most praised in Phaestus for her beauty.   1035
The two were similar in age and looks,
and had been taught together from the first.
     First love came unexpected to both hearts
and wounded them both equally—and yet
their expectations were quite different: 1040
Ianthe can look forward to a time
of wedding torches and of wedding vows,
and trusts that one whom she believes a man
will be *her* man. Iphis, however, loves
with hopeless desperation, which increases   1045
in strict proportion to its hopelessness,
and burns—a maiden—for another maid!
     And scarcely holding back her tears, she cries,
"Oh, what will be the end reserved for Iphis,
gripped by a strange and monstrous passion known   1050
to no one else? If the gods had wished to spare me,
they should have; if they wanted to destroy me,
they should have given me a natural affliction.
     "Cows do not burn for cows, nor mares for mares;
the ram will have his sheep, the stag his does,   1055
and birds will do the same when they assemble;
there are no animals whose females lust
for other females! I wish that I were dead!
     "That Crete might bring forth monsters of all kinds,
Queen Pasiphaë was taken by a bull,   1060
yet even *that* was male-and-female passion!
My love is much less rational than hers,

to tell the truth. At least she had the hope
of satisfaction, taking in the bull
through guile, and in the image of a cow,   1065
thereby deceiving the adulterer!

    "If every form of ingenuity
were gathered here from all around the world,
if Daedalus flew back on waxen wings,
what could he do? Could all his learnèd arts   1070
transform me from a girl into a boy?
Or could *you* change into a boy, Ianthe?

    "But really, Iphis, pull yourself together,
be firm, cast off this stultifying passion:
accept your birth—unless you would deceive   1075
yourself as well as others—look for love
where it is proper to, as a woman should!
Hope both creates and nourishes such love;
reality deprives you of all hope.

    "No watchman keeps you from her dear embrace,   1080
no husband's ever-vigilant concern,
no father's fierceness; nor does she herself
deny the gifts that you would have from her.
And yet you are denied all happiness,
nor could it have been otherwise if all   1085
the gods and men had labored in your cause.

    "But the gods have not denied me anything;
agreeably, they've given what they could;
my father wishes for me what *I* wish,
she and her father both would have it be;   1090
but Nature, much more powerful than they are,
wishes it not—sole source of all my woe!

    "But look—the sun has risen and the day
of our longed-for nuptials dawns at last!
Ianthe will be mine—and yet not mine: 1095
we die of thirst here at the fountainside.

    "Why do you, Juno, guardian of brides,
and you, O Hymen, god of marriage, come
to these rites, which cannot be rites at all,
for no one takes the bride, and both are veiled?"   1100

    She said no more. Nor did her chosen burn
less fiercely as she prayed you swiftly come,
O god of marriage.
                Fearing what you sought,
Telethusa postponed the marriage day
with one concocted pretext and another,   1105
a fictive illness or an evil omen.
But now she had no more excuses left,
and the wedding day was only one day off.

She tears the hair bands from her daughter's head
and from her own, and thus unbound, she prayed   1110
while desperately clinging to the altar:
"O holy Isis, who art pleased to dwell
and be worshiped at Paraetonium,
at Pharos, in the Mareotic fields,
and where the Nile splits into seven branches;   1115
deliver us, I pray you, from our fear!
    "For I once saw thee and thy sacred emblems,
O goddess, and I recognized them all
and listened to the sound of brazen rattles
and kept your orders in my memory.   1120
    "And that my daughter still looks on the light,
and that I have not suffered punishment,
why, this is all your counsel and your gift;
now spare us both and offer us your aid."
    Warm tears were in attendance on her words.   1125
The altar of the goddess seemed to move—
it *did* move, and the temple doors were shaken,
and the horns (her lunar emblem) glowed with light,
and the bronze rattles sounded.
                            Not yet secure,
but nonetheless delighted by this omen,   1130
the mother left with Iphis following,
as was her wont, but now with longer strides,
darker complexion, and with greater force,
a keener countenance, and with her hair
shorter than usual and unadorned,   1135
and with more vigor than a woman has.
    And you who were so recently a girl
are now a boy! Bring gifts to the goddess!
Now boldly celebrate your faith in her!
They bring the goddess gifts and add to them   1140
a votive tablet with these lines inscribed:

GIFTS IPHIS PROMISED WHEN SHE WAS A MAID
TRANSFORMED INTO A BOY HE GLADLY PAID

The next day's sun revealed the great wide world
with Venus, Juno, and Hymen all together   1145
gathered beneath the smoking nuptial torches,
and Iphis in possession of Ianthe.

BOOK X

The Songs of Orpheus

Orpheus and Eurydice

From there, dressed in his saffron mantle, Hymen
went on his way, traversed the boundless heavens
until he came to Thrace, where he'd been summoned
by the voice of Orpheus—to no avail,
for though the god appeared, he did not bring   5
the words that customary use has sanctioned,
nor countenances radiating joy,
nor omens of good fortune for the couple;
even the torch he carried merely sputtered,
emitting only tear-producing smoke,   10
not catching fire when he whirled it round.
    And the aftermath was even more unpleasant,
for as the bride was strolling through the grass,
attended by the naiads, she dropped dead,
bitten on her ankle by a snake.[1]   15
    When Orpheus had mourned sufficiently
in the upper air, he bravely went below
lest he should leave the underworld untried;
he made his way there by the Spartan Gates,[2]
and passing through the superficial forms   20
of those who had been buried up above,
he came to Proserpina and her spouse,
the ruler of this unattractive kingdom,
and master of the shades.
                The Thracian bard
plucked at his lyre and began to sing: 25
"Great god and goddess, appointed to govern in Hades,
into which every living creature relapses,
if it is rightful for me, if I am permitted
to shun all evasions, speaking the truth to you plainly,
know that I have not come down here to your kingdom   30
just for the view, or to chain up the three-headed Cerberus,
that monstrous child of Medusa, bristling with serpents;
my wife is the cause of my journey: she stepped on an adder
whose venom cut her life short as it spread through her body.
I won't deny that I wished to—and tried to—endure it,   35
but Love overcame me. Above, this god is quite famous;
whether he has the same status down here, I'm not certain,

---

1. A marriage tale with a happy ending concludes Book IX, and is followed at the beginning
   of Book X by a marriage tale ending tragically, though with comical abruptness.
2. The name of a cave in the southern Peloponnese believed to be one of the entrances to
   the underworld.

but even so, I would think him to be as well known,
for unless that tale of long-ago rape was invented,
the selfsame deity joined the pair of you, also! 40
If that's the case, then I, by all of these frightening places,
by mighty Chaos and by this realm of the silent, I beg you
to weave once again Eurydice's fate, done too swiftly.

"We are all owed to you wholly, and though we may linger,
later or sooner all hasten to this single dwelling. 45
Everyone heads for this place, the home that is final.
Your rule is the longest that any human encounters;
she will be yours by right and dwell down here also,
when her years are accomplished: I ask for her life as a favor,
but if the Fates should deny me the gift I am seeking 50
on behalf of my wife, be sure that I will remain here,
and you may take pleasure then in a double destruction."

These words, accompanied on the plucked strings,
so moved the bloodless spirits that they wept;
Tantalus did not seek the receding water, 55
and on his wheel lay Ixion, astounded;
the birds let go the liver, and the daughters
of Danaüs were resting by their urns,
while you, O Sisyphus, sat on your stone.[3]

Then, for the first time ever, overcome 60
by the effects of song, the Furies wept,
nor could Persephone reject his prayer,
nor he who rules the underworld deny him;
Eurydice was called up from her place
among the newly dead, and awkwardly 65
came forward, limping from her recent wound.

The Thracian bard accepted her, together
with the condition set for her release:
that he may not look back at all, until
he'd exited the valley of Avernus, 70
on pain of revocation of this gift.

He started out upon the soundless path
that rises steeply through dense fog and darkness
until they had come almost to the border
of the upper earth; here Orpheus, afraid 75
that she would fail him, and desiring
a glimpse of his beloved, turned to look:
at once she slipped back to the underworld,
and he, because he wanted to embrace her,
or *be* embraced by her, stretched out his arms— 80

---

3. Each of these enjoyed a respite from eternal punishment while Orpheus sang. The liver
belonged to Prometheus, and two birds endlessly devoured it, to punish him for the theft
of fire.

but seized on nothing, that unlucky man,
unless it was the abnegating air.
   And she now, who must die a second death,
did not find fault with him, for what indeed
could he be faulted for, but his constancy?   85
"Farewell," she cried out to him one last time,
and he had scarcely heard her cry before
she took her place again among the dead.
   The second time his wife died, Orpheus
collapsed into no different a stupor   90
than that which came upon that timid fellow[4]
who looked upon the triple-headed dog,
his middle throat encircled with thick chains;
that fellow's trembling did not cease until
his former nature did, as stoniness   95
arose and spread throughout his human frame;
or as Olenos, who, though innocent,
took on a fault wishing to seem guilty;
and you, luckless Lethaea, once so proud
of your great beauty, and once joined to him: 100
two hearts that beat as one are now transformed
into a pair of stones on humid Ida.
   Orpheus prayed, desiring in vain
to cross the river Styx a second time,
but was prevented by the border guard;   105
for seven days he sat by the river's banks,
unkempt, unshaven, and unfed, with naught
but care and sorrow for his nourishment;
complaining that the gods below were cruel,
he sought out lofty Rhodope and Haemus.[5]   110
   Three times the Sun had finished out the year
in Pisces of the waters. Orpheus
had fled completely from the love of women,
either because it hadn't worked for him
or else because the pledge that he had given   115
to his Eurydice was permanent;
no matter: women burned to have the bard,
and many suffered greatly from rejection.
Among the Thracians, he originated
the practice of transferring the affections   120
to youthful males, plucking the first flower
in the brief springtime of their early manhood.[6]

---

4. This and the two figures immediately following are unknown.
5. Two Thracian mountains.
6. Orpheus is credited with originating homosexual practices in Greece.

The Catalogue of Trees

There was a hill and on this hill there was
an open space, a level area
made green by all the grasses growing there.   125
    The place lacked shade, until that poet born
of heaven came to be in residence,
and plucking his resounding lyre strings,
he summoned many shade trees to his presence:
the oak tree sacred to great Jupiter,   130
a grove of poplars (once Heliades)
and the Italian oak, with deep green leaves;
soft linden, beech and laurel (still unwed)
with the tender hazel and the useful ash
(providing us with spears and javelins);   135
pine without knots, the acorn-laden ilex,
the genial plane tree and the maple too,
(unrivaled in the brilliance of its hue);
and river-dwelling willows, lotus trees,
thin tamarisk and boxwood evergreen,   140
and myrtle with its berries green and black,
viburnum with *its* berries gray and blue,
and you as well, O twining ivy, came,
along with tendriled vines and the vine-clad elm,
the mountain ash, the spruce, the arbutus   145
(encumbered with its fruit of brilliant red)
and victory's reward, the supple palm,
and the pine tree, bare to near its shaggy top,
so pleasing to Cybele, Mother of the Gods,
since her beloved Attis put aside   150
his manhood for that trunk in which he stiffened.[7]

Cyparissus

And present in the midst of this commotion
was the cone-shaped cypress, who, though now a tree,
was once a boy, beloved of that god
by whom the bow and lyre are both strung.[8]   155
    Dear to the nymphs of the Carthaean fields
was an enormous stag whose branching antlers
most generously shaded his own head.
They glowed with gilding, and around his neck
and on his shoulders lay a jeweled collar.   160

7. A nature goddess originally worshipped in Phrygia, Cybele and her cult were brought to
   Rome in the second century B.C. Attis was a Phrygian shepherd boy; Cybele fell in love
   with him but he wished to marry another. After the goddess drove him into a frenzy, he
   castrated himself and his spirit entered a pine tree.
8. Apollo.

A silver amulet tied to his brow
jiggled when he moved, and matching pearls
hung from each ear. Fearless by nature, he
would go into the homes of perfect strangers
and offer up his neck to their caresses.   165
    But he was pleased by you above all others,
Cyparissus, most beautiful of Ceans:
for it was you who led him to new pastures
and brought him to the fountain that he drank from
and wove the varied flowers through his antlers.   170
You, like a horseman, sat upon his back,
and joyfully you led him where you wished to,
guiding his tender mouth with purple reins.
    It was the middle of a summer's day,
and high up in the sky, the swollen claws   175
of the seashore-dwelling Crab baked in the heat;
the weary stag lay on the grassy ground,
absorbing the coolness of the woodland shade.
    Unwittingly, the boy Cyparissus
transfixed him with his deadly javelin,   180
and as he watched him die of his cruel wound
resolved that he himself should perish too.
    Phoebus tried everything to comfort him,
enjoining him to moderate his grief
and suit it to the nature of his loss;   185
the boy kept groaning nonetheless and begged
the finest (and the final) gift from heaven:
that he should be allowed to mourn forever.
    Enormity of grief had left him drained,
and now his limbs began to turn bright green,   190
and now the locks upon his snowy brow
became a crown of bristles as he turned
into a tree that sways but does not bend,
whose slender tips look up to starry heaven.
    The god, grief-stricken, told him, "You will be   195
mourned by myself, and others you will mourn,
and by your presence, you will signal grief."

The Songs of Orpheus

Such was the grove the bard had gathered round him,
and now, amidst the concourse of the birds
and the assembled beasts, he took his seat;   200
and after he had plucked the lyre strings
and felt the varied modes in harmony
(though each string had its own distinctive sound),
Orpheus began to raise his voice in song:

Proem

"O Muse, my mother,[9] let Jove inspire my poem,   205
for all things yield to Jove's power; on prior occasions,
I have sung the dominion of Jove, lifting my lyre
to deal with so weighty a subject: the fall of the Giants,
the bolts hurled victorious down on the fields of Phlegraea![1]
But now the task of my lyre requires a lighter   210
touch as I sing of young boys whom the gods have desired,
and of girls seized by forbidden and blameworthy passions.

Ganymede

"The king of heaven once burned with desire for Trojan
Ganymede; Jupiter found an identity pleasing
him more than even his own did: no bird but the eagle,   215
bearer of Jove's thunderbolt, could deserve this distinction.
Without delay, as his counterfeit wings beat the air, he
captured the boy, who, in spite of Juno's objections,
mixes his nectar and serves him above now in heaven.

Hyacinthus

"Phoebus loved *you*, Hyacinthus, and would have installed you   220
in heaven also, if cruel fate had permitted.
Nevertheless, you are made—in a fashion—immortal,
for just as often as springtime repulses the winter
and Aries assumes the place of watery Pisces,
you rise and break out in flowers upon the green earth.   225
    "My father, Phoebus, preferred you above all the others,
abandoning Delphi, his city at the earth's navel,
while he frequented the banks of the river Eurotas
and haunted unfortified Sparta,[2] paying no mind to
music and archery, skills that brought him great honor;   230
careless of his own pursuits, he happily carried
the nets, and held back the dogs, and played the good sport
by scrambling up the jagged ridges of mountains,
while his beloved's continual presence kept him afire.
    "The Sun stood halfway between the night driven off   235
and the night that was newly approaching; bodies shed garments
and glistened richly with olive oil, as the contestants
prepared themselves to engage in a match with the discus.
Phoebus threw first, sending the well-balanced object

9. Calliope, who poeticizes in Book V. This begins the second of the three poetic solos in the *Metamorphoses*.
1. Here the Giants attacked the gods and were defeated by Hercules.
2. The Spartans were so courageous that they did not need to fortify their city.

aloft to shatter the clouds arrayed in the distance;   240
after a long time, it fell back again to the hard earth,
displaying not only Apollo's great skill but his power.

"But the imprudent youth, driven by love of the contest,
had raced off ahead to capture the speeding discus,
which, when it landed, bounced up again and spun back   245
into your face, Hyacinthus. The selfsame pallor
now blankets the boy and the god who kneels to embrace him,
who gathers the fallen lad and attempts to revive him,
who stanches his wound, and who now, by the application
of healing herbs, tries to keep his soul from departing,   250
without success, for the wound defies the god's treatment.

"As when a poppy or violet grown in a garden
among the lilies (whose tongues are thick yellow and bristly)
breaks, and the flower's head shrivels, droops, and collapses,
unable to hold itself up, with downcast demeanor,   255
just so the dying boy's head, now lacking all vigor,
unable to bear its own weight, lies flat on his shoulder.

"'O Spartan lad, cheated out of your youth, you are fallen,
and the fault that I see in your wound is my own,' cried Phoebus.
'Your death is the cause of my self-reproach and my sorrow,   260
for my right hand must be charged with the crime of your murder,
and I alone am responsible for your destruction!
But where did I err, unless our pleasures were errors?
Where was I wrong, unless it was wrong to have loved you?
If only I were permitted to die or exchange my   265
life for your own! But even though Fate's law prevents this,
you will be with me always, my lips will never forget you!
You will be present both in my songs and my music,
and a flower will come into being, inscribed with my mourning;
later, a legend involving the boldest of heroes   270
will be conjoined to this flower and read in its markings.'

"The truth of Apollo's words appeared as he spoke them,
for look, where the boy's spilled blood, now staining the grasses,
stops being blood and at once a new flower springs up,
shining even more brightly than Tyrian purple,   275
and takes on the form, if not the color, of lilies.

"Phoebus (who was indeed the source of this honor),
still unsatisfied, now inscribed his own mourning
inside the flower, in the form of the letters AI, AI,
and left its petals marked with the cry of lamenting.[3]   280
Nor is his Sparta ashamed of Hyacinthus, for even
today, the city still honors him in the old manner,
by holding the Hyacinthian festival every midsummer.

---

3. The petals of the hyacinth were marked with the Greek letters *ai ai*, which to them was
the cry of lament. The hyacinth is also given to the hero Ajax in Book XIII (see p. 356).

The Propoetides and the Cerastae[4]

"But if you should ask Amathus, that Cyprian city
so rich in metals, if it were proud of its daughters   285
the Propoetides, it would deny them completely,
along with those folks who were once given horns on their foreheads,
and who, from then on, assumed the name of Cerastae.

"Before the gates of their city, there once stood an altar
to Jove the Welcome of Strangers; if any passed by it   290
who had not heard of the crime that had taken place there,
and happened to glance at the bloodstains, he would have reckoned
that priests had sacrificed tender young lambs or veal calves—
but a guest had been slain there! Enraged by this blasphemy, Venus
prepared to abandon her cities and farmlands on Cyprus: 295
'But how have these places so dear, how have these cities
sinned against me?' she asks. 'How have they offended?
Better that I should exile this impious people
or kill them—or choose something between these two fates:
what punishment serves my purpose better than changing   300
all of them into a different kind of a being?'

"While she was wondering what she would turn them all into,
she happened to glance at their horns and at once was reminded
not to change everything; leaving those parts as she found them,
the goddess transformed all that remained of these sinners,   305
their limbs and enormous torsos, into fierce bullocks.

"Nevertheless, the indecent Propoetides
dared to deny her divinity; in anger, Venus
made them the first, it is said, to sell their own bodies,
and as their shame ceased, and they lost the power of blushing,   310
they turned into stones—a very small difference, really.

Pygmalion[5]

"Pygmalion observed how these women lived lives of sordid
indecency, and, dismayed by the numerous defects
of character Nature had given the feminine spirit,
stayed as a bachelor, having no female companion.   315

"During that time he created an ivory statue,
a work of most marvelous art, and gave it a figure
better than any living woman could boast of,

---

4. Otherwise unknown, they would seem to fit into the second part of Orpheus's program, "girls seized by forbidden and blameworthy passions"; Pygmalion's avoidance of the female sex in the next tale is credited to his observance of their misdeeds. The word *Cerastae* in Greek means "wearing horns."
5. Ovid's tale of women made insensible is followed by a tale of an insensible woman given sensibility. Ovid's version of this story is the one that has endured to our time. In later versions, the woman is named Galatea.

and promptly conceived a passion for his own creation.
You would have thought it alive, so like a real maiden   320
that only its natural modesty kept it from moving:
art concealed artfulness. Pygmalion gazed in amazement,
burning with love for what was in likeness a body.
   "Often he stretched forth a hand to touch his creation,
attempting to settle the issue: *was* it a body,   325
or was it—this he would not yet concede—a mere statue?
He gives it kisses, and they are returned, he imagines;
now he addresses and now he caresses it, feeling
his fingers sink into its warm, pliant flesh, and
fears he will leave blue bruises all over its body;   330
he seeks to win its affections with words and with presents
pleasing to girls, such as seashells and pebbles, tame birds,
armloads of flowers in thousands of different colors,
lilies, bright painted balls, curious insects in amber;
he dresses it up and puts diamond rings on its fingers,   335
gives it a necklace, a lacy brassiere and pearl earrings,
and even though all such adornments truly become her,
she does not seem to be any less beautiful naked.
He lays her down on a bed with a bright purple cover
and calls her his bedmate and slips a few soft, downy pillows   340
under her head as though she were able to feel them.
   "The holiday honoring Venus has come, and all Cyprus
turns out to celebrate; heifers with gilded horns buckle
under the deathblow and incense soars up in thick clouds;
having already brought his own gift to the altar,   345
Pygmalion stood by and offered this fainthearted prayer:
'If you in heaven are able to give us whatever
we ask for, then I would like as my wife—' and not daring
to say, '—my ivory maiden,' said, '—one like my statue!'
Since golden Venus was present there at her altar,   350
she knew what he wanted to ask for, and as a good omen,
three times the flames soared and leapt right up to the heavens.
   "Once home, he went straight to the replica of his sweetheart,
threw himself down on the couch and repeatedly kissed her;
she seemed to grow warm and so he repeated the action,   355
kissing her lips and exciting her breasts with both hands.
Aroused, the ivory softened and, losing its stiffness,
yielded, submitting to his caress as wax softens
when it is warmed by the sun, and handled by fingers,
takes on many forms, and by being used, becomes useful.   360
Amazed, he rejoices, then doubts, then fears he's mistaken,
while again and again he touches on what he has prayed for.
She is alive! And her veins leap under his fingers!
   "You can believe that Pygmalion offered the goddess
his thanks in a torrent of speech, once again kissing   365

those lips that were not untrue; that she felt his kisses,
and timidly blushing, she opened her eyes to the sunlight,
and at the same time, first looked on her lover and heaven!
The goddess attended the wedding since she had arranged it,
and before the ninth moon had come to its crescent, a daughter   370
was born to them—Paphos, who gave her own name to the island.

Myrrha

"She had a son named Cinyras, who would be regarded
as one of the blessèd, if he had only been childless.
I sing of dire events: depart from me, daughters,
depart from me, fathers; or, if you find my poems charming,   375
believe that I lie, believe these events never happened;
or, if you believe that they did, then believe they were punished.
    "If Nature allows us to witness such impious misdeeds,
then I give my solemn thanks that the Thracian people
and the land itself are far away from those regions   380
where evil like that was begotten: let fabled Panchaea[6]
be rich in balsam and cinnamon, costum and frankincense,
the sweat that drips down from the trees; let it bear incense
and flowers of every description: it also bears myrrh, and
too great a price was paid for that new creation.   385
    "Cupid himself denies that his darts ever harmed you,
Myrrha, and swears that his torches likewise are guiltless;
one of the three sisters,[7] bearing a venomous hydra
and waving a Stygian firebrand, must have inspired your passion.
Hating a parent is wicked, but even more wicked   390
than hatred is this kind of love. Princes elected
from far and wide desire you, Myrrha; all Asia
sends its young men to compete for your hand in marriage:
choose from so many just one of these men for your husband,
so long as a certain one is not the one chosen.   395
    "She understood and struggled against her perversion,
asking herself, 'What have I begun? Where will it take me?
May heaven and piety and the sacred rights of fathers
restrain these unspeakable thoughts and repel my misfortune,
if this indeed *is* misfortune; yet piety chooses   400
not to condemn this love outright: without distinctions
animals copulate; it is no crime for the heifer
to bear the weight of her father upon her own back;
daughters are suitable wives in the kingdom of horses;
the billy goats enter the flocks that they themselves sire,   405
and birds are inseminated by those who conceive them:
blessèd, the ones for whom such love is permitted!

---

6. A fictional island near Arabia, famous for exotic spices.
7. One of the three Furies, who are referred to as "the serpent-coiffed sisters" at line 430.

"'Human morality gives us such stifling precepts,
and makes indecent what Nature freely allows us!
But people say there are nations where sons and their mothers,   410
where fathers and daughters, may marry each other, increasing
the bonds of piety by their redoubled affections.
Wretched am I, who hadn't the luck to be born there,
injured by nothing more than mischance of location!
    "'Why do I obsess? Begone, forbidden desires;   415
of course he is worthy of love—but love for a father!
So, then, if I were not the daughter of great Cinyras,
I would be able to have intercourse with Cinyras:
though he is mine, he is not mine, and our nearness
ruins me: I would be better off as a stranger.   420
    "'It would be good for me to go far away from my country,
as long as I could escape from my wicked desires,
for what holds me here is the passion that I have to see him,
to touch and speak to Cinyras and give him my kisses—
if nothing more is permitted. You impious maiden,   425
what more can you imagine will ever be granted?
Are you aware how you confuse all rights and relations?
Would you be your mother's rival? The whore of your father?
Would you be called your son's sister? Your brother's own mother?
Do you not shudder to think of the serpent-coiffed sisters   430
thrusting their bloodthirsty torches into the faces
of the guilty wretches that those three appear to and torture?
    "'But you, while your body is undefiled, keep your mind chaste,
and do not break Nature's law with incestuous pairing.
Think what you ask for: the very act is forbidden,   435
and he is devout and mindful of moral behavior—
ah, how I wish that he had a similar madness!'
    "She spoke and Cinyras, whom an abundance of worthy
suitors had left undecided, consulted his daughter,
ran their names by her and asked whom she wished for a
          husband;   440
silent at first, she kept her eyes locked on her father,
seething until the hot tears spilled over her eyelids;
Cinyras, attributing this to the fears of a virgin,
bade her cease weeping, wiped off her cheeks, and kissed her;
Myrrha rejoiced overmuch at his gesture and answered   445
that she would marry a man 'just like you.' Misunderstanding
the words of his daughter, Cinyras approved them, replying,
'May you be this pious always.' Hearing that last word,
the virgin lowers her head, self-convicted of evil.
    "Midnight: now sleep dissolves all the cares of the body;   450
Cinyras' daughter, however, lies tossing, consumed by
the fires of passion, repeating her prayers in a frenzy;
now she despairs, now she'll attempt it; now she is shamefaced,
now eager: uncertain: *What should she do now?* She wavers,

just like a tree that the axe blade has girdled completely,   455
when only the last blow remains to be struck, and the woodsman
cannot predict the direction it's going to fall in,
she, after so many blows to her spirit, now totters,
now leaning in one, and now in the other, direction,
nor is she able to find any rest from her passion   460
save but in death. Death pleases her, and she gets up,
determined to hang herself from a beam with her girdle:
'Farewell, dear Cinyras: may you understand why I do this!'
she said, as she fitted the noose around her pale neck.

    "They say that, hearing her murmuring, her faithful old nurse   465
in the next chamber arose and entered her bedroom:
at sight of the grim preparations, she screams out, and striking
her breasts and tearing her garments, removes the noose from
around the girl's neck, and then, only then, she collapses,
and weeping, embraces her, asking her why she would do it.   470

    "Myrrha remained silent, expressionless, with her eyes downcast,
sorrowing only because her attempt was detected.
But the woman persists, baring her flat breasts and white hair,
and by the milk given when she was a babe in the cradle
beseeches her to entrust her old nurse with the cause of her
        sorrow.   475
The girl turns away with a groan; the nurse is determined
to learn her secret, and promises not just to keep it:
    "'Speak and allow me to aid you,' she says, 'for in my old age,
I am not utterly useless: if you are dying of passion,
my charms and herbs will restore you; if someone wishes
        you evil,   480
my rites will break whatever spell you are under;
is some god wrathful? A sacrifice placates his anger.
What else could it be? I can't think of anything—Fortune
favors your family, everything's going quite smoothly,
both of your parents are living, your mother, your father—'   485
Myrrha sighed deeply, hearing her father referred to,
but not even then did the nurse grasp the terrible evil
in the girl's heart, although she felt that her darling
suffered a passion of some kind for some kind of lover.

    "Nurse was unyielding and begged her to make known
        her secret,   490
whatever it was, pressing the tearful girl to her bosom;
and clasping her in an embrace that old age had enfeebled,
she said, 'You're in love—I am certain! I will be zealous
in aiding your cause, never you fear—and your father
will be none the wiser!'

                        "Myrrha in frenzy leapt up   495
and threw herself onto the bed, pressing her face in the pillows:
'Leave me, I beg you,' she said. 'Avoid my wretched dishonor;

leave me or cease to ask me the cause of my sorrow:
what you attempt to uncover is sinful and wicked!'
"The old woman shuddered: extending the hands that now
      trembled 500
with fear and old age, she fell at the feet of her darling,
a suppliant, coaxing her now, and now attempting to scare her;
threatening now to disclose her attempted self-murder,
but pledging to aid her if she confesses her passion.
"She lifted her head with her eyes full of tears spilling over 505
onto the breast of her nurse and repeatedly tried to
speak out, but repeatedly stopped herself short of confession,
hiding her shame-colored face in the folds of her garments,
until she finally yielded, blurting her secret:
'O mother,' she cried, 'so fortunate you with your husband!' 510
and said no more but groaned.
               "The nurse, who now understood it,
felt a chill run through her veins, and her bones shook with tremor,
and her white hair stood up in stiff bristles. She said whatever
she could to dissuade the girl from her horrible passion,
and even though Myrrha knew the truth of her warning, 515
she had decided to die if she could not possess him.
'Live, then,' the other replied, 'and possess your—' Not daring
to use the word 'father,' she left her sentence unfinished,
but called upon heaven to stand by her earlier promise.
"Now it was time for the annual feast days of Ceres; 520
the pious, and married women clad in white vestments
thronged to the celebration, offering garlands
of wheat as firstfruits of the season; now for nine nights
the intimate touch of their men is considered forbidden.
Among these matrons was Cenchreïs, wife of Cinyras, 525
for her attendance during these rites was required.
And so, while the queen's place in his bed was left vacant,
the overly diligent nurse came to Cinyras,
finding him drunk, and spoke to him of a maiden
whose passion for him was real (although her name wasn't) 530
and praising her beauty; when asked the age of this virgin,
she said, 'the same age as Myrrha.' Commanded to fetch her,
nurse hastened home, and entering, cried to her darling,
'Rejoice, my dear, we have won!' The unlucky maiden
could not feel joy in her heart, but only grim sorrow, 535
yet still she rejoiced, so distorted were her emotions.
"Now it is midnight, when all of creation is silent;
high in the heavens, between the two Bears, Boötes
had turned his wagon so that its shaft pointed downward;
Myrrha approaches her crime, which is fled by chaste Luna, 540
while under black clouds the stars hide their scandalized faces;
Night lacks its usual fires; you, Icarus, covered

your face and were followed at once by Erigone,[8]
whose pious love of her father merited heaven.

"Thrice Myrrha stumbles and stops each time at the omen,   545
and thrice the funereal owl sings her his poem of endings;
nevertheless she continues, her shame lessened by shadows.
She holds the left hand of her nurse, and gropes with the other
blindly in darkness: now at the bedchamber's threshold,
and now she opens the door: and now she is led within,   550
where her knees fail her; she falters, nearly collapsing,
her color, her blood, her spirit all flee together.

"As she approaches the crime, her horror increases;
regretting her boldness, she wishes to turn back, unnoticed,
but even as she holds back, the old woman leads her   555
by the hand to the high bed, where she delivers her, saying,
'Take her, Cinyras—she's yours,' and unites the doomed couple.
The father accepts his own offspring in his indecent
bed and attempts to dispel the girl's apprehensions,
encouraging her not to be frightened of him, and   560
addressing her, as it happened, with a name befitting
her years: he called her 'daughter' while she called him 'father,'
so the right names were attached to their impious actions.

"Filled with the seed of her father, she left his bedchamber,
having already conceived, in a crime against nature   565
which she repeated the following night and thereafter,
until Cinyras, impatient to see his new lover
after so many encounters, brought a light in,
and in the same moment discovered his crime and his daughter;
grief left him speechless; he tore out his sword from the
          scabbard;   570
Myrrha sped off, and, thanks to night's shadowy darkness,
escaped from her death. She wandered the wide-open spaces,
leaving Arabia, so rich in palms, and Panchaea,
and after nine months, she came at last to Sabaea,[9]
where she found rest from the weariness that she suffered,   575
for she could scarcely carry her womb's heavy burden.

"Uncertain of what she should wish for, tired of living
but frightened of dying, she summed up her state in this prayer:
'O gods, if there should be any who hear my confession,
I do not turn away from the terrible sentence   580
that my misbehavior deserves; but lest I should outrage
the living by my survival, or the dead by my dying,
drive me from both of these kingdoms, transform me
wholly, so that both life and death are denied me.'

8. An example of a devoted father-daughter pair. This is a different Icarus: after his death,
    she hanged herself. Both were constellated, he as Boötes and she as Virgo.
9. Myrrha journeys east across the Arabian peninsula to the fictional island of Panchaea, which
    various Greek writers set in the Indian Ocean; from there she travels southwest to Sabaea
    (modern Yemen), where she contributes her name to one of its most important spices.

"Some god *did* hear her confession, and heaven answered   585
her final prayer, for, even as she was still speaking,
the earth rose up over her legs, and from her toes burst
roots that spread widely to hold the tall trunk in position;
her bones put forth wood, and even though they were still hollow,
they now ran with sap and not blood; her arms became branches, 590
and those were now twigs that used to be called her fingers,
while her skin turned to hard bark. The tree kept on growing,
over her swollen belly, wrapping it tightly,
and growing over her breast and up to her neck; she
could bear no further delay, and, as the wood rose,   595
plunged her face down into the bark and was swallowed.

"Loss of her body has meant the loss of all feeling;
and yet she weeps, and the warm drops spill from her tree trunk;
those tears bring her honor: the distillate myrrh preserves and
will keep the name of its mistress down through the ages.   600

"But under the bark, the infant conceived in such baseness
continued to grow and now sought a way out of Myrrha;
the pregnant trunk bulged in the middle and its weighty burden
pressed on the mother, who could not cry out in her sorrow
nor summon Lucina with charms to aid those in childbirth.   605
So, like a woman exerting herself to deliver,
the tree groaned and bent over double, wet from its weeping.
Gentle Lucina stood by the sorrowing branches,
laid her hands onto the bark and recited the charms that
aid in delivery; the bark split open; a fissure   610
ran down the trunk of the tree and its burden spilled out,
a bawling boychild, whom naiads placed in soft grasses
and bathed in the tears of its mother. Not even Envy
could have found fault with his beauty, for he resembled
one of the naked cherubs depicted by artists,   615
and would have been taken as one, if you had provided
him with a quiver or else removed one from those others.

Venus and Adonis (1)[1]

"Time swiftly glides by in secret, escaping our notice,
and nothing goes faster than years do: the son of his sister
by his grandfather, the one so recently hidden   620
within a tree, so recently born, a most beautiful infant,
now is an adolescent and now a young man
even more beautiful than he was as a baby,

---

1. Since the vocation of the goddess is to incite passion in others, it is perhaps not unseemly
   for her to be seen in passion's grip, as she is in this tale. Within the story of Venus and
   Adonis, Ovid has set the story of Atalanta and Hippomenes, one of his most exuberant
   narrative romps.

pleasing now even to Venus and soon the avenger
of passionate fires that brought his mother to ruin.   625
    "For while her fond Cupid was giving a kiss to his mother,
he pricked her unwittingly, right in the breast, with an arrow
projecting out of his quiver; annoyed, the great goddess
swatted him off, but the wound had gone in more deeply
than it appeared to, and at the beginning deceived her.   630
    "Under the spell of this fellow's beauty, the goddess
no longer takes any interest now in Cythera,
nor does she return to her haunts on the island of Paphon,
or to fish-wealthy Cnidus or to ore-bearing Amethus;[2]
she avoids heaven as well, now—preferring Adonis,   635
and clings to him, his constant companion, ignoring
her former mode of unstrenuous self-indulgence,
when she shunned natural light for the parlors of beauty;
now she goes roaming with him through woods and up mountains
and over the scrubby rocks with her garments hitched up   640
and girded around her waist like a nymph of Diana,
urging the hounds to pursue unendangering species,
hoppety hares or stags with wide-branching antlers,
or terrified does; but she avoids the fierce wild boars and
rapacious wolves and bears armed with sharp claws,   645
and shuns the lions, sated with slaughter of cattle.
    "And she warns you also to fear the wild beasts, Adonis,
if only her warning were heeded. 'Be bold with the timid,'
she said, 'but against the daring, daring is reckless.
Spare me, dear boy, the risk involved in your courage;   650
don't rile the beasts that Nature has armed with sharp weapons,
lest I should find the glory you gain much too costly!
For lions and bristling boars and other fierce creatures
look with indifferent eyes and minds upon beauty
and youth and other qualities Venus is moved by;   655
pitiless boars deal out thunderbolts with their curved tusks,
and none may withstand the frenzied assault of the lions,
whom I despise altogether.'
                            "And when he asked why,
she said, 'I will tell you this story which will amaze you,
with its retribution delivered for ancient wrongdoing.   660
    "'But this unaccustomed labor has left me exhausted—
look, though—a poplar entices with opportune shade, and
offers a soft bed of turf we may rest on together,
as I would like to.' And so she lay down on the grasses
and on her Adonis, and using his breast as a pillow,   665
she told this story, mixing her words with sweet kisses:

2. Places sacred to the cult of Venus.

Atalanta and Hippomenes

"'Perhaps you'll have heard of a maiden able to vanquish
the swiftest of men in a footrace; this wasn't a fiction,
for she overcame all contestants; nor could you say whether
she deserved praise more for her speed or her beauty.   670
She asked some god about husbands. "A husband," he answered,
"is not for you, Atalanta: flee from a husband!
But you will not flee—and losing yourself, will live on!"
        "'Frightened by his grim prediction, she went to the forest
and lived there unmarried, escaping the large and persistent   675
throng of her suitors by setting out cruel conditions;
"You cannot have me," she said, "unless you outrun me;
come race against me! A bride and a bed for the winner,
death to the losers. Those are the rules of the contest."
        "'Cruel? Indeed—but such was this young maiden's beauty   680
that a foolhardy throng of admirers took up the wager.
As a spectator, Hippomenes sat in the grandstand,
asking why anyone ever would risk such a danger,
just for a bride, and disparaging their headstrong passion.
However, as soon as he caught a glimpse of her beauty,   685
like mine or like yours would be if you were a woman,'
said Venus, 'her face and her body, both bared for the contest,
he threw up both hands and cried out, "I beg your pardons,
who only a moment ago disparaged your efforts,
but truly I had no idea of the trophy you strive for!"   690
        "'Praises ignited the fires of passion and made him
hope that no young man proved to be faster than she was
and fear that one would be. Jealous, he asked himself why he
was leaving the outcome of this competition unventured:
"God helps those who improve their condition by daring,"   695
he said, addressing himself as the maiden flew by him.
Though she seemed no less swift than a Scythian arrow,
nevertheless, he more greatly admired her beauty,
and the grace of her running made her seem even more lovely;
the breezes blew back the wings attached to her ankles   700
while her loose hair streamed over her ivory shoulders
and her brightly edged knee straps fluttered lightly; a russet
glow fanned out evenly over her pale, girlish body,
as when a purple awning covers a white marble surface,
staining its artless candor with counterfeit shadow.   705
        "'She crossed the finish line while he was taking it in, and
Atalanta, victorious, was given a crown and the glory;
the groaning losers were taken off: end of *their* story.
But the youth, undeterred by what had become of the vanquished,
stood on the track and fixed his gaze on the maiden: 710
"Why seek such an easy victory over these sluggards?

Contend with me," he said, "and if Fortune makes me the winner,
you will at least have been beaten by one not unworthy:
I am the son of Megareus, grandson of Neptune,
my great-grandfather; my valor is no less impressive   715
than is my descent; if you should happen to triumph,
you would be famous for having beaten Hippomenes."

"'And as he spoke, Atalanta's countenance softened:
she wondered whether she wished to win or to *be* won,
and asked herself which god, jealous of her suitor's beauty,   720
sought to destroy him by forcing him into this marriage:
"If *I* were judging, I wouldn't think I was worth it!
Nor am I moved by his beauty," she said, "though I could be,
but I *am* moved by his youth: his boyishness stirs me—
but what of his valor? His mind so utterly fearless?   725
What of his watery origins? His relation to Neptune?
What of the fact that he loves me and wishes to wed me,
and is willing to die if bitter Fortune denies him?

"'"Oh, flee from a bed that still reeks with the gore of past
    victims,
while you are able to, stranger; marrying *me* is   730
certain destruction! No one would wish to reject you,
and you may be chosen by a much wiser young lady!

"'"But why should I care for you—after so many have perished?
Now *he* will learn! Let him die then, since the great slaughter
of suitors has taught him nothing! He must be weary of living!   735
So—must he die then, because he wishes to wed me,
and is willing to pay the ultimate price for his passion?
He shouldn't have to! And even though it won't be *my* fault,
my victory surely will turn the people against me!

"'"If only you would just give it up, or if only,   740
since you're obsessed with it, you were a little bit faster!
How very girlish is the boy's facial expression!
O poor Hippomenes! I wish you never had seen me!
You're worthy of life, and if only *my* life had been better,
or if the harsh Fates had not prevented my marriage,   745
you would have been the one I'd have chosen to marry!"

"'She spoke, and, moved by desire that struck without warning,
loved without knowing what she was doing or feeling.
Her father and people were clamoring down at the racecourse,
when Neptune's descendant Hippomenes anxiously begged me: 750
"Cytherian Venus, I pray you preside at my venture,
aiding the fires that you yourself have ignited."
A well-meaning breeze brought me this prayer, so appealing
that, I confess, it aroused me and stirred me to action,
though I had scant time enough to bring off his rescue.   755

"'There is a field upon Cyprus, known as Tamasus,
famed for its wealth; in olden days it was given
to me and provides an endowment now for my temples;

and there in this field is a tree; its leaves and its branches
glisten and shimmer, reflecting the gold they are made of;   760
now, as it happened, I'd just gotten back from a visit,
carrying three golden apples that I had selected:
and showing myself there to Hippomenes only,
approached him and showed him how to use them to advantage.
　　"'Both of them crouched for the start; when horns gave the
　　　　signal,   765
they took off together, their feet barely brushing the surface;
you would have thought they were able to keep their toes dry
while skimming over the waves, and could touch on the ripened
heads of wheat in the field without bending them under.
　　"'Cries of support and encouragement cheered on the young
　　　　man;   770
"Now is the time," they screamed, "go for it, go for it, hurry,
Hippomenes, give it everything that you've got now!
Don't hold back! Victory!" And I am uncertain whether
these words were more pleasing to him or to his Atalanta,
for often, when she could have very easily passed him,   775
she lingered beside, her gaze full of desperate longing,
until she reluctantly sped ahead of his features.
　　"'And now Hippomenes, dry-mouthed, was breathlessly
　　　　gasping,
the finish line far in the distance; he threw out an apple,
and the sight of that radiant fruit astounded the maiden,   780
who turned from her course and retrieved the glittering missile;
Hippomenes passed her: the crowd roared its approval.
　　"'A burst of speed now and Atalanta makes up for lost time:
once more overtaking the lad, she puts him behind her!
A second apple: again she falls back, but recovers,   785
now she's beside him, now passing him, only the finish
remains: "Now, O goddess," he cries, "my inspiration,
　　　　be with me!"
　　"'With all the strength of his youth he flings the last apple
to the far side of the field: *this* will really delay her!
The maiden looked doubtful about its retrieval: I forced her   790
to get it and add on its weight to the burden she carried:
time lost and weight gained were equal obstructions: the maiden
(lest my account should prove longer than even the race was)
took second place: the trophy bride left with the victor.
　　"'But really, Adonis, wasn't I worthy of being   795
thanked for my troubles? Offered a gift of sweet incense?
Heedless of all I had done, he offered me neither!
Immediate outrage was followed by keen indignation;
and firmly resolving not to be spurned in the future,
I guarded against it by making this pair an example.   800
　　"'Now they were passing a temple deep in the forest,
built long ago by Echion to honor Cybele,

Mother of Gods,[3] and now the length of their journey
urged them to rest here, where unbridled desire
possessed Hippomenes, moved by the strength of my godhead.   805
There was a dim and cave-like recess near the temple,
hewn out of pumice, a shrine to the ancient religion,
wherein a priest of these old rites had set a great many
carved wooden idols. Hippomenes entered that place, and
by his forbidden behavior defiled it; in horror,   810
the sacred images turned away from the act, and Cybele
prepared to plunge the guilty pair in Stygian waters,
but that seemed too easy; so now their elegant pale necks
are cloaked in tawny manes; curved claws are their fingers;
arms are now forelegs, and all the weight of their bodies   815
shifts to their torsos; and now their tails sweep the arena;
fierce now, their faces; growls supplant verbal expression;
the forest now is their bedroom; a terror to others,
meekly these lions champ at the bit of the harness
on either side of the yoke of Cybele's chariot.[4]   820
    "'My darling, you must avoid these and all other wild beasts,
who will not turn tail, but show off their boldness in battle;
flee them or else your courage will prove our ruin!'

Venus and Adonis (2)

"And after warning him, she went off on her journey,
carried aloft by her swans; but his courage resisted   825
her admonitions. It happened that as his dogs followed
a boar they were tracking, they roused it from where it was hidden,
and when it attempted to rush from the forest, Adonis
pierced it, but lightly, casting his spear from an angle;
with its long snout, it turned and knocked loose the weapon   830
stained with its own blood, then bore down upon our hero,
and, as he attempted to flee for his life in sheer terror,
it sank its tusks deep into the young fellow's privates,
and stretched him out on the yellow sands, where he lay dying.
    "Aloft in her light, swan-driven chariot, Venus   835
had not yet gotten to Cyprus; from a great distance
she recognized the dying groans of Adonis
and turned her birds back to him; when she saw from midair
his body lying there, lifeless, stained with its own blood,
she beat her breasts and tore at her hair and her garments,   840
and leapt from her chariot, raging, to argue with grim Fate:
    "'It will not be altogether as you would have it,'
she said. 'My grief for Adonis will be remembered

3. Another of Cybele's titles.
4. The goddess was depicted enthroned between two lionesses.

forever, and every year will see, reenacted
in ritual form, his death and my lamentation;[5]   845
and the blood of the hero will be transformed to a flower.
Or were *you* not once allowed to change a young woman
to fragrant mint, Persephone?[6] Do you begrudge me
the transformation of my beloved Adonis?'

    "And as she spoke, she sprinkled his blood with sweet nectar,   850
which made it swell up, like a transparent bubble
that rises from muck; and in no more than an hour
a flower sprang out of that soil, blood red in its color,
just like the flesh that lies underneath the tough rind
of the seed-hiding pomegranate. Brief is its season,   855
for the winds from which it takes its name, the anemone,
shake off those petals so lightly clinging and fated to perish."

5. The Adonia, a cultic celebration of Adonis's death, was celebrated in Ovid's time.
6. Persephone had changed the nymph Minthe into the plant.

BOOK XI

Rome Begins at Troy

The Death of Orpheus

Meanwhile, as Orpheus compelled the trees
and beasts to follow him with suchlike songs,
and made the very stones skip in his wake,
behold: a raving mob of Thracian women[1]
with the pelts of wild beasts draped across their breasts   5
observed him from the summit of a hill
setting the words to music on his lyre.

    One of them tossed her hair in the light breeze:
"Look over there!" she cried. "The one who scorns us!"
And with no more ado, she cast her lance   10
at the vocalizing mouth of Apollo's seer;
it struck without wounding, being wreathed in leaves.

    Another's weapon was the stone she cast,
that even in midflight was overwhelmed
by words and music joined in harmony,   15
and, as though begging pardon for its mad daring,
fell at the poet's feet.

             Nevertheless,
the level of their mindless rage increased
and measure fled: mad fury was in charge,
but even so, their weapons would have been   20
made mild by the enchantment of his song,
had not the shrill clamor of Phrygian flutes,
the breaking tones of horns, the frenzied drums,
and the Bacchantes' applause and ululations
together overwhelmed his lyre's music;   25
when Orpheus no longer could be heard,
the stones were reddened with a poet's blood.

    Up until now, his voice had held in thrall
the countless birds, the snakes, the surging beasts
that were the indication of his triumph: 30
all these the Maenads savagely drove off,
then turned their bloody hands against the poet
and swarmed upon him as the birds will do,
when in the daylight they discern an owl
among them, dazed; or as when, in the arena,   35
on the morning of the games, the fated stag
is torn by dogs, and bleeds into the sand;
just so the Maenads search the poet out
and throw at him their wands wrapped in green leaves,

---

1. The Maenads, devotees of Bacchus; their enmity is depicted as a consequence of Orpheus's attitude toward women after Eurydice's (second) death.

not meant for such a use.
                Then some hurl clods,   40
and others, branches broken from the trees,
while others are still busy throwing rocks;
and, lest their madness lack for proper weapons
there happened to be oxen yoked nearby,
tilling the soil—and not too far from them,   45
some brawny peasants, breaking the hard ground,
sweating at their labors.
                But when these men saw
the Maenads surging toward them, they took off,
abandoning their work and implements;
scattered throughout the vacant fields now lay   50
their hoes and rakes and mattocks, which the Maenads
captured, and having torn apart the oxen
whose horns had threatened them, they hastened back
to finish off the seer, who, with raised hands,
spoke words unheeded for the first time ever,   55
his voice not moving them the slightest bit;
the sacrilegious women struck him down,
and past those lips—ah, Jupiter!—to which
the stones would listen and the beasts respond,
his exhaled ghost receded on the winds.   60

    For you now, Orpheus, the grieving birds,
the thronging beasts, the sharp, unyielding rocks,
the trees that often gathered for your songs,
and which, like men who tear their hair in grief,
have shed their leaves for you—all these now wept,   65
and it is said that rivers were increased
by their own tears, and water nymphs galore
distressed their tresses and dressed all in gray.

    His limbs lay scattered all about; his head
and lyre, as they glide on down your stream,   70
O Hebrus,[2] now (miraculously!) mourn;
the plaintive lyre makes some kind of moan,
the lifeless tongue moans on along with it,
the moaning riverbanks respond in turn.

    Now head and lyre are borne down to the sea   75
beyond their native stream, until they reach
the coast of Lesbos, near Methymna's walls:
here, as it lay at risk on foreign sands,
that head (its locks still dripping with salt spray)
was set upon by a ferocious snake;[3]   80
just as the serpent spread its jaws to strike,

2. The river in Thrace that carries the lifeless head of Orpheus down to the sea, where it
   comes to rest on the isle of Lesbos, famous for its poets, Sappho and Alcaeus.
3. An episode known only from Ovid's treatment of it here.

Phoebus at last appeared and drove it off,
then turned the serpent's open jaws to stone,
just as they were—and will forever be.

    The shade of Orpheus now fled below,   85
and recognized all he had seen before;
and as he searched through the Elysian Fields,
he came upon his lost Eurydice,
and passionately threw his arms about her;
here now they walk together, side by side,   90
or now he follows as she goes before,
or he precedes, and she goes after him;
and now there is no longer any danger
when Orpheus looks on Eurydice.

The Transformation of the Maenads

Nevertheless, Bacchus did not permit   95
the murder of his seer[4] to go unpunished,
and as he grieved for Orpheus, he bound
those Thracian women who had looked upon
that outrage: for now roots spring from the path
that each one walks upon, gripping her toes,   100
drawing them out and down into the earth,
as when a bird steps right into the snare
the skillful fowler cunningly conceals,
and sensing itself caught, it beats its wings
in agitated fear that only serves   105
to draw the noose more tightly round its leg;
just so, as each of them, fixed to the soil
in terror, vainly tries to get away,
is kept in place by the resistant roots,
and as she struggles upward, is drawn back,   110
and when she seeks her hands, her feet, her nails,
beholds the bark surmounting her trim calves;
and when her grieving hand would strike her thighs,
she strikes an oak; of oak is her breast made,
and oaken are the Maenad's shoulders, too;   115
you would have thought her knotty arms were branches—
and you would not have been at all mistaken.

Midas

Nor does this placate Bacchus, still so mad
that he removes himself from these same fields,
and, with a better crowd, sets out to find   120

---

4. Orpheus was more closely associated with Apollo than with Bacchus, and other accounts
   say that Bacchus incited the Maenads to murder Orpheus.

the vineyards of Mount Timolus and the banks
of the river Pactolus, which, in those days,
was water, not a stream of flowing gold,
nor envied for the value of its sands.[5]

    The usual throng of Satyrs and Bacchantes   125
accompanied the god—save for Silenus:[6]
staggering from age and inebriation,
he had been taken captive in Phrygia,
and led in chains of chaplets to King Midas,
who, with the Athenian king Eumolpus,   130
had once been taught the Bacchic mysteries
by Orpheus himself.
                On recognizing
his comrade and companion in the rites,
King Midas joyfully proclaimed a feast,
which lasted for ten days and nights together,   135
to celebrate his guest's arrival.
                     Now,
when Lucifer, on the eleventh day,
had driven off the ranks of stars above,
King Midas joyfully came to the fields
of Lydia, returning old Silenus   140
to Bacchus, who had been his foster child.

    The god, rejoicing in his safe return,
offered the king whatever he might choose,
a gratifying, although useless gift;
and destined to make evil use of it,   145
King Midas answered with, "Grant that whatever
my body touches will turn into gold!"
Bacchus assented to this harmful gift,
and granted him his wish—although he grieved
that Midas had not asked for something better.   150

    The Phrygian king took leave of him, rejoicing
in his misfortune—and as he went, essayed
the efficacy of his gift by touching
one thing and another: even he
could scarcely credit it, but when he snapped   155
a green twig from the low branch of an oak,
the twig immediately turned to gold;
he picked a stone up, and it did the same;
he touched a clod, and at his potent touch,
the piece of earth became a lump of ore;   160
ripe wheat-heads plucked produced a golden harvest,

---

5. Before Midas bathed in it, turning its waters to gold.
6. For Silenus, see note 5 on p. 92.

and when he took an apple from a tree,
you would have thought that the Hesperides[7]
had given it to him. His fingertips
brushed lofty columns, and they seemed to glow;   165
and when he washed his hands in water, why
the water would have gotten past Danaë:
All turns to gold! He scarcely could imagine!

    As he rejoiced, his servants set a table
with heaps of roasted meats and fresh-baked breads,   170
the gifts of Ceres; when he touched a loaf,
it hardened, and when Midas greedily
prepared to sink his teeth into his meat,
the teeth encountered golden dinnerware;
he mixed his Bacchic beverage with water,   175
and you could see him swallow liquid gold!

    Astounded by this strange catastrophe
of wretchedness in wealth, he longs to flee
its trappings—now despising what he'd prayed for.
Abundance was unable to relieve   180
his empty stomach or his burning throat;
so justly tortured by the hateful gold,
he raised his hands and gleaming arms to heaven:
"O Father Bacchus," he cried, "show your favor!
Though I have sinned, I beg you, grant me mercy,   185
save me from this ruinous extravagance!"

    The gods are gentle: when the king confessed
to having sinned, Bacchus repaired his case,
released him from the gift that he had given
to keep his pledge, and said, "Lest you remain   190
surrounded by the gold you wrongly wished for,
go to the stream that flows past mighty Sardis
as swiftly as you can, and climb upstream
until you come upon the river's source,
then plunge your head and body both at once   195
beneath the fountain that it burbles from,
and in that moment you will purge your crime."

    The king went where the god had ordered him;
the stream was colored by the force of gold
as it exchanged his body for the river;   200
and even now, the seed of that old vein
is taken up by the surrounding fields
whose soil, in hardness and in golden color,
still shows the influence of Midas' touch.

---

7. A trio of nymphs who guarded the golden apples that Juno gave to Jove on their wedding day.

Detesting wealth, he dwelled in woods and fields,   205
and worshiped Pan,[8] who haunts the mountain caves;
but he remained not altogether bright,
and as it happened once, now once again
his foolishness would do him injury.

    For Mount Timolus, looking out to sea   210
from his high peak, stands loftily between
the town of Sardis and little Hypaepa;
and there, while Pan was boasting to the gentle
nymphs of his skill at fingering the pipes
and playing melodies on waxen reeds,   215
he dared speak poorly of Apollo's gift
compared to his own—a boast which brought about
the uneven contest which Timolus judged.

    The aged judge was seated on his mountain,
and shook his ears free of the greenery;   220
a wreath of oak leaves bound up his dark hair,
and acorns dangled from his bulging temples.
At sight of Pan, the shepherd-god, he said,
"Court is in session: on with the proceedings."

    Pan made a noise on his outlandish reeds,   225
and that barbaric song charmed Midas (who
just happened to be present for the singing);
when Pan had finished, Mount Timolus turned
his face to Phoebus—and his forest followed.

    Apollo's golden locks were crowned with laurel   230
from Mount Parnassus, and his mantle, trimmed
with Tyrian purple, swept along the ground;
in his left hand, the god held up his lyre,
inlaid with precious gems and ivory,
and in his other hand he held the plectrum: 235
an artist, in his bearing and his manner.
And when his skillful thumb aroused the strings,
the judge, so taken by that sweetness, ruled
that Pan's reeds must be humbled by the lyre.

    The judgment that the sacred mountain gave   240
on the contestants was approved by all
but one man, Midas, who alone opposed it,
calling it unjust. Apollo could not bear
that ears so dull should keep their human shape,
and so he drew them out to greater length,   245
and stuffed them full of gray and shaggy hair,
and made them wobbly where they joined his head
and capable of moving back and forth;

8. A horned, goat-footed rural deity whose attempted violation of Syrinx is described in
Book I, *Pan and Syrinx*.

the rest stayed human: just in that one part
was Midas punished, whom the god compelled   250
to wear the ears of a lackadaisical ass.
     Now Midas, eager to alleviate
the shame upon his temples, tried to hide it
beneath a purple turban, but the slave
who barbered him took note of his disgrace,   255
and he, because he did not dare expose
the shameful sight, yet wished to speak of it,
and was unable *not* to bring it up,
went off a ways and dug himself a hole,
and in that hole he whispered quietly   260
what he had noticed about his master's ears,
and then concealed the vocal evidence
by shoveling the dirt back in the hole,
and, having filled it, silently slipped off.
     And on that spot, there started to spring up   265
a thickly planted grove of whispering reeds,
which, at year's end, when they had reached their growth,
betrayed their secret—stirred by the south wind,
they breathed the hidden words, and so revealed
the secret story of the master's ears.   270

The Perfidy of Laomedon[9]

Avenged, Apollo left Timolus, borne
through fluid air until he came to earth
in the land that Laomedon was ruler of,
on this side of the narrow Hellespont.
     Sigeum on the right, Rhodes on the left: 275
between them on a promontory stands
an ancient altar, consecrated to
the Thunderer, Jove of the Oracles;
and there Apollo watched as Laomedon
began the walls of his new city, Troy,   280
an undertaking of great magnitude,
which was not going well, the god perceived,
and which required very great resources;
so he and Neptune, father of the seas,
assumed the shapes of mortals and erected   285
walls there for the tyrant of Phrygia,
after arranging to be paid in gold.
     The work was soon accomplished, but the king
denied the debt, and in addition, swore

---

9. Greeks and Romans saw Laomedon's deceit as the source of Troy's later woes. The subsequent flood, the required sacrifice, and the rescue of the maiden have their parallels in
   Book IV, *Perseus and Andromeda*.

(the finishing touch put on his treachery!)   290
that he had never promised compensation.
"You will not get away with this unpunished,"
Neptune said, releasing all his waters
against the shores of avaricious Troy,
and drenched the land until it seemed a sea,   295
and overwhelmed the fields and ruined the crops.
   Nor did he think this punishment sufficient:
the daughter of the king must be surrendered
to a sea monster! It was Hercules
who freed her from the rocks that she was bound to,   300
and when he sought the horses he'd been promised,
the reward for his great service was denied;
so, for his prize, the hero took instead
the twice-perjured walls of vanquished Troy.
   And Hercules' companion, Telamon,   305
was given Hesione as his reward
for the role that he had taken in this action;
a goddess bride brought fame to Peleus,
who had no reason to be prouder of
his grandfather than of his father-in-law,   310
for Jove had many mortal grandchildren,
but only one had an immortal wife.

Peleus and Thetis

Old Proteus had prophesied to Thetis:
"Conceive, O water goddess: you will be
the mother of a youth who, in his prime,   315
will outperform the deeds of his own father,
and will be called the greater."
                                  For that reason,
lest the earth produce one greater than himself,
although the fire that he felt for her
was anything but tepid, Jupiter   320
shunned intercourse with Thetis, ordering
his grandson, Peleus, to take his place
in making love to her in word and deed.
   In Thessaly, there is a sickle-shaped
bay with two arms extending out to sea;   325
if it were deeper, it would be a port,
but the surface there lies just above the sand;
the shore is solid: footprints leave no trace,
and the sand is free of seaweed, firm to walk on.
   There is a myrtle grove nearby, whose trees   330
are thickly hung with their berries red and green,
and in the middle is a grotto, made
by nature or by art—it isn't easy

to say which of them has the greater claim,
but art would seem to.
Here you would often come,   335
Thetis, riding on your bridled dolphin,
and usually naked; here as you lay
disarmed by sleep, Peleus embraced you,
and after you rejected his desires,
resorted to force, wrapping both his arms   340
around your neck; and had you not employed
your customary arts, his audacity
would have won him what he was trying for:
but now you are a bird, which he holds fast,
and now a heavy tree that he must cling to;   345
you next appeared to be a spotted tigress,
which frightened him, so that he let you go.
  At which point, baffled Peleus entreats
the sea gods for their aid, offering wine
mixed with their element, and burning up   350
great clouds of incense and the guts of sheep,
till Proteus emerges from the deep:
"Peleus," he said, "you may obtain
what you desire in the way of bed,
if you do this: when she is fast asleep   355
in the unyielding cave, and unawares,
bind her in snares and chains to hold her close,
and do not let her work her wiles on you,
though she take on a hundred lying shapes:
press her, whatever she will be, until   360
she reassumes the form that she first had."
So Proteus spoke and quickly sank from sight
beneath the waves that covered his last words.
  Now in his tilted chariot, the Sun
was hastening down toward the western sea,   365
when lovely Thetis, leaving the deep water,
returned once more to her accustomed bed;
Peleus had just barely got a grip on
her virgin limbs, when she assumed new shapes,
continuing until she realized   370
her movements were constrained: she had been bound,
and both her arms were now securely pinned.
  She groaned and told him, "You would not have won
without the intervention of the gods,"
and then appeared to him in her own form,   375
and he achieved what he desired to,
and filled her womb with fabulous Achilles.[1]

---

1. Ancients believed that women's only function in conception was to nurture semen in
their wombs.

Daedalion

His son and wife proved Peleus to be
one of the fortunate, a man to whom,
if you ignore his butchery of Phocus,[2]   380
good only happens: stained with his brother's blood,
and driven from the palace of his father,
he found a refuge in the land of Trachin.

Here ruled, with great benevolence, the seed
of Lucifer, whose name was Ceyx,[3]   385
a son whose father's splendor shone in him,
though at that time he was unlike himself,
in mourning for a brother snatched away.

Exhausted by his cares and by his travels,
Peleus, with a few companions, entered   390
the city, after leaving flocks and herds
in a shaded valley just outside the walls,
and when permitted to approach the king,
extended, in the sign of supplication,
the olive branches wound around with wool,   395
and told him his and his own father's name,
concealing nothing other than his crime,
and lying about the reason for his flight;
he sought, in city or in countryside,
a competence.

        The ruler of Trachin   400
gently replied, "Even the common folk
find opportunities within our realm,
nor is our kingdom inhospitable;
your reputation and descent from Jove
provide another motive that unites   405
with our natural benevolence;
waste no more time with your petition, then:
you will have everything you ask us for,
just take your share of anything you see—
if only there were better to be seen!"   410
Then he broke down and wept.

            Moved by his grief,
Peleus and his companions asked its cause;
the king replied, "Perhaps you thought this bird
of prey, the terror of all other birds,
has been one always—but that isn't so: 415
he used to be a man, and so unchanging

---

2. Peleus, son of Aeacus, acting from envy of his half-brother, murdered Phocus with a discus; along with another brother, Telamon, he was banished from Aegina. Phocus was the
   son of Psamathe, a Nereid, who will be moved to vengeance against Peleus.
3. Ceyx is the son of Lucifer, the Morning Star, also known as Hesperus, the Evening Star.

are our characters that even then
his edgy bellicosity was noted,
as was his readiness to pick a fight—
his name? Daedalion. Like me, the son   420
of the god who calls Aurora to her duties
and exits from the heavens last of all;
my interests were in preserving peace
and being with my wife; my brother, though,
found pleasure only in ferocious war,   425
in subjugating by his strength of arms
rulers and their nations; now transformed,
he agitates the dovecotes of Boeotia!
  "Daedalion had a daughter named Chione,
endowed with beauty to a rare degree,   430
who had a thousand suitors by the time
she was old enough for marriage at fourteen.
  "It happened that Apollo was returning
from Delphi as it chanced that Mercury
was on his way back from Cyllene's heights: 435
both saw her at the same time, both caught fire.
Apollo deferred his longed-for satisfaction
until the nightfall, but the other one
would not delay: with sleep-inducing wand,
he touched the virgin's lips; its influence   440
made her lie down at once beneath the god
and bear his thrusts; Night spread the sky with stars;
came Phoebus in the guise of an old woman,
and he attained his long-delayed delight.
  "Now, when her time had come, a son was born   445
of the wing-footed god: Autolycus,
a thief with all his father's cleverness,
and able to persuade you white was black
and black was white; of Phoebus there was born
(for Chione had given birth to twins)   450
Philammon, later famous for his skills
as singer and musician.
       "Having delivered
a pair of twins and having pleased two gods;[4]
having a father who is powerful,
and a grandfather noted for his brilliance—   455
is this a guarantee of satisfaction,
or is such glory often just a trial?
  "Well, certainly, in this case, it was so,
for Chione, in her own estimation,

---

4. As Ovid indicates, Romans believed that one pair of twins could be fathered by two different men (or gods).

surpassed Diana in attractiveness,   460
and found fault with the goddess's appearance;
enraged, Diana answered, 'Deeds be my words!'
And without pausing, fitted to the string
of her curved bow an arrow and released it,
piercing, deservedly, Chione's tongue,   465
which lapsed into silence; neither voice nor word
ensued, as she attempted to speak out,
and blood and life both drained away from her.

    "Wretched, I took her in my arms and held her,
bearing my brother's sorrow in my heart,   470
attempting to console him with my words,
which had no more of an effect on him
than the murmuring of waves upon the rocks,
as he mourned for his daughter snatched away;
and when her father saw her body burning,   475
he tried four times to leap into the flames,
and after being thrown back the fourth time,
he fled in agitation, like a bullock
with a cloud of stinging wasps around his neck,
who plunges off the pathway.
                  "Even then   480
he seemed to run much faster than a man;
you would have thought his feet had put on wings,
as, in his eagerness to kill himself,
he outstripped all of us and gained the peak
of Mount Parnassus.
             "Apollo pitied him   485
when he had thrown himself down from the heights,
and changed him to the kind of bird that hovers
on unexpected wings; gave him a beak
and curving claws, but left his former courage
and strength out of proportion to his size;   490
he lives now as a hawk, at odds with all
the other birds he preys on savagely,
grieving himself, and a source of grief to them."

The Wolf of Psamathe

While Ceyx, the son of Lucifer, recounted
the marvel of his brother's transformation   495
to his rapt guest, the herdsman, Onetor,
came rushing in all breathlessly and cried,
"Peleus, Peleus, I bring you news
of a catastrophe!"
             And while King Ceyx
sat trembling in anxious expectation,   500
Peleus ordered Onetor to speak:

"I'd driven the weary cattle down to shore,"
he started and then started once again,
beginning with, "At that time when the sun
was highest, in the middle of his course,   505
with as much seen as there was left to see,
some of the cattle knelt on the yellow sands,
and rolling on their flanks, gazed out upon
the watery pastures; meanwhile, others roamed
unhurriedly here and there, and some   510
swam out and stood up to their necks in water.
      "There was a temple very near the sea,
not famous for its marble or its gold,
but built of thick-hewn timbers, in a grove
of ancient trees that shaded it, and sacred   515
to Nereus and the Nereids, his daughters
(a sailor who was drying out his nets
along the shore informed me that these are
sea deities); close to the temple grounds,
in a thick grove of willows, is a marsh   520
created by the back flooding of the sea;
now from this marsh, with an appalling noise,
a racket that upsets the neighborhood,
this very, very huge-sized animal,
a wolf, emerges from the marshy growth,   525
his jaws all dripping foam and clotted blood,
and his eyes blazing with their own red flames!
      "Driven by rage and hunger equally
(though rage seemed sharper), he attacked the herd,
not simply out of hunger, but to wreak   530
havoc upon the cattle that he slaughtered,
assaulting them as though they were his foes!
      "And some of us as well were badly wounded,
torn by his fangs as we attempted to
repel the beast, and given up for dead;   535
the shore, the shallow waters, and the swamp
reverberating with the groans of cattle
turned red with blood!
                          "Delay is ruinous,
nor does this matter let us hesitate!
While something yet remains for us to save,   540
let us unite and eagerly take arms,
and together bring the battle to the foe!"
      So spoke the rustic. Peleus kept calm,
despite his losses: mindful of his crime,
he realized that the grieving Nereid   545
intended them to be a sacrifice
to her son Phocus in the underworld.
      The king ordered his men to arm themselves

and to prepare for battle; when it seemed
that he too was preparing to go join them,   550
his wife, Alcyone, drawn by the tumult,
sped from her chambers with her hair undone,
undoing it still further in her flight,
and threw herself upon her husband's neck
and with her words and tears together begged   555
that he should send relief, not go himself,
and thereby save two lives by saving one.
　　And Peleus to her: "Put off, O Queen,
your dutiful and most becoming fear:
the aid that you have promised me is welcome,   560
but I do not intend to take up arms
against this hideous new apparition;
the powers of the sea must be appeased!"
　　A lighthouse stood atop the citadel,
a welcome sight to vessels in a storm,   565
which they ascended, and looking out, beheld
(and groaned to see), upon the bloody shore,
the slaughtered herd and devastating beast
with gore-stained jaws and bloody matted pelt.
　　Lifting his arms in invocation, Peleus   570
prayed to the sea-blue goddess, Psamathe,
and begged that she would end her enmity
and give him aid; the pleas of Peleus
left Psamathe unmoved until his wife
joined his prayers with her own, and then the goddess   575
relented and forgave him.
　　　　　　　　　　　But even when
commanded to desist his slaughtering,
the wolf continued, maddened by his bloodlust,
until, as he was clinging to the neck
of a wounded heifer, he was turned to stone;   580
his color changed, but all else stayed the same:
the change in color shows he is a wolf
no longer, and no longer to be feared.
　　The Fates, however, still did not permit
the exiled Peleus to stay in Trachin;   585
and so he wandered to Magnesia,
and here, from King Acastus, he obtained
an absolution for the murder he'd committed.

Ceyx and Alcyone (1)

His brother's transformation and some weird
portents that followed it left Ceyx perturbed   590
and eager to consult the oracles
that comfort men in their perplexity,

but on account of Phorbas and his brigands,
the road to Delphi was too dangerous,
so he prepared to undertake a journey   595
to Phoebus' shrine at Clarium instead.[5]
    Of course, before he did so, he consulted
you, most loyal Alcyone; at once
the marrow of your bones took a great chill,
your face turned white as boxwood, and your cheeks   600
were soaked with tears. Three times you tried to speak,
but could not manage it for weeping so,
as sobbing interrupted your complaints:
    "Dearest," she said, "what have I done amiss
to change your heart? Where is the consideration   605
that you have always showed me? Are you now able
to take your leave without a thought for me?
Does a long journey have such great appeal?
Does absence make me dearer to you now?
    "But I suppose you're traveling by land,   610
and though I will be sorry, I won't fear,
and my concern will be unmixed with dread.
The sea is terrifying, and that sad
image of the deep: a little while ago
I saw parts of a broken ship on shore,   615
and often, upon gravestones yet uncarved,
I've read the names of those about to die!
    "Don't put your confidence in the wrong place,
relying on your father-in-law, Aeolus,
who keeps the storm winds locked up in his prison,   620
and, when he wishes to, can calm the waves,
for once they break loose and reach open seas,
the winds are wholly uncontrollable,
and earth and sea alike are unprotected;
indeed, they even vex the clouds in heaven,   625
and shake the lightnings from them by collision!
The more I know the winds—I came to know them
from frequent observations as a girl
in my father's house—the more they frighten me!
    "But if your purpose, dear, will not be changed   630
by a thousand prayers, if you are fixed on going,
then take me with you, and most certainly
we will experience the storms together,
nor will I fear what I must undergo;
whatever will be, we will bear the same,   635
in the same ship, borne on the open sea!"
    Her starry husband[6] could not but be moved

5. Because he could get there by a journey at sea.
6. Starry, because the son of Lucifer.

by this lament of the daughter of Aeolus,
for an equal fire burned in his heart too;
however, he did not wish to abandon   640
the sea journey that he proposed to make,
nor let Alcyone share in its dangers;
his words poured forth, intended to console her,
but did not win consent until he added,
in order to alleviate her pain,   645
one last concession; it was this alone
that let his loving spouse give her permission:
    "Delay of any sort seems long to us,"
he said, "but by my father's light I swear
that if the Fates permit, I will return,   650
before the moon has filled his circle twice."
    When her hopes for his return had been renewed
by what he promised, he did not waste time,
immediately ordering his ship
brought out of dry dock down to water's edge   655
and suitably provisioned.
                        But at the sight,
as though the future had been told to her,
Alcyone was horrified once more,
and once again her tears began to flow,
and she embraced him most unhappily,   660
and managed only one word of farewell,
before she fainted. Even as the king
was searching for some pretext to delay,
the young men seated two by two in rows
drew the oars back to their powerful breasts,   665
cleaving the waters with long, even strokes.
    She raised her head, and leaning forward, fixed
her blurry gaze upon him where he stood
on the curved poop deck, waving back to her,
and she returned his signal till the ship   670
had gone so far she couldn't make him out;
but as long as she was able to, she followed
its path, until, when it was almost gone,
she watched the fluttering of its topmost sail;
when even this had disappeared from view,   675
she anxiously retreated to her chamber
and cast herself down upon her bed;
but empty bed and bedroom both renewed
her tears, by summoning to mind at once
that part of her now taken from her life.   680
    As soon as they had gotten out of harbor,
a breeze came up and made the rigging creak:
the oars were shipped, the yard run up the mast,

and the sails were spread to catch the rising wind.
 The ship sped through the sea, and now was far   685
from either shore—a little less, perhaps,
but certainly no more than halfway there—
when, as night fell, the swelling waves began
to whiten, and the east wind blew more fiercely:
"Lower the yard, now, now," cried the captain,   690
"tight reef the sail!" Those were his orders, but
the gale winds blew the words back in his face,
and no one's voice could possibly be heard
over the breaking waters.
      Nonetheless,
some hurry on their own to stow the oars,   695
some seal the rowlocks, others reef the sails;
here one is busy bailing out the ship,
sending the water back to where it came from,
and here one hastily secures the spars;
while this is happening in great confusion,   700
from every side, the winds are waging war
and agitating the indignant waves.
 The captain now admits to his own fear,
has no idea of what is happening,
what orders he should issue or enjoin: 705
his skill is nothing, in comparison
to the greater power of the fury's force.
 Men cry in panic, and the rigging creaks,
the surging waves resound, the thunder crashes:
the waves are high as mountains and appear   710
to reach up to the heavens, where they drench
the overhanging clouds with their wild froth;
and now the water gets its color from
the yellow sand stirred from the bottom, now
the water turns far blacker than the Styx,   715
or white with rolling sheets of hissing spume.
 The ship from Trachin was likewise beset
by these vicissitudes: now lifted up
as to a mountain's summit, she appears
to gaze down at the pit of Acheron;   720
now plunged beneath a curving wall of water,
she looks up from the underworld to heaven.
 The ship's sides, often battered by the blows
of surging waves, give out enormous crashes,
nor are those blows less resonant than when   725
the iron-headed ram or the catapult
makes tortured towers shake from its assault;
and as ferocious lions who gain strength
by going on attack will hurl themselves

onto the hunter's arms and leveled spears,   730
so, when the insurgent winds had roused the waves,
these were much higher than the highest part
of the tall ship they dashed themselves against.
    And now the hull, its covering of wax
all worn away, begins to spring its wedges,   735
providing entrance to the lethal waves:
see where the sheets of water pour in floods
from bursting clouds; it would have seemed to you
that all of heaven was sinking to the sea,
and the swollen sea was mounting to the heavens!   740
    Sails were rain-sodden, waters from above
were mixed in thoroughly with those below;
the stars were all put out, and blackest night
bore down with its own darkness and the storm's.
That darkness, nonetheless, was shattered by   745
the flickering thunderbolts that lit the sky
and made the raindrops glitter as they fell.
    Boldly the flood now sprang onto the ship,
and like a soldier, who, surpassing all
his many comrades, in the last assault   750
upon the walls of a beleaguered city,
after so many tries, achieves his aim,
and, fired by the love of praise, leaps over,
and one man holds the wall against a thousand;
just so, when nine successive waves have battered   755
the hull of that tall ship without success,
the tenth wave rushes in with greater force,
and does not end its struggle with the weary
vessel before it penetrates the wall
of the captured ship.
                Part of the sea was now   760
still trying to invade the craft, while part
had done so, and already was inside;
fear and confusion now were everywhere,
as in a city under siege, whose walls,
sapped from outside, are held fast from within.   765
    Skill fails, and courage sinks, and every wave
seems to bring with it one more way to die,
as it comes rushing on and breaking in;
this one is unable to stop crying,
that one's in a stupor; over here   770
is one who calls a funeral a blessing,
while here one lifts his unavailing arms
in vain to sightless heaven for its help;
one calls upon his brothers and his father,
and one upon his home and family,   775
and each upon what he has left behind.

But Ceyx is fixed upon his Alcyone,
and it is her name now upon his lips,
and yet, though she is all that he desires,
he nonetheless rejoices in her absence;   780
he wishes to behold his land once more,
and see, before his eyes are closed in death,
his palace, but in truth, he does not know
in which direction land and palace lie:
the waters boil in whirlpools, and the sky   785
is so completely hidden by dark clouds
that blackest night is doubled in its darkness.

   A whirlwind breaking in destroys the mast
and wrecks the rudder too; now the last wave,
like a conqueror rejoicing in his spoils,   790
rears up and looks down on the lesser waves,
and no more lightly than if one could tear
Mount Athos and Mount Pindus from their seats
and haul them both into the open sea,
that wave came crashing down upon the ship,   795
and by its weight and overwhelming force,
plunged it right to the bottom; with it went
most of its men, sucked down into that vortex,
and fated not to breathe the air again.

   But some still hang on pieces of the ship   800
that floated to the surface; here the hand
that used to hold the scepter clings to flotsam.
Ceyx calls upon his father and upon
the father of his wife—in vain, alas,
but now the name most often on his lips   805
is that of Alcyone, repeatedly
recalled to mind and called to, as he swam:
he prayed that he might float where she would find him,
and that his lifeless corpse could be entombed
by her devoted hands. And while he swam,   810
as often as the waves allowed him breath,
he murmured Alcyone's name to them
and to himself.

          But look now: towering
over the lesser swells, a giant bow
of blackest water breaks upon him now   815
and buries him beneath the shattered surface.

   That morning you would not have recognized
great Lucifer in his obscurity,
for even though he could not leave the sky,
he hid his face within the densest clouds.   820

   But Alcyone, meanwhile, unaware
of this disaster, counting down the nights,
makes haste now as she finishes the robes

that he will wear when he returns to her,
and those that she will wear herself as well,   825
at the homecoming that will never be.
    Devoutly, she sends clouds of incense up
to all the gods, but most of all to Juno,
before whose altar she prays on behalf
of her poor spouse, no longer in existence,   830
that he would be kept safe and would return
and would not find another woman—this
alone of all her prayers would find an answer.

The House of Sleep

But Juno could no longer bear to be
petitioned for someone already dead,   835
and wished to keep her altar from the touch
of hands that were unwittingly profaned;[7]
"Iris," she said, "most faithful messenger,
go to the soporific halls of Sleep
as swiftly as you can, and order him   840
to send a likeness of extinguished Ceyx
to Alcyone, sleeping, so that she
might learn the truth about her situation."
    The goddess spoke. Her messenger put on
a cloak dyed in a thousand varied colors,   845
and crossed the sky upon a rainbow's arc,
and sought, as ordered, the abode of Sleep,
concealed beneath a panoply of clouds.
    There is a hollow mountain near the land
of the Cimmerians,[8] and deep within   850
there is a cave where idle Sleep resides,
his special place, forbidden to the Sun
at any hour from the dawn to dusk;
the earth around it breathes out clouds of fog
through dim, crepuscular light.
                              No wakeful cock   855
summons Aurora with his crowing song,
no restless watchdog interrupts the stillness,
nor goose,[9] more keenly vigilant than dogs:
no wild and no domesticated beasts,
not even branches, rustling in the wind,   860

---

7. Ceyx is dead, and so his wife, though innocently unaware of it, will be in a state of ritual pollution until his funeral rites have taken place.
8. We are heading toward Rome: the Cimmerians lived on the western coast of Italy, near Campania, in caves so dark that Cimmerian darkness became proverbial. A perfect place for Sleep.
9. For vigilance of geese in ancient Rome, see note 7 on p. 50.

and certainly no agitated clamor
of men in conversation.
                    Here mute repose
abides, and from the bottom of the cave,
the waters of the sleep-inducing Lethe[1]
flow murmuring across their bed of pebbles.   865
   Outside, in front, the fruitful poppies bloom,
and countless herbs as well, that dewy night
collects and processes, extracting Sleep,
which it distributes to the darkened earth.
Doors are forbidden here, lest hinges creak,   870
no guardian is found upon the threshold;
but on a dais in the middle of the cave
a downy bed of blackest ebony
is set with a coverlet of muted hue;
upon it lies the god himself, at peace,   875
his knotted limbs in languorous release;
around him on all sides are empty shapes
of dreams that imitate so many forms,
as many as the fields have ears of wheat,
or trees have leaves, or seashore grains of sand.   880
   The maiden brushed aside these obstacles
before her as she entered; the god's home
was lit up by the splendor of her garments.
   But Sleep could scarcely lift his eyelids, weighed
down by his idleness: time after time   885
they slid back down again, and his chin bumped
against his breastbone as he nodded, till
he finally awakened from himself,
and hoisted himself up upon one elbow,
and recognizing Iris, asked her what   890
she had come there for.
                    The messenger replied,
"O Sleep, that gives your peace to everything,
most tranquil, Sleep, of all the deities,
the foe of care, the spirit's gentle balm
that soothes us after difficult employment,   895
restoring our powers for the morrow;
O Sleep, whose forms are equal to the real,
order an image in the shape of Ceyx
to go to Alcyone in her chamber
and represent the shipwreck that destroyed him.   900
Juno commands this."
                    Having carried out
her orders, Iris took her leave at once,

---

1. A river of the underworld, whose waters when drunk erased memories.

unable any longer to resist
the slumber she felt stealing through her limbs;
and so she fled, and swiftly journeyed back   905
upon that rainbow she had lately crossed.
    But from the nation of his thousand sons,
old Father Sleep arouses Morpheus,
skillful at simulating human form:
there wasn't any other of his children   910
as capable of copying the ways
men walked, or looked, or sounded when they spoke;
he did their clothing, too, and knew what words
they would most often use. He specialized
in human beings only: someone else   915
impersonated beasts and birds and serpents;
the gods refer to him as Icelon,
but human beings call him Phobetor.
A third, Phantasas, has another skill:
he imitates the soil and rocks and waves   920
and tree trunks, anything without a mind;
these show themselves at night to kings and leaders,
while others wander among common folk.
    The father passed these by and chose from all
his offspring Morpheus to do the task   925
Iris had ordered; having done so, he
repaired immediately to his couch
and closed his eyes; his chin fell to his breast:
time for old Sleep to get a little rest.

Ceyx and Alcyone (2)

Morpheus, meanwhile, flies on silently   930
through darkness, coming in no time at all
to the city of Haemonia, where he
removes his wings, assumes the face and form
of Ceyx, and turns up, pale as death and naked,
in the bedchamber of his wretched wife,   935
with his beard soaked, and matted, streaming hair.
    And then, profusely weeping, he leans over
their bed and says, "Do you not recognize
your Ceyx, my wholly pitiable spouse,
or have my features been so changed with death?   940
Another look—you'll recognize me then,
and find no husband but your husband's shade!
Your prayers, my Alcyone, went unanswered!
I am now dead! Don't hope for my return!
The cloud-gathering south wind seized my ship   945
on the Aegean, tossed it in high winds

until it broke apart; yours was the name
upon my lips, in vain, until I drowned.
    "No doubtful messenger announces this,
you hear no unreliable account: 950
but I myself am uttering these words,
the shipwrecked man who stands before you now!
    "Arise then, stir yourself, go shed your tears
and put on garments suitable for mourning:
do not let me go off to Tartarus, 955
that place of emptiness, without lament."
    Morpheus told her these things in a voice
that she could easily believe was his,
and seemed to be sincerely weeping too,
and gestured with his hands as Ceyx would do. 960
Weeping, Alcyone groans and moves her arms
in sleep: attempting to embrace his form,
she grasps the air instead, and cries out,
                          "Stay!
We'll go as one where you are hastening!"
    Awakened by the sound of her own voice 965
and by her husband's image, she attempts
to verify if it was really him
whom she has just observed; roused by her cries,
the servants had brought in a lamp, and she,
unable now to find him anywhere, 970
began to strike herself about the face,
and tearing at the robes upon her breast,
struck it as well, and without bothering
to let her hair down, started tearing it.
    And answered, when they asked what caused her grief, 975
"Alcyone is no one any more:
she died with Ceyx! No consolation, please!
He perished in a shipwreck: this I know,
for I have seen and recognized my man,
and stretched my hands to hold him as he fled! 980
    "He was a ghost—but even as a ghost,
he clearly was my husband. Nonetheless,
if you should ask, he did not *quite* appear
as normally he did, nor did his face
glow as it usually used to do. 985
    "I saw the doomed man standing pale as death
and naked with his hair still dripping wet:
look where he just now stood, right over here!"
    She searched to see if footprints still remained.
"And it was this which my divining mind 990
led me to fear when I implored him not
to leave, entrusting himself to the winds.

"But even though we both would now be dead,
I'd rather you had taken me along,
for going would have been more to the purpose: 995
I would not have to spend my life alone,
and we would not have separately died.

    "A part of me is dead; apart from it
I perish, tossed upon those very waves
that parted us! The sea does not have me?   1000
In having him, the sea has me as well!

    "My mind would be more cruel than the sea
if I should struggle to prolong my life,
attempt to overcome such wretchedness!
I will not fight against it, nor surrender   1005
you, my beloved, whom I must lament!

    "But rather I will come as your companion,
and if the same urn may not hold us both,
the letters carved in stone will let us mingle:
if not our bones, at least our names will touch!"   1010

    Grief forbade speaking further; weeping spoke
in place of words, beyond what words could say,
and groans that rose up from her broken heart.

    It was now dawn: she left her palace and
once again sought that sad place on the shore   1015
where she had stood and witnessed his departure,
and as she lingered there and told herself,
"He was right there when he released the cable,
and over here was where we kissed good-bye—"
while thinking of what had happened in that place   1020
and looking out to sea, she noticed, at a distance,
something that bobbed and floated on the water,
something resembling a human corpse;
at first she didn't know what it could be,
but after a while the waves drove it toward shore,   1025
and even though it was some distance off,
it was apparently a body—whose?

    She could not tell yet; nonetheless, because
it clearly was the victim of a shipwreck,
an omen stirred within her, and she cried,   1030
weeping as though for one unknown to her,
"Alas, poor man, whoever you might be,
and—if you have one—for your wife!"
                                            The waves
prodded the body nearer, and the more
she looked at it, the less composed she was,   1035
and now it had come close enough to shore
for her to recognize it, and she knew

it was her husband!
          "It is he," she cries,
and tears her hair, and tears her face and garments,
and reaches out with trembling hands to ask,   1040
"O dearest husband, now so pitiful,
is this the homecoming you promised me?"
    There was a breakwater along the shore
on which the anger of the sea was spent
and which it would exhaust itself attacking.   1045
She leapt from it—a miracle she could!
    And suddenly, Alcyone was flying;
beating the air with unexpected wings,
the saddened bird lightly skimmed the whitecaps,
and as she flew, her long and narrow beak   1050
gave out hoarse cries, as though of one grief-laden,
and when she reached his silent, bloodless corpse
with her new wings, embraced his cherished limbs
and gave him a cold kiss with her hard beak.
    Now, whether Ceyx could really feel that kiss   1055
or simply had his head raised by the current
was a matter of some popular debate;
no: he *did* feel it; and at length the gods
showed mercy and transformed them both; as birds,
their love and conjugal vows remain in force: 1060
they mate and rear their young; for seven days,
halcyon days, in winter, Alcyone
broods on a nest that floats upon the waves,
which at that time are still: Aeolus guards
the winds and keeps them in his custody,   1065
when, for his grandsons' sakes, he calms the sea.

Aesacus

Some old man watches them as side by side
they fly above the ocean's vast expanse
and praises their continuing devotion;
another man—or possibly the same—   1070
points to a long-necked diver and goes on:
    "This bird, which you see skimming on the waves,
trailing his slender legs, is royal too,
a child of kings, whose lineage goes back
uninterrupted—you could look it up—   1075
as far as Ilus and Assaracus,[2]
and Ganymede, abducted by great Jove,

2. Ilus was an early king, and Assaracus a prince, of the Trojans.

and Laomedon and aged Priam, who
achieved his destined end in Troy's last days;
this one was Hector's brother, and if he   1080
had not met his strange fate in early manhood,
his name might well be equal to that other's.

   "Hector, of course, was born to Hecuba,
but Aesacus was born in secrecy,
as folks say, in Mount Ida's undergrowth   1085
by the daughter of the two-horned Granicus,[3]
Alexiroë. He shunned city life
and lived apart from the glamour of the palace,
dwelling, by his own choice, in mountain caves
and in the unambitious countryside,   1090
and rarely sought the company of Trojans.

   "He was no bumpkin, though, and had a heart
susceptible to the delights of love,
and often through the forest he pursued
Hesperia, whom he had caught a glimpse of   1095
as she lay, after bathing, on the banks
of the river Cedren (who had fathered her),
drying her flowing tresses in the sunlight.

   "The nymph fled at the sight of Aesacus,
as frightened as the hind is of the wolf,   1100
or as the wild duck, taken by surprise
far from the shelter of his accustomed pond,
flies from the hawk; the Trojan hero followed,
sped by his love as she was by her fear.

   "But look: as she was fleeing him, a serpent   1105
that lurked there in the grass sank its curved fangs
deep in her foot and poisoned her at once;
her flight was ended even as her life;
the lover, maddened by his grief, embraces
her corpse and cries out, 'Shame on me!   1110
How I regret that I pursued you so!
I never feared any such thing as this,
or that my victory would cost so much!

   "'The snake and I are both responsible:
he for the bite that he has given you,   1115
and I for having given him the cause:
I'll be the greater criminal than he,
if, by my death, I cannot solace you!'[4]

   "And from a cliff that had been hollowed out
by the hoarse waves until it overhung   1120

---

3. Granichus was a river (god) in Bithynia, two-horned, as was Acheloüs before his fight
   with Hercules.
4. Note the similarity between Hesperia's death and that of Eurydice, whose consequences
   are felt by Orpheus at the beginning of this book.

the sea, he leapt—but Tethys pitied him
as he descended, and she broke his fall
so that he landed gently on the surface,
where she put feathers on him as he floated,
denying him the longed-for gift of death.   1125

  "The lover was indignant, being forced
to live against his wishes, and his spirit,
coerced into remaining in the seat
it longed to leave, could not endure to stay;
so as new wings appeared upon his shoulders,   1130
he flew aloft and once again attempted
to fling himself headlong into the sea.

  "His feathers broke his fall, and he, enraged,
dove straightway down, and plunging to the depths,
attempted to find out the way to death,   1135
continually and without success.

  "He's very thin now: Love has made him so.
His legs are lengthy, and his neck as well,
which keeps his head quite distant from his body.
He loves the water and approves his name   1140
[*mergus*] because [*as we once used to say*]
he *immerges* himself underneath its surface."

BOOK XII

Around and About the *Iliad*

Iphigenia on Aulis[1]

His father, Priam, mourned, quite unaware
that Aesacus still lived on borrowed wings:
and Hector and his brothers pointlessly
conducted funeral rites before a tomb
with the name AESACUS carved into the stone;   5
Paris had failed to show up for the service,
but afterward brought an abducted bride
and a long war back to his own country:[2]
a thousand ships and the whole Greek nation,
bound by their oath, came after in pursuit,   10
and would have promptly taken their revenge,
if fierce winds had not made the sea impassable,
and if Boeotia had not held the fleet
at the fishing port of Aulis; there, as they
prepared to offer sacrifice to Jove   15
in the manner of their country, and the ancient
altar was glowing with fresh-kindled flame,
the Greeks observed a dark-blue serpent winding
itself around a nearby pine tree's trunk.

 Eight fledglings nested high up in that tree,   20
and they, together with their mother, who
flew round her little lost ones, disappeared
into the serpent's gullet as he grabbed them!

 All were astounded save the prescient
augur, Thestorides,[3] who spoke the truth: 25
"Rejoice, O Greeks, for victory is ours!
Troy will be taken, though it will take time!"

 In his interpretation of events,
each of the nine birds was a year of war.
Their living predator, who coiled around   30
the leafy branches, was turned into stone
that had the serpent's form engraved on it.

 The north wind still blew fierce on the Aegean,

---

1. Ovid begins his account of the Trojan War by emphasizing the effect of the metamorphosis of Aesacus on his father and brothers; Paris is first mentioned as having failed to appear for the unnecessary funeral service, and then, almost as an afterthought, as the cause of the ensuing war. Ovid follows this with a second metamorphosis, that of the serpent turned into stone, and then with a brief account of the sacrifice of Iphigenia, which also ends in a metamorphosis of a kind, since at the last moment a deer is substituted for the maiden.
2. Paris's abduction of Helen, wife of the Greek Menelaus, provoked the Trojan War.
3. An augur was a Roman religious official who foretold events by interpreting signs and omens. Thestorides is another name for the seer Calchas, who appears in Homer's *Iliad*, Book I.

and military convoys kept to port:
some held that Neptune, having built its walls,   35
intended to protect the Trojan city,
but not Thestorides: not ignorant,
and not one to keep silent when he knew
that a virgin goddess's fierce wrath must be
placated by a mortal virgin's blood.   40
    And after piety had given way
to patriotics and the common good,
and kingship triumphed over fatherhood,
Iphigenia[4] waited at the altar,
prepared to sacrifice her spotless blood,   45
surrounded by her grief-stricken attendants;
the goddess suddenly was overcome,
yielded, and cast a cloud before their eyes;
and there, in the officiating throng
of bloody ritual and beseeching voices,   50
Diana substituted—so they say—
a deer for Iphigenia.
               Therefore, when
the goddess's cruelty had been appeased
by bloodshed and her anger (and the Ocean's)
had both subsided, the thousand ships discovered   55
a favoring wind, and after many trials,
at last they came to the Phrygian sands.

The House of Rumor

At the world's center is a place between
the land and seas and the celestial regions
where the tripartite universe is joined;   60
from this point everything that's anywhere
(no matter how far off) can be observed,
and every voice goes right into its ears.
    Rumor lives here; she chose this house herself,
well situated on a mountaintop,   65
and added on some features of her own;
it has innumerable entrances
and a thousand apertures—but not one door:
by day and night it lies completely open.
    It is constructed of resounding brass   70
that murmurs constantly and carries back
all that it hears, which it reiterates;
there is no quiet anywhere within,

---

4. The daughter of Agamemnon and Clytemnestra, whose story is told in some detail by Ulysses in Book XIII, *Ajax versus Ulysses*, p. 343.

and not a part of it is free from noise;
no clamor here, just whispered murmurings,   75
as of the ocean heard from far away,
or like the rumbling of thunder when
great Jupiter has made the dark clouds speak.
    Crowds fill the entryway, a fickle mob
that comes and goes; and rumors everywhere,   80
thousands of fabrications mixed with fact,
wander the premises, while false reports
flit all about. Some fill their idle ears
with others' words, and some go bearing tales
elsewhere, while everywhere the fictions grow,   85
as everyone adds on to what he's heard.
    Here are Credulity and Heedless Error,
with Empty Joy and Fearful Consternation;
and here, with Unexpected Treachery,
are Whispers of Uncertain Origin;   90
nothing that happens, whether here on earth
or in the heavens or the seas below,
is missed by Rumor as she sweeps the world.

Cycnus[5]

Rumor let it be known that a Greek fleet
replete with gallant soldiers was approaching;   95
its arrival—not unexpected—was observed
by the opposing Trojans, who defended
their shores and kept the enemy from landing;
and you were first to fall, Protesilaüs,
dispatched by Hector's spear; those early fights   100
cost the Greeks greatly as they came to know
what skill brave Hector had at slaughtering.
    Nor were the Phrygians exempted from
discovering how capably Achaeans
butchered *their* enemies, and soon the shores   105
grew red with blood; now Cycnus out of Troy,
the son of Neptune, cut his thousand down,
and now Achilles in his chariot
pressed on relentlessly against his foe,
flattening ranks of Trojans with each thrust   110
of his great spear, fashioned out of wood
from a tree harvested on Pelion;
and as he searched for Hector or for Cycnus,
met with the latter on the battlefield

---

5. This is the third Cycnus to be turned into a swan. Ovid is the only source for his story.

(for Hector's fate had been postponed ten years);   115
then urging on his horses, whose white necks
strained at the yoke, Achilles drove
his chariot straight for the enemy,
and shook his spear to threaten him, and cried,
"Young man, whoever you might be,   120
take consolation, dead, from knowing that
your slayer is Thessalian Achilles."
    So spoke the hero, and his weighty spear
followed directly on his utterance,
but though his cast was nothing less than certain,   125
the sharp point struck—and merely dinged the breast
of his opponent without harming him.
    "O goddess-born," the other one replied,
"for your celebrity has preceded you,
why do you marvel that we stand unscathed?"   130
(It was indeed a marvel to Achilles.)
"Neither the golden, horsehair-crested helmet
that you observe me wearing, nor the curved shield,
the burden that I bear on my left side,
serves any purpose other than adornment.   135
Mars also, for this reason, puts on armor!
Deprive me then, of my protective gear,
and I'll *still* walk away from here unhurt.
    "Breeding matters: it is good to be the son—
not of a Nereid—but of the one   140
who rules Nereus, his daughters—*and* the sea!"
    He spoke and cast his spear at the Achaean,
but it was fated just to strike his shield,
tearing through bronze and nine layers of hide,
and lodging in the tenth.
    　　　　　　　　　He shook it off   145
and hurled another back with his strong hand,
but once again did not inflict a wound
on the undamaged body of his foe,
nor did a third spear even land on Cycnus,
although he offered himself openly;   150
you will have seen a bull in the arena,
who, with his terrifying horns, pursues
the provocation of a scarlet cape,
only to discover that he's missed it:
Achilles, raging, was not otherwise.   155
    He checks his spear: is the tip still on? It is.
"My arm," he said, "that once was so very strong,
has lost its power—but only in this case?
—For surely, it was strong enough when I
was first to breech the walls at Lyrnesus,   160

or when this arm dyed Tenedos and Thebes,
Eetion's city, with their defenders' blood,
or left the Caïcus' swift current purple
from slaughter of the tribes along its shores,
or when Telephus—twice—felt my spear's heft![6]   165
    "And here as well, among so many dead,
these heaps of corpses piled up on the shore
which I have seen and made, this arm of mine
has done—and still can do—its mighty work!"
    He spoke as one who lacks all confidence   170
in the heroic deeds of yesterday,
and cast his spear directly at Menoetes,
one of the rank and file from Lycia,
and tore right through his armor and his breast.
    And as the dying foot soldier crashed down   175
headlong upon the heavy earth, Achilles
withdrew the spear from its hot wound, and said,
"This is the hand, and this, the very spear
with which I have just now gained victory,
and which I'll use on him in the same way,   180
and hope to get the same results again!"
    So speaking, he found Cycnus in the fray:
unerring ash struck unevading shoulder,
the left one, with a thud—then bounded off
as from a wall or from a solid cliff: 185
Achilles saw that Cycnus had been bloodied
where he had struck him and rejoiced—in vain:
there was no wound—it was Menoetes' blood!
    Then truly outraged, roaring like a madman,
Achilles leapt from his high chariot,   190
and seeking his invulnerable foe,
he drew his shining sword and closed with him;
he noticed that although the other's shield
and armor had been punctured by his blade,
it lost its edge on his unyielding body.   195
    Achilles could endure no more of this:
with shield and sword hilt as his weapons, he
assaulted him about the face and head,
blow after blow, until, as one gives way
the other one pursues, perturbs, keeps pressing him,   200
gives him no time to pull himself together.
    Fear seizes Cycnus, and his vision blurs;
the path he flees on is obstructed by
a boulder in the middle of the plain;

6. Achilles refers to various conquests of his before his arrival at Troy.

as he lies with his back pressed hard against it,   205
Achilles seizes him and whirls him round
and flings him heavily against the earth.

Then kneeling on his shield on Cycnus' breast,
he strips the thongs that tied his helmet on
beneath the chin, and wraps them round his throat   210
and strangles him.

                    Preparing to despoil
his conquered enemy, he notices
the armor that he seeks has been abandoned,
for Neptune took the body of his foe
and transformed Cycnus into that white bird   215
whose name, until quite recently, he bore.

Caeneus[7]

This effort, this contention, earned a rest
of several days, when arms were put away,
and on both sides, the combatants stood down;
as wakeful sentries paced the Trojan walls   220
and Argive trenches, the warriors relaxed.

Achilles, who had triumphed over Cycnus,
was pacifying Pallas with the blood
of a slain heifer; when its entrails were
ablaze upon the altars, and the reek   225
of burning flesh, so cherished by the gods,
had made its way to heaven, the immortals
received their portion, and the rest of it
was set out on the tables to be eaten.

The officers all took their ease, reclining   230
on couches where they stuffed themselves with meat
and drove away their cares and thirst with wine.
No lyres for this lot, no poetry,
no flutes of boxwood, pierced with many holes:
what pleases them is to extend the night   235
by telling stories of heroic deeds;
they reenact old wars, their own and others,
and are delighted to remember all
the dangers they've endured and gotten through:
what else has great Achilles to discuss?   240
What else is there to speak of in his presence?

The subject of their stories was, in fact,
his latest victory: the fall of Cycnus

---

7. The transformation of Caenis to Caeneus and his subsequent invulnerability allow Ovid
   to tease his audience with some unheroic notions about the mutability of gender, as he
   did in Book VIII, *Meleager and Althaea*, when the boyish maiden Atalanta performed better than most of the assembled heroes.

seemed quite a marvel to this gathering:
that any youth should have a body which   245
no spear could penetrate to wound,
and which, in fact, turned blunted steel away,
astounded all the Greeks—even Achilles.

But Nestor told them, "Cycnus was unique,
the only one in all your generation   250
who spurned the sword, impervious to wounds.
But I have seen Thessalian Caeneus—
oh, this was long ago—who could endure
a thousand blows without a single wound!

"Thessalian Caeneus, yes, indeed,   255
the one who used to dwell on Mount Othrys,
and once was famous for heroic deeds—
but what was most amazing about *him*,
was that he had been born . . . a *her*."

                                      Astonished
by such a marvel, his whole audience   260
implored him to continue with the story.
Achilles, among others, interjected:
"Do tell! For this entire company,
O fluent elder, source of sagacity,
is equal in its eagerness to learn   265
who Caeneus was, how he changed his sex,
in what campaign or battle did you know him,
and how was he defeated—if he was."

Nestor replied: "Though my extreme old age
is something of an obstacle to me,   270
and much of what I witnessed in my youth
I have forgotten, still I remember much,
and nothing stands out more in memory,
among so many acts of war and peace,
than this does. But if great expanse of years   275
makes one a living witness of so much
that happened, I have lived two centuries
already, and am living in my third!

"The daughter of Elatus was a maiden
named Caenis, celebrated for her beauty,   280
the most attractive of Thessalian women
in all the nearby cities, and in yours,
Achilles, for she grew up in your town.

"A host of suitors hoped in vain to wed her—
your father Peleus might have been one   285
had he not taken Thetis as his bride
already, or had they not been betrothed.

"But Caenis had no wish for any marriage,
and one day, as the story went, while she

was traveling alone along the shore,   290
the sea god, Neptune, forced himself on her.
        "And after he had taken his delight
by ravishing the maiden, he announced,
'Whatever you desire will be granted!
Fear no refusal; ask and it is given.'   295
(The story that I mentioned said this too.)
        "Caenis replied: 'The injury you've done me
requires a great wish to be set right;
that I might never suffer this again,
allow that I may be no more a woman,   300
and you will have fulfilled me utterly.'
        "The words she ended her prayer with were deeper
than those that she began it with, and seemed
as though they could be coming from a man.
And so it was: for Neptune had already   305
assented, and now gave much greater gifts:
that she should be impervious to wounds,
and never fall a victim to the sword.
        "Caeneus went off happily with these,
and spent his days in masculine pursuits,   310
wandering in the fields of Peneus,
delighting in his new phallicity.

The Lapiths and the Centaurs[8]

"Pirithoüs, the son of Ixion
the bold, wed Hippodame and invited
those cloud-born beasts,[9] the centaurs, to recline   315
at tables carefully arranged and set
in a grotto sheltered by high foliage;
the highest-born Thessalians were present,
and we ourselves; the palace hall rang out
with mingled sounds of festive merriment.   320
        "They had begun to sing the wedding hymn,
the torches were smoking up the atrium,
and the young maiden, outstanding in her beauty,
had just come in, surrounded by a crowd
of matrons and of newly married women.   325
        "We all congratulated Pirithoüs

---

8. From the fifth century B.C. the battle between the Lapiths and the Centaurs (half-men,
   half-horses) was a favorite for poets and artists: a struggle between Greek civilization and
   barbarian brutishness, heroic figures celebrating a solemn ritual versus "bimanous
   quadrupeds" incapable of holding their wine and restraining their passions.
9. When Ixion attempted to rape Juno, she told her husband about it. Jove substituted a
   cloud form for his wife, and after Ixion copulated with it, the cloud conceived and bore
   the race of Centaurs. Jove bound Ixion to a fiery wheel for all eternity.

on his new bride, which very nearly spoiled
the services by ruining the omen;[1]
for you, Eurytus, fiercest of the fierce
centaurs, with a heart inflamed by wine,   330
took fire at the entrance of the virgin,
and lust was doubled by inebriation.

      "The tables were all overthrown at once,
and the marriage feast was turned into a rout
as the new bride was picked up by the hair   335
and carried off! Eurytus seized Hippodame,
and the others seized the women that they fancied
or those that they were able to abduct,
and in no time at all the scene resembled
what happens when a city is despoiled.   340

      "Female shrieking filled the palace hall;
we rose up instantly, and Theseus
responded first: 'What senselessness impels you,
mad Eurytus, to harm Pirithoüs,
while I still live? Do you not understand   345
that in harming one, you harm the two of us?'

      "The hero fit his actions to his words,
driving the centaurs off and rescuing
the maiden from their hands. Aware that such
actions were indefensible with words,   350
the centaur rushed at Theseus and struck
his face and selfless breast with shameless hands.

      "It happened that an antique mixing bowl,
engraved elaborately, stood nearby;
though it was large, Theseus was larger,   355
and so the greathearted hero hoisted it
and smashed it into his opponent's face;
bits of his brain, gobbets of gore and wine
came vomiting from mouth and wound alike,
as he crashed backward on the blood-soaked sands.   360

      "His death enraged the bimanous quadrupeds,
who all together cried at once, 'To arms!'
Wine gave them courage and they fought at first
with flying cups and jars, and with curved basins;
the implements once found at dinner parties   365
were now appropriate to war and slaughter.

      "Amycus, son of Ophion, first dared
to rob the sanctuary of its gifts,
and snatching up a chandelier replete

---

1. Times for weddings were carefully chosen to ensure favorable omens; any departure from
   the ritual, as by premature congratulations, might offend the gods and bring misfortune
   on the couple.

with votive lamps all lit up for the wedding,   370
he lifted it up high above his head
as though he were about to sacrifice
a spotless bull, and brought it crashing down
on Celadon the Lapith, rendering
the wedding guest unrecognizable   375
in a welter of crushed bone. The eyes leapt forth
from the disfigured pudding of his face,
and his nose was driven back into his palate.
      "Amycus had *his* turn when Pellaeus,
dismantling a maple table leg,   380
used it to lay him flat upon the ground:
one blow fixed chin to breast, and then a second
dispatched him to the shades of Tartarus
in a fine mist of black blood and flying teeth.
      "Next up was Gryneus, who, as he stood   385
fiercely glaring at a smoking altar, asked,
'Why not use this?' And promptly hoisting it,
he hurled the huge high altar with its flames
into the middle of the Lapith throng
and flattened Broteas and Orios;   390
the mother of Orios was Mycale,
a witch, as people say, whose spells could bring
the moon, despite its struggling, to earth.
      "'You will not get away with that, if I
can find a weapon,' cried Exadius,   395
and found one in the antlers of a stag,
a votive offering fixed to a pine.
He plunged the horns into Gryneus' eyes
and gouged them out; one to an antler clung,
the other dribbled down his beard and hung   400
suspended in a mass of clotting gore.
      "But look: right from the middle of the altar,
Rhoetus snatches up a blazing brand
of plum-tree wood, and whirling it around
on his right side, he smashes in the head   405
of Charaxus, all covered in blond hair,
which catches fire instantly and burns
as swiftly as a grainfield in a drought,
and the boiling blood that issues from that wound
gives out a terrifying hissing noise,   410
just as a heated bar of iron does
when the blacksmith removes it from the furnace
with his pincers and then thrusts it in a vat
of water where it hisses and it sizzles.
      "Distressed, he brushed the leaping flames away   415
from his unkempt hair, and tore a threshold stone

out of the earth, and hoisted that great weight,
more suitable for oxen, on his shoulders;
too heavy to be launched against a foe,
it fell—he dropped it—on a friend, Cometus,   420
who happened to be standing near, and crushed him.
   "Rhoetus could not keep from chortling:
'Oh, bravely done,' he said, 'and may the rest
of your side do as well as *you*, I pray!'
He charged again, still wielding his charred brand,   425
and struck at him repeatedly, until
his skull was broken into many pieces,
which sank into the jelly of his brain.
   "The winner then went up against Euagrus,
Dryas, and young Corythus; when the latter,   430
a lad who'd only just begun to shave,
lay flattened out, Euagrus asked, 'What glory
will you receive for murdering a child?'
   "Rhoetus didn't give the man a chance
to say another word: fiercely he thrust   435
his glowing torch into the other's mouth,
while he still had it open from his speech,
and drove it deeply down into his breast!
   "And you, cruel Dryas, he pursued as well,
whirling his flaming torch about his head,   440
but not, in your case, with the same results:
for as that serial slaughterer came on,
rejoicing in his rampage, you transfixed him
with a blackened stake where neck and shoulder join.
   "Rhoetus groaned and then, with all his might,   445
he wrenched the stake from his unyielding bone,
and dripping with his own blood, ran away;
and with him fled Orneus, Lycabas,
and Medon, whose right shoulder had been wounded;
and Thaumas fled along with Pisenor   450
and Mermeros, till recently the winner
in footraces against any contender,
but now disabled by a wound himself;
and Phobus, Melaneius, and Abas,
hunter of boars, and Asbolus the augur,   455
who had attempted, unsuccessfully,
to argue against their going into battle;
to Nessus, worried about being wounded,
he spoke these reassuring words: 'Don't worry:
stay where you are—your fate reserves you for   460
the bow of Hercules!'
                "But Eurynomus,
Lycidas, Areos, and Imbreus

did not escape: Dryas destroyed them all
in combat, face to face; your fatal wound
was frontal too, Crineus, even though   465
you took it fleeing him: for you looked back
and his spear nailed you right between the eyes.
      "Aphidas lay asleep, inertly clutching
his cup of wine and water mixed together,
stretched at his ease upon a bearskin throw,   470
and would not stir, no matter all the tumult;
and from a distance, Phorbas spotted him,
not answering (in vain!) the call to arms,
and fitting javelin to sling, he said,
'One Beaujolais-and-River-Styx to go!'   475
      "At once he hurled his spear at the young man,
and as he lay there with his head flung back
the iron-tipped ash drove right through his throat;
death took him unawares, and from his wound
the black blood flowed onto the couch he lay on   480
and filled the cup he clung to till the end.
      "I saw Petraeus struggling to wrench
an acorn-laden oak out of the ground;
with both his arms he'd managed to surround it,
and shook it back and forth until it tottered,   485
and just as he had almost got it loose
the spear of Pirithoüs tore through his ribs
and pinned his straining breast to the firm oak.
      "Men praise the valor of Pirithoüs
for slaying Lycus and for Chromis too,   490
but neither of those deaths gave him the glory
that slaying Dictys and Helops did: Helops
was pinned by a javelin that went right through
his temple, from the right ear to the left,
and Dictys, as he fled Pirithoüs   495
in fearful haste, toppled over the edge
of a mountain with two peaks, plunging headlong
until a giant ash tree broke his fall,
and left its fractured branches decorated
with loops of his intestines.   "Aphareus   500
was fixing to avenge him, struggling
to hurl the rock he'd broken off a mountain,
and as he struggled with it, Theseus
got in the first shot with his club of oak
and broke the huge bones of his elbow joint;   505
and then, with neither time nor inclination
to wound the helpless creature any further,
he leapt upon the back of tall Bienor,

accustomed to no rider but himself,
and locking knees against the centaur's ribs,   510
with his left hand, he clutched him by the hair,
and with his knotty cudgel smashed his face
and trashy mouth and shattered his thick skull.

"And with that club, he flattened Nedymnus
and Lycopes, skilled with the javelin,   515
and Hippasos, whose breast was covered by
his uncut beard, and Ripheus, who loomed
above the tallest trees, and Thereus,
who caught bears on the peaks of Thessaly
and fetched them back still living and indignant.   520

"No longer could Demoleon endure
the stunning victories of Theseus;
he had been struggling with all his might
to tear an ancient pine tree from the ground,
but when he could not, he just broke it off   525
and sent it flying at his enemy;
and when he saw it coming, Theseus
moved out of range, upon advice of Pallas—
or so he would prefer us to believe.

"That tree still did some damage as it fell,   530
for it sheared off the breast and left shoulder
from Crantor's neck—remember him, Achilles?
That fellow was your father's armor-bearer,
given to him as a guarantee of peace
by Amyntour, king of the Dolopians,   535
when Peleus defeated him in battle.

"At sight of him so horribly disfigured,
Peleus cried out from far away,
'Crantor, most pleasing of all youths, accept
this sacrifice sent to the underworld!'   540
With all the strength of his right arm, he hurled
his ash-wood spear against Demoleon:
it tore right through the basket of his ribs
until it shuddered, biting into bone.

"With difficulty, he plucked out the shaft,   545
but the spear tip still adhered within his lung;
grief gave him courage; wounded though he was,
he reared up on his hind legs and struck out
with deadly forehooves at his enemy.

"Peleus stood beneath that hammering   550
and took it on his helmet and his shield,
protecting his torso, readying his thrust,
then lunging forward, as with one swift blow
he pierced a human and an equine breast.

"That man, before he slew Demoleon,   555

had already slain Hyles and Phlegraeos,
both at a distance; and at hand to hand,
Iphinous and Clanis; Dorylas was next,
who wore a wolf-skin cap upon his head,
and armed himself, not with a deadly spear,   560
but with a pair of bull's horns, dripping blood.

    "Said I to him (for courage gave me strength!),
'See how my iron yields before your horns,'
and hurled my javelin. Since he could not duck it,
he raised his right arm to ward off the wound: 565
his forehead and his hand were nailed together.

    "On being struck, he made a great commotion,
but he was quite disabled by his wound,
and Peleus was standing close to him
and used his sword to open up his belly;   570
that fierce, unbridled beast bounded forward
and spilled his entrails out upon the ground,
and what spilled out of him, he trod upon,
and what was trodden on was burst asunder
and tangled in his legs until he fell,   575
his belly emptied of its viscera.

    "Nor did your beauty save you in that battle,
Cyllarus, if we grant that your kind may
be beautiful; his beard, just growing in,
was golden in its color, like the hair   580
that fell straight from his shoulders to his flanks.
He had a gratifying vigor of expression,
and you would praise all of his human parts
—his graceful neck, his shoulders, hands, and torso—
as equal to an artist's masterpiece.   585

    "Nor could his equine attributes be faulted
as inferior to the *man's* beauty:
provide him with a proper head and neck
and he would be a worthy mount for Castor!
His back so well adapted for the saddle,   590
his breast so muscular! In color, black,
and blacker even than the blackest pitch,
save for his legs and tail, which were both white.

    "Many there were, among the centaur folk,
who sought him for a lover; only one,   595
Hylonome, succeeded, captured him,
the comeliest of females in that tribe
of savages who dwelled in the deep woods;
and by alluring him and loving him
and whispering sweet nothings in his ear,   600
maintained her own exclusive hold on him;
and by her refinement—insofar as one

can speak of such a thing among her kind—
for she would run a comb through her long tresses,
and twine them with rosemary, violets, 605
or roses—even lilies, now and then;
and twice a day she washed her face beneath
the waters of a font near Pegasa,
that leapt and tumbled from a sylvan height,
and twice a day she bathed in that same stream; 610
and never would you find Hylonome
dressed unbecomingly, in anything
but well-matched pelts, all carefully selected
and draped across her left side from the shoulder.

  "Their love was mutual; together, they 615
roamed through the mountains and explored the caves;
now they were at the Lapith feast together,
and stood by one another, fiercely fighting;
from the left side, there came a javelin
(I don't know whose) that entered you, Cyllarus, 620
just at the sternum: a slight wound to the heart,
but heart and body all the same grew cold,
after the weapon was removed.
                                             "At once
Hylonome knelt by her dying lover,
and pressed her hand against the bleeding wound 625
and placed her lips on his, and so attempted
to keep his soul from exiting his body;
but when she realized that he was dead,
she took the spear with which he had been slain,
and saying something that I couldn't hear 630
because of the great clamor there, she fell
upon it and in death embraced her lover.

  "And even now there stands before my eyes
Phaeocomes, who killed half a dozen lions
and tied their skins together to protect 635
his human and his horsey parts at once;
he hurled a tree trunk which two teams of oxen
could scarcely budge; it cracked Tectaphos' pate,
shattered the broad dome of his skull, and pressed
his fluid brains till they exuded through 640
his mouth, his sinuses, his eyes and ears,
as when the whey pours through the oaken basket
leaving the curds behind, or as when grapes
beneath the press drip through the slender sieve,
and juice is squeezed out through the narrow openings. 645

  "But as he knelt to strip the dead man's arms
(your father knows this story well, Achilles)
I thrust my sword up through his testicles

from underneath! Chthonius as well,
and Teleboas fell before my sword: 650
the one had as his weapon a forked stick,
the other had a spear, and with that spear
the creature wounded me—you see the mark?
Why, even to this day, I bear the scar!

    "Those were the days when *I* should have been sent   655
to take Troy by myself! Those were the days
when I could have—not overwhelmed great Hector,
but fought him to a draw by force of arms.
But Hector, in those days, was not yet born
or was a boy, and now it is too late: 660
old age has taken much away from me.

    "Why should I tell you of the victory
of Periphas over the half-and-half
Pyraethus? Why should I renew once more
the deed of Ampyx, who ran his spear haft through   665
the forehead of that quadruped Echeclus?
Or tell how Macareus hurled a crowbar
at Pelethronian Erigdupus,
and laid him flat? And well do I recall
how the hunting spear that left the hand of Nessus   670
was buried in the balls of Cymelus!

    "Nor would it have seemed credible to you
that Mopsus, the son of Ampycus,
was nothing other than a soothsayer,
for by his spear the centaur Hodites   675
was stretched out as he tried, in vain, to speak,
with his tongue fixed to his chin and chin to throat!

    "Caeneus had already slaughtered five:
Styphelus first, then Bromus, Antimachus,
Elymus, and axe-wielding Pyracmos;   680
I don't recall the manner of their deaths,
for I took note just of the names and numbers.

    "Then Latreus charged out upon the scene,
gigantic in his limbs and body both,
and wearing armor taken from Halesus,   685
whom he had slain; even though middle-aged,
with graying hair, he still had youthful vigor.

    "Conspicuously bearing shield and helmet
and a Macedonian lance, he rode
between the front lines, showing off to both,   690
and circled tightly, beating on his shield,
while arrogantly adding to the wind:
'Are you supposed to be my match, *Caenis*?
In my eyes, you will always be a woman,

you'll always be *Caenis* to me,' and such: 695
'Consider well what you are by your birth
and by what you have gone through: go, take up
the colander and milk pail, twist the threads
across your thumb—leave war to men!'
    "While Latreus was boasting in this manner,   700
Caeneus hurled a spear into his side,
extended for his gallop, where the man
and horse were joined; raging with his pain,
he struck the young man's unprotected face
and saw his lance rebounding in the way   705
a hailstone does when it strikes against a roof,
or a pebble when it bounces from a drumhead:
then Latreus closed in on him and tried
to slip his sword into the other's side,
too hard to penetrate. 'Still you won't escape,   710
for even though my weapon's point is dull,
it has an edge, with which you will be slain!'
    "So he told him, and holding his weapon flat
in his long right arm, lunged at the other's balls.
It was as though his blade had struck on marble,   715
for with that blow, it shattered into pieces!
    "Caeneus, unscathed, paused for effect before
his astonished enemy a while, then said,
'Now let me try *your* body with *my* blade!'
and thrust his sword into the other's side   720
up to the hilt, then blindly twisted it
around to make a wound within the wound.
    "Outraged, the quadrupedal bimanites
rushed up screaming, hurling all their spears
against a single target, Caeneus: 725
their blunted weapons fell, but he remained
unbloodied and unbowed by all their blows.
    "They were astounded by this miracle.
Monychus cried out, 'What a great disgrace
that our nation is overwhelmed by one   730
not quite a man—and yet he *is* a man,
while *we* seem more like what *he* used to be,
the fault of our indecisiveness.
    "'What purpose in these monstrous limbs of ours?
And why is it that we have double strength?   735
Wherefore in our natures do we join
the strongest beings in a single force?
I can't believe a goddess was our mother,
or that we are the sons of Ixion,
who had the greatness to attempt the rape   740

of lofty Juno—while we are conquered by
an enemy who used to be a mare!

"'Then let a whole mountain worth of boulders
and a forest full of tree trunks be the missiles
we use to crush the life right out of him!   745
Let the sheer mass of it cut off his breath
and let its weight do for a fatal wound!'

"He spoke, and as it happened, came upon
a tree trunk that had been uprooted by
the fearsome power of the mad south wind,   750
and hurled it at his formidable foe;
so many others followed his example
that in no time, Mount Othrys was denuded,
and Pelion was left without its shade.

"Buried beneath that monstrous heap of trees,   755
Caeneus seethed with rage and lifted up,
on his broad shoulders, the whole timber pile;
but even so, once the enormous burden
had covered up his lips and then his head,
he found it was impossible to breathe,   760
and gasping, he attempted (though in vain)
to raise his buried head up, and so scatter
the forest heaped upon him; and as he moved,
he seemed like Mount Ida (visible from here)
when its green slopes are shaken by an earthquake.   765

"His end is still a matter of dispute:
some claim his body sank beneath the weight
of all those trees into the underworld;
Mopsus denies this, for he saw a bird
on golden wings rising from the center   770
of that great pile into the yielding air,
and I beheld the very same myself,
for the first time then, and never afterward.

"As Mopsus watched him in his graceful flight
around the camp and heard his beating wings,   775
attending with his eyes and with his spirit,
he cried out to him, 'Glory of the Lapiths,
once greatest of all men, but now a bird
unparalleled, Caeneus, fare thee well!'

"The story rests on his authority.   780
Grief added to our rage: it sickened us
to think that one man should be vanquished by
so many enemies; we did not cease
expressing grief with our steel until the night
had fallen; half of our enemies were dead,   785
and those still left alive had taken flight."

Periclymenus

And hearing Nestor's story of the battle
between the Lapiths and the half-wild centaurs,
Tlepolemus, indignant that his father
was being silently passed over, said: 790
"One moment, Senior, for a senior moment
astonishes: how could you possibly
forget to praise the deeds of Hercules,
when I have often heard my father speak
of the cloud-born quadrupeds he overcame?"[2]   795
    Nestor rebuked him sharply: "Why must you
compel me to remember wrongs again,
unearthing sorrow that the years have buried,
those injuries that make me hate your father?
God knows that he has done deeds past belief,   800
and all the earth speaks only of his merits,
which I, if I were able to, would gainsay:
Deiphobus does not find praise from us,
nor Polydamas, no—not even Hector;
for who will sing the praises of a foe?[3]   805
    "That father you're so proud of sacked Messene,
and devastated without cause the towns
of Elis and Pylos; yes, Hercules
destroyed *my* home by fire and by sword.
I shall not speak of others whom he slew,   810
but we were the dozen sons of Neleus,
distinguished youths; all twelve of us were slain
by the strength of Hercules, except for me.
    "The deaths of all those others could be borne,
but that of Periclymenus was weird;   815
his grandfather Neptune had given him
the power to transform himself at will
to any shape and then resume his own.
    "Now when his repertoire had been exhausted
to no avail, he changed into that bird   820
who in his talons bears the thunderbolt,
and is most pleasing to the king of heaven;
that bird, with all the strength of his strong wings,
curved beak, and talons, tore the hero's face.

2. The anger of Hercules's son over Nestor's omission of any account of his father's deeds in this battle allows the latter to tell his own story of how Hercules killed eleven of his brothers, including Periclymenus, slain after taking the form of an eagle.
3. Three Trojan heroes: Deiphobus was a prince who married Helen after Paris died; Polydamas was at last killed by Ajax, after slaying many Greeks; Hector was the great champion of the Trojans, slain by Achilles.

"Then Hercules took all too certain aim   825
with his great bow, as risen to the clouds
the bird hung, hovering and motionless,
and the hero's arrow struck him in the side,
where his wing began. The wound was minor,
but sinews which were severed by the arrow   830
were paralyzed and could not aid his flight.
He lost his purchase on the yielding air,
and plunged headlong to earth, and when he struck,
the arrow in his wing was driven through it
into his breast and then right through his throat.   835
    "Now then, most admirable admiral
of the fleet from Rhodes, what reason do I have
to sing your father's praises? Nonetheless,
I seek no further vengeance for my brothers
than to ignore the deeds of Hercules;   840
but our friendship—yours and mine—is solid."
    When Nestor had brought his story to an end
so courteously, the wine was sent around
once more, and then they rose up from their couches;
the remainder of the night belonged to sleep.   845

The Death of Achilles

But the god who rules the waters with his trident
still felt paternal sorrow for his son
Cycnus, who had been changed into a swan,
as he lamented the death of Phaëthon,
and exercised his unremitting wrath   850
on manslaying Achilles, whom he hated.
    War had been waged for almost ten years now,
and Neptune urged Apollo's intervention:
"O most obliging of my brother's sons,
with whom I built Troy's ineffectual walls,   855
do you not groan at sight of that citadel
so soon to fall? And do you not lament
for the many thousands slain defending it?
And of those many, whom I will not speak of,
does not the shade of Hector rise from below,   860
his corpse appearing just as when Achilles
shamefully dragged him round the Trojan walls?
    "But he who has a greater thirst for blood
than even Mars himself, the pillager
of our handiwork—Achilles—he still lives!   865
Give him to me, and I will make him feel
what I can do with my three-pronged spear!
    "But since I am not permitted to engage

my enemy in combat hand to hand,
the task is yours: slay him with an arrow,   870
unseen and unexpected."
                    So Apollo,
agreeing with his uncle, gave assent,
and in a cloud, came to the Trojan front,
where, in the midst of slaughter, he discerned
Paris, lackadaisically shooting   875
his arrows at anonymous Achaeans.
    Revealing his divinity to him,
Apollo said, "Why do you waste your barbs
on nobodies? If you have any care
for your own people, take aim at Achilles,   880
and so avenge his slaughter of your brothers!"
    And with these words, he showed him where Achilles
was devastating Trojans with his spear,
and made him turn his bow in that direction,
and with his own death-dealing hand, he guided   885
that certain arrow to its fated target.
    Not since the death of Hector had old Priam
a cause for celebration; now he had:
that you, Achilles, conqueror of many,
are overcome by an unheroic   890
adulterer who snatched a Grecian's wife![4]
Better that you were slain in battle by
an Amazon, wielding her double axe.
    Now he who was the terror of the Trojans,
the glory and protector of the Greeks,   895
invincible Achilles, has been burned
upon the pyre; one god and the same
armed this great hero and consumed him quite;
now he is ashes: and the little left
of great Achilles scarcely fills an urn,   900
although his living glory fills the world.
That glory is the measure of the man,
and it is this that is Achilles' essence,
nor does he feel the emptiness of death.
    His very shield—that you should be aware   905
whose it once was—now instigates a battle,[5]
and for his arms, arms are now taken up.
None of the lesser leaders, such as Ajax,

---

4. The death of Achilles at the hands of a very unheroic Paris allows Ovid once again to question the heroic ethos, and raise again, in the next two lines, the issue of gender and courage.
5. The death of Achilles now leads us into Book XIII, which begins with the struggle over his arms.

the son of Oileos, or Diomedes,
or Menelaüs dares to lay a claim,   910
nor any of the other leaders, more
distinguished for their age and experience;
only Ajax, the son of Telamon,
and Ulysses are bold enough to do so.
    Now Agamemnon, to spare himself the thankless   915
burden of deciding on this issue,
ordered the Argive leaders to assemble
in the middle of the camp, and hear the case,
and come to a decision by themselves.

BOOK XIII

Spoils of War and Pangs of Love

Ajax versus Ulysses[1]

The leaders were seated while the common grunts
stood round them in a circle. Ajax rose,
the master of the seven-layered shield,
now barely able to contain his anger.
    He looked back at the fleet along the shore,   5
then pointed to it, fiercely glowering:
"By Jupiter, it is appropriate
to plead my case before these ships," he said,
and fitting that I clash here with Ulysses,
who did not hesitate to yield them up   10
to Hector's torches—which I held at bay,
then put to flight![2]
                 "There's more security
in flinging lies than fighting hand to hand.
But I'm as slow to speak as he to act;
I am his master on the battlefield,   15
as he is mine—when it comes to talking.
    "Nor is it necessary, fellow Greeks,
that I remind you once again of my great deeds,
for you have seen them: let Ulysses tell
his stories of events that went unwitnessed,   20
which none but night, it seems, was privy to.
    "I realize I seek a great reward,
but having such a rival is demeaning
and cheats me of the honor I am due:
Ajax cannot be proud to win a prize,   25
no matter how substantial, that Ulysses
can have the expectation of receiving;
he has already gotten his reward,
for when his claim has been rejected, he
can boast that he and I were fairly matched!   30
    "But even if my courage were in doubt,
my lineage would prove superior
to his, for I am the son of Telamon,
who, under Hercules, once captured Troy,
then sailed to Colchis for the Golden Fleece;   35

---

1. The debate between these two Greek heroes of the *Iliad*, representing brawn versus brains, rude strength against mental agility, does not occur in Homer, though many of the events referred to by the characters take place in the *Iliad*. The protagonist of Homer's *Odyssey* meets Ajax in the underworld, where he unsuccessfully attempts to placate the spirit of the fallen hero. The liveliness of the debate reminds us that Ovid studied law before he presented himself as a poet. Indeed, the last point that Ajax makes in his argument is one that Ovid borrowed from one of his own teachers of rhetoric.
2. An allusion to events described in the *Iliad*, Book XV.

Telamon's father was Aeacus, the stern judge
of the silent underworld, where Sisyphus
is forced to push a huge rock up a hill.
Since Jupiter, the highest god in heaven,
acknowledges Aeacus as his son,   40
I am the great-great-grandson of great Jove!
      "But this connection should not advance my cause
unless I am related to Achilles:
and he's my cousin![3] I seek a cousin's arms!
And why do you, O son of Sisyphus,   45
and most like him in lies and thievery,
seek to associate Aeacus' line
with the name of an unrelated family?[4]
      "Is it because I freely took up arms
that arms are now denied me? Is the better man   50
the one who was the last to go to war,
who sought to shirk the action by feigned madness,
till someone who was cleverer than he,
but not as self-serving, Palamedes,
exposed this coward's trickery and forced him   55
to take up the very weapons that he shunned?[5]
Shall he now have the best of arms, who wished
no arms at all? Shall I go without honor,
deprived of my own cousin's worthy gifts,
because I was the first to go to battle?   60
      "Would that Ulysses had been *truly* mad,
or that we had believed him: either way
the fellow never would have come to Troy
and driven us to crimes! You, Philoctetes,
would not have been—to our shame—abandoned   65
on Lemnos, where, they say, you hide yourself
in woods and caves, and move the rocks to groans
with curses you call down upon Ulysses,[6]
well merited, and not—if there are gods—
called down in vain! And he who took the oath   70
to fight in our cause, a leader who
inherited the bow of Hercules,

---

3. Ajax's father Telamon was the brother of Peleus, father of Achilles.
4. Some accounts claim that Sisyphus, famous for his wiliness and cunning, was Ulysses'
   true father, having had intercourse with his mother Anticlcia before she married Laertes.
5. Palamedes exposed Ulysses when he feigned madness to avoid having to go to the Trojan
   War. When a vengeful Ulysses falsely accused Palamedes of treachery against the Greeks,
   Palamedes was executed. The story does not occur in Homer.
6. Philoctetes, the archer who carried the bow and arrows that Hercules entrusted to him
   on his funeral pyre, was bitten by a snake on the isle of Lemnos on his way to the Trojan
   War. After the stench from his wound became unbearable to his comrades, they abandoned him there on advice of Ulysses. At this point in the war, Greek seers had revealed
   that it could not be won unless Philoctetes and his weapons were brought to Troy.

now perishes of hunger and disease,
is clothed and nurtured by the birds brought down
with arrows fate intended for the Trojans!   75
　　"No matter: he still lives, at least—because
he chose not to accompany Ulysses,
unlike unfortunate Palamedes,
who would prefer to have been left behind,
and would be living now—or would have died   80
without dishonor; for Ulysses here,
reacting to the exposure of his madness,
accused him of betraying our cause,
and as his proof of this fictitious crime,
produced the gold which he himself had hidden!   85
And so, by means of exile or by murder,
he has reduced the strength of our forces;
that's how he fights, and why he must be feared.
　　"Although his eloquence surpasses Nestor's,
the man will never manage to persuade me   90
that abandoning old Nestor[7] was no crime:
for when, exhausted by extreme old age
and held back by his wounded mount, he begged
Ulysses' aid, his friend deserted him;
not only I, but Diomedes too,   95
is well aware of this: he called to him
repeatedly and seized him as he fled,
reproaching him for his timidity!
　　"The gods, however, even out the scales:
behold, Ulysses is in need of aid,   100
who did not offer it; he who once left
another must himself be left behind;
a precedent that he himself has set.
He cries to his companions for relief;
arriving, I observe him trembling, pale,   105
all discomposed by his impending doom;
I plant my massive shield in front of him
and save—no praise is due—his worthless life.[8]
　　"Will you keep on contesting me? If so,
let us return, then, to the battlefield,   110
to the enemy, your wound, your constant fear:
crouch down again behind my shield and argue!
But once I had relieved him of the danger,
he took off on those legs he couldn't stand on—
his 'wound,' remember? No laggard here!   115

7. An episode described in the *Iliad*, Book VIII.
8. *Iliad*, Book XI.

"Hector shows up and leads the gods to battle,[9]
and where he charges, not just you, Ulysses,
are terrified, but even brave men too,
so great a fear that warrior inspires.
And while he was rejoicing in a string   120
of bloody victories, I laid him low
with a great rock I hurled from quite a distance;
when he sought someone out for single combat,
I was the only one to undertake it;
you prayed the lot would fall to me, Achaeans,   125
and your prayers were answered. If you would learn
the fortunes of that battle, know that I
survived it undefeated by great Hector!

"Look where the Trojans rush out of their city,
carrying iron, fire, and the force of Jove   130
against our helpless fleet! Where's glib Ulysses?
A thousand ships,[1] the hope of your return,
and who protected them but me, alone!
Give me the armor in exchange for them!

"In truth, if I may say so, it's the prize   135
that seeks association with *my* glory,
and would be honored much more than would I—
for it's the armor would be given Ajax,
not Ajax the armor.
                        "To my heroic deeds
Ulysses should compare the way he dealt   140
with Rhesus, Dolon, and Helenus,
his capture of the statue of Athena:[2]
none of these deeds was done in the light of day,
and none without his Diomedes' help;
but if, on such weak merits, you decide   145
to give the armor, then divide it up
and give the larger share to Diomedes!

"What use does someone like Ulysses—who
conducts maneuvers secretly, unarmed,
relying on his cunning to deceive   150
a careless foe—what use has he for armor?
The rays reflecting from the golden helmet
would spoil his ambush and reveal him hiding;
nor could his head support the weight of it,
not any more than his unwarlike arm   155
could heft the spear shaft grown on Pelion;

9. A synthesis of several different episodes from the *Iliad*: Books VII, XIV, and XV.
1. According to tradition, Helen's face launched the thousand ships of the Greek fleet that
sought to bring her back to Greece.
2. The deaths of Dolon and Rhesus occur in Book X of the *Iliad*; the story of the capture of
the statue of Athena is told in non-Homeric Greek sources.

nor is the shield,[3] engraved to represent
the world in all its vastness, suitable
for his left hand—the timid, thieving one!
    "Indecent man, why do you ask for gifts   160
that cannot but enfeeble you? Gifts which,
if ever by some error on the part
of the Achaeans, were presented to you,
would not inspire terror in our foe,
but greed to strip such prizes from your corpse!   165
    "And flight, most timid one, your only gift,
and the one in which you *do* surpass us all,
will be impeded for you by that burden.
    "To all these reasons let us add one more:
your shield, so rarely used, is still brand new,   170
while mine, which bears a multitude of scars,
is urgently in need of a replacement.
    "And finally, what need is there for words?
Let us be seen in action: send the armor
back to our foe, then order its recapture,   175
and give it to the one who rescues it."[4]
Ajax concluded: an approving murmur
broke out among the soldiers standing there.
    Ulysses rose, paused briefly, and looked up
to gaze upon the leaders,[5] then began   180
to speak the words they had been waiting for,
ingratiating in his eloquence.
    "If our prayers had triumphed—yours and mine,
my fellow Greeks—there'd be no doubt at all
as to the winner of this important match,   185
and you would have your armor, now, Achilles,
and we would now have you; but since his fate
unfairly must deny him to you, to me—"
and here he made as though to wipe his eyes,
"the one who should relieve him of his armor   190
is the one who brought him to relieve the Greeks.
    "I don't want my opponent here to profit
simply because he seems to be (and is)
just a bit slow—or that I should be harmed
for being clever, or for having used   195
my cleverness to your advantage always;
my eloquence now takes its master's side,

---

3. The marvelous shield of Achilles, the gift of Hephaestus to Achilles' mother Thetis,
   described in Book XVIII of the *Iliad*, is passed over rather quickly here. Ulysses will bring
   it up again to significant effect later.
4. The argument that Ovid took from his teacher, Marcus Porcius Latro.
5. It is the leaders who will decide the issue, not the common soldiers, whose virtues Ajax
   both appeals to and embodies.

but it has often spoken up for you;
I would not have it garner any envy,
for each should do his best with his own gifts.   200
    "My race and family, the famous deeds
of famous ancestors are not my own;
since Ajax raised this issue, though, by claiming
that Jove was *his* great-grandfather, I
have to reply that he was also *mine*,   205
the founding father of *my* father's line:
my father was Laertes; Arcesius,
the son of Jupiter, was his; and nowhere
in my father's line was anyone convicted
of criminal offenses, or condemned   210
to exile; moreover, on my mother's side,
Mercury adds his luster to our name;[6]
my lineage, on both sides, is divine!
    "But the reason why I ask you for these arms
is not because of my more noble birth   215
(owing to my mother) nor because
my father was innocent of fratricide:[7]
this case must be decided on its merits;
that Telamon and Peleus were brothers
should not advantage Ajax: not origin,   220
but honor ought to be considered here
in seeing which of us deserves the plunder!
    "For if inheritance is linear,
Achilles had a father, Peleus,
and a son, Pyrrhus: so where is there a place   220
for Ajax in Achilles' family?
Let the arms be sent to Phthia or Scyros![8]
Teucer was a cousin of Achilles,
no less than Ajax: does *he* seek the armor,
and if he did, would he be like to win?   230
    "Plain speech is what is called for in this contest;
I have done more than words can manifest,
yet I will try to tell my deeds in order.
    "Achilles' mother, an immortal nymph,
foreseeing the destruction of her son,   235
attempted to disguise him as a woman:
though her deception took in everyone,
including Ajax, it was I who introduced
some arms that would arouse a manly spirit

---

6. Anticleia was the daughter of Autolycus (a notorious liar and trickster, whom Ulysses pointedly omits from the family tree) and the granddaughter of Mercury.
7. Ulysses implies that Telemon, Ajax's father, was guilty of the murder of his half-brother Phocus. In Book XII Ovid goes along with the usual version, which has Peleus responsible for the murder.
8. The birthplace of Achilles in Thessaly, and the island where his son Pyrrus lived, respectively.

among the items in the women's quarters;   240
although he was still dressed up as a maiden,
at once Achilles grasped the spear and shield:
'O goddess-born,' I said, 'Troy waits for you,
a city destined for destruction—why
do you prevent yourself from sacking it?'   245
I seized his hand, inspired and possessed him,
then sent that brave man off to do brave things.
    "So everything that *he* did was *my* doing;
my spear defeated Telephus in battle,
whom *I* restored, when he entreated *me*;   250
if Thebes has fallen, *I* deserve the thanks,
and you can credit *me* with Lesbos and
the cities of Apollo: Tenedos,
Chryse, and Cilla; give me Scyros too,
and grant that it was *my* right arm alone   255
reduced the walls of Lyrnesus to rubble,
and—not to speak of other actions—*I*,
and no one else, gave you the only man
able to destroy the warlike Hector; yes,
through *me* that famous hero met his end!   260
I seek these arms then, in exchange for those
by which the hidden hero was discovered;
I gave him arms while he was living; now,
after his death, I ask them back again.
    "When one man's troubles spread to all of Greece,   265
and a thousand ships were idling at Aulis,
all waiting for a wind that wouldn't come,
or when it came, came from an adverse quarter,
our leader, Agamemnon, was commanded
by an unyielding oracle to offer   270
his blameless daughter as a sacrifice
to fierce Diana; this he would not do,
since, in that king, there was a father, who
in his great anger cried out against heaven;
I was the one that, with ingenious speech,   275
turned the kind parent into the public man
(and I confess it here and beg your pardon,
Agamemnon), although I found it hard
to plead my case before a biased judge.
    "He was persuaded, for the common good,   280
and by his high command, and by his brother,
to temper his affection for his daughter
with a concern for doing the right thing.
    "They sent me also to the mother,[9] who
would not hear reason, but must be deceived   285

9. Clytemnestra.

by cunning—and if Ajax had been sent,
those ships would still be waiting for a breeze!
    "As your ambassador to Ilium,
I went into the Trojans' Senate House,
which was still full of heroes in those days,   290
but I, as ordered, pled the cause of Greece;[1]
I charged Paris with abduction, and demanded
that they give Helen and the plunder back;
Priam and Antenor were moved by my speech,
but Paris, his brothers, and accomplices   295
were scarcely kept from laying their indecent
hands on me—Menelaüs—you know this!
That was the first day when I shared your dangers.
    "It would take far too long for me to tell
of all the services that I performed   300
as an advisor and as engineer
during the course of that long, drawn-out war.
    "After the first engagements, the enemy
for a long time stayed within their city,
and so no opportunity for combat   290
presented itself; at last, and not before
the tenth year, did we do battle with our foe:
and what had you been doing all this time,
who have no expertise *except* in battles?
What use were you?
                    "Would you know what *I* did?   310
I set up ambushes and dug a trench
around our fortifications; furthermore
I gave encouragement to our allies,
so that they could endure the tedium
of such a long engagement; I advised   315
on how to keep us armed and well provisioned,
and served on other missions as required.
    "But look: deluded by a phantasm[2]
appearing in his sleep at Jove's command,
the king gives orders to give up the war,   320
orders which he defends as being Jove's:
so now let Ajax put an end to this,
let Ajax now insist on Troy's destruction,
and fight, since he is such a warrior!
    "Why doesn't he restrain them, and provide   325
a bulwark where the wavering could rally?
That wouldn't be too much for such a braggart!
But he was busy fleeing: ashamed, I saw
you turn your back and raise disgraceful sails!

1. An episode mentioned in the *Iliad*, Books III and XI.
2. From the *Iliad*, Book II.

"At once I cried out, 'Men, what are you doing?   330
What madness now incites you to run off
just when the city is within our grasp?
What will we have to show for these ten years,
what can we carry home except disgrace?'
    "And I said other things like that as well,   335
for disappointment gave me eloquence,
which turned them from the ships and brought them back.
    "Then Agamemnon called for an assembly[3]
of the Greek alliance, still panic-stricken;
not even then was Ajax bold enough   340
to make a peep, although Thersites dared
to mock the kings with insubordination—
but thanks to me, he didn't get off lightly![4]
I got up and exhorted them once more
to take the battle to our enemy,   345
replacing their lost courage with my speech.
From then on, whatever acts of bravery
Ajax may claim in truth belong to me,
who dragged him back from his intended flight.
    "And lastly, Ajax, who among the Greeks   350
has praise for you and seeks your company?
But Diomedes has joined his cause with mine
in all his actions; I have his approval,
and he can always count on his Ulysses—
and that is something, to be singled out,   355
chosen from all the Greeks by Diomedes!
    "Nor was I picked by lottery to go:
but careless of the dangers posed by night
and by our enemy, I took out Dolon,
who was scouting us, as we were scouting him;   360
but not before I'd gotten him to tell me
the battle plans of the dishonest Trojans.
    "I understood their strategy completely
and had no need for more discoveries:
I could return to certain commendation,   365
but not content with that, I made my way
to the tents of Rhesus; there, in his own camp,
I slaughtered him and his whole retinue.
    "A victor now, with all I'd prayed for won,
I proceeded in a captured chariot   370

3. Ulysses, not Agamemnon, summoned the Greeks to assembly in the *Iliad*, Book II; either
   this is an unlikely memory lapse on Ovid's part, or Ulysses, knowing just who is going to
   make the decision about the armor, sees a purpose in flattering Agamemnon about his
   qualities of leadership.
4. Thersites was an insolent coward who advocated abandoning the war and was humiliated
   and beaten by Ulysses.

in imitation of a joyful triumph;
the enemy insisted on those horses
as that night's price; deny the arms to me
and let Ajax be the more generous!

   "Why should I tell again of how my sword   375
brought devastation to the rank and file
of Sarpedon, the Lycian commander?
Or how I slew a bloody multitude:
Coeranos, the son of Iphitus,
and Alastor and Chromius I killed,   380
and Alcander, and Halius and Noëmon,
and Chersidamas and Thoön as well,
and Charopes and Ennomos, pursued
by Fates implacable, and others who
were not as famous, but who nonetheless   385
my strong right arm left broken on the ground
beneath the walls of Troy.

                   "O citizens,
I have my scars, and they are glorious
for where I've gotten them—but do not trust
in empty words: look on them for yourselves,"   390
he said, uncovering himself to them.

   "My breast," he said, "has always been engaged
in this great cause of yours. But Ajax here
has paid out nothing for so many years
in blood shed for his comrades that he's earned   395
a body free of scars!

                "So what if he brings up
how he defended the whole Grecian fleet
against the might of Troy and Jove combined?
I grant it: let him have the credit owed
his great accomplishment; but he should not   400
take all the glory; some belongs to you,
for Patroclus, as great Achilles, drove
the Trojans back and saved the fleet from burning.

   "He even thinks himself the only one
who dared trade spears with Hector on the field,   405
ignoring the king, the rulers, and myself;
he was but ninth in our chain of command,
and only won the task by lottery.
What was the outcome of this fight of yours,
bravest of warriors? Hector withdrew,[5]   410
unblemished even by the slightest scratch!

5. *Iliad*, Book XIII.

"It grieves me to think back to our sorrow
when Achilles, bulwark of the Greeks, was slain.
The tears that I shed then did not prevent me
from lifting him and carrying him off   415
upon these shoulders—yes, indeed—I bore
the body of Achilles on these shoulders,
and at the same time bore his armor off—
a deed I am now striving to repeat.

   "I've shown the strength to bear so great a weight,   420
and have the spirit to appreciate
the honor you confer upon the bearer:
am I to think that this was the ambition
of his immortal mother for her son,
that these exquisite gifts, the consummate   425
masterworks of the gods' own armorer,
were meant to grace a rude and brainless soldier?

   "He has no understanding of the world
depicted on the shield, its sea and lands
and stars arranged in patterns high in heaven,   430
the Pleiades, the Hyades, the Bear
who is exempt from setting in the ocean,
and opposite, Orion's gleaming sword:
he grasps at armor that his mind *can't* grasp.

   "Does he not realize that in blaming me   435
for hiding from the rigors of the war,
and for arriving after it began,
he deprecates great-spirited Achilles?
If pretense is a crime, then we're both guilty,
and if delay is culpable, then my   440
offense is lessened: I arrived here first!
My devoted wife and his devoted mother
kept us from leaving, but after those first days
were given them, the rest were given you;
and though I were unable to refute   445
the crimes I'm charged with—well, I could care less,
since those are faults I share with such a man,
and by Ulysses' ingenuity
was Achilles found; but Ajax looked around
and nowhere a Ulysses could he see.   450

   "Nor should it shock us that his stupid mouth
should so abuse me, for you also are
the targets of his indecent reproaches.
Can it be baseness for me to accuse
Palamedes unjustly, but correct   455
for you to find him guilty of the charges?
Palamedes could not defend himself

against so great a crime; his guilt was proven,
and you not only heard that guilt proclaimed,
but saw it in the evidence produced![6]   460
    "Nor is it my fault that Philoctetes
languishes on Lemnos: you consented;
defend your action. Yes, I persuaded him
to go on leave and to absent himself
from the rigors of the journey to the war,   465
and try to ease his awful state with rest.
He listened to me—and he's still alive!
So my advice was not just well intended,
but in its outcome was successful too,
though only my intentions really mattered.   470
    "And now that our augurs have decided
that Philoctetes has to be brought here
before the city can be overcome,
don't give this task to me: it would be better
if Ajax went—for by his eloquence,   475
he'll calm the raging fury of the man,
and by some cleverness or skillful trick
will bring our Philoctetes back to us!
    "The Simoïs will start to flow upstream,
Mount Ida will stand bare of foliage,   480
and Greece send war relief to Troy, before—
if my mind ever gives up on your cause—
the wit of Ajax does the Greeks some good!
    "O bitter Philoctetes, it is right
that you should hate me so ferociously,   485
and heap your endless curses on my head,
and long, in misery, to drink my blood,
if ever chance should give me up to you,
doing to me in spades as I did you.
    "Despite your enmity, I would set out   490
and try to bring you back with me to Troy;
if Fortune favors, I would have your bow,
just as I had that Trojan seer I captured,
just as I found the oracles, revealing
the fate of Troy, just as I carried off   495
the image of Minerva from its shrine
within the city of our enemy—
does Ajax now compare himself to me?
    "The Fates forbade the city to be captured
without that image: where was bold Ajax then?   500
Whatever happened to his boastful speech?

---

6. Sophistry on the part of Ulysses, who manufactured the evidence by which Palamedes
was convicted, thus making it impossible for him to defend himself.

Why was he frightened? How does Ulysses dare
to venture out beyond the sentry line,
entrusting his own safety to the night,
and facing opposition, enters Troy,   505
and penetrates its citadel and steals
the goddess from her altar, and then brings
the captured image past our enemies?
    "And had I not accomplished all of this,
the bull-hide shield of seven thicknesses   510
that our Ajax carries on his left arm
would have been worn in vain, for on that night
I guaranteed our victory at Troy:
I overcame Pergama[7] when I made it
possible to overcome the city!   415
    "Allow me, Ajax, to express the thought
your scrunched up face and muttering convey:
'*Part of his glory goes to Diomedes!*'
Of course it does: nor were *you* all alone
when you braced your shield before the Grecian fleet;   520
you had a host beside you: I but one.
    "Unless he knew that fighting has less value
in warfare than strategic capability,
and that the prize by right should not be given
merely to an indomitable arm,   525
Diomedes would also rise to claim it,
and lesser Ajax, and Eurypylus,
Andraemon's son, and Idomeneus,
and his own countryman, Meriones,
and Agamemnon's brother, Menelaüs,   530
would also seek it; all of them, however,
though strong of hand, my equals on the field,
have yielded to my insight and my counsel.
    "Your arm is purposeful in war, but lacks
the wisdom that my counsel can provide;   535
you have meer strength, but not my intellect;
lacking my foresight, you know only *how*,
not *when* to fight; that is my special skill,
and the task which our leaders picked me for;
you represent the body, I the mind,   540
and as an oarsman to an admiral,
or as a GI to a general,
so much are you inferior to me,
because, in our bodies, our hands
are of far lesser value than our brains: 545
in them resides the vigor of our lives.

---

7. Another name for Troy.

"Now you, O leaders, should award the prize
to your faithful guardian, considering
the many years which I have loyally spent
in anxious care for these concerns of ours,   550
as compensation for my services.
     "My labor now is ended: I've removed
the obstacle of the resistant Fates,
and I have taken lofty Troy for you
by making possible the city's capture.   555
     "Now, by the hopes that we all have in common,
and by the walls of Troy, fated to topple,
and by those gods I've recently removed
from our foe, and by whatever else
is left to do with wisdom and with daring   560
before Troy falls, remember all I've done!
     "And if you *still* won't give the arms to me
(he pointed to the image of Minerva)—
give them to her!"
                    The leadership was moved,
and the outcome showed what eloquence could do: 565
the skillful man bore off the hero's armor,
while the other one, who had so often stood
alone against great Hector and endured
iron and fire and the wrath of Jove,
discovered a passion he could not withstand: 570
the undefeated man was overcome
by the anger that he turned against himself.
     He seized his sword and turned to face them all:
"But surely this, at least, is mine," he said.
"Or will Ulysses take this from me too?   575
I must employ it now against myself,
and the blade so often stained with Trojan gore
must now be steeped in its own master's blood,
lest anyone but Ajax conquer Ajax!"
     He, when he finished speaking, drove that sword   580
into his previously unscarred breast,
up to the hilt—and none was strong enough
to draw the weapon out, until the force
of his own blood expelled it, and the earth
was stained with its color; from patches of green turf   585
there sprang a purple flower, which before
had sprung from the mortal wound of Hyacinthus;
and on its petals, letters were inscribed,
appropriate both to the man and boy,
spelling a hero's name, a cry of woe.[8]   590

8. Ovid reminds us that the youth Hyacinthus and the warrior Ajax share the hyacinth
   flower. In Greek, Ajax was Aias, which resembles the earlier *ai ai*. The flower refered to in
   modern times as the hyacinth does not have any such markings on its petals.

The Sorrows of Hecuba[9]

Ulysses then set sail for the isle of Lemnos
(the realm of Thoas and Hypsipyle,
where once a famous massacre took place)[1]
to carry back the arrows of Hercules;
and after he had brought them and their master,   605
Philoctetes, back to the Greek forces,
the final blow of that long war was struck. . . .
    Troy was ablaze, the flames not yet subsided;
Jove's altar was still drinking the thin blood
of aged Priam, and Apollo's priestess,   600
drawn by her hair, raised unavailing hands
in silent supplication; Trojan women,
while they still could, embraced the images
of native gods—until triumphant Greeks
dragged their appealing plunder from the temples.   600
    Astyanax[2] was flung off of that tower
from which his mother would point out to him
his father on the battlefield, defending
his reputation and ancestral realm.
    And now the north wind urged them to depart;   610
the sails flapped noisily against the masts
and the mariner had whistled up a breeze.
"Farewell, O Troy, for we are carried off,"
they cry, kissing the earth as they relinquish
their still-smoldering homes. Last to embark—   615
a pitiable sight—was Hecuba,
discovered at the princes' sepulchers,
clutching the tombs and kissing their dry bones;
Ulysses broke her grip and dragged her off,
but she hid Hector's ashes in her bosom,   620
and left locks of her white hair on his tomb,
her hair and tears a pointless offering.
    There is, across the way from where Troy was,
a country that the men of Thrace inhabit;
here was the wealthy court of Polymestor,   625
to whom, O Polydorus, your father Priam,
entrusted you in secret to be raised
far from the fighting: a wise decision,
had he not sent you off with a great treasure,
provoking avarice and ensuring evil.   630

9. Hecuba, wife of Priam and queen of Troy, survives its fall. Ovid's source here is Euripedes'
   tragedy *Hecuba*. The "manly" courage of suffering women as victims of the heroic ethos is
   one of Ovid's themes here and in the next three tales.
1. Venus, angered by the indifference of the women of Lemnos, afflicted them all with a foul
   odor; their men sought comfort from captive women, and the Lemnians murdered their
   fathers and husbands, save for Hypsipile, who hid her father, Thoas.
2. The very young son of Hector and Andromache.

When Troy collapsed, the impious Thracian king
savagely cut the throat of his young charge,
and then, as though to show that crimes could be
eliminated just as easily
as victims are, the corpse of Polydorus   635
was tossed down from a cliff into the sea.

  Awaiting quiet seas and a steady wind,
Agamemnon gave orders that the fleet
was to be moored along the Thracian coast;
quite unexpectedly, the ground split open,   640
and there emerged the ghost of great Achilles,
as large, and in his form as threatening
as in that time when, like a wild man, he
went after Agamemnon with his sword
and challenged him for his unjust behavior:[3]   645
  "O Greeks," he said, "do you depart for home
heedless of me? My body lies decayed,
as are the thanks you owe me for my service!
This cannot be: so that my sepulcher
may not go without honor, let my shade   650
be pleasured by the death of Polyxena."

  He finished speaking, and the Greeks obeyed
his unforgiving ghost: torn from the arms
of her mother Hecuba, for whom the maiden
was almost the only comfort she had left,   655
that fierce, unfortunate, unfeminine
virgin was brought directly to the grave
and sacrificed upon that ominous tomb.

  And after she had been brought to the altar,
and realized that she would be the victim   660
of this cruel sacrifice, not even then
did she forget herself; but when she saw
Neoptolemus waiting, blade in hand
and eyes fixed on her countenance, she said,

  "The time has come to spill my noble blood;   665
let there be no delay: plunge your blade now
into my throat or breast," and she bared both,
"for you may rest assured: Polyxena
does not desire to live as a slave!

  "My only wish is that my death somehow   670
could be unnoticed by my mother,
for her awareness of it spoils the joy

---

3. Ovid recalls the conflict recounted in Book I of the *Iliad*, when Agamemnon demanded
that Achilles surrender to him his slave Briseis, his share of the booty of war, thus precip-
itating the action of the *Iliad*.

that I would take in it—although her life,
and not my death, should really make her tremble!
   "Do not press close around me now, if what   675
I ask of you is just: let no man's hand
defile a maiden's honor by its touch,
lest I go to the Styx unwillingly!
My death will be more acceptable to him,
whoever he is, whom you propitiate,   680
if I endure it willingly.[4] But if
any are moved by these last words of mine—
no captive maid but Priam's daughter asks!—
then let my mother have my body back
without a ransom; let her tears, not gold,   685
redeem my corpse for its sad funeral:
when she was able to, she gave you gold."

   The tears that she was able to restrain
flowed in abundance from the eyes of those
who heard her speak; and even as he plunged   690
his blade into the breast she offered him,
the priest himself, though with reluctance, wept.

   Her knees gave out, and she slid to the ground,
a resolute expression on her face
right to the end—and as she fell took care   695
to cover up those parts that should be hidden
and served the honor of her chastity.

   The Trojan women took her body up,
once more lamenting another child of Priam,
the many victims given by one house;   700
and they mourned you, who, until yesterday,
had been the king's consort and queen-mother,
the image of an Asia in its prime—
now, even for a captive, you appear
especially unfortunate. Ulysses,   605
in his triumph, would surely not have wished
you to be his, except that you gave birth
to Hector, who would not have chosen *him*
to be his mother's master and her lord!

   She bathed her daughter's corpse now with the tears   710
that she had shed so often for her country,
her children, and her husband; she poured those tears
into her daughter's wound, and kissed her face
and beat her own breast, accustomed to the gesture,

---

4. In many cultures, including those of Greece and Rome, sacrifice, whether human or
   animal, was pleasing only if the victim was willing, or at least perceived to be so by those
   offering the victim. Polyxena does not know to whom she is being sacrificed.

and as she plucked her hair in bloody clumps,   715
these words, and even more than these, she cried:
    "O daughter, the last grief of your poor mother,
what else is there still left for me to lose?
The wound that you were given is my own,
lest I should ever lose a child of mine   720
without it being murdered—and yet you,
because you were a woman, I imagined,
would be safe from the sword—but even so,
as a woman, you too have perished by it,
killed as so many of your brothers were,   725
the victims of Achilles, who has bereft
the Trojan people and their helpless queen.
    "But after he had fallen to the arrows
of Paris and Apollo, I said, 'Surely
Achilles is no longer to be feared!'   730
Now more than ever I had cause to fear him!
The very ashes in his sepulcher
despise our race, and even from the grave
we feel the enmity that he still bears us!
I have been fruitful for Achilles' sake!5   735
    "Great Troy has fallen, and the public woe
has ended in calamity—yet it *has* ended:
for me alone the story still continues,
my ship of sorrow holds its steady course.
    "So very fortunate till recently,   740
in children, in their marriages, my husband—
now destitute, an exile, sundered from
my family's remains! Penelope
will soon display me to her women friends
on Ithaca, and tell them, as I weave   745
my daily quota, 'This is Priam's queen,
and noble Hector's celebrated mother.'
    "Now after all the others have been lost,
you who were left to alleviate my grief
have now been sacrificed upon his tomb!   750
The child that I gave birth to has become
an offering made to Achilles' ghost!
Why do I linger here, unyielding? To what end
is my old age, rich only in its years?
    "O cruel gods, why draw my lifetime out,   755
unless to show me even further grief?
For who could think that Priam could be called
fortunate after Troy had been demolished?
Only your father's death was fortunate,

---

5. The lines that Ovid's critics felt went over the top.

my daughter, for he did not see you die,   760
leaving his life and kingdom both at once.
    "But surely you, a princess of the blood,
would have your funeral rites as dowry
and lie in state among your ancestors?
No, this is not the fortune of our house: 765
your only offerings will be my tears,
your burial, upon a foreign beach!
    "We have lost everything—yet there remains
what may allow me to continue living
a little while: her mother's favorite,   770
my youngest once, and now my only son,
my Polydorus, sent to the Thracian king
on these same shores. But why do I delay
to wash this cruel wound with water
and bathe your face, still splattered with your blood?"   775
    She finished speaking and went down to shore,
tottering with age, and in her grief
tearing her white hair: "O women of Troy,
fetch me an urn," the luckless one commanded,
intending to draw water from the sea,   780
she found instead the body of her son
washed onto shore, disfigured by the open
wounds carved in it by Thracian implements.
    The Trojan women screamed, but Hecuba
was silent in her grief, which had devoured   785
the tears and the cry that sprang up deep inside her;
she stood stone still and fixed her angry gaze
now on the ground and now upon the heavens,
and sometimes staring at her dead son's face
and sometimes, and more often, at his wounds,   790
as surging rage armed and instructed her.
    Yet even in her fury, she behaved
as though she were still queen, and fixed her mind
and her imagination on revenge;
and as a mother lioness, whose cub   795
is taken from her, follows its spoor back
to find the enemy it cannot see,
so Hecuba, when anger mixed with grief,
forgot her years, but not her bravery,
and went directly to the Thracian king,   800
for this cruel murder had been his idea,
and asked him for an audience, pretending
that she would give him gold that she had long
kept hidden for her son. Deceived by this,
and by his customary avarice, the king   805
came in secret and implored her thus:

"Give your son the treasure, now, Hecuba,
for everything you give will go to him,
as everything you've so far given has,
I swear by all the gods."
                    She stared at him   810
ferociously as he foreswore himself,
and swelling with the flames of indignation,
she seized him, calling to the captive women,
and sank her fingers in his faithless eyes,
and plucked them out—for anger gave her strength—   815
then plunged her hands, stained with his foul blood,
into the places where his eyes had been
(for they were there no more) and plucked *them* out.
    The Thracians were enraged by this disaster
which befell their king, and started to throw stones   820
and spears at Hecuba; growling, she snapped
at the stones they threw at her, and even though
her jaws were meant for words, she started barking
when she attempted speech. Because of this,
the place has taken (and still takes) its name   825
[in Greek, *Cynossema*: Sign of the Dog]
from the place where Hecuba, remembering
the evils of that distant time, would howl
across the Thracian grasslands mournfully.[6]
    The Trojans and her enemies, the Greeks,   830
were likewise moved by what became of her,
as were the gods in heaven, all of them,
even the one who is the bride and sister
of Jupiter, for Juno, too, denied
that Hecuba deserved to end like this.   835

Memnon

Although she had supported them with arms,
Aurora had no time to sympathize
when Troy and Hecuba both came to ruin.
    The goddess had a care closer to home;
a private grief tormented her, the loss   840
of her son Memnon, whom she had just seen
Achilles murder with his deadly spear
on the Phrygian fields; and, as she watched,
the reddish color of the dawn grew pale
and clouds spread over the entire sky.   845

---

6. Ovid seems not to follow the tradition in which Hecuba is actually transformed into a
dog; rather, he has her wandering the neighborhood, howling like one in her grief. A rare
case in which he avoids a likely metamorphosis.

Aurora was unable to look on
as her son's body fed the final flames,
but didn't think it inappropriate,
just as she was, and with her hair unbound,
to fling her arms around the knees of Jove   850
and supplement her speech with flowing tears:
"Although I am inferior to all
the other gods that dwell in shining heaven
(my temples being few and far between),
I nonetheless approach you as a goddess,   855
but not to ask you for more festal days
on earth below, for temples or for altars
ablaze with the bright flames of sacrifice:
nevertheless, if you would just consider
all that I do (though I am just a woman),   860
the services I undertake for you,
when, with new light, I sever night from day,
you'd say that I deserved to be rewarded.

"But my present situation and concern
is not to ask for honors I deserve: 865
I come because I am bereft of Memnon,
who bravely (but in vain) bore arms for Priam,
and, still a youth, was slain by bold Achilles,
for so you wished it. Now I pray that you,
ruler supreme of all the gods in heaven,   870
grant him some honor, a solace for his death
and consolation for his mother's wound."

Jupiter nodded, as the towering
pyre collapsed into its leaping flames,
and thick, black smoke clouds blotted out the day,   875
as when a water nymph exhales a fog
that can't be penetrated by the sun;
black embers flying up accumulate
into one body, which, thickening, takes shape,
drawing warmth and animation from the fire;   880
lightness provides it with a pair of wings,
and birdlike at first, but very soon a bird
in fact, it flies off noisily among
innumerable sisters like itself,
all of them having the same origin.   885
Three times they flew around the blazing pyre,
and their mournful cries in harmony arose
and filled the air; on their fourth circuit, they
divided into two opposing camps
which waged ferocious war against each other,   890
employing their sharp beaks and curved talons
until they had worn out their wings and breasts;

and then, as sacrifices to the dead,
these ashy creatures fell back to the earth,
remembering the hero that they sprang from.   895
    The unexpected offspring took their name
from their creator: they are the *Memnonides*,
or *children of Memnon*; when the sun has crossed
the zodiac, their combat is renewed:
they fight and die in mourning for their parent.   900
    So others wept while Hecuba was barking,
but Aurora was intent on her own grief,
and even to this day she sheds her tears,
the morning dew that falls upon the world.

The Daughters of Anius

Nevertheless, the Fates did not allow   905
the hopes of Troy to perish with the city:
Aeneas, the heroic son of Venus,
brought out the sacred objects in his arms,
and likewise sacred, the venerable burden
of his father, Anchises.[7] These were the spoils of war   910
that pious man selected from his wealth,
and with his son Ascanius, he bore
in his fleet of refugees from Antandros
and from pernicious Thrace, so lately stained
with the blood of Polydorus; winds and tides   915
favored his voyage, and he soon arrived
at Delos, the city of Apollo, which
he entered with his cohorts.
                        There Anius
the king, who served Apollo as high priest,
received him in his temple and his palace   920
and showed him the city, with its famous shrine
containing the two trees Latona gripped
while she was giving birth to the twin gods.
    Here they gave incense to the altar's flame,
then doused it with an offering of wine,   925
and after sacrificing cattle, burned
the entrails, as was customary, then
went back into the palace and reclined
on piles of carpets and refreshed themselves
with gifts of Ceres and with flowing wine.   930
    Devout Anchises asked, "Priest of Apollo,
am I mistaken in my recollection,
or did you not have four daughters and a son
when I first came to visit in your city?"[8]

7. Aeneas escapes from Troy after its fall, as Virgil recounts in the *Aeneid*, Book II.
8. Ovid fabricates Anchises's former visit as a bridge to the story that follows.

Anius shook his head, bound with white ribbons,   935
and sadly answered him: "You are not wrong,
O greatest of heroes, for you saw me then
as the father of five children, of whom now
(such the inconstancy of human life!)
I am almost entirely bereft;   940
what aid can I expect from my absent son,
who holds the land of Andros (named for him)
in his father's place, and rules there as its king?

"Apollo gave him the gift of prophecy,
but Bacchus gave a gift to my four daughters   945
greater than they could have prayed or hoped for:
whatever any of these maidens touched,
turned into grain, or wine, or olive oil:
a profitable metamorphosis!

"When Agamemnon, the great scourge of Troy,   950
learned of this gift (lest you should think that we
had not experienced your trials), he
at once resorted to the use of force,
dragged the reluctant girls from my embrace
and ordered them to use their heavenly gift   955
to supply provisions for the Argive fleet.

"Each of them fled where she was able to:
two of the girls sought refuge in Euboea,
the other two, in Andros with their brother.
The Greeks arrived and threatened him with war   960
unless he gave them up: the ties that bind
in piety were overcome by fear,
and he surrendered them for punishment:
a brother's pardonable cowardice,
for he had no Aeneas to defend   965
his Andros, and no hero like great Hector,
who helped you to endure for ten long years.

"Now as the Greeks were forging manacles
to bind my daughters, they all raised their arms
to heaven, and together they cried out,   970
'O father Bacchus, deliver us from this!'

"The author of their gift delivered them—
if you can call it a delivery
to lose your human form in some strange way—
I couldn't understand then how they lost it,   975
nor am I able to explain it now.
But I *do* know how this evil came to end:
they put on plumage and became the birds
attending Venus, your immortal consort:[9]
my daughters were all changed to snow-white doves."   980

9. Venus and Anchises were lovers; Aeneas is the fruit of their union.

The Daughters of Orion

And there were more such stories until dinner
concluded and they sought their beds.
                                        At daybreak,
the oracle of Phoebus bade them seek
their ancient mother and related shores;
the king presented gifts on their departure: 985
a scepter to Anchises, and a robe
and quiver to Ascanius his grandson;
a goblet to Aeneas which a guest
had brought back from Aionia for the king.

    The precious goblet was the handiwork   990
of Alcon of Hyleus,[1] who had engraved
a lengthy narrative along its side.
The scene: a city having seven gates,
by which the viewer knows that it is Thebes;
funeral services were taking place   995
before the city walls: at sepulchers,
flames leapt into the air from blazing pyres
and mothers with bared breasts and unbound hair
proclaimed their grief; and even water nymphs
wept at the ruin of their dried-out springs;   1000
the trees were all bare and goats gnawed dry rocks.

    But look, where in the middle of the city,
the daughters of Orion, both of them,
are exhibiting unwomanly behavior:[2]
this one exposes her throat to the blade,   1005
while that one bares her breast to the cast spear;
they sacrifice themselves to save their people;
then with great ceremony, they are borne
through the city's crowds, to where they are cremated.

    And to prevent their family's extinction,   1010
twin boys (whom fame has named the Coronae)[3]
spring from the still-warm ashes of the virgins;
these lads at once join in the services
commemorating their maternal cinders.

    These figures had been brilliantly depicted   1115
around the outside of that ancient bronze;
its lip was decorated with a rough
border of gold-engraved acanthus leaves.
Nor did the Trojans offer gifts less worthy:
they gave Apollo's priest an incense box,   1020
a saucer, and a crown of gold and gems.

---

1. Whether or not his creation is imaginary, Alcon himself was a real silversmith.
2. Ovidian irony: like Polyxena, they are showing the courage in the face of death that only men are supposed to muster.
3. A word that meant *crowns*.

From there, recalling that Teucrians
sprang from Teucer,[4] they sailed off to Crete,
but couldn't bear for long the wrath of Jove
and left that island of a hundred cities,   1025
eager to reach the shores of Italy.
Fierce storms of winter tossed their ships about,
and when at last they came to the deceitful
harbor of the Strophades, Aëllo,
a Harpy, terrified them with her threats.[5]   1030
      And then to Samos, where Neritos dwells,
and Ithaca, the kingdom of Ulysses
the deceitful; they sailed past both of these,
and saw Ambracia, contested by the gods,
with its image of a judge turned into rock,   1025
but better known now for Apollo's deeds;[6]
they saw Dodona, of the talking oaks,
and Chaonia's bay, where once the threatened sons
of King Molossos managed to escape[7]
the impious flames on wings that they both sprouted.   1040
      They next sought out the Phaiakhian's land,
felicitous for its abundant orchards,
and landed in Epirus at Buthrotos,
a town that was a replica of Troy,
and ruled by Helenus, a son of Priam;   1045
thanks to the prophecies of the Phrygian seer,
they were aware of what the future held for them,
and after that, they came to Sicily.
      That island has three capes that run to sea
in three directions: Pachynus is turned   1050
to the rainy south, while Lilybaeum faces
the gentle western breezes; Pelorus
looks north and sees the Great and Lesser Bears,
two groups that never set beneath the sea.
      By strength of oar and by the favoring tides,   1055
the Teucrians arrived and beached their fleet
at nightfall on the sands of Messana:

---

4. Teucrians was another name for Trojans: Teucer was an ancient king of Troy who had
   originally come from Crete.
5. Aëllo was one of three Harpies, winged monsters with women's faces, vultures' bodies,
   and savage claws. Foul-smelling, they spoiled anything they touched with their filth and
   excrement.
6. The transformed judge is unknown. On the Gulf of Ambracis was the promontory of
   Actium, an important place in the founding myth of the Augustan dynasty: home of a
   temple to Apollo, it was the site of the decisive battle between the forces of Cleopatra and
   Marc Antony against Octavian, who became Augustus.
7. Prophetic oaks sacred to Zeus were found at Dodona; when robbers attacked the family of
   Molossus, famed for his piety, and threatened to burn down his house, the god turned
   them all into birds and let them fly off.

Scylla assails the whole coast on the right,
and, on the left, unsleeping Charybdis;
the latter devours and regurgitates   1060
the ships that she has captured, while the former
is girdled with wild dogs from the waist down.

    She has a virgin's face, and, if our poets
are not to be completely disbelieved,
was once a maiden ardently pursued   1065
by many lovers, all of whom she scorned,
finding among the sea nymphs (who adored her)
a shelter from unwanted male attentions,
where she could boast of outmaneuvered swains.

    And there once, while she offered Galatea   1070
her hair to groom, that lovelorn Nereid,
sighing repeatedly, told her this tale:

Polyphemus, Galatea, and Acis

"Without a doubt, O virgin, you attract
men of refinement, those of a better class,
whom you can brush off without any fear   1075
of consequence; but I, although the daughter
of two immortals, Nereus and Doris,
and although guarded by a throng of sisters,
could not escape from the undesired
attentions of the Cyclops without grief."   1080
A flood of tears kept her from saying more.

    The other smoothly scrubbed away the tears
from Galatea's eyes and soothed her, saying,
"Tell me the reason for your sorrow, dear,
do not conceal it—I'm a faithful friend!"   1085
    And Galatea answered Scylla so:
"Acis, the son of Faunus and a nymph,
gave pleasure to his parents, but gave me,
a pleasure even greater, to be sure:
we were inseparable. At sixteen,   1090
he was a gorgeous boy, whose tender cheeks
displayed the faintest down: I felt for him
exactly what the Cyclops felt for me:
incessant longing. Nor, if you had asked,
would I have been capable of telling you   1095
whether my detestation of the Cyclops
meant more to me than did my love of Acis:
for they were equal!

               "O Venus most benign,
how powerful a governance is thine!

"For see where that wild creature which the woods   1100
are terrified to look upon, the host
no stranger ever safely sees, the one
who disregards Olympus and its gods,
now realizes what love's all about,
and as he burns with powerful desire,   1105
entirely ignores his rocks and flocks;
you give attention now to your appearance,
Polyphemus, and now you take a rake
against your matted locks, and are well pleased
to trim your shaggy beard with a great scythe,   1110
observing your hirsuteness in a pool
and practicing an ardent swain's expressions.[8]

"Your love of slaughter and bloodthirstiness
now disappears, and ships can come and go
in perfect safety.

    "Meanwhile, Telemus,   1115
son of Eurymus, an unerring seer,
had landed here on Sicily, near Etna.

"He said to terrible Polyphemus,
'That eye of yours, the only one you've got,
and which you wear in the middle of your head,   1120
is going to be taken by Ulysses!'

"The Cyclops laughed and said, 'O foolish seer,
you are entirely mistaken here:
another has already taken it!'

"So he dismissed the one who tried in vain   1125
to warn him, and set out with heavy heart,
walking with leaden steps along the shore
or turning back, exhausted, to his cave.

"A sloping, wedge-shaped cliff juts out to sea,
washed evenly on both sides by the waves: 1130
the brutal Cyclops scrambled to its top
and sat down in the middle of the rock,
soon followed by his sheep, now leaderless.

"And after placing by his feet the pine
he used as walking stick—though others might   1135
employ it as the yardarm of a ship—
he took his pipes made from a hundred reeds,
and piped away: the mountains felt it keenly,
and the waters, too; a rock concealing me,
I lay in the lap of my darling Acis,   1140
whence I could hear, so very far away,

---

8. Polyphemos, the Cyclops, had been represented by Homer and Virgil as a savage cannibal
 and by Theocritus and Virgil again as a comical lover. Ovid was the first to combine these
 two representations.

words of the song the Cyclops sang to me,
and kept them afterward within my mind:
   "'O Galatea, whiter than the snowy white
flowers that decorate the privet hedge,   1145
richer in blossoms than the meadow is,
taller, more slender than an alder tree,
brighter than crystal, more skittish than a kid,
smoother than a seashell on the shore
worn by the ceaseless motion of the waves,   1150
more pleasing than the shade in summertime
or sun in winter, swifter than the deer,
and even more remarkable to see,
far more conspicuous than the tall plane tree;
clearer than ice, sweeter than ripe grapes,   1155
softer than swans' down or the curdled milk,
and, if you would not always flee from me,
more beautiful than an irrigated garden.
   "'Yet you, the very selfsame Galatea,
are fiercer than an untamed heifer is,   1160
harder than oak, more feigning than the sea,
tougher than willow wands or bryony,
less movable than the rock I'm sitting on,
rougher than rapids, prouder than a peacock,
fiercer than fire, bitterer than thistles,   1165
grumpier than a nursing mother-bear,
more unresponsive even than the ocean,
less apt to pity than a stepped-on snake,
and, finally, the worst of all your faults,
the one that I most wish to rid you of: 1170
not only swifter than the deer pursued
by the baying pack, but even swifter than
the winds and the swiftest breezes in the air!
   "'If only you would get to know me well,
you would regret your giving me the rush,   1175
condemn yourself for holding out against me,
and do your best to keep a catch like me:
a large part of this mountain is my own;
I have my caves, cut from the living rock,
protected from excessive summer heat   1180
and winter's chill; my apples strain their branches,
and yellow grapes are hung upon their vines
like lumps of gold, and purple ones as well:
to serve you, maiden, there will be both kinds;
and in the summer, you yourself will gather   1185
delicious strawberries in wooded shade,
in autumn, cherries, and the sweet black plums,
and not just those, but the big yellow ones,
which have the color of fresh new wax.

"'Nor will you lack, with me as your mate,   1190
chestnuts and fruit of the arbutus tree,
and orchards will be placed at your disposal.
    "'This flock is mine entirely, and many
others are out there grazing in the valley,
many I have in the woods, and many more   1195
are penned in stables deep within my caves;
and if you were to ask, I could not say
how many sheep are mine, for only paupers
can tally up the number of their flocks;
but don't trust me when I sing my own praises: 1200
just look around you here and trust your eyes,
see how these sheep can scarcely get around,
with their teats hanging down between their shanks.[9]
    "'The little lambs are kept warm in their folds,
as are an equal number of small goats.   1205
The milk I get from them is snowy white,
and part of it is kept for drinking fresh,
and the rest of it is made into my cheeses.
    "'You'll get no ordinary gifts from me,
and nothing that is easily obtained,   1210
like deer, and hares, and goats, and pairs of doves,
or a bird's nest lifted off a treetop:
on a mountainside, I found a pair of twins,
too like for you to tell one from the other—
playmates for you! Cubs of the shaggy bear!   1215
I cried out, when I found them, "For my mistress!"
    "'Come on now, Galatea, now's the time
to lift your pretty head above the waves!
Come on now, don't despise my offerings!
I have a good opinion of myself: 1220
lately I saw my image in the water,
and my appearance pleased enormously.
    "'Just look how big I am! Not even Jove—
this Jupiter that you go on about,
who you say governs heaven—is as big!   1225
Abundant hair hangs over my fierce face
and shoulders, shading me, just like a grove;
but don't think me unsightly just because
I am completely covered in dense bristles:
unsightly is the tree that has no leaves,   1230
the horse without a mane; birds have their plumage
and sheep are most attractive in their wool,
so facial hair and a full body beard
are really most becoming in a man.

9. Robert Lowell: "[Polyphemos] pleads his suit in a long, touching, absurd song filled with dairy products."

"'In the middle of my forehead is one eye,   1235
as large in its appearance as a shield:
what of it, then? Does not the mighty Sun
see everything that happens here on earth?
And as for eyes, he too has only one!

"'And furthermore, my father Neptune rules   1240
your waters; I present him as a gift
to be your father-in-law—if you will only
have pity on my prayers and supplications!

"'For only you do I bow down before,
despising Jupiter and heaven too,   1245
and his all-penetrating thunderbolt!
I fear you, Galatea, and your wrath,
far more ferocious than Jove's armaments!

"'But I could bear your scorn more patiently
if you fled everyone—though you do not: 1250
how can you spurn the Cyclops, but love Acis,
preferring his embraces to my own?
Well, he may please himself for all of that,
but what I don't like is, he pleases *you,*
Galatea—just let me at the guy,   1255
he'll learn that I'm as strong as I am big!
I'll tear his living gut out and I'll scatter
his body parts in fields and in your waters,
so you can mingle with his mangled limbs!

"'I burn indeed, and your offense against me   1260
blazes within more fiercely than a fire:
I feel as though Mount Etna in eruption
has been transported into my own breast,
and none of this makes any difference
to how you feel about me, Galatea!'   1265

"And after uttering these vain complaints,
he stood erect (for I saw everything),
and as a bull whose cow is snatched away,
unable to stand still, goes wandering
through forests and familiar fields, until   1270
that wild one catches sight of me with Acis,
and we both unaware and fearless too:

"'I see!' he cried out, 'and I will see to it
that this fond coupling will be your last!'
And these words spoken in a frightening voice,   1275
such as an angry Cyclops ought to have,
that left Mount Etna shaken to its core.

"In fear, I dove into the nearby waters,
while my Sicilian hero turned and fled,
crying out, 'Galatea! Help me! Please!'   1280

and 'Help me, parents! Admit into your kingdom
the son who otherwise will be soon dead!'
   "The Cyclops followed, pausing just to fling
a portion that he'd broken off the mountain,
and even though the barest corner struck him,   1285
it nonetheless crushed Acis altogether.
I (who could do but as the Fates permitted)
caused Acis to assume ancestral powers.
   "Bright purple blood streamed from beneath the rock,
and in a little while the redness faded   1290
until it turned the color of a stream
swollen from the first rainstorms of spring,
then shortly afterward completely cleared.
   "The boulder that the Cyclops threw cracked open,
and from within, there sprang a living reed   1295
of noble size; and from the hollow rock
there came the sound of waters leaping up,
and marvelous! there suddenly emerged,
from the middle of that womb, a tender youth
whose fresh new horns were wreathed in streaming rushes,   1300
and who, though larger than he used to be,
and with a face now of immortal blue,
was Acis, changed into a river god,
whose waters kept the name he had before."

Scylla and Glaucus

When Galatea finished with her story,   1315
the company of Nereids dissolved
and went off swimming in the placid waters.
Not Scylla, though: the maiden did not dare
entrust her body to the liquid depths,
but wandered naked on the thirsty beach   1310
or swam, when she was weary, in a pool
secluded and remote, to cool her limbs.
   But look, where other limbs, so lately changed
(near Anthedon, a town set in Boeotia),
belonging to a strange new resident   1315
of the deep sea, skim now across its waves:
Glaucus is here—and brought to a standstill
by his desire at first sight of her,
he says whatever comes into his mind
that he thinks might be able to prevent her   1320
from fleeing him; but she flees anyway,
fear speeding her, until she comes to rest
atop a mountain very near the shore,

a massive mountain, facing out to sea,
which rose up till it gathered in a peak   1325
of shaded woods that hung out over it:
here, in a place of safety, Scylla stopped,
not knowing whether he was god or monster,
admiring his color and the hair
descending past his shoulders to his back,   1330
where at his groin began a fish's tail.

He senses her discomfiture, and says,
while leaning on a rock that stood nearby,
"Maiden, I am no monster, no wild thing;
I am, in fact, a god of these same deeps,   1335
and of no less authority to govern
than Proteus or Triton or Palaemon.

"Before that, I was, nonetheless, a mortal,
but so bound to the ocean, to be sure,
that even then I schooled myself in it: 1340
now I would draw in nets laden with fish,
and now, while sitting on a rock, employ
my rod and line.   "There is a strip of beach
adjacent to green meadows: on one side,
the waves, and on the other, fields,   1345
undamaged by the grazing of horned cattle,
or depredations made by sheep or goats;
no busy bee has gathered flowers here,
no festive wreathes were ever taken hence,
and grasses never felt the sickle's sweep.   1350

"I was the first to stop there on that turf,
while my wet fishing lines were drying out
and I examined my catch of the day,
all laid out in a line along the shore,
the fish that chance had swept into my nets   1355
or whom credulity brought to my hooks.

"Now comes what sounds like fiction, I admit,
but what advantage would I gain by feigning?
Lying on the grass, my plunder from the surf
began to stir, and flipped from side to side,   1360
as all at once, they strove to leave the earth
and get back to the water. While I watched,
dumbfounded and incapable of moving,
they fled, the lot of them, abandoning
the shore and their new master for the sea.   1365

"I stood stock-still in wonder a long time,
asking myself how such a thing could be;
was it some god—or something in the grass?
'How could mere grass,' I asked, 'be strong as that?'

"I plucked some and I ground it in my teeth,   1370
and scarcely had I gulped that unknown liquid,
when suddenly my heart began to pound,
and my whole sensibility was taken
with the desire for another element,
which I could not resist for long: 'Farewell,   1375
O earth, which I will nevermore return to,'
I said, and plunged beneath the ocean's waves.
     "The sea gods welcomed me, pronounced me fit
to join their honorable company,
and asked the Ocean and his consort, Tethys,   1380
to take away whatever still remained
of my mortality; and this they did
first, by the recital of a hymn, nine times,
to purge me of my evil; then they bade
me to immerse myself a hundred times   1385
in just as many rivers; when I did,
the rivers that flow on from every part
poured all their cleansing waters on my head.
     "I can recall what happened up to this point,
and repeat it to you; this I recollect,   1390
but I don't understand the rest of it.
When I awoke, my body and my mind
were both much changed from what they once had been:
I saw then for the first time my green beard,
and my long hair, which spreads across the waves,   1395
and my broad shoulders, and my sea-blue arms
and legs which vanish in a fish's tail.
     "But where's the benefit of my new form,
and that the sea gods are all pleased with me—
what point is there to my divinity,   1400
if you have not been touched by all of this?"
     And so he spoke, and had much more to say,
and would have said it, had not Scylla fled;
then he, enraged by her rejection, went
to the wondrous halls of Titan's daughter, Circe.   1405

BOOK XIV

Around and About with Aeneas

Glaucus

Now he[1] who dwells among the swelling waves
left Etna, perched upon the Giant's Neck,[2]
and left the Cyclops' fields, that were unused
to rake and plow and unbeholden to
the oxen yoked together in matched pairs;[3]   5
Messana, too, he left behind, and left
the walls of Rhegium, on the far side
of that shipwrecking strait which separates
the shores of Sicily and Italy.

    From there, with mighty strokes propelling him   10
across the Tyrrhene Sea, Glaucus arrived
at the grass-covered hills and fabled halls
inhabited by many varied beasts,
where Circe,[4] daughter of the Sun, held sway.

    No sooner had he seen her and exchanged   15
greetings, when he urgently implored her:
"Have pity on a god, I beg you, goddess,
for you alone can cure my passion—if
you find me worthy! The strength of magic herbs
is better known to no one than to me,   20
for they have utterly transformed my life!

    "What caused my madness? This: one glimpse of Scylla
on the Italian coast, off Sicily!
It would be much too shameful to repeat
the promises that she dismissed with scorn,   25
the vows and the endearments she rejected!

    "But if there is some power found in charms,
then by all means, recite a charm for me;
or, if herbs should be of greater potency,
rely on those you know as efficacious;   30
I am not asking to be healed and whole,
to have this burden lifted from my heart,
but that these flames should burn *her* in some part."

    Such flames burned no one more than they burned Circe,
(either because of her own inclinations   35
or by the agency of Venus, acting
in retribution for the Sun's exposure
of her own indiscretion once, with Mars)[5]

1. Glaucus.
2. The part of Sicily that is above the corresponding part of the buried giant Typhoeus.
3. The Cyclops was a herdsman, not a farmer.
4. Circe was the aunt of Medea (see Book VII), and like her a magician skilled in the phar-
   macological arts, and with no strong moral principles governing their use.
5. A reference to Book IV, *Mars and Venus*.

and who responded to his plea with this:
    "You would do better to pursue someone   40
as ready and as willing as yourself,
someone who reciprocates your passion.
    "For you were worthy once (most certainly!)
of being asked, and, take my word for it,
if only you will give a girl some hope,   45
you will assuredly be asked again.
    "Don't think that you are lacking in appeal,
for I, a goddess, the daughter of the Sun,
the mistress of strong drugs and incantations,
I pray that you will have me! Only spurn   50
the one who spurns your passion, and return
the love of one who loves you: let one deed serve
two women as they each of them deserve."
    Glaucus responded to her proposition:
"The leaves of trees will spring out of the ocean,   55
and seaweed will be found on mountain ranges,
before my love for Scylla ever changes."
    The goddess was offended; even though
she could not injure him, another god
(nor did she wish to, being so in love),   60
yet stung by his rejection, she concocted
at once a mess of horrifying herbs
and poison potions; as she blended these,
she murmured certain charms of Hecate's,
then dressed herself in a cloak of azure hue,   65
and passing on through throngs of cringing beasts,
she left her palace, seeking Rhegium,
across the straits directly from Messana,
and made her way over the roiling waters
as if she walked upon the solid earth,   70
her bare feet dry as she skimmed the tops of waves.
    There was a little pool, curved like a bow,
that Scylla found appealing for its quiet;
here she restored herself from midday heat,
when the sun was high and shadows disappeared.   70
    Circe got here before the maiden did,
and fouled that place with poisons that produced
prodigious monsters; juice of noisome roots
she sprinkled there, and three times nine times spoke
the dark and winding words of incantation,   80
her lips well practiced in the magic arts.
    Arriving, Scylla sinks into the pool
up to her waist, and when she first beholds
her private parts deformed into the shapes
of barking dogs, cannot believe them *her*,   85

and in her fear, attempts to drive them off,
and then flees from their gaping wantonness;
but what she flees is drawn along with her,
and reaching down to touch herself below,
discovers not her thighs and legs and feet,   90
but that those parts of her have been replaced
by gaping mouths, like those of Cerberus;
she stands on rabid dogs and on the backs
of beasts beneath her, and her private parts
are girded with a ring of monstrous shapes.   95
    Her lover Glaucus wept at this and fled
from having any more to do with Circe,
whose use of potent herbs was too aggressive.
    Scylla remained where she was standing, though,
and when the opportunity arose   100
for her to show the hatred she bore Circe,
she carried off Ulysses' men as plunder,[6]
and would have done the same to the Trojan ships
had she not been transformed into a rock
before their coming—a rock that stands there still,   105
deep in the water, shunned by navigation.

Aeneas Wanders

When the Trojans had passed Scylla and Charybdis,
and were quite near the shores of Italy,
a head wind drove them to the Libyan coast,
where Dido took Aeneas to her heart   110
and home, but was unable to endure
a separation from her Phrygian mate;
and on a pyre built to counterfeit
the sacred rites, she fell upon his sword:
and she, who had been tricked, tricked everyone.[7]   105
    And fleeing that new city in the sands,
Aeneas once again returned to Eryx,
the royal residence of his true friend
Acestes; here, at Anchises' tomb
he honored his father with gift offerings.   120
    And setting out again in ships that Iris,
the messenger of Juno, almost burned,
he soon sailed past the Aeolian isles,
and the lands that reek of burning sulfur,
and the rocky islets haunted by the Sirens,   125

---

6. An episode recounted in the *Odyssey*, Book XII.
7. Ovid's brief and ambivalent recapitulation of Virgil's account of the passionate and tragic
relationship of Dido and Aeneas is deliberate and ironic.

the daughters of Acheloüs; and then,
once he had lost the helmsman of his ship,
he coasted past Inareme and Prochyte,
and Pithecusae on its barren hill,
an island named for its inhabitants.   130
    For to be sure, the father of the gods,
enraged by all the fraud and perjury
and criminality of the Cercopians,
transformed their men into misshapen creatures,
so that they should seem unlike human beings   135
and yet appear quite similar as well,
with shortened limbs and flattened, pushed-back noses
and faces deeply lined with old-age furrows;
and with their bodies cloaked in yellow hair,
he sent them off to dwell in these abodes,   140
but not before he took from them the use
of their congenitally lying tongues,
yet left them with the power to complain,
in raucous, strident noises, of their lot.[8]

The Sibyl[9]

When he had sailed past these and left behind   145
the walls of Parthenope on his right,
there, on his left side he beheld the tomb
of Misenus, Aeolus' tuneful son,
and the fertile lowlands' sedgy marsh
on the coast of Cumae, where he stopped and entered   150
the cave of the superannuated Sibyl
to pray that he might journey through Avernus
for consultation with his father's shade.
    For a long time, the Sibyl kept her gaze
fixed on the ground, but when the god within   155
had stirred her to frenzy, she raised her eyes to his:
"It is a great thing that you ask of me,"
the Sibyl said, "O man of mighty deeds,
whose strength and piety have been essayed
by sword and fire and are well esteemed.   160
    "So put aside your apprehension here,
Aeneas: what you ask for will be granted;
and with me leading, you will come to know

8. The name of the tribe clearly comes from the Greek word for tail, *kerkos*: since *cercopithecus* was the Latin word for a long-tailed monkey, the Cercopians must have been changed into simians of some sort.
9. The Sibyl of Cumae was the most famous of her kind, one of an indeterminate number of women prophets. She lived in a cave thought to be one of the entrances to the underworld. For a more elaborate treatment of Aeneas's visit (though one that lacks the Sibyl's own very interesting story), see Virgil's *Aeneid*, Book VI.

the Elysian abodes and that extraordinary
kingdom within whose borders you will find   165
the shade of your dear father: nothing prevents
such access to the man of excellence."
     She spoke and showed him, deep within the wood
of Proserpina, a shining golden branch
and ordered him to break it from its tree.   170
Aeneas did as he was told and saw
the underworld's formidable resources,
and his ancestral spirits, and the shade
of that great-spirited and venerable man,
father Anchises. He carefully observed   175
the laws and customs of the places there,
and learned what dangers he himself would face
in the wars to come.[1] And afterward,
as he retraced his steps in weariness,
struck up a conversation with his guide,   180
to alleviate the journey's tedium.
     And while they were returning through dim twilight
on that dreadful road, Aeneas said to her,
"Whether you are yourself a goddess, or
are one who is most pleasing to the gods,   185
you will seem always most divine to me.
I will avow that my opportunity
to tour the underworld and leave it alive
has been your gift to me; and in exchange,
when I return to where the air is fresh,   190
I will erect a temple and establish
a cult that will burn incense in your honor."
     The Sibyl took a deep breath and responded,
"I am no goddess—and no mere mortal
is worthy of the gift of sacred incense!   195
But lest you err by ignorance, know that
eternal life *was* offered to me once,
if I would yield my maidenhead to Phoebus,
who, while he thought I would submit to him,
attempted to seduce me with fine gifts: 200
     "'Select, Cumaean virgin, what you wish,
and you will have whatever it may be.'
     "I pointed to a piled-up heap of sand
and asked a gift that would prove meaningless:
that I should have as many years of life   130
as sand grains in the pile. My words escaped
before I'd thought to say, *'unaging* years.'
He gave the years and promised endless youth

---

1. Wars fought with the inhabitants of Italy.

if I would let him love me—but I spurned
the gifts of Phoebus and remained a maid.   210
    "My better days have turned their back on me,
and scant old age with palsied step draws near,
which I must suffer for a long, long time,
for seven centuries have been accomplished,
and three more yet remain to me before   215
my years are equal to those grains of sand:
three hundred harvestings of grape and grain.
    "A time will come when many days reduce
my body to near nothing, and old age
whittles my limbs to where they scarce can bear   220
their meager burden; nor will I then seem
to have inspired love in a god's breast;
Phoebus himself perhaps will not remember,
or may deny that he desired me:
these are the changes I will come to bear,   225
but when I am no longer visible,
I will be recognized by my voice still,
according to the promise of the Fates."
    So while they journeyed up that sloping road,
the Sibyl told her story to Aeneas;   230
they exited the underworld at Cumae,
and there Aeneas offered customary
sacrifices, then landed on the shore
that, as yet, did not bear his nurse's name.[2]

Cyclops Revisited[3]

Macareus, companion of Ulysses,   235
had lingered here, weary of wandering.
He recognizes Achaemenides,
who had so long ago been left behind
on rocky Etna, and who, now discovered
so unexpectedly among the living,   240
causes astonishment: "What luck, what god
has saved you, Achaemenides?" he asked.
"What is a Greek doing on a Trojan ship,
and what land are you seeking in this vessel?"
    Now like himself, no longer clad in rags   245
that thorns had torn and then had pinned together,
Achaemenides answered him with this:

2. Ovid's little joke on Virgil: in Book VI of the *Aeneid*, Virgil gives the place-name, Caieta,
   then explains in Book VII how it got its name from Aeneas's wet nurse. Ovid has trouble
   letting go of this: he refers to it again in line 622 and in Book XV, line 882.
3. Having seen the Cyclops as hapless lover, we now see him as cannibal. Macareus is Ovid's
   own invention, just as Achaemenides is Virgil's.

"May I behold Polyphemus again,
his gaping jaws awash in human blood,
if I prefer my home and Ithaca   250
to *this* ship, or if I should venerate
Aeneas less than I do my own father;
nor would I ever, though I gave my all,
be able to discharge my debt to him!
        "I speak, I breathe, I look up at the stars   255
in heaven, always mindful, always grateful!
His gift was that I did not end my life
in the Cyclops' mouth—that if I *should* die now,
I'd have another grave besides his gut!
        "What feelings came to me—or would have come,   260
had dread not left me numb to all sensation—
when I beheld you make for the open seas!
I wanted to cry out to you, but feared
to give myself up to the enemy:
Ulysses' outcry nearly sank you all!   265
I saw a boulder broken from the mountain
and hurled into the middle of the water!
I saw him flinging out enormous rocks
with his great arms, as from a catapult,
and feared that wind and waves would sink your ship—   270
having forgotten I was not on board.
        "But after you had fled from certain death,
the groaning Cyclops prowled all over Etna
and shook the trees to search them with his hands,
and blindly hurled himself against the rocks,   275
and stretching his misshapen arms out seaward,
he damned all Greeks entirely and said,
        "'If only by some chance that knave Ulysses
were brought back here—or any of his men
on whom I might now ventilate my rage,   280
whose guts I might devour, and whose lives
might be extinguished in my strong right hand,
whose blood might run in rivers down my throat,
whose shattered limbs might quiver in my jaws—
little or nothing would my blindness seem!'   285
        "This and much more he said, just as ferocious,
while pale-faced horror gripped me at the sight
of those grim features, stained with recent slaughter!
Those hands! The empty socket of that eye!
That beard, now stiff with human gore! Those limbs!   290
        "My death was right before my very eyes,
although it was the least of all my troubles,
for now I reckoned that I would be caught,

that my own viscera would merge with his:
I couldn't get that image from my mind,   295
how I had seen two of my companions
snatched up, their bodies dashed against the ground
three or four times, before he crouched above them,
and like a shaggy lion at his prey,
had crammed his belly with their guts, their flesh,   300
the marrow of their bones, their twitching limbs!

    "A tremor seized me: there I stood, stock-still,
my face a funeral as I watched him chew
and spit out remnants of his bloody feast
and vomit gobbets mixed with sour wine,   305
and I pictured the same fate in store for me
and hid myself away for many days,
trembling at every sound I heard,
fearing my death and wishing but to die,
and living off of acorns, grass, and leaves,   310
helpless, alone, abandoned to my death,
until, after a long time had gone by,
at a great distance, I beheld a ship,
and begging with dumb gestures for relief,
I raced down to the shore: I touched their hearts   305
and a Trojan ship allowed a Greek on board!

Circe Revisited

"But you, most welcome comrade, tell your adventures—
what leader, what companions went with you
when you entrusted yourself to the sea?"

    Macareus told them of how Aeolus,   320
son of Hippotes, ruled the Tyrrhene Sea,
imprisoning the winds: he gave Ulysses
a gift worth mentioning: a bag of winds,
and aided by the breezes it contained,
he sailed nine days until he came in sight   325
of the desired land. But at first light
of the tenth day, his crew was overcome
by greed and envy: after reckoning
the bag was full of gold, they loosed the string
that bound it up and were blown all the way back   330
across the waves until their ship regained
the harbor of Aeolus the king.[4]

    "And after that," Macareus went on,
"we came to Formiae, in ancient times
founded by Lamus the Laestrygonian;   335
Antiphates was ruler in this kingdom.

---

4. As recounted in the *Odyssey*, Book X.

I was dispatched to him with two companions,
and barely managed, after taking flight,
to save myself and one of my two men:
the other's blood was smeared across the faces   340
of the inhospitable Laestrygonians.

    "Antiphates pursued us as we fled,
urging his forces on: they came together
and hurled great rocks and timbers after us
and sank our men and sank our ships as well.   345
Ulysses and I, however, got away
on one of them.

            "We mourned our lost companions
and with much lamentation found that land
which, at a distance, you can see from here—
believe me when I say that from a distance   350
is the best way to see it!

              "O goddess-born,
most righteous man of all the Trojan race
(whom I may not describe as 'enemy,'
now that the war is over), heed my warning:
avoid the shores of Circe!

             "We landed there,   355
but with Antiphates still fresh in mind
and the barbaric Cyclops, we refused
to leave our ships; so men were picked by lot
whose task was to approach her secret palace.

    "The lot sent me and loyal Polites   360
as my companion with Eurylochus
and Elpenor (who was too fond of wine)
and eighteen others to the walls of Circe;
as soon as we'd arrived there and were standing
upon the threshold of her palace,   365
a thousand wolves, she-bears, and lionesses
came rushing at us, frightening us all;
our fears were groundless, for they meant no harm
and even joined us, followed in our tracks,
wagging their tails and fawning just like dogs,   370
until we were received by her attendants
and brought through marble courtyards to their mistress,
who sat upon her throne within an alcove
in a robe of purple and a golden veil.

    "Nymphs joined with Nereids in serving her,   375
their nimble fingers plucking at no wool
nor deftly spinning it to useful thread:
instead, they went through piles of herbs and flowers
and sorted plants out into separate baskets;
she supervised the work that they were doing,   380
who knew the purpose of every leaf,

and how to blend ingredients together,
and weighed and measured them out carefully.
　　"When she had noticed us and made us welcome,
she gazed upon us warmly and gave signs   385
that our prayers were going to be answered.
She ordered her attendants to prepare
refreshments at once: they produced a drink
of roasted barley, honey, and strong wine
with curds of milk, whose sweetness would conceal   390
the drops of juice she furtively slipped in.
　　"We took the cups the goddess offered us,
and when we'd thirstily consumed it all,
the goddess touched each of us with her wand
atop our heads. It shames me, yet I'll say it: 395
bristles began to sprout all over me,
and I lost my ability to speak:
instead of words I only managed grunts,
my face was turned completely to the ground,
and I could feel my mouth becoming hard   400
and turning into an extended snout—
my neck grew thick with wrinkles, and that part
which only recently had held the cup
was now creating hoof prints in the dirt!
I was enclosed in a pigsty with all those   405
likewise transformed—so potent was that drink!
　　"We saw that just one man, Eurylochus,
persisted in his shape: he alone had shunned
the proffered cup; had he not done so,
I would still be among that herd of porkers,   410
nor would he have been able to inform
Ulysses of our tragic situation,
nor he have come to Circe, seeking vengeance.
　　"Peace-bearing Mercury had given him
a white flower, which the gods call *moly*:[5]   425
it springs up from the soil out of black roots.
With this, and with the deity's instructions
to keep him safe, he entered Circe's palace:
he too was offered the deceitful cup,
but struck away the wand with which she tried   420
to stroke his hair, and terrified the witch
with his drawn sword.
　　　　　　　　"And afterward, when they
had pledged their faith and shaken hands on it,
and she had taken him to be her spouse,
he made her, for his dowry, restore us;   425

---

5. Homer's word for Circe's flower in the *Odyssey*, Book X. Its identity is unknown.

then we were sprinkled with the healing juices
of an unknown herb, and tapped upon the head
with the other end of her enchanted wand,
and words were spoken to undo the words
that had been spoken to make us the herd.   430
    The more she sang, the more upright we stood;
bristles dropped off, and our cloven hooves
were turned back into feet, and our shoulders
and upper arms resumed their normal shapes;
weeping, we clung to our weeping leader,   435
embraced him and threw our arms about his neck,
but nothing said until we all had thanked him.
    "We lingered there with Circe for a year,
and in that time I witnessed many things
and took in much by listening: for instance,   440
this story told me privately, by one
of her four slaves, assigned to sacred rites.

Circe and Picus[6]

"One day, while Circe dallied with Ulysses,
this woman that I mentioned pointed out
a statue of white marble which depicted   445
a youth with a woodpecker on his head;
it had been placed in a temple of its own
and was distinguished by its many wreathes;
but who the marble figure represented
and why it had its cult here in this temple,   450
and why the bird, were things I wished to know!
    "'Listen to this, Macareus,' she said,
'and learn how powerful my mistress is;
apply yourself to what I have to say:
    "'Picus, the son of Saturn, was the king   455
of Ausonia, and one who understood
the purpose of the cavalry in combat.
His manly form was as you see it here,
but if you could have seen the living man,
you would have found the truth superior   460
to its depiction by an artist's hand.
He hadn't yet gone four times to the games
they celebrate at Elis twice each decade.[7]
    "'He turned the heads of all the dryads born
in the mountains of Latium, and was pursued   465
by water nymphs and by the naiads who

---

6. *Picus* is the Latin word for woodpecker.
7. Another way of saying that he was not yet twenty.

haunt Tiber's stream, as well as those beside
the waters of Numicius and Anio,
brief-running Alma, swiftly flowing Nar,
and Farfarus, hidden under its shade trees,   470
and those as well within the woody pool
of Scythian Diana and its nearby lake.[8]
    "'All these he spurned, attracted just to one,
a nymph, delivered on the Palatine
(or so the story went) to Venilia,   475
and fathered by the double-facing Janus;
when she had reached the marriageable age,
she was betrothed to Picus, much preferred
to all other suitors.
                    "'She was exquisite
not just for beauty, but the art of singing,   480
and for which she was given the name Canens:[9]
she moved the trees and rocks, and tamed the beasts
and stilled great rivers with her lovely voice;
she charmed the birds right back into their tree.
    "'And while his wife was singing prettily,   485
Picus of Latium set out from home
to hunt the wild boar native to that region;
dressed in a purple tunic trimmed with gold,
he pressed his legs against his horse's back,
holding a pair of spears in his left hand.   490
    "'The daughter of the Sun had quit those fields
that bore her name—Circeaen—and had come
to these same woods, out to collect fresh herbs
on the abundant hillsides. From within
a thicket, she caught sight of him: at once   495
astounded, she let fall her gathered herbs;
she blushed, and that bright color penetrated
right to the very marrow of her bones.
    "'As soon as she had pulled herself together
and had recovered from the shock of passion,   500
she was about to tell him what she wanted
but wasn't able to get near enough,
so swift his steed, so great his entourage.
    "'"Not even on the wind could you escape me,
not if I know my powers and myself,"   505
said Circe, "not if I still know my herbs,
not if my charms have not abandoned me!"

---

8. All of the rivers mentioned are Italian tributaries of the Tiber. At Lake Nemi in the Sabine
   hills was the grove consecrated to Scythian Diana, a sanctuary whose priest took office by
   murdering the former holder of the office. "Scythian" was synonymous with "barbarous."
9. Canens personifies song; her name derives from the Latin *canere*, to sing.

"'She spoke and formed an incorporeal
image of a wild boar and ordered it
to start across the trail before the king,   510
then to appear to plunge into a thicket
full of fallen trees, where the woods were densest,
impenetrable to a man on horseback.

   "'Swiftly dismounting from his frothing steed,
Picus, all unaware, sought out his prey,   515
pursuing an illusion through deep woods,
without companions.

                "'Circe now began
to utter certain prayers and incantations,
addressing unknown gods with unknown charms,
which would allow her to conceal the moon   520
and hide her father's face behind rain clouds.

   "'Then, by the recitation of her prayers,
the sky grew dark, fog rose up from the earth,
and the king's companions wandered all amazed,
unable to protect him in his danger.   525

   "'The hour and the setting are arranged:
"Oh, by your eyes," she cried, "which have taken mine,
and by your figure, O most beautiful,
which has converted me, a goddess, even,
into a suppliant, I implore you   530
to assuage my passion's fires and accept
the all-seeing Sun as your father-in-law,
nor harshly spurn the Titan's daughter, Circe!"

   "'She spoke; he savagely rejected her:
"Whatever you are," he said, "I am not yours;   515
I have been captured by another,
who holds, and will hold me, I pray, forever,
nor will I violate my marriage vows
to Canens, daughter of immortal Janus,
as long as fate allows her to be mine."   540

   "'And when the Titan's daughter realized
that her oft-repeated pleas had come to naught,
she said, "You will not stroll away from here,
returning to your Canens: no, you will learn
just what a woman scorned in love can do,   515
for Circe is a loving woman, scorned!"

   "'Then, after turning three times to the west
and three times to the east, she cast three spells
and struck the young man three times with her wand;
he fled, but was amazed to find himself   550
running more swiftly now than usual;
he saw the feathers on his body, and, enraged
to find himself so suddenly transformed

into this new, unprecedented kind
of bird in his own woods of Latium,   515
he pecked at the rough oaks with his hard beak,
and angrily left wounds on their long limbs;
his wings took on the scarlet of his tunic,
the golden clasp he wore upon it changed
into bright feathers; a band of yellow gold   560
encircled his neck; and now, but for his name,
nothing remained of Picus from before.

    "'Meanwhile, his comrades, who, with hue and cry
had searched the fields and not discovered him,
came upon Circe (for she'd cleared the air   565
and let the sun and winds disperse the clouds)
and rightly they accused her of her crime
against the king, demanding his return,
and making preparations to attack her
with their fierce weapons.
                "'Instead, she sprinkled them   570
with noxious drugs and poisonous concoctions,
and summoning up Night and all his gods,
that dwell below in Erebus and Chaos,
she called upon the goddess Hecate
with long-drawn ululations.
                  "'Astonishing   575
to say it, but the woods leapt from their place,
the earth shuddered, the nearby trees turned white,
and clumps of grass were stained with drops of blood;
stones seemed to bellow and wild dogs to bay,
the earth appeared to writhe with poison serpents,   580
and ghostly forms to flutter all around.

    "'Astounded by these monstrous apparitions,
his comrades turned into a fearful mob;
she touched their faces—trembling, terrified—
with the magic wand by which these youths were changed   585
into a great variety of beasts;
and not a one of them kept his old shape.[1]

    "'Phoebus, descending, had already bathed
the Spanish coast beyond the Western Gates,
and the spouse that Canens sought with eyes and heart   590
was nowhere to be found: slaves and subjects
hastened through the forest, bearing torches;
nor did it seem sufficient to the nymph
to weep and tear her hair and beat her breast
(though she did all of these), but she herself   595
rushed off and wandered madly through the woods.

---

1. Circe's technique and its results recall the very similar work of her niece, Medea, as practiced earlier in Book VII.

"'Six days and nights observed her wandering
through hills and valleys just as Chance proposed,
without food or sleep; the Tiber was the last
to see her, worn by grief and wandering,   600
laying her body down on its long bank;
and there she poured her heart out in her grief,
words mixed with tears in ever-fainter tones,
as when it happens that the swan will sing
his elegy himself before he dies.   605
    "'At last, attenuated so by grief
that in her bones the marrow turned to water,
she melted down and vanished on the breezes;
the place has kept alive her legend's fame,
however, bearing even now the name   610
of the nymph Canens, given by the Muses.'
    "Many such things I saw and heard about
during that long year's time, in which we grew
accustomed to our inactivity:
once more we were commanded to set sail;   615
Circe warned us of all that lay ahead:
a long journey on an uncertain path
and danger everywhere on that cruel sea.
I must confess that I was terrified,
and when we reached this shore, I stayed behind."   620

Acmon Transformed

So Macareus ended his account,
and the ashes of the wet nurse of Aeneas,
sealed in a marble urn, were then interred
in a grave with these brief verses on the stone:

WITHIN, THE ASHES OF CAIËTA LIE: 625
MY FOSTER CHILD, KNOWN FOR HIS PIETY,
SNATCHED ME FROM GREEK FLAMES, THEN CREMATED ME
WITH FITTING RITES AND GREAT PROPRIETY

    The lines that bound them to the grassy shore
were loosed, and treachery left far behind   630
in the abode of that disreputable goddess:
they sought the wooded grove where gloomy Tiber
sends his sand-laden waters to the sea;
he[2] won the throne and daughter of the king
of Latium, though not without a struggle,   635

2. Aeneas.

for Turnus, raging, battled for the bride
he had been previously promised, and
war with a fierce race was undertaken,
as Etruria united against Latium,
and for a long time a hard victory   640
was sought in the anxiety of arms.
    Both sides increased the size of their own forces
with help from foreigners, and many men
guarded the Rutulian and Trojan camps.
Aeneas sued successfully for aid   645
from King Evander, although Venulus
was disappointed on *his* mission to the city
of the exiled Diomedes: he had founded
a great-walled city in Apulia,
the realm of Daunus, and he held the lands   650
his bride had brought him as her dowry.
    But after Venulus, at the behest of Turnus,
had gone to him and asked him for his help,
Diomedes answered that he lacked the troops,
and was unwilling to commit himself   655
or the forces of his father-in-law, either;
nor did he have a nation of his own
that he could mobilize: "Lest you should think
that my excuses to you are fictitious,
I will recount my bitter woes again,   660
though each recital must renew my grief.
    "When Ilium's high towers had been burned,
and Troy had toppled into the Greek flames,
and after Ajax (who alone deserved
the punishment that all of us received   665
because he took a virgin from a virgin)[3]
had sinned against Minerva, we poor Greeks
were taken by the winds and strewn all over
the hostile sea, whose wrath (and heaven's too)
we bore in the forms of rainstorm, darkness, lightnings,   670
till finally, the blow to end all blows:
the promontory at Caphereus![4]
    "I will not long delay you, setting out
our woes in the order they occurred:
just say that even Priam would have wept   675
to see how Greece was faring at that time!

3. Diomedes argues that the Greeks should not have been punished for the crime of Ajax (son of Oileus), who raped Cassandra, the virgin priestess of the virgin goddess Minerva, and whom Minerva slew with a thunderbolt borrowed from Jove.
4. Where King Naplius, to avenge the death of his son Palamedes at the hands of Ulysses and Diomedes, set a burning torch on a mountain, luring the Greeks to shipwreck.

"Warlike Minerva kept me safe, however,
and delivered me from the tumultuous waves
into another sorrow, even worse:
I was expelled from my ancestral fields   680
as kindly Venus settled an old score
with fresh new pain; and so oppressive were
the toils at sea and wars on land I bore
that often I would call men fortunate
who had been drowned in the storm we all endured   685
or had been shipwrecked on Caphereus,
and wished myself to have been one of them.
        "My comrades had endured the very worst
that wars and storms could offer, and they begged
that our wandering should have an end;   690
but Acmon, an excitable young man,
made even more so by these trials, said,
        "'Is there still something you have not endured,'
he asked, 'some grief you might decline to bear?
What is there that is left for her to do,   695
if she should wish to do more than she has?
As long as we fear something worse may come,
prayer has its place—but when the short straw's drawn,
we put our fears behind us and below,
and hopelessness releases us from care.   700
        "'So *let* her hear me saying this—so what?
So *what* if she despises, as she does,
all of the men who serve with Diomedes,
since all of us despise her attitude:
her high-and-mightiness seems scarcely high,   705
as far as we're concerned!'
                            "Provocative,
those words of Acmon, and they angered Venus,
and brought her old anger back to life again.
        "His bitter words pleased very few of us,
and the majority rebuked Acmon,   710
who learned, when he attempted to reply,
that his throat and voice were both attenuated,
his hair had changed to feathers, and new plumage
concealed his recently remodeled neck;
his arms accepted even larger feathers,   715
and his sharp elbows turned gracefully to wings;
his feet were given over to webbed digits,
and his face hardened to inexpressive horn
that ended in a sharply pointed beak.
        "Lycus, Idas, Rhexenor, Nycteus,   720
and Abas, too, all stared at him in wonder,
and while they wondered, took on the same shape;

the greater part of them were changed to birds
and flew up all together as one flock,
encircling the oarsmen on flapping wings: 725
and if you wish to know what kind of bird
they had so swiftly been transformed into,
I'd have to say that though they weren't swans,
they much resembled them, though these were white.
    "And now that I am the son-in-law of Daunus,   730
I hold—just barely—this new-founded town
and these dry fields with what few men are left."
Here Diomedes finished his account.

The Wild Olive Tree

Venulus left the realm of Calydon,
the realm of Peucetia and the fields   735
of Messapia, where he saw a cave
hidden in the forest dense and misty,
a screen of waving reeds that grew before it.
    Goat-footed Pan now holds it as his own,
but at one time it was the lair of nymphs   740
who had been driven off in terror by
the unexpected apparition of
an Apulian shepherd. But soon after,
the nymphs regained their lost composure, and,
with nothing but contempt for their pursuer,   745
they went back once again to nimble-footed
choral dancing.
           Still the shepherd mocked them
with boorish imitations of their dancing,
and barnyard insults, and obscene expressions;
nor would he close his mouth until a tree   750
sprang from his throat and covered up his face;
indeed, he is a tree now: by his fruits
you may know what kind, for the sour berries
of the wild olive show his language plain,
whose bitterness has entered into them.   755

The Transformation of Aeneas' Ships[5]

When the ambassadors returned with word
that the Aetolians refused to fight,
the Rutulians waged war without their help,
as they had planned, and both sides shed much blood.
    But look! Where Turnus flings his greedy torches   760
at hulls of pine, and ships spared by the waves

---

5. Another episode from the *Aeneid*, Book IX.

are terrified by fire! Vulcan now
burns pitch and wax and other foods for flames,
which leap from mast to mast, and the wooden thwarts
in the curved hulls are wreathed in acrid smoke!   765
    Then the Holy Mother of the Gods[6] recalled
that these pines had been felled upon the summit
of Mount Ida, and at once she filled the air
with the tintinnabulation of her cymbals
and the shrill ululation of her boxwood flutes;   770
and lightly carried through the parting air
in a chariot drawn by her familiar lions,
the goddess cried, "Your sacrilegious hand
flings torches at these ships to no avail,
Turnus, for I will rescue them from danger: 775
I will not let your hungry flames devour
limbs that were mine, that grew in my own groves!"
    The goddess was still speaking when it thundered,
and the thunder was immediately followed
by dancing hailstones mixed with falling rain;   780
and the winds, like brothers in a civil war,
brought tumult and confusion to the air
and to the waves, so suddenly increased.
    Cybele then selected one of these
to break the ropes that held the Trojan fleet,   785
then plunged their burning hulls deep underwater:
the wood lost firmness and turned into flesh;
the curved prows changed to heads; oars turned to toes
and swimming legs; what had been sides still were,
and keels remained, though they were changed to spines;   790
lines softened into locks, sail yards to arms,
and the ships' cerulean color stayed the same;
vessels that once were frightened by the waves
are naiads now and gambol in the water;
despite their hard beginnings on a mountain,   795
they now frequent the waves, untroubled by
old memories of their peak experience.
    They do remember, though, their lives as ships,
and the dangers they so often faced at sea;
on which account, they often lend a hand   800
to guide the keels of storm-tossed ships—unless
those ships should happen to belong to Greeks;
still mindful of the fall of Troy, they hate
that race entire, and rejoiced to see
the floating wreckage of Ulysses' ship,   805

6. The goddess Cybele. Her fondness for the pines may have something to do with the legend of Attis, her resistant lover who became one.

as they rejoiced to see the wooden vessel
of Alcinoüs transformed into stone.[7]

The Heron

There was a hope that when the fleet had been
endowed with life as water nymphs, this wonder
would have inspired fear in the Rutulians,   810
and make them end the war; but war continued,
since both sides each had gods supporting them,
and courage, which is just as good as gods;
they went on fighting not for a dowered kingdom,
not for the scepter in your father's hand,   815
nor for you, even, fair Lavinia:
they fought to win and to avoid the shame
of having to surrender; finally,
Venus saw that the arms which she'd provided
brought her son victory; now Turnus fell,   820
and with him fell the city of Ardea,
called powerful while he lived to protect it,
but when the fire of barbarians
reduced it to a heap of tepid ashes,
there flew out from the middle of that mass   825
a swift-winged bird not previously known,
flapping its wings above the cinder heap;
its cry, its scrawniness, its sickly pallor
were fitting for a city that is captured,
and it has even kept the city's name: 830
[*ardea* is the Latin name for heron]
Ardea mourns itself with beating wings.

The Deification of Aeneas

The manly excellence Aeneas showed
compelled the gods, including even Juno,
to put an end to their old enmity;   835
and now with Julus[8] well set up and rising,
it was the proper time for our hero
to enter heaven; Venus had approached
the deities, soliciting approval,
and threw her arms about her father's neck: 840
     "Father," she said, "you've always been most kind;
now I beseech you to be even more so,
and for the sake of my own flesh and blood,
your grandson too, grant him divinity;

7. An episode from the *Odyssey*, Book XIII.
8. Another name for Aeneas's son Ascanius, and one that links him to his putative descendant, Julius Caesar.

however small a portion does not matter,   840
as long as you give something! It is enough
that he has once seen the Unlovely Realm,
that he has once traversed the river Styx!"⁹
  The gods gave their assent, and even she,
Jove's consort, now appeased, beamed her approval.   850
The father of the gods said, "Both of you,
the seeker and the one for whom it is sought,
deserve the gift of immortality,
and so, my daughter, take what you would have."
  Venus thanked him and then was carried off   855
on the light breezes in a chariot
drawn by her team of yoked and harnessed doves
to the Laurentian coast, where the Numicius
weaves its way through a curtain of tall reeds,
then spills its waters in the nearby sea.   860
  She bade the river-god to take Aeneas
under the surface of his silent stream
and cleanse him of all mortal deficits;
he did as she commanded, bathing him,
and having purged him of his mortal dross,   865
restored his best, immortal part to him.
  His mother purified Aeneas' body,
anointing it with heavenly perfumes,
and touched his lips with sweet ambrosia
and nectar both, so he became a god,   870
known to the Roman folk as Indiges
[a name that means both "native born" and "needy"],
who honor him with altars and with shrines.
  Ascanius (also known as Julus)
ruled Latium and Alba after him,   875
and then there followed Silvius, whose son,
Latinus, took an ancient name and scepter;
distinguished Alba followed Latinus,
and Epytus came next, and after him
came Capetus and Capys (who came first,   880
but these my Latin meter has reversed);¹
then Tiberinus followed them, who drowned
in the Tuscan stream to which he gave his name;
his sons were Remulus and fierce Acrota;
the elder, Remulus, was struck by lightning   885
as he was imitating its effect;
Acrota, somewhat less brave than his brother,
yielded the scepter to Aventinus, who

9. A reference to Aeneas's earlier visit to the underworld.
1. Ovid jokingly complains that the metrical demands of the Latin hexameter line will not
   allow him to list these two rulers in chronological order.

was buried on the hill where he held sway,
and to which he has given his own name;   890
then Proca ruled the race that dwells in Rome.[2]

Pomona and Vertumnus (1)[3]

Under his rule, Pomona flourished there,
unrivaled in her skill at gardening
among the Latin wood nymphs of her time;
nor was there any other who was more   895
devoted to the nurturing of fruit trees,
from which she had her name: not one for woods
or rivers, she loved open country best,
and branches laden with abundant fruit;
she was not one to grip a javelin,   900
but used instead a pruning hook to suppress
the exuberance of nature and restrain
the trees from branching out in all directions;
or she would graft a slip onto a tree,
whose sap would rise into the foreign nursling;   905
she would not let them thirst; her flowing streams
would irrigate the threads of their parched roots.
    This was her love, to which she was devoted,
and the other kind, that Venus knows about,
held no attractions for her; indeed, fearing   910
the possibility of rustic rape,
she closed herself within her orchard's walls,
from which she barred all forms of manliness.
    What did her many suitors—the young Satyrs,
fit for a dance or two; the pack of Pans,   915
with pinecones decorating their wee horns;
Sylvanus, who acts younger than he is;
and that divinity whose look or hook
(I mean Priapus)[4] frightens off all thieves—
what did her many suitors leave undone   920
in unsuccessful efforts to attain her?
    Vertumnus loved her more than all of them,
but he had no more luck with her than they did.
How often did he show up in the likeness
of an unpolished hired hand at harvest,   925
carrying a basket full of wheat—
indeed, the very image of a reaper!

2. A list of the legendary early kings of Rome.
3. Their names—hers from *pomum*, fruit; his from *ver/autumnus*, spring/fall—reveal the
   plot: Can a Latin wood nymph, the goddess of fruit trees, find happiness with an Etruscan deity of changing seasons?
4. A rustic Italian deity, Sylvanus was usually represented as a man on top, goat below. Priapus was the ithyphallic son of Venus and Bacchus. Both of these rural divinities presided
   over orchards and gardens.

At other times, Vertumnus would appear
wearing a still-green wreath of new mown hay
around his temples, and would seem to be   930
one of the mowers turning grass to dry;
or show up with an ox goad in his hand,
and so much like a drover you would swear
that he had just unyoked his weary oxen;
given a pruning hook, he seemed to be   935
off on his way to shaping trees or vines;
up on a ladder, you would think that he
was picking apples with the other men;
in the same way, a sword made him a soldier,
a fishing rod made him a fisherman: 940
in short, his many changes of appearance
allowed him frequent access to her presence,
and great delight in gazing at her beauty.
    He went so far as to put on a wig
of gray hair and to wrap around his head   945
a gaudy turban like those that women wear,
and leaning on a walking stick, he entered
her garden, where he marveled at the fruit.
"But you," he said, "are so much more impressive!"
and showered her with kisses of a kind   950
that ancient ladies are not wont to give.
    He sat down on the ground beneath the trees
and looked up at those branches bent with fruit,
the weight of autumn. There was a splendid elm
across from these, adorned with shining grapes;   955
he glanced at it approvingly, and said,
    "Now if that tree trunk were to stand unwed,
untrained to any vine, it would not be
of any worth to us, but for its leaves;
likewise the vine, which has been joined to it,   960
rests on the elm tree; if it had not been,
it would be lying flat upon the ground:
however, the example of this tree
makes no impression on you, for you flee
the joys of sex, nor do you care to wed.   965
    "But how I wish you would, for you would have
suitors more numerous than Helen had,
or she for whom the Lapiths went to battle,
or the wife of too long tarrying Ulysses!
    "And even though you run away from them,   970
resisting those who come here seeking you,
a thousand men desire to possess you,
and gods and even demigods as well,
every god up in the Alban hills!

"But if you would be wise and marry well,   975
then lend an ear to what this old crone says,
who loves you more than all the others do,
and more than you could easily believe:
spurn all those many others, but accept
Vertumnus as the sharer of your bed: 980
I guarantee that he's the one for you,
and no one knows him better than I do,
as well—I daresay—as he knows himself!

"He isn't one to wander round the world,
but lives alone here in your neighborhood;   985
nor is he like so many other suitors,
who fall in love with everyone they see:
you are his first love and will be his last,
and he will give his years to you alone.

"And add to these the fact that he is young   990
and unaffectedly attractive too,
and that he has a gift for changing shape,
for taking on whatever form he wishes,
and that he will do anything you want,
even if you should ask for everything!   995

"Your interests are likewise similar,
for he is always the first there to enjoy
the fruit it is your pleasure to provide!
But it is not the fruit found in your trees
that he desires, nor the pleasing herbs   1000
that grow within the confines of your garden,
nor is it anything, in fact, but you!
Take pity on his passion and believe
that his own prayers are coming through my lips.

"Reflect a moment on the vengeful gods,   1005
how Venus, who frequents Mount Ida, hates
the unyielding heart, and have a proper fear
of Nemesis, whose wrath is unforgiving!

"And so that you may fear these all the more,
I will tell you a story that is quite well known   1010
on Cyprus, for my years make me a source
of useful wisdom; from it you should learn
to modulate your wishes and be mild.

Iphis and Anaxarete

"Iphis, a young man drawn from lowly stock,
caught sight of Anaxarete, a woman   1015
descended from the ancient race of Trojans:
the flames of passion scared him to the bone.

"For a long time, he struggled with his feelings,
but after reason failed to overcome

his madness, he appeared upon her threshold,   1020
and as a suppliant, he now confessed
his mad infatuation to her nurse,
praying that she would not be hard on him,
by the hopes that she had for her tender charge;
then he went on to servant after servant,   1025
and fawning on them anxiously, he sought
their help in getting close to his desire;
often he had them carry his love letters,
and sometimes he would hang upon her door
garlands of flowers wet with the dew of his tears,   1030
and lay his tender flanks on her hard threshold,
despondently reproving the barred door.
   "But she, who was more cruel than the storms
arising at the setting of the Kids,[5]
harder than steel that has been tempered by   1035
Noricum[6] fires, or like a great stone
still clinging to its roots, she spurned and mocked him,
and adding insults to that injury,
the fierce contempt of her response deprived
her suitor of his last remaining hope.   1040
   "Iphis, unable to endure for long
the torment of his grief, spoke his last words
in a message he delivered at her door:
'You win, Anaxarete, and no longer
must you endure my tiresome pursuit: 1045
now grant yourself a triumph, and rejoice:
sing hymns and gird your brow with shining laurel!
You win indeed; now I will freely die,
and you, unyielding one—go celebrate!
   "'But certainly, you will be forced to praise   1050
some aspect of my love that pleases you,
compelling you to speak of my good points—
remember that I loved you while I lived,
and that in dying and in losing you
the light of my life has been twice put out.   1055
   "'Nor will you learn of my death secondhand:
for I myself—undoubtedly—will be there,
a presence visible, so you may glut
your cruel eyes upon my lifeless corpse!
   "'If it is true that you, O gods, observe   1060
the acts of mortals, then remember me—
for I desire nothing more from you—
and see that I am spoken of for ages,

---

5. Two stars in the constellation Auriga, whose rising and setting were believed to be associated with storms.
6. Noricum, a region between the Danube and the Alps, was famous for its iron.

and that the time subtracted from my life
is added to my fame!'
              "So Iphis spoke   1065
with streaming eyes, and raising his pale arms
to those doorposts he'd often crowned with wreaths,
affixed his noose onto the highest beam:
   "'O cruel and unkind,' he said, 'are you
well pleased by this bouquet?'
              "He thrust his head   1070
into the noose and turned in her direction,
and then, misfortunate, the burden of
his lifeless corpse hung by his broken neck.
   "Dying, the convulsive motions of his feet
against the door made sounds that sounded like   1085
someone outside demanding to be let in,
and when the door was opened in response,
the shocking deed revealed itself: her servants
cried out, and took the young man down—too late.
   "They brought him to his mother's house (his father   1080
was dead already); she embraced her son
and tried to warm his lifeless limbs with hers,
and after she had given voice to grief
and did the things that grieving parents do,
she led a throng of mourners through the city   1080
escorting his pale corpse to its cremation.
   "By chance that sad procession passed before
the very home of Anaxarete,
and stirred by an avenging deity,
the sounds of bitter mourning struck her ears;   1090
in spite of herself, she was moved, and said,
'Let us go see this mournful funeral.'
Going inside, she went upstairs and stood
at an open window: scarcely had she glimpsed
the corpse of Iphis laid out on his bier,   1095
when her eyes hardened and her cold blood ran
in terror from her body: she attempted
to step back from the sight, but her feet froze;
when she attempted to avert her face,
she was unable to; and very soon   1100
the stoniness that for so long a time
had been within her heart spread through her body.
   "And lest you should consider this a fiction,
there is a statue, even to this day,
at Salamis, the image of this lady: 1105
and a temple of foresightful Venus[7] too.

---

7. The island of Salamis was famous for the worship of Venus Prospiciens, who was both
   foresighted and far-seeing.

"So, my dear nymph, you should be ever mindful
of these events, and put aside, I pray,
your proud resistance to a lover's plea,
lest the late spring frost nip your budding fruit,   1110
or swift winds tear the flowers from the bough."

Pomona and Vertumnus (2)

After the god, disguised as an old woman,
had argued well, although to no effect,
he changed himself back into a young man,
appearing to the maiden just as brightly   1115
as does the Sun, when its resplendent face
prevails against the dim opposing clouds
and shines undimmed in all its radiance;
he was prepared to take her then by force,
which proved unnecessary, for the nymph   1120
was taken by the figure of the god,
and felt within a corresponding wound.

A Roman Spring

Amulius (known as the Oppressive)
next governs Italy, by force of arms;
and after him comes ancient Numitor,   1125
whose grandson aided him in getting back
the kingdom he had lost; the city's walls
are founded on the feast day of the shepherds;
King Tatius and the Sabine senators
wage war on Romulus; having betrayed   1130
the path that leads up to the citadel,
Tarpeia justly perishes[8] beneath
the weapons piled upon her by the Sabines,
who are now busy shushing one another,
and silently as wolves are sneaking up   1135
upon the Romans, overcome by slumber;
the Sabines try the gates, which Romulus
had closed and bolted firmly; nonetheless,
Saturnia unfastens one of them,
and draws the gate back on its silent hinges;   1140
Venus alone knew that the bolt had fallen
and would have put it back and locked the gates,
but one god is unable to rescind

---

8. A woman who betrayed Rome, asking for what the Sabine soldiers wore on their arms as
   her reward; instead of giving her their golden bracelets, they buried her alive under the
   weight of their shields.

the actions of another.
                    Near the shrine
of Janus is an icy spring of water,   1145
possessed by the Italian water nymphs;
Venus asked them if they would help her out,
and they did not refuse her just request,
opening the fountain to its fullest.
    The pass of Janus was still open then,   1150
and never had the waters closed it off;
the nymphs put yellow sulfur underneath
their fountain and then heated it until
the boiling veins were full of smoky pitch; -
by these and other means, steam penetrated   1155
throughout the fountain: water which had dared
quite recently to challenge alpine chill
was ready now to stand up against fire!
The twin gate posts smoked with boiling mist
and the gates which had been opened up in vain   1160
before the unyielding Sabines were now blocked
by this new spring, which gave the Romans time
to arm themselves; then Romulus set forth,
and Roman earth was strewn with mingled corpses,
Romans and Sabines, for the impious sword,   1105
indifferent to kinship, mixed the blood
of husbands with the fathers of their wives.
    But finally, they chose to end the war
instead of fighting to the bitter end,
and Tatius[9] agreed to share the throne.   1170

The Deification of Romulus

Tatius died, and you set out the laws
equitably to Romans and to Albans,
O Romulus.[1] Doffing his helmet, Mars
addressed the author of all gods and men:
    "The time has come, O father, since the state   1175
of Rome has been established on a sound
foundation, and does not depend upon
a single man to serve as its protector—[2]
the time has come for you to grant the gift
promised to me and to your worthy grandson: 1180
that he should be released from earthly bonds
and taken up to heaven and installed

---

9. A Sabine who agreed to be ruler in Rome.
1. The legendary founder of the city of Rome, who established its walls on the Palatine hill.
2. Perhaps an indiscreet line for a poet to take in the time of Augustus.

as one of the immortals; this you promised
in a council where the other gods were present,
and I took note of your inspiring words,   1185
which memory allows me to repeat:
    "'There will be one that you will carry up
to the blue vault of heaven.' This you said;
now ratify the promise that you gave."
    Jove the omnipotent gave his consent,   1190
first darkening the air with thunderclouds,
then frightening the world with lightning bolts.
    Mars realized that the apotheosis
he had been promised was now ratified
by this event, and leaning on his spear,   1195
he vaulted up into his chariot,
whose steeds both strained against the bloody yoke,
and flogging them to action with his whip
descended headlong through the air until
he set down on the wooded Palatine,   1200
where he abstracted Romulus from the earth
as he was giving out his royal decrees
to the Roman people; his mortal parts
dissolved as he was borne up through the air,
as a leaden bullet fired from a sling   1205
is worn away as it traverses the sky;
and now a beauty that is heavenly,
more worthy of the couches of the gods,
transforms him as he turns into Quirinus,
adorned in a white robe with purple seam.   1210
    His wife, Hersilia, was mourning him
when Juno ordered Iris to descend
upon a rainbow and console her thus,
and carry these instructions to the widow:
    "O glory of the Latins and the Sabines,   1215
most worthy to have been the wife and queen
of such a man as Romulus has been,
and now most fit to be Quirinus' spouse,
leave off your lamentations: would you see
your husband once again? Then come with me   1220
into that grove, bright green upon the hill
named after Quirinus;[3] within it lies
the shaded temple of the Roman king."
    Iris obeyed, descending to the earth
upon her rainbow and made Hersilia   1225
hearken to the message she was given;

---

3. Another name given to Mars by the Romans; here, the name supplied to the deified
   Romulus after his apotheosis.

and she, with downcast eyes and modest look,
responded to the messenger of Juno:
   "O goddess, for I know that you are one,
although I cannot say which one you are—   1230
lead on, lead on: show me my husband's face,
for if the Fates should let me see it once,
then I would say that I have gone to heaven."
   Without delay she went with Iris to
the hill of Romulus, and there a star   1235
slipped from the vault of heaven down to earth;
Hersilia, whose hair burst into flames,
ascended with that star into the air;
Rome's founder there receives her, takes her hand
within his own, and gives her a new name   1240
along with her new body; she is called
Hora, and as a goddess now is joined
to her immortal Quirinus forever.

BOOK XV

Prophetic Acts and Visionary Dreams

Numa (1)

In the meantime, a ruler capable
of bearing such responsibilities
and of succeeding Romulus is sought;
Fame accurately prophesies the fitness
of the distinguished Numa[1] for the throne;   5
and he, not satisfied by his command
of Sabine thought and practices, conceived
a larger project in his receptive mind,
striving to master universal knowledge.

The love he had for this activity   10
drove him to leave his capital of Cures,
and travel to a distant city, famed
for its hospitality to Hercules.

Myscelus and the Founding of Crotona

Numa asked who had founded this Greek city
on the Italian coast, and an old man   15
who knew the ancient legends well responded.
"They say that Hercules, the son of Jove,
returning from his journey to the ocean,
enriched by herds of Spanish cattle,[2] landed
felicitously at Lacinium;   20
and while his cattle grazed the tender grass,
he enjoyed the home and hospitality
of Croton, a great man, beneath whose roof
he found refreshment from his lengthy labor.

"As he was leaving, he said, 'In the future,   25
this place will be a city of your offspring.'
That promise, as it happened, was fulfilled:
there was a certain man named Myscelus,
the son of Alemon of Argus, who
in his day was most pleasing to the gods.   30

"One night, as he lay sleeping heavily,
Hercules stood above him with his club
and said, 'Go now and leave your native land:

---

1. According to legend, Numa Pompilius reluctantly succeeded Romulus as king of Rome. A
   member of the Sabine tribe, his mind was cultivated and wide-ranging as Ovid suggests
   here. Romulus and Numa provide the first part of a Roman frame that will be completed
   in the last lines of Book XV by Julius Caesar and his adopted heir, Augustus.
2. The tenth of Hercules's twelve labors was to kill the monster Geryon of Gadez (now
   Cadiz) and steal his blood-red cattle. After doing so, Hercules landed on Lacinium, a
   promontory on the coast of Italy.

seek the remote and rocky straits of Aesar,'
and threatened Myscelus quite vividly   35
if he did not obey; and after that,
the vision and the god both disappeared.
    "The son of Alemon leapt out of bed
and silently reviewed his recent dream,
and struggled for a long time with its meaning: 40
the god commanded his departure, but
the law prohibited his setting forth;
death was the penalty for anyone
who wished to change his homeland for another.
    "The bright Sun had concealed his shining face   45
far underneath the surface of the Ocean,
and darkest Night had wreathed her head with stars,
when once again that selfsame god returned
delivering the selfsame admonition,
and threatening, unless the man obeyed,   50
worse punishments, and even more of them.
This terrified him: he at once prepared
to move his household to another region.
    "Word got around about it in the city,
and he was brought to trial for his malfeasance.   55
The prosecution rested: no defense:
no need to call on any witnesses;
the poor wretch raised his face and hands to heaven:
'O you who by twelve labors merited heaven,
help me, I pray,' he cried, 'for it is you   60
who are the instigator of my crime!'
    "Back in those ancient times, white or black pebbles
were used to show one's innocence or guilt;[3]
and that was how the court proceeded then
in handing down the sentence: every pebble   65
placed in the unforgiving urn—was black!
But when they turned it over to count up
the pebbles, every single one of them,
without exception, had been changed to white!
    "The judgment against Myscelus had been   70
reversed by Hercules, and he was saved;
he thanked Amphitryon's heroic son
and then sailed across the Ionian Sea,
bypassing Neretum, Sybaris, and Tarentum;
nor did he linger by the bay of Siris,   75
Crimese, or the coast of Apulia;
and scarcely had he gotten past those lands

3. Jurors were each given one white and one black pebble. When rendering a verdict, they
   passed by an urn and dropped in the white if they believed the defendant innocent, black
   if guilty.

which look upon those waters, when he found
the end that had been destined for his journey,
the mouth of the river Aesar.

            "Not far away   80
there was a mound of earth: beneath it lay
the sacred bones of Croton; on this site,
as he had been commanded to, Myscelus
established his new city, which he named
for the one who had been buried in the tomb."   85
    Such were the origins of that region
and of the Greek city built in Italy,
according to dependable tradition.

The Teachings of Pythagoras[4]

There was a man who had been born on Samos,[5]
but fled his native island and its rulers,   90
freely choosing to become an exile
out of his hatred for despotism;
and this man was allowed to understand
the thought of gods, off in remotest heavens;
his inner sight exposed what Nature kept   95
from human view; and when he had at last
exhaustively examined all there was,
would lecture to improve the people's minds;
a silent multitude stood marveling
at the erudition of his discourse   100
upon the origin of the universe,
on the laws of Nature and causality,
what God is, and where the snow comes from,
and whether lightning is produced by Jove
or by the winds that tear apart the clouds;   105
what causes earthquakes and what keeps the stars
from flying off, and other hidden things;
he was the first to censure man for eating
the flesh of animals and was the first
to preach this learnèd, but not widely held   110
doctrine, in these words from his own lips:
    "Mortals, refrain from defiling your bodies with sinful
feasting,[6] for you have the fruits of the earth and of arbors,

---

4. As we have seen, Ovid inserts a "poetic" solo in his poem every five books. The pre-Socratic Greek philosopher Pythagoras (c. 580–c. 490 B.C.) was born on Samos and moved to Crotona, where Numa studied with him. Pythagoras should be regarded as one of Ovid's characters, not as his spokesman.
5. An island in the Aegean Sea.
6. Most Romans ate some meat, though few were vegetarians. Many of Ovid's contemporaries spent a significant portion of their lives in amphitheaters where the violent slaughter of beasts was a main event.

whose branches bow with their burden; for you the grapes ripen,
for you the delicious greens are made tender by cooking;   115
milk is permitted you too, and thyme-scented honey:
Earth is abundantly wealthy and freely provides you
her gentle sustenance, offered without any bloodshed.
Some of the beasts *do* eat flesh to allay their own hunger,
although not all of them, for horses, sheep, and cattle   120
feed upon grasses; but those of untamable nature—
Armenian tigers, furious lions, wolves and bears, too—
these creatures take pleasure in feasting on what they have
          slaughtered.
    "What an indecency, mingling entrails with entrails,
fattening one on the flesh from another one's body,   125
saving the life of one by another's destruction!
Surrounded by all of this wealth, so freely provided
by Earth, the best of all mothers, you wholly ignore it,
choosing to mangle sad flesh with your cruel teeth, and
delighted again to act out the rites of the Cyclops,   130
unable ever to placate your stomach's voracious
desires until, at last, you have murdered another!
    "That time long since past, which we now refer to as 'golden,'
was blessed in the fruit of its trees, and in its wild herbs,
and in the absence of blood smeared on men's faces.   135
In that time, the birds flew through the air without danger,
the fearless rabbit went wandering over the meadows,
and the fish was not brought to the hook by its credulous nature.
All lived without ambushes; none had a fear of deception,
and peace was everywhere. But after that bringer of trouble,   140
whoever he was, who envied the lion his dinner,
had crammed his greedy gut with the flesh from a body,
he led us down the wrong path; for it may be that iron
was first stained with the warm blood of the beast that he
          butchered;
this would not have been a crime had the creatures attacked us,   145
for I say that any such beasts may be rightfully murdered,
but those that we must destroy should never be eaten!
    "Crimes even greater emerged from that one: the sow is
thought to have merited death as a ritual victim
because she uprooted new crops with her snout, thus depriving   150
farmers of hope for the year; the goat was led to the altar
to pay with his life for the sin of devouring Bacchus;[7]
these two, then, died for offenses that they had committed.
But what did *you* ever do, sheep, to merit *your* murder?
—You who were born to serve man with milk from your udders   155
and with the soft wool wherewith we make our garments—

7. By eating grapes from the vine.

your life is surely more useful to us than your death is!
And what have *you* done, poor ox, so soulful and guileless,
innocent simpleton, born but to bear our labors?
Wholly unmindful, unworthy the gift of the earth's fruits   160
is one who, after releasing him from the weight of the harness,
strikes down the worker with whom he had broken the hard field
as many times as it had given him harvests,
and chops with his axe at that neck worn out by exertion.

    "Nor is it enough that *man* had committed such misdeeds: 165
the gods were charged with them too, were believed to take
      pleasure
in dealing death out to the labor-bearing young bullock!
Since that which makes him so pleasing is what will most harm him,
a victim distinguished in figure and quite without blemish,
his horns gilded, trailing bright ribbons, is led to the altar,   170
where he, without comprehending them, listens to prayers,
and observes the barley he helped to cultivate sprinkled
between his horns: perhaps even sees in the basin,
held under his head by the priest, the knife blade reflected
a moment before his blood is spilled into the water.   175

    "At once they tear out the guts from the still-living creature,
and scrutinize them in search of some heavenly purpose!
So great is the human hunger to eat what's forbidden,
you mortals will dare even to feed upon this! Don't you do it,
I beg you! Pay close attention to my admonition,   180
and when you devour the flesh of your fresh-butchered cattle,
taste it and know you are eating your labor's companion!

    "A god is directing my speech: I will speak as inspired,
revealing, as though I were Delphi, the secrets of heaven,
disclosing mysteries known but to the illumined;   185
I will sing of great issues, never before now uncovered
by earlier thinkers and hidden until the present,
for it delights me to travel up into the heavens,
delights me to leave the earth's insipid abode, and
riding on clouds, mount to the capable shoulders   190
of Atlas, where I can look down on those wandering mortals,
lacking in reason, anxious and fearful of dying,
and from there, exhort and encourage them by unrolling
the scroll upon which Fate is inscribed in succession.

    "O people stunned with the icy terror of dying,   195
why do you fear the Styx? Why are you frightened of phantoms
and names that mean nothing, the empty blather of poets,
foolish hobgoblins of a world that never existed?
Here is what happens after you die: your body,
whether consumed on the pyre or slowly decaying,   200
suffers no evil; souls cannot perish, and always,
on leaving their prior abodes, they come to new ones,

living on, dwelling again in receptive bodies;[8]
in the time of the Trojan war, I remember quite well
that I was Panthoüs, son of Euphorbus, and wounded   205
once in the breast by a spear cast by Lord Menelaüs;
recently, while in the temple of Juno on Argos,
I recognized the shield that I bore on my left arm![9]

"Everything changes and nothing can die, for the spirit
wanders wherever it wishes to, now here and now there,   210
living with whatever body it chooses, and passing
from feral to human and then back from human to feral,
and at no time does it ever cease its existence;
and just as soft wax easily takes on a new shape,
unable to stay as it was or keep the same form,   215
and yet is still wax, I preach that the spirit is always
the same even though it migrates to various bodies.

"And so, at the risk of repeating myself, I exhort you,
lest your devotion be vanquished by the greed of your bellies,
stop this expulsion by slaughter of spirits so like you,   220
this practice of feeding one creature on blood from another.

"And since I am already embarked upon this great sea,
have given full sails to the wind, hear me out: nothing
endures in this world! The whole of it flows, and all is
formed with a changing appearance; even time passes,   225
constant in motion, no different from a great river,
for neither a river nor a transitory hour
is able to stand still; but just as each wave is driven
ahead by another, urged on from behind, and urging
the next wave before it in an unbroken sequence,   230
so the times flee and at the same time they follow,
and always are new; for what has just been is no longer,
and what has not been will presently come into being,
and every moment's occasion is a renewal.[1]

"Do you not see how the nighttime turns toward the daylight,   235
and how a radiant shining comes after night's darkness?
Nor is the sky at midnight unchanged in appearance
when dazzling Lucifer rides in upon his white horse,
and that too is changed, when Aurora, the herald of sunlight,
brightens the world as she hands it on over to Phoebus,   240
whose heavenly shield is brilliantly red when he lifts it
from under the earth in the morning, and also at sunset,
when it is replaced, but turns a pale white at its zenith,
where the air is clearer and free of the earth's infection.

8. Pythagoras believed in the reincarnation of souls.
9. The Trojan shield would be hanging in the temple as a gift of thanks to the goddess. Note
   her Roman name, however.
1. Pythagoras's belief in incessant metamorphosis differs from the usually irreversible and
   punitive metamorphoses that Ovid so often describes.

Nor does nocturnal Diana[2] appear the same always: 245
for if she is waxing, she will be less today than tomorrow,
and less tomorrow than she is today, if she is waning.
    "But really, do you not see how the year has four seasons
in imitation of how we pass through our lifetime?
For tender and milky and most like a child is the early   250
Spring, when the world is freshly green and lacking in vigor,
swelling with moisture, a hopeful sign for the farmer.
Everything flowers then, and the fields are a riot of color,
although as yet there is no real strength in the foliage.
Spring is replaced by the Summer, a more robust season,   255
which in its vigor resembles a hardy young man;
no other time is richer or warmer than *this* one.
Autumn steps in and the ardor of youth is replaced by
a milder maturing, a time between younger and older,
when the thinning hair begins to go gray at the temples;   260
then Winter's old age approaches us, lame and trembling,
and whatever hair it still happens to have has been whitened!
    "Our bodies, too, are always incessantly changing,
and what we were, or are, is not what we will be,
tomorrow: once we were seeds, the hope of our fathers,   265
and lay concealed in the womb of our first mother;
creative Nature willed otherwise: took us in hand, and
out of the narrow confines of mother's expanded
viscera, sent us forth into the open air, homeless!
The infant lay powerless, blinking his eyes at the light, and   270
shortly began to walk like a beast on all fours,
and then learned to stand, although still weak-kneed and trembling,
and needing to grasp at whatever could aid its endeavor;
this changes into the swift and powerful stage of first youth,
and then middle age, which, when its service is ended,   275
glides down the path of decline that leads us to old age,
which undermines and demolishes all of the strength of
those earlier stages: contemplating the shoulders
and arms that once, with their masses of muscle, resembled
those of great Hercules, Milon, the heavyweight champion,   280
now weeps to see them hanging so useless and flabby;
Helen too weeps at the wrinkles seen in her mirror
and asks herself why she was—twice!—seized by a lover.[3]
    "Devouring Time! Envious Age! Working together,
you bring all to ruin: in your unhurried consumption,   285

2. The moon.
3. Milon of Cromona was a legendary boxer and strongman. A disciple of Pythagoras, he saved his master's life when the roof of a temple collapsed, by holding it up until the philosopher could escape. Helen's first abductor was Theseus; she had a child by him and was then rescued by her brothers and brought back to Sparta. After marrying Menelaüs, she was carried off to Troy by Paris, thus providing the motive for the Trojan War.

the world is ground down, and everything perishes slowly.
Even what we call the elements do not endure, and
if you pay heed, I will show you the changes they go through.
    "Four genitive substances make up the eternal cosmos;
two of them, which we call earth and water, are heavy,   290
and of their own weight will sink right down to the bottom;
but the other two, air and fire (purer than air is),
are weightless and will rise up if nothing suppresses them.
Though they are spatially distant, each element rises
out of another, and into that other, collapses;   295
when earth is unbound, for example, it changes to water,
then, as it loses its moisture, it once again changes,
this time to wind and air, and, as it grows thinner,
bursts into flame and rises through heaven as fire;
from there the way is reversed, and in the same order;   300
fire, condensing, turns into air, which turns into water,
and fluid water, changing to earth, becomes solid.
    "Nothing persists without changing its outward appearance,
for Nature is always engaged in acts of renewal,
creating new forms everywhere out of the old ones;   305
nothing in all of the cosmos can perish, believe me,
but takes on a different shape; and what we call birth is
when something first changes out of its former condition,
and what we call death is when its identity ceases;
things may perhaps be translated hither and thither;   310
nevertheless, they stay constant in their sum total.
    "I truly believe that nothing may keep the same image
for a long time; the age of gold yields to iron,
and often places will know a reversal of fortune.
For with my own eyes, I have seen land that once was quite solid 315
change into water, and I have seen land made from ocean;
seashells have been discovered far from the seashore,
and rusty anchors right on the summits of mountains;
a former plain was converted into a valley
by rushing waters, whose force has leveled great mountains; 320
and a onetime marshland has been turned into a desert,
while thirsty sands have been transformed into marshland.
    "Here Nature allows a new spring of water to surface,
there closes one off; and shaken by underground tremors,
rivers leap out of the earth, or shrink and are swallowed.   325
So then, when Lycus sinks in the ground through a fissure,
he comes up from under again, far away, totally altered;
now the Erasinus, swallowed, glides underground, hidden
till it emerges and flows through the fields of Argolis;
they say that Mysus regrets his former existence,   330
and, having chosen a different course, is the Caïcus;
and the Amenanus flows through the Sicilian desert,

sometimes disappearing, whenever its sources dry up.
Once the Anygras was potable; now no one will touch it,
not since the centaurs, riddled by Hercules' arrows,   335
bathed there to clean out their wounds—or else the poets
who tell us this story are truly not to be trusted.
Haven't the formerly sweet waters of the Hypanis,
sourced in the Scythian mountains, turned bitter and brackish?

   "Antissa, Pharos, and Tyre once were surrounded   340
by water, but none of those cities now is an island;
folks around Leucas say it was once part of the mainland,
but now it's encircled as well; and they say that Messana
was joined to Italy, until the ocean's waves shattered
their borders, and left them completely divided by water.   345
If you seek Buris and Helice, those Achaean cities,
you will discover them both underwater, and even
today the sailors still point out their wavering towers
and overwhelmed walls; near Troezen, ruled by Pittheus,
there is a steep and treeless hillock, which once was level   350
but now is rounded; for—it's a terrible story—
the bestial force of the winds, sealed up in their cavern,
seeking to exhale and vainly striving for freedom—
and since there was not the slightest crack in their prison
through which their breath could break out, they made the
   earth bulge,   355
as when one exhales one's own breath into a bladder
or blows up a goatskin; that was a permanent groundswell,
now like a hillock, which, over the years, has grown harder.

   "I will refer to a few of the many such instances
that I have heard of or witnessed—why, isn't water   360
itself subjected to taking and giving new shapes?
At midday, your waters, O spring of Ammon, are frigid,
but warm in the morning and evening. They say the Boeotians
can set wood on fire by dumping it into the water
when the moon is in its last phase, and the Thracian Cicones   365
have a river which, if you drink from it, turns your intestines
to stone and changes whatever it touches to marble;
closer to home, those neighboring rivers, the Crathis
and the Subaris, turn hair into gold or silver;
even more strange are those streams that not only alter   370
the body, but have an effect upon the mind too;
who hasn't heard of the indecent pool of Salmacis,[4]
or of the Ethiopian lakes? Any who swallow
their waters either go mad or go into a coma;
whoever quenches his thirst at the spring of Clitorius   375
will give up wine in favor of its purer fluid,

---

4. See Book IV, *The Fountain of Salmacis*.

whether there is some intrinsic strength in the water
which counters the heat of the wine, or, as legend would have it,
the son of Amythaon, after relieving the frenzied
daughters of Proetus with potent herbs and enchantments,   380
cast the means of purgation into the river,
making the hatred of wine a part of its nature.
The Lyncestrian river acts in the opposite manner,
for whoever drinks even a tiny amount of it
staggers as though he had swallowed his wine undiluted.   385
There is a place in Arcadia formerly known as
Pheneus, whose inconsistent stream is mistrusted:
don't drink it at night, for that is when it is harmful,
while it is harmless if it is drunk in the daytime;
so streams or lakes will have, at one time or another,   390
these or some other effects.
                              "There was a time when Ortygia
moved about on the ocean, but now she stays still;[5]
when the Argonauts sailed, they found the Symplegades fearful,
twin rocks exploding with spray when they crashed together,
but now, fixed in place, they form a motionless windbreak.   395
     "Nor will Mount Etna, her sulphurous ovens now blazing,
always be fiery, nor was she fiery always.
For if the earth is animal-like in its nature,
then it lives and it has many places that fire exhales from,
and the earth changes those places with every eruption,   400
sealing some caverns off as she opens up others.
     "Or if the winds that are penned up deep inside caverns
fling rocks against other rocks or at matter containing
the seeds of fire, a blaze will be started from friction,
but the caves will cool down when the winds are no longer
          blowing;   405
and if the fire is caused by the nature of asphalt
and yellow sulphur that burns with a very thin flame,
when the earth no longer furnishes food for that fire
and cannot sustain it, and it has been worn out for ages,
then Nature herself must suffer a want of nutrition   410
and will not be able to endure such a great famine;
abandoned herself, she will abandon her fires.
     "In Macedonia, there are supposed to be men whose
bodies get covered completely with delicate feathers
when they have plunged nine times in the pool of Minerva.   415
I find that hard to believe, but among the Scythians,
women are said to achieve results much the same by
sprinkling a magical potion all over their bodies.

5. Another name for the isle of Delos, the once-floating island, where Apollo and Diana
were born to Latona. See Book VI, *Latona*.

"Nevertheless, if trust in such strange situations
may be adduced from examples already proven,   420
do you not see that when corpses decay from the heat or
from length of time, they turn into wee tiny beasties?
Here is a common experiment: bury some bullocks
slain by the priests, and from their decaying intestines,
the flower-culling bees will be born:[6] rural in nature,   425
as are their parents, inclined to hard labor and prudent.
Buried in earth, the bellicose horse breeds out hornets;
if you remove a crab's curved claws from its body
and bury them in the earth, from the interred portion
a scorpion emerges to menace you with its bent tail;   430
we know that worms which quite commonly (ask any farmer)
cover green leaves with their white threads will change to
butterflies, emblems of spirit departing from body.

"Mud contains seeds which generate frogs, at first legless,
though soon they develop limbs that equip them for swimming,   435
and so that these same limbs can be used for long-distance leaping,
their hind legs are always much greater in length than their
        forelegs.
Nor is the bear cub, when newly brought forth by the she-bear,
other than bear-pulp: by her own purposeful licking,
the mother bear shapes it and forms it in her own image.   440
Do you not see how the larva of bees, makers of honey,
so well protected within their hexagonal chambers
of wax, are born without any limbs on their bodies,
and only later develop legs and the wings used for flying?
The peacock of Juno, with stars in its feathery tail, or   445
the arms-bearing eagle of Jove, the doves dear to Venus,
or any others within the entire bird kingdom:
who could believe that such wonders emerged out of eggshells,
unless he already knew how they came into being?
And there are those who believe that when men have been
        buried   450
and their spines decay, the marrow turns into a serpent.

"Each of these lives is brought forth out of another,
but there is one bird which can renew its own being;
Assyrians call it the Phoenix; it lives not on grasses
and grains but on incense and on the essence of balsam.   455
As soon as five hundred years of his life are completed,
employing his talons and unsullied beak, the old Phoenix
builds his own nest in the top of a tremulous palm tree.
Once it is covered completely with sweet-smelling branches
of nard and mezereon, myrrh and pieces of cinnamon,   460

6. It was commonly thought in the ancient world that bees were born from, and nested in, the bodies of dead cattle.

he lies down upon it, expiring over the odors.
Out of the corpse of his father, there springs a young Phoenix
(or so people say) destined to live the same life span.
When age gives him strength to carry such weighty burdens,
he lightens that of the palm tree by taking his nest down   465
and bearing his cradle, along with the tomb of his father,
through the light air until he comes to the city
of Hyperion and piously places his burden
before the sacred doors of Hyperion's temple.[7]

　　"Should you think this is at all surprising or novel,   470
you'll find the hyena a marvel for changing her gender:
females, when they are mounted, turn into males, and
there's also a creature, nourished on air and light breezes,
that takes on the color of whatever substance it touches.

　　"Defeated India offered wine-bringing Bacchus   475
a tribute of lynxes, and it is said that their urine
turns into stones which the air instantly hardens.
So too with coral, which waves like a grass underwater,
but being exposed to the air turns instantly rigid.

　　"Day will be ended with Phoebus bathing his weary   480
horses at sunset in the deep ocean, before I
manage to put into words how everything changes
into new forms: we can even see the times changing,
as one nation gains in strength while another collapses:
once Troy was great, rich in its wealth and its heroes,   485
and able to go on bleeding both for ten years;
now brought to earth, she has nothing to show but her ruins,
no wealth besides that which lies in her burial chambers.

　　"Sparta was famous, mighty Mycenae once flourished,
even as Athens, even as Thebes of the Towers;   490
Sparta is worthless now, lofty Mycenae has toppled,
what but the name remains of the Thebes of Oedipus?
What but the name remains of Pandion's Athens?[8]

　　"Fame now informs us that Dardanian Rome[9] is rising,
even now building a deep and enormous foundation   495
close to the Tiber that flows from the Apennine mountains:
therefore, she changes her form by increasing, and shortly
will be the boundless world's capital! So say the prophets,
so say the oracles also. Indeed, I remember
Helenus, the son of Priam, telling Aeneas,   500

---

7. Heliopolis, in Egypt.
8. Greek city-states, once powerful, but in Ovid's time politically insignificant. Sparta was
   conquered by Rome in 146 B.C. Mycenae was important from 1600 to 1200 B.C., but
   went into decline thereafter. Thebes, the city founded by Cadmus, became the most
   important of Greek city-states by the fourth century, and then was destroyed by Alexander
   the Great in 335 B.C. Oedipus was its king. Pandion was the legendary king of Athens and
   the unhappy father of Philomela and Procne. By Ovid's time, Athens was no longer a
   political power.
9. Dardanian because of its Trojan origin.

bitterly weeping and doubtful about his survival,
back when the matter of Troy was beginning to crumble,
'O goddess-born, if you will pay careful attention
to my foretelling, while you live, Troy will not perish!
Fire and iron will give way as you carry your city   505
forth from the ruins, until, together, you come to
a more hospitable, even though foreign, site than your homeland.
   "'I now see the city destined for Priam's descendants:
never has there ever been one as great, or one greater
than this one is,[1] never will there be one in the future!   510
Princes besides him will maintain her power for ages,
but he, the offspring of Julius, will make her the mistress
of all creation! And when he is no longer useful
on earth, the powers above will rejoice in his presence,
for heaven will be his reward and his destination.'   515
   "Helenus foretold all of this to Aeneas, encumbered
by his household gods, and I recall it quite clearly,
and I rejoice in the walls of my relatives rising,
a welcome result of the conquest of Troy by the Argives!
   "However, lest I should wander far off in digression,   520
and my forgetful steeds stray from their course on the racetrack,
heaven and everything under it will take on new forms,
as will the earth too, and everything here upon it,
as even we will, for we are a part of it also,
not merely bodies, but wingèd spirits, and able   525
to shelter in beasts, to lodge in the breasts of cattle;
bodies which once may have given refuge to parents
or brothers, or any joined to us by obligation,
or men like ourselves, to be sure, should be safe and respected,
not crammed into our guts like a Thyestean banquet![2]   530
   "What a slippery slope he descends, who slits a calf's throat
able to listen unmoved to its piteous mooing,
for he prepares himself to murder a human!
Or who can butcher a kid, whose terrified bleating
so resembles the cries of our children! Or eat a chicken,   535
whom we have fed from our hand? Is this less than a murder?
How does it differ? What is the end that it leads to?
   "Let the bull plow and in time let him die of old age,
and let the sheep arm you against the freezing north wind,
and let the goat give herself to the hands at her udders!   540
Hang up your nets, nooses, snares, and artful deceptions,
completely! Do not betray the poor bird with a limed twig,
nor drive the deer into nets with forms made of feathers,
nor hide a treacherous dinner upon a barbed hook!

---

1. Augustus. The philosopher's understanding of the transitory nature of everything is difficult to reconcile with his claims for the unsurpassable perfection of Augustan Rome.
2. Atreus, the brother of Thyestes, once served him the limbs of his own son at a banquet.

Kill any that harm you, but make sure *only* to kill them;   545
don't stain your mouths with their blood; be nourished more gently."

Numa (2)

They say that Numa, having taken these
and other such instructions to his heart,
returned to his own nation and submitted
to the desire of the Roman people   550
that he should be the ruler of their state;
successful in his marriage to a nymph,
and wisely guided by the Muses, he
instructed the Romans in the sacred rites,
and led that previously warlike folk   555
into the practice of the arts of peace.

Egeria and Hippolytus[3]

In old age, when his life and governance
were ended, people of all classes mourned;
his wife, Egeria, was so distracted
by grief that she left Rome altogether,   560
withdrawing to Aricia's wooded dale,
where her loud groans and lamentations hindered
the celebration of Diana's rites.
       How often all the nymphs of grove and pool
admonished her and offered consolation!   565
How often did Hippolytus address her:
"Enough!" he cried. "For yours is not the only
misfortune that deserves to be lamented!
Reflect on situations like your own,
and you will find your own more bearable.   570
I wish that I had nothing of that kind
to offer for your comfort, but I do:
       "If you have heard about Hippolytus
at all, you know that the credulity
his father gave to the perversity   575
of his stepmother brought him to his death.
It will astonish you to learn that I—
though I can hardly prove it—I am he.
       "In vain the daughter of Queen Pasiphaë
once tempted me to shame my father's bed   580
and then imputed her foul lusts to me

---

3. Hippolytus, son of Theseus, was falsely accused of rape by his stepmother Pasiphaë. Fleeing his father's wrath, he was destroyed by the god Neptune, whom his father had summoned to punish him. In one legend, he is restored to life by the goddess Diana, and
   identified with the Italian god Virbius (twice a man).

(either from fear that she would be discovered
or else from her displeasure with rejection);
and though I had done nothing to deserve it,
my father ordered me to leave the city,   585
placing a fatal curse upon my head.
    "Banished, I headed in my chariot
for Troezen, and had made it to the shore
of the Bay of Corinth, when the sea rose up
and a huge mass of water, like a mountain,   590
seemed to arch up and hover over me
till, at its highest point, it split in two,
and when those waters burst, a roaring bull
was driven forth, and rearing on hind legs,
it spewed salt water from its nose and mouth!   595
    "But I was still too occupied with thoughts
of my mistreatment to be terrified,
as my attendants were, when suddenly
my warlike horses turned toward the waves,
their ears pricked up, they shook at what they saw,   600
then dragged my chariot in headlong flight
along the rocky coast; in vain I strive
to guide them, dragging on the foam-flecked reins;
bent over backward in my hurtling car,
I test my own against their frenzied strength,   605
and would have won, had not my turning wheel,
striking a tree stump, shattered into pieces;
had you been there, you would have seen my limbs
entangled in the reins, my viscera
drawn from my living body and bestrewn   610
about the tree to the accompaniment
of breaking bones, as trunk and limbs were severed,
and my poor body was strung out between
the tree trunk and my team, still galloping;
when I exhaled my last, nothing at all   615
was left of me for you to recognize,
for everything was just one single wound.
    "And have *you* got the nerve, nymph, to compare
my sufferings with those that you've endured?
I had to journey to the underworld   620
and warm my limbs in river Phlegethon,[4]
and would not have been brought to life again
had not Apollo's son, Aesculapius,
revived me with his artful remedies;
when his strong herbs and simples had restored me   625
(against the will of Pluto), Cynthia,

---

4. One of the rivers of the underworld, its waters burned.

lest envy be encouraged by this gift,
cast a thick cloud and wrapped it all around me;
so that I would be safe, and could be seen
without endangerment, she added years   630
to those I had already, and she altered
the features of my face past recognition;
long she debated whether Crete or Delos
would have me, but deciding finally
that neither of them suited, placed me here   635
and ordered me to put my old name by,
which might remind me too much of my horses.[5]
'And you,' she said, 'who were Hippolytus,
will now be Virbius, the very same.'

    "And in this grove I have dwelt ever since,   640
one of the lesser deities, protected from
misfortune by the godhead of my mistress,
and recognized as Cynthia's attendant."

    But another's woes could not alleviate
the lamentation of Egeria,   645
who, situated at a mountain's base,
dissolved in tears, until the goddess Phoebe,
impressed by the devotion of her sorrow,
transformed her body into a chill fountain,
and of her limbs made streams that will not die.   650

Tages; The Spear of Romulus; Cipus

This strange event astonished all the nymphs
and Hippolytus was similarly stunned,
as was the plowman of Etruria
when in his field he saw the fateful clod—
on its own, moving without being touched,   655
and then exchanging *its* form for a man's,
before it opened its unaccustomed mouth
to speak of what would happen in the future!
The locals called him Tages; he first taught
the skill of prophecy to the Etruscans;   660
no less astounding than when, once upon a time,
Romulus saw the spear shaft he had cut
upon the Palatine put forth green leaves
and stand, not with its head fixed in the ground,
but newly rooted: no weapon now: a tree   665
providing unanticipated shade
to those who flocked beneath it, marveling;
or as when Cipus, looking in the water,

---

5. Because the name Hippolytus contains the Greek word for horse, *hippos*.

saw horns upon his head,[6] which he believed,
erroneously, to be an illusion,   670
for they were real, as he discovered when
he touched what he could see upon his forehead;
and then, accepting what he saw was there,
as a victor returning from a vanquished foe,
he raised his eyes and hands in prayer to heaven: 675
   "O gods, whatever this should prove to be,
this wonder, if it prove to be propitious,
may it be so for the Roman folk and nation;
but if misfortune, may it fall on me."
   Then Cipus built an altar out of turf,   680
where he burned incense to placate the gods,
and poured out wine from a libation dish,
and in the entrails of a slaughtered sheep
(still quivering) he sought to comprehend
the meaning of the horns upon his head.   685
   As soon as Tages, the Etruscan seer,
had looked into this matter, he could see
great deeds astir, but somewhat murkily;
yet when he raised his sharp eyes to the horns
on the head of Cipus, he saluted him: 690
   "Hail, King Cipus! To you and to your horns
the land and towers of Latium will bow!
Hasten to enter those wide-open gates!
The Fates would have it so, and you will be
received as king and rule securely there,   695
forever!"
               Cipus walked back to the city,
averting his grim visage from its walls:
"O may the gods keep all that far from me!
Better, much better, that I spend my days
in endless exile from my home," he said,   700
"than that the Capitol see me as king!"
   He spoke and called together an assembly
of the people and its leaders in the senate,
but not before he covered up his horns
with peaceful laurel; standing on a mound   705
constructed by the soldier-citizens,
he offered prayers up to the ancient gods
according to the rites, and then he said,
   "There is one here who will become your king
unless you drive him from your city now;   710

6. Psychoanalytically interesting: Cipus discovers horns (*cornua*) on his head, which symbolize a suppressed desire for a crown (*corona*); his name is an anagram for *Picus*, the
woodpecker, and his case would inevitably remind a Roman of Julius Caesar, who also
spurned a crown three times, but who did not retire peacefully to the country.

I will not tell you what the person's name is,
but by this sign you may discover him:
he bears a pair of horns upon his forehead!
The augur indicates that if you let this man
enter Rome, you will be reduced to slaves.   715
He might have broken through your open gates,
had I not stood against him, even though
no one is closer to him than am I:
oh, keep him from your city, citizens,
or if he merits it, put him in chains,   720
or end your fear of destined tyranny
by slaying him!"
                         A murmuring arose
among the folk assembled there, as when
a sharp wind whistles through the girded pine
or like the ocean's waves, heard from afar—   725
but out of all their troubled murmuring
a single cry emerged, "Who can it be?"
And they examined one another's foreheads
in search of the horns that he had spoken of.

    Then Cipus spoke again and this time said,   730
"The one that you are seeking has been found,"
and as the crowd attempted to restrain him,
removed the crown of laurel from his head,
exhibiting the horns that marked his brows.

    All looked down in dismay and groaned as one,   735
and then—who could believe this?—with reluctance,
they looked upon that fame-deserving head,
and so that it should not lack further honor,
they placed the laurel crown back on his head.

    But since you could not come inside the walls,   740
the leaders, Cipus, gave you as a gift
of honor as much land as could be worked
by a team of oxen yoked up to a plow
from sunrise to sunset; those horns of yours,
transformed into a work of art, have been   745
inscribed in bronze upon the temple's gates,
and there they will remain throughout the ages.

Aesculapius[7]

O Muses, who attend upon the bards,
reveal (for you have knowledge of these things,
nor do the ages, stretching out forever,   750
betray your memories) that place from whence

---

7. The god of healing. In a time of plague, Romans brought his cult to their city in the form
   of a giant serpent.

the island bathed in the deep Tiber's stream
once brought Apollo's son by Coronis,[8]
and worshipped him among the gods of Rome.
    A dire plague once blighted Latium   755
and men lay wasted from the grim disease.
Exhausted by too-frequent funerals,
and seeing that their labors and the skills
of their own healers had all come to naught,
it was the aid of heaven that they sought,   760
in Delphi, at the center of the earth,
the shrine and oracle of Phoebus, where
they prayed that he would show by prophecy
his own intention to deliver them
from wretchedness and end the city's woes.   765
    The laurel tree, the shrine, and the quiver
held by the god at once began to tremble,
and from the tripod deep within the shrine
there came a voice that filled their hearts with fear:
O Romans what you seek here what you seek   770
you should have looked for in a closer place
and should now look for in a closer place
the task of lessening your wretchedness
is not that of Apollo but his son
go with good auspices and seek my child   775
    Obedient to the orders of the gods,
the prudent senators soon ascertained
the city that the son of Phoebus lived in,
and sent an emissary under sail
to search for the coast of Epidaurus.   780
    Soon as the curved keel scraped against the beach,
they went to the assembly of the Greeks,
begging as a gift the god whose power,
according to the prophecy of Phoebus,
would put an end to Roman funerals;   785
the Greeks were much divided on this issue,
with some opposed to holding back the aid,
while many favored keeping the god there,
not sending help or letting go of the godhead.
    While they debated, evening came on,   790
extinguishing the latest lights of day,
and darkness cast its shadow on the world;
the health-restoring god now seemed to stand
before your couch, O Roman, as you slept,
just as he used to look in his own temple,   795

8. For the prequel, see Book II, *The Raven and the Crow*.

holding a rustic staff in his left hand,
and with his right hand stroking his long beard,
as from his gentle heart arose these words:
    "Be unafraid, for I will leave my image
and come with you: now carefully observe   800
the snake that winds itself around my staff,
so you will recognize its shape on sight,
for this is what I will change myself into,
although I will appear to be much larger,
as heavenly bodies will, in transformation.   805
And with his voice, the god (and sleep) departed,
and with the flight of sleep came kindly night,
for Dawn had chased away the burning stars.
    Unsure of what to do, the senators
assembled at the temple of the god   810
whose aid they sought and urged him with their prayers
to indicate, by supernatural signs,
where he himself desired to reside.
    They had just finished when the golden god,
transformed into a snake with a high crest,   815
forewarned them of his presence there by hissing;
at his arrival, the entire temple,
its statues and its altars and its doors,
its marble pavement and its gilded roof,
began to tremble; and right in the center   820
he slowly rose until he stood breast high;
his eyes, like fire flicking, swept the room
and left them shaking; but a priest (whose hair
was bound with a white ribbon) recognized
the presence of divinity and cried: 825
    "The god is here, the god is here among us!
Silence your tongues and keep your spirits still,
you who are present! O god most beautiful,
grant that this vision be a blessing on
these people here who worship at your rites!"   830
    Those who were present reverenced the god
as they were ordered to, and everyone
repeated what the priest said; and the sons
of Aeneas also carried out the rites,
performing them with fervor and devotion.   835
    The god then nodded his assent to them,
and shook his heavy crest and hissed three times,
and then, as he descended those smooth steps,
he turned back, looking at the ancient altars
he was about to leave, and then saluted   840
the home that he was so accustomed to
and the temple he had dwelt in for so long.

The great god slithered out and down the streets
strewn with scattered blossoms, through the town,
until he had snaked his way right to the harbor,   845
which was protected by a curved embankment.
    He halted there, and looking most benign,
seemed to dismiss his crowd of devotees
before he went aboard the Roman vessel,
which felt the heavy presence of the god   850
and was pressed down by his immortal form;
the offspring of Aeneas were delighted,
and after sacrificing on the shore
their flower-decorated ship left harbor.
    A light wind drove the ship along: the god   855
conspicuously lay athwart the stern
and gazed down at the sea's reflective blue
as he was borne through the Ionian Sea,
and on the sixth day came to Italy,
passing Lacinia (where Juno's temple is)   860
and Skylaceum; Iapygia next,
and then their oars sped them between the rocks
of Amphrysia on the left, and the steep
cliffs of Cocinthia hard on the right;
Rometheum, Caulona, and Narycia   865
were next, and then the Sea of Sicily
and the constricted straits of Pelorus;
then the Aeolian isles and copper-rich
Temesa; Leucosa, and the warm
rose gardens of Paestum; past Capreae   870
(the promontory of the wise Minerva),
Surrentum, whose soft hills are rich in vines,
and Herculaneum, conceived (along
with Stabia and Parthenope, too)
as charming playgrounds for the idle rich,   875
and after to the Sibyl's shrine at Cumae,
and then to Baeae (where the hot springs flow)
and then Liternum, rich in mastic trees,
and the mouth of the Volturnus, clogged with sand,
and Sinuessa, famed for snowy doves;   880
Minturna, famous for its illnesses,
and the land named for someone's foster nurse;
the palace of Antiphates, the town
of Trachin, situated in a marsh,
and Circe's territory, and the shore   885
of Antium, a sweep of polished sand.
    They put in here, because the seas were rough;
the god unfolded himself from the ship,
great rolls of serpent gliding down the beach

to slip into the temple of his father   890
there on the sands.
            When the sea was calm again,
the god from Epidaurus left the shrine
where he had been hospitably received
by a kindred deity, and went back aboard,
dragging his scaly body through the sands;   895
and after winding himself round the rudder,
he placed his head upon the ship's high stern,
where he reposed until the ship reached Castrum
and the sacred city of Lavinium
and the mouth of the Tiber.
                   Here everyone   900
came pouring out to greet the deity,
the fathers and the mothers of the city
and the virgins who attend the shrine of Vesta,
saluting the new god with a joyful clamor.
And as the ship sailed swiftly up the Tiber,   905
from altars set in rows along both banks
came clouds of fragrant incense, and the blood
of victims warmed the sacrificial knives;
he enters Rome now, the world's capital,
and gliding to the topmost of the mast,   910
inclines his head now this way and now that,
in search of an appropriate abode.
And where the Tiber separates to flow
in two parts equally around that place
known as the Island, the serpent-shaped son   915
of Phoebus left the ship, and, once again
assuming the form that he displays in heaven,
brought an end to the bereavement of
the city by restoring it to health.

The Apotheosis of Julius Caesar

That one approached our altars as a stranger,   920
but Caesar is a god in his own city,
raised up to heaven, changed into a star
blazing so brilliantly, not by his own
remarkable success in war and peace,
not by the battles that were crowned in triumph,   925
nor by his service to the commonwealth,
nor yet by glory that hastened to his side;
but rather by his offspring, for no deed
has Caesar done that stands out more than this:
he is the father of our own Augustus![9]   930

---

9. Ovid caps this curious argument with an inaccuracy that any Roman would have noticed:
   Augustus was Caesar's great-nephew, adopted as his heir.

For truly, it was less significant
to subjugate the Britons on their isle,
or lead his vessels up the reedy Nile
to victory; and less to have subdued
Iuba, the king of the Numidians,   935
and Pontus, boasting yet of Mithridates;
and less indeed to have been granted some
of the many triumphs that he merited;
all these are far, far less significant
than to have begotten such a man![1]   940
And you, O gods, by placing him in charge,
have showered blessings on the human race!   ·
     That such a man might not be born a mortal,
his father must be made into a god;
the golden mother of Aeneas saw this   945
as clearly as she saw the sordid plotting
of armed conspirators, bent on the destruction
of her own high priest. Venus grew quite pale,
and told the gods, as she encountered each,
"Just look at all the plots arrayed against me,   950
the many treacheries that seek to slay
the last descendant of my Trojan Julus!
     "Am I the only god to be forever
vexed by such justified anxieties?
For even now the Calydonian spear   955
of Diomedes wounds me, and the walls
of ill-defended Troy come crashing down,
and I can see my son's long wandering
in exile and his struggle with the sea,
his journey to the silent underworld   960
and war with Turnus, or, to speak the truth,
with Juno, rather. But why do I recall
these ancient injuries against my people?
This new fear drives all former fears from mind!
     "Behold where sinful blades are being sharpened!   965
Prohibit this, I pray, prevent this crime,
or else the blood of Vesta's sacred priest
will soon put out the fires on her hearth!"[2]
     Care-ridden Venus cried out all these woes
through heaven, and although the gods were moved,   970
they could not break the stern decree of Fate,
though they were able to provide at least
unambiguous signs of approaching grief:
they say that wars broke out high in the heavens

1. An enumeration of Julius Caesar's various military victories.
2. Julius Caesar had been *pontifex maximus*, but in Ovid's time, the pontifex was also
   regarded as a priest of Vesta. The goddess Vesta was worshipped as a fire tended by the
   Vestal Virgins, whose extinction would bring disaster to Rome.

where storm clouds clashed, and horns and trumpets sounded   975
alarms that brought terror to the hearts of men
and warned them of the evils soon to come;
a dismal sun now shed its lurid light
upon the agitated lands below,
and torches seemed to blaze among the stars;   980
often great drops of blood fell from the clouds,
the morning star turned dark, and its complexion
was stained as though by flakes of iron rust;
now Luna's chariot seemed smeared with blood;
and the Stygian owl hooted mournful omens   985
in a thousand places; in a thousand places,
ivory statues wept; in sacred groves
they say that threats and cries of woe were heard.
There were no victims found acceptable,
and livers warned of tumult soon to come;   990
and in the forum and around men's homes,
and in the temples, dogs would howl at night;
the silent dead would wander, it is said,
and earthquakes shook the city with their tremors.
Nor could those premonitions from the gods   995
overcome fate or human treachery,
and unsheathed swords were brought into the senate,
for there was nowhere else in all the city
for such a dreadful murder to take place.
    Then Venus struck her breast with both her hands,   1000
and made to gather Caesar in a cloud,
as Paris once was borne from Menelaüs,
and as Aeneas from Diomedes.
    Her father said, "My dear, are you preparing
to alter his inevitable fate   1005
all by yourself? It is permitted you
to enter the Hall of Records kept by the Fates;
there you will find the labor of the ages,
the universal script, in bronze and iron,
which does not fear that clashes in the sky   1010
or lightning's rage will bring it down to ruin,
for it will be eternally secure.
    "Here you will find, inscribed on adamant
that will not perish ever, your son's fate:
and I myself have read and noted it,   1015
and I will now expound on it to you,
so you may understand what is to come.
The one that you are mourning has accomplished
the time he was allotted here on earth;
the debt that he has owed to life is paid.   1020

"So that he may set out on his career
as a god in heaven, worshipped here on earth,
you will assist him, working with his son,[3]
who as the heir to Caesar's name and title
will bear alone the burden this imposes,   1025
and as the chief avenger of his murder
will have our full support in all his wars:
under his leadership, the vanquished walls
of Mutina, besieged, will sue for peace;
Pharsalia will suffer from his blows,   1030
and Philippi once more be drenched in gore;
the one called 'great' will drown off Sicily;
a Roman general's Egyptian wife
will rue that poor connection, and will fall,
her threat that our Capitol would kneel   1035
to her Canopus having proven false.[4]

"But why should I enumerate to you
the foreign lands and people situated
on either ocean—when whatever land
is habitable will belong to him?   1040
The sea as well will be his very own.

"And having given universal peace
to humankind, his fresh attentions turn
to Roman laws, where justly legislating,
himself a model for all citizens,   1045
he guides their actions; and looking to a time
ahead and future generations, he
will bid the son born of his blameless wife[5]
to carry his own name and burdens too;
but not until his years and services   1050
are equal in number, not until old age,
will he at last reach his divine abode
and join the stars he is related to.[6]

"Meanwhile, do as I tell you; go, take up
the spirit from his father's murdered body,   1055
so that forevermore the deified
Julius will look down upon the forum
and Capitol from his own lofty temple."

---

3. Augustus, again described as Julius Caesar's son.
4. Military landmarks after the death of Julius Caesar on the way to the triumph of Augustus, as Octavian eliminated first the Republican conspirators, then the son of Caesar's rival Pompey, Sextus Pompeii, called "the Great," and finally Marc Antony and Cleopatra.
5. Ovid has in mind Augustus's stepson, born to his wife Livia by her first husband, and who, after adoption, would be known as Tiberius Julius Caesar Augustus. After Augustus's death he ruled in Rome from A.D. 14 to 37.
6. Like Julius Caesar, Augustus too will be deified.

No sooner had he spoken when the goddess
slipped back into the senate house unseen   1060
and took the still-fresh soul from Caesar's body,
which she would not let vanish in the air,
and carried it up to the stars in heaven;
and as she did so, she could see it glowing
and feel it start to kindle in her bosom: 1065
she let it go; and as it flew through space
trailing fire, it flickered like a star.

  Observing now the good deeds of his son,
Caesar admits that he has been surpassed,
and is delighted to have lost to him.   1070
And though the son will not allow *his* deeds
to be regarded as above his father's,
Fame (which obeys no will except its own)
raises him up, despite his own desire;
in this, and this alone, defying him: 1075
so Atreus gave way to Agamemnon,
Aegeus to Theseus, Peleus to Achilles,
and finally, as no inapt example,
so Saturn, in the later light of Jove:
for Jupiter rules kingdoms up above   1080
as well as air and sea and earth below;
on earth Augustus rules, and like great Jove
he is our father and our governor.

  O gods, I pray you, comrades of Aeneas,
before whom sword and fire both yielded sway,   1085
and O you local gods of Italy,
Indigetes, and noble Quirinus,
Father of Rome, and Gravidus,
the father of invincible Quirinus,
and Vesta (to whom Caesar was devoted),   1090
and you Apollo, worshipped beside Vesta,
and Jove whose temple rises high upon
Tarpeia's rock, and all the other gods
a poet ought to call on in his prayer,
late be that day and not in our time   1095
when he, Augustus, ruler of the world,
departs from it, and rises to the stars,
and absent, is attentive to our prayers.

The Poet of the Future[7]

My work is finished now: no wrath of Jove
nor sword nor fire nor futurity   1100

---

7. Fittingly, Ovid ends a Book full of visions and prophecies with a very accurate vision of his
  own future reception and reputation.

is capable of laying waste to it.
Let that day come then, when it wishes to,
which only has my body in its power,
and put an end to my uncertain years;
no matter, for in spirit I will be   1105
borne up to soar beyond the distant stars,
immortal in the name I leave behind;
wherever Roman governance extends
over the subject nations of the world,
my words will be upon the people's lips,   1110
and if there is truth in poets' prophesies,
then in my fame forever I will live.

Contexts

BERNARD KNOX

Ovid in His Time and Ours[†]

Publius Ovidius Naso[1] (the last name, "Nose," was a family inheritance from an ancestor who presumably had a big one), though admired by Shakespeare,[2] was distrusted in the nineteenth century as an immoralist and dismissed for most of the twentieth as a lightweight, but is now back in favor. He was all the fashion in his own time, too, and that time has some intriguing resemblances to our own. It was an age of peace that succeeded generations of war and also one that saw the obsolescence of the stern moral code that had made the early Roman republic a nation of dedicated farmer-soldiers and faithful, fertile wives.

In Ovid's day divorce had become commonplace in upper-class Roman circles, abortion not infrequent, families small, and adultery generally condoned. Ovid, who proclaimed himself "the well-known recorder of his own amorous follies," justified that title by devoting well over two thousand lines of elegiac couplets (the standard meter of Latin love poetry) to a witty chronicle of the ups and downs of his long affair with a married woman, including her abortion and his seduction of her maid. Not content with this he went on to write *The Art of Love*, an instruction book for young men on where in Rome to find women and how to seduce them, in which at one point he announced his satisfaction with the age in which he lived. "Let others delight in the good old days; I am delighted to be alive right now. This age is suited to my way of life."[3]

---

† From Ovid, *Metamorphoses*, trans. Charles Martin (New York: W. W. Norton, 2004). Reprinted by permission of the author.
1. Ovid uses this name when he refers to himself in his poems; *Ovidius*, with its first three syllables short, could not be fitted into either hexameter or the second line of the elegiac couplet.
2. In *Love's Labour's Lost* (IV.ii), Holofernes dismisses a poetic love letter addressed by Biron to Rosaline as lacking in "the elegancy, facility, and golden cadence of poesy. . . . Ovidius Naso was the man. And why indeed 'Naso' but for smelling out the odoriferous flowers of fancy, the jerks of invention?"
3. *Ars Amatoria* III, 121–22. *Ovid: The Erotic Poems*, trans. Peter Green (New York: Penguin, 1982), 217.

The word here roughly translated as "way of life"—*moribus*—is, as so often in Ovid, a significant allusion. It is an unmistakable and mocking echo of a famous line of Ennius, the epic poet who, two centuries earlier, had celebrated the great days of the early republic, the wars against Carthage, and the conquest of the eastern Mediterranean: *Moribus antiquis res stat Romana virisque*—"By its ancient way of life and its men the Roman state stands firm." Ovid goes on to make perfectly clear why he is so happy to be living now. It is not because of "the stubborn gold we mine, or the rare shells gathered/ For our delight from foreign shores,/ . . . but for/Refinement and culture, which have banished the tasteless/Crudities of our ancestors."[4] One important aspect of "refinement and culture," Ovid took it for granted, was sexual license. "In the old days," he had remarked in his earlier poem, the *Amores*, "it was different. Those Sabine women stuck to/One husband apiece. But then *they* didn't wash."[5]

Unfortunately for Ovid, Octavian, the adopted son of Julius Caesar, who in 30 B.C., after the defeat and death of Antony and Cleopatra, had become the master of the Roman world, was intent on turning the clock back. Using powers granted him by a subservient Senate, he established a whole legislative program designed to restore the old Roman family values. Octavian himself, before he assumed the titles of Augustus and *pater patriae*, had been no plaster saint. He had divorced his wife, Scribonia, to marry Livia while she was still pregnant by her divorced husband, and, according to Suetonius, he had even before that had a remarkable career as a libertine. He was also the author of a six-line epigram abusing Antony and his wife Fulvia so explicitly obscene that Martial (who quotes it in full)[6] cites Augustus as his precedent for his own "witty little books" stuffed with epigrams that Byron labeled "nauseous." But there is no moral reformer more fanatical than a reformed rake, and these severe laws, though not always strictly enforced, were there on the books to be used if needed. One of them made adultery a crime punishable by expulsion from Rome; another restricted advancement on the administrative-military ladder to high office, the *cursus honorum*, to married men with three children.

Augustus must have been infuriated by the popularity of poems that, as Peter Green puts it, "presented adultery as a high-class social game,"[7] but it was not until 8 A.D. that he took action, not just expelling Ovid from Rome but sending him all the way to Tomi on the

4. *Ars Amatoria* III, 122ff.
5. *Amores* I, 8.39–40; *Ovid: The Erotic Poems*, 98.
6. Book XI. 20. In the Loeb Classical Library's original edition of the *Epigrams* (1925) this one (like many another) was translated into Italian. In the new edition edited by D. R. Shackleton Bailey it is turned into plain English.
7. *Ovid: The Erotic Poems*, 44.

Black Sea, a Fort Apache of the Roman frontier, where, according to Ovid, showers of poisoned arrows could come over the walls at any moment. One of the two reasons for this harsh sentence, Ovid informs us in one of the many poems written in exile, was a poem—presumably *The Art of Love*—which, however, he defends in a long letter addressed to Augustus as no worse than the love elegies written by Tibullus and Propertius or for that matter than Virgil's *Aeneid*, in which Aeneas, the ancestor of Rome's founder, joins in illicit union with Dido. The other reason he gives for his punishment is an *error*, a word with a semantic range stretching from "mistake" to "madness"; whatever he did (or failed to do) probably had some connection with the many court intrigues sparked by the vexed problem of the succession to Augustus or with the sexual scandal that resulted in the exile of Augustus' daughter Julia.

The Art of Love had been in circulation for some eight years when Ovid was forced to leave Rome. In those years he worked on two long poems. One of them was the *Fasti*, a celebration of the recurring religious fesitvals of the Roman calendar and the myths connected with them.

But this was not the only poem Ovid worked at in the years before the imperial edict consigned this playboy of the Roman World to the outer darkness of the frontier. He also produced a major work which, he announced in its closing lines, was his warrant for eternal fame: "Wherever Roman power rules over conquered lands I shall be read, and through all centuries, if poets' prophecies speak truth, I shall live." The poem was known by the title *Metamorphoses*,[8] a Greek word meaning "changes of shape"; its opening lines proclaim its theme—"My mind is intent on singing of shapes changed into new bodies." In the *Metamorphoses*, by far the most ambitious of his poems (and also the longest—over 12,000 lines divided into fifteen books), he abandoned the elegiac couplet, the metrical form used in all his other extant work. For the *Metamorphoses* he chose the hexameter, the line in which Homer sang of the wrath of Achilles and the wanderings of Odysseus, which Ennius adapted for the Latin language in his celebration of the great wars of the early republic, and Virgil shaped to majestic music for his tale of Aeneas and the origins of Rome.

It was a meter Ovid had once publicly rejected. The opening couplet of his first collection, the *Amores*, presents a comic apology for not celebrating the wars of Augustus in hexameter verse. He was about to do so—"Arms and the violence of war were to be my theme, in solemn meter, the subject suited to the verse. My second line was

---

8. Ovid never uses the word, but later writers (Seneca, for example) refer to the poem under this title.

as long as the first." But he was thwarted—"Cupid, they tell me, burst out laughing, and slyly docked it of one foot." The first word of the poem—*arma*—a deliberate echo of Virgil's *Arma virumque*, makes even more pointed Ovid's expression of his disinclination to celebrate the glories of the Augustan age in epic verse. And now that he has abandoned the verse form of which he had made himself the supreme master, the theme he chooses for his new medium has little to do with heroic action or the Roman national tradition.

Initially, it seems much broader; he begins with the original great metamorphosis, the emergence of our universe from primeval chaos, a magnificent account of the Creation based on the writings of the Stoic philosophers, which suggests perhaps that his model is neither Ennius nor Virgil but Lucretius, whose great poem *De Rerum Natura* expounds in epic verse the doctrines of Epicurus. The next metamorphoses, however—the passage of the human race through the changes from Golden through Silver and Bronze Ages to the Age of Iron, suggest Hesiod as the model. But at this point Ovid charts his own path with the story of Lycaon, the tyrant whose savagery and contempt for the gods so enrages Jupiter that he changes him into a howling wolf.

This is the first of a long and dazzling succession of transformations, over 250 of them. People are changed into animals, birds, fish, insects, flowers, plants, trees, rivers, fountains, rocks, mountains, islands, and stones; stones are turned into people as are ants; men are changed into women and vice versa; and, in one famous case, a statue is changed into a woman. The stories are told with such graceful charm and wit, and sometimes with a *terribilità* worthy of Dante at his most infernal, that they have been appropriated by poets and artists ever since. Shakespeare plundered Medea's appeal to Night and Hecate for the great speech in which Prospero abjures his "rough magic" and burlesqued one of Ovid's most famous tales as "the most lamentable comedy and cruel death of Pyramus and Thisbe." Bernini, in a miraculous metamorphosis of his own, transformed into marble the limbs of Ovid's Daphne as they become trunk, twig, and leaf of the laurel.

In the first six books the transformations are for the most part the result of divine action. Daphne becomes a laurel tree to escape Apollo's pursuit and Syrinx a reed to escape Pan. Io is changed into a cow in an attempt on Jupiter's part to conceal his coupling with her from Juno. Callisto is changed into a bear by Diana because she has been made pregnant by Jupiter. Coronis becomes a crow to escape rape by Neptune. Arachne is changed into a spider for challenging Minerva to a spinning contest—and so on. In the next six books, though the actual transformation has to be the work of a god, it is the result of human passion and crime.

So far, the myths Ovid has been using, and often radically recasting, are Greek, but toward the end of Book XIV Roman myth takes over as Aeneas starts on his long journey to Italy, though his progress is often interrupted by more Greek stories—Galatea, Polyphemus, Glaucus—before he reaches his destination and, his mission accomplished, is changed into a god. But before the final metamorphosis— the spirit of Julius Caesar changed into a star—Numa, the Roman lawgiver king who succeeded Romulus (also changed into a star), goes to visit the Greek mystic and philosopher Pythagoras, who, in a 400-line speech, explains to him the nature of the universe and our lives. It is a majestic sermon on the instability not only of the universe but also of our own identities, for, according to Pythagoras, the individual spirit does not perish, but after the death of the body enters some other shape. This transition from metamorphosis to metempsychosis, together with Pythagoras' eloquent diatribe against eating animal flesh, casts an intriguing backward light on the transformations of human beings into animals in the poem, suggesting perhaps that when we see a cow, instead of thinking of meat we should see the animal as an Io transformed, just as we should see a stag as Actaeon, a bear as Callisto, and that when we instinctively move to crush a spider we should remember Arachne.

There is a further resonance to Pythagoras' great speech. Though toward the end of his long litany of impermanence he foresees Rome's dominance of the world and the deification of Augustus, he does not promise permanence. There is no exception to the rule *Nihil est quod perstet in orbe*—There is nothing in the world that does not change. There are other passages, too, that remind us of Ovid's incurable habit of writing poems "with double or even triple meanings." When Jupiter, after changing Lycaon into a wolf, decides to annihilate the whole human race, he calls a council of the gods to announce his decision. Though they were all worried about the consequences ("Who would bring incense to their altars?"), they approved, "some with speeches that sharpened Jupiter's anger, some in silence."

Ovid's epic model is of course the divine councils in the *Iliad* and *Odyssey*, where, however, disagreement is often expressed and the will of Zeus sometimes (though never openly) opposed. Here, as William S. Anderson points out in his illuminating commentary, "it becomes clear that Jupiter plays the role of Augustus and that the gods are the obsequious senators for whom, a century later, Tacitus expressed such contempt. This poetic Council and its mythical subject suddenly have contemporary repercussions, which generates a mixture of tone that is provocatively elusive."[9] Ovid makes sure that his readers will not miss the point by his description of the council's location: "This is the place which, if such audacity be permitted, I would not hesitate to call the Palatine Hill of the wide

heaven"—the area where the Roman aristocracy, including Augustus, maintained their stately homes. Just to make everything perfectly clear Ovid adds that the lower-class gods (he actually calls
them the *plebs*) live somewhere else.

But in the main body of the poem, framed by the account of Creation and Flood at the beginning and the discourse of Pythagoras
toward the end, Ovid avoids such "contemporary repercussions"; he
is the master storyteller who enchants the reader by the variety and
strangeness of his tales of passion, violence, and young love as he
makes his swift and often surprising transitions from one to another.
Many of them speak directly to the concerns of the modern reader;
they have, to quote the editors' introduction to *After Ovid: New
Metamorphoses*,[1] "direct, obvious, and powerful affinities with contemporary reality. They offer a mythical key to most of the more
extreme forms of human behavior and suffering, especially ones we
think of as especially modern: holocaust, plague, sexual harassment,
rape, incest, seduction, pollution, sex-change, suicide, hetero- and
homosexual love, torture, war, child-battering, depression and intoxication form the bulk of the themes." Noting that "Ovid is once
again enjoying a boom," they invited a number of poets to translate
an episode, ending up with forty-two contributions from Britain, Ire-
land, America, Australia, and New Zealand.

The result is a surprising and fascinating anthology of modern
variations on Ovidian themes, some faithful (after their fashion),
some ranging from eccentric to outrageous, all of them impressive.
Seamus Heaney offers a moving version, in subtly rhymed couplets,
of Orpheus' quest for Eurydice and his death at the hands of the
Maenads. C. K. Williams, in his trademark long Whitmanesque
lines, gives us a version of the death of Hercules which owes more to
Sophocles' *Trachiniae* (which he translated) than to Ovid. The late
(and much lamented) Amy Clampitt contributed a graceful adaptation of the tale of Medea's transformation from love-struck girl to
betrayed and vengeful wife. Michael Longley tackles no less than
seven of Ovid's episodes, among them the rustic idyll of Philemon
and Baucis, in which he stays close to the original, and a wild but
charming Irish adaptation of the story of Phoenix, which begins: "I'll
hand to you six duck eggs Orla Murphy gave me. . . ."

Alice Fulton's contribution is a thirty-one-page extravaganza based
on the 113 lines Ovid devoted to the story of Apollo and Daphne, fea-
turing an Apollo who "favored snapbrim hats, alligator shoes/and
sharkskin/suits from Sy Devore's Hollywood men's store. . . ." Kenneth

9. *Ovid's Metamorphoses, Books 1–5*, ed. with a commentary by William S. Anderson (Norman: U of Oklahoma P (1977), 168.
1. Ed. Michael Hofmann and James Lasdun (London, 1994).

Koch serves up a rollicking ballad of Jove and Io—"Her youthful beauty caused in Jove such ache that 'Me, oh! my, oh!'/He cried, 'she must be mine!' . . ." Simon Armitage's short version of Jove's affair with Europa will send American readers to their dictionaries looking (sometimes in vain) for the meaning of such Northern English dialect words as stirk and stot, bezzle and plodge. There is a short poem by our own former poet laureate, Robert Pinsky, which is not so much a translation of Ovid as an intriguing poem about Ovid and poetic creation. And there are four excerpts by England's poet laureate, Ted Hughes: a fine version of the first 300 lines—Creation, Four Ages, Flood, Lycaon—together with the long episodes of the deaths of Pentheus and Adonis and a shorter tale, that of Salmacis and Hermaphroditus.

Hughes has now combined these four selections with twenty more to form a volume: *Tales from Ovid*.[2] It contains about one third of the text, including most of the well-known tales, though those of Orpheus, Jason and Medea, Cephalus and Procris, Baucis and Philemon, as well as the contents of Books XIII to XV, are missing. Hughes is of course an accomplished and powerful poet and the deep sympathy with and imaginative recreation of animal life and feeling that is such a marked feature of his work serves him well here. As, for example, in his version of the fate of Actaeon, who, returning from the hunt with his hounds, accidentally stumbles on the virgin goddess Diana as she bathes naked in a pool. Infuriated at being exposed to male gaze, she reaches behind her for an arrow, but she has left her weapons on the shore.

> No weapon was to hand—only water.
>
> So she scooped up a handful and dashed it
> Into his astonished eyes, as she shouted:
> "Now, if you can, tell how you saw me naked."
>
> That was all she said, but as she said it
> Out of his forehead burst a rack of antlers.
> His neck lengthened, narrowed, and his ears
> Folded to whiskery points, his hands were hooves,
> His arms long slender legs. His hunter's tunic
> Slid from his dappled hide. With all this
>
> The goddess
> Poured a shocking stream of panic terror
> Through his heart like blood. Actaeon

---

2. *Tales from Ovid*, trans. Ted Hughes (New York: Farrar, Straus and Giroux, 1997).

Bounded out across the cave's pool
In plunging leaps, amazed at his own lightness.
And there

Clear in the bulging mirror of his bow-wave
He glimpsed his antlered head,
And cried: "What has happened to me?"

No words came. No sound came but a groan.

This loose stanza form served Hughes, with varying line lengths throughout the book, for a collection of episodes that combine, as one English critic has put it, "his feeling for drama with a tough, brawny language." Unfortunately the language is apt at times to become much too brawny, to the point in fact where it is utterly alien to the style and spirit of the original. Ovid's description of the wickedness of mankind in the Iron Age concludes with the phrase Victa iacet pietas—Piety (which includes respect for duty to one's fellows as well as to the state and the gods) lies conquered. In Hughes's version these three words turn up as: "The inward ear, attuned to the Creator,/Is underfoot like a dog's turd." Even if one manages to accept the inward ear being underfoot, that dog's turd is too much. Ovid is absolutely incapable of introducing such an object into his verse. He can be terrifying as well as beguiling, sexually suggestive as well as discreetly allusive, comic as well as tragic, but he is always elegant.

Sometimes Hughes does more than add a discordant detail of his own. When Pentheus mocks the prophet Tiresias, "he jeered," Hughes writes,

at this dreamer.
"Dreams," he explained,
"Which this methane-mouth
Tells us are the dark manifesto
Of the corrector,
In fact are corpse-lights, the ignes fatui,
Miasma from the long-drop
and fermenting pit
Of what we don't want, don't need,
And have dumped.
They rise from the lower bowel. And lower."

If you look for the source of this brawny language in Ovid you will find no trace of it whatsoever. In fact in Ovid Pentheus is not even given direct speech; Ovid reports simply that "he laughed at the prophetic words of the old man and taunted him with his darkness, the loss of his sight." Hughes's versions, for all their merits, are to be read with caution; some of their most striking passages have no warrant in the text.

Tales from Ovid also suffers from the disadvantage that it is a selection of stories from a work in which the means employed to ensure continuity are often as intriguing as the stories themselves. Continuity is what Ovid prays for in his poem; he asks the gods to look kindly on his enterprise and "bring the poem uninterrupted down from the first beginnings of the world to the present day." Since what he is about to launch into is a collection of hundreds of stories, some short, some long, selected from Greek and Roman mythology because they end in a metamorphosis, this sounds like a tall order, even for gods. But they comply. Though the poem is divided into fifteen books, these books, unlike those of Virgil's *Aeneid*, are not artistic unities, each with its dramatic opening and significant closure. On the contrary, time after time, a story runs over from one book to the next. The poem is a seamless whole, an uninterrupted progress from start to finish, from the creation of the world to the final metamorphosis of the spirit of the murdered Julius Caesar into a star. And one of the many pleasures offered to the reader stems from the subtlety, variety, and often surprising wit of the transitions from one tale to another.

Sometimes one tale is embedded in another, in the style of *The Arabian Nights*. Mercury, for example, sent by Jupiter to get rid of Argus, the hundred-eyed guardian Juno had set to watch Io, puts him to sleep with the story of Syrinx, the nymph changed into a reed, and then cuts off his head. When, after the Flood and the creation of the new human race, other forms of life emerged, one was an enormous serpent called Python, which Apollo killed. To commemorate his victory he established the Pythian Games, at which the prize for the winners was a crown of oak leaves. Every one of Ovid's readers knew that it was a crown of laurel leaves, and he hastens to explain that the laurel tree had not yet come into existence. That was the result of Apollo's pursuit of Daphne, who was the daughter of a river god. All the other river gods came to console her father for his loss, except Inachus, who had himself lost a daughter—Io, transformed into a cow.

She eventually regained human shape and bore Jupiter a son, Epaphus, who became a great friend of Phaethon, the son of Helios, the sun god. Phaethon persuaded his father to let him drive the chariot but lost control of the horses and came too near the earth. Jupiter put a stop to his ride with a thunderbolt and then came down to survey the damage. He ran into Callisto, a nymph companion of the goddess

Diana, seduced her, and made her pregnant; when Diana saw her
condition she changed the girl into a bear. The skill with which these
transitions are managed, providing surprise time after time in the
long series, is one of the most delightful features of the poem; anything short of a full version gives the reader short weight.

This point is emphasized in the preface to David Slavitt's translation
of the whole text.[3] "As a translator," he writes, "I take all kinds of liberties, but I am strict in my observance of length and scale, which I
take to be significant artistic decisions that any new poem ought to
respect and re-create. The sweep of this work, the change in its
moods and rhythms, the way in which the heart of the poem turns
out to be in the transitions, some of them quite arbitrary and fortuitous, are what have impressed me and what I have tried to convey."
    Convey the sweep of the work he does, as the poem rolls on in the
polished "English hexameters" modeled on but lighter than those
developed by Richmond Lattimore for his translation of the *Illiad*.
They are impressive, as the following excerpt will demonstrate. It is
a passage in which the youth goddess Hebe has just rejuvenated her
husband Iolaus. As she starts to swear that she will never do the
same thing for anybody else, Themis prevents her, with a prophecy
packed with mythical examples of future rejuvenations that may
puzzle modern readers by its cryptic allusiveness. The excerpt also
makes clear what Slavitt meant by the phrase "all kinds of liberties."

. . . Themis, the Hours' mother and Mistress
of Seasons and Years, prevented this ill-considered gesture.
And now we get Themis' list of myths in which time stands still,
moves around, plays tricks . . . not stories but only allusions,
some of them clear, and others oblique or coy. Our attention
wanes, as the voice—of Themis? Ovid?—falters and drones.
Tired perhaps? We strain to follow its murmur and feel
frustration, even annoyance. Why has he thus betrayed us?
Is this a place he'd have fixed had the gods not sent him away
(or, to keep to the pattern, turned him from darling to exile,
the victim of Caesar Augustus' whim)? But there is a way
to read this passage and turn time back. We are children again,
hide in the hall at the top of the stairs and strain to hear
the phrases that float up from our parents' conversations.
Greedy for what we can catch, we hold our breath to listen
and to comprehend their words and the world's unpleasant secrets
from which they have tried to protect us as long and as well as
    they could.

3. *The Metamorphoses of Ovid*, trans. David R. Slavitt (Baltimore: Johns Hopkins U.P., 1994).

The question is one of trust, which Ovid invites or tests.
Have we learned in these pages to yield to his moods and moves,
    to read
with that mixture of love and awe we felt many years ago
in the upstairs hall? The subject, at any rate, is the business
of youth and age, how the gods can turn back the clocks—not
    often,
but every now and again. We get Amphiarius' story. . . .

At this point Slavitt gives us a highly selective version of what
Themis said (omitting Amphiarius, to whom Ovid devotes ten lines)
and proceeds with the words "We are back on track now. . . ." But
we are not. He regales us with seven more lines of editorial comment—"This story, a somewhat mannered performance,/is one of
those nice rhetorical set pieces Ovid loved . . ."—before settling
down to the lurid story of Byblis' passion for her brother Caunus.
Slavitt speaks eloquently in his introduction of the reader's (and the
translator's) reaction to the poem as a "leap of sympathy, intuition,
understanding, and, finally, collaboration." But this seems to go
beyond collaboration; it is in fact editorial intervention, or perhaps
intrusion would be a more accurate description.

Fortunately such passages are rare. No one can deny the merits of
Slavitt's version. His English hexameter is a great success—a supple,
fluid, and versatile medium that does Ovid's loosening of the Virgilian line full justice. And at his best he is very good indeed. Here,
for example (and for comparison with Hughes), is his version of the
metamorphosis of Actaeon.

Without her quiver of arrows, she makes do with splashing his
    head
with water she kicks in his direction in playful anger—
or is it real? He has no idea! His wits have left him.
Utterly dumb, he can barely comprehend her words
as she speaks to him: "Now, that you've seen a naked goddess, go
and tell whomever you will, or whomever you can. . . ." On his
    head,
where the water drops landed, his horns are already sprouting out
in a rack of impressive antlers that spread out from the crowns
of mature stags. His ears are sharpening into pointed
excrescences, while his hands are pointing, becoming hoofs,
and his arms are turning to forelegs. His skin is a hide, and his
    heart
is cold with terror. He looks down into the water's surface
sees what he has become, then turns in panic and runs
faster than he has ever been able to run. He attempts

to vent his rage at what's happened, give voice to his woe, but words
fail, have fled. . . .

Ovid, as the editors of *After Ovid* remarked, is once again enjoying a boom. There is at least one more translation of the *Metamorphoses* under way; excerpts from it have appeared in literary magazines[4] and the finished version is to be published by Norton. It is by Charles Martin, a well-known poet[5] and also the author of a brilliant translation of Catullus, which was reviewed in these columns some years ago.[6] Like Slavitt, he avoids breaks in the narrative and stanza form, using one line throughout, an elegantly varied version of the standard English pentameter. Here is the fate of Actaeon:

. . . [Diana] managed to turn sideways and look back
as if she wished she had her arrows handy—
but making do with what she had, scooped up
water and flung it in Actaeon's face,
sprinkling his hair with the avenging droplets,
and adding words that prophesied his doom:
"Now you may tell of how you saw me naked,
tell it if you can, you may."
                              No further warning:
the brow which she has sprinkled jets the horns
of a lively stag; she elongates his neck.
narrows the tips of his ears to tiny points,
converts his hands to hooves, his arms to legs,
and clothes his body in a spotted pelt.
Lastly the goddess endows him with trembling fear:
that heroic son of Autonoe flees,
astonished to find himself so swift a runner.
But when he stopped and looked into a pool
at the reflection of his horns and muzzle—
"Poor me!" he tried to say, but no words came. . . .

This is not only more faithful to Ovid than either of the other two versions (Slavitt's "in playful anger—or is it real?" and Hughes's "hunter's tunic slid from his dappled hide" are both additions) but also captures an important feature of the original which the others have missed. They attribute the original action, the sprinkling of the water, to Diana, but after that the transformation is described as a process, a sort of organic growth. Martin uses active verbs; each

4. *The Tennessee Quartely* (Fall 1995); *Edeatic Literary Forum*, vol. 7, no. 1 (1997).
5. He is the author of *Steal the Bacon* (1987) and *What the Darkness Proposes* (1996), both published by the Johns Hopkins University Press.
6. "A Dangerously Modern Poet," *The New York Review*, December 3, 1992, 19–23.

detail of the transformation is a separate action on the part of the goddess. And this is true to Ovid's text, where a remarkable repetition, the -at ending of the verbs—*dat, dat, cacuminat, mutat, velat*— she *gives* him the horns, *gives* length to his neck, *points* his ears, *changes* his forearms to legs, and *covers* his body with a pelt—presents the stages of Actaeon's transformation as the whiplash blows inflicted by divine fury. Martin's complete text is clearly something to look forward to with high expectations.

I wrote those words in 1998, and now at last we have the whole of Ovid's masterpiece in Charles Martin's translation, which surpasses in its brilliance and accuracy even my high expectations. From the very first lines the general reader recognizes the expertise of a translator who is also a widely admired poet, and the scholar admires the skill of a poet who is also a scholar and literary critic. But the translation's prime virtue is its irresistible readability; its flowing, melodious lines sweep you on from the end of one story into the beginning of the next, from the creation of the world to Ovid's final claim: that after his death he will be "immortal as the name I leave behind/ . . . my words will be upon the people's lips . . . then I will live forever in my fame." It is a claim that over the centuries proved true, and Martin's splendid version of Ovid's masterpiece will give it a fresh lease on life for a long time to come.

SENECA THE ELDER

Seneca the Elder (ca. 55 B.C.–40 A.D.), a contemporary of Ovid's, was a historian who put together, at the request of his sons, a survey of Roman oratory in two collections, the *Controversiae* and the *Suasoriae*. He was the source for several interesting anecdotes about Ovid that cast light on his attitude toward his own work and talent.

Two Anecdotes of Ovid[†]

Controversiae 2.2.12

In his use of language, [Ovid] practiced restraint—except in his verses, and here he was not ignorant of his blemishes, but rather cherished them. An example will make this clear: Once, when he was asked by some friends if he would remove three of his lines, he

---

[†] Adapted by Charles Martin from *The Elder Seneca: Declamations in Two Volumes*, trans. M. Winterbottom (Cambridge: Harvard UP, 1974), vol. I, 325; vol. 2, 265.

reciprocated by asking that he be allowed to propose three lines which they would not be permitted to touch. This seemed a fair rule; they separated, and his friends wrote down the verses they wanted removed, while he wrote down those he wanted to save. The verses on his sheet were the same as the verses on theirs. One of the spectators, Albinovanus Pedo, said that the first of these lines was

Semibovemque virum semivirumque bovem;[1]

The second was

Et gelidum Borean egelidum Notum[2]

From this it appears that this man of great genius was not deficient in discernment, but lacked the spirit to restrain his poetic license. He would sometimes say that a face was made more attractive by the presence of a mole.[3]

Controversiae 9.5.17

The speaker Montanus has this defect, that he ruins his aphorisms by repetition. Because he is not content to say a thing well once and for all, he winds up not saying it well at all. And on account of this and some other similarities between the orator and the poet, Scaurus would say that Montanus was the Ovid of orators, for Ovid too did not know how to leave well enough alone.

To give just one example of what Scaurus called Ovid's "Montanisms," when Polyxena was taken to the tomb of Achilles to be sacrificed, the poet has Hecuba say

The very ashes in his sepulcher
Despise our race.

He might have been satisfied with that, but he added

Even from the grave
We feel the enmity that he still bears us.

Nor was he satisfied with that, but added

I have been fruitful for Achilles' sake.

Scaurus spoke the truth when he said that it is no less a virtue to know how to stop speaking as to know how to speak.

1. "A man half bull and a bull half man."
2. "The gelid north wind and the tepid south wind."
3. Seneca does not provide us with the third line.

Influences, Anxious and Benign

Ovid was of course influenced in his writing of the *Metamorphoses* by a variety of Greek and Roman poets, including the archaic Greek poet Hesiod, the sophisticated Alexandrian Callimachus (perhaps closest to his own sensibility), and his Latin predecessor Lucretius. Perhaps the strongest influence on his work was the poetry of his near contemporary Virgil, with whose epic poem the *Aeneid* Ovid clearly had a love-hate relationship.

Here are two earlier versions of the creation of the universe, a theme which Ovid treats in Book I of the *Metamorphoses*. The first is that of Hesiod, an eighth-century B.C. Greek poet who gave his version of the creation in his didactic poem *Works and Days*.

HESIOD

From Works and Days[†]

Or if you will, I'll briefly and expertly
tell you another tale: place it in your heart—
how gods and mortal men sprang from one source.
First, the immortal gods on Mount Olympus
created the golden race of mortal men   5
who lived when Cronos reigned above in heaven.
They lived like gods, suffering no sorrow,
far from all toil and grief; they did not know
wretched old age; with never-failing limbs,
they partied and they feasted, free from care.   10
Dying, it was as if they had fallen asleep,
and all good things were theirs, for, uncompelled,
the earth supported them without their toil.

---

† Adapted by Charles Martin from *Hesiod, the Homeric Hymns, and Homerica*, trans. Hugh G. Evelyn-White (Cambridge: Harvard UP, 1914), lines 106–201.

They dwelled in ease and peace upon their lands,
rich in their flocks and loved by the immortals. 15
    But after earth had covered up this race,
they still live here as pure and kindly spirits
who keep men safe, deliver them from harm,
and roam the world, enveloped in dark mist,
watching for fraudulence in law courts 20
and cruel deeds; they also dispense wealth,
for this royal right belongs as well to them.
    The gods upon Olympus next created
a second, far less noble, race of silver,
unlike the golden race in form or spirit. 25
A worthy mother spent a hundred years
keeping her simpleton at home to play,
but once they came into maturity
their foolishness would cut their sad lives short,
who could not keep from harming one another,— 30
nor would they worship the immortal gods,
nor sacrifice upon their holy altars
as is the proper custom everywhere.
Then Zeus in anger did away with them,
who would not honor the Olympians. 35
    But when the earth had covered them as well,
though mortal, they were still considered spirits,
and honored, though they are of second order.
    Then Zeus created a third generation,
A race of bronze, sprung from spears of ashwood, 40
in no way like that of the silver age,
but terrible and strong. Men to be feared,
as hard as adamant, they cherished warfare
and deeds of violence; they ate no bread.
Great was their strength, invincible the hands 45
which grew on strong limbs thrusting from their shoulders.
Their armor was of bronze, their houses too,
as were their tools—there was no iron then.
These were destroyed by their own hands and went
off to the cold and crumbling underworld, 50
unsung, for dreadful as they surely were,
black Death snatched them out of the sun's bright light.
    But when the earth had covered these up too,
Zeus made another on the fruitful earth—
the fourth race was both nobler and more righteous, 55
a godlike race of heroes, demigods,
the race before our own, on the vast earth.

Some were destroyed in warfare's savage battles,
some in the land of Cadmus when they fought
before the walls of seven-gated Thebes   60
to carry off the flocks of Oedipus;
and some, whom war transported overseas
to fall at Troy for gold-haired Helen's sake;
a moiety death's end enshrouded there.
On others of them, Zeus, however, granted   65
a living and a place to live, apart
from men, and made them dwell at the world's end.
And there they live untouched by any sorrow
on isles of the blessed, by swirling Ocean's shore,
blissful heroes for whom grain-yielding earth   70
bears harvest honey-sweet three times a year,
far from the gods, and governed there by Cronos,
for Zeus the father freed him from his bonds.
And these last equally have honor and glory.

Then Zeus made yet another race, the fifth,   75
who still inhabit the abundant earth.
O would that I were not among their number!
—Had died before, or had been later born!
For now it truly is a race of iron,
With never any rest from toil and troubles   80
In daytime, or from suffering by night
when gods shall trouble them with cares and woe.
But even grief comes not unmixed with joy.
And Zeus will end this final race as well
when they are born with gray hair on their temples,   85
when fathers disagree with their own children,
and children with their fathers; guest with host,
comrade with comrade; when brothers will
not be as dear to brothers as before.
Men will no longer honor their old parents,   90
will carp at them and chide them bitterly,
so hard their hearts, so fearless of the gods.
They will not repay their parents for the cost
of raising them, for might shall be their right,
and one man sack the city of another.   95
No favor for the man who keeps his oath
or for the just or good man; men will rather
praise the evildoer and his violent dealing.
Strength will be right, and reverence will cease;
the wicked will hurt the worthy with false words,   100
then swear an oath that what he said was true.

And foul-mouthed Envy with a scowling face,
delighting in evil, will be ever-present.
    Respect and Retribution, their sweet forms
wrapped in white robes, will flee the wide-pathed earth   105
forsaking mankind for the deathless gods;
just bitter sorrow will be left for men,
and there will be no bulwark against evil.

TITUS LUCRETIUS CARUS

Another version of the creation that Ovid clearly drew upon was that of his Roman predecessor Titus Lucretius Carus (95 B.C.–55 B.C.), whose social and literary relationships are largely unknown, but whose epic poem *De rerum natura* (On the Nature of Things) Ovid clearly admired. Lucretius's version of the creation comes from Book V of his epic.

From De rerum natura[†]

Now I'll describe how the chaotic motes,
The turbulent atoms, met, somehow to form
The basic order of the earth, the sky,
The deep, the courses of the sun and moon.
Never suppose the atoms had a plan,   5
Nor with a wise intelligence imposed
An order on themselves, nor in some pact
Agreed what movements each should generate.
No, it was all fortuitous; for years,
For centuries, for eons, all those motes   10
In infinite varieties of ways.
Have always moved, since infinite time began,
Are driven by collisions, are borne on
By their own weight, in every kind of way
Meet and combine, try every possible,   15
Every conceivable pattern, till at length
Experiment culminates in that array
Which makes great things begin: the earth, the sky,

† From Lucretius, *The Way Things Are: The De Rerum Natura of Titus Lucretius Carus*, trans. Rolfe Humphries. Copyright ©1969 by Indiana University Press. Reprinted with permission of Indiana University Press.

The ocean, and the race of living creatures.
No sun with lavish light was visible then   20
Wheeling aloft, no planets, ocean, sky,
No earth, no air, no thing like things we know,
But a strange kind of turbulence, a swarm
Of first beginnings, whose discordances
Confused their intervals, connections, ways   25
And weights and impacts, motions and collisions;
And so the battles raged, because these forms
Were so dissimilar, so various
They could not rest in harmony, nor combine
In any reciprocal movements. But at last   30
Some parts began to learn their separate ways—
Like elements joined with like, in some such way
As to effect disclosure—a visible universe
With parts arranged in order, as the earth
Was sundered from the lofty sky, as ocean   35
Spread with its waters kept in proper bounds,
As the pure fires of heaven knew their place.

At first, no doubt of it, the bodies of earth,
Being heavy and thick matted with each other,
Met in the middle, took the lowest places   40
And as they came together and adhered
More tightly, they squeezed out those particles
Which formed the sea, the stars, the sun, the moon,
The walls of the world, for every one of these
Was made of elements more smooth and round,   45
Much tinier than motes of earth. So ether—
Wherever there might be openings in the mesh—
Found its way upward, and its lightness trailed
Fire as it rose. In just this way we see
In morning's ruddy sunlight over lawns   50
Jewelled with dew the veils of mist arising
From pool or river, and it seems to us
The earth is almost smoking. All this air,
Ascending frail, thickens aloft, and weaves
A canopy of cloud across the sky.   55
So, long ago, the light diffusible ether
In compact circular denseness curved its way
In all directions, spread abroad, and held
All other things in its embracing fold.
Then sun and moon were born, and went their rounds   60
Between the earth and sky, with neither earth

Nor sky appropriating either sphere.
They were not heavy enough to sink and settle
Into the earth, nor light enough to float
Up to the ether, but their course was set   65
Between the two; between the two they turn
Like living bodies, their existence keeping
A time, a place, as parts of the great world.
Their motion and their fixity resemble
Our own in this respect: that we can move   70
Some of our bodily members while the rest
Remain in quietude.

                    When sun and moon
Departed, earth sank suddenly, where now
The blue-green reach of sea extends; earth's hollows
Filled with salt water, and day after day   75
The more the tidal force of air, the rays
Of sun beat down on earth with frequent blows,
Compressing it from width to narrowness,
Its nature all compact, so much the more
By the salt sweat exuded from its body   80
Its ooze increased the sea, the swimming plains;
And, likewise all the more, uncounted motes
Of heat and air escaped, rose far from earth,
Crowded the shining reaches of the sky,
Valleys and plains subsided, mountains loomed   85
To lofty heights, for the crags could not sink down
Nor all the parts descend to equal depth.

So, then, the weight of earth solidified,
And all the heavy sludge of all the world
Settled like lees or wine-dregs in a cask.   90
Then sea, then air, then all the fiery realm
Of ether, with translucent particles,
Was purified, lightnesses varying
From lightnesses, till the most delicate
Floated, most frail, above the highest breath   95
Of the least air, above all whirlwind force,
Unmingling with all turbulence of storm,
Smoothly the calm direction of its fire
Gliding along, like to the Pontic sea
Keeping the even tenor of its way.   100

For earth to rest in the middle of that realm
We call the universe, its weight must be

Diminished little by little, must decrease,
Must have some other substance underneath
Joined with it from the start, must have, above,   105
Some other, forming one organic whole.
This neither hinders nor depresses air
Any more than a man's limbs weigh him down, or his head
Is an overload to his neck, any more than we feel
Our whole weight bearing down upon our insoles;   110
Whereas any foreign matter, imposed from without,
Is a vexatious nuisance, however small
Its actual heft may be. The difference lies
In the innate capacity of things.
So earth is not some foreign body, thrust   115
All of a sudden on resentful air,
But from the outset of the universe
An integral part thereof, as surely so
As our own limbs and organs seem to us.
When the earth shudders at some cataclysm,   120
The atmosphere above is also shaken,
And this could not ensue unless the earth
Were somehow fastened and bound to air and sky.
They are joined, they cling together by common roots,
They have always been so joined and so united.   125
You've seen the like in the way the spirit's essence,
Frail and invisible, sustains the weight
Of our bodies, however heavy they may be.
They have always been so joined and so united.
What else but power of spirit lifts the body   130
Of the high-jumper up and over the bar?
By now you do see, don't you, how a frail
Nature can be most powerful, conjoined
With a substantial body, as the air
Combines with earth, as our own power of mind   135
Joins with our physical natures?

* * *

CALLIMACHUS

In Ovid's opinion, Callimachus (fl. third century B.C.)—poet, grammar-
ian, and chief librarian of the Alexandrian library—was a writer of wit
rather than genius. Still, his influence on Ovid was subtle and profound:
His use of elegiac couplets and his serial poems, exploring the same

topic or situation by means of different examples, provided Ovid with
the technique for early poems (his *Heroides*) and late (the *Tristia*). Callimachus's defense of the epyllion, a brief mythological epic on erotic
themes, strongly influenced Ovid's *Metamorphoses*. His "Hymn to
Demeter" deals with the same unpleasant character that Ovid treats in
Book VIII, *Erysichthon and His Daughter*, p. 226.

Hymn VI: To Demeter[†]

Chant as the wicker moves in procession:
"Hail, great Earth Mother, Lady of Grain!"
Chant, O my sisters, but if you are not an initiate,
Watch from the ground, not from rooftop or height,
Child, woman, or flowing-haired girl—not then nor when   5
We spit from dry mouths in the ritual fast.
Hesperos watches from the clouds for its coming,
Hesperos who alone convinced Deo to drink
When she searched for the footprints of her ravaged daughter.
How could your feet carry you, Lady, to the West,   10
The black men, the gloomgolden apples! You did not
Drink, eat, or bathe the whole time you traveled.
Three times you crossed the silverslipping streams
Of Akhéloös and each of the perpetual rivers.
Three times by Kallíkhoros Spring you sat down,   15
Parched on the ground without drinking water,
Nor did you eat or bathe in the pool.

But we will not speak of what brought tears to Deméter.
Prettier to tell how she gave cities fair laws,
How she was the first to cut straw, bind   20
Holy sheaves, and put the oxen to tread them
When she taught Triptólemos the good art of farming.
A prettier poem, and a grim warning to all,
To tell how she wasted the son of Triópas.

The Pelásgians still lived in Old Thessaly then   25
And had made for the goddess a beautiful grove
With trees so close scarcely an arrow could pass,
Pine and great elms, sweet apples and pears,
And water foamed up in the trenches like amber.

† From *Callimachus: Hymns, Epigrams, Select Fragments*, ed. and trans. Stanley Lombardo
and Diane Rayor. © 1987 The Johns Hopkins University Press. Reprinted with permission of The Johns Hopkins University Press.

She was mad for the place, loved it like Eleusis   30
Or Triopa, or Enna. But fortune turned sour
For the clan of Triópas, and Erysíkhthon lost
His sense of good judgment. He armed twenty retainers
With axes and hatches, great hulks of men
Who could lift a whole town, and stampeded them into   35
Deméter's holy grove. A poplar grew there,
A tree that kissed the blue sky: woodnymphs played
In its shadow at noon. It was the first to be hit
And keened to the others a cadenza of pain.
Deméter knew her holy wood was in danger. She cried out   40
In anger, "Who is felling my beautiful trees?"
And appeared on the scene disguised as Nikíppê,
Her public priestess by the city's appointment,
A poppy clenched in her hand, the key of office
Slung over her shoulder, and dealt with him gently,   45
Trying to reason with the sacrilegious oaf:

"My child, why are you cutting the trees of the gods?
Stop this, my son. Your parents hoped better for you.
Cease, and order your men to desist, before Lady Deméter
Becomes angry with you for destroying her shrine."   50

He looked at her with a scowl more ferocious
Than a birth-raw lioness gives to a hunter
In the Tmárian hills: No glare is more baleful.
"Out of my way, or I'll bury this axe in your chest!
This timber will roof me a fine drinking hall   55
Where my friends and I will feast forever."
An ugly speech from the lad, and Nemesis duly

Recorded his words. Now Deméter's anger
Transcended speech: she was the Goddess once more,
Her feet firm on terra, her head level with Olympos.   60
The men were half-dead with fear when they saw the grim
Lady, and ran away leaving bronze axes in oaks.
She let them go, a despot's mere underlings
And addressed instead their ponderous lord:
"O yes, yes, you dog, go build a hall   65
For feasting with friends. Your feasts will come fast now."

And with these words she wrought Erysíkhthon's doom,
Infecting him with a virulent hunger, a caloric
Morbidity, an astringent disease that puckered his innards,

An appetite unabated no matter how much he ate. 70
Twenty servants prepared his dinner, and twelve
Poured the wine (Dionysos always supports Deo's grudges:
What affronts Deméter affronts the Wine God as well).
His mortified parents invented every excuse
Not to send him to dinner parties. The sons of Órmenos 75
Summoned him to Athena's Itónian Games.
His mother demurred: "He's not home. He just went
to Krannon to collect a debt of twenty oxen."
Polýxo came, Aktórian's mother, with a wedding invitation
For Triópas and son. Fighting back tears, the lady replied: 80
"Triópas will come. Erysíkhthon a boar wounded
Up on Mount Pindos. He's been nine days in bed."
The poor woman loved her son. Why shouldn't she lie?
Another neighbor was giving a feast: "I'm sorry,
But Erysíkhthon left the country today." Another marriage: 85
"A discus hit Erysíkhthon," or "He fell off his horse,"
Or "He's out on Mount Othrys counting his sheep."

While inside the house the incessant gourmand
Ate round the clock, and the more he ate,
The more his stomach somersaulted for more. 90
It was as if the victuals were poured in the sea
And the abyss didn't burble a bubble of thanks.
Like snow on Mount Mimas, like a wax doll in the sun,
He melted to sinews. Nerve-strings and bones
Were all that remained. His mother cried, his sisters 95
Both groaned, as did his old nurse and ten faithful servants.
Old man Triópas pulled his white hair and addressed
To Poseîdon, his putative father by Kanáke, the nymph,
Words that Poseîdon affected not to hear:

"Some patriarch you are! Look at your grandson! 100
Better Apollo should shoot him and I lay him to rest.
My son the ox-eater. So cure him—you're a god—
Or take him and feed him yourself! My pantry's exhausted,
My stables are empty, my cooks have all quit!
He's eaten the wagon mules, the cow that his mother 105
Was fattening for Hestia, the thoroughbred, the war-horse,
Even the cat—and such a mouser he was!"
So long as Triópas's estate had supplies,
Only the walls were aware of the scandal.
But when his teeth had weeviled to the house's depths, 110
The king's son was reduced to sitting at crossroads
Begging for crusts, leftovers, and garbage.

May I never be friends with your enemies, Goddess,
May no wall unite us. I loathe bad neighbors.

Sing, maidens, and join the chant, mothers: 115
   "Hail, great Earth Mother, Lady of Grain!"
And as four white horses carry the basket,
May the wide-ruling goddess whiten our harvest
And so preserve us through white winter and spring
And the white heat of summer. As we walk the city   120
Without sandals or snoods, so may our heads
Be safe from all harm and our feet protected.
As we carry baskets filled with gold grain,
So may we be showered with gold.

                              The uninitiated
May follow as far as the Prytaneîon,   125
The initiates to the goddess's shrine,
But those who are heavy with age or with child
Or the women in pain may come just as far
As their knees will allow: Deméter will give them
As full a share as if they had come to the temple.   130

Hail, Goddess, and save this city,
Keep it harmonious and prosperous ever,
Bring good things home to us from the fields,
Feed our cattle, bring us more flocks,
Bring us ears of grain, bring in the harvest!   135
And nourish peace, Goddess, so that he who plows
May also reap.
                    And be gracious to me, Goddess,
Thrice prayed for, Great Queen.

VIRGIL

Publius Virgilius Maro (70 B.C.–19 B.C.) was the most important living poet in Rome when Ovid was a young man. Virgil's epic, the *Aeneid*, was both an inspiration and a source of anxiety to Ovid, and he parodies Virgil and satirizes his hero Aeneas in the *Metamorphoses*. In the first passage below, Virgil expresses Juno's cosmic rage at Aeneas's escape from destruction after the fall of Troy; Ovid's reductive response to this sequence can be found in Book III, *Juno, Jove, and Semele* (p. 72). In the second passage, the epic dignity Virgil ascribes to a council of the

gods in *Aeneid*, Book X, should be contrasted to Ovid's more uproarious
council in the *Metamorphoses* Book I, *Lycaon's Feast*, p. 10.

From The Aeneid[†]

From Book I

* * *

Scarce out of sight of Sicily, they spread
Their sails with joyous hearts, and over the sea
With brazen prows were plunging through the foam,
When Juno, the eternal wound still fresh
Within her breast, thus with herself communed:—   5
"Shall I who have begun, desist, overcome,
Nor avert from Italy this Trojan king?
The Fates forbid, indeed! Shall Pallas[1] burn
The fleet of the Greeks, and drown them in the sea,
All for the crime and furious lust of one,   10
Ajax, Oïleus' son? She, from the clouds,
Snatched the swift fire of Jove, and hurling, smote
The ships, and scattered them, and upturned all
The sea with winds; and he, by whirlwinds seized,
And breathing flames from his transfixèd breast,   15
On a sharp rock impaled. But I, who move as
Queen of the gods, Jove's sister and his spouse,
So many years with one sole race wage war.
And who henceforth will worship Juno's power,
Or suppliant at her altars lay his gifts?"   20

From Book X

Meanwhile the omnipotent Olympian doors
Are opened, and the father of the gods
And sovereign of men holds a council
Within his starry courts, from where above
He sees the spreading lands, the Trojan camp,   5
And Latian tribes. The double-folding gates
Receive the gods; they sit; then Jove thus speaks:—

† From *The Aeneid*, trans. Christopher Pearse (Cranch New York: Barnes and Noble Classics, 2007).
1. The goddess Minerva.

"Celestial Powers, why is your purpose thus
Turned backward, and why with these hostile minds
Do you contend? No token of assent   10
I gave, that Italy and the Trojan race
Should clash in war. Why this discordant strife
Against my decree? What fears persuaded these
Or those to draw the sword and rush to arms?
The lawful time will come for war—let none   15
Anticipate the day—when on the towers
Of Rome, fierce Carthage through the opened Alps
Shall bring destruction. Then, for war and spoils
Your hatred shall be free. But now hold off,
And willingly conclude our destined league."   20

Thus briefly Jupiter; but not so brief
The words of golden Venus, who replied:—
"O Father, O eternal power of men
And their affairs! for whom is there beside
That we can now implore? Do you not see   25
How these Rutulians insult; how, borne
Conspicuous on his steed amid the ranks,
Flushed with success, Turnus is rushing on?
Their guarded ramparts now protect no more
The Trojans; but within their very gates   30
And mounded walls the battle rages still;
And with their blood the trenches overflow.
Æneas, absent, knows nothing of this.
And will you never suffer that this siege
Be raised? Once more their enemies now threaten   35
Their rising Troy and with another host.
Once more against the Trojans comes the son
Of Tydeus, from Ætolian Arpi sent.
For me, I truly believe, new wounds
Are yet in store; and I, your offspring, still   40
Must await a contest with mortal arms.
If without your consent, against your decree
The Trojans come to Italy, for this
Let them atone, give them no aid; but if,
Obedient to so many answers given   45
From the celestial and infernal realms,
They came, how now can any one pervert
Your high commands or frame the fates anew?
Why call to mind the burning of their fleet
On the Sicilian shore?—the furious winds   50
Raised from Æolia by the king of storms?—

Or Iris, through the clouds dispatched to earth?
Now even the forces of the underworld
She moves—this region yet remained untried—
And, suddenly let loose on upper realms,   55
Allecto through the Italian cities raves.
I care no more for empire: this we hoped
While Fortune stood our friend. Let those prevail
Who you will have prevail. If upon earth
There be no spot your rigid spouse accords   60
Unto the Trojans, then, O Sire divine,
I do beg of you, by the smoking ruins
Of Troy demolished, let me send away
Ascanius safe; let my grandson survive.
Yes, let Æneas upon unknown seas   65
Be tossed, and follow whatsoever course
Fortune may grant; but give me power to shield
His son, and save him from the direful war.
Amathus, Paphos, and Cythera are mine,
And mine the mansion of Idalia.   70
Here let him pass his life, and lay aside,
Inglorious, his arms. Let Carthage rule
Ausonia with oppressive sway. From him
The Tyrian cities shall receive no check.
What profit had Æneas to have escaped   75
The pest of war, and through the Grecian flames
To have fled, and on the ocean and the land
Borne so many perils to the uttermost,
While Latium and a Pergamus revived
The Trojans seek? Better for them to have built   80
Upon their country's ashes, and the soil
Where Troy once was. Give back, O Sire, I beg,
To these unhappy ones their Simöis
And Xanthus, and again let them endure
The sufferings of Troy."

                      Then, stung with rage,   85
The royal Juno spoke: "How is it that you
Force me to break my silence deep, and thus
Proclaim in words my secret sorrow? Who
Of mortals, or of gods, ever constrained
Æneas to pursue these wars, and face   90
The Latian monarch as an enemy?
Led by the fates he came to Italy;
Be it so; Cassandra's raving prophecies
Impelled him. Was it we who counseled him
To leave his camp, and to the winds commit   95

His life? or to a boy entrust his walls,
And the chief conduct of the war? or seek
A Tuscan league? or stir up tribes at peace?
What god, what unrelenting power of mine,
Compelled him to this fraud? What part in this   100
Had Juno, or had Iris, sent from heaven?
A great indignity it is, indeed,
That the Italians should surround with flames
Your new and rising Troy, and that their chief,
Turnus, should on his native land maintain   105
His own, whose ancestor was Pilumnus,
Whose mother was the nymph Venilia.
What is it for the Trojans to assail
The Latins with their firebrands, and subdue
The alien fields, and bear away their spoils?   110
Choose their wives' fathers, and our plighted brides
Tear from our breasts? Ask with their hands for peace,
Yet hang up arms upon their ships? Your power
May rescue Æneas from the Greeks and show
In place of a live man an empty cloud;   115
Or change his ships into so many nymphs.
Is it a crime for us to have helped somewhat
The Rutuli against him? Ignorant
And absent, as you say, Æneas is;—
Absent and ignorant then let him be.   120
You have your Paphos, your Idalium too,
And lofty seat, Cythera. Why then try
These rugged hearts, a city big with wars?
Do we attempt to overturn your loose
Unstable Phrygian state? Is it we or he   125
Who exposed the wretched Trojans to the Greeks?
Who was the cause that Europe rose in arms
With Asia, or who broke an ancient league
By a perfidious theft? Did I command,
When the Dardanian adulterer[2]   130
Did violence to Sparta? Or did I
Supply him weapons, and foment the war
By lust? You should have then had fear for those
Upon your side; but now too late you bring
Idle reproaches and unjust complaints."   135
So Juno pleaded; and the immortals all
Murmured their various sentences; as when
The rising breeze caught in the forest depths,

2. Paris.

Muttering in smothered sighs and undertones,
Foretells to mariners the coming storm.   140
Then the Omnipotent Father, who rules over
The universe, begins. And while he speaks,
The lofty palace of the gods is hushed,
The fixed earth trembles, and the heights of air
Are silent; then the Zephyrs fold their wings,   145
And the great Ocean smoothes his placid waves.
"Hear then, and fix my words within your minds.
Since it is not permitted that a league
Between the Trojan and the Ausonian powers
Be made, and since your discord finds no end,   150
Whatever fortune falls today for each,
Whatever hope each one may build for himself,
Or Trojan, or Rutulian, he with me
Shall know no difference; whether through the fates
The Latians hold the Trojan camp besieged,   155
Or through Troy's fatal error, and mistake
Of doubtful warnings. Nor do I exempt
The Rutuli. To each his enterprise
Will bring its good or ill. Jove is the same
To all alike. The Fates will find their way."   160
By his Stygian brother's river-banks, the gulfs
And torrents of black pitch, he sealed his vow,
And bowed his head, and all Olympus shook.
Here ended speech. Then from his golden throne
Jove rose, and in the midst of all the gods   165
Attending, through the Olympian portals passed.

* * *

CHARLES MARTIN

Ovid's *Metamorphoses* and Pantomime Dancing†

A question to begin with: "Why metamorphoses?" By which I mean, why should a poet in Ovid's position—immensely successful, highly popular, at the height of his powers—write a poem of epic length, consisting of 250 (give or take a few) metamorphic transformations? The epic would be a natural temptation for such a poet, but why the metamorphoses? Did he actually believe that it was possible for men to change into beasts, women into laurel bushes, gods into whatever

---

† Reprinted by permission.

form they chose? If not, then what meaning did metamorphosis have for Ovid? What led the poet to imagine the work that he created?

One very likely source of inspiration for Ovid was the art form called pantomime dancing, which had originated in Greece centuries earlier, but enjoyed a great revival in Rome during the years of Augustus. A synthetic form like opera, pantomime dancing combined music, song, and interpretive dance into a single performance art. In Ovid's time, it was performed by organized troupes, each consisting of a dancer, a singer, and a chorus, and a non-singing actor plus musicians, playing a variety of wind, string, and percussion instruments. The art they created was essentially narrative: the dancer, whose supple body was the center of everyone's attention, mimed a story, while the actors and singers, accompanied by the musicians, delivered the libretto and supported the dancer's interpretation.

Much of what we know about pantomime dancing comes from a dialogue by Lucian, a second-century Greek writer, called *On the Dance*, in which he both described and defended this art form against those who thought it morally and aesthetically inferior to tragedy and comedy. One of the heads on which he defended it was the professional training of the dancer, whose brief had to include a knowledge of the entire mythological history of the world, for the subject of pantomimic dancing was always a story from Greek, Roman, or Egyptian mythology: "Beginning with Chaos and the primal origin of the world, he must know everything down to the story of Cleopatra the Egyptian." (Lucian 37) From Chaos to Cleopatra pretty much describes the range of Ovid's *Metamorphoses*, and Lucian goes on to enumerate, as necessary for a dancer to know how to perform, most of the stories that Ovid retells, including quite a few that deal with metamorphoses of one kind or another, such as the transformation of Cadmus into a serpent and Callisto into a bear: moreover, the dancer "will not fail to know all the fabulous transformations, the people who have been changed into trees or beasts or birds, and the women who have been turned into men; Caeneus, I mean, and Tiresias, and their like." (Lucian 57)

In pantomime dancing, we have a synthetic form that is devoted to narrative. One scholar of the art, Ismene Lada-Richards, describes it as "a fully integrated spectacle, a 'hybrid' mode of performance. Very much like opera today, pantomime was 'a spectacle of excess,' a lavish multi-media extravaganza." (Lada-Richards 13) A penchant for excess, wretched or otherwise, has been one of the elements that define the word "Ovidian" from his time to ours. Ovid's *Metamorphoses* may be described as an epic poem, but as many critics have noted, not only does it slip out of any standard definition of epic, its strange synthesis is composed of many other literary genres. In *The World of Ovid's* Metamorphoses, Joseph B. Solodow sees in the poem not only characteristics of the epic, but of the epyllion (a brief epic of a few hundred lines), tragedy (with its dramatic monologues), forensic oratory (of the kind that Ovid studied as a young man), hymns, Roman erotic elegy, pastoral, and epigram. (Solodow 18–23) Ovid's conception of epic is Protean, refuses definition, and constantly reminds us of its synthetic nature, its relationship to other artistic and literary genres, such as opera and, indeed, pantomimic dance, with which it shares not only a penchant for indefinableness, but a commitment to narrating the great stories of Greco-Roman mythology. The dancer who can transmit these tales through his body, the center of everyone's attention on the stage, finds his equal in the poet who has mastered all of the same myths and who finds himself at the center of his poem as narrator of the *Metamorphoses*.

While I cannot adduce any Ovidian ticket stubs (or copies of the Roman equivalent of *Playbill*) to support my case, Ovid appears to have been not only familiar with pantomime dancing, but to have understood and approved of the erotic implications of the art. In his *Ars Amatoria* (*The Art of Love*), he advises the lover to pursue the object of his desire unremittingly, wherever she goes:

> *Nec sine te curvo sedeat speciosa theatro. . . .*
> *Et plaudas, aliquam mimo saltante puellam:*
> *Et faveas illi, quisquis agatur amans.*

Nor let her sit in the round theater, her fair looks by you unheeded. Applaud when an actor portrays some woman in his dance, and favor whoever be the lover that is played. (Ars, I. 497 and 501–2: Loeb, 47–48).

Here Ovid clearly implies that the lover's sympathy with the erotic nature of the dance will make him more attractive to the object of his intentions.

Later, in Book II of his *Tristia*, the collection of poems that he wrote from exile, Ovid defends himself to Augustus against the charge of licentiousness by arguing that bawdry is permitted in the theater and that Augustus himself has been an amused spectator at such performances. In the course of his defense, he incidentally describes a connection between his own poetry and the dance:

> *Et mea sunt populo saltata poemata saepe,*
> *Saepe oculos etiam detinuere tuos.*

My poems too have often been presented to the people with dancing, often they have even beguiled thine own eyes. (Tristia II. 519–20: Loeb 94–95)

The context here suggests that he is describing a less sophisticated kind of mimery than pantomime dancing, but such is clearly not the case in Tristia V. vii, when he writes to a friend about the apparently welcome news that his poems are enjoying a theatrical presentation back in Rome:

> *Carmina quod pleno saltari nostra theatro,*
> *Versibus et plaudi scribes, amice, meis,*
> *Nil equidem feci—tu scis hoc ipse—theatris,*
> *Musa nec in plausus ambitiosa mea est.*

As for your news that my [poems] are being presented with dancing in a crowded theater, my friend, and that my verses are applauded—I have indeed composed nothing (you yourself know this) for the theater; my Muse is not ambitious for [ovations]. (Tristia, V. vii, 25–28: Loeb 236–237.)

Roman attitudes toward intellectual property were a good deal more casual than ours, so Ovid may not have been asked permission for his work to be performed on a Roman stage. It is also possible that Ovid is pretending not to have known about the performances as a matter of discretion: for after all, why was the audience applauding the work of a man whom Augustus had banished? Ovid is silent about which of his poems are being performed; the Loeb editor notes, "Probably scenes adapted from the *Heroides*, etc., to the purposes of ballet and pantomime." (Lucian 237) It sounds very clearly like pantomime, but we have no way of knowing which poems they were. Considering Lucian's description of the subject matter of pantomime as everything from Chaos to Cleopatra, the dancers might very well have been performing parts of *Metamorphoses*, and once again, Ovid's silence here may be a matter of discretion.

As we have seen, Ovid's epic and pantomime dancing are both synthetic forms, dealing with the same kinds of narrative events, with, at the center of each, a knowing narrator. The resemblances do not stop there. Pantomimic dancing differed from the performance of tragedy and comedy in one very important way: its emphasis on spectacle, which Aristotle described in his *Poetics* as the least artistic part of tragedy: "The tragic effect is quite possible without a public performance and actors; and besides, the getting up of the Spectacle is more a matter for the costumier than the poet." (*Poetics*, Chapter 6, 15.) Karl Galinsky, who first noticed the relationship between pantomimic dancing and Ovid's poem in his *Augustan Culture*, argues that since scenes in the dance were excerpted from complete tragedies, they "were taken out of their context and the tragic impact of the total drama thus disappeared. The tendency was reinforced by an emphasis on the most sensational and visually gripping episodes; Oedipus's blinding, for instance, relegated like other such acts of violence to a messenger's speech in Greek drama, was now shown in performance." (Galinsky 265)

Such acts of violence, performed onstage by a pantomimic dancer, would no doubt have disgusted and horrified some members of the audience. Others would have found immoral—Lucian uses the word *effeminate*—the fact that a male dancer would impersonate female characters. Male actors impersonated women in Greek drama as well, but no doubt the highly stylized conventions of the form shielded the spectator from most of the implications of that kind of impersonation, while in pantomimic dancing there was no escape from the gender-bending sight of a beautiful male body becoming, on stage, the body of a woman. There is considerable anecdotal evidence supporting the idea that the body of the pantomimic dancer was an object of intense erotic fascination for the Roman audience.[1] Though some would have found it scandalous, the vivid sensuality of the dance, liberated from the former constraints of representation, along with its sophistication as an art form, are exactly those elements that would have made it appealing to Ovid and to members of his circle.

Metamorphosis was at the heart of this revived performance art, and it would hardly be surprising that at least one member of its audience found it an inspiration for his own art, which, after all, is characterized by its graphic nature, its devotion to spectacle: one sees Ovid's poem as much as one hears it. One of the rare times when he employs a messenger to describe "offstage" events occurs in Book XI, when one comes to Peleus to tell him about the wild beast marauding his cattle. Other episodes, like the savage violation of Philomela by Tereus in Book VI and the dismemberment of Pentheus by the enraged Bacchae in Book III, are described by the poet in graphic, violent detail. Greek tragedy would have banished these from the stage, but pantomime dancing would have made them familiar to the poet and his audience, would have accustomed them to expect the graphic representation of a great variety of mythological tales, many culminating in onstage metamorphoses.

Galinsky adduces other likely ways in which pantomimic dancing might have influenced Ovid:

> The emphasis on single scenes in the *Metamorphoses*, the narrator's bravura performance, his sophistication, the constant shifts and changes, and the graphic, visual appeal of many scenes, all have their counterparts in the pantomime. Conversely, the pantomimic qualities of episodes like that of Narcissus (3.339–510) are striking.

1. See, for example, Lada-Richards, chapter 5, "Pantomimes and Their Body Dangerous."

Indeed, one can easily imagine Ovid's *Narcissus* being performed onstage.

Certain other aspects of Ovid's art in the *Metamorphoses* may owe much to the pantomimic dance. Dancers performed in broad daylight, in an open theater which could not rely either on a curtain or a blackout for a change of scene. As Ismene Lada-Richards says, typically

> a single, usually male dancer . . . acted out successively by means of dancing all the characters in a given pantomime plot . . . so that, in a danced adaptation of, say, the Dionysiac story dramatised in Euripedes' *Bacchae*, he would impersonate in turn Dionysus, Teiresias, Cadmus, the Messenger and the frenzied Agave. . . . How exactly the transitions between the roles were effected we do not know, but it is possible that an instrumental and vocal interlude entertained the spectators while the dancer changed his mask in order to "become" the next character. (40–41)

If transitions between stories were something of a challenge for the dancer, who must slip out of one character and almost immediately slip into another, they were no less challenging for Ovid, who has to do exactly the same thing. The poet described his work in l. 1 as a *carmen perpetuum*, a continual poem. There are no clear divisions between stories or between the books that constitute the poem. Stories do not begin and end so much as they are transformed, morphing from one tale to another on a principle often more familiar to the poet than to his audience. The books that make up the *Metamorphoses* typically offer at the end no closure, only a cliffhanger to be continued in the next book, where, in some way, the continuation will resolve itself into another story before long.

For example, Book VI begins with a reference back to the theme of the story that ended Book V, the need for humans to show respect for the immortal gods. From there, it moves into a metamorphic story full of visual appeal and dancerly gestures: the tale of Arachne, the weaver from a humble background, whose overweening pride leads her to deny that her gift comes from the goddess Minerva, whom she challenges in a contest of skills at the loom. When the goddess appears in response to the girl's taunt, she first "disguises herself as a crone:/puts on a wig of counterfeit grey hair/and, with a staff to prop her tottering limbs, / begins to speak . . ." (lines 38–41) Her appearance is a kind of dance, accompanied by her speech in praise of old age and respect for the gods. When Arachne rejects the goddess's approach contemptuously, she meets with a dramatic revelation:

> The goddess answered her with, "She has come,"
> and casting off the image of old age,

revealed herself as Pallas; the Phrygian
matrons and the nymphs bowed down before her. (lines 62–65)

While Ovid is usually (and justly) praised for his brilliant description
of the colors in the tapestries woven by the two antagonists, that
description is accompanied by equally graphic references to the
hands and fingers of the contestants, who

> . . . draw the slender threads of the warp between
> the horizontal crossbeams of the yoke;
> the warp is separated with a reed,
> and dexterous fingers, busy at the shuttle,
> draw woof through warp, then tap it into place
> with the comb's notched teeth.
>   Then they go to it,
> hitching their robes up underneath their breasts,
> their well-instructed fingers swiftly flying . . ." (lines 78–85)

Well-instructed fingers were also essential to the pantomimic
dancer's art: Our sources are unanimous about the pantomime's
ability to "speak," "display," or even "write" with his hands." (Lada-
Richards 44) Ovid's tale concludes with a scene that is brilliantly
gestural: the wrath of the goddess as she beats the girl with her shuttle; Arachne's attempt to hang herself, and her final punishment,
when the goddess sprinkles her

> . . . with the juice of Hecate's herb,
> and at the touch of that grim preparation,
> she lost her hair, then lost her nose and ears;
> her head got smaller and her body, too;
> her slender fingers were now legs that dangled
> close to her sides; now she was very small,
> but what remained of her turned into belly,
> from which she now continually spins
> a thread, and as a spider, carries on
> the art of weaving as she used to do. (lines 190–208)

Arachne's tale is followed in Book VI by another story of overweening pride: that of Niobe, the queen who imagines herself as
superior to the goddess Latona because of the greater number of her
offspring. We first see Niobe at her proudest, and because Ovid is
writing a *carmen perpetuum*, he must provide a transition that will
inventively link these two stories of mortal pride and deific retribution, while allowing us to traverse the great distance between the
two characters, one a maiden from a humble background, the other

a haughty matron and ruler. Just as in the dance, one character must be shed as another is put on. How does Ovid do it? By providing us with a transition that seems very much the equivalent of the musicians vamping until the pantomimic dancer was ready for his next character:

> Now all of Lydia is in an uproar
> and farther to the east, the story spreads
> from town to town through Phrygia,
> until the great world speaks of nothing other
> than Arachne's fate.
>   Before her wedding day,
> when she was living in Maeonia,
> Niobe knew this girl; nevertheless,
> the punishment her countrywoman suffered
> did not convince Niobe to defer
> to the immortals, and to treat with them
> as with superiors. (VI. 209–19)

Can it be that the inventive transitions that link together so many of Ovid's stories in the *Metamorphoses* are based on the "forms changed to new bodies" that he observed watching the dance?

The questions we began with about whether Ovid believed or did not believe in the real possibility of metamorphosis cannot be answered in a naïve way. There was after all another art form in which a figure as learned in mythology and as skillful as Ovid in bringing it to life for his audience, demonstrated the possibility of metamorphosis every time he stepped onto the stage. The pantomime's performance no doubt helped Ovid to see metamorphosis—the instability of formal arrangements in the natural, social, and aesthetic spheres—as the constant but ever-shifting ground of his art. What he would do with it became his poem.

Works Cited

Galinsky, Karl. *Augustan Culture: An Interpretive Introduction*. Princeton: Princeton UP, 1996.

Lada-Richards, Ismene. *Silent Eloquence: Lucian and Pantomime Dancing*. London: Duckworth, 2007.

Lucian of Samosata. *Lucian, Volume V*. Trans. A. M. Harmon, Loeb Classical Library, Cambridge: Harvard UP, 1936–37.

Solodow, Joseph B. *The World of Ovid's* Metamorphoses. Chapel Hill: U of North Carolina P, 1988.

CRITICISM

J. W. MACKAIL

[A Work of Such Wide Importance]†

Interspersed in the *Art of Love* are a number of stories from the old mythology, introduced to illustrate the argument, but set out at greater length than was necessary for that purpose, from the active pleasure it always gives Ovid to tell a story. When he conceived the plan of his *Metamorphoses*, he had recognised this narrative instinct as his special gift. His tragedy of *Medea* had remained a single effort in dramatic form, unless the *Heroides* can be classed as dramatic monologues. The *Medea*, but for two fine single lines, is lost; but all the evidence is clear that Ovid had no natural turn for dramatic writing, and that it was merely a clever *tour de force*. In the idea of the *Metamorphoses* he found a subject, already treated in more than one Alexandrian poem, that gave full scope for his narrative gift and his fertile ingenuity. The result was a poem as long, and almost as unflagging, as the *Odyssey*. A vast mass of multifarious stories, whose only connection is the casual fact of their involving or alluding to some transformation of human beings into stones, trees, plants, beasts, birds, and the like, is cast into a continuous narrative. The adroitness with which this is done makes the poem rank as a master-piece of construction. The atmosphere of romantic fable in which it is enveloped even gives it a certain plausibility of effect almost amounting to epic unity. In the fabulous superhuman element that appears in all the stories, and in their natural surroundings of wood, or mountain, or sea—always realised with fresh enjoyment and vivid form and colour—there is something which gives the same sort of unity of effect as we feel in reading the *Arabian Nights*. It is not a real world; it is hardly even a world conceived as real; but it is a world so plausible, so directly appealing to simple instincts and unclouded senses, above all so completely taken for granted, that the illusion is, for the time, all but complete. For later ages, the *Metamorphoses* became the great text-book of classical mythology; the legends were understood as Ovid had told them, and were repro-duced (as, for instance, throughout the whole of the painting of the Renaissance) in the spirit and colour of this Italian story-teller.

For the metre of the *Metamorphoses* Ovid chose the heroic hexame-ter, but used it in a strikingly new and original way. He makes no attempt, as later poets unsuccessfully did, at reproducing the richness

† From Mackail, *Latin Literature* (London: J. Murray, 1895).

of tone and intricacy of modulation which it had in the hands of Virgil. Ovid's hexameter is a thing of his own. It becomes with him almost a new metre—light, brilliant, and rapid, but with some monotony of cadence, and without the deep swell that it had, not in Virgil only, but in his predecessors. The swift, equable movement is admirably adapted to the matter of the poem, smoothing over the transitions from story to story, and never allowing a story to pause or flag halfway. Within its limits, the workmanship is faultless. The style neither rises nor sinks with the variation of subject. One might almost say that it was without moral quality. Ovid narrates the treachery of Scylla or the incestuous passion of Myrrha with the same light and secure touch as he applies to the charming idyl of Baucis and Philemon or the love-tale of Pyramus and Thisbe; his interest is in what happened, in the story for the story's sake. So, likewise, in the rhetorical evolution of his thought, and the management of his metre, he writes simply as the artist, with the artistic conscience as his only rule. The rhetorician is as strong in him as it had been in the *Amores*; but it is under better control, and seldom leads him into excesses of bad taste, nor is it so overmastering as not to allow free play to his better qualities, his kind-liness, his good-humour, his ungrudging appreciation of excellence. In his evolution of thought—or his play of fancy, if the expression be preferred—he has an alertness and precision akin to great intellectual qualities; and it is this, perhaps, which has made him a favourite with so many great men of letters. Shakespeare himself, in his earlier work, alike the plays and the poems, writes in the Ovidian manner, and often in what might be direct imitation of Ovid; the motto from the *Amores* prefixed to the *Venus and Adonis* is not idly chosen. Still more remark-able, because less superficially evident, is the affinity between Ovid and Milton. At first sight no two poets, perhaps, could seem less alike. But it is known that Ovid was one of Milton's favourite poets; and if one reads the *Metamorphoses* with an eye kept on *Paradise Lost*, the intellectual resemblance, in the manner of treatment of thought and language, is abundantly evident, as well in the general structure of their rhetoric as in the lapses of taste and obstinate puerilities (*non ignoravit vitia sua sed amavit* might be said of Milton also), which come from time to time in their maturest work.

The *Metamorphoses* was regarded by Ovid himself as his master-piece. In the first impulse of his despair at leaving Rome, he burned his own copy of the still incomplete poem. But other copies were in existence; and though he writes afterwards as though it had been published without his correction and without his consent, we may suspect that it was neither without his knowledge nor against his will; when he speaks of the *manus ultima* as wanting, it is probably a mere piece of harmless affectation to make himself seem like the author of the *Aeneid*.

The actual achievement of Ovid was to perfect and popularise a poetical form of unusual scope and flexibility; to throw a vivid and lasting life into the world of Graeco-Roman mythology; and, above all, to complete the work of Cicero and Horace in fixing a certain ideal of civilised manners for the Latin Empire and for modern Europe. He was not a poet of the first order; yet few poets of the first order have done a work of such wide importance.

DIANE MIDDLEBROOK

A Roman in His Prime[†]

20 March A.D. 4, aet. 46

Even before the sun begins to draw its first bright lines across the temple facades at the summit of the Capitoline Hill, a torch's light falls between the columns of a portico at the back of a handsome family home in a nearby street.[1] In single file, members of the household emerge from under the portico and walk slowly across their garden toward a small altar, dimly visible in the pre-dawn light. At the head of the procession, swathed in white, is the poet Publius Ovidius Naso: a short, slight man who moves with easy dignity in the voluminous toga that he has drawn up over his head to cover his dark hair and shield his eyes from distractions. This is his forty-sixth birthday, 20 March in the year 4. Behind him, dressed in woolen finery,[2] is the young wife he married a year ago, and behind her, his stepdaughter, ten years old, cloaked against the chilly damp of early spring. Maintaining a deferential separation from the family group, household slaves carry the equipment for a birthday ritual: a plate of warm cakes covered with a cloth, a pitcher of honey, a small precious box of saffron, a silver libation bowl filled with wine. Well to the rear is one who expertly brandishes a flaming torch, feeding it with air.

Roman citizenship under Augustus has turned many old customs into required religious observances. The birthday of the Roman paterfamilias is one of them, and Ovid's household has made extensive preparation. Much earlier that morning, the slaves had been out clipping long-stemmed blossoms from the garden, by torchlight. They have braided

---

† Copyright © 2009 by the Estate of Diane Middlebrook. Reprinted by permission of Georges Borchardt, Inc.

1. Recalling his last night in Rome, Ovid describes his house as adjoining the buildings on the Capitoline Hill: *"hanc ego suspiciens et ad hanc Capitolia cernens / quae nostro frustra iuncta fuere Lari"* (*Tristia*, hereafter referred to as "T," 1.3.29–30 in A. L. Wheeler, trans. *Ovid, VI, Tristia. Ex Ponto*, rev. G. P. Goold [Cambridge: Harvard UP, 1996]).

2. Ovid, *Ars Amatoria* 3.179–80.

flowers and foliage into fragrant garlands and draped them around the tufa altar that stands before a painted niche in the garden wall. On the altar platform, faggots and scraps of tinder stand ready to be set ablaze.

Arriving at this altar, Ovid gestures for the torch, and as he lights the tinder, the painting in the garden niche springs to life: an image of two dancing youths—the household Lares—flanking the figure of a man togaed and veiled like Ovid himself, but accompanied by guardian serpents.[3] *This is an artist's rendering of a* genius natalis, *the god who protects the fertility, the continuity, of the family,*[4] *and Ovid now reenacts the ritual he learned by watching his father perform it year after year in his rural childhood home.*[5] *Casting saffron on the fire he summons and praises the Genius in the ceremonial language sanctioned by tradition, while the flame fattens and crackles, and a rich scent rises from the altar. Then Ovid lifts the god's portion from the warm plate of cake, drizzles it with yet more honey, and lays pieces on the fire. While the flames lick at the offering, he petitions the Genius to keep all of the members of his household at peace with one another and safe from every kind of harm. Now he tilts the libation bowl over the fire, and as the wine hisses, the coiling smoke wavers, hesitates, and finds an updraft: it streams straight toward the morning stars that watched over his birth forty-six years ago. Ovid completes his prayer with a phrase that just might be a joke about the god's nose. The precociously clever little girl laughs, as she was meant to do. Ovid hands around the remaining honeycakes, while the first light of dawn streaks the sky overhead. This has been the best year of his life.*

3. The iconography of the Lares and the Genius is described and illustrated in David Orr, "Roman Domestic Religion: The Evidence of the Household Shrines," in *Aufstieg und Niedergang der Romischen Welt: Geschichte und Kultur Roms im Spiegel der neueren Forschung.* Vol. II, ed. Hildegarde Temporini and Wolfgang Haase (Berlin: Walter De Gruyter & Co., 1978), 1557–91. Though Orr's examples are taken from houses in Pompeii, he quotes Ovid on the costuming of the Lar (*"libate dapes, ut, grati pignus honoris / nutriat incinctos missa patella Lares,"* Fasti 2.633–4), which suggests a consistency of representation between Rome in Ovid's time and the houses of Campania.
4. "The origins of the cult of the Genius are shrouded in the mists of time, but there is no doubt that the Genius is one of the oldest features of Roman religion, related to the words *gignere* and *gens.* Whether it represents the divine embodiment of a man's power to beget, or whether it is the spirit that begat a person, is disputed. In its enlarged sense it stands for the sum of one's vitality, energy, and capability of enjoyment, in short for his personality and his higher, inner self" (Michael Speidel and Alexandra Dimitrova-Milčeva, "The Cult of the Genii in the Roman Army and a New Military Deity," in *Aufstieg und Niedergang der Romischen Welt,* 1543).
5. That Ovid was accustomed to conducting the traditional birthday ritual, we know from poems he wrote in exile on the Black Sea. On one of his birthdays, he addresses his *genius natalis* scornfully: "Thou awaitest, I suppose, thine honour in its wonted guise: a white robe hanging from my shoulders, a smoking altar garlanded with chaplets, the grains of incense snapping in the holy fire, and myself offering the cakes that mark my birthday and framing kindly petitions with pious lips." Ovid, T 3.13.13–18, Loeb 151.

Ovid, born in 43 B.C., was passing a civic milestone on this forty-sixth birthday. As a high-caste Roman with voting rights, he had now attained official seniority as a citizen; henceforth he would be exempt from certain duties he owed the state.[6] But Ovid had also passed a number of personal milestones in recent years,[7] as it is possible to deduce from his poetry. The classicist Peter Green, who spent a lifetime working on Ovid's texts, has been able to tease a complete account of Ovid's life out of the briefest of comments and asides in Ovid's writing. According to Green's calculations, the death of Ovid's father occurred around the year 1 A.D., and made Ovid a wealthy man: he was the only heir to the family estate, his older brother having died at age twenty. The death of his father also appears to have provided psychological release to Ovid, along with the security of wealth. He ended a gadabout bachelor life, and married for the third time. Ovid had married for the first time when he was around sixteen years old, an unsuccessful match that apparently ended in divorce. He waited about a decade to marry his second wife,[8] who apparently died fairly young, and bore him a daughter who had married young, and now lived abroad with her husband and children—the continuity of his family had been secured. Ovid's third wife was possibly in her early twenties when they married, Green estimates, and the many verses in which he addresses her from exile suggest that she was an ideal companion, deeply loved. Her name does not appear in his poetry, but he does tell us a good deal about her social affiliations, and we can observe that Ovid had married up. His wife was in some way attached to the household of a wealthy aristocrat named Paullus Fabius Maximus, an intimate of Augustus and a patron of the arts. She also endowed his life with the lively-minded stepdaughter that Ovid would call Perilla in his poems from exile.

The extraordinary happiness of Ovid's private life in the year 4 was matched by, even surpassed by, extraordinary fame. He was far and away the best known and most admired poet in Rome.[9]

Ovid had made his name by writing love poetry, beginning while he was still in his teens: a series of books of loosely linked poems that explored various aspects of romantic and sexual passion, written in the first person. *Amores*—on falling in love—was followed by

---

6. "At forty-six a man ceased to be a 'junior' when voting in the centuries at elections and became a 'senior,' and this normally signified the end of his liability for military service, though he might still be called up to serve up to the age of fifty. At sixty he was exempt from jury service" (J. P. V. D. Balsdon, *Life and Leisure in Ancient Rome* [New York: McGraw-Hill, 1969], 169; citing Livy).
7. For this and the other details about Ovid's biography in this paragraph, I am indebted to the work of Peter Green. See his "Introduction" in *Ovid: The Erotic Poems* (New York: Penguin, 1982), esp. 36–44.
8. Green, 30.
9. "Feted and continuously successful for almost thirty years, Ovid had been without a rival since the death of Horace." Denis Feeney, "I Shall Be Read," *London Review of Books* 17 August 2006, 13.

Ars Amatoria, a witty seduction manual, and by *Remedia Amoris*, on curing oneself of love: all delivered in the voice of a witty, sophisticated narrator; and *Heroides*, a collection of verse epistles in the voices of women famously abandoned by their lovers. But Roman literary culture classified poetry in a well-differentiated hierarchy according to subject matter and meter, and on both counts, love occupied a middling position. So Ovid's several books of love elegies, brilliant and accomplished as they were, ranked by genre far below the most important poem yet written by a Roman: the *Aeneid* of Virgil, the epic narrative based on the legendary military history of the founding of Rome. Virgil's epic, completed the year of his death in 19 B.C., now stood among the glories of literature, proving that Rome had at last matured as a culture (always, the point of comparison was Greek culture). Moreover, the *Aeneid* achieved a significant political aim. It made a coherent account of Rome's destiny as the civilization built on the ruins of the Trojan War, and its action culminated in a prophetic affirmation of the present regime in Rome, in which Augustus, the adopted heir of Julius Caesar, had finally ended the civil wars and brought lasting peace and prosperity.

But Ovid had confidence in his own powers and in his own point of view, which was deeply opposed to every kind of militarism. Now a mature man in complete command of his talent, he had conceived of not one but *two* ambitious works in which he was attempting to change the way Romans might think about their history without glorifying military combat and victory. One was, inevitably, an epic. It was titled *Metamorphoses*, and its general subject was the transformation of human beings by the will of the gods. The other poem, *Fasti*, was an exposition of Roman beliefs and religious practices structured on the Roman calendar of festivals. Both poems made innovative use of established literary forms, by applying them to the "wrong" subject matter: *Metamorphoses* was an epic without a hero;[1] *Fasti* was a quasi-didactic poem written in elegiac meters—the medium of love poetry. Threaded into each was a cleverly deployed insistence that love,[2] not war, was the great enterprise of human

---

1. Elaine Fantham lists Ovid's precedents: Naevius, *Punic War*; Ennius, *Annals*, both epics; and the Hellenistic miniature epic (*epyllion*) which often incorporated smaller tales as foil; she mentions examples by Catullus as well as lost poems by Ovid's friends Calvus and Cinna; a final model was Callimachus's collection "of short, allusive self-contained" poems arranged for balance and contrast. See *Ovid's Metamorphoses* (New York: Oxford UP, 2004), 6–7.
2. Regarding *Fasti*, see Barchiesi's reading of Book 4, the civilizing influence of Venus, which produced the first poem, a love song sung outside the closed door of a *puella* who had refused him (the genre is *paraklausithyron*). "Literature, and rhetoric too, originates from the situation of the *paraklausithyron* (love poem written outside the closed door of a woman who refuses the lover): and Venus is the goddess who has provided the necessary means and art. This is elegiac imperialism; the *paraklausithyron* and love poetry in general, the elegy, have been promoted to the rank of the initial stage of literature, and are traced back to Venus" (Alessandro Barchiesi, *The Poet and Prince: Ovid and Augustus*, U of California P, 1997, 58–59).

beings, from the very beginning of recorded time. And each contained a lively-minded narrator with a distinctive role to play in each of the poems.

Both of these projects were already well underway on that birthday morning, and we can reasonably assume that, once the birthday ritual was finished and the ritual clothing and objects laid away, Ovid devoted some time to working on these new poems, and that he returned to his garden to do so; it was his favorite place to write.[3]

Before he settles into his morning work, Ovid likes to make a propri-etary circuit of this garden. The early morning air is fresh and cool, an aid to deliberation. Ovid makes all of the decisions about this garden himself, and from the time he settled in his Roman house has been actively involved in its planning and cultivation.[4] Finding a position in which the necessary plants can flourish requires an intimate knowl-edge of every inch of the available ground; unlike the broad acres of his villa, where an orchard and a vineyard flourished in open fields, the city garden is a walled and porticoed extension of the house. Sun-light must be shrewdly deployed within this enclosure, which mea-sures nine meters at the back end, seven meters on the longer side.[5] The garden must supply food for the table, medicines for those who live and work in the house, and floral materials for the many domestic occasions on which garlands and chaplets are required. The challenge is to create a resource in which the beauty conceals the usefulness.

The most prominent feature in Ovid's garden is the wide circle of planting at its center, punctuated by a slow-trickling fountain attractive

---

3. In *Tristia* 1.11.35–44, Ovid says he is writing on the tossing deck of a ship, en route from Rome to his exile in Tomis, his "paper sprayed by the dark waters," and adds "kindly reader . . . grant me the more indulgence should these verses be—as they are—poorer than your hopes. They were not written, as of old, in my garden . . ." (*non haec in nostris, ut quondam, scripsimus hortis*). *Tristia* 4.8.25–27 again refers to his gardens: "T'were time for me to breathe no foreign air nor slake my parching thirst with Getic water, but now at my leisure to withdraw into the gardens I once had" (*sed modo, quos habui, vacuos secedere in hortos*).

4. Evidence for Ovid's active participation in gardening occurs in his memories of working on the grounds of his villa: " . . . *those gardens lying on the pine-clad hills which the Clo-dian and Flaminian roads survey—them I tilled for I know not whom, in them I used to guide (nor am I ashamed to say it) the spring water upon the plants; somewhere, if they still live, there are certain trees also planted by my hand," Ex Ponto* (hereafter "EP") 1.8.43–48, in Loeb, 309; also, he comments on his wish to have a plot of ground to till in exile: "*tis pleasant to spend one's time tilling the fields,"*EP 2.7.69.

5. I am basing this description of Ovid's garden and house, arbitrarily, on the plan of the Casa del Principe di Napoli in Pompeii, which is described in Andrew Wallace-Hadrill, *Houses and Society in Pompeii and Herculaneum*, 47–50, and Plate 5. The arrangement and distribution of rooms would ideally suit the poet's occupation; the size of the house, though on the small side (about 230 square meters, whereas a house of "medium" size would run 250–650 square meters [Pedar Foss, "Watchful Lares: Roman Household Organization and the Rituals of Cooking and Eating," in *Domestic Space in the Roman World: Pompeii and Beyond*, ed. Ray Laurence and Andrew Wallace-Hadrill [Portsmouth, RI: JRA, 1997], 207, 211]), has nine well-separated rooms with good sources of light; and the actual house in Pompeii has elegant decoration, suggesting habitation by a well-established owner.

to birds. The strongly-marked circular shape provides emphatic symmetry to a space that is surrounded by the somewhat haphazardly-shaped rooms of his house. On this early morning at the vernal equinox, strong light is just now edging down the columns of the portico; soon its warmth will release the fragrance of herbs growing in a corner plot where it captures the morning light and is shaded from the midday sun. This is where Ovid begins his inspection. Basil, marjoram, chives, and mint flourish amid lettuces and bristling leeks and newly-burgeoning fronds of fennel: the dinner salad will be harvested from this efficient little triangle of earth. He next turns his attention to the large glazed earthenware container positioned within sight of honored guests in the dining room that opens onto the portico. Ovid had chosen the planting for this ornamental basin himself, months ago, with early-blossoming annuals that were needed for the day's ceremonies. Hyacinths, anemones, narcissi will capture the light and rustle in the breeze of late afternoon, their vivid colors drawing the eyes of the diners, a few of whom will recognize that these blossoms are literary references, too: they are characters in Ovid's new poem, hapless victims of transformation by the callous gods. From other flower beds, less in sight, more of the same flowers will be plucked and braided with myrtle into chaplets for the dinner guests. And from the shadiest areas of ground, mint and ferns and verbena will be gathered and strewn on the dining room floor to be crushed by the diners' feet as they enter, mingling those delicate scents with the stronger notes of the diners' perfumes.[6]

Ovid steps back under the portico that separates the garden from the house, and runs a critical gaze along the newly-trimmed box hedge that gives sharp definition to the flower beds flanking the walls. Finally, he lets his eye linger on a shapely tree standing in an antique stone vessel at the tip of the circle, on an axis with the room that houses his library. This is his garden's most recent acquisition: a laurus nobilis, *its slim trunk as straight and smooth as the columns that form his portico, its crown a dense sphere of glossy leaves. For Ovid, the laurel is both a finishing touch in the garden he has been landscaping with deliberate care for several years, and a dramatic character in* Metamorphoses, *on which he is now ready to go to work. A wooden couch spread with rugs and cushions has been moved into position between columns of the portico, alongside a table piled with fresh wax tablets. He has been working on this story for several days, and new lines are already forming in his head as he settles into place and takes up his stylus.*

Ovid's epic poem *Metamorphoses* is highly entertaining, like the rest of his work. It ingeniously threads together hundreds of myths that

---

6. Andrew Dalby discusses the importance of "aromatics" in the Roman household, and as a particular feature of dining. See *Empire of Pleasures: Luxury and Indulgence in the Roman World* (London: Routledge, 2000), esp. 244–47.

tell of the ways the gods seize on the lives of human beings, and transform them. But it has quite a startling opening, for an epic poem:

> My spirit impels me to speak of bodies changed into new forms: gods, inspire my beginnings—for you have changed even those—and draw my song without breaks from the first beginning of the world to my own times.[7]

It is conventional for the epic poet to open with a greeting of his Muse—here, a brisk "gods, inspire my beginnings"—and then to announce the subject of the epic in twenty-five words or less, as Ovid does in these lines. However, "bodies changed into new forms" cannot by any stretch of the imagination qualify as an epic action. There is no plot—no historical conflict to be commemorated, no charismatic hero, no victories or defeats—just a rough timeline: from the beginning of the world until now. Moreover, Ovid was going to have to solve the problem of making a silk purse out of a literary ragbag: there are about 250 transformation tales in the completed *Metamorphoses*, some short, some very long.

Ovid's solution was to put the epic in the mouth of a strong, omnipresent narrator. He uses the opening of *Metamorphoses* to situate all of his audience—you, the gods; and you the reader—in our proper places vis-à-vis this storyteller. Ovid deferentially acknowledges that the gods are listening to this story; but its true audience is human beings. We are not immortal, and we live in bodies that are all too susceptible to transformation by influences beyond our control. We are subject to transforming accidents—such as inadvertently catching the eye of a god. And we are also changed incessantly from within, through processes that are entirely invisible to us. We grow up; some of us are deformed; others are host to alien life forms—diseases and disfiguring disorders of every kind; most of us grow old and lose our looks; all of us die. The narrator keeps all of these characteristics of the human audience in mind, and the audience of gods as well, and plays on the anxieties they prompt.

Incessant resourcefulness is the heroic characteristic in this narrator. He presents himself in the first-person at the very beginning of the poem and remains a lively presence throughout: signposting, taking sides, cautioning, drawing back in dismay, and generally keeping us aware that there is, ultimately, a single teller of all these tales. He frequently appears at the point where one tale ends and another begins. An example occurs in "Diana and Actaeon," in

---

7. *Metamorphoses* 1.1–4. This clumsy translation captures the inflection of the gods' intervention on *Ovid's* beginnings, which is emphasized in recent criticism. Translation by Andrew Feldherr, "Metamorphosis in the *Metamorphoses*," in *The Cambridge Companion to Ovid*, ed. Philip Hardie (Cambridge UP, 2002), 164.

which the princely hunter comes upon the grotto where the goddess retreats from the hunt to bathe with her band of nymphs. Actaeon sees Diana naked, and she punishes him by transforming him into a stag. He is chased down and killed by his own hunting dogs. The narrator introduces this tale with solemn moralizing:

> Of a surety man's last day must ever be awaited, and none be counted happy till his death, till his last funeral rites are paid.

Yet at the end of the tale, the narrator comments that news of Actaeon's fate aroused conflicting attitudes in the hearers:

> Common talk wavered this way and that: to some the goddess seemed more cruel than just; others called her act worthy of her austere virginity; both sides found good reasons for their judgment.[8]

Both the narrator's introduction and the views expressed by "common talk" are given three lines each: the narrator may try to contain the story's power within a narrative chain of explanatory connections, but the action told will always take hold in imaginations prepared to defend positions that differ from his own.

The poem's powerful immediacy flows from the existential predicament of this narrator: the gods may or may not help; it will be human ingenuity alone that enables him to arrive at "my own times." This phrase gives away a subtle feature of the poem's ambitiousness. By that phrase (*ad mea tempora*) Ovid cleverly includes the Now of both the writing and of the reading: the moment of the encounter of the eyes with this phrase, on whatever day of whatever year it occurs.

Given the scope of Ovid's ambition, it would have been perfectly fitting, on this significant birthday in his life, for him to spend the morning hours putting the finishing touches on one of the internal masterpieces of *Metamorphoses*, the tale of Phoebus Apollo and Daphne.

> Now, the first love of Phoebus was Daphne, daughter of Peneus, the river-god. It was no blind chance that gave this love, but the malicious wrath of Cupid . . .

This story is ostensibly about the origin of the laurel wreath that was awarded to winners of the Pythian games in ancient days: an athletic competition among the Greeks, known to Roman antiquarians; the games were dedicated to Apollo. Ovid explains this background in the overture to this tale:

> At these games, every youth who had been victorious in boxing, running, or the chariot-race received the honor of an oaken

8. *Metamorphoses* 3.135–37, 253–55.

garland. For as yet the laurel-tree was not, and Phoebus was wont to wreathe his temples, comely with flowing locks, with a garland from any tree.[9]

Otherwise, Ovid makes little use of any previous literary or cultural tradition in shaping this story: it is entirely his invention.[1] The tale is set on the slopes of Parnassus. Apollo—an adolescent in the story—is bragging to Cupid about his expertise with the bow and arrow. Cupid decides to teach him a lesson. He flies to the peak of Parnassus and shoots Apollo with a gold-tipped arrow that condemns Apollo to fall helplessly in love. Then Cupid shoots a leaden arrow into a young nymph named Daphne, who is roving the woods nearby, snaring game; the leaden arrow repulses love.

Apollo, who has never been in love, is enflamed by the sight of Daphne and attempts to chase her down, comically appealing to her better judgment: "You don't know who you are running from," he tells her, listing all the attributes and powers and geographical locations that would be associated with Apollo—and, seemingly, discovering them himself as he enumerates them. But Daphne flees from Apollo, paying no attention to his eloquence. By the time they reach the river Peneus, Apollo is closing in. Daphne, who is the daughter of the river's god, throws up her arms, pleading that her father Peneus release her from the beauty that has caused Apollo's lust. She changes into a laurel tree just as Apollo's hands reach her breasts: he can feel her heart pounding under the bark. Stymied in his desire for consummation, Apollo attains her for another purpose:

> Since you cannot be my wife, you will be my tree: there will always be you on my hair, you on my lyres, you, laurel, on my quivers . . . and as my head is youthful, my hair unshorn, you too be always dressed in a perpetual glory of leaves.[2]

Stirred to motion, Daphne, now voiceless, seems to nod her assent.

A plot outline cannot do justice to the psychological acuity of the telling of this tale, in which Ovid provides a psychosocial frame for Apollo's development into the god of lyric poetry. It requires four points of view: the naïve boy, Apollo, just coming into sexual awareness; the slightly older boy, Cupid, who instigates Apollo's sexual initiation by playing a brutally competitive practical joke; the inno-

---

9. *Metamorphoses* 1.452–54, 448–51.
1. According to William S. Anderson's commentary on *Metamorphoses*, "This highly polished story is essentially Ovid's free invention . . . Earlier versions of Apollo's love for Daphne existed, but they seem to have been late Hellenistic creations, and they were set in the area of Laconia in the Peloponnesus, not in Thessaly. *Parthenius* 15 summarizes their narratives, which differed substantially, in detail, theme, and tone from the account here produced. Ovid uses Apollo to develop a thematic representation of male erotic desire, an obviously flawed kind of love." See Anderson, 190.
2. *Metamorphoses* 1.557–58; translation adapted from Rolfe Humphries.

cent bystander, Daphne, who remains unknowable to Apollo; and the omniscient narrator, who can read the minds of all the others. Most significantly, this narrator gives us a good deal of information about Daphne: especially about her relationship to an indulgent father, and about her desire not to become a wife, not ever.

Most prominent in the psychological complexity of this story is the triumphalism of young Apollo, his claim that the transformation of Daphne into a tree would make her "ever green"—immortal.

> Phoebus loved her in this form too and, with his right hand
>   upon her trunk,
> felt her breast still trembling under the new grown bark,
> and, putting his arms around her branches as if they were
>   her limbs,
> he gave his kisses to the wood; but the wood shrank from
>   the kisses.
> The god responded, 'But, since you cannot be my wife,
> you will at least be my tree. There will always be
> you on my hair, you on my lyres, you, laurel, on my quivers.
> You will be present for the Latin leaders, when the joyful cry
> proclaims the Triumph and the Capitol beholds the long
>   procession.
> At Augustus' porch too, a most faithful guardian
> before the doors will you stand and behold the oak between,
> and, as my head is youthful, my hair unshorn,
> you too be always dressed in a perpetual glory of leaves.'
> Paean had finished; the laurel assented with her branches
> that had just been made, and seemed to nod her top like a head.[3]

The story does not blame Apollo for the callow self-aggrandizement in these lines; it understands him. "Apollo and Daphne" shows us a boy discovering through feeling and action his own powers—then finding words for them, beginning with his boast of prowess with the bow. The stakes are higher than Apollo knows, for Cupid is slightly older and already practiced in malice. That is fitting: Apollo's challenger should have hidden strengths because Apollo needs to discover rather than exercise his developmentally empowered gifts. Cupid says "maybe" Apollo's powers are greater than his own, then smites Apollo with unrequitable desire. This is, paradoxically, exactly the condition which enables Apollo to outgrow being a mere braggart, and become a poet. Attempting to convince Daphne that she doesn't know who she is running away from, he enumerates the

---

3. *Metamorphoses* I, trans D. E. Hill (Wiltshire: Aris & Phillips, 1985).

elements of his divine patrimony, and as he does so moves toward the rhetoric of command. In the brief course of the story, he acquires the power of turning feelings into words, and also acquires mastery of the full range of what words can do. His words have no power whatsoever over the heart and mind of Daphne, however. His is the power of art, which he begins to exercise after losing her. She has already been turned into a tree when he turns her into a metaphor, and thus possesses her forever.

The narrator gives us insight into the other hearts and minds in this story, too. Cupid, though he plays only a small role, is an important god: the son of Venus, her agent in the world of nature, his "arrow" is the instinct of lust. But in this story he is first and foremost the competitive adolescent male. He already knows a lot about sex, and Apollo doesn't (or so we gather from the opening lines of the tale: "The first love of Phoebus Apollo was Daphne"). Cupid means to infatuate Apollo and thus win the glory of possessing the stronger bow and arrow—the reader can easily find a phallic symbolism here. And it takes a competitive young male to test another competitive young male.

> The son of Venus said to [Apollo], 'Let your bow, Phoebus, pierce all,
> mine shall pierce you; and, by how much all creatures yield to god, by so much is your glory less than mine.'
> He spoke and after forcing through the air with beating wings eagerly settled on Parnassus' shadowy peak
> and from his arrow-bearing quiver plucked two shafts of opposite effects; one routs love, the other brings it on.
> Golden is the one that brings love and gleams at its sharp tip;
> blunt is the one that routs love and has, under its reed stem, lead.
> This one the god fixed in the Peneid nymph, but with the other he drove through Apollo's bones, wounding him to the marrow.

And at the center of the story is Daphne herself, struggling with an inner life uncomprehended by all of the males in the story, except the narrator. Daphne wishes to have no lover, wishes not to enter into her heterosexuality, which is to say, to give up to a male her reproductive capacities. It is what her father wants from her; but if she stays infantile she will not have to hand it over on his behalf. She too discovers something in the chase: the desirability of her body. That is what she wants to give up. She can never give up her subjectivity; as it is swallowed up by the bark we are made to understand that an interior life continues in the tree, silent except for the power of its gestures: the ambiguous sighing of its leaves as the wind moves its branches.

Finally, there is the point of view of Peneus, Daphne's father. The death or loss of a young person produces a different kind of grief from that of the loss of an older person, and that dimension is given its emotional weight by the thunder of the waterfall in the heart, so to speak, of another god, Daphne's father. The "constant roar . . . returned from the distance" is the last sound we hear from the story, the wordless but expressive response to his daughter's loss, the ironic counterpart to the fluency in which the young Apollo revels.

In addition to the psychology of the characters, "Apollo and Daphne" contains an account of the psychology of the lyric poem as a genre in Western literature: a genre that is essentially commemorative, the art made necessary by the human experience of loss. "Apollo and Daphne" is the only one of Ovid's tales in which a god is shown to have a developmental history comparable to that of a human being. Apollo displays that development in the increasing maturity of his command of language. At the outset, he is a boy-god acquiring mastery of his powers, and he brags. Chasing Daphne while he pours his heart out, his rhetoric grows increasingly sophisticated. Finally, unable to possess her in any other way, Apollo makes a godlike command: let the laurel be my tree. In effect, Apollo puts Daphne through yet another metamorphosis, from tree into poetic symbolism. "My hair, my lyres, my quiver will always hold you," he tells her. It is a radiantly expressive chain of associations, transferring his arousal by Daphne from the hairs on his body to the strings on his lyre, and keeping the power of love's influence on him always ready at hand in his quiver.

One implication of this tale is that even an immortal god would have to undergo these particular kinds of pain—longing, rejection, abandonment—to become the god of poetry. At that final moment in the story Ovid applies to Apollo the epithet *Paean*, which is the name associated with Apollo's powers as a healer, but it also the term for a mode of song: a victory chant of joy and triumph. Making the *paean* in his final lines, we might say, is an act of sublimation in which Apollo's frustrated desire is driven upward into formal beauty, and the lost body of the girl is fixed forever in a generic form—this line in *Metamorphoses* is the source of Petrarch's name for the idealized lady in his sonnets, Laura. And not the least interesting thing about the tale of Apollo and Daphne is that last glimpse Ovid gives us of the silenced woman, whose leafy head nods in a movement that the god interprets as compliance. When she has been transferred from life into emblem she speaks no more in her own person.

It is not difficult to see that this story is at least partly shaped by an autobiographical retrospect. Apollo in this tale is the prototype of the kind of poet, and possibly the kind of young man, that Ovid became in his youth, a sexual swordsman and celebrant of love. But

Apollo is too young to understand everything the poem understands about the violent male drive, and the frustration of that drive, both of which lie behind the evolution of elegiac verse. The metamorphosis of Apollo is Ovid's complex tribute to the tradition of poetry-making which was his chosen mode of participating in the work of civilization: writing the poetry of love, not war. But in Ovid's life, writing love elegy was only the beginning of the career that had led, in middle age, to the work of *Metamorphoses*.

Yet how does the writing of such a poem, impressive as its artfulness may be, constitute an act of political resistance? To answer that question, we have to take a sidestep into *Fasti*, the other poem Ovid may have been working on in his garden that morning, and take a look at the vegetation.

By the time Ovid was writing *Metamorphoses* and *Fasti*, Augustus had been emperor for more than twenty years, and Ovid's world was thronged with images saturated by Augustan propaganda. Both of Ovid's projects, it may be speculated, had the aim of picking the locks on official symbolisms, and letting the imprisoned complexity escape back into the social world where ideas were exchanged and new meanings made. Ovid accomplished this by situating both poems in an irreducibly subjective framework — the mind of an individual who is curious about what went *before*.

In *Fasti*, this artistic aim is overt. *Fasti* was a general name for feast days in the Roman calendar which perpetuated the old Roman religion. One of the earliest moves Augustus had made as *princeps* was the "restoration" of religious priesthoods that had fallen into disuse. This policy had a political basis: appointing priests from among the now disenfranchised patricians—and inventing new priesthoods to multiply the opportunities for appointment—helped salvage their social standing, while providing Augustus with what one skeptical scholar has labeled "advertising." The *nobiles* "were now brigaded for public pageantry. Wearing their vestments and emblems, the priests went on parade. They offered vows and sacrifices, inaugurated the monuments of war and peace, advertised the prince and his dynasty." The *nobiles* complied with pleasure; togas were the apparel required of public servants within the precincts of Rome; the priests alone were now permitted to break the rule against wearing uniforms or other regalia. "To belong to an exclusive club confers value on a life devoid of talent or denied public recognition; and it is pure delight when membership brings arcane knowledge."[4] Moreover, This was the political environment within which Ovid undertook to write the poem he titled *Fasti*. Ovid had collected an enormous database of scholarly references to the ancient Roman cults that were currently being repackaged for public

4. Ronald Syme, *The Augustan Aristocracy* (New York: Oxford UP, 1986), 6.

consumption, by imperial decree, in the name of "reconstituting" the "old ways" of Roman life. The archival sources Ovid consulted were prodigious, and mainly dry as dust. As a way of dramatizing his material, Ovid sets himself up in *Fasti* as a kind of investigative journalist, who, in the interest of fact-checking, closes his books and goes straight to the most authoritative sources: the gods themselves. This narrator is an entirely different kind of personality from the speaker in *Metamorphoses*—shamelessly nosy, a bit naïve, tiresomely persistent, often on the verge of going too far. Ovid establishes this character immediately, in his poem for the first day of January:

> With notebook in hand I was pondering these topics
>   When my house seemed brighter than a moment before.
> Then holy Janus, an amazing sight with those two heads,
>   Suddenly met me face to face.
> Frightened out of my wits, I felt my hair stand on end
>   And suddenly an icy chill gripped my heart.
> With a staff in his right hand, and a key in his left, the god
>   Uttered these words with his forward mouth:
> Don't be afraid, illustrious poet of the calendar; learn
>   What you want, and take my words to heart.[5]

God of doorways, Janus faces both forward and backward. Ovid makes cartoonish comedy out of this peculiar arrangement. Presumably, Janus speaks from his "forward" mouth because he wishes to set the record straight, for posterity. The god is gruff and plain-spoken, as befits an old-timer, but patient, too, and the interview gets Ovid's project off to a good start. The past is hard to exhume—it exists in rumors and legends and partial works of history; and most Romans do not occupy themselves, as Ovid does, by spending long hours in libraries almost every day, reading old books. Instead, Romans are now being rallied to patriotic piety by streamlined teaching stories about founding fathers who have been elevated into divinity; stories, moreover, that point to all of Roman history as culminating in the fortunes of the current Emperor.

Ovid's ingenious self-presentation in *Fasti* as a self-appointed investigator is an oblique challenge to this imperial narrative. The gods he interviews are, amusingly, aware of his "illustrious" reputation as a writer, and don't mind granting him the interview he seeks—canny celebrities themselves, each sees the advantage in serving as a source for his ambitious project.

---

5. Betty Rose Nagle, trans., *Ovid's Fasti: Roman Holidays* (Bloomington: Indiana UP, 1995), 1.93–102.

The most significant of these interviews, for our purposes, occurs at the opening of April, the month associated with Venus. Ovid greets the presiding goddess like an old friend: "Kindly mother of love, requited or slighted, indulge me." Indeed, she knows him well.

> She turned her face in this poet's direction.
> "What do you want with me? Surely you were singing a
>   grander song.
> Have you got that old wound in your sensitive heart?"

No, he hasn't fallen in love again, Ovid explains; but yes, as a matter of fact he does have a new project, "a grander song," one that he associates with his maturity:

> In my earlier years, as was proper, I dallied innocently;
>   Now my horses are running on a bigger track.

Venus gives her blessing, in effect crowning him with foliage from the tree sacred to herself:

> Stirred by this, she gently touched my temples with myrtle
>   From Cythera, and said, "Complete the work you've begun."[6]

As we have seen in "Apollo and Daphne," the wreath conventionally associated with the god of poetry, and thus with poetry itself, is the laurel.[7] But, Ovid tells us in *Metamorphoses*, that was because Apollo himself began appropriating the laurel as a symbol of victory, on the day he failed to win Daphne; *Fasti*, along with *Metamorphoses*, looks back to those days before the laurel *belonged* to Apollo. The inquiring narrator acquires his information from Janus, who recalls the time before Rome became an empire, and foreign incense began to be imported for use in religious rituals. In the good old days, Janus tells him,

> "Altars were content to give off smoke from Sabine juniper,
>   And laurel crackled loudly as it burned.
> Whoever had violets to weave in a garland of meadow
>   Wildflowers, that was a wealthy man."[8]

---

6. *Fasti* 4.1–18.
7. This act of blessing resonates with an earlier passage in Ovid's poetry: the end of *Amores*, Book 1. Finishing this, his inaugural book, in a gust of self-congratulation, Ovid preens himself on having become a poet rather than a lawyer or a politician: "What I seek is perennial fame, / Undying world-wide remembrance . . . To me may golden Apollo proffer a cup, brimming over, from the Castalian spring / And a wreath of sun-loving myrtle."
8. *Fasti* 1.343–346.

The use of laurel in ceremonies, that is, dated back to Roman pre-history. And laurel trees had stood since time immemorial at the entrances to such archaic shrines as the Temple of Vesta and the Regia, the historic home of Roman kings, and later at the office of the *pontifex maximus*, the chief priest of Rome. It was customary to replace these prestigious trees annually, at the beginning of the new year.[9]

Under the Augustan Principate, the ancient symbolisms of the laurel tree, along with the symbolisms of oak, were being absorbed into the iconography of the emperor himself. When Octavian received the title "Augustus" from the Senate in 27 B.C. in recognition of his service to the state in ending the civil wars, a pair of laurel trees were planted at the entrance to *his* official home, and an oak wreath—a military honor traditionally awarded for rescuing a fellow citizen or a comrade in battle[1]—was hung above the door. According to the archeologist Paul Zanker, those venerable symbols soon became a kind of logo for Augustus. The "pointy, sharp-edged leaves, so ideally suited to ornamental fantasies, sprouted all over the place—from coins and architectural decoration to small painted panels with bucolic scenes. . . . laurel and oak leaves became widely understood as synonyms for 'Augustus' and gradually lost their original meaning."[2]

So when Ovid undertook to write his commentaries in *Fasti* on the ancient vegetation used in sacrifices, or on the affiliation of newly-planted laurel trees with the most sacred institutions in Roman life, his decisions must be seen partly as an effort to exert a counter-pressure against the overwhelming pressure of imperial iconography. That is why the gesture he attributes to Venus, when she brushes his temples with myrtle, can be viewed as a significant signal to the reader. The term *tempora* has two meanings: not only the *temples* of the head in which Ovid is shaping the poem, but the *times* in which he lives while writing it.[3] Venus was explicitly the Muse of Ovid's youthful poetry. Now that he has outgrown that phase of his

---

9. Under the old Roman calendar, which was revised by Julius Caesar, the year began in March, as Ovid reminds in *Fasti*: "To convince yourself that the Kalends of March was once New Year's Day, / you can turn your attention to the following evidence. / The laurel which has stayed a full year by the flamens' houses / is removed, and new foliage is highly regarded. / Then the king-priest's door is green when Apollo's tree is replaced. / The same happens at the door of the old ward-hall. / So that Vesta too may shine decked with fresh leaves, / The gray laurel withdraws from her Trojan hearth." *Fasti* 3.135–42.

1. Zanker (see next note) says comrade (93). Adkins says citizen. (Lesley and Roy A. Adkins, *Handbook to Life in Ancient Rome* [New York: Oxford UP, 1998], 91.)

2. Paul Zanker, *The Power of Images in the Age of Augustus*, trans. Alan Shapiro (Ann Arbor: U of Michigan P, 1990), 94.

3. *Tempora cum causis Latium digesta per annum . . . canam*, "The dates—and their origins—arranged through the Latin year . . . of that I'll sing." Nagle trans. "*Tempora*" is also the first word in the *Fasti*, where it means time itself as the Romans experience it, organized in distinctive ways. See Barchiesi, *Poet and Prince*, 58.

creative life, he sees her authority as different—wiser, more generous—from what he imagined earlier. And, he says, she has lent that
authority of her inspiration to the "grander song" of his maturity, in
which "my horses are running on a bigger track." His epic, *Metamorphoses*, he means, written in a meter which has more syllables than
the elegiac verse in which *Fasti* is composed (and thus occupies a
wider "track" on the scroll). But he also appears to mean that the
goddess of love blesses the ambitious agenda of both *Metamorphoses*
and *Fasti*, poems of resistance to the military ethos of Rome.

Ovid's departures from the best-known sources in "Apollo and
Daphne,"[4] for example, sharpen the focus of political implications
embedded in the poem, by weighting the image of Apollo with
youthful brashness, and with desire to acclaim his power through a
symbolism of unearned self-importance: Apollo binds his own head
with laurel once he gains the insight that he can make a song out of
Daphne, though the girl is gone for good. However, the governing
point of view in the story is not the god's but the poet's, and *his*
temples—we can reasonably infer—are wreathed with myrtle.
"Apollo and Daphne" is quite evidently a keynote poem in *Metamorphoses*, written by a poet who has outgrown the game of sexual conquest: an account of how, in a civilized world, poetry is the art
motivated by love and created as compensation for the inescapabil-
ity of change.

*Ovid's seat has been moved a couple of times during his long morning
of work, keeping pace with the gradual incursion of the sun into the
walkway of his portico. Late into the morning a slave carried from
the house a wide cloth curtain and hung it from the pole stretched in
the upper space between two columns, for shade. From time to time, a
slave brought a cool drink from the kitchen: sometimes water sweet-
ened with honey, sometimes water sharpened with vinegar. Ovid's con-
centration did not waver. He has written steadily, without needing to
consult his notes; like most educated Romans he has a trained memory, and carries much in his head, but in any case, it was wise to stay
with the momentum of the meter he had set going like a metronome in
his body. But he had a good reason to press forward with his writing
that day—he has decided he will read "Apollo and Daphne" to his dinner guests.*

*Now the piece is finished, and Ovid rises for a stretch. His garden is
his clock: the position of the sun tells him it is the sixth hour, time for
a stroll to the bath house for some exercise and a good soaking. He*

---

4. Robert Graves provides a version in which Mother Earth rescues Daphne and bears her
   away to Crete, where she became known as Pasiphae; he cites Apollodorus 1.7.9 and
   Plutarch, *Agis* 7 as his sources. Graves, *The Greek Myths*, vol. 1, 78.

summons his amanuensis, who will convert the rapidly-written cursive
on the high-piled stack of wax tablets into neat columns on a papyrus
scroll. His dinner guests will begin to assemble in the late afternoon.
He must be rested and fresh when they arrive.

Wax tablets were a writer's preferred medium for drafting new work;
revisions and corrections could more easily be entered than on
papyrus. The tablets were thick pieces of wood, a frame with carved
recesses into which beeswax was poured. The name book—*liber*—
dated to the days when Romans wrote on thin leaves of wood: *liber*
was also the Latin word for bark. This etymology is captured in Ovid's
story of "Apollo and Daphne." At the outset of her metamorphosis,
"her soft sides were begirt with thin bark" (*mollia cinguntur tenui
praecordia libro*),[5] a stage of her transformation into the subject of
Apollo's art. Bark remained in use as a writing material, but the surface of beeswax was a great technological improvement, allowing not
only for second thoughts but for complete re-use of the tablet, which
could be scraped clean. Writing was incised in the wax with a stylus
made of hard metal or bone. The tablets could be made into sets by
stringing them together through holes drilled in the outer edge.

   The writing on Ovid's wax tablet would be transferred to papyrus,
which could be manufactured in the home. Pith taken from the
stem of the papyrus plant was slit vertically into thin strips and laid
out on the vertical; then a layer of strips was superimposed horizon-
tally on the first layer, and sometimes a third layer parallel to the
first. The assemblage was dampened, and the layers pounded
together; the plant exuded a gum that sealed them firmly. After drying, the surface was polished. The sheets, measuring about 16
inches (0.4 m) wide and 9 inches (0.23 m) high, were then pasted
into rolls about 33 feet (10 m) long.[6] The scribe would transfer
Ovid's writing from the wax tablets to a scroll in vertical columns
separated by a margin, with larger margins at the top and bottom of
the scroll. A wooden roller with finial knobs might be attached to
each end of the roll to assist the process of reading; it would be
unrolled with the right hand and rolled up with the left. The title of
the work was written at the end of the scroll, where it was less susceptible to damage. It was customary to attach a strip of parchment
to the outer end of the roll, bearing the author's name. The scroll
was best stowed in a pigeonhole, with this identifying tag dangling in
plain sight.

   By the time Ovid became a writer, a private library was not an
unusual feature in the house of a wealthy man. One of the excavations at Herculaneum suggests what Ovid's library might have looked

5. *Metamorphoses* 1.549.
6. Paraphrased from Adkins, 208–09, and the *Oxford English Dictionary*.

like: the so-called Villa of the Papyri contained a chamber about three meters square, opening onto the colonnade that was its light source, and lined with bookshelves reaching to above eye level, with a freestanding bookcase in the middle of the room fitted with shelves on both sides, piled with rolls of papyri.[7] In the best libraries, the scrolls were organized in alphabetical order by author, and the library's holding was catalogued. Ovid would have used his servants to make presentation copies of his own work, when he was ready to put it into circulation, and then it would have appeared in libraries as well as in private hands. Once a writer had released a book, anyone might copy it.[8] Books would be traded among friends for that purpose; some popular titles could also be acquired from booksellers. A writer such as Ovid, heavily dependent on reference works, was likely to have put a well-trained slave in charge of his collection, and a separate library would have been an essential feature of his house.

In his poems from exile, Ovid tells us that he had two homes: a city house and a country villa; he also mentions the locations. Great excitement ensued in the year 2000 when archeologists claimed they had identified a mosaic floor and remnants of walls belonging to Ovid's villa, while excavating a site for borough council offices—lines from his poetry were quoted by the archeologists as evidence that they were digging at the correct address.[9] We have no way of knowing exactly where Ovid's house inside the city was located, much less what his house looked like; it has been by now compacted with the debris of centuries and buried to a depth of eighteen feet beneath the skin of Roman topography. But knowing Ovid's occupation, status, and wealth, and the general neighborhood of his Roman house, makes it possible to offer some educated guesses about its layout and decoration.

Roman domestic architecture was, helpfully, codified by the ideals of the architect Vitruvius, who wrote a book that is still in print today. The Roman house, or *domus*, described by Vitruvius was longer than it was wide, and axial in plan. It began at the door opening from the street, progressed through an atrium—usually, an area open to the light of the sky, with a basin to catch rainwater—and stopped at the *tablinum*, or office of the *paterfamilias*, which lay just beyond the atrium; smaller rooms for working and sleeping might flank the walls on either side of the atrium. In the homes of families whose members had achieved consular status, this reception area would be furnished with the death-masks of ancestors. The

---

7. Lionel Casson, *Libraries in the Ancient World* (New Haven: Yale UP, 2001), 74.
8. Casson, 77.
9. See news story dated 20 September 2000, http://users.pandora.be/daedalus/Ovid/ Ovid'sLoveNestFound.htm.

display would communicate the family's social significance to a visitor, at once.

Any stranger might enter a Roman *domus* and proceed through the atrium and arrive at the *tablinum* with the reasonable expectation of being able to hold a conversation with its master. But beyond the *tablinum* would be the area of the house into which a visitor had to be invited. This area could be glimpsed through a window at the back of the *tablinum*: it showed the garden. A necessity in a Roman house, the garden was a source of light and air and food, and an expression of the Roman sense of connection to the rural past. Often, the garden would be surrounded by a peristyle, or covered walkway; where space was restricted, a partial colonnade would serve. But whatever its scale, the garden was private space, related to the rooms or room in which the host entertained at dinner: the *triclinium*, or "three-couch dining area." A distinction was always strongly marked in a Roman house, informing the visitor about this fundamental separation of the space: the parts that anyone might enter, and the parts that required an invitation.

The excavations at Pompeii reveal a range of variations on this axial scheme. Pompeii itself was laid out on a grid, and, as in a neighborhood built by Eichler, the relative sameness of the basic floor plan makes the variations easy to read. One especially interesting set of variations can be viewed in the rendering of the House of the Prince of Naples, located in Pompeii Regio VI.[1] The house had some grand neighbors. The House of the Vetii occupied the corner lot, six doors away; the House of the Golden Cupids anchored the corner lot directly across the road from the Vetii. Both contained lavishly decorated rooms which have been widely studied. The House of the Prince of Naples was squeezed into the dense middle of the block, and at 290 square meters, was not grand. It had a floor plan that would have been highly congenial to Ovid's way of life, and can serve as an example of the sort of house he might have chosen for himself in Rome.

Here is the plan. The house is two storeys high. From the street, a visitor enters a small atrium open to the sky, with an *impluvium* to capture rain water, and a marble table. On the right, a porter sits near the narrow stairway leading up to the second floor, which is of little interest: cubicles used as bedrooms and storage are located upstairs. It is the ground floor that interests us. Beyond the atrium, the kitchen and storage area lies to the right, in the dusky corner of the house. A latrine would have been set in this same area, to make efficient use of the kitchen's waste water. On the left, lit all day by

---

1. The House of the Prince of Naples is located at Regio VI, 15,7–8. See teaching website with partial plan of Pompeii Regio VI: www.indiana.edu/~leach/c409/regio6.html.

windows opening onto the garden, stands Ovid's reception room, and behind that a small room that houses his library.

The walls in several of these rooms would have been frescoed, since most Romans with the means to do so made a considerable investment in the decoration of their homes. Let us assume that Ovid's ownership dates back to his second marriage, around 16 B.C., when a new style of decoration was just becoming fashionable. Ovid was apparently interested in painting. It is said that—through his social acquaintance with the emperor's daughter Julia, during her marriage to Agrippa—Ovid's circle of acquaintances included artists influential in setting the style for domestic decoration under the Emperor, the so-called "Third Style."[2] A passage of *Fasti* indicates that Ovid was familiar with the tools of the decorators' trades; among the artisans who should pay homage to Minerva as their patron, Ovid writes, are the engravers (presumably of silver and gold tableware), painters in encaustic, stonemasons, and—poets: for, "The goddess of a thousand crafts, she is surely a goddess of poetry."[3] That is, Ovid did not separate literature from other kinds of "craft." Moreover, his tales are distinctively visualized. The vivid detail in which he renders scenes, settings and characters in the *Metamorphoses* made him a popular source for Renaissance painters when they began to seek subject matter outside Biblical sources.

Ovid can't be given credit for his influence on the Renaissance, but he can be seen to have placed his imprint on interior decoration in his own day. Despite the fact that mythological material was widely distributed in the Roman Empire, it appears that some of the images found in the best-preserved houses in Pompeii and Herculaneum were influenced by Ovid's *Metamorphoses*.[4] For example, the House of M. Lucretius Fronto in Pompeii, which was decorated at a very high level of skill and thoroughness, contains a panel representing the story of Pyramus and Thisbe, which was not known before Ovid's telling. Other paintings in the house reinforce the impression that Ovid had an influence: a Narcissus; a sequence involving Ariadne; and possibly the painting of Mars and Venus in a bedchamber.

In the decorative system of the Third Style, each wall was divided into three strongly-marked areas (the base; the large middle zone; and the upper zone); the middle zone was again divided into large

---

2. John R. Clarke, *The Houses of Roman Italy, 100 B.C.–A.D. 250: Ritual, Space, and Decoration* (Berkeley: U of California P, 1993), 55. The painter identified, though not by name, is described by the art historian Peter H. Blanckenhagen, as "a painter of the most elegant and sophisticated set at the Imperial court where Ovid and his taste ruled supreme." This seems to me an exaggeration based on Blanckenhagen's observation that the painter used mythological subjects.

3. *Fasti* 3.831–33, trans. Nagel. Ovid's lines: "*quique moves caelum, tabulam coloribus uris, / quique facis docta millia saxa manu. / mille dea est operum: certe dea carminis illa est.*"

4. See Clarke, 146–63.

rectangular panels separated by slim architectural and botanical elements. At the center of the large panels would hang what appeared to
be a painted "canvas" depicting, usually a scene from mythology or
literature, like those described above.

The production of these elaborate design elements required
applying all of the paint to damp plaster, and was the occupation of
specialists. It would have required substantial advance planning.
The pictorial workshops had patterns based on pre-existing works,
and sometimes made pastiches of these.[5] Clients apparently exercised choices in the matter and, possibly, at times commissioned
new images. The work of some of the painters was extraordinarily
accomplished, as the excavations at Pompeii and Herculaneum
reveal. The skillful composition, the beauty of draperies and settings, the liveliness of the bodies, and the adroit storytelling combine to give these images lasting fascination.

What if Ovid himself had commissioned paintings based on *Metamorphoses* for the decoration of his reception rooms? If he did, it
seems likely that Ovid would have engaged the service of artists
capable of clever special effects, such as the painter of "Narcissus"[6]
in the House of the Vetii, a striking composition that includes a
reflection of the face of Narcissus, crazed by the water in the pool
where, according to Ovid's story, he will drown. Or possibly the more
ambitious painter of "Thetis and Hephaestus," a scene from the
Iliad:[7] Hephaestus is forging armor for Achilles, while his mother
Thetis looks on; her image is reflected in the shield. *Metamorphoses*
too has some spectacular—literally—tales in which the communica-
tion is made by artisans, using another medium than speech.

*By the ninth hour of the day, freshly bathed and shaved, and dressed in
a new tunic and short cloak, Ovid is ready to receive his friends. It is
never possible to predict the time a guest will arrive for dinner. But
someone is bound to arrive at the early end of the conventional gathering hour, so he has given himself plenty of time to inspect the preparations while there is still a possibility of giving additional instructions to
the slaves.*

*Ovid takes pleasure in circumnavigating the private areas of his
house. He had overseen the decoration himself, and is especially proud
of his dining room. Entering the triclinium through the wide portal
that separates the diners from the garden, he pauses to enjoy the vivid
frescoes. These illustrate the metamorphosis of the girl Arachne into a
spider.*

5. See Clarke, 157.
6. House of M. Lucretius Fronto (Pompeii V. 4.a). See Clarke, fig. 79, 160.
7. Pompeii IX.1.7. Ernesto De Carolis, *Gods and Heroes in Pompeii* (Los Angeles: The J. Paul Getty Museum), 45.

The largest wall is segmented into three panels—a large central panel flanked by two narrower ones—dedicated to the goddess Minerva, whom the Greeks called Pallas Athena. In the narrow, more vertical panels, Minerva appears upright. On the left, she is depicted greeting one of her sisters, the Muse Urania, at the site of the Hippocrene on Mount Helicon—by legend, a fountain created by the hoof of Pegasus; in this image Minerva displays the glory of her armor. On the right, a symmetrical image shows her in the disguise of a shabby old woman accosting the talented weaver Arachne, a young woman of lowly birth who has attracted Minerva's wrathful attention by claiming to be a better craftswoman than Minerva herself, the patroness of weaving. The central panel shows the contest to which Minerva has challenged Arachne. Minerva, no longer disguised, has flung off her armor and hitched up her robes to free herself for action at the loom, where she crouches facing Arachne, who works at an identical loom. The female figures are seen in angled profile, and their working posture brings them into equivalency: no longer does the angry goddess tower over the defiant girl. On either side of them, watching the action, recline the nymphs who have been designated judges of the contest. The lower half of each loom shows a slice of the tapestry that each has just begun to weave.

The two remaining walls of the room depict the finished tapestries, just as Ovid has described them in Metamorphoses. Minerva's tapestry depicts the legend of how she became the patron deity of Athens by winning a contest with Neptune while the other Olympian gods looked on with solemn attention; and she embellishes the four corners of the tapestry with images of mortals brought low by their audacity. Then she encloses her work in a border of olive wreath, the tree sacred to herself. Minerva's artistic style is perfectly classical: the figures centered, balanced and framed, and the content didactic.[8]

Arachne's tapestry boils with swirling energies: her theme is the libidinous self-indulgence of the Olympian gods who conceal themselves in metamorphic shapes in order to prey on mortal women. Episodes from previous books of the Metamorphoses are reenacted in Arachne's tapestry, only now they are presented from the point of view of an angry girl. "She added how, in a satyr's image hidden, Jove filled lovely Antiope with twin offspring; how he was Amphitryon when he cheated thee, Alcmena; how in a golden shower he tricked Danaë; Aegina, as a flame; Mnemosyne, as a shepherd . . ."[9] Ironically, Arachne borders her passionate visual denunciation in a wreath of flowers and ivy.

In Metamorphoses, Ovid says that Minerva could find no flaw in Arachne's work[1] and, enraged rather than impressed by Arachne's

8. William S. Anderson's commentary on Metamorphoses, 160.
9. Metamorphoses 6.110–114.
1. Metamorphoses 6.129–130.

successful artistry, the goddess shredded Arachne's tapestry and began beating her on the head with a shuttle. Arachne tried to escape by hanging herself, but the goddess intervened: she shrank Arachne into the form of a spider. But Ovid did not commission a painting of that episode. In his dining room, the story ends with each of the two glorious "tapestries" occupying a wall of its own, for the delectation of opinionated Romans. Nonetheless a spider motif can be detected in the weblike ornamental traceries on panels surmounting the frescoes in the upper zone of the walls, and in an obscure corner, a small nondescript painted spider seems to hang suspended.

The room's décor never fails to stimulate exactly the kinds of conversation Ovid hopes for: political fulminations, technical disputes and disquisitions, literary gossip, even scholarly footnotes. The three dining couches have been positioned on the diagonal in the room, the better to afford the diners a view of the garden, and each couch will afford a different angle on the paintings as well. Empty at this moment, the triclinium has almost the look of a stage set: its black and white mosaic floor agleam, the rugs and pillows where the diners will recline a soft tumble of luxuries, the early-spring garden beyond lit to perfection by the declining sun, the shade deepening.

In planning his birthday dinner, Ovid would have demonstrated the way his own tastes reflected his membership in a social class. Ovid was born into a family with longstanding Roman citizenship whose members regularly qualified to become *equites*: a class of men who had won advancement not by birth, as did the patricians, but through the accumulation of wealth.[2] He had higher than usual social status among the Augustan poets. Only his friend the poet Sextus Propertius held social rank this high;[3] in contrast, Virgil was the son of a landowner prosperous enough to educate him well; and Horace was the son of a freedman. Roman culture was prejudiced against all occupations except law, business, soldiering and farming,[4] so Ovid's decision to step permanently into the shade placed him—contentedly—among the outsiders.

The conventional Roman dining room had space for nine people; Ovid's small guest list would have included the men whose company he most enjoyed. The socialite financier Atticus, Ovid's favorite companion for theater-going, was a likely guest; Julius Hyginus, keeper of the Palatine Library[5] where Ovid was a frequent visitor,

2. Peter Green clarifies that "despite Ovid's own remarks on the subject, this honour was not hereditary"; admission to the rank of *equites* required "a minimum capital reserve of 400,000 sesterces." Introduction to *Ovid: The Erotic Poems*, 17.
3. Green, 32.
4. Green, 32.
5. Green, 37.

might have been included too. Among the poets would have been Brutus and Celsus, unknown today except as recipients of Ovid's affectionate epistles from exile. As a courtesy to Ovid's wife an invitation would have been extended to her highborn protector Paullus Fabius Maximus and his wife Marcia. Almost certainly Ovid's patron Marcus Valerius Messalla Corvinus would have been invited, as might his wife, if he had a wife; Messalla had recognized Ovid's talent while Ovid was still a youth, and fostered his career wholeheartedly ever since.

Perhaps because this is a special occasion, the guests arrive promptly, remove their street shoes, put on their decorative slippers,[6] and gather in the garden, where a garlanded table has been set up for pouring mulsum, the honeyed wine always served as an aperitif. The accompanying slaves carry gifts, and these are arranged on the serving table for inspection. The wealthy Fabians' tribute is a heavy silver mixing bowl for wine. Atticus has brought Ovid a small bronze sculpture of a chimera with a lion's head, a goat's body, and a serpent's tail, to bring him good luck in his work on Metamorphoses. *Brutus and Celsus had commissioned together an encaustic portrait of Ovid—so that later in life he could remember his good looks, they joked. Julius Hyginus had found a rare work of Greek mythology on one of his recent voyages to make acquisitions for the library, and had it copied for Ovid: it is a little known version of the story of Narcissus.[7] Messalla brought a sun dial for the garden, along with verses commemorating their long friendship.*

Before they enter the triclinium, a slave hands each guest a freshly-prepared chaplet of flowers, and arranges it to advantage on each head. Now that the wine has begun to work its way with them, high spirits take over; Ovid has written, in Fasti, *"no serious business is conducted by the brow that wears a wreath / and waterdrinkers don't wear flower chains."[8] The wine drinkers make no protest. Then, upon entering the triclinium they remove their slippers and hand them to the slave who accompanies them, and who will wait in attendance crouched at their feet.*

Each of the three long couches in the triclinium hold three guests, who recline on their left elbows, supported by a firm cushion. The couches are placed in the form of a U *with a serving table in the center. As host, Ovid will occupy the far end of the couch on the left as they enter the room; his guest of honor, Messalla, will recline to Ovid's*

6. Balsdon, 41.
7. Dr. Dirk Obbink reported that scholars working on a collection of ancient materials known as the Oxyrhynchus Papyri had recently discovered "a poem about Narcissus that appears to have been the basis for Ovid's poem on the same subject." Sarah Lyall, "A Historical Discovery? Well, Yes and No," *The New York Times*, 30 May 2005, B1, B6.
8. *Fasti* 5.140–141.

left on the middle couch. The others find their own places, the women
next to their husbands.

Once they are settled, Ovid welcomes them warmly, but briefly. He
knows that his guests are hungry; most Romans eat only this one large
meal every day. He summons the staff to begin serving. Each diner will
hold a plate in the left hand and spoon food onto the plate with the
right hand. All of the food will have been cut into bite-size pieces,
since it is meant to be eaten with the fingers.[9]

A Roman meal was served in three courses, at which a large number
of diverse dishes were presented. Since Romans took pride in growing their own food for the table, Ovid's country villa may have supplied much of the food that evening, determining the menu. The
substantial appetizer course, or *gustum*, would include raw and
cooked vegetables, mushrooms, smoked cheese, olives, and an egg
dish; because this was a fancy meal, oysters and other shellfish
might be added. The main course was called the *mensa prima*, and
featured meat, with accompanying side dishes of vegetables, and
strongly flavored sauces. The dishes for the *mensa prima* were usually brought around in successive services—a choice of from two to
seven dishes, from which the guests would select.[1] The featured
dish at this early spring meal might have been a roast of young kid.
Game birds or pullets, boar or roast pig, or specialty dishes such
as stuffed sow's udder, would have filled out the *mensa prima*. The
dessert, or *mensa secunda*, consisted usually of nuts and fruit, both
dried and fresh. Remnants of food would not be left on the plate but
tossed on the floor for the slaves to remove.[2]

The Roman banquet was a stylized affair. Ovid drew on its features in writing one of the most often quoted parts of *Metamor-*
phoses, "Philemon and Baucis." An elderly couple, they live in rustic
poverty, and are visited in their hut one day by Jupiter and Mercury
in disguise, who have been treated inhospitably while wandering the
earth unrecognized. The old folks welcome them kindly, and invite
them to dine. Every step in the preparation and serving of the meal
is described, and every detail is meant to convey that the couple are
well-versed in the customs of hospitality but subsist at a level of dep-
rivation that would make a Roman shudder. Philemon prepares a
dish of cabbage and bacon, for example, as the *mensa prima*:

> She took a cabbage which her husband had brought from the
> well-watered garden and lopped off the outside leaves. Mean-
> while the old man with a forked stick reached down a chine of

9. Giacosa, 22–23.
1. Balsdon, 42.
2. Giacosa, 24.

smoked bacon, which was hanging from a blackened beam, and cutting off a little piece of the long-cherished pork, he put it to cook in the boiling water. Meanwhile they beguiled the intervening time with their talk and smoothed out a mattress of soft sedge-grass placed on a couch with a frame and feet of willow. They threw drapery over this, which they were not accustomed to bring out except on festal days; but even this was a cheap thing and well-worn, a very good match for the willow couch. The gods reclined. The old woman, with her skirts tucked up, with trembling hands set out the table. But one of its three legs was too short; so she propped it up with a potsherd. When this had leveled the slope, she wiped it, thus leveled, with green mint. Next she placed on the board some olives, green and ripe, truthful Minerva's berries, and some autumnal cornel-cherries, pickled in the lees of wine; endives and radishes, cream cheese and eggs, lightly roasted in the warm ashes, all served in earthen dishes. After these viands, an embossed mixing-bowl of the same costly ware was set on together with cups of beech-wood coated on the inside with yellow wax. A moment and the hearth sent its steaming viands on [i.e., the dish of cabbage and bacon], and wine of no great age was brought out, which was then pushed aside to give a small space for the second course. Here were nuts and figs, dried dates, plums and fragrant apples in broad baskets, and purple grapes just picked from the vines; in the center of the table was a comb of clear white honey. Besides all this, pleasant faces were at the board and lively and abounding goodwill.[3]

The old couple notice that the mixing bowl of wine keeps filling of it own accord, and become suspicious about the identity of their guests. Wine was an important element in a Roman dinner. It was drunk throughout the meal, though sparingly; and it was mixed with water, usually three parts water to one part wine.[4] In a well-staffed Roman house, looking after the supply of wine would have been the responsibility of the *cellarius*; in addition to decanting and mixing, and, in winter, heating the wine, the *cellarius* would often add seasonings such as fennel seed or other fragrant spices or herbs to the filter through which the wine was being decanted.[5] Different kinds of wines would be served with the successive courses. Guests continued to sip *mulsum* with the first course, the *gustum*; at the *mesa prima*, they would switch to unsweetened wine. Many well-to-do Romans were connoisseurs and maintained wine cellars; a Greek wine called Chian commanded high prices; among the Italian wines,

3. *Metamorphoses* 8.645–678. Loeb.
4. Giacosa, 193.
5. Giacosa, 193.

Falernian and Nomentanum were admired.[6] At the *mensa secunda* a sweet raisin wine called *passum* was sometimes offered.[7]

Romans enjoyed fragrances, and were surrounded by them at the dinner table. Not only the wreaths they wore, and the herb-strewn floor that surrounded them—like Philemon's mint-scrubbed table, a source of pleasure for the nose—but also the personal fragrances with which both men and women adorned themselves would mingle in the warm atmosphere of the room where they reclined. Guests would sometimes bring a bottle of scented oil, to reapply in the pauses between courses.[8] Dinner was a leisurely affair once the guests had taken the first edge off appetite by partaking of the *gustum*. Not only did the courses arrive in dramatic sequences, the service was often punctuated by entertainment: musical interludes, or, possibly a performance by the house *lector*, the slave whose work was reading aloud to the family and to guests.

At Ovid's table, conversation is the main attraction, and nothing is permitted to impede it, during dinner. But at the end of the meal, he announces that he wishes to extend the evening with a recitation from his new poem. He invites the guests to rise and stretch and refresh themselves while the slaves clear away the last scraps of the mensa secunda *and sweep the floor. Then the* cellarius *will bring a fresh supply of wine, purchased specially for this occasion. The dinner guests will reassemble, with additional guests invited specifically to share this* convivium. *"Apollo and Daphne" will make its public debut, a milestone in Ovid's life, and, he hopes, in the life of his writing.*

"Apollo and Daphne" was, he trusted, a ravishing story about falling helplessly in love—resembling the richest poems of Amores, *but achingly imbued with the vantage of middle age. And it was also a prime example of the subversive strategy by which Ovid's art was meant to counter the overwhelming influence of imperial authority. The stories in* Metamorphoses *have in common that they might be able to trigger, in the Roman reader, the twin anxieties of living under imperial rule: the fear of control, and the fear of the loss of control. The gods, as literary characters, served as devices in which to release in the reader a cascade of fantasies, all requiring identification with the human being who was the object of power's malice and its whim. There was nothing so crude as allegory in* Metamorphoses; *it bore no messages in its teeth, and could be enjoyed at the most superficial level of attention, because of the pace and wit of its storytelling. But readers accustomed to fixing an inquisitive gaze upon those who governed*

6. Balsdon, 43–44.
7. Giacosa, 194–95.
8. Griffin, 10–12; Dalby, 246.

them would recognize a deeper intention in Metamorphoses. *It was offering an artful challenge to imperial mythmaking, shrewdly enticing the reader to comprehend the instability of power, even the highest. At age forty-six, he had reached the height of his powers, as he well knew. And now more than ever, he was performing the work he was born to do.*

ITALO CALVINO

Ovid and Universal Contiguity†

On high in the sky there is a Way, which one sees when the night is clear. It is called Milky, and it catches the eye because it is so white. Here the gods pass by on their way to the dwelling of the great Thunderer, at the palace. To right and left, with open doors, are the atria of the nobles, forever crowded. The populace lives dispersed in other places. The most powerful and illustrious gods have here established their dwelling at the front [*a fronte potentes/caelicolae clarique suos posuere penates*]. If the expression did not seem irreverent, I would dare to say that this place is the Palatine of the great heaven.

Thus, as the beginning of the *Metamorphoses*, to introduce us to the world of the celestial gods, Ovid starts by making it so similar as to be identical to everyday Rome, with regard to layout, division into social classes, and matters of custom (the throng of *clientes*, for instance). And religion also: the gods keep their penates in the houses where they dwell, which implies that the sovereigns of heaven and earth also devote a cult to their little household gods.

Comparison does not imply irony or belittling. We are in a universe in which the forms densely pack the allotted space, constantly exchanging qualities and dimensions, and the flux of time is filled with a proliferation of stories and cycles of stories. Terrestrial forms and stories echo celestial forms and stories, but each entwines the other by turns in a double spiral. The contiguity between gods and human beings—related to the gods and the object of their compulsive loves—is one of the dominant themes of the *Metamorphoses*, but this is no more than a particular instance of the contiguity between all the figures and forms of existing things, anthropomorphic or otherwise. Fauna, flora, mineral kingdom, and firmament embrace within their

† From *The Uses of Literature: Essays*, trans. Patrick Creagh (San Diego: Harcourt Brace Jovanovich, 1986). Reprinted by permission of Harcourt Houghton Mifflin.

common substance what we are accustomed to think of as human, in the sense of an aggregate of bodily, psychological, and moral qualities.

The poetry of the *Metamorphoses* is rooted above all in these indistinct borderlands between diverse worlds, and as early as book II it seizes an extraordinary opportunity in the myth of Phaëthon, who dares to take the reins of the sun chariot. The sky appears in this as absolute space, abstract geometry, and at the same time as the scene of a human adventure rendered with such precision of detail that we do not lose the thread for an instant, as it carries emotional involvement to an agonizing pitch.

This is not merely precision in the most concrete and material facts, such as the motion of the chariot swerving and bumping because of the unusual lightness of the load, or the emotions of the clumsy young charioteer, but in the visualization of idealized patterns, such as the map of the heavens. I should say at once that this is only apparent precision, one of contradictory facts that convey their effect when taken one by one, and even in terms of general narrative impact, but cannot weld together into a coherent vision. For example, the sky is a sphere traversed by roads going up and going down, recognizable by the wheel ruts, but at the same time the sky is whirling in the opposite direction to the sun chariot. It is suspended at a dizzying height above the lands and the oceans that are seen in the background. At one time it appears as an overarching vault in the loftiest part of which the stars are fixed, at another as a bridge that carries the chariot over the void, causing Phaëthon to be equally terrified of going on or turning. back: "*Quid faciat? Multum caeli post terga relictum/ante oculos plus est. Animo metitur utrumque.*" It is an empty wilderness (and therefore not the sky city of book I: "Do you think, perhaps, that there are sacred woods and cities of gods and temples rich with gifts?" asks Phoebus), a wilderness populated by the figures of ferocious beasts that are only *simulacra*, shapes of constellations, but no less menacing for all that. There one discerns an oblique track, halfway up, that skirts the South Pole and the Bear; but if one swerves off the road and is lost among the precipices, one ends up falling beneath the moon, to scorch the clouds and set fire to the earth.

After the ride through the heavens, suspended in space, which is the most engrossing part of the story, there begins the grandiose description of the earth on fire, of the boiling sea with the bodies of seals floating on it belly up. One of the classic passages of Ovid as a depictor of catastrophe, this is a twin to the flood in book I. All around Alma Tellus, Mother Earth, the waters recede. The shriveled springs attempt to turn back and seek refuge in the maternal womb (*"fontes/qui se condiderant in opacae viscera matris"*). And the earth, with singed hair and eyes bloodshot from the ashes, implores Jove with what little voice is left in her parched throat, warning him that if the poles catch fire even the palaces of the gods will crumble. (The terrestrial or the celestial poles? It has also been suggested that this means the axis of the earth, which Atlas can no longer hold because it is incandescent. But the poles at that time were an astronomical notion, and besides, the next line clearly states *"regia caeli."* Was the sky palace really up there, then? How is it that Phoebus left it out and Phaëthon didn't come across it? Anyway, such contradictions are found not only in Ovid: in Virgil and the other supreme poets of antiquity, it is also hard to get a clear idea of how the ancients really "saw" the skies.)

The episode culminates in the wrecking of the sun chariot by a thunderbolt from Jove, in an explosion of shattered bits and pieces: *"Illic frena iacent, illic temone revulsus/axis, in hac radii fractarum parte rotarum. . . ."* (This is not the only traffic accident in the *Metamorphoses*: another high-speed skid off the road is that of Hippolytus, in the last book of the poem; the wealth of detail in relating *this* disaster passes from mechanics to anatomy, with descriptions of the rending of the bowels and severed limbs.)

This interpenetration of gods, men, and nature does not imply an unequivocal hierarchical order, but an intricate system of interrelations in which each level can influence the others, though to differing extents. Myth, in Ovid, is the field of tension in which these forces clash and balance. Everything depends on the spirit in which the myth is related. Sometimes the gods themselves recount the myths in which they are involved, as moral examples intended as warnings to mortals; at other times mortals use the same myths to challenge or argue with the gods, as do the daughters of Pierus or Arachne. Or it may be that there are some myths that the gods love to hear told, and others they prefer to have silenced.

The daughters of Pierus know a version of the Titans' ascent to Olympus seen from the point of view of the Tirans, including the terror of the gods as they are put to flight (book V). They recount it after challenging the Muses in the art of storytelling, and the Muses come back with another series of myths that re-establish the viewpoint of Olympus. Then they punish the mortals by turning them into magpies. A challenge to the gods implies irreverent or blasphemous intentions in the story.

Arachne the weaver challenges Minerva in the art of the loom and makes a tapestry depicting the sins of the libertine gods (book VI). The technical precision with which Ovid describes the working of the looms in this challenge might suggest a possible identification of the poet's work with the weaving of a tapestry in various shades of purple. But which? That of Athena-Minerva, in which we see the grandiose figures of Olympus with their traditional attributes, while in tiny scenes at the four corners of the web, framed by olive leaves, are depicted four divine punishments inflicted on mortals who have challenged the gods? Or that of Arachne, in which the insidious seductions of Jove, Neptune, and Apollo, which Ovid has already recounted at some length, reappear as sarcastic comments among garlands of flowers and festoons of ivy (not without the addition of some delightful details, such as Europa, carried across the sea on the bull's back, lifting her feet so as not to get them wet: ". . . *tactumque vereri / adsilientis aquae timidasque reducere plantas*")?

Neither one nor the other. In the vast catalogue of myths that the entire poem in fact is, the myth of Athena and Arachne may in its turn contain two smaller catalogues aimed in opposing ideological directions: one to induce holy terror, the other to incite people to irreverence and moral relativity. Anyone who inferred from this that the poem as a whole should be read in the first manner (since Arachne's challenge is cruelly punished) or in the second (since the poetic rendering favors the guilty victim) would be making a mistake. The *Metamorphoses* aim to represent all that is worth telling of what has been passed down by literature, and with all the force of images and meanings that this implies, without deciding between the various keys in which it can be read—in accord with the ambiguity that is proper to myth. Only by giving a place in the poem to all the stories or implied stories that flow in every direction, that push and shove to channel themselves into the well-ordered expanse of his hexameters, can the author of the *Metamorphoses* be sure of presenting no partial design, but rather a living multiplicity that excludes no god known or unknown.

The case of a new, foreign god, not easy to recognize as such, a scandalous god clashing with each and every model of beauty and virtue, is amply exemplified in the *Metamorphoses* in the case of Bacchus-Dionysus. It is his orgiastic cult that the devotees of Minerva, the daughters of Minyas, refuse to join, continuing to spin and card wool on the days of the Bacchic festivals and alleviating their long labors by telling stories. Here, then, is another use for storytelling, which in lay terms is justified as pure entertainment (*"quod tempora longa videri / non sinat"*) or as an aid to productivity *"utile opus manuum vario sermone levemus"*), but which is also pleasing to Minerva, *melior dea* for those industrious girls disgusted by the orgies and dissipation of the cults of Dionysus that were fast spreading through Greece after triumphing in the East.

It is certain that the art of storytelling, so dear to the hearts of weaving women, is linked to the cult of Athena-Minerva. We have seen this in the instance of Arachne, who for scorning the goddess was turned into a spider; but we see it also in the opposite case, that of an excessive cult of Athena which led to the other gods being neglected. In fact, in book IV the daughters of Minyas, also guilty of being too certain of their talents, too exclusive in their worship (*"intempestiva Minerva"*), are punished horrendously by being changed into bats by the god who knows not labor but drunkenness, who listens not to stories but to impetuous, dark song. To avoid being changed into a bat himself, Ovid was extremely careful to leave all the doors of his poem open to gods past, present, and future, indigenous and foreign; to the East, which exerted pressure on the world of fable from beyond the bounds of Greece, and to the Augustan restoration of the Roman spirit, which weighed upon the contemporary political and intellectual situation. But he was not able to convince the nearest and most "executive" god, Augustus Caesar, who transformed him forever into an exile, an inhabitant of distant places—Ovid, who longed to bring everything together into one close-knit whole.

From the East ("from some ancestor of the *Thousand and One Nights,"* says L. P. Wilkinson) he got the romantic tale of Pyramus and Thisbe (which one of the daughters of Minyas chooses from a list of tales of the same mysterious origin), with its wall that opens a way for whispered words to pass but not for kisses, with the night flooded with moonlight beneath the bright mulberry tree—a tale destined to cast its reflections as far as the midsummer of the Elizabethan age.

Also from the East, by way of the Alexandrian romance, Ovid obtained the technique of multiplying the space within the poem by means of stories inserted into other stories and thereby increasing the impression of density, of intricacy, of being packed in. An example is the forest in which a wild-boar hunt intrudes into the destinies of illustrious heroes (book VIII), not far from the whirlpools of the Achelous, which halt the survivors of the hunt on their way home. They are welcomed to the dwelling of the river-god, who represents an obstacle as well as a refuge, a pause in the action and an opportunity for reflection and storytelling. Since one of the hunters is Theseus, eager to know the origin of everything he sees, and another is Peirithoüs, insolent and unbelieving (*"deorum/spector erat mentisque ferox"*), the river feels encouraged to tell some wonderful stories of metamorphosis, and is then emulated by his guests. Thus, in the *Metamorphoses*, new incrustations of stories are constantly being added, as on shells that might bring forth a pearl. In this case the pearl is the humble idyll of Philemon and Baucis, which embraces a whole minutely delineated world and moves at a totally different pace.

It should be said that Ovid only occasionally makes use of these structural complexities. The passion that dominates his compositional talents is not arrangement but accumulation, along with the varying of perspective and changing of pace. Thus, when Mercury wishes to bring sleep to Argus, whose hundred eyelids never close all at once, and begins to recount the metamorphosis of the nymph Syrinx into a clump of reeds, one part of her story is told in detail, another summed up in a single phrase; the rest is left moot when the god falls silent as soon as he sees that all of Argus's eyes have yielded to sleep.

The *Metamorphoses* are above all the poem of rapidity. Everything has to happen at high speed, strike the imagination; every image has to overlap another image, come into focus, and then vanish. This is the principle of the cinema: each line, like each frame, must be full of visual stimuli in motion. The abhorrence of the vacuum dominates both space and time. For page after page all verbs are in the present, so that everything is happening before our eyes; events pursue each other, and anything distant is rejected. When Ovid wishes to change pace, the first thing he does is to change not the tense of the verbs but the person, switching from the third person to the second, which means introducing the character whom he is just going to speak about and addressing him directly as "you"; "*Te quoque mutatum torvo, Neptune, invenco. . . .*" The "present" resides not simply in the tense of the verb, but in the very presence of the character who is being called up to the eyes. Even when the verbs are in the past, the vocative suddenly closes the gap. This method is often used when several subjects are performing parallel actions, to avoid the monotony of making lists. If he has spoken of Tityus in the third person, then Tantalus and Sisyphus are summoned with the vocative "You." Even plants have a right to the second person ("*Vos quoque, flexipedes hederae, venistis*"), and no wonder, seeing that they are plants that move like human beings, and run toward the sound of the lyre of the widowed Orpheus, crowding together into a dense bed of Mediterranean flora (book IX).

There are also times—and the one I mentioned just now is one of them—when the story has to slow down, change to a calmer gait, render the passage of time as if it were suspended, and depict a vague distance. What does Ovid do in such cases? To make it clear that the story is not in any hurry, he stops to gaze at the most minute details. For example, Philemon and Baucis are welcoming some unknown visitors (the gods) to their humble dwelling. "*Mensae sed erat pes tertius impar:/testa parem fecit; quae postquam subdita clivum/sustulit, aequatem mentae tersere virentes. . . .*": "But of the three legs of the table one is too short. A bit of pottery corrects that;

slipped underneath, it gets rid of the incline, and the tabletop is then cleaned with leaves of green mint. And on it they put olives of two colors, sacred to chaste Minerva, and autumnal dogberries steeped in liquid juice, and endives and radishes and some curdled milk, and eggs carefully turned on ashes that are not too hot: and all in earthenware dishes" (book VIII).

It is by making his picture ever richer in detail that Ovid achieves an effect of rarefaction, and a pause. For Ovid's way is always to add, never to remove; to go in for more and more detail, never to become blurred and vague. This method achieves different results according to the intonation. In this case it is quiet and sympathetic to humble things, but elsewhere it is agitated and eager to saturate the wonder of the fable with objective observation of real natural phenomena. For instance, Perseus fights with the sea monster whose back is encrusted with shells, laying Medusa's head, bristling with snakes, face down on a rock, but only after covering the rock with a layer of seaweed and underwater plants, so that her face does not have to suffer contact with the gritty sand. Seeing the foliage turn to stone on touching Medusa, the nymphs amuse themselves by making other twigs undergo the same transformation. This is the origin of coral, which is soft underwater but petrifies on contact with the air. Thus Ovid concludes this fantastic adventure in an etiological key, in keeping with his taste for the bizarre forms in nature.

A law of the greatest internal economy dominates this poem, which on the surface is devoted to unbridled extravagance. It is the economy proper to metamorphosis, which demands that the new forms should recover the materials of the old ones as far as possible. After the flood, during the transformation of stones into men (book I), "if there was in them a part damp with some moisture, or earthy, this came to serve as the body; what was solid, unable to bend, changed into bone; those that were veins remained, with the same name." Here the economy extends to the very name: *"quae modo vena fuit, sub eodem nomine mansit."* What most catches the attention about Daphne (book I) is her disheveled hair (so much so that Phoebus's first thought on seeing her is "Think, if she were to comb it!" (*"Spectat inornatus collo pendere capillos/et 'Quid, si comantur?' ait"*), so that in the flowing lines of her flight she is already predisposed toward metamorphosis into a plant: *"in frondem crines, in ramos bracchia crescunt/pes modo tam velox pigris radicibus haeret. . . ."* Cyané, in book V, merely takes her dissolution into tears to the last degree (*"lacrimisque absumitur omnis"*), until she turns into the little lake of which she was the nymph. And the Lycian peasants (book VI) who hurled insults at the vagabond Latona (who wanted to quench the thirst of her newborn twins) and fouled the lake waters by stirring up the mud, were already not much different from the frogs into which they were then changed by just retribution. Enough that the neck should disappear, the shoulders join to the head, the back turn green and the belly a dirty white.

This technique of metamorphosis has been studied by Shcheglov in a very clearly stated and convincing essay.

> All these transformations are concerned with physio-spatial traits that Ovid was in the habit of isolating even apart from metamorphosis ("hard stone," "long body," "curved back"). . . . Thanks to his knowledge of the properties of things, the poet makes transformation take the shortest route, for he knows in advance what man has in common with the dolphin, what he lacks, and what he has more of in comparison. The essential thing is that, thanks to the representation of the entire world as a system of elementary properties, the process of trans-formation—this improbable and fantastic phenomenon—is reduced to a series of comparatively simple processes. The event is no longer represented as a fable, but as a set of habitual and likely facts: growth, diminution, hardening, softening, curving, straightening, compression, rarefaction, etc.[1]

Ovid's writing, as defined by Shcheglov, would contain the coldest and most rigorous model, or at least program, of Robbe-Grillet. It goes without saying that such a definition does not exhaust all that we can look for in Ovid. But the important thing is that this way of describing objects *objectively* (whether animate or inanimate), "as different combinations of a relatively small number of basic, utterly simple elements," corresponds to the one certain philosophy of the *Metamorphoses*: "that of the unity and kinship of all that exists in the world, things and living beings alike."

With the cosmogonical account in book I and Pythagoras's profes-sion of faith in the last book, Ovid attempted to endow this philos-ophy of nature with a theoretical system, perhaps in competition with his remote predecessor Lucretius. A lot has been argued about what weight to give these pronouncements, but maybe the only thing that counts for us is the poetic coherence of Ovid's way of expressing his world: this swarm and tangle of events that are often similar yet always different, in which he celebrates the continuity and mobility of all that is.

Ovid has not yet finished the chapter on the origins of the world and the primordial catastrophes when he starts in on the series of

1. Scheglov, Yu. K. "Some Features of the Structure of Ovid's *Metamorphoses*" in *Russian Poetics in Translation* 2 (Oxford: Oxford UP, 1976), 50–65.

love affairs of the gods with nymphs or mortal girls. The love stories (which make up the most vivid part of the poem, the first eleven books) reveal a number of constants. Love here is love at first sight, an impelling demand, without psychological complications, and one that cries out for immediate satisfaction. Since the creature desired usually refuses and flees, the motif of a chase through the woods is recurrent. Metamorphosis can occur at different moments, either as a disguise on the part of the seducer, or as an escape for the trapped girl, or else as a punishment meted out to the victim of seduction by some jealous goddess.

Compared with the continual pressure of male desires, cases of female initiative in love are relatively rare, but in compensation they are more complex, not matters of momentary whim but of the passions, bearing a greater psychological depth (Venus in love with Adonis, for instance). They often involve a morbid erotic element (the nymph Salmacis, who in embracing Hermaphroditus melts into a bisexual creature). In a few cases we have illicit passions, incestuous (like the tragic characters of Myrrha and Byblis; the way in which the latter's passion for her brother is revealed to her, her dream, her suffering—these make up one of the finest passages of Ovid as a psychologist), or homosexual (Iphis), or criminally jealous (Medea). In the heart of the book the stories of Jason and Medea open up enough space for a genuine novel, with the interweaving of adventure, dark passions, and the "black" grotesque of witches' potions that will later reappear in *Macbeth*.

The passage without intervals from one story to the next is underlined, as Wilkinson observes, by the fact that the end of a story rarely coincides with the end of one of the books into which the poem is divided. Ovid may even begin a new story when he has only a few lines left until the end of a book. This is partly the old expedient used by writers of serials, who whet the reader's appetite for the next installment; but it is also a sign of the contiguity of the work, which would not have been divided into books if its length had not necessitated a certain number of scrolls. We are thus given the impression of a real and coherent world in which there is an interaction between events that are usually considered in isolation.

The stories may resemble one another, but they never repeat one another. Not for nothing is the most heartbreaking story the one (in book III) concerned with the unrequited love of the nymph Echo— condemned to the repetition of sounds—for the youth Narcissus, condemned to gaze upon his own image "repeated" in the watery mirror. Ovid races through this forest of love stories, all similar and all different, pursued by the voice of Echo reverberating among the rocks: *"Coeamus! Coeamus! Coeamus!"*

NORMAN O. BROWN

Daphne, or Metamorphosis[†]

Metamorphosis, or Mutabilitie. *Omnia mutantur.* Mutation
everywhere. *The Book of Changes.*

ॐ

Metamorphosis, or transubstantiation: we already and from the first
discern him making this thing other. His groping syntax, if we attend,
already shapes:

Fac nobis hanc oblationem ascriptam, ratam, rationabilem, accept-
abilem, quod figura est corporis et sanguinis Christi. Make for us this
offering consecrated, approved, reasonable, and acceptable, which
is a figure of the body of Christ. *Mutando perde figuram.* Transub-
stantiate my form, says Daphne.

> D. Jones, *Anathemata*, 49.
> Auerbach, "Figura," *Scenes from the Drama of European Literature*, 60, 235.
> Ovid, *Metamorphoses*, I, l. 547.

ॐ

Metamorphosis, or symbol-formation; the origin of human culture. A laurel branch in the hand, a laurel wreath on the house, a
laurel crown on the head; to purify and celebrate. Apollo after slaying the old dragon, or Roman legions entering the city in triumph.
As in the Feast of Tabernacles; or Palm Sunday. The decoration, the
mere display is poetry: making this thing other. A double nature.

> Leviticus 23:40.
> Mannhardt, *Antike Wald und Feldkulte*, 1:296–298.

ॐ

Daphnephoria, carrying Daphne. A ceremony of Apollo carrying
Daphne, with a choir of maidens. They decorate a piece of olive wood
with laurel branches and all kinds of flowers; at the top is tied a bronze
ball with smaller balls hanging from it; at the middle they tie another
ball not so big as the one on top, with purple ribbons attached; the
lower part of the wood they cover with saffron-colored cloth. The ball
at the top signifies the sun; the lower one, the moon; the lesser balls,
the stars; and the ribbons, the cycle of the year. The Daphne-bearer is
made like unto Apollo himself, with hair flowing, and wearing a golden
crown, and clothed in a shining robe that reaches down to his feet.

> Nilsson, *Griechische Feste*, 164–165.

ॐ

518

One branch is the spring. *Pars pro toto*: the tree is a symbol.

ะ.

The metamorphosis is a trope, or turning: a turn of phrase or figure of speech. *Corpus illud suum fecit "hoc est corpus meum" dicendo, "id est, figura corporis mei."* He made it his own body by saying, "This is my body, that is, the figure of my body." Every sentence is bilingual, or allegorical: saying one thing and meaning another. *Semper in figura loquens.* Every sentence a translation. Of bread and wine, this is my body. Or, of my body, this is a house and this is a steeple.

Tertullian in Auerbach, "Figura," 31.

Salutati, *Epistolario* 4:235: poetry is a *facultas bilinguis, unum exterius exhibens, aliud intrinseca ratione significans, semper in figura loquens.* Cf. Dante, letter to the Can Grande.

ะ.

Saying makes it so. Poetry, the archetypal fiat; or creative act.

ะ.

Poetry, the creative act, the act of life, the archetypal sexual act. Sexuality is poetry. The lady is our creation, or Pygmalion's statue. The lady is the poem; Laura is, really, poetry. Petrarch says that he invented the beautiful name of Laura, but that in reality Laura was nothing but that poetic laurel which he had pursued with incessant labor.

Petrarch letter in Wilkins, "The Coronation of Petrarch," *The Making of the Canzoniere*, 26.

ะ.

To love is to transform; to be a poet. Together with Apollo's help, the aim is to see, amazed, our lady sitting on the grass, making with her arms a thick shade; as in Pollaiuolo's painting. She is the gentle tree whose shade made my weak genius flower.

Petrarch, *Rime*, XXXIV, LX.

ะ.

To love is to transform, and be transformed. The lover must be flexible, or fluxible. There are a thousand shapes of girls, their figures, or *figurae*; the lover, like Proteus, will now melt into flowing water, will be now a lion, now a tree, now a bristling boar.

Ovid, *Ars Amatoria*, I, ll. 759–762.

ะ.

To transform and be transformed. Love and the lady transform him, making out of living man a green laurel, which through the frozen season still loses not its leaves.

Petrarch, *Rime*, XXIII, l. 39.

&

    Apollo's laurel-bough
    That sometime grew within this learned man—

The first stage of spiritual deliverance in yoga is to discover in oneself the tree; the upright surge of the spinal column. Wisdom in Ecclesiastes 29:17: like a cedar I am exalted in Lebanon, and like a cypress on Mount Zion. *Sapientia* is a lady; the *anima* in all of us; the *aura* in Laura. The lady and the lover are one tree.

J. Onimus, "La poétique de l'arbre," *Revue des Sciences Humaines* 101 (1961): 107.
Ovid, *Metamorphoses*, VII, l. 813.

&

The metamorphosis of sexuality: sublimation.

    The gods that mortal beauty chase
    Still in a tree did end their race.

Instead of the girl, the laurel. *Hanc quoque Phoebus amat.* Orpheus sings, and a tree goes up; in pure sublimation. Or are they one and the same, the tree and the girl, Laura—*remanet nitor unus in illa*—or the tree and the girl and the song. The tree is in the ear; or is it a girl that makes herself a bed in my ear.

Rilke, *Die Sonette an Orpheus*, I, nos. i–ii.
Ovid, *Metamorphoses*, I, ll. 552–553.

&

From the sensual ear to the spirit ditties of no tone. The spiritualization of the senses; a purification. The laurel purifies. Laurel leaves; Laura laves. Daphne is art, or through art, the still unravished bride. In sublimation the sexuality is not consummated—

    Bold Lover, never, never canst thou kiss,
    Though winning near the goal—yet, do not grieve;
    She cannot fade, though thou hast not thy bliss;
    For ever wilt thou love, and she be fair!

M. B. Ogle, "The Laurel in Ancient Religion and Folklore," *American Journal of Philology* 31 (1910): 287–311.

&

The still unravished bride. The struggle stilled. The mad pursuit is deathly still. The chase arrested. The immobile running girl, with no carnal motion.

Ovide Moralisé, I, l. 3178.

≈

The chase arrested, the chase goes on forever. As in those gothic novels described by Leslie Fiedler: "Through a dream landscape, usually called by the name of some actual Italian place, a girl flees in terror. . . . She escapes and is caught; escapes again and is caught; escapes and is caught. . . . The Maiden in flight representing the uprooted soul of the artist . . . the girl on the run and her pursuer become only alternate versions of the same plight. . . . Each is a projection of his opposite—*anima* and *animus*."

Fiedler, *Love and Death in the American Novel*, 107, 111.

≈

The still unravished bride, the ever-green. A virginal viridity.

Ovide Moralisé, I. l. 3108.

≈

Ever-green is golden: *grün des Lebens goldner Baum*. The *aurum* in Laura; a golden crown. The alchemical gold of sublimation. The green girl is a golden girl.

Goethe, *Faust*, I, l. 2039.

≈

Ever-green is ever-burning. Daphne a fire-brand; the laurel is full of fire. The branches of that tree which antiquity dedicated to the sun in order to crown all the conquerors of the earth, when shaken together give out fire. The laurel is the burning bush, the Virgin Mary; ardent busshe that did not waste. In the office of the Virgin: *rubum quem viderat Moyses incombustum conservatam agnovimus tuam laudabilem virginitatem*. In the bush that Moses saw burning but unconsumed we recognize the conservation of thy glorious virginity.

Eusebius, *Praeparatio Evangelii*, III, §112: the laurel sacred to Apollo, ὅ πυρὸς μεστόν τὸ φυτόν.
Bacon in Bachelard, *The Psychoanalysis of Fire*, 69–70.
Greene, *Early English Carols*, no. 199.
E. Harris, "Mary in the Burning Bush," *Journal of the Warburg Institute* 1 (1937–1938): 281–282 (Froment triptych, 1476).
L. Réau, *Iconographie de l'Art Chrétien*, vol. 2, part 1, p. 187.
Daphne, δαΐς(δαίω). Cf. H. Boas, *Aeneas' Arrival in Latium*, 98.

≈

Vel rubus incombustus humanitas Christi a divinitate non absorpta; vel ecclesia probata vel turbata tribulatione non consumpta. Or the bush is the humanity of Christ not devoured by his divinity; or the church tried or troubled but not consumed by tribulation.

Harris, "Mary in the Burning Bush," 286.

ॠ

May she become a flourishing hidden tree. *Virgo, virga,* the rod out of the stem of Jesse. The maiden is a may, a May-branch; thy moder is a may.

> He cam also stylle
> There his moder lay
> As dew in Aprille,
> That fallyt on the spray.

Yeats, "A Prayer for My Daughter."
Greene, *Early English Carols,* nos. 172, 182.

ॠ

The symbolic equation Girl = Tree; the symbolic equation Girl = Phallus. The virginity is virility; the viridity is virility. We harden like trees.

> I loathe the lewd rake, the dress'd fopling despise:
> Before such pursuers the nice virgin flies;
> And as Ovid has sweetly in parables told,
> We harden like trees, and like rivers grow cold.

O. Fenichel, "The Symbolic Equation Girl = Phallus," *Collected Papers.*
Lady Mary Wortley Montague, "The Lover: A Ballad."

ॠ

Mascula virgo; going against the grain of her sex. Daphne was a huntress, like Diana; and the only boy she ever loved was a boy disguised as a girl.

S. Sontag, *Against Interpretation,* 279.
Parthenius, *Narrationes Amatoriae,* no. 15.

ॠ

Metamorphosis into a tree. The sublimation is at the same time a fall, into a lower order of creation; an incarnation. The way up is the way down. The sublime Apollo is desublimated, descends; in love with human nature he takes on human, all-too-human form—the hound of heaven, *ut canis in vacuo leporem cum Gallicus arvo*—to be united with the Virgin. And what she finally gives him is wood, the maternal material. The Virgin is his mother; Osiris, Adonis, born of a tree. In her womb he puts on wood; in her womb he is surrounded with wood, crowned with the laurel, embraced by the Virgin.

Ovid, *Metamorphoses*, I, l. 533.
Ovide Moralisé, I, ll. 3245–3250.

ॐ

What she finally gives him is the wood of the cross.

The gods that mortal beauty chase
Still in a tree did end their race.

In a tree or on a tree. Sublimation is crucifixion. Even so shall the Son of Man be lifted up. There is a Coptic tapestry fragment from a fifth-century tomb showing the tree-girl, naked and sexed, handing to Apollo a flower which is a cross. Ovid says, *oscula dat ligno*. He kisses the cross.

In the Louvre Museum.
Ovid, *Metamorphoses*, I, l. 556.

ॐ

She is his mother; the Great Mother; the naked goddess rising between two branches.

E. Neumann, *The Great Mother*, 241–256.

ॐ

She is his mother; she may have been a whore. Laura, Laurentia; some say she was the nurse of Romulus and Remus; others say she was a whore.

Freud, "A Special Type of Choice of Object Made by Men," *Collected Papers* 4:199.
Varro, *De Lingua Latina*, V. § 152; VI, § 23.

ॐ

From the vagabond maiden to the family tree: she settled down; in the Laurentian land. Laura becomes Lar. On Augustus' doorstep—

postibus Augustis eadem fiddissima custos
ante fores stabis.
like some green laurel
rooted in one dear perpetual place.

Vico, *New Science*, § 533.
Cato, *Originum*, Frag. no. 10.

Ovid, *Metamorphoses*, I, ll. 562–563.
Vergil, *Aeneid*, VII, ll. 59–62.

&

Metamorphosis into a tree. A fall, into the state of nature. The spirit, the human essence, hides, buried in the natural object; "projected." Great Pan is dead. Ovid's *Metamorphoses*, the death of the gods, and the birth of poetry.

Schiller, "Die Götter Griechenlands."

&

Dead and buried. The Muses as museum; art as sarcophagus

> with brede
> Of marble men and maidens overwrought.

Like the laurel, promising immorality.

&

Promising immortality, or awaiting resurrection. Not dead but sleeping. The maiden is not dead, but sleepeth. The tree is the sleeping beauty. She made herself a bed in my ear and went to sleep. And everything is her sleep.

Matthew 9:24.
Rilke, *Die Sonette an Orpheus*, I, no. ii.

&

To waken the spirit from its sleep. Orpheus or Christ, saying to stem and stone,

> trees
> And the mountain-tops that freeze—

Maiden I say unto thee, arise.

Shakespeare, *Henry VIII*, act 3, scene 1.
Luke 8:54.

&

We shall not all sleep, but we shall all be changed. The resurrection is the revelation of the sons of God. In the Apocalypse

> Daphne hath broke her bark, and that swift foot
> Which th' angry Gods had fast'ned with a root
> To the fix'd earth, doth now unfettered run
> To meet th' embraces of the youthful Sun.

Running to meet the son from whom she originally fled. *Nescis, temeraria, nescis quem fugias*.

Romans 8:19.
Carew, "The Rapture."
Ovid, *Metamorphoses*, I, ll. 514–515.

৯

The triumphant laurel. *In hoc signo vinces*. Be thou faithful unto death and I will give thee a crown of life. A crown of glory that fadeth not; a golden crown. The laud in Laura. The laurel on Caesar's brow; the coronation of Petrarch, the poet laureate. The emperor, the poet, and the triumphant lover:

> Ite triumphales circum mea tempora laurus!
> vicimus, in nostra est, ecce, Corinna sinu.

Revelation 2:10; 1 Peter 5:4.
Danielou, "The Palm and Crown," *Primitive Christian Symbols*.
Kantorowicz, "On Transformations of Apolline Ethics," in *Selected Studies*, 399–408.
Wilkins, "The Coronation of Petrarch," *The Making of the Canzoniere*.
Isidorus, *Etymologiarum Lib.*, XVII, vii. *Laurus a verbo laudis dicta. . . . Apud antiquos autem laudea nominabatur . . . ut in auriculis, quae initio audiculae dictae sunt, et medidies quae nunc meridies dicitur.*
Ovid, *Amores*, II, no. xii, ll. 1–2.

৯

To restore to trees and flowers their original animality; their original spirituality; their original humanity. Erasmus Darwin in the Proem to his *Loves of the Plants*: "Whereas P. Ovidius Naso, a great necromancer in the famous court of Augustus Caesar did by art poetic transmute Men, Women, and even Gods and Goddesses, into Trees and Flowers; I have undertaken by similar art to restore some of them to their original animality, after having remained prisoners so long in their respective vegetable mansions."

E. Sewell, *The Orphic Voice*, 228.

৯

The Spirit is human; the invisible reality is human. *Ecce homo; ecce Daphne*. Instead of a stone or tree displayed, a statue; a transfiguration of the stone or tree, disclosing the human essence.

৯

The final metamorphosis is the humanization of nature. It is a question of love: the transformation of the Bear into a Prince the moment the Bear is loved. The identification is a change of identity; the magic is love.

Novalis, in Hartman, *The Unmediated Vision*, 135.
Ficino, *Commentarium in Convivium Platonis de Amore*, chapter VI, § 10; cf.
F. Yates, *Giordano Bruno and the Hermetic Tradition*, 127.

ta

Overcoming the distinction between *Naturwissenschaft* and *Geisteswissenschaft*: "I know what it is to look like a tree but I cannot know what it is to be a tree."

I. Berlin, "The Philosophical Ideas of Giambattista Vico," *Art and Ideas in Eighteenth-Century Italy*, 172.

The Tree

Ezra Pound

I stood still and was a tree amid the wood,
Knowing the truth of things unseen before;
Of Daphne and the laurel bow
And that god-feasting couple old
That grew elm-oak amid the wold.

ta

A Girl

Ezra Pound

The tree has entered my hands,
The sap has ascended my arms,
The tree has grown in my breast—
Downward,
The branches grow out of me, like arms.

Tree you are,
Moss you are,
You are violets with wind above them.
A child—so high—you are,
And all this is folly to the world.

A spiritualization of nature; an invisible spirit in the tree—

Casting the body's vest aside
My soul into the boughs does glide.

The transfiguration is a transmigration.

ta

As Karl Marx said, the humanization of nature is the naturalization of man.

> The gods that mortal beauty chase
> Still in a tree did end their race.

The tree is the teleological end, the *eschaton*. We shall all be changed, in the twinkling of an eye. Resurrection is metamorphosis, from the natural to the supernatural or spiritual body. It is raised a spiritual body. Casting the body's vest aside. The harps that we hung on the willow trees, the organs, are our natural bodies, the sexual organizations.

K. Marx, "The Philosophic-Economic Manuscripts."
G. H. Hartman, "Marvell, St. Paul, and the Body of Hope," *English Literary History* 31 (1964): 175–194.
Methodius, in Rahner, *Greek Myths and Christian Mystery*, 317.

ⵗ

The supernatural body reunites us with nature; with rocks and stones and trees. It gives us the flower body of Narcissus, or the tree body of Daphne. Love's best retreat. It is the resurrection of nature in us; nature transformed into invisible spirit. As Rilke says, Earth, is that not what you want, to rise again, invisible, in us. *Unsichtbar in uns zu erstehen.*

Rilke, in Heller, *The Disinherited Mind*, 169.

ⵗ

Love's best retreat. The spiritualization of sensuality is love: a great triumph over Christianity, says Nietzsche. Sensuality is not abolished, but fulfilled.

> No white nor red was ever seen
> So amorous as this lovely green.

Kaufmann, *Nietzsche*, 202.

ⵗ

The reconciliation of spirit and nature; the opposition of sexuality and sublimation overcome. When our eyes are opened, we perceive that in sexuality the object is not the literal girl; but the symbolic girl, the tree. It is always something else that we want. The object is always transcendent.

ⵗ

"Up till now—as is right—my tastes, my feelings, my personal experiences have all gone to feed my writings; in my best contrived phrases

I still felt the beating of my heart. But henceforth the link is broken between what I think and what I feel. And I wonder whether this impediment which prevents my heart from speaking is not the real cause that is driving my work into abstraction and artificiality. As I was reflecting on this, the meaning of the fable of Apollo and Daphne suddenly flashed upon me: happy, thought I, the man who can clasp in one and the same embrace the laurel and the object of his love."

A. Gide, *The Counterfeiters*, trans. D. Bussy, 83–84.

ཀ

The humanization of nature—not in some single herb or tree. In all the flowers and trees. Hierophanies everywhere.

> Each herb and each tree,
> Mountain, hill, earth and sea,
> Cloud, Meteor and Star,
> Are Men Seen Afar.

Blake, letter to Butts, October 2, 1800.

ཀ

In the meantime, the whole creation groaning. In the meantime, vision is to perceive the tree as Parthenon or maiden's chamber; to perceive the Caryatid in the pillar. To hear the silent speech, or under the bark the beating of a heart. To catch the trembling of her head—

> tremere omnia visa repente
> liminiaque laurusque dei.

Glimpses that can make us less forlorn.

Vergil, *Aeneid*, III, ll. 90–91.

To make the tree speak. I am leafy speafing. The oracular tree, or tree of dreams. The sylvan historian, telling a leaf-fringed legend. The *silva* or garden of verses. These trees shall be my book. Book is beech in German (*Buch* and *Buche*); a tree on which we carve our mistress's name. The maidens stray impassioned in the lettering leaves. Laura is really poetry.

Joyce, *Finnegans Wake*, 619.
Fulgentius, *Mitologiae*, I, § 14.
Eliade, *Patterns of Comparative Religion*, 284.
Curtius, *European Literature and the Latin Middle Ages*, 337.

ཀ

Thus, the whole story from Genesis to Apocalypse in any event; in any metamorphosis. Therefore it is important to keep changing the subject. The subject changes before our very eyes. It is important to keep changing our mind—

> The mind, that ocean where each kind
> Does straight its own resemblance find.

The mind, or the imagination, the original shape-shifter: Thrice Greatest Hermes.

ॐ.

Leo Spitzer said that "in Christian art earthly images easily appear to melt away and vanish. There is a parallel in modern 'poetics by alchemy' exemplified by the practice of a Góngora, who may lead us by metaphors from a maid adorning herself for marriage to Egyptian tombstones; or we may think of the famous passage in which Proust, by the use of metaphors, transforms lilac into fountain—or of Valéry's *Cimetière marin*, that sea cemetery which becomes successively a roof covered with white pigeons, a temple of Time, a flock of sheep with a shepherd dog, a multicolored hydra; all this," says Spitzer, "is based on the same Christian poetics of kaleidoscopic transformation of symbols." A Christian transfiguration, or a pagan orgy: a Bacchanalian revel of categories in which not one member is sober; a protean flux of metamorphosis. As in *Finnegans Wake*.

L. Spitzer, "Classical and Christian Ideas of World Harmony," *Traditio II* (1944), 426.

ॐ

Not everyone can play *Finnegans Wake*. But professors can. James Joyce is the apostle unto the professors. And the message is: Let's play. Or, let's practice metamorphosis. Or, let's change the subject.

ॐ

In any case it is necessary to have faith. To believe what the Bible tells us. Only beleaf. The Bible; *Le Livre*; it is all one book. Literature is as collective as the unconscious; private authorship or ownership is not to be respected. It is all one book, which includes the gospel according to Ovid, Saint Ovid the Martyr (*Ovide Moralisé*), and Petrarch, and Marvell, and Keats, and Rilke, and Yeats, and Gide, and Pound. And also the ravings of every poor Crazy Jane. Every poor schizophrenic girl is a Delphic priestess; or a Daphne, saying, "I am that tree." "That's the rain—I could be the rain. That chair—that wall. It's a terrible thing for a girl to be a wall." It's a terrible thing for a girl to be a Delphic priestess. In the cave the priestess raves: she still resists the brutal god, to shake from her hapless breast his breast; all the more his pressure subjugates her wild heart, wears down her rabid mouth, shapes her mouth into his mouthpiece.

R. D. Laing, *The Divided Self*, 217.
Vergil, *Aeneid*, VI, ll. 77–80.
L. K. Born, "Ovid and Allegory," *Speculum* 9 (1934): 362–379.

ૐ

It is all one book; blossoms on one tree,

>   Characters of the great Apocalypse
>   The types and symbols of Eternity.

One tree, in kaleidoscopic metamorphosis.

Wordworth, *Prelude*, VI, ll. 637–639.

[Added, July 1990]
>   we that were wood
>   when that a wide wood was
>
>   In a physical Universe playing with
>
>   Words
>
>   Bark be my limbs my hair be leaf
>
>   Bride be my bow my lyre my quiver

Susan Howe, "Pythagorean Silence," *The European Trusts* (Los Angeles: Sun and Moon, 1990), 17.

Persons, Places, and Personifications in the *Metamorphoses*

Ovid takes omnivorous delight in including names in the *Metamorphoses*, so that his poem abounds with references to characters and places of only marginal significance to its action. The reader may wonder why we are given the names of every walk-on (or, more accurately, die-on) character from the battle between Perseus and Andromeda's disappointed suitors or the violent struggle between the Lapiths and the centaurs. And must we have such a detailed itinerary of the progress of Aesculapius from Epidaurus to Rome? By the frequent naming of unimportant characters, Ovid undercuts the reader's expectation of epic unity with the suggestion that every name has its story, all equally worthy of mention if not of development. He also questions the hierarchy of epic values and the immortality that the epic poet traditionally conferred, by giving everyone the Roman equivalent of fifteen minutes of fame and by revealing that all heroes are very much the same, and often somewhat less heroic than previously indicated.

The tales that Ovid tells are not discrete and self-contained, in the way that modern short stories often are. They are very often family tales, involving figures whose fates are connected to those of a distant ancestor or not-so-distant relation. The human universe is made up of stories told; those stories are all part of one story, and so the way in which one tale is succeeded by another in the *Metamorphoses* is part of what Ovid means by the title of his poem.

In the entries below, I have tried to supply useful information about the more important places and names of the *Metamorphoses*, especially information about familial relationships, since this information can often lead the reader to a tale that opens up into many other tales, related by character, theme, or structure. Minor characters and those about whom little or nothing more is known, as well as places unimportant to the story or already familiar to the modern reader, have been excluded.

531

Each entry gives the first reference as it occurs in the translation, by book and line.

Acestes, Sicilian king; friend of Aeneas, XIV.119

Achaea, Region in the Peloponnese or Greece itself, V.447

Achaemenides, Companion of Ulysses; rescued from the Cyclops by Aeneas, XIV.237

Acheloüs, River and shape-shifting river god, father of the Sirens, V.727

Acheron, River in the underworld or the underworld itself; father of Ascalaphus, V.714

Achilles, Son of Peleus and Thetis; greatest Greek hero of the Trojan War, VIII.434

Acis, Lover of Galatea; son of Faunus; slain by jealous Cyclops, XIII.1087

Acmon, Companion of Diomedes, XIV.691

Acoetes, Shipmaster; devotee of Bacchus, III.750

Acrisius, Father of Danaë; grandfather of Perseus; king of Argos who opposed the worship of Bacchus, III.721

Acropolis, Citadel of Athens, II.997

Actaeon, Grandson of Cadmus; son of Autonoe; slain by Diana, III.183

Adonis, Son of Myrrha and Cinyras; lover of Venus, X.635

Aeacus, Son of Jove and Aegina; ruler of island named after his mother, VII.676

Aeetes, King of Colchis, an Asian nation east of the Black Sea; father of Medea; guardian of the Golden Fleece, VII.458

Aegaeon, Son of Neptune; a hundred-armed giant, II.12

Aegeus, Son of Pandion; king of Athens and father of Theseus, VII.571

Aegina, Mother of Aeacus by Jove; also the island named after her, VI.158

Aeneas, Son of Anchises and Venus; father of Ascanius; Trojan hero; legendary founder of Rome; became Indiges after his apotheosis, XIII.907

Aeolus, Father of Athamas; god of the winds, I.364

Aesacus, Son of Priam and the nymph Alexiroë, XI.1084

Aesculapius, Son of Apollo and Coronis; god of healing, XV.623

Aeson, Father of Jason; restored to youth by Medea, VII.161

Aetolia, Country in middle Greece, XIV.757

Agamemnon, Son of Atreus; brother of Menelaüs; husband of Clytemnestra; father of Iphigenia, Orestes, and Electra; king of Mycenae; Greek leader during the Trojan War, XII.915

Agave, Daughter of Cadmus; mother of Pentheus, III.932

Agenor, Son of Neptune; father of Cadmus and Europa; king of Tyre, II.1179

Aglauros, Daughter of Cecrops; envious sister of Herse, II.776

Ajax, (1) Son of Telamon; one of the greatest of Greek heroes of the Trojan War, XII.913; (2) Son of Oileos; rapist of Cassandra; slain by Minerva, XII.908

Alcithoë, One of the storytelling daughters of Minyas, IV.1

Alcmena, Mother of Hercules, VI.157

Alcon, Boeotian designer of goblet depicting the deeds of Orion's daughters, XIII.991

Alcyone, Daughter of Aeolus; wife of Ceyx; changed into halcyon, VII.569

Alpheus, River and river god; infatuated by Arethusa, II.333

Althaea, Wife of Oeneus; mother of Deianira and Meleager, VIII.611

Ammon, Egyptian deity identified with Jove, IV.918

Amphion, Husband of Niobe; father of fourteen; builder of Theban walls, VI.264

Amphissus, Son of Dryope, IX.517

Amphitryon, Husband of Alcmena; putative father of Hercules, VI.156

Amulius, Usurper of Alba Longa from his brother, Numitor, XIV.1123

Anapis, Sicilian river and god; lover of Cyane, V.585

Anaxarete, Maiden of Cyprus who spurned Iphis, XIV.1015

Ancaeus, Arcadian at the Calydonian boar hunt, VIII.444

Anchises, Lover of Venus, by whom he fathered Aeneas, IX.620

Andraemon, Husband of Dryope, IX.485

Androgeos, Son of Minos, whose death in Athens he avenges, VII.656

Andromeda, Daughter of Cepheus and Cassiope; rescued by Perseus, IV.918

Anius, King and priest of Apollo on Delos, XIII.918

Antaeus, A giant, IX.274

Antigone, Changed to a stork by Juno, VI.132

Antiphates, King of the Laestrygonians, XIV.336

Anubis, Dog-headed Egyptian god, IX.997

Aphrodite, *See* Venus, IV.531

Apis, Sacred ox worshiped by Egyptians, IX.999

Apollo (aka Phoebus and Delius, the latter from his birthplace, on Delos), Son of Jove and Latona; twin brother of Diana; the sun god, I.629

Arachne, Daughter of Idmon; rival (in weaving) of Minerva, VI.8

Arcadia, Region in the Peloponnese, I.304

Arcas, Son of Jupiter and Callisto, II.646

Ardea, Rutulian city; a heron sprang from its ashes, XIV.821

Areopagus, Site of the highest council of the Athenians, VI.99

Arethusa, Nymph of Elis; loved by Alpheus; became a spring, V.577

Argonauts, Band of Greek heroes, led by Jason, who set sail from Greece to Colchis in search of the Golden Fleece, VII.2

Argos, City in the Peloponnese, I.834

Argus, Hundred-eyed monster guarding Io; slain by Mercury, I.869

Ariadne, Daughter of Minos; abandoned lover of Theseus, VIII.238

Arne, Woman of Siphnos who betrayed her homeland for gold, VII.668

Ascalaphus, Son of Acheron and Orphne who betrayed Proserpina, V.712

Ascanius (aka Julus), Son of Aeneas and Creusa; first king of Alba Longa, XIII.912

Astraea, Goddess of justice, I.203

Astyanax, Son of Hector and Andromache; slain by Greeks, XIII.606

Atalanta, (1) Participant in Calydonian boar hunt and loved by Meleager, VIII.449; (2) Boeotian maiden famous for her speed in running, X.672

Athamas, Son of Aeolus; husband of Ino, III.728

Athena, *See* Minerva, II.1145

Athos, Mountain in Macedonia, II.289

Atlas, A Giant; son of Iapetas; a mountain in North Africa; supported the weight of the heavens on his shoulders, I.945

Atreus, Son of Pelops; father of Agamemnon and Menelaüs; king of Mycenae, XV.1077

Attis, Phrygian shepherd; beloved of Cybele, X.150

Augustus, Nephew of Julius Caesar adopted as his son; first Roman emperor; identified by Ovid with Jove, I.285

Aulis, Boeotian harbor where the Greeks gathered before sailing to Troy, XII.14

Aura, A fatal breeze, VII.1155

Aurora, Wife of Tithonus; mother of Memnon; goddess of the dawn; infatuated by Cephalus, II.155

Ausonia, Region of southern Italy or Italy itself, XIV.456

Auster, The south wind, I.92

Autolycus, Son of Mercury and Chione; grandfather of Ulysses; husband of Erysichthon's daughter, VIII.1043

Autonoe, Daughter of Cadmus; mother of Actaeon; sister of Semele; aunt of Pentheus, III.250

Avernus, The underworld or its entrance at lake of same name in Campagna, V.714

Bacchantes, Devotees of Bacchus, III.904

Bacchiadae, Royal family of Corinth, V.573

Bacchus, Son of Jove and Semele; god of wine, III.407

Baucis, Pious old woman; wife of Philemon, VIII.890
Belides, The fifty daughters of Danaus, forty-nine of whom murdered their husbands on their wedding nights, IV.633
Bellona, Sister of Mars; goddess of war, V.226
Boeotia, Region in central Greece, I.432
Boötes, Constellation in the northern sky, II.237
Boreas, The north wind, I.90, VI. 987
Bubastis, Egyptian goddess similar to Diana, IX.998
Busiris, Egyptian king; serial murderer of strangers; slain by Hercules, IX.271
Byblis, Daughter of Miletus and Cyanee; twin sister of Caunis, whom she desires, IX.661

Cadmus, Son of Agenor; brother of Europa; husband of Harmonia; father of Semele, Autonoe, and Agave; founder of Thebes, III.6
Caeneus, Thessalian boy; born a girl, Caenis, VIII.427
Caenis, Thessalian girl who is turned into a boy, Caeneus, XII.280
Caesar, Julius (aka Julius), Roman soldier and statesman who traced his origins back to Venus and Anchises; ambition to rule Rome led to his assassination in 44 B.C.; civil war followed, and his adopted nephew Augustus emerged as first Roman emperor, I.281
Caïcus, River in Mysia, a country in Asia Minor, II.323
Caiëta, Aeneas' old nurse; the place in Italy where she is buried, XIV.625
Calliope, Mother of Orpheus and Muse of poetry, V.503
Callirhoë, Daughter of Acheloüs; wife of Alcmaeon, IX.602
Callisto, Daughter of Lycaon; mother of Arcas, II.563
Calydon, Aetolian city; home of the hero Meleager, VI.593
Canens, Daughter of Janus and Venilia; wife of Picus, XIV.481
Canopus, An Egyptian city, XV.1036
Capaneus, One of the Seven against Thebes, IX.588
Caphereus, Promontory on the Euboean coast, XIV.672
Cassiope, Wife of Cepheus; mother of Andromeda, IV.1005
Castalian grotto, Site of a spring on Parnassus sacred to Apollo, III.18
Castor, Son of Tyndareus and Leda; twin brother of Pollux; one of the Gemini, XII.589
Caunus, Son of Miletus and Cyanee; twin brother of Byblis, IX.661
Cayster, River in Lydia, noted for its swans, II.337
Cecrops, Founder of Athens; father of Herse, Pandrosos, and Aglauros, II.770
Cenchreïs, Wife of Cinyras; mother of Myrrha, X.525

Centaurs, Sons of Ixion and a Juno-shaped cloud; bimanous quadrupeds, half man and half horse, IX.146

Cephalus, Grandson of Aeolus; husband of Procris; a prince of Athens, VI.986

Cepheus, Ethiopian king; Andromeda's father, IV.917

Cephisus, River in Phocis; father of Narcissus, I.511

Cerastae, Horned Cypriots; turned into bulls by Venus, X.288

Cerberus, Three-headed watchdog of the underworld, IV.616

Cercyon, King of Eleusin, an Attic city, who challenged strangers to wrestle and killed the losers; slain by Theseus, VII.627

Ceres (aka Demeter, in Greece), Sister of Jove; mother with him of Proserpina; goddess of agriculture, V.158

Ceyx, King of Trachin, a city in Thessaly; husband of Alcyone, XI.385

Chaos, Formless matter from which the cosmos was shaped, I.9

Chariclo, Water nymph; mother of Ocyrhoë, II.886

Charybdis, Whirlpool between Italy and Sicily, VII.99

Chimaera, Lion-headed, goat-bodied, snake-tailed, fire-breathing monster, VI.486

Chione, Daughter of Daedalion; loved by Apollo and Mercury; mother of Philammon and Autolycus, XI.429

Chiron, Wisest of centaurs; raised Aesculapius, II.875

Cinyras, Father of Myrrha and of her son, Adonis, VI.139

Cipus, Legendary Roman praetor, XV.668

Circe, Daughter of the Sun and the sea nymph Perse; a magician unlucky in love, IV.284

Cithaeron, Mountain in Boeotia, II.298

Clymene, Mother of Phaëthon and the Heliades; wife of Ethiopian Merops, I.1048

Clytie, Loved Apollo; changed to a flower, IV.286

Corinth, City of Greece on the Isthmus of Corinth, II.320

Coronae, Two boys who sprang from ashes of Orion's daughters, XIII.1011

Coronis, Nymph beloved of Apollo; mother of Aesculapius, II.750

Crocus, Youth who died of love for Smilax; changed into a flower, IV.392

Croton, Host of Hercules; man for whom the Italian city of Crotona is named, XV.23

Cumae, Colony on coast of Campagna; home of the Sibyl, XIV.150

Cupid, Son of Venus and Mars; god of love, I.631

Cures, Principal city of the Sabines; home of Numa, XV.11

Cyane, Water nymph whose objections to the rape of Proserpina saw her changed into a fountain, V.577

Cyanee, Mother of Byblis and Caunis, IX.657

Cybele, Phrygian mother of gods; lover of Attis, X.149

Cyclopes, Race of savage one-eyed giants; employed by Vulcan in thunderbolt production; Polyphemus was one of them, I.359

Cycnus, (1) Self-sacrificing son of Sthenelus; changed to a swan while mourning Phaëthon, II.496; (2) Petulant son of Apollo and Hyrie; changed to a swan by Apollo after leaping from a cliff, VII.521; (3) Invulnerable son of Neptune and Canace; changed to a swan by his father after being slain by Achilles, XII.106

Cyllarus, Centaur beloved of Hylonome, XII.578

Cyllene, Mountain in Arcadia; birthplace of Mercury, I.302

Cynthia, *See* Diana, XV.626

Cynthus, Mountain in Delos; birthplace of Diana, II.296

Cyparissus, Youth beloved of Apollo; changed to cypress, X.167

Cythera, Island in the Aegean sacred to Venus, IV.402

Daedalion, Son of Lucifer; brother of Ceyx; father of Chione, XI.420

Daedalus, Father of Icarus; uncle of Perdix; Athenian architect, VIII.219

Danaë, Daughter of Acrisius; mother of Perseus by Jove, who came to her as a golden shower, IV.837

Danaüs, Father of the Belides, X.58

Daphne, Daughter of Peneus; Apollo's first love; changed to laurel, I.628

Daphnis, Phrygian shepherd boy, IV.384

Daulis, City in Phocis, V.403

Deianira, Daughter of Oeneus and Althaea; sister of Meleager; wife of Hercules, VIII.777

Deiphobus, Son of Priam; a Trojan hero, XII.803

Delius, *See* Apollo, V.485

Delos, Island in the Cyclades that sheltered Latona when she gave birth to Apollo and Diana, III.773

Delphi, City in Phocis; home of Apollo's oracle, I.712

Demeter, *See* Ceres, VI.160

Dercetis, Syrian goddess; mother of Semiramis, IV.74

Deucalion, Son of Prometheus; husband of Pyrrha; saved from Jove's flood, I.439

Dia, Old name for island of Naxos, VIII.243

Diana (aka Phoebe and Cynthia), Daughter of Jove and Latona; twin brother of Apollo; goddess of chastity, hunting, childbirth, and the moon, I.671

Diomedes, Greek hero at Troy; companion of Ulysses, XII.909

Dis, Son of Saturn; brother of Jove and Neptune; husband of Proserpina; king of the underworld, IV.602

Dodona, City in Epirus famed as site of Jove's oracle and sacred oaks, VII.888

Dolon, Trojan spy captured by Ulysses and Diomedes, XIII.141

Doris, Daughter of Oceanus and Tethys; wife of Nereus; mother of Nereids, II.13

Dryads, Wood nymphs, VIII.1053

Dryope, Mother (by Apollo) of Amphissus; husband of Andraemon; changed to tree by water nymph, IX.480

Echinades, Islands formed when Acheloüs grew angry with indifferent nymphs, VIII.846

Echion, Husband of Agave; father of Pentheus; survivor sprung from dragon's teeth sown by Cadmus, III.157

Echo, Wood nymph deprived by Juno of power to initiate conversation; in love with Narcissus, III.470

Egeria, Nymph; wife of Numa, XV.559

Elis, City and region in the western Peloponnese, II.941

Elpenor, Comrade of Ulysses, XIV.362

Elysian Fields, Abode of the blessed in the underworld, XI.87

Enipeus, River in Thessaly, VI.165

Epaphus, Son of Jupiter and Io, I.1034

Epidaurus, City in Argolis sacred to Aesculapius, III.357

Epimetheus, Brother of Prometheus; father of Pyrrha, I.540

Erebus, Another name for the underworld, XIV.573

Erectheus, King of Athens; father of Orithyia and Procris, VI.982

Erichthonius, Son of Vulcan and Mother Earth; raised by Minerva; a legendary Athenian ruler, II.766

Erigone, Daughter of Icarus; constellated as Virgo, VI.178

Erysichthon, Cut down the sacred tree of Ceres, VIII.1042

Eryx, Mountain on Sicily sacred to Venus, II.296

Etruria, Country in central Italy; home of Etruscans, XV.639

Europa, Daughter of Agenor; taken by Jove; mother of Minos and Rhadamanthus, III.3

Eurus, The east wind, I.84

Eurydice, Wife of Orpheus, X.43

Eurylochus, Companion of Ulysses, XIV.361

Eurynome, Mother of Leucothoë, IV.290

Evander, Founded city of Pallanteum in Latium; aided Aeneas, XIV.646

Evippe, Wife of Pierus; mother of the Pierides, V.442

Fates, Three sisters (Clotho, Atropos, and Lachesis), originally Greek but known to the Romans as the Parcae; said to have unlimited power over gods and men, whose destinies they inscribed on tablets of bronze, I.355

Faunus, Deity of the woods; identified with Pan, VI.473

Furies, Three sisters (Alecto, Tisiphone, and Megaera), originally Greek, but known to the Romans as the Furiae; goddesses of vengeance, who torture the guilty in the underworld and sometimes drive the living to madness and frenzy, I.335

Galanthis, Servant of Alcmena; changed into a weasel, IX.447

Galatea, Sea nymph; lover of Acis; pursued by Polyphemus, XIII.1070

Ganymede, Boy beloved of Jove, X.214

Gargaphie, Grove and spring in Boeotia sacred to Diana, III.194

Gemini, Castor and Pollux, twin sons of Tindareus and Leda; later constellated as the Twins, VIII.526

Geryon, Monster with three bodies; slain by Hercules, IX.275

Giants, Race of monsters born from Mother Earth who challenged Jove and the Olympian gods; defeated by him in the course of the Gigantomachy, or fight with the Giants, they were imprisoned under the earth, often in volcanic areas, I.206

Glaucus, Mortal changed into sea god; infatuated by Scylla, VII.334

Gorgon, Any of three daughters of Phorcys whose gaze turned men to stone; Medusa, principally, who was slain by Perseus, IV.847

Graces, Roman *Gratiae*; beautiful nymphs attendant on Venus, VI.614

Granicus, Father of Alexiroë; river and river god in Asia Minor, XI.1086

Haemus, Thracian man changed into mountain of same name for taking name of Jove, II.293

Harmonia, Daughter of Mars and Venus; wife of Cadmus; mentioned but not named in IV.776

Harpies, Winged goddesses, half bird, half maiden; makers of mischief, VII.6

Harpocrates, Egyptian god of silence, shown with finger on mouth, IX.1000

Hebe, Fatherless daughter of Juno; Hercules' wife in heaven, IX.581

Hebrus, River in Thrace, II.342

Hecate, Goddess of underworld and enchantments, VI.199

Hector, Son of Priam and Hecuba; father of Astyanax; greatest Trojan hero, XI.1080

Hecuba, Wife of Priam; mother of Hector, Polyxena, and Polydorus, XI.1083

Helen, Daughter of Leda and Jove (or Tyndareus); cause of Trojan War, VII.504

Helenus, Prophetically gifted son of Priam, XIII.141

Heliades, Daughters of the Sun and Clymene, whose grief for their brother Phaëthon sees them changed into poplars, their tears into amber, II.454

Helicon, Mountain in Boeotia sacred to the Muses, II.293

Hercules, Son of Jove (or Amphitryon) and Alcmena; husband of Deianira and Hebe; father of Tlepolemus; greatest of Greek heroes; granted immortality by Jove, VII.509

Hermes, *See* Mercury, IV.531

Herse, Daughter of Cecrops; beloved of Mercury, II.774

Hersilia, Wife of Romulus; became Hora after her apotheosis, XIV.1211

Hesperides, Daughters of Night (or of Atlas and Hesperis); guardians of a tree of golden apples, XI.163

Hesperus, Evening star, V.611

Hippodame, Wife of Pirithoüs, XII.314

Hippolytus, Son of Theseus and the Amazon Hippolyte; dies and is reborn as Virbius, XV.566

Hippomenes, Son of Megareus; the youth who outraced Atalanta and wed her; changed into a lion by Cybele, X.682

Hora, *See* Hersilia, XIV.1242

Hyacinthus, Spartan youth; loved by Apollo, X.220

Hydra, Water serpent, a dragon-like monster, II.907

Hyllus, Son of Hercules and Deianira; husband of Iole, IX.412

Hylonome, She-centaur; beloved of Cyllarus, XII.596

Hymenaeus, God of marriage, VI.614

Hymettus, Mountain in Attica, VII.1001

Hypaepa, Town in Lydia; home of Arachne, VI.20

Hyperion, One of the Titans; father of the sun god or the Sun himself, IV.267

Hyrie, Lake in Boeotia, named for mother of petulant Cycnus, VII.520

Iacchus, Another name for Bacchus; the ritual cry of his worshipers, IV.24

Ianthe, Betrothed of Iphis, IX.1033

Iapetas, One of the Titans; father of Atlas and Prometheus, IV.863

Icarus, (1) Son of Daedalus, VIII.269; (2) Father of Erigone; constellated as Boötes, X.542

Ida, Mountain near Troy, II.291

Idmon, Father of Arachne, VI.13

Ilium, Another name for Troy, XIII.288

Inachus, Father of Io; Thessalian river and river god, I.806

Indiges, *See* Aeneas, XIV.871

Indigetes, A term used for local gods and heroes, XV.1087

Ino, Daughter of Cadmus; wife of Athamas; foster mother of Bacchus; aunt of Pentheus; deified as Leucothoë, III.403

Io, daughter of Inachus; raped by Jove; changed to a heifer; worshiped in Egypt as Isis, I.809

Iolaüs, Nephew of Hercules; restored to youth by Hebe, VIII.436

Iole, Maiden loved by Hercules; wed by his son Hyllus, IX.210

Iphigenia, Daughter of Agamemnon and Clytemnestra; sacrificed by her father at Aulis or saved by Diana, XII.44

Iphis, (1) Daughter of Ligdus and Telethusa; changed to young man by Isis, IX.964; (2) Cypriot youth who loves Anaxarete, XIV.1014

Iris, Goddess of the rainbow; messenger of Juno, I.374

Isis, An Egyptian deity, the deified Io, IX.1112

Ithaca, Island in the Ionian Sea; home of Ulysses, XIII.745

Itys, Son of Tereus and Procne, VI.628

Ixion, Lapith king; father of Pirithoüs and the centaurs; punished in underworld for attempted rape of Juno, IV.631

Janus, Two-faced Roman god of entrances, bridges, and archways, XIV.476

Jason, Son of Aeson; lover of Medea; leader of the Argonauts, VII.9

Jove (aka Jupiter), Son of Saturn; husband of Juno; ruler of heaven, I.147

Julus, *See* Ascanius, XIV.836

Julius, *See* Caesar (Julius), XV.512

Juno (aka Saturnia), Daughter of Saturn; sister, wife, and queen of Jove, I.374

Jupiter, *See* Jove, I.158

Laestrygonians, Ancient Italian tribe; reputedly cannibals, XIV.335

Lapiths, People of Thessaly who engaged in famous battle with centaurs, XII.374

Latinus, Father of Lavinia, XIV.877

Latium, Italian region whose capital became Rome, XIV.465

Latona, Daughter of the Titan Coeus; mother (by Jove) of Apollo and Diana, VI.232

Lavinia, Daughter of Latinus; wife of Aeneas, XIV.816

Learchus, Son of Athamas and Ino; slain by his frenzied father, IV.704

Leda, Wife of Tyndareus; mother (by Jove-as-swan) of Castor and Pollux, VI.153

Lesbos, Island in the Aegean, II.822

Leuconoë, One of the storytelling daughters of Minyas, IV.229

Leucothoë, (1) Daughter of Orchamus and Eurynome; beloved of Phoebus, IV.272; (2) name given to the deified Ino, IV.742

Liber, An Italian god of wine; identified with Bacchus, III.681

Lichas, Servant of Hercules; changed into a rock, IX.234

Ligdus, Father of Iphis, IX.967

Liriope, Water nymph; mother of Narcissus, III.441

Lotis, Nymph changed into a lotus tree, IX.504

Lucifer, Father of Ceyx; the morning star, II.158

Lucina, Goddess of childbirth, V.443

Lycaon, King of Arcadia; father of Callisto; changed into a wolf, I.225

Lycurgus, Thracian king opposed to the worship of Bacchus, IV.38

Lydia, Country in Asia Minor, II.336

Lyncus, Scythian king turned into a lynx, V.832

Macareus, Companion of Ulysses, XII.667

Maeander, Father of Cyanee, the mother of Byblis and Caunis; a famously winding river and a river god, II.326

Maenads, Frenzied followers of Bacchus, XI.31

Maeonia, Old name for Lydia, III.751

Manto, Daughter of Tiresias and herself a prophet, VI.229

Mars, Son of Jove and Juno; god of war, III.42

Marsyas, Satyr who challenges Apollo to a musical contest, VI.574

Medea, Daughter of Aeetes; a magician; in love with Jason, VII.20

Medusa, Daughter of Phorcys and Keto; raped by Neptune, she was turned by Athena into a monster whose snake-girded head became a weapon that petrified those who saw it; decapitated by Perseus, her streaming blood produced Pegasus and Chrysaor, IV.899

Meleager, Son of Oeneus and Althaea; Calydonian hero, VIII.379

Melicertes, Son of Athamas and Ino; changed into the sea god Palaemon, IV.712

Memnon, Son of Aurora and Tithonus; slain by Achilles, XIII.841

Memnonides, Birds that sprang from the ashes of Memnon, XIII.897

Menelaüs, Son of Atreus; brother of Agamemnon; husband of Helen, whose abduction by Paris instigates the Trojan War, XII.910

Mercury, Son of Jove and Maia; father of Autolycus; messenger of Jove, I.953

Merops, Ethiopian king; husband of Clymene; putative father of Phaëthon, I.1060

Messana, City in Sicily, XIII.1057

Midas, Phrygian king of dubious intellect, XI.129

Miletus, Son of Apollo; father of Byblis and Caunis, IX.648

Milon, Legendary athlete, XV.280

Minerva (aka Pallas Athena), Daughter of Jove; goddess of wisdom and technical skill; virgin warrior; patron of Athens, II.781

Minos, Son of Europa (by Jove-as-bull); husband of Pasiphaë; father of Androgeos and Ariadne; warlike king of Crete, VII.653

Minotaur, Monster born of Pasiphaë by a bull; kept in the labyrinth that Minos ordered Daedalus to build; slain by Theseus, VIII.215

Minyas, King of Orchomenus, a city in Boeotia; his daughters opposed the worship of Bacchus, IV.1

Mithridates, King of Pontus vanquished by Pompey, XV.936

Mnemosyne, Mother (by Jove) of the nine Muses, V.389

Morpheus, Son and messenger of Sleep, XI.908

Mother Earth, Roman Terra; the earth goddess; daughter of Chaos; wife of Uranus; mother of the Giants, I.215

Muses, Nine daughters of Zeus and Mnemosyne, goddess of Memory, charged with inspiring various kinds of poetry, as well as dance, history, and astronomy, V.369

Mycenae, City in Argolis; home of Agamemnon, VI.592

Myrmidons, Race of men created by Jove from ants, VII.934

Myrrha, Daughter of Cinyras who fell in love with him; mother (by Cinyras) of Adonis, X.387

Myscelus, Son of Alemon; founder of Crotona, XV.28

Naiads, Water nymphs, goddesses of rivers and springs, I.890

Narcissus, Son of river god Cephisus and water nymph Liriope, III.446

Nature, A process responsible for giving form to Chaos, I.8

Naxos, Largest of the Cyclades, III.821

Neleus, Son of Neptune; king of Pylos; father of Nestor, II.953

Nemesis, Greek goddess; a personification of the righteous indignation of the gods, who punishes men for their presumption and arrogance, III.523

Neoptolemus, Son of Achilles, XIII.663

Neptune, Son of Saturn; brother of Jove and Dis; trident-bearing god of the waters, I.381

Nereids, Sea nymphs; daughters of Nereus and Doris, I.417

Nereus, A sea god; father of the Nereids, I.256

Nessus, Centaur slain by Hercules for attempted rape of Deianira, IX.145

Nestor, Son of Neleus; oldest of Greek heroes during the Trojan War, VIII.441

Niobe, Daughter of Tantalus and Dione; wife of Amphion; mother of fourteen, all slain by Apollo and Diana, VI.215

Nisus, King of Megara; father of Scylla; vanquished by Minos, VIII.9

Nixi, Three Roman goddesses protective of women in labor, IX.433

Nonacris, Mountain in Arcadia, I.955

Numa, Second Roman king, XV.5

Numidians, Tribe in North Africa vanquished by Julius Caesar, XV.935

Numitor, King of Alba; deposed by brother, Amulius; restored by his grandsons, Romulus and Remus, XIV.1125

Nyctimene, Daughter of Epopeus; changed into an owl, II.819

Nysa, Site of a cave in India where the infant Bacchus was sheltered, III.405

Oceanus, God of the ocean; husband of Tethys, II.704

Ocyroë, Daughter of Chiron and Chariclo; changed into a mare, II.885

Oedipus, Theban king who solved the riddle of the Sphinx, VII.1087

Oeneus, King of Calydon; father of Meleager and Deianira; husband of Althaea, VIII.382

Oeta, Site of a mountain range in southern Thessaly, I.433

Olympus, Mountain in Thessaly; home of the gods, I.211

Ops, Italian deity; goddess of abundance; wife of Saturn, IX.728

Orchamus, Father of Leucothoë, IV.294

Orion, (1) Constellated Giant, VIII.287; (2) Theban man famed for self-sacrificing daughters, XIII.433

Orithyia, Daughter of Erectheus; seized by Boreas, VI.991

Orpheus, Son of Apollo (or Oeagrus) and the Muse Calliope; husband of Eurydice; famed Thracian poet and musician, X.4

Orphne, Nymph of the underworld; mother (by Acheron) of Ascalaphus, V.713

Osiris, Husband of Isis; Egyptian god of fertility, IX.1003

Ossa, Mountain in Thessaly, I.212

Othrys, Mountain in Thessaly, II.296

Pactolus, River in Lydia famed for its gold, VI.23

P-Airides, *See* Pierides, V.867

Palaemon, *See* Melicertes, IV.741

Palamedes, Exposed Ulyssess feigned madness to the Greeks and was later falsely accused by him, XIII.54

Palatine, Hill in Rome, favored by the upper classes, I.242

Pallas Athena, *See* Minerva, III.124

Pan, Goat-footed god of woods and shepherds; a faun, I.967

Pandion, King of Athens; father of Procne and Philomela, VI.610

Paphos, Son of Pygmalion and his statue; gave his name to Cypriot city, X.371

Paris, Son of Priam and Hecuba; brother of Hector; lover of Helen, XII.6

Parnassus, Mountain in Phocis; sacred to Apollo and the Muses, I.436

Parthenon, Famous temple of Athena on the Acropolis in Athens, II.987

Pasiphaë, Daughter of the Sun; wife of Minos; mother (by him) of Phaedra and Ariadne; mother (by a bull) of the Minotaur, VIII.183

Pegasus, Winged horse born from Medusa's blood, IV.1072

Peleus, Son of Aeacus; brother of Telamon; half brother of Phocus; husband of Thetis; father of Achilles, VII.682

Pelias, Half brother of Jason's father, Aeson, whom he deposed; sent Jason on quest for Golden Fleece, VII.418

Pelion, Mountain in Thessaly, I.212

Pelops, Son of Tantalus; brother of Niobe; slain by his father and offered as a feast to test the gods, VI.579

Penelope, Wife of Ulysses, VIII.443

Peneus, Thessalian river and river god; father of Daphne, I.629

Pentheus, Son of Echion and Agave; Theban king who opposed worship of Bacchus, III.662

Perdix, Nephew of Daedalus; changed by Minerva into a partridge, VIII.363

Pergama, Trojan citadel or Troy itself, XIII.514

Periclymenus, Grandson of Neptune; shape-shifting brother of Nestor; slain (in the form of an eagle) by an arrow of Hercules, XII.815

Perimele, Nymph loved by Acheloüs; changed by him into an island, VIII.849

Persephone, See Proserpina, V.640

Perseus, Son of Jove and Danaë; Greek hero who slew the Medusa and rescued Andromeda, IV.836

Phaëthon, Son of Clymene and Phoebus (or Merops); took father's chariot for his last ride, I.1039

Pharsalia, Region in Thessaly where Julius Caesar defeated Pompey in 48 B.C., XV.1030

Philemon, Pious old husband of Baucis, VIII.890

Philippi, Macedonian city where Octavian (later Emperor Augustus) and Marc Antony defeated Brutus and Cassius, conspirators who slew Julius Caesar, XV.1031

Philoctetes, Son of Poeas; companion of Hercules; abandoned on isle of Lemnos by the Greeks at the beginning of the Trojan War, IX.341

Philomela, Daughter of Pandion; sister of Procne; raped by Tereus, VI.648

Phineus, (1) Uncle and betrothed of Andromeda, V.11; (2) Blind seer; Thracian king tormented by Harpies, VII.3

Phlegethon, River in the underworld, V.719

Phocis, Region in Greece between Boeotia and Aetolia, I.432

Phocus, Son of Aeacus and the Nereid Psamathe; half brother of Peleus and Telamon, VII.683

Phoebe, *See* Diana, I.661

Phoebus, *See* Apollo, I.468

Phoenix, Legendary self-resurrecting bird, XV.454

Phorcys, Father of the Gorgons, IV.1056

Phrygia, Country in Asia Minor; original site of the worship of Cybele, VI.64

Phylius, Lover of Cycnus, VII.524

Picus, Son of Saturn; husband of Canens; king of Latium; changed by Circe into a woodpecker, XIV.455

Pierides (aka P-Airides), Nine daughters of Pierus; changed into magpies by the Muses, V.857

Pierus, Father of nine daughters known as the Pierides, V.441

Pindus, Mountain range in Thessaly, I.787

Pirene, A spring in Corinth, II.320

Pirithoüs, Son of the Lapith king Ixion; friend of Theseus, VIII.424

Polydorus, Son of Priam and Hecuba; betrayed and slain by the Thracian king Polymestor, XIII.626

Polymestor, Thracian king whose murder of Polydorus was avenged by Hecuba, XIII.625

Polyphemus, Cyclops who loved Galatea and slew Acis, XIII.1108

Polyxena, Daughter of Priam and Hecuba; sacrificed to the shade of Achilles, XIII.651

Pomona, Wood nymph of Latium wooed by Vertumnus, XIV.892

Pontus, Kingdom in Asia Minor on the Black Sea, XV.936

Priam, Son of Laomedon; husband of Hecuba; last king of Troy, XI.1078

Priapus, God of procreation and gardens, IX.505

Procne, Daughter of Pandion; sister of Philomela; wife of Tereus; mother of Itys, VI.612

Procris, Daughter of Erectheus, the Athenian king; wife of Cephalus; sister of Orithyia, VII.990

Procrustes, Robber who famously compelled victims to lie on eponymous bed, then stretched or lopped their limbs to fit, VII.625

Prometheus, Son of Iapetus; father of Deucalion; created mankind out of clay, I.112

Propoetides, Women of Amathus who, despising Venus, were turned by her into prostitutes, then into stones, X.286

Proserpina (aka Persephone), Daughter of Jove and Ceres; wife of Pluto; queen of the underworld, V.558

Protesilaüs, First Greek slain in the Trojan War, XII.99

Proteus, Shape-shifting sea god, II.11

Psamathe, Mother of Phocus; slain by Peleus; a Nereid, XI.571

Pygmalion, Cypriot sculptor whose ivory maiden lived to marry him, X.312

Pylos, city in Elis; Nestor's home, II.947

Pyramus, Lover of Thisbe, IV.87

Pyreneus, Thracian king who attempted to violate the Muses, V.400

Pyrrha, Daughter of Epimetheus; wife of Deucalion, I.483

Python, Monstrous serpent slain by Apollo, I.608

Quirinus, *See* Romulus, XIV.1209

Rhadamanthus, Son of Jove and Europa; brother of Minos, IX.638

Rhegium, Italian seaport opposite Messana, XIV.7

Rhesus, Thracian king allied with Priam; slain by Ulysses and Diomedes, XIII.141

Rhodope, Man changed by Jove for his impious presumption into a mountain in Thrace frequented by Orpheus, II.297

Romulus, Son of Mars and Ilia; brother of Remus; husband of Hersilia; known after death as Quirinus, XIV.1130

Rutulians, Latins, whose hero was Turnus and whose city was Ardea, XIV.644

Sabines, People of central Italy, neighbors of the Romans, XV.7

Salmacis, Nymph enamored of Hermaphroditus who gave her name to a pool of water in Caria, IV.397

Samos, Island in the Aegean; birthplace of Pythagoras, VIII.309

Sardis, Capital of Lydia, XI.192

Saturn, Son of Heaven and Mother Earth; husband of Ops; father of Jove, Juno, Neptune, and Dis, by whom deposed and confined to underworld, I.55

Saturnia, *See* Juno, XIV.1139

Satyrs, Goat-footed libertarians; companions of Bacchus, I.266

Scylla, (1) Daughter of Nisus; infatuated with Minos, VIII.20; (2) nymph wooed by Glaucus; changed into monster, then a rock between Italy and Sicily, VII.101

Scythia, Region in Asia and southeastern Europe; home of nomadic Scythians, I.89

Semele, Daughter of Cadmus; mother by Jove of Bacchus, III.330

Semiramis, Queen of Babylon, IV.90

Seriphos, Island in the Aegean, V.352

Sibyl, Priestess of Apollo living at Cumae, XIV.151

Sidon, Phoenician city; birthplace of Mercury; home of Cadmus and Europa, II.1153

Silenus, Satyr, tutor, and companion to Bacchus, IV.51

Simoïs, River near Troy, XIII.479

Sinis, Greek robber slain by Theseus, VII.628

Sirens, Daughters of Acheloüs and one of the Muses; transformed unjustly and incompletely into birds, whose irresistible song lured sailors to their deaths, V.730

Sisyphus, Son of Aeolus; punished for theft in the underworld, IV.629

Smilax, Nymph beloved of Crocus; changed into a flower, IV.392

Sphinx, Riddle-posing Theban monster, vanquished by Oedipus, VII.1088

Stellio, Boy changed into a lizard by Latona for his presumption, V.632

Styx, River in the underworld or the underworld itself, I.1019

Symplegades, Two rocky islands in the Euxine, or Black Sea, that clashed together when ships passed between them, XV.393

Syrinx, Arcadian nymph; loved by Pan; changed into pipes of Pan, I.956

Tages, Etruscan god who was changed from clod of earth to man and who taught soothsaying to his people, XV.659

Tagus, Spanish river famous for its gold, II.335

Tantalus, Son of Jupiter; father of Niobe and Pelops; punished in the underworld for attempting to deceive the gods by serving them Pelops at a feast, IV.626

Tarpeia, Roman woman who attempted to betray Rome to Sabines, XIV.1132

Tartarus, The underworld, I.55

Tatius, Sabine king who first warred against Romulus, then ruled jointly with him, XIV.1129

Telamon, Son of Aeacus; king of Aegina; brother of Peleus; half brother of Phocus; Greek hero who accompanied Hercules in the capture of Troy; joined with the Argonauts and the heroes of the Calydonian boar hunt, VII.682

Telethusa, Wife of Ligdus; mother of Iphis, IX.984

Tempe, Thessalian valley through which the river Peneus runs, I.786

Tereus, Thracian king; husband of Procne; father of Itys, VI.605

Tethys, Sea goddess; wife of Oceanus, II.93

Teucer, Son of Telamon and Hesione, XII.228

Thaumas, Father of Iris, IV.659

Thebes, City founded by Cadmus in Boeotia, III.63

Themis, Daughter of Heaven and Mother Earth; goddess of justice, I.443

Thersites, Greek soldier berated by Ulysses for his verbal abuse of leaders, XIII.341

Theseus, Son of Aegeus; father of Hippolytus; husband of Phaedra; Greek hero who slew the Minotaur, VII.575

Thessaly, Country in the northeastern part of Greece, I.784

Thetis, Sea nymph daughter of Nereus and Doris; wife of Peleus; mother of Achilles; a Nereid, XI.313

Thisbe, Beloved of Pyramus, IV.88

Thrace, Country to the northeast of Macedonia, II.328

Tiber, River running through Rome, II.344

Tiberinus, King of the Albans, XIV.882

Timolus, Mountain and its presiding deity in Lydia, II.290

Tiresias, Theban seer who spent seven years as a woman, III.415

Tisiphone, One of the three Furies, IV.650

Titans, Family of primordial gods; children of Uranus and Gaea; overthrown and replaced by the Olympians, VI.275

Tithonus, Husband of Aurora; father of Memnon, IX.616

Tityos, A Giant punished in the underworld for attempting to rape Latona, IV.625

Tlepolemus, Son of Hercules, XII.789

Triptolemus, Greek king used by Ceres to disseminate knowledge of agriculture, V.827

Triton, Son of Neptune; a fish-tailed sea god, I.457

Troezen, City in Argolis, VI.597

Turnus, King of the Rutulians; enemy of Aeneas, XIV.636

Typhoeus, Giant; struck by Jove's lightning bolt, he lay buried beneath Sicily, I.391

Ulysses, Son of Laertes; husband of Penelope; Greek hero famed for his endurance and verbal cleverness, XII.914

Urania, One of the nine Muses, V.378

Venus, Roman goddess of love; daughter of Jupiter and Dione, or, as Greek Aphrodite, sprung from the foam of the sea; husband of Vulcan; mother of Cupid (by Mars) and of Aeneas (by Anchises), I.643

Vertumnus, Etruscan god of changing seasons and fruitfulness, XIV.922

Vesta, Roman goddess of the hearth, XV.903

Virbius, *See* Hippolytus, XV.639

Vulcan, Son of Juno, husband of Venus; armorer of the gods, II.7

Xanthus, River near Troy, II.325

Zephyr, The west wind, I.87

Selected Bibliography

• Indicates works included, adapted, or excerpted in this Norton Critical Edition.

Anderson, William S., ed. *Ovid's Metamorphoses, Books 6–10*. Norman: U of Oklahoma P, 1972.

Anderson, William S., ed. *Ovid's Metamorphoses, Books 1–5*. Norman: U of Oklahoma P, 1997.

Armstrong, Karen. *A Short History of Myth*. Edinburgh: Canongate, 2005.

Barchiesi, Alessandro. *The Poet and the Prince: Ovid and Augustan Discourse*. Berkeley: U of California P, 1997.

Barkan, Leonard. *The Gods Made Flesh: Metamorphosis & the Pursuit of Paganism*. New Haven: Yale UP, 1986.

Barton, Carlin A. *Roman Honor: The Fire in the Bones*. Berkeley: U of California P, 2001.

Beye, Charles Rowan. *Ancient Epic Poetry: Homer, Apollonius, Virgil*. Ithaca: Cornell UP, 1993.

• Brown, Norman O. *Metamorphosis and/or Apocalypse*. Berkeley: U of California P, 1991.

• Calvino, Italo. *The Uses of Literature: Essays*. Trans. Patrick Creagh. San Diego: Harcourt Brace Jovanovich, 1986.

Calvino, Italo. *Six Memos for the Next Millennium*. Cambridge: Harvard UP, 1988.

• Cranch, Christopher Pearse, trans. *The Aeneid*. New York: Barnes and Noble Classics, 2007.

• Evelyn-White, Hugh G., trans. *Hesiod, the Homeric Hymns, and Homerica*. Cambridge: Harvard UP, 1914.

Fränkel, Hermann. *Ovid: A Poet Between Two Worlds*. Berkeley: U of California P, 1945.

Galinsky, Karl. *Ovid's Metamorphoses: An Introduction to the Basic Aspects*. Berkeley: U of California P. 1975.

Galinsky, Karl. *Augustan Culture: An Interpretive Introduction*. Princeton: Princeton UP, 1996.

Graves, Robert. *The Greek Myths*. Baltimore: Penguin Books, 1955.

Green, Peter, trans. *Ovid: The Erotic Poems*. New York: Penguin, 1982.

Hardie, Philip, ed. *The Cambridge Companion to Ovid*. Cambridge: Cambridge UP, 2002.

Harmon, A. M., trans. *Lucian*, Loeb Classical Library. Cambridge: Harvard UP, 1936–37.

Hine, Daryl, trans. *Works of Hesiod and the Homeric Hymns*. Chicago: U of Chicago P, 2005.

Hofmann, Michael, and James Lasdun, eds. *After Ovid: New Metamorphoses*. London: Faber and Faber, 1994.

Hopkinson, Neil, ed. *Metamorphoses, Book XIII*. Cambridge: Cambridge UP, 2000.

Hughes, Ted, trans. *Tales from Ovid*. New York: Farrar, Straus and Giroux, 1997.

• Humphries, Rolfe, trans. *The Way Things Are: The* De Rerum Natura *of Titus Lucretius Carus*. Bloomington: Indiana UP, 1969.

Kossman, Nina, ed. *Gods and Mortals: Modern Poems on Classical Myths*. New York: Oxford UP, 2001.

Lada-Richards, Ismene. *Silent Eloquence: Lucian and Pantomime Dancing*. London: Duckworth, 2007.

Lattimore, Richmond, trans. *Hesiod: The Works and Days, Theology, The Shield of Heracles*. Ann Arbor: U of Michigan P, 1978.

Lefkowitz, Mary, R. *Greek Gods, Human Lives: What We Can Learn from Myths*. New Haven: Yale UP, 2003.

Lendon, J. E. *Empire of Honour: The Art of Government in the Roman World*. New York: Oxford UP, 1997.

• Lombardo, Stanley, and Diane Rayor. *Callimachus: Hymns, Epigrams, Select Fragments*, Baltimore: Johns Hopkins UP, 1988.

Mack, Sara. *Ovid*. New Haven: Yale UP, 1988.

• Mackail, J. W. *Latin Literature*. London: J. Murray, 1895.

Miller, Frank Justus, trans. *Ovid*: Metamorphoses, Third Edition, in Six Volumes. Rev. G. P. Goold. Cambridge: Harvard UP, 1977–1984.

Morford, Mark P. O., and Robert J. Lenardo. *Classical Mythology*, Sixth Edition. New York: Longman, 1999.

Mozley, J. H. *Ovid: The Art of Love, and Other Poems*, Second Edition. Rev. G. P. Goold. Cambridge: Harvard UP, 1979.

Nisetich, Frank, trans. *The Poems of Callimachus*. New York: Oxford UP, 2001.

Otis, Brooks. *Ovid as an Epic Poet*. Cambridge: Cambridge UP, 1966.

Ruden, Sarah, trans. *The* Aeneid *of Vergil*. New Haven: Yale UP, 2008.

Showerman, Grant, trans. *Ovid*: Heroides; *and* Amores. Rev. G. P. Goold. Cambridge: Harvard UP, 1977.

Simpson, Michael. *Gods and Heroes of the Greeks: The Library of Apollodorus*. Amherst: U of Massachusetts P, 1976.

Slavitt, David R., trans. *The* Metamorphoses *of Ovid*. Baltimore: Johns Hopkins UP, 1994.

Solodow, Joseph B. *The World of Ovid's* Metamorphoses. Chapel Hill: U of North Carolina P, 1988.

Stallings, A. E., trans. *Titus Lucretius Cams: De Rerum Natura*. New York: Penguin, 2007.

Terry, Phillip, ed. *Ovid Metamorphosed*. London: Chatto & Windus, 2000.

Warner, Marina. *Fantastic Metamorphoses, Other Worlds: Ways of Telling the Self*. New York: Oxford UP, 2002.

• Wheeler, A. L., trans. *Ovid, VI, Tristia. Ex Ponto*. Rev. G. P. Goold. Cambridge: Harvard UP, 1996.

Wilkinson, L. P. *Ovid Surveyed*. Cambridge: Cambridge UP, 1962.

• Winterbottom, M., trans. *The Elder Seneca Declamations*. Cambridge: Harvard UP, 1974.